Actions and Events

Actions and Events

Perspectives on the Philosophy of Donald Davidson

Edited by

Ernest LePore and Brian P. McLaughlin

Basil Blackwell

First published 1985

Basil Blackwell Ltd
108 Cowley Road, Oxford OX4 1JF, UK

Basil Blackwell Inc.
432 Park Avenue South, Suite 1505,
New York, NY 10016, USA

British Library Cataloguing in Publication Data

Actions and Events: perspectives on the philosophy of Donald Davidson
   1. Davidson, Donald, 1917–
   I. Le Pore, Ernest   II. McLaughlin, Brian
128'.4'0924   B945.D3

   ISBN 0–631–14451–X

   Bibliography: p.
   Includes index.
   1. Davidson, Donald, 1917–   —Essays on actions and events—Addresses, essays, lectures. 2. Act (Philosophy)—Addresses, essays, lectures. 3. Events (Philosophy)—Addresses, essays, lectures. I. LePore, Ernest, 1950– . II. McLaughlin, Brian.
B105.A35D3736   1985   128'.4   85–4064
ISBN 0–631–14451–X

Library of Congress Cataloging-in-Publication Data
Main entry under title:

Actions and events.

   Bibliography: p.
   Includes index.
   1. Davidson, Donald, 1917–   —Essays on actions and events—Addresses, essays, lectures. 2. Act (Philosophy)—Addresses, essays, lectures. 3. Events (Philosophy)—Addresses, essays, lectures. I. LePore, Ernest, 1950– . II. McLaughlin, Brian.
B105.A35D3736   1985   128'.4   85–4064
ISBN 0–631–14451–X

Typeset by Photo·Graphics, Honiton, Devon
Printed in Great Britain by TJ Press Ltd, Padstow, Cornwall

This volume is dedicated to our mothers:

to Flora McLaughlin
and
to the memory of Erminia Santangelo LePore

Contents

List of Contributors   x

Preface
DONALD DAVIDSON   xi

Introduction
ERNEST LePORE AND BRIAN P. McLAUGHLIN   xii

Part I   Intention and Action   1

Actions, Reasons, Causes, and Intentions
ERNEST LePORE AND BRIAN P. McLAUGHLIN   3

1   Davidson's Theory of Intention
    MICHAEL BRATMAN   14

2   Davidson on Intentional Action
    GEORGE M. WILSON   29

3   Davidson on Intentional Behavior
    FREDERICK STOUTLAND   44

4   The Nature and Scope of Rational-Choice Explanation
    JON ELSTER   60

5   Fishing the Red Herrings Out of the Sea of Moral Responsibility
    PETER A. FRENCH   73

6   Questions About Motivational Strength
    IRVING THALBERG   88

7   Davidson on Moral Conflict
    FRANK JACKSON   104

8   Rhyme and Reason: Reflections on Davidson's Version
    of Having Reasons
    ANNETTE C. BAIER   116

9   Reply to Annette Baier: Rhyme and Reason
    DAVID PEARS   130

10   Deception and Division
    DONALD DAVIDSON   138

Part II   Event and Cause   149

The Semantics of Action, Event, and Singular
Causal Sentences
   ERNEST LEPORE   151

11   Events and Reification
        W. V. O. QUINE   162
12   Reply to Quine on Events
        DONALD DAVIDSON   172
13   Actions and Events Despite
     Bertrand Russell
        JAMES D. McCAWLEY   177
14   Adverb-Dropping Inferences and the
     Lemmon Criterion
        JONATHAN BENNETT   193
15   A Decompositional Approach to Modification
        JERROLD J. KATZ, CLAUDIA LEACOCK AND YAEL RAVIN   207
16   Underlying Events in the Logical Analysis of English
        TERENCE PARSONS   235
17   How Not to Flip the Prowler: Transitive Verbs of Action and the
     Identity of Actions
        LAWRENCE BRIAN LOMBARD   268
18   Causal Relata
        DAVID H. SANFORD   282
19   Aspectual Actions and Davidson's Theory of Events
        HECTOR-NERI CASTAÑEDA   294
20   Causation and Explanation: A Problem in Davidson's View on
     Action and Mind
        DAGFINN FØLLESDAL   311
21   Adverbs and Subdeterminates
        RODERICK M. CHISHOLM   324

Part III   Philosophy of Psychology   329

Anomalous Monism and the Irreducibility of the Mental
   BRIAN P. McLAUGHLIN   331

22   Psychophysical Laws
        JAEGWON KIM   369
23   Functionalism and Anomalous Monism
        JOHN McDOWELL   387
24   Davidson's Unintended Attack on Psychology
        ALEXANDER ROSENBERG   399
25   Why Having a Mind Matters
        MARK JOHNSTON   408
26   Against the Token Identity Theory
        TERENCE HORGAN AND MICHAEL TYE   427
27   Physicalism, Events and Part–Whole Relations
        JENNIFER HORNSBY   444

28 Davidson and Sartre
        ESA SAARINEN   459
29 Rational Animals
        DONALD DAVIDSON   473
30 Animal Interpretation
        RICHARD JEFFREY   482
Bibliography   488
Index   498

Contributors

Annette C. Baier, University of Pittsburgh.
Jonathan Bennett, Syracuse University.
Michael Bratman, Stanford University.
Hector-Neri Castañeda, Indiana University.
Roderick M. Chisholm, Brown University, Providence, Rhode Island.
Donald Davidson, University of California, Berkeley.
Jon Elster, University of Oslo.
Dagfinn Føllesdal, University of Oslo.
Peter A. French, Trinity University, Texas.
Terence Horgan, Memphis State University.
Jennifer Hornsby, Corpus Christi College, Oxford.
Frank Jackson, Monash University, Victoria, Australia.
Richard Jeffrey, Princeton University.
M. L. Johnston, Princeton University.
Jerrold J. Katz, The City University of New York.
Jaegwon Kim, University of Michigan.
Claudia Leacock, The City University of New York.
Ernest LePore, Rutgers University, New Jersey.
Lawrence Brian Lombard, Wayne State University, Michigan.
James D. McCawley, University of Chicago.
John McDowell, University College, Oxford.
Brian P. McLaughlin, Rutgers University, New Jersey.
Terence Parsons, University of California, Irvine.
David Pears, Christ Church College, Oxford.
W. V. O. Quine, Harvard University.
Yael Ravin, The City University of New York.
Alexander Rosenberg, Syracuse University.
Esa Saarinen, University of Helsinki.
David H. Sanford, Duke University, Durham, North Carolina.
Frederick Stoutland, St Olaf College, Minnesota.
Irving Thalberg, University of Illinois at Chicago.
Michael Tye, Northern Illinois University.
George Wilson, The Johns Hopkins University.

Preface

When Ernie LePore asked me if I would like to participate in an informal conference on my work I was pleased and flattered. He suggested a weekend, with six or ten participants. Of course I agreed. I did not know what I was in for. Within a month things were out of control. Ten had grown to dozens, whole symposia with chairpersons and organized replies began to loom, and there was talk of concurrent sessions. In the end there were even dancing women and men. It became clear that my work was not to be the focus but the excuse for an extraordinary philosophical enterprise.

As the present volume testifies, everyone gained by the transformation. There was a gain in breadth, for many aspects of the problems raised by actions and events could be discussed, and relations between these problems explored. There was a gain in depth, since a host of attitudes and ideas could be brought to bear on the central topics under discussion. Above all, there was the intellectual stimulation produced by days of good talk devoted to a unified field of subjects by a large number of congenial and imaginative people.

Analytic philosophy is not, of course, either a method or a doctrine; it is a tradition and an attitude. The contributors to this book work in many disciplines, come from many universities, have widely differing views, and write in various styles. The analytic tradition is only one among several, but that thinkers with such a variety of talents and tastes can work cooperatively and productively within it, as here, is a reassuring tribute to the continuing vigour of the analytic attitude.

The editors of this volume have done me, and anyone interested in my work, a rare service: in their introductions to the major divisions of the book they have provided original and comprehensive discussions of the problems with which I have been concerned, they have surveyed difficulties in my views and criticisms which have been directed against them, and when they could they have offered improvements. Thus they have created an invaluable setting in which to read the essays that follow.

I have often been accused of making too much of the 'principle of charity' in my writing. But noticing the generous and positive spirit in which the editors and other contributors to this volume treat my work, I am inclined to agree with Alexander Pope:

In faith and hope the world will disagree,
But all mankind's concern is charity.

Donald Davidson

Introduction

Donald Davidson teaches philosophy at the University of California, Berkeley. In spring, 1985, a conference devoted to discussing his work was held at Rutgers University (New Brunswick, New Jersey). More than 500 scholars from various disciplines representing 26 countries participated in 70 sessions squeezed into four days. Topics covered in these sessions included Davidson's views on freedom to act, weakness of the will, practical reasoning, intentions, actions, events, causal relations and explanations, the nature of mental events, the scope, limits and nature of decision theory, radical interpretation, knowledge, justification, indirect and direct quotation, truth, reference, meaning, malaprops, conventions, and metaphor. This list is neither exhaustive, nor self-explanatory, but it does indicate some of the areas Professor Davidson has investigated, and gives an idea of the breadth of his contributions to contemporary discussion of crucial issues in many academic disciplines.

Almost all of the essays in this book were presented at the Davidson Conference and it is intended to be a companion to Davidson's *Essays on Actions and Events* (1980). [A second volume, intended to be a companion to Davidson's *Inquiries into Truth and Interpretation*, (1984) is forthcoming.] This volume divides into three sections corresponding to the three sections of *Essays on Actions and Events*: intention and action, event and cause, and philosophy of psychology. Each section begins with an introductory essay which provides an overview of Davidson's ideas in the context of current discussion about the issues which he raised. Each introductory essay is followed by essays which develop in some detail a response to some of Davidson's contributions to various topics of each section.

The first section contains papers about the nature of rational explanation, the relationship between reasons and actions, the relationship between intentions and actions, the concept of agency, freedom and weakness of the will, and the relationship between the will and irrationality. This section also includes an essay by Davidson entitled "Deception and Division" in which he presents his current view concerning self-deception.

The second section contains papers concerned with the nature of events, causal relationships, and the logical form of action and singular causal statements. The final section contains papers about the relationship between the mental and the physical, the scientific status of psychological and psychophysical explanations. Several of the papers discuss Davidson's formulation of anomalous monism.

Many people and institutions supported the Conference, and thus contributed to this volume. The following members of Rutgers University deserve special thanks: Peter Klein, Chairperson of the Philosophy Department; Phyllis Cohen, Director of the Voorhees Assembly Board; Reneé Weber, Director of the Council for Integrated and Cross-Disciplinary Studies; Mary Hartman, Dean of Douglass College; John Yolton, Dean of Rutgers College; David Mechanic, Dean of the Faculty of Arts and Sciences; Kenneth Wolfson, Dean of the Graduate School; Kenneth Wheeler, Provost. We are most grateful to Elizabeth Woodward and David Cayer of Research and Sponsored Programs, and to the President of Rutgers University, Edward Bloustein.

Individuals from outside of Rutgers University who deserve special thanks are: Bas van Fraassen, Gilbert Harman, Barry Loewer, Colin McGinn, and David Rosenthal. Of course, it goes without saying that an enormous debt is owed to Donald Davidson for his help throughout.

We also wish to thank Carol Busia from Basil Blackwell and also Kim Pickin, our publisher, for her patience and assistance.

Loretta Mazlen Mandel, best of all imaginable assistants, we cannot thank enough. Without her neither the Davidson Conference nor this volume would have been possible.

This project was generously supported by the National Endowment for the Humanities; the National Science Foundation; the Exxon Educational Foundation; the New Jersey Committee for the Humanities; Rutgers University Research and Sponsored Programs; the Dean's offices of Douglass and Rutgers Colleges, its Faculty of Arts and Sciences, the Graduate School of Rutgers University, Rutgers University Cost Sharing Fund and the Douglass College Fellows.

Ernest LePore
Brian P. McLaughlin
Rutgers University

Part I

Intention and Action

Actions, Reasons, Causes, and Intentions

Ernest LePore and Brian P. McLaughlin

Our purpose here is to present some major themes of Davidson's views on action and intention and to trace the development of these views.[1] Since the focus in most of the following papers in this section is the nature of rationalizing explanations, we shall concentrate on Davidson's views on the latter. Other matters will be discussed only if they bear on this topic. We begin with Davidson's discussion of rationalizing explanations in his seminal paper 'Actions, Reasons, and Causes' (hereafter, ARC). Then we shall trace some changes his views have undergone since ARC.

One way we understand intentional actions is by understanding their purpose or purposes. The purpose or purposes of an action are those the agent had in performing the action. We understand an agent's purpose in acting in a certain way by understanding the agent's reason for so acting. The sort of reason in question is the sort an agent can *have* for acting. So much was common ground between Davidson and his intended audience in ARC.[2]

ARC opens with the question, What is the relation between a reason and an action when the reason explains the action by giving the agent's reasons for performing the action? Davidson labels this explanatory relationship 'rationalization': a reason explains an action by rationalizing it. And a reason rationalizes an action when, and only when, the agent so acts for that reason. Prior to ARC, something close to a consensus had formed that this relationship was not causal. Discussion tended to center around why it could not be causal and the consequences of its not being so. Davidson's central purpose in ARC is 'to defend the ancient – and commonsense – position that rationalization is a species of causal explanation' [3]. He defends this thesis by defending (1) and (2):

---

[1] Essays (1)–(5) of Davidson's *Essays on Actions and Events*, Oxford University Press, 1980. All pagination in this essay is from that volume.
[2] Charles Taylor, *The Explanation of Behavior*, Routledge & Kegan Paul,1964; R.S. Peters, *The Concept of Motivation*, London, 1958; William Dray, *Laws and Explanation in History*, Oxford, 1957.

(1) In order to understand how a reason of any kind rationalizes an action it is necessary and sufficient that we see, at least in essential outline, how to construct a primary reason [4].

(2) The primary reason for an action is its cause [4].

Both (1) and (2) employ the technical term 'primary reason'. A primary reason is a pair of mental states. One state in such a pair is a belief state, the other a pro-attitude. Pro-attitudes include 'desires, wantings, urges, promptings, and a great variety of moral views, aesthetic principles, economic prejudices, social conventions, and public and private goals and values *insofar as these can be interpreted as attitudes of an agent* directed towards actions of a certain kind' [4, emphasis ours]. 'Attitude' does yeoman service here for short-lived mental states such as a fleeting desire to look in the rear view mirror of one's car as well as long standing mental states such as wanting to succeed in all one's endeavours. 'Pro-attitude' is a term of art introduced by Davidson for the various sorts of mental states that can combine with certain beliefs to constitute reasons for acting. Davidson expresses sympathy, without endorsing, the view that wanting is the genus of pro-attitude. But whether wanting is such, desiring to act in a certain way, wanting to, having an urge to, feeling prompted to, thinking one ought to, feeling obliged to, and the like, can all be reasons – though not always good reasons, and rarely by themselves sufficient ones – for so acting. They all count as pro-attitudes. The belief component of a primary reason can either be a belief that acting in a certain sort of way promotes whatever one has a pro-attitude towards, or it can be a belief about a particular action that it is of the kind toward which one has a pro-attitude. One can rationalize an action by citing a primary reason for which it was performed. When one does, one must, of course, cite a belief about a specific action taken. Suppose, for example, Paul takes a sip of coffee. The primary reason why he so acted may be that he wanted to take a sip of coffee and believes his action is his taking a sip of coffee.

A primary reason rationalizes an action when, but only when, it is a reason why (or for which) the agent so acted. Davidson offers thesis (3) as a necessary condition for a primary reason being a reason why an agent acted.

(3) R is a primary reason why an agent performed the action A, under description d, only if R consists of a pro-attitude of the agent towards actions with a certain property, and a belief of the agent that A, under the description d, has that property [5].[3]

The condition cited in (3) is not sufficient for R's being a primary reason why an agent performed the action A. One can have a pro-attitude towards actions of a certain kind, perform an action of that kind, believe one is performing an action of that kind, and yet not perform it for that reason; so that the primary reason is not a reason why one performed the action. One may have performed it for some other reason. Paul may want to do something enjoyable, believe of

---

[3] For present purposes, talk of actions under descriptions can be recast in terms of talk of actions instantiating types of actions. For further discussion, cf. Davidson [193–5].

some action of his that it is enjoyable, but not have performed the action because it is enjoyable. The reason why he performed it may be that he believes his job requires it and wants to do what his job requires. That he finds the action enjoyable may have nothing to do with *why* he performs it. As Davidson notes, 'central to the relation between a reason and an action it explains is the idea that the agent performed the action *because* he had the reason' [AE:9, emphasis Davidson's]. Paul did not read the article he assigned to his students because he wanted to do something enjoyable and found his reading the article enjoyable. Rather, Paul read the article he assigned to his students because he wanted to do his job and believed his reading it was part of his job.

Davidson maintains that R is a primary reason why X did A only if X did A because X had primary reason R. Moreover, he maintains that pending a better alternative account, the 'because' in this statement is best understood as expressing a causal explanatory relationship. Agent X did A because X had primary reason R only if X's having R is a cause of X's Aing. This is why Davidson asserts thesis (2). Any primary reason for which an action is performed is a cause of the action. According to Davidson, since rationalizing explanations that cite primary reasons explain actions by citing primary reasons that are *causes* of those actions, thesis (4) is true.

(4) A rationalization that cites a primary reason is a species of causal explanation.

The conditions cited in theses (2) and (3) are, perhaps, necessary for a primary reason's being a reason why an agent acted, but they are not sufficient. A primary reason for acting in a certain way can cause an agent to act in that way and yet not be the reason for which the agent so acted, and so not rationalize his action. Paul wants to trip on the rug because he believes that by doing so he will amuse his friends and he wants to amuse his friends. These thoughts so distract Paul that he trips on the rug. Paul wanted to trip on the rug, and while it was happening believed that he was tripping on the rug. He even believes while it is happening that it will amuse his friends. His desire to trip was a cause of his tripping. So, he had a primary reason for tripping on the rug that caused him to trip on the rug. But this primary reason does not rationalize his tripping since it is not a reason for which he tripped. There is no primary reason for which he tripped since his tripping was just something that happened to him. It might be claimed that this is not a case that shows the conditions cited in theses (2) and (3) are not sufficient because the event in question is not an action. And, afterall, we are concerned with whether the conditions are sufficient for a primary reason's being the reason why an agent *acted*. Indeed, it is not a counterexample for just this reason. But the following case is.

Suppose Paul wants to ingest something fattening and believes that by drinking milk he would be ingesting something fattening. Suppose further his want and belief cause him to conjure up an image of his drinking milk and that this image in turn causes him to recall that his doctor recommended that he drink a glass of milk daily because he is short of calcium. So, because he wants to do what the doctor ordered, and believes he can do so by drinking milk, he drinks a glass of milk. His wanting to ingest something fattening and his belief that by drinking milk he would be ingesting something fattening are causes of his drinking milk and constitute a primary reason for drinking milk. But this belief and want do not constitute a primary reason *for which* Paul drank milk. He did not drink milk because he wanted to ingest something fattening. He is generally avoiding ingesting fattening foods since the doctor also has told him that he must lose weight. He would not have drunk milk had he not believed that the doctor had ordered it. He drank the milk because the doctor ordered it. This case is one in which the agent has a primary reason R for performing an action of kind A, intentionally performs an action of kind A, and in which R is a cause of his intentionally performing the action. But R is not a reason for which he performs A. Davidson acknowledges that further conditions are needed in order to state jointly necessary and sufficient conditions. But in ARC he postponed this task since his primary concern there was to establish theses (1)–(4).[4]

Theses (1)–(4) comprise a causal theory of action. This theory differs in important ways from earlier causal theories of action. According to many such theories, intentionally Aing is invariably caused by a volition, such as a willing to A, or an intention to A[5]. Davidson's causal theory invokes beliefs and pro-attitudes. But while one must have a pro-attitude towards Aing in order to intentionally A, there is no specific kind of pro-attitude required. He acknowledges that when we act intentionally we act with an intention. But he claimed that while the locution 'acting with an intention to A' has the outward form of a description, it is syncategorematic, and cannot be taken to refer to an entity, state, disposition, or event [8]. The function of the locution 'He Aed with the intention to B' is to redescribe the action of Aing in terms of one of its causes since 'with the intention to B' goes proxy, or does duty, for any of the wide variety of pro-attitudes towards Bing. In ARC Davidson maintains:
duty, for any of the wide variety of pro-attitudes towards Bing. In ARC Davidson maintains:

(5) There are no intentions. When we act intentionally, we act with an intention, but the locution 'with the intention of' is syncategorematic.

Davidson's theory also differs from earlier causal theories that required there be laws covering the explanans and explanandum of rationalizing explanations.[6]

---

[4] A large portion of ARC is devoted to defending Thesis (2) against various arguments, quite popular then, that purported to show that reasons could not be causes of the actions they rationalize. The arguments are too many and varied to be properly treated here, but we note in passing that they were inspired by remarks of Wittgenstein's and/or certain interpretations of Human strictures on causation. Each argument purported that a necessary condition for two items to causally interact could not be satisfied by reasons and actions. For our purposes here suffice it to say that Davidson replied to the leading arguments of this sort by showing in each case either that reasons and actions indeed satisfy the necessary condition in question or that the would-be necessary condition for causal interaction was not in fact one.

[5] Cf., e.g. H.A. Prichard, 'Acting, Willing, Desiring,' in *Moral Obligation* (Oxford, England, 1949).

[6] For example, Carl Hempel, 'Rational Action,' *Proceedings and Addresses of the American Philosophical Association*, October, 1962; cf., especially the section "Rational action as an explanatory model concept".

He acknowledges that singular causal connections require laws. But he distinguishes two readings of the requirement. 'It may mean that "A caused B" entails some particular law involving the predicates used in the descriptions 'A' and 'B', or it may mean that "A caused B" entails that there exists a causal law instantiated by some true descriptions of A and B' [16]. The second alternative is weaker than the first in that it is implied by, but does not imply, the first. Davidson maintains that 'only the second version … can be made to fit with most causal explanations; it suits rationalizations equally well' [17]. Causal connections require laws, but 'the laws whose existence is required if reasons are causes of actions do not, we may be sure, deal in concepts in which rationalizations must deal' [17]. He says:

> If the causes of a class of events (actions) fall in a certain class (reasons) and there is a law to back each singular causal statement, it does not follow that there is any law connecting events classified as reasons with events classified as actions – the classifications may even be neurological, chemical, or physical [17].

Rationalizations that cite primary reasons do not invoke laws. But they are no different in this respect from most ordinary causal explanations (e.g., causal explanations couched in our everyday non-technical vocabulary).

Of course, not every causal explanation is a rationalizing explanation. What differentiates this species from its genus? Recall that a rationalization which cites a primary reason thereby cites a cause of acting that is also a reason for so acting. If one has a reason for acting, then one has, in a sense, some grounds for so acting. Thus, it is not surprising that Davidson says: 'if rationalization is, as I want to argue, a species of causal explanation, then justification … is at least one differentiating property' [9]. Rationalizing explanations provide some justification for the action they explain, at least some justification from the agent's point of view (i.e., given the agent's values). Davidson remarks that 'there is a certain irreducible – though somewhat anaemic – sense in which every rationalization justifies: from the agent's point of view there was, when he acted, something to be said for the action' [AE:9].[7] What makes a primary reason a reason for acting in a certain way is that it provides the agent with a rationale or grounds for so acting, at least given the agent's values.

What is the relationship between a primary reason and a course of action in virtue of which the former provides the agent with a rationale for engaging in the latter? In ARC [9] Davidson maintains that the relationship is a logical relationship between the reason and the course of action that can be represented by a *practical syllogism*. The conclusion of the practical syllogism is that the course of action has a certain desirability characteristic. That it has a desirability characteristic is alleged to follow deductively from the propositional contents of the belief and pro-attitude constitutive of the primary reason for this course of action.

Davidson does not provide an example of a practical syllogism in ARC. But

---

[7] However, our point of view cannot differ too greatly from the agent's if we are able to rationalize the agent's actions. Cf., essays (9)–(14) in Davidson's *Inquiries into Truth and Interpretation*, Oxford University Press, 1984, for more on this constraint.

let us consider an example similar to one he offers in 'Intending' [85–86]. Suppose Paul wants to improve the taste of the stew and believes that by adding sage to the stew, he will improve its taste. This want and belief provide him with a rationale for adding sage. According to Davidson, this is so in virtue of a relationship between propositions that can be represented by a practical syllogism. The minor premise is provided by the belief: (a) by adding sage to the stew, he will improve its taste. The major premise is provided by the pro-attitude. One suggestion is: (b) he does something that improves the taste of the stew. Davidson rejects this suggestion on the grounds that it does not follow from (a) and (b) that adding sage to the stew has any desirability characteristic. He claims that the propositional expression of a pro-attitude must include the attitude of approval of the agent: otherwise, it will not follow from the premises that adding sage to the stew has any desirability characteristic. Proposition (b) does not include the attitude of approval of the agent. Davidson takes the propositional content of Paul's desire to be: (c) any action of his is desirable insofar as it will improve the taste of the stew. Proposition (c) is the major premise of the syllogism. Davidson's position in ARC is that from (c) and (a) it follows deductively that: (d) his adding sage to the stew is desirable in that it will improve the taste of the stew.

Davidson maintains that sometimes the conclusion of a practical syllogism corresponds to the action as rationalized by a primary reason. This obtains when the primary reason is a reason for which a particular action is performed. In such cases:

(6) The propositional contents of the primary reason for an action are deductively related to a proposition to the effect that the action has a certain desirability characteristic (where the desirability characteristic varies from one sort of pro-attitude to another).

When we seek a rationalizing explanation for a particular action, thesis (3) requires that the belief that partly constitutes the primary reason why the particular action was performed be a belief *about* that particular action, that is, about the act token. Thus, a belief such as the belief that by adding sage to the stew he will improve its taste cannot figure as a component of a primary reason for a particular action, according to (3), since it is not *about* any particular action. Thus, the practical syllogism which accounts for the logical relationship between a particular action and the primary reason for this particular action, must contain both a belief about the particular action and a proposition to the effect that the particular action is desirable insofar as it is an action of a certain kind. So, for example, corresponding to (b) and (d) will be (b′) and (d′) respectively:

b′. This act of adding sage to the stew will improve its taste
c′. This act of adding sage to the stew is desirable inasmuch as it improves the taste of the stew.

As Davidson conceives of practical syllogisms, their conclusions express only *a* reason for an action. There may, of course, be reasons against; so while a reason, the reason need not be conclusive. Davidson acknowledges this but claims:

> The practical syllogism exhausts its role in displaying an action as falling under one reason; so it cannot be subtilized into a reconstruction of practical reasoning, which involves the weighing of competing reasons [ARC:16].

Consider now thesis (1) that in order to understand how a reason of any kind rationalizes an action it is necessary and sufficient that we see, at least in essential outline, how to construct a primary reason for the action. Why does Davidson give primary reasons such a prominent role in his account of rationalizing actions? It is useful in explicating (1) to coin the term 'primary rationalizing explanation,' where such an explanation is one that rationalizes an action by citing a primary reason for which it was performed. Thesis (1), then, can be recast as follows:

1′ To understand how a reason of any kind rationalizes an action it is necessary and sufficient that we understand, at least in essential outline, how to construct from the rationalization in question a primary rationalizing explanation of that action.

On the face of it, this thesis seems false. Often, the reason we cite in rationalizing an action is neither a primary reason nor a component of one. We can explain actions by citing non-psychological facts ('He pulled the car over because the police officer told him to'), character traits ('He wants the money because he is greedy'), moods ('He was curt because he was in a bad mood'), purposes ('She left at 8.00 in order to catch the 8.15 train'), bodily sensations ('He took the wool sweater off because he felt itchy'), expectations ('He kept looking through the window because he expected to see the car pull up any minute'), civil laws ('He drives within the speed limit because the law requires it'), and in many other ways. These explanations count as rationalizations in that they explain by citing a reason the agent had for so acting. But none of these reasons for acting is a primary reason. So, the rationalizations in question are not primary rationalizing explanations.

According to (1′), though, we understand the sorts of rationalizations illustrated above when we understand that the agent had some pro-attitude towards the actions of the sort in question, some appropriate belief about his action, and that the agent so acted because he had the belief and pro-attitude. We may, of course, rationalize an action without knowing a specific pro-attitude or belief that constituted a primary reason the agent had for so acting. But, for example, 'when we learn that a man cheated his son out of greed, we do not necessarily know what the primary reason was, but we know there was one, and its general nature' [9]. We know its general nature because we know the sorts of desires, longings, urges, and so on, greedy people are prone to have, and that such desires, longings, etc., can join with beliefs to result in acts of greed. For further illustrations note that we can rationalize an action by citing the fact that the agent was itchy because we understand that being itchy is an unpleasant sensation, one that people tend to want to relieve, and that people tend to do things, they deem otherwise acceptable, to relieve unpleasant sensations. Non-psychological facts, such as the fact that the police officer ordered the person to pull over, might rationalize why the person pulled over, only if we suppose that the person believed, suspected, thought, etc., the police officer ordered this, and wanted, felt obliged to, or thought he ought to, etc., do what was ordered. Non-psychological facts can rationalize an action only if they are in some way psychologically registered by the agent. In short, rationalizing explanations explain actions, in part, in virtue of their being backed up by primary rationalizing explanations of those actions. For this reason, Davidson maintains that:

(7) Every action has at least one primary rationalizing explanation.

Primary rationalizing explanations are necessary for non-primary reasons to succeed in rationalizing actions. We can rationalize an action without knowing a primary reason for which it was performed; but we must know that there was a primary reason and what, in general outline, that primary reason was.

Unintentional actions, it may seem, are not performed for primary reasons. Mary might shoot her father *because* she thought he was a burglar. When we say that she shot her father because she mistakenly believed he was a burglar we explain her action. Yet Mary did not have a primary reason for shooting her father. She had no pro-attitude towards shooting her father at all.

This line of criticism is ineffective against Davidson because he maintains that the intentional/unintentional distinction does not divide actions into two separate and distinct classes. Rather, he holds that *every* action is intentional under *some* description and unintentional under others. Since every action, including Mary's shooting her father, is intentional under some description, he can hold to thesis (7) in the face of the would-be counter-example simply by noting that the action will have a primary rationalizing explanation, at least under a description under which the action is intentional. Thus understood thesis (7) can be recast as:

(8) Every action, under some description, has at least one primary rationalizing explanation.

To sum up, a primary rationalizing explanation explains an action by citing a primary reason for which it was performed. A primary reason is a pair of mental states, one element of which is a belief, the other of which is a pro-attitude. What makes a primary reason a reason for an action is a logical relationship, expressed by a practical syllogism, between the propositional contents of the belief and pro-attitude constitutive of the primary reason and a proposition to the effect that the action has a certain desirability characteristic. What makes a primary reason a reason for which an agent acted is, in part, a causal connection between the belief and pro-attitude constitutive of the primary reason and the action. So, primary rationalization is a species of causal explanation. When one acts intentionally, one acts with an intention. But 'with an intention' is syncategorematic, doing duty for any of the various pro-attitudes. Finally, every action has a primary rationalizing explanation; and non-primary rationalizing explanations explain only in virtue of their being backed up by primary rationalizing explanations.

Theses (1)–(8) comprise most of the central tenets of ARC. Davidson's views have changed somewhat over the years. In what follows, we shall trace the evolution of his thought.

In his Introduction to *Essays on Actions and Events*, Davidson notes three changes in his views. One change [xiii] is essentially this. When he wrote ARC, he thought it would be relatively easy to supplement theses (2) and (3) so as to state noncircular necessary and sufficient conditions for a primary reason's being the reason for which an agent performed an action. One popular attempt to specify the further needed conditions is to place constraints on the way the primary reason causes the action. A primary reason for acting in a certain way is the reason for which an agent so acted when, but only when, the primary reason causes the action *in the right kind of way*. The problem is seen as how to specify the right kind of way non-circularly.[8] Davidson argues in "Freedom to Act" that this cannot be done. He offers reasons for thinking that a non-circular specification of the right kind of causal connection for action is impossible. [He also does so in 'Psychology as Philosophy,' 232–3]. Moreover, he despairs of stating an *analysis* of 'a primary reason's being the reason for which an agent performed an action'.

For present purposes, one point to note is that even if an analysis of a primary reason's being a reason why an agent acted is not possible, (1)–(8) may still all be true. Theses (2) and (4) mention causation. But (2) requires only that a necessary condition for a primary reason's being a reason why an agent performed an action is that the primary reason is a cause of the action. Thesis (4) asserts that rationalization based on a primary reason is a species of causal explanation. But, as we understand him, Davidson maintains this because he maintains that primary reasons must be causes of the actions they rationalize.

Davidson notes a second change of view [xxii]. He says:

> In Essay 2, I come out against the view espoused in Essay 1 [ARC], that the propositional expressions of the reasons for action are deductively related to the proposition that corresponds to the action as explained by reasons.[9]

The view Davidson comes out against in WOW is the view espoused by thesis (6).

In WOW Davidson distinguishes between two *kinds* of evaluative propositions: *prima facie* and *unconditional evaluative* propositions. The evaluative propositions that express the propositional contents of pro-attitudes that figure as components of primary reasons are *prima facie* evaluative propositions. The content of Paul's desire to improve the taste of stew is "any action of his that will improve the taste of the stew is desirable *insofar* as (or *given that*) it will improve the taste of the stew". This expression of the content of Paul's desire, Davidson notes, does not have the logical form of a universalized conditional, say, "For any action x of his, if x improves the taste of the stew, then x is desirable insofar

---

[8] Cf., e.g., C. Peacocke *Holistic Explanation*, Cambridge University Press, 1979.

[9] Essay 2 is Davidson's 'How is weakness of the will possible?' (hereafter, WOW).

as it will improve the taste of the stew". Instead, Davidson thinks its logical form is best displayed by using a *prima facie* operator that relates pairs of (open or closed) sentences. Let 'pf' represent '*prima facie*'. The content of Paul's desires has the logical form 'pf (an action is desirable/it will improve the taste of the stew)'. 'pf(A/B)' should be read as 'A is *prima facie* desirable given that B'. Davidson notes that probably there is something to be said for, and something to be said against, actions of any kind. So, the major premise of a practical syllogism must be a *prima facie* proposition. But, then, so must the conclusion. This is a proposition to the effect that the action has a certain desirability characteristic, and so it will be the *prima facie* proposition, 'pf (this adding of sage to the stew is desirable/it will improve the taste of the stew)'. Given that these propositions have these logical forms, the relationship between the propositional contents of a primary reason and the proposition to the effect that the action has a desirability characteristic is not an inference licensed by first order quantification theory. This, we take it, is what Davidson means by saying that the relationship is not deductive. (Of course, Davidson does not show that the relationship cannot be captured in some logical system other than first order logic.)

Davidson also marks the following change in his views [xiii]:

> When I wrote Essay 1 [ARC] I believed that of the three main uses of the concept of intention distinguished by Anscombe (acting with an intention, acting intentionally, and intending to act), the first was the most basic. Acting intentionally, I argued in Essay 1, was just acting with some intention. That left intending, which I thought would be simple to understand in terms of the others. I was wrong. When I finally came to work on it, I found it the hardest of the three; contrary to my original view, it came to seem the basic notion on which the others depend; and what progress I made with it partially undermined an important theme in Essay 1 – that 'the intention with which the action was done' does not refer to any entity or state of any kind.

The theme that is partially undermined here is the one expressed by (5). In 'Intending,' Davidson acknowledges that there are intentions not accompanied by action. One might have the intention to build a squirrel house and never act on it. Intentions are mental states we can occupy. So, the first sentence in (5) is false. This leads Davidson to reconsider the nature of intentional action. Sometimes we have intentions and when the time comes we act on them. So, intentional action and intending to act are intimately related.

Davidson maintains that intentions have contents which can be expressed by all-out evaluative propositions. Such propositions are ones to the effect that an action is better than its alternatives. Thus, these are not *prima facie*. One may wonder how future directed intentions can have all-out evaluative propositions as their contents. It may seem wildly irrational to judge that *any* future action of a certain sort is more desirable than any alternative. Let the future action be going to the store. One might do this by stealing a car. But surely one might not judge this unconditionally desirable. Davidson acknowledges all this. But he claims that future directed intentions are made in the light of one's beliefs about what the relevant future will be like. The idea, then, is this: given what one believes the relevant future will be like, one judges that doing A in the relevant future is flat out desirable (or more desirable than its alternatives). According to Davidson, such is the nature of future directed intentions.

Several queries arise: Does the fact that there are intentions show that 'with the intention of' is not syncategorematic? Are the contents of intentions all-out evaluative propositions? Must an action always correspond to an all-out proposition? Each of these questions is taken up by one or more of the contributors. But a couple of brief remarks concerning the first query are in order to help prepare the way for their discussion.

Suppose that there are intentions. That there are does not undermine the view that 'with the intention of' is syncategorematic. The locution 'with an intention' does seem to do duty for any of the various pro-attitudes.[10] Thesis (5) consists of two sentences. The point then is that the first sentence is false, while the second is true. Finally, there is a reason (which Davidson does not mention) for thinking that intentionally Aing is not just acting with the intention to A. One can act with the intention to A without intentionally Aing. Paul can go to Europe with the intention of returning in two weeks without its being the case that he intentionally returns in two weeks. He may never return.

---

[10] We owe this point to Michael Bratman. We thank him for his help.

1

Davidson's Theory of Intention

MICHAEL BRATMAN

In an important and fascinating series of papers, spanning a decade and a half, Donald Davidson has sketched a general theory of intention, a theory that tries to explain what it is to do something intentionally, what it is to intend to do something later, and how these two phenomena are related.[1] In this paper I say what this theory is, argue that it faces a pair of serious difficulties, and diagnose these difficulties as rooted in an overly limited conception of the role of intentions and plans in practical reasoning.

1 *Davidson's theory: main ideas*

Davidson begins with intentional action. In his classic paper 'Actions, reasons, and causes' he sketches the following general view. Intentional action is action that is explainable, in the appropriate way, by appeal to the agent's reasons for action. The reasons that explain intentional actions are appropriate pairs of the agent's desires (and other 'pro-attitudes' and beliefs). When one acts *for* a certain reason an appropriate desire–belief pair *causes* one's action. Suppose, for example, that I intentionally go to Davies Hall, because I want to hear Pavarotti sing and believe going to Davies Hall would be a way of doing this. Since I act *for* this reason, the pro-attitude and belief *cause* my action.

This conception of intentional action makes no essential appeal to any distinct state or event of *intending* to go to Davies Hall that intervenes between my desire–belief pair and my action. The intentionality of my action lies, rather, in its *relation* to my desire–belief pair.

This is a compromise position. On the one hand it insists that in explaining actions in terms of their reasons we are citing *causes* of those actions. So it rejects radical suggestions to the contrary – typically rooted in strong behavioristic assumptions – offered by Anscombe, Melden, and others.[2] On the

---

[1] These papers are all reprinted in his recent collection, *Essays on Actions and Events*, (Oxford University Press, New York, 1980). The crucial papers for my purposes here are 'Actions, reasons, and causes', 'How is weakness of the will possible?,' and 'Intending.' Page references are to this collection.

[2] For references, see Davidson's initial footnote in 'Actions, reasons, and causes.'

other hand, in seeing the intentionality of action as solely a matter of its relation to the agent's desires and beliefs, Davidson rejects the *volitional* conception that frequently accompanies causal theories. On a volitional conception of, for example, an intentional arm-raising, a volition in favor of so acting is, as Davidson says, 'an event that is common and peculiar to all cases where a man intentionally raises his arm.'[3] Further, on such a conception this volitional event plays a crucial causal role in the arm-raising. While embracing a causal theory of the relation between reason and action, Davidson explicitly denies that there is any such volitional event involved in the causation of intentional arm-raisings.

Now, even granting that when I act for a reason my reason is a cause of my action, there will also be some sort of *logical* relation between my reason and my action. In his later paper on weakness of the will, 'How is weakness of the will possible?', Davidson tries to characterize this logical relation in terms of a general conception of practical reasoning.[4] The guiding idea is that the reason for which I act provides me with premises from which I could have reasoned to a conclusion which corresponds to my action.

Consider again my intentionally going to Davies Hall because I want to listen to Pavarotti sing. This pro-attitude provides one premise for my potential reasoning, and my belief that going to Davies Hall is a way of doing this provides another. The premise provided by my belief is just *what* I believe: the proposition that going to Davies Hall is a way of listening to Pavarotti. The premise provided by my pro-attitude is not, however, so easily arrived at. *What* I want is *to listen to Pavarotti* or, perhaps, *that I listen to Pavarotti*. But, on Davidson's view, the relevant premise is neither of these, but rather the *prima facie evaluative proposition* that any act of mine would be desirable, *insofar as* it is an act of listening to Pavarotti. Davidson supposes that such an evaluative proposition is the 'natural expression'[5] of my pro-attitude.[6] Finally, my intentional action corresponds, on the theory, to an 'unconditional' (or, as he later says in 'Intending,' 'all-out') – rather than a merely prima facie –evaluative proposition that my action is desirable. This unconditional evaluative proposition can, on the theory, be represented as a non-deductive conclusion of an

---

[3] Ibid., p. 13.

[4] The main ideas of this conception are also usefully discussed in 'Intending.' In what follows I draw on that discussion as well.

[5] Ibid., p. 86.

[6] Davidson's explanation of this prima facie evaluative proposition leans on a supposed parallel with inductive-statistical explanations, as they are understood by C. Hempel in *Aspects of Scientific Explanation* (The Free Press, New York, 1965), pp. 376–403. While I am convinced by Davidson that there is some important parallel here, I am unsure about the details of his treatment of this parallel. As Hempel emphasizes, inductive–statistical explanations involve two distinct concepts of probability: statistical probability, and inductive probability. The former is used in the major premise of such explanations, the latter characterizes the *relation* between premises and conclusion of the explanation. Davidson's main idea is to treat 'prima facie' as relating premises and conclusion of practical syllogisms. In this respect, 'prima facie' is seen as analogous to inductive probability. But Davidson also understands the major premises of such practical syllogisms as using the concept of prima facie. Given the analogy with probability, this suggests that there is a notion of prima facie analogous to that of statistical probability. But the problem is that we seem to have only a *single* notion of prima facie, in contrast with the probabilistic case. This disanalogy between the two cases does not emerge clearly in Davidson's discussion, because the distinction between two concepts of probability is lost in his formalism. (See 'How is weakness of the will possible?', p. 38.)

argument whose premises are provided by my pro-attitude and belief. In intentionally going to Davies Hall I accept this all-out evaluative conclusion.

This signals a modest retreat from the rejection of a volitional conception. On this later version of Davidson's theory, there *is* an element 'common and peculiar to all cases' of intentional concert-going, namely: the acceptance of an all-out evaluation that the concert-going being performed is desirable.[7] But this retreat is not a capitulation, for Davidson supposes that when I intentionally go to the concert my acceptance of this all-out evaluative proposition in favor of my action need not be distinct from my very act of going. This is why he says that on his theory 'Aristotle's remark that the conclusion [of a piece of practical reasoning] is an action remains cogent.'[8] And, of course, if my acceptance of this all-out conclusion is not distinct from my action, it cannot be a cause of my action.[9]

My all-out evaluative conclusion has two further features it is important to note. First, it is at least implicitly comparative. It assesses my action favorably in comparison with the other options I actually considered (which in some cases may only include the option of refraining from so acting).[10]

Second, my all-out evaluation is about the *particular* act of concert-going I am now performing. In this respect it differs from my initial pro-attitude, which was in favor of actions insofar as they were of a certain *type* (e.g. concert-going). Davidson's view seems to be that desirability is, strictly speaking, always a property of particular actions, rather than of types of actions.[11] Different

---

[7] 'Evaluation' is ambiguous between the evaluative proposition accepted, and the acceptance of that proposition. So I will only use this term when the context clearly disambiguates.

[8] 'How is weakness of the will possible?', p. 39.

[9] Given Davidson's metaphysics of action as presented in 'Agency' in *Essays on Actions and Events*, however, my acceptance of this conclusion *could* cause the upshot in terms of which the action is described. Thus, my acceptance of an all-out conclusion in favor of raising my arm may cause my arm's rising. This suggests that Davidson's theory *is* compatible with a volitional theory in the spirit of H.A. Prichard, 'Acting, willing, and desiring,' in *The Philosophy of Action*, ed. A.R. White (Oxford University Press, Oxford, 1968).

[10] As I urged in 'Practical reasoning and weakness of the will,' *Nous*, 13 (1979), pp. 153–70, I think that at this point the theory encounters serious difficulties with weak-willed intentional conduct. But here I am interested in other matters. The implicitly comparative nature of these all-out evaluations is clearer in Davidson's earlier discussion in 'How is weakness of the will possible?' than in his later discussion in 'Intending,' where he typically uses the apparently non-comparative predicate 'is desirable.' Suffice it to say here, in defense of my interpretation of these all-out evaluations as implicitly comparative, that if they really were non-comparative the problem of agglomerativity, discussed below, would arise even more immediately. It would be immediately clear that one could have future-directed all-out evaluations both in favor of going to the concert and in favor of not going.

[11] Davidson's main discussion of this feature of all-out evaluations is in 'Intending,' pp. 96–7. In this discussion he seems to me not to separate two different issues. First, there is the issue of when there can be *demonstrative reference* to a particular action. Here Davidson supposes that there can be no demonstrative reference to an event in the future. Second, there is the issue of what the property of desirability is a property *of*. Here Davidson's view is, I take it, that it is always a property of *particular* acts. As I see it, it is this second view that is critical to his discussion of future intention.

What about an all-out *comparison* that my action is better than certain alternatives? What does such a comparison compare my particular act *to*? The answer, I take it, is that it compares my particular act to other particular acts *of different types*, where the relevant types are determined by the alternatives I have considered.

instances of a given type of action may well vary in their desirability. Some ways of going to the concert (e.g. by hijacking a cab) will be quite undesirable. Only when we are given a particular action are we given something which is either desirable or not (relative to the agent's values).

We have so far seen the main outlines of Davidson's theory of intentional action. A theory of intentional action cannot, however, stand alone. It needs to be related to a plausible conception of future intention – intending (or, having an intention) now to do something later. After all, both phenomena in some sense involve *intent*; our theory needs to say in what sense.

I may now have various reasons – appropriate desire–belief pairs – in favor of going to the concert tomorrow. But such desires and beliefs do not suffice for an intention to go. What is the nature of the new state I am in when I come to intend to go?

Davidson's strategy here is to *extend* his account of the role of all-out evaluations in intentional action to the future-directed case. In just having reasons for acting in a certain way I only accept certain prima facie evaluative propositions. When I actually act for those reasons – and so act intentionally – I accept an appropriate all-out evaluative proposition. Similarly, on Davidson's theory, when I come to intend to go to the concert tomorrow I come to accept a future-directed all-out evaluative proposition in favor of going to the concert then: my future intention is this all-out evaluation. By extending his theory of intentional action in this way Davidson can ensure that future intention, like intentional action, can be a conclusion of practical reasoning. And he can exhibit a common feature in the two cases of intent.

However, Davidson sees a problem with this strategy. As we have seen, in the case of intentional action the involved judgment of all-out desirability is about a particular action; desirability is a property of particular acts, not of types of acts. But when I intend to go to the concert tomorrow I have in mind no single, particular act of concert-going. And there may well never be in the world an actual, particular concert-going to judge desirable. So, how could my intention be an all-out evaluation?

Granted, I could judge that *any* particular act of concert-going would be desirable, for such a judgment would still only ascribe desirability to particular acts.[12] But this would normally be an insane judgment. Some concert-goings – e.g., those that involve hijacking a cab – will surely be undesirable. Future intention should not require insanity.

Davidson's solution to this problem is couched in terms of a different example – that of intending to eat a sweet in a moment. Here is what he says:

> It would be mad to hold that any action of mine in the immediate future that is the eating of something sweet would be desirable. But there is nothing absurd in my judging that any action of mine in the immediate future that is the eating of something sweet would be desirable *given the rest of what I believe about the immediate future*. I do not believe I will eat a poisonous candy, and so that is not one of the actions of eating something sweet that my all-out judgment includes. (emphasis in the original)[13]

---

[12] As John Perry has emphasized to me in conversation.
[13] 'Intending,' p. 99.

Returning to our example, when I intend to go to the concert I judge that any act of mine that is both a concert-going and *whose other features are all consistent with my beliefs* would be desirable. I believe that I would not go to the concert by hijacking a cab. So the undesirability of going that way does not stop me from holding that any concert-going of mine that *is* consistent with my beliefs would be desirable. And that is just what I hold when I intend to go.

2 *Davidson's theory: belief conditions on intention*

We have now seen the main features of Davidson's theory of intentional action and future intention. On the latter theory, my beliefs provide a critical background for the all-out evaluations which are my future intentions. As Davidson puts it, my future intentions are 'conditioned by my beliefs.'[14] But having said this it remains unclear just what these beliefs must be. So let us ask just what I must believe for me to intend to go to the concert tonight.

Consider three candidates for necessary conditions for such a future intention:

(1) My going to the concert is consistent with my beliefs.
(2) I believe I will be able to go.
(3) I believe I will go.

Davidson sees his theory as imposing 1 as a requirement on my intention. He says that 'wishes for things that are not consistent with what one believes' cannot be intentions, for that is 'ruled out by our conception of an intention'.[15] His reasoning seems to be that if, in our example, my going to the concert is inconsistent with my beliefs, then there 'can be no judgment that such an action consistent with [my] beliefs is desirable. There can be no such intention.'[16]

What about 2? Note that 2 is not entailed by 1. It *is* necessary for 1 that I do not believe I will not be able to go. But my going may be consistent with my beliefs even though I do not actually believe I will be able to go. So we need to ask whether, on the theory, 2 is also required for intention.

I find Davidson's remarks on this issue unclear. At times he seems to think that 2 is indeed required.[17] But this cannot be his considered view. Let me note three reasons why.

---

[14] Ibid., p. 100.

[15] Ibid., p. 101.

[16] Ibid., p. 101. I am puzzled by this, for it seems that in such a case there *can* be a judgment that any concert-going act consistent with my beliefs would be desirable. Indeed, if this is ordinary universal quantification, it seems that the theory is in danger of saying that, once I believe I will not go, I get an intention to go by default. This suggests that Davidson is *adding* to his account of my future-directed all-out evaluation in favor of *A*-ing, the further condition that my *A*-ing be consistent with my beliefs. In any case, in what follows I will assume Davidson's interpretation of my future-directed all-out evaluation in favor of *A*-ing as requiring that my *A*-ing be consistent with my beliefs.

[17] For example, at one point he describes a future intention as a judgment in favor of 'something I think I can do' (ibid., p. 101).

The first concerns Davidson's discussion of 3. Grice and Harman have both argued that 3 is necessary for my intention.[18] In Grice's example I think I may well be in jail by tonight, and for that reason do not believe I will go to the concert. Grice claims that I then do not intend to go, but only, perhaps, hope to go or intend to go if I can.

Davidson disagrees. He claims that in such a case I still may intend to go, though it might be misleading for me simply to report this intention without mentioning my worries about jail. Now in such a case I surely will not satisfy 2. The whole point of the example is that I believe I may well be in jail, and for that reason do not actually believe I will be able to go to the concert. At most, I will not believe I will not be able to go, and so be in a position to satisfy 1. Since Davidson insists that in such a case I may still intend to go, he must not see 2 as necessary for my intention.

Second, in his discussion of Grice's paper Davidson seems to commit himself to the view that future intention cannot be subject to a stronger belief requirement than is intentional action.[19] So, for Davidson to accept 2 as a condition on my future intention, he would also have to suppose that to *A* intentionally I must believe, while I am *A*-ing, that I can *A*. But Davidson himself has an example that shows that this latter view is not plausible. I might try to make ten carbon copies of a paper on my typewriter while doubting that I can. Nevertheless, if I actually do make ten copies, if my success is due to my relevant skills, and if making ten copies is also my goal in acting[20] then I *intentionally* make ten copies. This shows that intentional action does not require a belief that one can so act. So, given his assumption about the relation between belief requirements on intentional action and future intention, Davidson cannot accept 2 as a condition on my future intention.

There is, finally, a third reason why Davidson must reject 2 as necessary for my intention. To explain this I need to touch on Davidson's approach to the distinction between simple and conditional intentions.

3 *Davidson's theory: simple and conditional intention*

Suppose my going to the concert is consistent with my beliefs, but I do not actually believe I will be able to. Perhaps I just do not know whether there will be any tickets left. I ask myself: would any concert-going act, consistent with my beliefs, be desirable?

There is an initial problem in answering this question. Let us call a condition whose presence I believe to be required for my being able to *A* an *enabling*

---

[18] H.P. Grice, 'Intention and uncertainty', *Proceedings of the British Academy*, 57 (1971), pp. 263–79; G. Harman, 'Practical reasoning,' *Review of Metaphysics*, 29 (1976), pp. 431–63.

[19] See his remarks in 'Intending,' p. 92. Let me note that in my view this assumption is quite dubious. It seems quite likely that I need a stronger belief about my ability to *A* to intend now to *A* later, than I do just to give *A* a try when the time comes.

[20] These last two qualifications are mine, not Davidson's, but I think they are needed to make the example convincing. I was convinced of the need for the second qualification by Harman's discussion in 'Willing and intending,' in R. Grandy and R. Warner (eds), *Philosophical Grounds of Rationality* (Oxford, forthcoming).

condition for A-ing. In our example, the availability of tickets is an enabling condition of my going to the concert. This condition is consistent with my beliefs, but not guaranteed by them. So among those future situations which are consistent with my beliefs there will be some in which this enabling condition will hold, and some in which it will not. When I try to answer my question, do I consider all of these future situations, or only those in which the appropriate enabling conditions obtain?

I think Davidson must suppose that I need consider only those future situations in which I *can* go to the concert. After all, there will be no *un*desirable concert-goings in those other situations, consistent with my beliefs. In answering my question, then, I limit my attention to futures consistent with my beliefs *and* in which obtain all enabling conditions for going to the concert. I limit my attention, for example, to those cases in which there are tickets left and ask whether, in such cases, my going would be desirable. I do this even if some enabling conditions, though consistent with my beliefs, are not guaranteed by my beliefs.

Suppose I conclude that any such concert-going act, consistent with my beliefs, would be desirable. And suppose I reach this conclusion even though some enabling conditions for my going – e.g., the availability of tickets – are not guaranteed by my beliefs. Do I *simply* intend to go; or do I have only the *conditional* intention to go if I can?

I think it is clear that Davidson's answer is that I simply intend to go; for consider his remarks about 'genuine conditional intentions':

> Genuine conditional intentions are appropriate when we explicitly consider what to do in various contingencies; for example, someone may intend to go home early from a party if the music is too loud. If we ask for the difference between conditions that really do make the statement of an intention more accurate and bogus conditions like 'if I can' ... it seems to me clear that the difference is this: bona fide conditions are ones that are reasons for acting that are contemporary with the intention. Someone may not like loud music now, and that may be why he now intends to go home early from the party if the music is too loud. His not being able to go home early is not a reason for or against his going home early, and so it is not a relevant condition for an intention.[21]

On Davidson's view, then, mere enabling conditions are not 'bona fide' conditions for 'genuine conditional intentions', for they are not 'reasons for acting that are contemporary with the intention.' The availability of tickets is, by itself, no reason for my going to the concert, though it is an enabling condition for my going. Of course, to intend to go I cannot believe such enabling conditions will *not* be present; for then I would not satisfy 1. But even if I do not actually believe they will all be present I may still have a simple intention to go.

In our example, then, I simply intend to go to the concert, despite my lack of belief in the availability of tickets. But then 2 cannot be necessary for my future intention.

---

[21] 'Intending,' pp. 94–5.

4 *The Buridan problem*

I now want to consider two interrelated problems for Davidson's theory. The first problem is an analogue of the old problem of Buridan's Ass. Buridan wondered how an ass, midway between two piles of hay judged equally desirable, could intentionally go to one.[22] Our problem concerns the possibility of *future* intention in the face of equally desirable future options.

Suppose I know I can stop at one of two bookstores after work, Kepler's or Printer's Inc., but not both. And suppose I find both options equally attractive. I judge all-out that any act of my stopping at Kepler's would be just as desirable as any act of my stopping at Printer's Inc., given my beliefs. Does it follow from Davidson's theory that I have both intentions? neither intention?

These questions highlight an unclarity in Davidson's discussion. An all-out desirability judgment in favor of *A*-ing is implicitly comparative. But there are weak and strong comparisons. A *weak* comparison would see *A*-ing as at least as desirable as its alternatives; a *strong* comparison sees *A*-ing as strictly more desirable than its alternatives. Which sort of comparison does Davidson's theory require for future intention?

There is a dilemma here. If all that is required is a weak comparison, then in the present case I both intend to go to Kepler's and intend to go to Printer's Inc. But this seems wrong. Recall that I know I cannot go to both stores. So I cannot, on Davidson's view, intend to go to both. But then, if I were to have each intention, I would be in a position in which I (rationally, we may suppose) intend to *A* and intend to *B*, but cannot intend to do both.

This violates a natural constraint on intention. Rational intentions should be *agglomerative*. If at one and the same time I rationally intend to *A* and rationally intend to *B* then it should be both possible and rational for me, at the same time, to intend to *A and B*. But if all that is required for future intention is a weak comparison, then intentions will not be agglomerative in this way.

Granted, many practical attitudes are not agglomerative. I might rationally desire to drink a milkshake for lunch and rationally desire to run four miles after lunch, and yet find the prospect of doing both appalling. But this is one way in which intentions differ from ordinary desires. Rational intentions are agglomerative, and this fact should be captured and explained by our theory.

This suggests that Davidson should insist that to intend to *A* I must hold a strong comparative evaluation in favor of *A*. Thus I neither intend to go to Keplers, nor intend to go to Printer's Inc. So, in the present case, agglomerativity is not threatened.

But now we have our Buridan problem. It seems that I can just decide on which bookstore to go to, while continuing to see each option as equally desirable. Such a decision provides me with an intention which does not correspond to a strong comparative evaluation. I might just decide to go to Kepler's, even though I do not judge all-out that so acting would be strictly

---

[22] For a useful discussion of such cases see E. Ullmann-Margalit and S. Morgenbesser, 'Picking and choosing,' *Social Research*, 44 (1977), pp. 757–85. I was first led to consider the relevance of such cases to Davidson's theory by a remark of Saul Kripke's.

more desirable than going to Printer's Inc. But the intention I thereby reach does not satisfy the demands of Davidson's theory as we are now interpreting it. In trying to avoid the horn of agglomerativity, Davidson's theory is threatened by the horn of a Buridan problem.

5 *A further problem with agglomerativity*

The second problem is that even if future intention requires a strong comparative evaluation, Davidson's theory still will not ensure that rational intentions are agglomerative. This results from the weak belief condition on intention.

An example will make my point. I have for a long time wanted to buy copies of *The White Hotel* and *The Fixer*, and know I will be at a bookstore this afternoon. Further, I know the bookstore will have one or the other of these novels in stock, but not both. Unfortunately, I do not know which one will be in stock.

I ask: would any act of my buying *The Fixer* be desirable, given my beliefs? In answering this I limit my attention to possible futures consistent with my beliefs and in which all enabling conditions – including the condition that *The Fixer* is in stock – obtain. And, let us suppose, I reasonably judge that any such act of buying *The Fixer* would be strictly better than its alternatives, and so, in the relevant sense, desirable. Note that the relevant alternatives here will include buying no novel, but will not include buying *The White Hotel*. This is because the latter is not open to me in any future which is both consistent with my beliefs and in which I can buy *The Fixer*. In this way I reach a simple intention to buy *The Fixer* this afternoon.

By an analogous route I might also reasonably judge that any act of my buying *The White Hotel* that is consistent with my beliefs would be desirable, thereby reaching an intention to buy *The White Hotel*.

Of course, in each case I do not believe all the required enabling conditions will obtain. But on Davidson's account that does not turn my intentions into mere conditional intentions to buy *The Fixer/The White Hotel* if I can. Rather, I both intend to buy *The Fixer* and intend to buy *The White Hotel*. And on Davidson's account both intentions might be perfectly reasonable.

But recall that I believe I cannot buy both novels. So it is not possible for me to intend to buy both. We are led to the result that though I rationally intend to buy *The Fixer*, and rationally intend to buy *The White Hotel*, it is not even possible for me to intend both to buy *The Fixer* and to buy *The White Hotel*. On Davidson's theory rational intentions may fail to be agglomerative. And that seems wrong.

6 *Intention and practical reasoning*

I now want to try to diagnose the source of this pair of difficulties. My conjecture is that both difficulties are in large part rooted in Davidson's conception of just what facts a theory of future intention must account for. In particular, I think Davidson's theory is constrained by an overly weak conception of the role of future intentions in further practical thinking.

To my knowledge, Davidson says almost nothing about this role. His picture seems to be that the basic inputs for practical reasoning about what to do – either now or later – will just be the agent's desires and beliefs. Such reasoning, when concerned with the future, can issue in future intentions. And these intentions are fundamentally different sorts of states than the desires and beliefs on which they are based. But there is no significant, further role for these intentions to play as inputs into one's further practical thinking. Future intentions are, rather, mere spin-offs of practical reasoning concerning the future.

This is an attenuated conception of the role of intention in practical reasoning. It receives support from Davidson's *strategy of extension*, the attempt to extend the materials present in his account of intentional action to an account of future intention. In intentional action, there is no temporal interval between all-out evaluation and action. So there is no room for further practical reasoning in which that all-out evaluation can play a significant role as an input. When we extend the notion of an all-out evaluation to the future-directed case, it will then be easy to overlook the possibility that *future* intentions *will*, at least typically, play such a role.

I believe that this limited conception of the role of future intentions in practical reasoning fails to accommodate the facts; for such intentions typically play an important role in our practical thinking. Moreover, I suspect that Davidson's acceptance of this limited conception may well account for his failure to be concerned with the pair of problems I have emphasized.

Let us begin with my first point. A theory of future intentions needs to explain why we ever *bother* to form them. Why don't we just cross our bridges when we come to them? One answer is that we want to avoid the need for deliberation at the time of action. But, more importantly, we form future intentions as parts of larger plans whose role is to aid *coordination* of our activities over time. Further, we do not adopt these plans, in all their detail, all at once. Rather, as time goes on we add to and adjust our plans. As elements in these plans, future intentions force the formation of yet further intentions and constrain the formation of other intentions and plans. For example, they force the formation of intentions concerning means, and constrain later plans to be consistent with prior plans.[23] This means that they play a significant role in our further practical thinking, in the ongoing creation and adjustment of our plans – a role Davidson neglects.

My second point is that Davidson's neglect of this role may well account for his neglect of the pair of problems I have emphasized. This is because this (neglected) role is a major source of the facts about future intentions that generate these problems.

Let us call the role my future intentions play in constraining and influencing the further construction and adjustment of my plans in pursuit of coordination, their *coordinating role*. Rational intentions will be capable of playing this role

---

[23] I discuss these and related ideas further in 'Taking plans seriously,' *Social Theory and Practice*, 9 (1983), pp. 271–87, and in 'Two Faces of Intention,' *Philosophical Review*, 93 (1984), pp. 375–405.

well. To do this they must be capable of being part of an overall plan that can successfully coordinate the agent's activities. So rational intentions are to be agglomerative.

Further, the search for coordination of my activities over time may sometimes require me to settle in advance on one of several options judged equally desirable. Perhaps in order to get on with my plans for the day I must settle now on one of the bookstores, despite their equal attractiveness. Or, having settled on a bookstore I must settle on a means to getting there, even if there are several equally desirable routes.

So, the coordinating role of future intentions underlies the further facts about future intentions that have been the basis of my pair of criticisms. This coordinating role both imposes a demand for agglomerativity and creates a need for the ability to settle in advance on one of several options judged equally desirable. If one's conception of the facts to be explained about future intention does not include this coordinating role, it may be easy for it also not to include these further facts.

My conjecture is that this is what happens to Davidson's theory. He begins with an attenuated conception of the role of intention in practical reasoning, a conception partly supported by his strategy of extension. This attenuated conception blocks from view the facts about agglomerativity and Buridan cases which I have emphasized, and allows Davidson to accept a theory that does not accommodate these facts. If this is right, Davidson's difficulties with agglomerativity and the Buridan problem are symptoms of a deeper problem. They are symptoms of an overly limited conception of the role of intentions and plans in rational motivation and practical reasoning.[24]

Appendix: Davidson's alternatives

When this paper originally appeared, it was accompanied by a useful reply from Professor Davidson.[25] There is much in Davidson's reply that merits discussion. But in this brief appendix I want to focus primarily on his reply to the problem raised in section 5 of my paper, for this reply raises interesting issues about the concept of an alternative. To anticipate: I distinguish three increasingly strong notions of an alternative, the weakest being the one Davidson embraces in his reply. I argue that the two weaker notions allow Davidson to escape my problem only at the cost of other difficulties. The third notion avoids these other difficulties but not my original problem.

My problem concerned an example in which I knew that either I would be able to buy *The Fixer* or I would be able to buy *The White Hotel*, but that I would

---

[24] I want to thank Robert Audi, Myles Brand, John Dupre, Dagfinn Føllesdal, John Perry, Howard Wettstein, and members of a Spring 1982 Stanford seminar, given jointly by John Perry and me, for their helpful comments and criticisms concerning this paper.

[25] My paper originally appeared, together with Davidson's 'Reply to Michael Bratman,' in *Essays on Davidson: Actions and Events*, ed. B. Vermazen and M. Hintikka (Oxford University Press, Oxford, 1985). I want to thank Oxford University Press for allowing my paper to be reprinted here, together with this new appendix.

not both be able to buy *The Fixer* and also be able to buy *The White Hotel*. My criticism was that on Davidson's theory I might reasonably both intend to buy *The Fixer* and intend to buy *The White Hotel*. As Davidson agrees in his reply, this would be an 'unwelcome result.'[26]

A natural view about this example is that my intentions are *conditional*: to buy *The Fixer if it is in stock*, and similarly with *The White Hotel*. But this view is ruled out by Davidson's account of conditional intentions; and Davidson's belief condition on simple (i.e., non-conditional) intentions is too weak to block simple intentions to buy each book. Davidson might have avoided my criticism by changing these aspects of his theory,[27] but that is not what he does. Instead he argues that the 'unwelcome result' does not follow from his theory.

Davidson has two arguments for this. The first begins with the claim that on his theory my buying *The Fixer* and my buying *The White Hotel* really are alternatives to each other. Here is what he says:

> [Bratman] imagines that he covets two books, *The Fixer* and *The White Hotel*, believes only one will be in stock, and knows not which. In this situation, he claims, buying *The White Hotel* is not an alternative to buying *The Fixer* since according to my analysis 'the latter is not open to me in any future which is both consistent with my beliefs and in which I can buy *The Fixer*.'[28] The trouble lies in the last phrase: on my analysis it would not be included. Since each purchase is consistent with his beliefs, each purchase is an alternative to the other.[29]

Since each purchase is an alternative to the other, I cannot (barring confusion) judge of each purchase that it is strictly the best of my alternatives. So I cannot intend to buy each book.

Davidson's second argument involves introducing a further option: buying the available book. He writes:

> If Bratman believes only one of the books he wants will be available, among the relevant options he can consider are: buy the available book, buy *The Fixer*, buy *The White Hotel*, buy *The Fixer* only, buy *The White Hotel* only, and buy neither. Under the circumstances, the first option is the one Bratman will rank highest, and it will determine his intention.[30]

So, Davidson thinks that my alternatives include not only buying *The Fixer* and buying *The White Hotel*, but also buying the available book. It is the latter that I should rank highest, and so, Davidson supposes, it is only the latter that I should intend.

On the first argument I cannot both intend to buy *The Fixer* and intend to buy *The White Hotel*, since each purchase is an alternative to the other. On the second argument I will neither intend to buy *The Fixer* nor intend to buy *The White Hotel*, since I will instead judge the alternative of buying the available

---

[26] Ibid., p. 198.
[27] As John Searle remarked in his comments on my paper at the Rutgers Conference.
[28] In quoting me Davidson has inadvertently switched the reference of 'the latter'.
[29] 'Reply to Michael Bratman', p. 198.
[30] Ibid., p. 199.

book to be best. Do these arguments succeed in blocking the unwelcome result?

They do, but at the cost of making Davidson's account of intention unacceptable for other reasons. To see why, consider Davidson's notion of an alternative. It seems clear that in his reply Davidson supposes that a type of action is an alternative of mine if my so acting is consistent with my beliefs.[31] That is why he supposes that buying *The Fixer*, buying *The White Hotel*, and buying the available book are all alternatives of mine. Let us call an alternative in this sense a *Davidsonian alternative*.

This is a very weak notion of an alternative. You can see this by noting two points. First, different Davidsonian alternatives of mine may be, by my lights, compatible with each other: It may be consistent with my beliefs that I perform *both* of two different Davidsonian alternatives. For example, both eating yogurt and thinking about my paper are Davidsonian alternatives of mine; yet I know I can think while I eat. Again, it is consistent with my beliefs that I both buy the available book and buy *The Fixer*. Yet they are both Davidsonian alternatives of mine. Second, I may know of my Davidsonian alternatives *A* and *B* that I will not be both able to *A* and able to *B*. Indeed, that is what I know about my Davidsonian alternatives of buying *The Fixer* and buying *The White Hotel*.

Now, Davidson wants to 'identify an intention to perform an action with an all-out judgment that any such action is more desirable than any alternative.'[32] The notion of alternative here presumably is just that of a Davidsonian alternative. And Davidson is right to insist that so interpreted his theory has the consequences he says it has: I cannot (barring confusion) intend to make each purchase; and if I do rank buying the available book highest I will neither intend to buy *The Fixer* nor intend to buy *The White Hotel*. But now the problem is that this account of intention has the other unwelcome consequence that it frequently rules out intending each of two *compatible* Davidsonian alternatives. If I prefer thinking about my paper to eating yogurt, it rules out my both intending to eat and intending to think, though I know I can do both. Perhaps it will be replied that the alternative I will rank highest will be eating while thinking, and so that is what I will intend. But then, on the theory, I will intend to eat while thinking, without intending to eat. And that seems wrong.

So if the notion of alternative at work in Davidson's account is that of a Davidsonian alternative, the theory avoids my problem at the cost of others. Still, it may be suggested that there is a stronger notion of an alternative that Davidson can use in his theory, a notion that avoids my problem but does not incur such costs. Let us see.

Consider a slightly stronger sense of 'alternative', which I will call the *weak, relational* sense. *A* is an alternative to *B* for agent *S* in this weak, relational sense just in case each is a Davidsonian alternative for *S*, but their joint performance is *not* a Davidsonian alternative for *S*. This notion of an alternative is relational in a way in which Davidson's is not; for it involves a relation between an act type and another act type to which it is an alternative. However, it is still a rather

---

[31] Throughout I assume that the alternatives in question are alternatives *for the same occasion* – for example, the occasion of my arrival at the bookstore. In my formulations of different conditions of 'alternative-hood' I suppress reference both to this occasion and to the time at which the relevant beliefs are held.

[32] 'Reply to Michael Bratman,' p. 198.

weak notion of an alternative, for it does not require that *S* believe (or that it be true) that he is or will be able to do each. My buying *The Fixer* and my buying *The White Hotel* are alternatives to each other in this weak, relational sense. However, neither is a weak, relational alternative to my buying the available book, since the joint performance of buying *The Fixer* (*The White Hotel*) and buying the available book *is* a Davidsonian alternative for me.

Suppose now that the notion of alternative at work in Davidson's account of intention is this weak, relational notion. An intention is an all-out judgment that a certain type of action is better than its weak, relational alternatives. This blocks the second argument. Since my buying the available book and my buying *The Fixer* are not weak, relational alternatives to each other, nothing stands in the way of my intending each. But it also seems to allow for a forceful version of the first argument. Since each purchase is a weak, relational alternative to the other, the account of intention has the consequence that I cannot (barring confusion) intend each.

But, again, there are other costs. Suppose I prefer *The White Hotel* to *The Fixer*. I judge buying *The White Hotel* to be more desirable than any of its weak, relational alternatives – including the alternative of buying *The Fixer*. But I make no such favorable judgment about buying *The Fixer*. So, on the present reading of Davidson's theory, I will non-conditionally intend to buy *The White Hotel* but not intend to buy *The Fixer*. Nor will I conditionally intend to buy *The Fixer* if it is in stock, since that is ruled out by Davidson's treatment of conditional intentions. So I will non-conditionally intend to buy *The White Hotel*, but have no intention to buy *The Fixer*.

But this seems wrong. Given my belief that it is equally likely that either will be in stock, my preference for *The White Hotel* should not create such an asymmetry in my intentions concerning the different purchases.

It might be thought that Davidson should reply with an even stronger notion of alternative, namely: for *B* to be an alternative relevant to the intention to *A* it must not only be a weak, relational alternative to *A*, it must also be such that it is consistent with the agent's beliefs that he will be both able to *B* and able to *A*. But this prevents the unwelcome asymmetry only at the cost of returning us to my original problem. Since on this theory buying *The Fixer* and buying *The White Hotel* are no longer alternatives to each other, the theory will now have the consequence that I may reasonably both intend to buy *The Fixer* and intend to buy *The White Hotel*.

I am unable, then, to discover a notion of alternative for use in Davidson's theory of intention that enables Davidson to avoid all unwelcome results without change to his theory.

I close with a brief response to Davidson's reply to my 'Buridan problem.' Davidson writes:

> sometimes we have to decide even when we can find no obvious grounds for decision. But if there is reason to reach some decision, and there are no obvious or intrinsic grounds for decision, we find extrinsic grounds. Perhaps I flip a coin to decide. My need to choose has caused me to prefer the alternative indicated by the toss; a trivial ground for preference, but a good enough one in the absence of others.[33]

---

[33] Ibid., p. 200.

In this way Davidson maintains that when, in my example, I plump for going to Kepler's I must reach a *strong* all-out evaluation in favor of Kepler's over Printer's Inc.

I remain sceptical, for the reason given by Ullman-Margalit and Morgenbesser.[34] Consider the suggestion that I toss a coin. Why does heads 'indicate' Kepler's rather than Printer's Inc.? Presumably because I have made this arbitrary assignment, rather than the equally desirable alternative assignment. So we still have a decision that seems unaccompanied by a strong, comparative evaluation, namely: my decision to assign 'heads' to Kepler's. Must I judge all-out that this assignment is strictly better than its alternative? The problem seems only to have been pushed back.[35]

---

[34] 'Picking and choosing,' pp. 769–70.

[35] Thanks to John Dupre for his helpful comments on the penultimate draft of this appendix. Work on this appendix was assisted by a grant from the American Council of Learned Societies under a program funded by the National Endowment for the Humanities, as well as by support from the Center for the Study of Language and Information. I thank both for their support.

2

Davidson on Intentional Action

GEORGE M. WILSON

Donald Davidson's 'Actions, reasons, and causes' undoubtedly marks a prominent turning point in analytical theory of action. It appeared at a time when there was a substantial consensus that an agent's reasons for acting could not be among the causes of his actions performed for those very reasons. In particular, it was widely believed that there was a knockdown argument to this conclusion based upon the purported existence of a 'conceptual connection' between reasons and actions, a quasi-logical connection that was supposed to exclude causation from the field. Davidson's article achieved two results whose correctness and importance remain unscathed. First, he laid bare much of the poverty and obscurity that infected the 'conceptual connection' arguments then being circulated. Second, he made poignant the question, 'If reasons can't be causes, how then do they explain actions?' He correctly pointed out that there were no tolerably clear answers to this query forthcoming from the crowd of non-causalists. Actually, these two achievements stand together. If one supposes that one knows *a priori* that reason explanations of action can't be causal, then one can explore the ramifications of this dramatic discovery without worrying overmuch about the absence of a detailed account of how, alternatively, these explanations do work. But when the *a priori* conviction begins to wane, the philosophical void looms as more embarrassing. Davidson's classic essay encouraged such a waning and suggested thereby that maybe reasons had better be causes after all.

In this paper, I wish to re-examine this central line of thought in 'Actions, reasons, and causes' and to argue that *there is* a plausible non-causalist view that Davidson's considerations do not at all exclude.[1] Indeed, I will try to show that

---

[1] In the first two-thirds of this paper I attempt to restate the central issue of the last two chapters of my monograph *The Intentionality of Human Action* (North-Holland, Amsterdam, 1980). Although the general line of argument remains the same, I have changed or modified some specifics. More importantly, perhaps, I have tried to state what I take to be the main issue in a more direct, less cluttered, and more intuitive fashion. In doing so, I have sacrificed some precision, a number of qualifications, and a range of developments to be found in the earlier work. But I hope that the overall *force* of my argument is clearer here. The remainder of the paper is wholly new, but it could not have been easily formulated without the material that precedes it.

the old debate, in a somewhat new form, deserves to be re-opened. Toward the end of the paper I will comment on some of his more recent thoughts on intentional action as they appear in the article 'Intending', explaining why the modified views expressed there seem not to touch the fundamental issue that I want to be raising for a new round of sustained reflection.

It is important, I think, to take some care in describing the issues that divide a causalist like Davidson from a non-causalist like, e.g., the Melden of *Free Action*. The question between them *cannot* be this: if an agent φ's for some reason R, does it follow that (in some sense or other) the agent's having R caused him or her to φ? It is of some significance here to recall that the term 'cause' does have a variety of different uses. A person may have to show cause for something she did or various facts about her situation may give her some cause for acting in a certain way. In these uses, 'cause' seems to mean something like 'ground' or 'rational basis' and, as such, they seem distinct from uses making reference to the notorious connection between fire and smoke. Therefore, the non-causalist can and probably should allow that if the agent φ'd for reason R, then her having R did cause her to φ, while holding that the consequent of this conditional has roughly the following sense: the agent (in virtue of R) had cause to φ and performed the relevant act of φing for the sake of achieving or promoting that very cause. We will return to this thought in a moment.

But then, how should the controversy between the causalist and the non-causalist be stated? Well, it seems clear that Davidson himself holds and various non-causalists deny the following thesis: if an agent φ'd for reason R, then the agent's state of having R as a reason was a cause or causal condition of the relevant concrete act of φing. Or again, suppose that M is the bodily movement or series of bodily movements that the agent performed in φing at the given time. Then Davidson holds and non-causalists deny that if the agent acted for reason R, then his state of having R was a cause or causal condition of those very movements M. (Naturally, if, like Davidson, one identifies the act of φing with the movements, then the two theses come to the same thing.) In these formulations, the causality that is appealed to appears as a relation between events and/or particular occurrences of states and therefore ought to be the 'Humean' causation of the physical sciences.

Moreover, it *is* precisely for theses such as these that Davidson presents the well-known argument of 'Actions, reasons, and causes.' Here are a couple of central and characteristic passages from that article.

> Talk of pattern and contexts does not answer the question of how reasons explain action .... One way we can explain an event is by placing it in the context of its cause; cause and effect form the sort of pattern that explains the effect, in a sense of 'explain' that we understand as well as any. If reason and action illustrate a different pattern of explanation, that pattern must be identified.[2]

Or again, a little later, 'Failing a satisfactory alternative, the best argument for a

---

[2] 'Actions, reasons, and causes,' reprinted in *Essays on Actions and Events* (Oxford University Press, New York, 1980), p. 10.

causal scheme like Aristotle's is that it *alone* promises to give an account of the "mysterious" connection between reasons and actions.'[3] In these and related remarks, Davidson is presenting the non-causalist with a certain precise challenge. He points out that if the agent's reason for φing was to ψ, then it must be that the agent φ'd on that occasion *because* he wanted to ψ—or, because he had some other pro-attitude toward ψing. (I will ignore the associated instrumental belief for the time being.) However, this last explanatory statement will not be true unless there was some connection between the agent's wanting to ψ and his particular act of φing, a connection *in virtue of which* the desire explains *why* he φ'd. Or we can state this in a slightly different way. We feel that it should be possible to understand *how* the fact that the agent wanted to ψ explains (when it does) why he φ'd on the given occasion. And this means, at a minimum, that there must be some definite relation that holds between his wanting to ψ and his act of φing which makes the explanatory claim true. So, what relation or connection could this be? Having raised this question sharply and with a proper emphasis on its key importance, Davidson goes on to point out that (1) event-causation *is* a connection of the required kind, and (2) if no 'satisfactory alternative' can be specified, then rationalizations of action presuppose that desire and act must be causally linked. Finally, it is clear that Davidson holds that no such satisfactory alternative is to be found. Thus he states, in summary, 'If, as Melden claims, causal explanations are "wholly irrelevant to the understanding we seek" of human action, then we are *wholly without an analysis* of the "because" in "He did it because ..." where we go on to name a reason.'[4] This I take to be the central positive argument of 'Actions, reasons, and causes.'

It is at this juncture that the issues become murkier and more difficult. For, to make a start at this, it can certainly seem as though there *is* an alternative that Davidson does not consider. Moreover, it is an alternative suggested by much in Anscombe's *Intention* and by some remarks in Melden, Charles Taylor, and others. Indeed, the heart of the alternative I have in mind is found pretty explicitly in Daniel Bennett's 'Action, reason, and purpose.'[5] But I will formulate the view in my own fashion. If a person comes to have a certain desire, then it is natural to say that a certain type of action, event, or state of affairs has become for her a potential *objective*. If she wants to ψ, then she views her ψing in the future as being at least logically possible and as being in some way and to some degree desirable. Thus, that she is to ψ is for her a potential end, goal, or, once more, a potential objective. And now, if she actually goes on to φ *because* she wants to ψ (where this gives a reason), then that she is to ψ becomes for her an actual objective *of her act of φing*. That is, her act of φing is performed *for the purpose of* bringing about the type of ψing that she desires. Her act of φing and, in particular, the bodily movements she executes in that φing, are performed *in order to* realize the objective embodied in her desire. And yet, doesn't this provide the sort of alternative that the non-causalist requires? Can't it be claimed that the relation '——— was for the purpose of satisfying ...' should

---

[3] Ibid., p. 11.
[4] Ibid., p. 11.
[5] Bennett's article is in *Journal of Philosophy*, LXII (1965), pp. 85–95.

stand in place of event-causation as *the* explanatory connection between an action and a desire that rationalizes it?

I have formulated all of this in a tentative fashion, for it is certain that Davidson would reject this last proposal as *not* offering a 'satisfactory alternative' to his causalist account. It is not, I think, that Davidson would not accept the thrust of the early remarks in the previous paragraph. Rather, it is that it seems a clear part of the overall conception of 'Actions, reasons, and causes' that the 'teleological connectives' in:

$$\text{The act of } \phi\text{ing was } \textit{for the purpose of } \psi\text{ing}$$

and:

$$\text{That act was performed } \textit{in order to } \psi$$

are *themselves* to be explicated (within the domain of intentional action) in terms of a causal relation between the action and the agent's having the relevant primary reason. Hence, a teleological statement of these and related forms is supposed to *strictly entail* that the act of ϕing was caused by the agent's pro-attitude toward ψing. It is easiest to see how 'Actions, reasons, and causes' commits itself fairly explicitly to such a reductive thesis if we first link these present uses of the teleological connectives with certain kinds of propositions about the agent's intentions in acting.

Certainly, talk about the purpose of a specified intentional act is inextricably tied to the concept of the intention the agent had *in* performing that very act. Although 'purpose' and 'intention (in action)' are not synonyms in this domain, they run as a pair across the relevant discourse. For example, if a person performed a certain movement of his hand for the purpose of flipping the switch, then it will be the case that *in* performing that very movement, he intended to flip the switch. And if the person flipped the switch in order to turn on the light, then he flipped the switch *with* the intention of turning on the light. In general, when we are dealing with intentional action, a statement like:

$$\text{He } \phi\text{'d for the purpose of } \psi\text{ing}$$

can be exchanged in favor of:

$$\text{In } \phi\text{ing, he intended to } \psi$$

or, in most cases:

$$\text{He } \phi\text{'d with the intention of } \psi\text{ing.}[6]$$

---

[6] Although most uses of 'A ϕ'd with the intention of ψing' will purport to give a reason why A ϕ'd, there are plenty of exceptions to this. It may be true that Gloria ate her dinner with the intention of going to the movies afterwards but false that going to the movies (after dinner) was among the reasons why she ate her dinner. I have included the 'with' locution here since this is the form that Davidson tends to employ when his remarks touch upon intention in action.

Now, despite some obscurity of formulation, it seems unquestionable that in 'Actions, reasons, and causes' Davidson envisaged the existence of some causalist analysis of statements about an intention an agent had in acting or with which he acted at the time in question. Consider, for example, the following well-known and somewhat gnomic passage. 'The expression "the intention with which James went to church" has the outward form of a description, but in fact it is syncategorematic and cannot be taken to refer to an entity, state, disposition, or event. Its function is to generate new descriptions of actions in terms of their reasons.[7] The force of this, I assume, is to claim that 'He φ'd with the intention of ψing' is to be analyzed as (roughly) 'He performed an act of φing which was caused (in the right way) by his desire to ψ and his belief that φing was a means of ψing'. In this way, the apparent reference to something called 'an intention' would disappear under an analysis conceived in this fashion.

This idea that there is or should be some causalist reduction of the concept of intention or purpose in action is crucial to the program of 'Actions, reasons, and causes.' If the idea is right, then the non-causalist account of reasons for action that I sketched a few pages earlier cannot be satisfactory and the Davidsonian argument that I rehearsed there will, as far as I can see, be sound. But we should not become confused. The soundness of that central argument presupposes the existence of the causalist reduction and does not argue for it. Indeed, it seems to me that Davidson's work on action contains no argument to show that intention and purpose in action can be explicated along the envisaged lines. At any rate, the enlightened non-causalist should dispute this claim. For him or her, the attempt to provide such an analysis is to be regarded as a misbegotten effort to convert explanations which are primitively grounded upon purpose and intention in action into a kind of ersatz causal explanation.

We can better understand what is at stake in the controversy I am trying to delineate if we take the topic of 'intention in action' a step or two further. The first step is this. Suppose that a person performs a certain definite movement of her hand and, *in* doing so, she intended to flip the switch. Then it follows from this assertion that she intended *of this very movement* that it flip the switch. And, if *in* flipping the switch, she thereby meant to turn on the light, then it follows that she performed some act of flipping the switch and intended *of that act* that it (by flipping the switch) was to make the light turn on. In other words, ascription of an intention in action essentially involves an ascription of intention which is *de re* with respect to some individual act of the action-type which the agent has been said, in that ascription, to have performed. Therefore, minimal analysis of ascriptions of intention in action seem to lay bare a patently *de re* use of 'A intends (act) x to φ' which has, beyond its being *de re*, quite a special set of semantical properties. That is, the form in question is satisfied (if at all) by an act which is:

(1) performed by the agent A, and
(2) occurs at the time of the ascribed intention, and

---

[7] Davidson, 'Actions, reasons, and causes', p. 8.

(3) consists of *voluntary* behavior (e.g., voluntary movements) of A's; and where
(4) the existence and intentional character of this behavior are matters of which
A is immediately aware without observation – in Anscombe's sense of that
phrase.

Since this is important for my present concerns, let me clarify and lay stress
upon these features which I take to be so peculiar and central to ascriptions of
intention in action. First, in saying of a relevant use of 'A intended of (act) x that
it φ', that it is *de re*, I have in mind at least the following: (1) intuitively, a definite
singular term in place of 'x' genuinely makes reference or purports to make
reference to an action of A's, and (2) existential generalization at that position is
accordingly valid. This, of course, assumes that quantification into that position
makes sense. However, the logical situation here is complicated, as Daniel
Bennett and others have observed, by the fact that the 'x' position seems
normally to be referentially *translucent*. That is, the inference from, e.g.,

> Bruno intended of his act of flipping the switch that it turn on the
> light

together with:

> his act of flipping = his act of alerting the burglar

to the conclusion:

> Bruno intended of his act of alerting the burglar that it turn on the
> light

seems to be, in general, invalid. The trouble arises, I think, from the following
fact. The most natural reading of an unregimented English form like:

> A intended his act of φing to ψ

is:

> A intended of his act of φing that it *thereby* ψ,

where the latter means:

> A intended of his act of φing that it, by φing, ψ.

Thus, in the little argument above, it is natural to think that we are going from
the true claim that Bruno intended of his act that it, by flipping the switch, turn
on the light to the false conclusion that Bruno intended of that act that it, by
alerting the burglar, turn on the light. My view is that the normal translucency
of these contexts is to be explained thus as analogous to the translucency of the
subject position in Quine's:

Giorgione was so called because of his size.

If we guard against implications of the normal ellipsis in 'A intended (act) x to φ', the argument with which we began seems fine to me.

Of course, in saying this, I am assuming that there is a literal, non-elliptical use of:

> Bruno intended of his act of alerting the burglar that it, by flipping the switch, turn on the light

which contains 'his act of alerting the burglar' in a purely *transparent* position and where the thought expressed can be true where Bruno simply alerted the burglar by turning on the light and did this by flipping the switch. But some would deny this. Notice, however, that such a person would have to deny that 'his act of alerting the burglar' is equivalent to 'the act of his which alerted the burglar.' There is nothing odd in the statement:

> Bruno intended of the act of his which alerted the burglar that it, by flipping the switch, turned on the light.

In a similar vein, I believe that there are various devices that cancel whatever oddness may seem to attach to the form of ascription now under scrutiny. For example:

> Bruno intended of his act which – as things turned out – was an act of alerting the burglar that it, by flipping etc.

sounds to me equivalent to its counterpart with 'the act of his which alerted the burglar.' Actually, I suspect that the intuition that Bruno simply can't be intending of his act of alerting the burglar that it flip the switch etc. rests on the common idea that 'the act of alerting the burglar' must refer to the whole causal activity between, say, the movements Bruno then performed and the onset of alertness in the burglar. Like Davidson, I think this is wrong, but, in any case, for someone with this view the problem at hand does not arise since the original identity statement will be, for such a person, false. These remarks on this topic are probably too brief, but it seems worth saying *something* here since this matter of translucency has obscured the fundamental *de re* character of ascriptions of intention in action.

In the second place, I want to emphasize that it is not merely the *de re* nature of these ascriptions that gives them their peculiar semantical status. The content of a hope or of a desire about my actions is likely to be general, i.e., I want to perform some act of φing or I hope that I will do some φing. But, there are also ascriptions of hope and desire that are, in a similar way, *de re* with respect to an action of the agent cited. Thus, John wants this present gesture of his to be noticed and Alice hopes concerning this act of kicking of hers that it will knock over the chair. Nevertheless, ascriptions of intention in action differ greatly from such *de re* ascriptions of pro-attitudes. John can also (if, for example, he observes it) hope concerning Alice's kicking that it knock over the lamp, and she may be in a position to share his desire about his gesture that it be noticed. But John and Alice cannot strictly *intend* of the other's action that *it* be such-and-such or so-and-so. Further, John may hope and desire about some purely involuntary movement of his that it has some agreeable consequence, but he can't *intend* of such a movement anything at all. Having a desire or hope concerning some voluntary or involuntary act of mine or another's is simply the having of a pro-attitude toward a certain type of states of affairs which essentially involves the specific action in question. I take up some sort of favorable view toward the relevant type of situation in which that action figures.

However, to say that I intend of my action that it has a certain effect or character is to convey something more than that I have some special *positive view* of the possible consequences of an act of mine. The more, unfortunately, is easier to state than to analyze. An ascription of intention in action conveys that the action – or the bodily movements in which the action consisted – was *directed* by its agent *toward* the achievement of some objective that he had in mind. It was *aimed at* bringing about a desired state of affairs; it was *guided* by the agent *toward* some end he valued.[8] In fact, it is just this central aspect of the concept of an intention in action that links it so directly to the concept 'a purpose of a specific action.'[9] When I hope or desire of my involuntary trembling that it have some positive result, that act of trembling does not have a purpose for me just because no exercise of my bodily control has made it the case that the trembling is aimed by me at the realization of an objective that I have in view.

Actually, I think the concept of 'intention' adds still another very difficult idea. If a person in a delirium, unthinkingly and unaware of what he is doing, reaches out for a familiar glass of water beside his bed, then it does seem true that the movement of his hand was directed and aimed at securing the glass – it had just that purpose for him. Still, I think, the very same movement was not *intended* by him to secure the glass. And this is because he was not conscious either of the act itself or of the purpose that it had. The concept of an intention in action requires that the action or movement be *consciously* directed or *consciously* aimed at the objective in question. I wish I knew how this qualification about consciousness of and in action is to be explained, but it is enough for current purposes if it is agreed that it is among the bases of our notion of intention in action.

At #647 in the *Philosophical Investigations*, Wittgenstein says, 'What is the natural expression of an intention? – Look at a cat when it stalks a bird; or a

---

[8] My views here share a certain important kinship with those of Harry Frankfurt in 'The problem of action,' *American Philosophical Quarterly*, Vol. 15 (1978), pp. 157–62.

[9] This link seems a special case of the still broader tie between the concept of 'having a purpose' and the concept of 'being directed at an end' where these concepts apply to processes and activities quite generally. Thus, I take it that there is a trivial equivalence between, e.g., 'The pumping of my heart has the purpose of maintaining the circulation of my blood' and 'The pumping of my heart is directed at maintaining the circulation of my blood.' Of course, we don't suppose that the pumping is directed by my heart or by any agent, let alone that is *consciously* directed by some agent. My thought is only that the biological concept of 'direction toward an end' and the concept of 'intention in action' belong to the same specifically 'teleological' *family* of concepts. For some more on this, see chapter VII of *The Intentionality of Human Action*.

beast when it wants to escape!'[10] From our present vantage point, I would gloss this remark as follows. We *see* in the stalking movements of the cat and in the restless prowling of the beast the fact that the behavior is directed by the creature at the obvious objective in each instance. These are paradigms for us of goal-directed activity and our concept of intention in action has a fundamental grounding in such cases. It is here that we find the foundations, such as they are, of the concept of animal and of human agency. For surely it is an important part of what it is to become a human agent that one forms the ability to guide and regulate one's behavior in a manner appropriate to the content of one's desires and to the circumstances as one believes them to be. One is able, for example, to coordinate the various segments of a stretch of activity in such a way that, given one's beliefs about the way things are, the sequence of actions can be expected to realize some objective that one holds. Except for the simplest acts serving the simplest basic functions, this involves the mastery of a great number of motor skills. Beyond this, one develops the capacity for calculating the probable consequences of a course of action in a perceived situation and to integrate, with seeming appropriateness, the physical interventions that one makes with the calculations that back them. That is, we also master an increasing repertoire of variously sophisticated physical *and* mental behavior and learn how to employ interrelated combinations of this behavioral repertoire in getting what we want. All this, of course, is more than familiar, but it reminds us of the terrain upon which the concept of an intention in action finds its first and most salient points of application.

I have lingered a bit upon these matters because they will allow me to explain (I hope) more clearly some observations I want to make about Davidson's early views about intentional action and its explanation. First, I have already claimed that Davidson is committed to there being a certain type of causalist analysis of the teleological connectives when they are invoked on the subject of intentional action. And, I have further asserted that this is tantamount to proposing such a causalist analysis of the concept of an intention in action. When we ask, 'Why did A ϕ?', making the assumption that he did so intentionally, our question could be recast as a specific question about the intention he had in ϕing. We take for granted that he performed some act of ϕing which was intended to ϕ and we ask for a *further* intention (if any) that he had in performing that act. This means, it seems to me, that we ask for a further description of the *specific* intention he had in performing that particular act. Our 'why' question is, in effect, just this: He performed an act of ϕing and he intended of that act that it, by ϕing, was to do *what*? This also casts light, I think, on the role of the agent's relevant instrumental belief in such an explanation. In saying or otherwise conveying about the agent that she intended of her act that it, by ϕing, was to ψ we do not simply presuppose that she believed that an act of ϕing would or might lead to ψing. We presuppose much more specifically that she believed *of her actual act* that it, by ϕing, would or might be ψ. It is this belief that conditions, so to speak, the very existence of the ascribed intention in action and therefore is a necessary ground of the relation upon which the explanation essentially depends. As such, it need not and probably cannot be a cause of the

---

[10] Ludwig Wittgenstein, *Philosophical Investigations* (Macmillan, New York, 1953), p. 165e.

action which is its subject. In any case, if someone asks, for instance, 'Why did she flip the switch?', it is a direct answer to this to say, 'She (thereby) intended to turn on the light.' And, in giving this answer, we not only redescribe the action, but we also give a fuller redescription of an intention she had in performing it.

If the core of my recent discussion is sound, then the project of analysis to which Davidson is committed in 'Actions, reasons, and causes' aims at making good the thesis that there is some causalist reduction of the use of 'A intends of act x that it φ' which I have been trying to describe. Moreover, I think we can roughly summarize the conceptual situation this creates in the following way. As I have claimed earlier, it is not just that these ascriptions of intention in action are *de re* with respect to an agent's action. I want to say that they are, in a certain sense, *quasi-de se* as well. That is, if I make a *de se* ascription of belief to a person A, then I ascribe to him a belief which is *de re* about himself *and* my words entail that, in holding that belief, he conceives of himself in a certain privileged, 'first-person' kind of way. Analogously, if I ascribe an intention in acting to A, then I ascribe to him an intention which is *de re* about his action and my words entail that he is acquainted with and is in control of the relevant behavior also in a privileged and 'first-person' kind of way. This then is the very special concept which is purportedly to be analyzed in terms of some elaboration of the idea that the behavior in question must be caused by some general desire of the agent in conjunction with a suitable, general instrumental belief. Putting things in this way, we see what we have – a project essentially similar to more familiar attempts to reduce *de re* and even *de se* ascriptions of belief to *de dicto* ascriptions of belief which have been subjected to a range of further, restrictive conditions. Indeed, I've argued elsewhere that, not only are the projects largely the same, but that Davidson's approach to intention in action is closely parallel to some of the more notable strategies utilized when the topic is belief.[11]

My own conviction is that none of these reductive projects can succeed. For our present problem – the status of intention in action – my negative conclusion is not something I think that I can prove. There are, naturally, an indefinite number of possible elaborations of the causalist's basic analysis and I don't see how all are to be sweepingly ruled out. Nevertheless, I can use the considerations developed thus far to explain why my scepticism is so deep and broad. There is, of course, a well-known range of counterexamples to causalist analyses which various authors have devised. We are now in a position to characterize the basic fact that this range of counterexamples seems to reveal.

Here, as one reminder, is an example that Davidson himself has given.

> A climber might want to rid himself of the weight and danger of holding another man on a rope, and he might know that by loosening his hold on the rope he could rid himself of the weight and danger. This belief and want might so unnerve him as to cause him to loosen his hold, and yet it might be the case that he never *chose* to loosen his hold, nor did he do it intentionally.[12]

In our terms, the climber did not intend of the relevant movement of his fingers

---

[11] See *The Intentionality of Human Action*, pp. 188–9.
[12] 'Freedom to act,' in *Essays on Actions and Events*, p. 79.

that it released the rope from his hands and no other type of effect, for that matter, was thereby intended either.

There are other examples which work in somewhat different ways, but what all the different kinds of counterexamples conspire to show is this. If, as I have been suggesting, the central problem is to analyze the relevant use of 'A intended of x that it φ' then there seems to be more wrong here that an incidental infelicity of formulation. It is granted on all sides than an appropriate pair of desire and instrumental belief can, in proper circumstances, be a cause of a range of wholly involuntary responses: e.g., blushing, sweating, fainting, and uncontrollable crying. But such responses always could include involuntary movements performed by the agent. What is more, it is always possible – no matter how unlikely it may be – for one of these involuntary movements or series of movements to satisfy *purely by accident* the descriptive content of the antecedent of the instrumental belief that rationalizes it. This will remain true no matter how much one tries to restrict the scope or character of what that content may be. The general consequence of this fact is that causalist analyses seem, in the end, to do *nothing* to mark the difference between, on the one hand, a mere behavioral effect of a desire–belief pair that satisfies a designated content by sheer happenstance and, on the other, a piece of behavior which is genuinely intended by its agent to achieve or promote an end. Finally, I think that the ultimate source of this failure is the specific failure to capture the very special idea that intentional action is continuously and consciously directed by the agent at a desired or valued end. Causalism leaves the matter of the agent's sentient control of his intentional action in relation to an objective entirely out of the picture. It also ignores, it seems to me, the fact that intention in action is a relation that can answer suitable 'why' questions on its own.

Of course, it has become standard practice to require that the causation operate 'in the right way.' And perhaps some kind of non-question-begging substance can be given to this notion. But doing so is bound to be at least difficult. The right way must be enough to ensure that the agent's state of having a certain reason causes his behavior to have the content of the desire as its target in a manner that accords with or seems to the agent to accord with the content of the instrumental belief. The prospects of finding a type of causal route that can offer this sort of guarantee seem grim to me.

I hasten to add that, at least since 'Actions, reasons, and causes,' Davidson has shared my grim outlook on this topic, although, no doubt, his diagnosis of the underlying troubles would be different. In 'Freedom to act,' before giving the counterexample I just quoted, he says, 'What I despair of spelling out is the way in which attitudes must cause actions if they are to rationalize the action.'[13] And, after sketching the causalist account in the article 'Intending,' he grants, 'We would not, it is true, have shown how to *define* the concept of acting with an intention; the reduction is not definitional but ontological.'[14] What puzzles me in all this is the following. Given the admitted non-existence of any such worked-out reduction (whether definitional or not), what then is the basis of the continuing assumption that reasons must be causes of intentional action and so

---

[13] Ibid., p. 79.
[14] 'Intending,' in *Essays on Actions and Events*, p. 88.

that there must be causing which is in 'the right way'? Once again, I will not attempt to canvas the possibilities, but my central point has been this. *If* that basis is given by the original central argument in 'Actions, reasons, and causes,' then those grounds are radically inadequate in the absence of the once hoped-for reduction. The failure of the reduction guarantees that an alternative, based on intention in action, does certainly exist. It is my impression that this point has not been clear, and it has not been appreciated that the alternative generated by intention in action recaptures a view that some earlier non-causalists were eager to defend.

By the time of his 1978 paper 'Intending,' Davidson's perspective on these issues has become more complex.[15] In that essay he reaffirms, although with reservations, his familiar causalist position, but he also indicates that in the course of his discussion he will introduce a substantial modification of his earlier treatment of intentional action. For instance, he asserts, 'Our inability to give a satisfactory account of pure intending [of having a general intention for the future] on the basis of our account of intentional action thus reflects back on the account of intentional action itself. And I believe the account I have outlined [the old one] will be seen to be incomplete when we have an adequate analysis of pure intending.'[16] In the remainder of the present essay, I wish, in short fashion, to raise some questions about how the proposed modification is to be understood.

The chief aim of Davidson's paper is to give a positive account of general intention for the future, and I will say nothing here about the success or failure of that aim. However, one point should be clear. It is *not* a thesis of Davidson's paper that the earlier view of intentional action (and, thus, intention in action) is to be modified by substituting general future-directed intentions in the place of desires and other pro-attitudes within the original model. For one thing, Davidson is willing to allow, correctly I think, that there are cases of intentional action where no relevant general intention makes an appearance. Second, simply replacing desires etc. as causes with general intentions does nothing to improve substantively the bleak prospect for a causalist analysis that I have already sketched.

Actually, I take it that the principal innovation in 'Intending' is specified in this passage: 'With respect to the first point, finding an account of intending that would mesh with our account of intentional action, we devised a satisfactory way of relating the two concepts, but only by introducing a new element, an *all-out judgment*, into the analysis of intentional action.'[17] So the question becomes: what is an all-out judgment and how is it employed to modify the basic causalist account of intentional action?

With reference to the first half of this question, Davidson states,

> It is a reason for acting that the [type of] action is believed to have some desirable characteristic, but the fact that the action is performed represents a further

---

[15] Some aspects of the view sketched in 'Intending' are anticipated in 'How is weakness of the will possible?' (reprinted in *Essays on Actions and Events*).

[16] 'Intending,' p. 88.

[17] Ibid., p. 101.

judgment that the desirable characteristic was enough to act on – that other considerations did not outweigh it. The judgment that corresponds to, or perhaps is identical with, the action cannot, therefore, be a *prima facie* judgment; it must be an all-out or unconditional judgment which, if we were to express it in words, would have a form like 'This action is [simply or unconditionally] desirable.'[18]

A little earlier, we have been told,

> Some actions [of a set desired type], even all of them, may have plenty else wrong with them. It is only when I come to an actual action that it makes sense to judge it as a whole as desirable or not; up until that moment there was no object with which I was acquainted to judge. Of course, I can still say of the completed action that it is desirable insofar as it is this or that, but in choosing to perform it I went beyond this; my choice represented, or perhaps was, a judgment that the action itself was [simply] desirable.[19]

Obviously, these new singular all-out judgments bear an interesting relation to some of the things that I have already claimed about intentions in action. Such a judgment like such an intention is, so to speak, *de re* with respect to some action which the agent is then performing and with which he or she is, in some appropriate style, acquainted. Further, the all-out judgment involves viewing the particular action in the light of an objective or a range of objectives that the agent favors at the time of the acting. In the light of those objectives and a perspective on the surrounding circumstances, the view of the action is, to repeat, expressed by a statement like 'This action is *überhaupt* desirable' or 'This action is worth doing.'

Some of these remarks suggest, as a strongest interpretation, that the making of such an all-out judgment about a piece of behavior x is actually to be *identified* with an intention in the performance of x. (This strong interpretation is particularly suggested by the fact that a general intention for the future is unambiguously identified with a certain type of all-out judgment, and that proposal is largely motivated through an analogy with the role played by an all-out judgment about a particular concrete action.) Indeed, if we supposed that an all-out judgment has or can have a form like 'This action x, if or given that it φs, is simply worth performing,' then the making of that judgment – the holding of that view – might be identified with intending of x that it is φ. On this line of thought, we would no longer have a causalist analysis of intention in action; this is now directly explicated by the singular all-out judgments. Still, we would continue to have a causalist theory of *how* pro-attitudes and beliefs explain, when they do, an intentional act of φing. This would now run roughly as follows: the attitudes must cause (perhaps through a conscious or unconscious course of practical reasoning) *both* the behavior that constitutes the act *and* the all-out judgment about that act.

It is easiest to introduce the sort of difficulty that I find with such a possible account by means of a simple example. Suppose that I am at the eye-doctor's,

---

[18] Ibid., p. 98. In 'How is weakness of the will possible?' Davidson seems to use 'unconditional' in much the way he later uses 'all-out.' Here I use both terms interchangeably.

[19] 'Intending,' p. 97.

and he is probing at my left eye with strange instruments. In the face of an especially threatening poke I blink involuntarily. Finally, just at the tense instant when I feel the onset of the blink, I judge, in the light of my fear for my eye, my doubts about the doctor's aptitude, etc., that 'This act of blinking is overall desirable – it is, in these circumstances, simply worth performing.' Naturally, *if* this and similar cases are acceptable, then the first part of our little theory can't be right: intentions in action can't, in general, be identified with all-out judgments about the action. Moreover, given our earlier discussion, the intuitive reason for this would be familiar. The concept of an all-out judgment does not include the idea of agent guidance of behavior in relation to an objective that he has in mind.

However, it may well be that this example implicitly distorts the concept of an all-out judgment that Davidson wants to use. There is much in his paper that suggests that a true all-out judgment is *only* made in the performance of an intentional action or in a conscious attempt to perform the action in question. (For example, in the last quote given, the claim that the agent's '*choice*' of an action 'represents or perhaps is' an all-out judgment may indicate this stronger interpretation.) Thus, from this point of view, the most that an agent could judge about an involuntary action of hers would be, e.g., a *prima facie all-things-considered judgment*. But to get to a genuine all-out judgment about behavior x the agent has to perform x with some intention. This contention, of course, blocks the previous would-be counterexample, but it does so, I would have thought, at a significant price. For now intention in action is being used to explain what it is for a singular judgment of *überhaupt* desirability to be all-out or unconditional rather than the other way around. Why not say that a singular all-out judgment about x is simply a judgment of overall desirability *upon which the agent is acting* in performing x? But this will mean, it seems to me, that the agent intends of x that it has those consequences judged overall worth achieving in those circumstances. This complaint does not harm, for instance, the use of the all-out judgments to tell us much about the nature of practical reasoning, but it does render dubious the hope that have a new account, from within a causalist framework, of the nature of intention in action.

There are a number of weaker interpretations of Davidson's reflections upon all-out singular judgments. For example, one might decide to allow that such judgments can conceivably be made about a piece of involuntary behavior. But then, one will try the following: a person intends of x that it φ just in case he makes the envisaged all-out judgment about x *and* both x and the judgment are caused through a course of practical reasoning. However, leaving a host of other issues aside, we must ask in the most general way, 'What kinds of reasoning about action count as "*practical*"'? If practical reasoning is defined as reasoning of such-and-such a type which must have either intentional action or the formation of a general intention as its upshot and conclusion, then the new analysis will have travelled in another circle. And if practical reasoning includes suitable reasoning from desires, values, and beliefs to *prima facie* judgments about the overall desirability of a situation that an agent, as it were, merely confronts, then the circle is broken, but, also, my overall desirability judgment at the eye-doctor's is derived from practical reasoning in this wider sense. Admittedly, my involuntary blinking was not caused by that practical reasoning, but it is easy to construct an example (like the one quoted from Davidson earlier) that does the job. On the basis of some sly and libidinous practical reasoning, Pierre forms the intention of touching Claire's knee by shifting the position of his hand in a certain way. The forming of that decisive intention so fills him with lust, embarrassment, and nervousness that this turmoil causes a movement of his hand that answers nicely to the kind of movement he intended to perform. Noting the happy trajectory of his hand, he judges the movement to be overall desirable and more. Further, the practical reasoning may well be a cause of that judgment since the reasoning may involve various provisional conclusions of desirability (on the way to the intention) that have a role in determining the *überhaupt* desirability judgment about the movement which is finally made. Of course, one wants to protest that neither the movement nor the judgment were caused by the practical reasoning 'in the right way,' but this is where we have been before.

It is probably useless, in this context, for me to speculate further about how these remarks of Davidson's might be read, so I close with this summary statement. I have wished, in the present discussion, to sound as a major theme the importance of questions about the nature and function of the concept of 'intention in action.' Because of this concept's close connection with the idea of a purpose of an action, and, therefore, with possible answers to a certain reading of the question 'Why did the agent do so-and-so?', intention in action gives some promise of an alternative to causalist views. The kind of non-causalist I've described accepts that promise and denies both that this concept and the teleological explanations it generates can be reduced to the causation of action by an agent's general attitudes. Davidson, as we saw, once claimed that intention in action is 'no thing at all, neither event, attitude, disposition, or object.' With this the non-causalist might agree while insisting that it *is* a genuine relation between an agent, action, and a type of state-of-affairs held good or desirable by the agent, i.e., it is a genuine relation which takes the place of event-causality in certain familiar teleological explanations that we give.

In 'Actions, reasons, and causes,' Davidson's views about intention in action are pretty plainly reductive, and I have argued that nothing points to and much points against the availability of the envisaged reduction. In his later writings on action, the situation is more complicated and less clear because of the presence of what he himself describes as a 'new element' – the singular all-out judgment of desirability. I have just expressed some of my puzzlement about how these judgments are to be conceived, how they are supposed to relate to intentions in action, and how they are to function as an 'element' in reason explanations of intentional action. The simple fact is, I believe, that we need from Davidson a longer and more elaborate telling of this particular tale. Moreover, in the absence of this elaboration my reaction here remains sceptical. Davidson asks not to be held too closely to his choice of the term 'judgment.' So we might try, e.g., 'perceiving,' 'evaluating,' 'viewing' the action 'as overall desirable.' To my mind, all such possibilities refer too exclusively to the mere holding of some 'attitude' about the action and thereby miss the crucial fact that the action itself, in intentional action, is directed, guided, aimed by the agent at an object of his heart's desire.

3

Davidson on Intentional Behavior

FREDERICK STOUTLAND

Introduction

It is just over twenty years since Davidson's 'Actions, reasons, and causes' was published. That was an enormously influential paper: in 1963 the majority of philosophers working in the so-called analytic tradition rejected a causal analysis of intentional behavior; now the majority assume that a causal analysis *must* be correct. That change is largely due to Davidson, and while recent causal analyses often differ from his in significant ways, all are indebted to his work.

Davidson himself has gone beyond 'Actions, reasons, and causes' in many ways, not only by developing themes only hinted at there but by arguing new ones. The most significant of these is the idea that the mental is anomalous and that psychology, therefore, is autonomous in the sense that it 'cannot employ the same methods, or be reduced to, the more precise physical sciences'.[1]

I have never been persuaded by the causal analysis of action, and a major reason for continuing in this perverse point of view has been Davidson's own subtle discussion of psychological concepts and their relation to the physical, which seems to me to provide good reasons for giving up the causal analysis.

Davidson is not unaware of this kind of reaction. 'What apparently arouses the most doubt and opposition,' he writes, 'is my attempt to combine the view that psychological concepts have an autonomy relative to the physical with a monistic ontology and a causal analysis of action.'[2] This is precisely the kind of doubt I have and which I shall press in this paper, not arguing against what I take to be Davidson's fundamental point of view, both in philosophy of action and philosophy of language, but arguing that that point of view fits badly with a causal analysis of action and with a materialist ontology.

In section 1 I sketch Davidson's causal analysis of action, which, in rejecting implausible assumptions held by traditional causal analyses, made possible the revival of causal analyses in general. In section 2 I develop difficulties in

---

[1] Donald Davidson, *Essays on actions and events* (Clarendon Press, Oxford, 1980), p. 240.
[2] Ibid., p. 240.

Davidson's own causal analysis. In section 3 I argue that a materialist ontology for action makes a causal analysis appear more plausible than it is, but that a materialist ontology should be rejected.

1 *Davidson's causal analysis of intentional behavior*

By a causal analysis of intentional behavior I mean one which makes it a necessary condition of behavior's being intentional that it be caused by a mental event. By a mental event I mean an event describable in mental terms – which takes a mental description. I shall use 'mental description' as Davidson does: 'A description of the form "the event that is M" ... is a *mental description* ... if and only if the expression that replaces "M" contains at least one mental verb essentially.'[3] Mental verbs are verbs that express propositional attitudes – like believing, hoping, intending, wanting – and, therefore, in their normal use set up non-extensional contexts.

As Davidson points out, the mental in this sense applies not only to such 'inner phenomena' as beliefs and desires but also to intentional behavior. This is certainly the case when we are dealing with behavior which the agent had reasons for performing – behavior for which a rationale can be given in terms of the agent's attitudes – since a description under which such behavior is intentional must have some kind of necessary connection with descriptions of the agent's reasons. These descriptions of behavior, therefore, also set up non-extensional contexts and meet the criterion for being mental. This is as it should be, given, as Davidson puts it, that 'the distinguishing feature of the mental is not that it is private, subjective, or immaterial, but that it exhibits what Brentano called intentionality.' We might, therefore, better speak, not of mental descriptions, but of intentional or psychological descriptions.

Putting it this way lets us see the causal analysis of intentional behavior as part of the larger project of explaining the role and status of the intentional in our account of the world, a project that has preoccupied philosophy since modern physical science de-intentionalized nature. The causal analysis belongs in the tradition inaugurated by Descartes, which argues that behavior takes only physical descriptions unless it is caused by events which themselves already have intentional or psychological descriptions. Davidson's account of the latter sort of events is not Cartesian, but his account of intentional behavior is, and it is this which I reject and which I think Davidson ought to reject, given the other things he says about these matters.

With much of what Davidson says about intentional behavior I have no quarrel. Consider an agent who swings a stick in order to injure someone, and who succeeds, but who also inadvertently breaks a window. I should say, as Davidson would say, the following about this case: (1) that the agent's behavior is a single action describable in at least three ways; (2) that the agent's behavior is intentional under the descriptions 'swinging a stick' and 'injuring someone,' but not under the description 'breaking a window'; (3) that, nevertheless, the agent did break a window because that behavior is intentional under other

---

[3] Ibid., p. 211.

descriptions; (4) that his behavior is intentional under the descriptions 'swinging a stick' and 'injuring someone' because he not only had reasons for acting that way but acted *for* those reasons; (5) that his behavior was not intentional under the description 'breaking a window' since there is no suitable way to connect that description by principles of practical reason to the agent's beliefs, desires, or other attitudes; (6) that these descriptions would not apply to the agent's behavior straightforwardly unless certain causal relations obtained – for example, unless his behavior caused someone to be injured and caused a window to break.

More generally, I agree with Davidson on the following: (1) that actions are particulars, describable in many ways, not universals or states of affairs; (2) that the fundamental (though I think not the only) mark of intentional behavior is that it is performed for a reason; (3) that there is a significant difference between someone merely having a reason and acting, and his acting *because of* that reason; (4) that the connection between an agent's reasons and actions performed for these reasons requires principles of practical reason; (5) that the principles of practical reason are holistic, interpretative, inescapably normative, and not expressible in causal laws. Psychology is, therefore, autonomous relative to the physical.

These theses, however, do not add up to a causal analysis of action. To get that we must *add on* a thesis not entailed by these, namely, that an agent acts *because* of a reason only if the reason causes his behavior. Davidson has made this central to his causal analysis, arguing that the essential difference between an agent's acting for reasons and his having those reasons but not acting on them is that when he acts for reasons, the reasons cause his behavior. Given that the fundamental mark of *intentional* behavior is that it is performed *for* reasons, then we have the thesis that behavior is intentional only if it is caused by the agent's reasons. More precisely: behavior is intentional under a description only if the behavior is caused by beliefs, desires, or other attitudes, descriptions of which yield, by principles of practical reason, the description under which the behavior is intentional. The thesis is a very strong one: it is not saying merely that reasons are causes of behavior but that an item of behavior performed for a reason is not intentional under a description unless it is caused by just those reasons whose descriptions yield the description under which the behavior is intentional. This requires that every item of intentional behavior have just the right cause.

I speak of this as an add-on thesis for Davidson because, in affirming the autonomy of psychology, he denies that the principles of practical reason are causal laws. The connection between reason descriptions and descriptions of behavior is neither expressible in nor entails any specific causal laws. Hence, to admit the distinction between reasons agents merely have and reasons they act on is not thereby to be committed to a causal analysis of this distinction.

For what we might call the 'traditional causal analysis' this thesis is not an add-on thesis, for the connection between reason descriptions and descriptions of behavior in the traditional theory was made by causal laws. On that version, to say that someone had a reason for acting under a certain description would be to say that anyone with such a reason would, everything else being equal, perform an act of that description. If the agent merely had a reason but did not act because of it, then everything was not equal: there were other causal laws applicable to the agent's behavior which took precedence. The very concept of reasons was explicated in terms of causal laws, so that the distinction between merely having a reason and acting because of one entailed a difference in the causal laws that actually governed behavior. For the traditional theory the concept of a reason for action was a *nomic* concept, and the descriptions under which behavior was intentional were also nomic.

The main reason for the revival of causal analyses was Davidson's argument that they do not have to take this traditional form. On the one hand, his powerful arguments for the autonomy of psychology undermined many critics of the causal analysis, who were arguing precisely for the normative and holistic character of the principles of practical reason and against the claim that there were causal laws connecting reasons with descriptions under which behavior is intentional. Most of the arguments over the traditional causal theory of action had centered on whether there were such laws, its advocates saying there were, its critics saying there were not. Davidson sided with the critics, borrowing their arguments and adding his own – in particular his argument that causal laws must be formulated in physical terms, so that the attempt to formulate causal laws in psychological terms is hopeless, the concept of a reason for action not being nomic. This argument is a splendid contribution to philosophy of action, tied in as it is with Davidson's philosophy of language, which gives it wide significance.

On the other hand, Davidson argued that it did not follow from this limitation on causal laws that reasons could not cause behavior. Both the critics and the defenders of the traditional theory thought that it did follow: that was the point of the so-called 'logical connection argument' – that the non-causal character of the principles of practical reason ruled out causal connections. In undermining this argument, Davidson showed that both critics and defenders of the traditional analysis were missing the point in thinking that it mattered whether or not there were causal laws connecting reason descriptions with psychological descriptions of behavior. Even if there were no causal laws of this type, the particular events to which these descriptions applied may have other descriptions related by causal laws. Such descriptions, Davidson argued, must be physical, so that if reasons cause behavior, both must have physical descriptions, and in *that* sense be physical.

I shall not dispute what Davidson says about causality nor his claim that the absence of (known) causal laws is compatible with reasons causing behavior. Every item of behavior presumably has a physical description. Moreover, given a man who, say, wants to injure someone, there may be a physical description true of this man if and only if he wants to injure. Moreover, it may be true that there are causal laws connecting physical descriptions of his behavior with physical descriptions of his reasons.

But even if this were true, we would still not have Davidson's causal analysis of intentional behavior. For that requires not merely that reasons cause behavior but that an item of behavior performed for a reason is intentional under a description only if caused by the very reasons which yield that description by practical reason. The most that has been shown so far is that the impossibility of psychological causal laws is not incompatible with reasons causing behavior since there may be physical laws covering both the reasons and the behavior. But it does not follow that behavior performed for a reason is intentional *only if* there are physical laws which connect a reason with behavior whenever the behavior is performed for that reason. That necessary condition can't be met, but fortunately it isn't necessary.

2 *Criticisms of Davidson's causal analysis of intentional behavior*

Rejecting the *traditional* causal analysis of intentional behavior, while maintaining that behavior takes a psychological description only if caused by the right mental events, implies that behavior takes a given psychological description only when it also takes a physical description nomically related to physical descriptions of those mental events. The distinction between behavior which is intentional under a description and behavior which is not, in other words, is the distinction between behavior to which a specific physical law applies and behavior to which it does not apply. The same is true of the distinction between behavior performed for a reason and behavior not performed for that reason.

There are two dimensions to distinguishing between behavior which is intentional under a description and behavior which is not (or between behavior performed for a reason and behavior not performed for a reason). The first is the *evidence* we have for applying the distinction in a particular case – for actually determining if behavior is intentional or if an agent acted for a reason. The second is the *truth conditions* for the distinction – the necessary conditions for an agent's behavior being intentional or for a reason being his reason for acting. Davidson's causal analysis should require an appeal to physical laws in both cases. Our evidence that an agent's behavior is intentional should include reference to physical laws. And a necessary condition for behavior being intentional should be the presence of an appropriate physical law. There are difficulties in both cases; let me consider the case of evidence first.

An appeal to physical laws is not part of our evidence for determining whether an agent acts for a reason or whether his behavior is intentional under a description yielded by that reason. In determining whether a person has acted for a reason, we normally take his word for it: if he says he swung the stick in order to injure a man, we normally do not question that. If we do, we ask him to reflect further, and if he changes his mind we normally accept that. But accepting a person's word, either directly or after reflection, means that physical laws are playing no role. There is no first-person authority with respect to causal relations on the assumption that causality entails the existence of a physical law.

Davidson admits first-person authority about such things as reasons for action. He grants, for example, that we have special authority about what we are proud of: 'The fact that claims to know what one is proud of can be wrong ... does not show that we do not have special authority with respect to them,' even though judgments about pride include a causal element: 'It is necessary that someone's being proud that p be caused by (among other things) a belief that p.'[4] And presumably this also implies a physical law.

---

[4] Ibid., p. 289.

In accounting for this first-person authority, he appeals to his theory of interpretation and the central role of the principle of charity – that interpreting linguistic behavior necessarily presupposes that most of the sentences people hold true are true. Thus he writes, 'The source of this authority springs from the nature of human interpretation of human thoughts, speech, intentions, motives and actions. ... People are in general right about the mental causes of their emotions, intentions, and actions because as interpreters we interpret them so as to make them so. We must, if we are to interpret at all'.[5]

While sympathetic with Davidson's theory of interpretation, I do not believe this argument accomplishes its purpose. For the principle of charity implies that people are *generally* right in what they believe. It does not imply that people have special authority in beliefs about themselves – that their beliefs about themselves have a status their beliefs about others do not. The principle of charity makes no distinction between beliefs about oneself and beliefs about others.

While beliefs about oneself present the most obvious difficulties here, beliefs about others cannot be disconnected from them: even when we overrule a person's self-attributions, they do not lose their status. For overruling means that we think self-deception is at work, and self-deception sets up a complex relation between beliefs about another person and that person's belief about himself, such that our belief about the other person *is* the belief the person would accept about himself if he were not self-deceived. Appeals to physical laws play no role in determining what belief that is.

At the same time we can in general know the descriptions under which someone's behavior is intentional without his telling us. Even here the most common case is not one where we make an *inquiry*. We observe what people are doing intentionally and why, and this is not merely guessing. We acquire this ability in learning the language, and it enables us to determine when persons have acted intentionally and why, independently of knowledge of the physical laws governing their behavior.

When we do have to *inquire* into what a person's intentional behavior is we push these same considerations in an extended and systematic way. They are, as Davidson has emphasized, interpretative, holistic, and normative. They are interpretative because we do not in general begin with an accepted description of what the agent's intentional behavior is and ask for his reasons, or begin with an accepted understanding of his reasons and then seek out his behavior. We have to seek out both at once, modifying our descriptions of behavior in the light of possible reasons, articulating our account of reasons in the light of descriptions of behavior. They are holistic because, as Davidson puts it, 'Beliefs and desires issue in behavior only as modified and mediated by further beliefs and desires, attitudes, and attendings, without limit.'[6] They are normative because 'There is no way psychology can avoid consideration of the nature of rationality, of coherence, and consistency. ... [It] cannot be divorced from such questions as what constitutes a good argument, a valid inference, a rational plan, or a good reason for acting.'[7] All of this proceeds in psychological terms, for only behavior psychologically described is evidence for an agent's reasons,

[5] Ibid., p. 290.
[6] Ibid., p. 217.
[7] Ibid., p. 241.

and only psychological descriptions of his reasons bear on psychological descriptions of his behavior.

I'm not clear whether Davidson really thinks that appeals to physical causation are part of our evidence for determining when behavior takes a psychological description. He often emphasizes the disparate nature of the evidence for psychological and physical descriptions. When he discusses actual cases, appeals to physical causes play no role. While he says such things as that 'causality and rationality go hand in hand,'[8] this is never worked out to show how physical causality plays a role in determining when an agent has acted for a reason or when behavior is intentional. His clearest statements speak in terms of the overall coherence of the psychological descriptions themselves, and this rules out physical causality in favor of rationality – 'rationality both in the sense that the action to be explained must be reasonable in the light of the assigned desires and beliefs, but also in the sense that the assigned desires and beliefs must fit in with one another'.[9] Appealing to wider and wider psychological descriptions of an agent may not always determine whether he acted for a reason, and it may leave it problematic whether he acted intentionally, but it is the only kind of evidence we have.

Yet Davidson never wavers in his claim that ascribing a reason for action involves not only 'rationality considerations' but also causation. This passage from 'Psychology as philosophy' is characteristic: 'Two ideas are built into the concept of acting on a reason (and hence the concept of behavior generally): the idea of cause and the idea of rationality. A reason is a rational cause.'[10]

Perhaps this is not meant as a claim about evidence at all, but as a claim just about truth-conditions, that is, a claim about a necessary condition for the truth of a sentence saying that an agent acted for a certain reason or that his behavior was intentional under a description. Perhaps it is meant as a claim, for example, simply about the differences between the truth-condition of (1) S swung the stick because he wanted to injure the man, and (2) S swung the stick, and although he wanted to injure the man, he did not do so for that reason.

Clearly there are differences in the truth-conditions of these two sentences. I would say they are complex – as complex as the considerations to which we appeal in actually making the distinction – and that we cannot articulate them in a general formula. Given this way of construing Davidson's analysis, however, there must be *underneath* these complex considerations *the* difference between these two cases: the truth-conditions for (1) must include a causal relation between the agent's desire and his behavior, the truth-conditions for (2) must not. The truth-conditions for (1), therefore, must include a causal law connecting *physical* descriptions of the agent's desire and behavior, whereas the truth-conditions for (2) must not.

Construing Davidson's causal analysis as just about truth-conditions, however, raises a new difficulty. For if appeals to physical causation are not part of our evidence for determining when an agent acts for a reason, then our evidence

---

[8] Ibid., p. 290.
[9] 'Thought and Talk' in *Inquiries into truth and interpretation* (Clarendon Press, Oxford, 1984), p. 159.
[10] *Essays on actions and events*, p. 233.

will consist only of psychological descriptions of his attitudes and behavior. But the truth-conditions for psychological descriptions require, on this analysis, physical descriptions of the agent's attitudes and behavior: it will be true that he acted on a desire only if there are causal laws connecting physical descriptions of that desire and that behavior. The difficulty is the *connection* between the psychological descriptions which serve as evidence that the agent acted for a certain reason and the physical descriptions which specify corresponding truth conditions: can there be the kind of connection which enables the psychological description to serve as evidence for the physical truth conditions without which the behavior is not intentional?

Given the autonomy of psychology, I do not see how there can be, for no psychological description is related by causal law to any other description, least of all to any physical description. The mental, Davidson says, is anomalous; psychological descriptions are not nomic. And Davidson does not envisage any other general connection between physical and psychological descriptions. But this entails that there *cannot* be an explanation of why an event which has a particular psychological description also has any particular physical description. There can be no general connection between the two. Knowing that an attitude has a certain psychological description, therefore, is irrelevant to knowledge of whether it has a suitable physical description, that is, one which enters into a relevant causal law. So whether an attitude has a physical description related by causal law to physical descriptions of the agent's behavior is not anything we can have reason to believe, no matter how much we know about psychological descriptions of the agent. And this means that psychological descriptions of an agent cannot serve as evidence for the physical causation Davidson makes a truth-condition for an agent's having acted on a reason. On this analysis behavior might be intentional even though no one, not even the agent, had the slightest reason for thinking it was. We may be dark to ourselves but we aren't that dark.

I can think of two responses that might be made to this, but neither appears adequate. The first is that I have made the dichotomy between evidence and truth too extreme by overlooking certain generalizations about reasons and behavior, which play an important role in practical reasoning. These generalizations, falling short of being causal laws, do not violate the physical character of causality by being psycho-physical laws, but they, nevertheless, serve to bring together psychological evidence and physical truth conditions.

Thus Davidson writes in 'Mental events':

> If an event of a certain mental sort has usually been accompanied by an event of a certain physical sort, this often is a good reason to expect other cases to follow suit roughly in proportion. The generalizations that embody such practical wisdom are assumed to be only roughly true.... Their importance lies mainly in the support they lend singular causal claims and related explanations of particular events. The support derives from the fact that such a generalization, however crude and vague, may provide good reason to believe that underlying the particular case there is a regularity that could be formulated sharply and without caveat.[11]

---

[11] Ibid., pp. 218ff.

Generalizations do play a role in practical reasoning, but they will not resolve the difficulty I have raised here. The problem is that generalizations of this type, if they hold true of an agent who acts because of a desire, will also hold true of an agent who merely has the desire but does not act because of it. Appealing to generalizations about desires and behavior – about how persons with certain desires are apt to behave in certain ways, and so on – may enable us to make reasonable predictions about what agents are apt to do on certain occasions. But these generalizations will not, by themselves, discriminate between when an agent has a desire and acts because of it and when he has it and does not act because of it, simply because any generalization which falls short of being a causal law will apply equally to both occasions and hence will give us no reason to believe that physical laws underlie the one but not the other. The gap between the truth of a sentence ascribing a reason for action and its evidence remains as wide as ever.[12]

The traditional analysis avoided this problem, because it argued that there were intrinsic causal differences between attitudes an agent has on an occasion when he acts because of them and those he has when he does not act because of them. They are intrinsic to the attitudes because these causal differences involve causal laws in which psychological terms figure directly, and the occasions are distinguished by the ways such causal laws intersect on the agent. For the traditional analysis, in other words, psychological descriptions were nomic. This avoids the objection I am making, but at the price of accepting those features of the traditional analysis which Davidson rightly rejects.

The second response is that I ignore the relevance of the principle of charity – that 'people are in general right about the mental causes of their emotions, intentions, and actions because as interpreters we interpret them so as to make them so.'[13] I argued earlier that this will not account for the special authority persons have with respect to beliefs about themselves, but perhaps it can play a role in the more general case we are considering here.

Let us grant the principle of charity, and let us grant that it implies that in general we are right in our ascriptions of intentional behavior. The response I am considering argues that if the truth of such ascriptions requires that the behavior be caused by reasons, then we must also in general be right about when behavior is caused by reasons and, hence, when there are physical causes at work.

This looks like an outrageously broad use of the principle of charity to argue for the plausibility of a *philosophical* theory. But even if it isn't, this use of the principle does not give us what we need. It will, at best, give us reason to think that behavior is, in general, governed by causal laws, which is not something I am denying. It may even give us reason to think there is some sort of general correspondence between physical and psychological descriptions of the sort cognitive-science people explicate in terms of the relation between syntactic and semantic dimensions of a formal language. But Davidson's analysis requires something much stronger – not merely that there are physical causes

---

[12] I have developed this argument in 'Oblique causation and reasons for action' in *Synthese, 43* (1980), pp. 351–67.

[13] *Essays on actions and events*, p. 290.

of behavior and not merely that there is a general correspondence between physical causes and psychological descriptions – but that there are *suitable* physical causes for each *particular* case. For his position is that when an agent has acted for a reason, there must be a physical description of that very reason and a physical description of that behavior *which are related by causal law*. We need not, and normally will not, know what these descriptions are, but unless the reason and behavior are such that there is a law connecting physical descriptions of them, the reason was not the reason for the agent's behavior.

The point is that Davidson holds that psychological descriptions are true of behavior only if suitable – generally unknown – physical descriptions are also true of it, namely, descriptions connected by causal law with physical descriptions of the agent's reasons. It is also his position that there is no law-like connection between psychological descriptions and physical descriptions. This is ruled out by the disparate nature of the psychological and the physical. What has to be guaranteed are suitable links between *particular* psychological and *particular* physical descriptions. This is not something that can be guaranteed by a general principle, certainly not one as general as the principle of charity. That can at best guarantee that there are some physical descriptions or other, not that there are the particular law-governed ones needed for the behavior to be intentional under the descriptions yielded by the agent's reasons.

The criticism I have been making is complex; let me summarize it. Davidson's view amounts to the claim that events are causes only in virtue of their having certain properties – namely, properties which figure in causal laws – nomic properties. His view that all causal laws are physical means that only *physical* properties are nomic. A reason cannot, therefore, cause an action in virtue of its psychological properties, for those are non-nomic; there are no nomological ties between the psychological and the physical. But if a reason causes an action only in virtue of its physical properties, then the psychological as psychological has no causal efficacy, so that the connection between the psychological and the physical is accidental: it is an accident that any event should have, on the one hand, the property of being, say, a desire, and, on the other hand, any causally relevant (i.e., physical) property.[14]

Let me suggest one final objection to this, namely, that it will make the problem of wayward causal chains intractable. For that problem arises for the causal theory because an agent can have a reason for acting which causes his behavior not qua reason but qua something else, for example, qua stimulant of emotional disturbance. In this case, although the reason caused the agent's behavior, his behavior was not intentional because the reason did not cause it in the right way.

But on Davidson's view an agent's reason *cannot* cause his behavior in the right way because it cannot cause it qua reason; it can cause it only qua physical event since it is only in virtue of physical properties that events are causes.

---

[14] For this way of putting the point and for controversy over it see Ted Honderich, 'The argument for anomalous monism', *Analysis* 42.1 (January, 1982), Peter Smith, 'Bad news for anomalous monism?' *Analysis* 42.4 (October, 1982), and Honderich's reply in *Analysis* 43.3 (with more to come in *Analysis*).

3 *The ontology of intentional behavior*

The argument so far has been directed against the causal analysis of action, and it has proceeded largely in terms of premisses which Davidson himself accepts. What I called the add-on thesis about the role of causation in intentional behavior is not implied by other parts of Davidson's philosophy nor does it fit well with them. The question arises as to why the add-on thesis. Davidson in fact gives little argument for it; the only one developed is that without causation we *cannot* distinguish between an agent acting because of a reason and his having a reason but not acting because of it, but this is not very strong. Most of Davidson's discussion is directed rather to showing *how* causation can play a role, on the assumption that it *must*. And this is characteristic of much recent work in philosophy of action: it is assumed that a causal analysis must be correct, the problem being to work out the details. But why this assumption that a certain philosophical thesis *must* be right?

One reason is failure to distinguish adequately between a monistic ontology for action and a materialist ontology. Davidson claims to be a materialist; I shall argue that an adequate ontology should be monist but not materialist, which doesn't mean it should be idealistic either. My concern is not with inner states but with intentional behavior itself; even intentional behavior, I shall argue, should not be construed in a materialist way.

Obviously all intentional behavior has a physical description. But to agree that behavior has a physical description is not to accept materialism, any more than to agree that all intentional behavior has a psychological description is to accept idealism. Even to agree that everything in the world has a physical description is not to be materialist. For, on the one hand, as Davidson has argued, one who subscribes to that might also agree that everything in the world has a psychological description,[15] but that would not be to accept idealism. On the other hand, philosophers who by any criterion are not materialist could accept the claim that everything has a physical description. Descartes, for example, could allow that a soul is truly describable as that which is, or was, or could be, intimately related to a body, and this is a description in physical terms. A thought could then be described as a mode of the soul, and thus acquire a physical description. Even Berkeley might allow that everything has a physical description: he thinks that some collections of ideas are truly describable as stars or human bodies, and he could use this as a starting point to cook up physical descriptions of all ideas.

Materialists must claim more than that everything has a physical description. Although they need not claim that things are nothing but physical, they must give physical terms some kind of privileged role relative to psychological terms. This privileged role is often expressed by using physical terms to say what something *consists in*. In philosophy of action materialism is the idea that what action consists in is certain physical events – for Davidson peripheral movements of the body. I want to look at Davidson's idea that 'our primitive actions … mere movements of the body – these are all the actions there are.'[15]

---

[15] Cf. *Essays on actions and events*, pp. 211ff.
[16] Ibid., p. 59.

What does it mean to say that action consists in bodily movements? The idea is that only bodily movement descriptions – or more generally, physical descriptions – identify the descriptum for action descriptions *all by itself, by reference to nothing else.* Other descriptions – in particular psychological descriptions – describe the behavior *by reference to* something other than the behavior – for example, by reference to its causes or effects. Only physical descriptions are, we might say, *intrinsic*; only they describe behavior by reference to nothing else. Psychological descriptions are extrinsic; they describe behavior relative to other things.[17] As Davidson puts it, 'To describe an action as one that had a certain purpose or intended outcome is to describe it as an effect; to describe it as an action that had a certain outcome is to describe it as a cause.'[18] To describe an action neither as a cause nor as an effect requires a physical description, which, describing an action in terms of itself alone – intrinsically – describes what action consists in.

This means that physical descriptions are given the privileged role of identifying the particular about which we can raise the question whether *it* is intentional under a description. Psychological descriptions are secondary in that they describe an item of behavior, which is intrinsically physical, in terms of something extrinsic to it, namely, its causes or effects. Hence Davidson's claim that 'Our primitive actions ... mere movements of the body – these are all the actions there are. We never do more than move our bodies; the rest is up to nature.'[19]

This notion that only physical descriptions are intrinsic and play the privileged role of identifying the particular which is the descriptum for other descriptions is, I believe, mistaken. What is at stake here is the question of the individuation of action and the central role that plays in ontology. I agree with Davidson that actions are particulars which take various descriptions. Thus if we speak of the agent who swung the stick, deliberately injuring a man, but inadvertently breaking a window, we have given three descriptions of one action, and we can form the true identity statement: swinging the stick is identical with injuring the man and identical with breaking the window. But doing this presupposes that we have identified *an* action, that is, that we have at least one term that enables us to *count* how many actions of that kind the agent performed on that occasion, and to conclude that he acted only once in accomplishing those things. There is no problem in this case, for these psychological descriptions contain count terms; we can count how many times he swung the stick, or how many times he injured the man, and thus identify *the* action to which the various descriptions apply.

To give physical descriptions the privileged role of saying what action consists in, however, is to assume that bodily movement terms play the primary role in identifying *an* action as *the* particular to which various psychological descriptions apply. Bodily movement descriptions do usually contain count terms; we can count how many times a man's arm moves in such and such a way, or how many times his hand closed, and so on. But the way bodily

---

[17] For this way of putting things see J. Hornsby's *Actions* (Routledge & Kegan Paul, London, 1980).

[18] *Essays on actions and events*, p. 48.

[19] Ibid., p. 59.

movement terms count particular events and the way psychological terms count particular events are different, and they do not normally yield the same results. The question is whether in identifying *an* action as *a* particular to which various descriptions apply, it is bodily movement terms or psychological terms which play the privileged role.

Clearly psychological terms do. The point is obscured if we consider relatively simple behavior like swinging a stick. We count one swing of the stick, we also count one movement of the arm; the terms yield the same result. But if we consider more complex behavior, like buying a ticket, or writing a letter, or driving from Minneapolis to Chicago, the point is clearer. Consider driving to Chicago. How many times did I do that last month? Once. What was my reason? To see the exhibit at the Art Institute. My driving to Chicago is describable also in other ways: as fulfilling my desire to see the exhibit, as trying out my new car, as amusing myself for eight hours. These are all psychological descriptions of *an* action.

This action also has a purely physical description – a description in bodily movement terms. But no matter what bodily movement terms we choose, if they let us count at all, they will count *many* bodily movements. Even if there is a bodily movement term we could cook up which would count only one bodily movement in driving to Chicago, the point is that it would be cooked up. It would not identify the bodily movement about which anyone would raise the question whether *it* is intentional under some description. The particular about which we raise that question can be identified only by some such description as 'the drive to Chicago last month,' and that is not a bodily movement description.

The same point can be made for simple actions. For when an agent is moving his arm to swing a stick, he engages also in much other behavior. He moves his head and feet, he swings his other arm, he clenches his teeth. These are all parts of his behavior at the time. To identify *an* action, which is such that *it* has a physical description, assumes a description which contains a count term which yields one action of that kind. Such a description will be psychological. Indeed normally it will be a description under which the behavior is intentional. This is a primary reason for the plausibility of arguing (as Davidson does) that we speak of action of any kind – intentional or not – only if the behavior has a description under which it is intentional. For speaking of action requires speaking of *an* action, and speaking of *an* action assumes we have identified *one* descriptum, and that normally requires a description under which the action is intentional.

Once we have identified an action, we can construct a physical description which describes it. But the physical description will in the usual cases include count terms which count several descripta, not one. The action will be *an* action only when counted in terms of psychological descriptions. As far as action is concerned, therefore, physical descriptions are secondary to psychological ones. Physical descriptions do not give what action consists in; they have to be tailored to psychological descriptions, not the other way around. We don't have to give up a monistic ontology for intentional behavior, but we should give up materialism, for we should reject the idea that intentional behavior consists in bodily movements.

Why does it seem so compelling to give physical descriptions the privileged role of saying what action consists in? Why does it seem so natural to think of intentional behavior as just movements of the body, where this means more than the platitude that all behavior can be described in bodily movement terms? The main reason, I suggest, is a widespread claim about how to formulate the fundamental question in philosophy of action. Thus Donagan: 'The theory of action began with the question, "In virtue of what are certain bodily movements by human adults human actions, and others of the same kind by infants and brute animals not?"'[20] He goes on to say that 'We need an answer, not to "What did he do?", which is properly answered by a narrative, but to "In what did his action consist?" to which a proper answer would be a description of the movements of his body.' Once the question is put this way, the issue has been begged. For this way of putting the question *assumes* that we have already picked out bodily movements as *one* descriptum (which may or may not have psychological descriptions), and that is precisely to *assume* that descriptions in bodily movement terms are privileged: they are the descriptions which identify the descriptum to which psychological descriptions also apply. It is this assumption which should be rejected: the bodily movements associated with action are not *a* descriptum except by reference to a psychological description. Our normal descriptions of the behavior of infants and brutes are also psychological descriptions under which their behavior could be (or perhaps is) intentional, hence the possibility of formulating the fundamental question of action theory as one about what distinguishes bodily movements which are, from those which are not, intentional. But the question as normally posed assumes that bodily movement descriptions yield *a* descriptum to which psychological descriptions may or may not apply, and there is no reason to give physical descriptions that privileged role.

That this assumption is made in the very way the question is posed also accounts (at least in part) for the sense that the causal analysis of intentional behavior *must* be right. For the assumption that physical descriptions identify what actions consist in is also the assumption that the only intrinsic descriptions of behavior are physical. Psychological descriptions *must*, therefore, describe behavior by reference to something external to the behavior being described, and the distinction between behavior which is intentional under a description and behavior which is not *must* be made in terms of something extrinsic to the behavior. But if descriptions of an agent's behavior as intentional, or psychological descriptions generally, *must* be in terms of something extrinsic, the only plausible alternative is that the description be in terms of the behavior's causes, and that is just the causal analysis.

It is the assumption behind this which should be rejected. Since there is no good reason to think that only physical descriptions identify what an action consists in, there is no good reason to think that only physical descriptions are intrinsic. Psychological descriptions can be intrinsic – they need not describe behavior by reference to something extrinsic to the behavior being described.

[20] Alan Donagan, 'Philosophical progress and the theory of action', *Proceedings of the American Philosophical Association*, 55 (1981), pp. 25–52, at p. 45.

Given this, the causal analysis no longer appears to be the only plausible alternative.

But are psychological descriptions, some of them anyway, intrinsic, describing an action in terms of itself and (in particular) not by reference to its causes or effects? As far as causes are concerned, in describing an agent as, say, intentionally injuring someone, we are not committed to any particular claim about what caused his behavior. We may be committed to many open-ended claims about his behavior *not* having certain sorts of causes, but neither the evidence nor the truth-conditions for psychological descriptions require, in general, that the behavior have any particular causes. To say that is just to reject the causal analysis. I have not refuted that analysis, but I think I have both shown that it has serious problems and uncovered a source for the compulsion that it *must* be correct in spite of whatever problems it has.

What about effects? Does a psychological description of an agent as intentionally injuring someone necessarily describe an action in terms of its effects? It is true that 'injuring someone' will not describe an agent's behavior unless his behavior caused an injury. And in *that* sense it is true that we have described his action in terms of *its* effects. But that is not the decisive sense, for, again, we have the 'it,' and what account do we give of that? A person's behavior on any occasion causes many things, most of which do not enter into descriptions of his actions. Moreover, even if his behavior had not resulted in an injury, 'injuring someone' would still give us the description under which his behavior was intentional if we just insert the word 'try': his behavior was intentional under the description 'trying to injure.' This is the move we make whenever action is unsuccessful – we say that someone tried. So although 'injuring someone' does not describe an agent's behavior unless an injury was its effect, it is not actually having an injury as an effect which gives that description its central role, for 'injuring' will be an essential part of a description of the agent's behavior (part of the description 'tried to injure') even if he was quite unsuccessful in an attempt to injure someone. That there are causal conditions for 'injuring someone' to describe an agent's behavior does not, therefore, entail that his action is being described in terms of *its* effects, for it is a necessary condition of there being a single descriptum here that the description apply to the agent's action, even if that causal condition is not met, as a part of the description of what he was trying to do. That's just the function of the word 'try': to allow psychological descriptions their central role in individuating behavior, even when the behavior fails to have its intended outcome.[21]

---

[21] This account of 'try' is meant as an alternative to Hornsby's in *Actions*, who argues that the only intrinsic description of an action is in terms of trying to act in that way. She begins with the true premise that whenever I set out to perform an action A and fail, then it is true that I tried to A. She concludes than when I succeed in A-ing, it must, therefore, also be true that I tried to A (with descriptions of my action other than as 'trying to A' being in terms of the *effects* of my trying). But the conclusion does not follow, for there is no reason to assume (indeed it is false) that what occurs when I fail to A must also occur when I succeed in A-ing. My own account may also be seen as a defense of G.H. von Wright's distinction between *result* and *consequence* as developed, for example, in his *Explanation and understanding* (Cornell University Press, Ithaca, 1971). This distinction has the great advantage (for ethics, for example) of allowing for an action, such as injuring a man, that

These criticisms of Davidson's ontology do not, I believe, undermine the central points of his philosophy. What they do is push one step further his claims about the autonomy of psychology. These claims require, as Davidson has emphasized, recognition of the fundamental difference between psychological and physical terms, a difference which rules out psycho-physical laws, and which entails that psychological *kinds* (properties) are fundamentally different from physical *kinds* (properties). My criticisms imply that this difference between the psychological and the physical should be extended to the level of particulars, and that we should recognize that the psychological not only classifies differently from the physical but also individuates differently. The former implies the rejection of type-identity materialism, the latter involves the rejection of token-identity materialism. For token-identity materialism assumes that physical individuation is privileged, and psychological individuation is secondary. There is no good reason to think that is true in general: the individuals of psychology are as irreducible to the individuals of physics, as the kinds of psychology are to the kinds of physics.[22] We can continue to defend monism without defending materialism of any kind.

---

the man's being injured, an event which occurs outside of the agent's body, is intrinsic to the act (von Wright would call it the result of the act) and not (as Davidson says) merely a consequence of the act in terms of which we describe it. See also my 'Philosophy of action: Davidson, von Wright, and the debate over causation' in *Contemporary philosophy: a new survey, Vol. 3* (Martinus Nijhoff, The Hague, 1982), pp. 45–72.

[22] For a similar conclusion see John Haugeland, 'Weak Supervenience' in *American Philosophical Quarterly*, Volume 19, Number 1 (January, 1982), pp. 93–103.

4

The Nature and Scope of Rational-Choice Explanation

JON ELSTER

How do rational-choice explanations explain? What are their limits and limitations? I want to discuss these questions in three steps.[1] In section 1 the topic is the more general category of intentional explanation of behaviour. Section 2 adds the specifications needed to generate rational-choice explanation. Section 3 considers more closely the power of rational-choice theory to yield unique deductions. In particular, this concerns the possible non-unicity and even non-existence of optimal choice.

1 *Intentionality*

To explain a piece of behaviour intentionally is to show that it derives from an intention of the individual exhibiting it. A successful intentional explanation establishes the behaviour as *action* and the performer as an *agent*. An explanation of this form amounts to demonstrating a three-place relation between the behaviour (B), a set of cognitions (C) entertained by the individual and a set of desires (D) that can also be imputed to him. The relation is defined by three conditions, that form the topic of this section.

First, we must require that the desires and beliefs are *reasons* for the behaviour. By this I mean:

(1) Given C, B is the best means to realize D

The presence of such reasons is not sufficient for the occurrence of the behaviour for which they are reasons. An actor might be asked to shudder as part of a scene. Even with the requisite beliefs and desires, he might find himself unable to shudder at will. More importantly, even if the behaviour does occur, the reasons do not suffice to explain it. The sight of a snake on the set might cause the actor to shudder involuntarily. This also holds if we assume

[1] I thank Marcelo Dascal, Dagfinn Føllesdal and Michael Root for their comments on an earlier version of this paper.

that the actor is in fact able to shudder at will, viz. if his intention to shudder is preempted by the sight of the snake. We must add, then, a clause ensuring that his behaviour was actually caused by his intention to behave in that way:

(2) C and D caused B

The reasons, that is, must also be causes of the action which they rationalize.[2] To see why this is also insufficient, we must look into the ways in which beliefs and desires can act as causes. Consider a rifleman aiming at target. He believes that only by hitting the target can he achieve some further goal that he values extremely highly. The belief and the desire provide reasons for a certain behaviour, viz. pulling the trigger when the rifle is pointed towards the target. They may, however, cause him to behave quite differently. If he is unnerved by the high stakes, his hand might shake so badly that he pulls the trigger at the wrong moment. If he cared less about hitting the target, he might have succeeded more easily. Here the strong desire to hit the target acts as a cause, but not *qua* reason. To act *qua* reason, it would at the very least have to be a cause of the behaviour for which it is a reason.

Now consider Davidson's well-known example:

> A climber might want to rid himself of the weight and danger of holding another man on a rope, and he might know that by loosening his hold on the rope, he could rid himself of the weight and the danger. This belief and want might so unnerve him as to cause him to loosen his hold, and yet it might be the case that he never *chose* to loosen his hold, nor did he do so intentionally.[3]

Here conditions (1) and (2) are fulfilled, yet the beliefs and desires do not cause the behaviour *qua* reasons. The example differs from that of the rifleman in that the beliefs and desires of the climber cause the very same behaviour for which they are reasons, but is similar in that they do not cause it *qua* reasons. It is a mere accident that in the case of the climber they happen to cause the very same behaviour for which they are reasons. Hence we must add:

(3) C and D caused B *qua* reasons

As in other cases, we may ask by virtue of which features the cause produced its effect. When the falling of the stone leads to the breaking of the ice, we point to the weight of the stone, not to its colour, to explain what happened. When the desire of the rifleman causes him to miss the target, we point to something like psychic turbulence or emotional excitement, not the strength of the desire. The latter reflects the agent's evaluation of the importance of the goal, compared to other goals that he might entertain. Hence the strength of the desire is primarily relevant for its efficacy *qua* reason, and only to the extent that the desire causes behaviour *qua* reason for the behaviour is its strength also relevant for its causal efficacy. The emotional halo surrounding the desire is irrelevant for its efficacy

---

[2] Here, as elsewhere, my debt to Donald Davidson's work will be obvious.
[3] D. Davidson, *Essays on Actions and Events* (Clarendon Press, Oxford, 1980), p. 79.

qua reason, but may influence its efficacy *qua* non-rational cause. To be sure, these are loose and metaphorical manners of speaking. We do not yet have a good language for getting emotions and their relevance for action into focus. Yet I take it that no one would deny the phenomenological reality of the facts I am describing, or the need for something like clause (3) in order to exclude a certain kind of accidental coincidences, just as clause (2) was needed to exclude another kind of coincidence.

Although these clauses would have to be satisfied in a fully satisfactory intentional explanation, we usually make less stringent requirements. An analogy would be the detective story that proceeds by inquiring into motive and opportunity. When a person engages in a certain kind of behaviour, we already know that he had the opportunity. If he did it, he could do it (in one sense of 'could'). If in addition we find that he had a motive and also knowledge of the opportunity, we usually conclude that we have found an intentional explanation of the behaviour, even if the kind of coincidences excluded by clauses (2) and (3) might conceivably have been operating. In some special cases we might want to reduce the likelihood of the first kind of coincidence, by also establishing that the agent had the ability to perform the behaviour in question, e.g. the ability to shudder at will or the ability to hit a target. While this does not fully eliminate the possibility of coincidence, it does so for most practical purposes. The point is that satisfaction of clauses (2) and (3) requires us to scrutinize the actual mental machinery at work, which is something we are only exceptionally able to do. By contrast, establishing motive, opportunity, knowledge and ability is a much easier task (which is not to say that it is at all an easy one).

The non-sufficiency of clause (1) in establishing an intentional explanation is related to the difference between explaining and predicting action. If (1) were sufficient for explanation, we could also use it for prediction. There is, however, no regular lawlike connection between having certain desires and beliefs on the one hand, and performing a certain action on the other.[4] However, just as for practical purposes clause (1) goes a long way towards explaining behaviour, one may with some practical confidence predict that motive, opportunity, etc. will result in action. The present paper, nevertheless, is mainly concerned with first-best explanation.

2 *Rationality*

Rational-choice explanation goes beyond intentionality in several respects. For one thing, we must insist that behaviour, to be rational, must stem from desires and beliefs that are themselves in some sense rational. For another, we must require a somewhat more stringent relation between the beliefs and desires on the one hand and the action on the other.

Minimally, we require that:

(4) The set of beliefs C is internally consistent

---

[4] Ibid., ch. 11.

(5) The set of desires D is internally consistent

One might think that these are required not just for rational-choice explanation, but for intentional explanation more generally. If, for instance, there is *no* way of realizing a given desire, because it is internally inconsistent, how could anyone choose the *best* way to realize it? The answer, of course, is that the agent must believe that the desire is feasible. This belief, in turn, is internally inconsistent. For the belief that a certain goal is feasible to be consistent, there must be some possible world in which it is feasible. And that implies that there must be some further world in which it is realized, contrary to the assumption. Yet purposive action may spring from such inconsistent mental states. Someone may believe that the best way of trisecting the angle by means of ruler and compass is by first drawing a certain auxiliary construction. That drawing can then be explained in terms of the logically inconsistent goal of trisecting the angle in this way, and the belief that the goal is feasible and best attained by first taking that step. If this is not an intentional explanation, nothing is, but we might not want to call it a rational-choice explanation.

True, this example is controversial, because the implicit notion of rationality might seem to be too stringent. In fact, it seems to confuse irrationality with lack of mental competence. To this one may answer that while there need not be anything irrational in wanting to bring about a goal that happens to be logically inconsistent, rationality requires that we should be aware of the possibility that it might not be feasible. To believe, unconditionally, in the feasibility of a certain mathematical construction can be irrational, regardless of its actual feasibility. This, however, pertains to the well-groundedness of the belief, not to its internal consistency; I return to this issue below. There are, however, other and more clearcut examples of actions deriving from internally inconsistent desires or beliefs. The belief 'It will rain if and only if I do not believe it will rain' is logically inconsistent,[5] yet people might decide, on the basis of this belief, to bring their umbrella along for a trip across the Sahara. Also one may cite the less exotic phenomena of intransitive preferences, inconsistent time preferences, subjective probabilities over exhaustive and exclusive events that do not add up to 1, etc.[6]

One might want to demand more rationality of the beliefs and desires than mere consistency. In particular, one might require that the beliefs be in some sense substantively well grounded, i.e. inductively justified by the available evidence. This, to be sure, is a highly problematic notion; yet here I assume throughout that it is a meaningful one. The analysis of rational belief then closely parallels that of intentional action. Again there are three conditions to be satisfied:

(1b) The belief must be the best belief, given the available evidence

---

[5] It is inconsistent because there is no possible world in which the belief is both true *and believed* (J. Hintikka, *Knowledge and Belief*, Cornell University Press, (Ithaca, N.Y., 1961)).

[6] Cp. J. Elster, *Sour Grapes*, Cambridge University Press, (Cambridge, 1983), ch. I, for more details.

(2b) The belief must be caused by the available evidence

(3b) The evidence must cause the belief 'in the right way'

Of these, the first condition presupposes some rather strong rule of inductive inference. The second is needed to rule out the possibility that one has hit on the best belief merely by accident. It may be possible, for example, to arrive by wishful thinking at the belief which also happens to be the best.[7] The third condition is needed to exclude the possibility that by considering the evidence one might arrive at the belief which is in fact warranted by it – but by an incorrect process of reasoning. There could, for instance, be several compensating errors in the method of inference.[8] Once again, we may make the distinction between this first-best analysis of rational belief-formation, and the less demanding condition that only (1b) be satisfied.

Given the satisfaction of (1b), (2b) and (3b), the belief is explained by its well-groundedness with respect to the available evidence E. One might want to make this part of the definition of rational-choice explanations:

(W) The relation between C and E must satisfy (1b), (2b) and (3b)

For reasons set out in section 3, this proposal is incomplete. It needs to be supplemented by a condition about how much evidence it is rational to collect.

Could one, similarly, demand substantive rationality of the desires? If so, what requirements would one want to impose on the rational formation of desires and preferences? Although I believe it possible to suggest the beginning of an answer to these questions, the results are not sufficiently robust to be reported here.[9] We do need, however, an additional condition on the relation between desires and behaviour. This is designed to exclude akratic behaviour, or weakness of the will.

Consider the man who wants to stop smoking, and yet yields to temptation when offered a cigarette. In accepting it, he behaves in conformity with conditions (1) through (5). He desires to smoke: a perfectly consistent goal. He believes that he is offered a cigarette, not just a plastic imitation. Hence the best way to realize his desire is to accept it, which he does. This, however, gives only part of the picture. The account mentions that there are reasons for smoking, but omits the reasons against smoking. When discussing intentional explanation, I implicitly used an existential quantifier: there exist a set of beliefs and a

---

[7] This is contested by D. Pears, *Motivated Irrationality* (Oxford University Press, Oxford, 1984), ch. 5. He argues that motivated, irrational belief formation always takes the form of a failure to correct an irrational belief, not the positive form of directly producing it; hence there is never any superfluous irrationality. I disagree, but the point is not essential to my argument, since there are other ways in which a belief might be caused by something else than the available evidence. A person might be hypnotized into forming a belief for which he also has good evidence, without having formed the belief prior to the hypnosis, since we do not usually put together the pieces of information in our mind unless there is a need to do so.

[8] R. Nisbett and L. Ross, *Human Inference: strategies and shortcomings of social judgment* (Prentice-Hall, Englewood Cliffs, N.J., 1980), pp. 267–8.

[9] See Elster, *Sour Grapes*, ch. I.3.

set of desires that constitute reasons for the action and that actually, *qua* reasons, cause it. But these need not be all the reasons there are. The agent may have a desire to stay in good health that would provide a reason for not accepting the offer. Moreover, he might think that this desire outweighs the immediate wish to smoke: all things considered, he had better reject the offer. And yet he might take it. To exclude such akratic behaviour from being considered rational, we must add the following condition:

(6) Given C, B is the best action with respect to the full set of weighed desires

There are various accounts of how akratic behaviour comes about. To my mind, the most plausible is offered by Donald Davidson, who argues that it occurs because of faulty causal wiring between the desires and the action.[10] The weaker reason may win out because it blocks the stronger ones from operating; or the stronger reasons might lose because they cause another behaviour than that for which they are reasons. In either case, condition (1) fails to hold for the full set of desires. The action is intentional, but irrational.

Is there a cognitive analogy to condition (6)? This would have to be part of condition (1b). By considering only part of the evidence, one might form a belief that is the best relative to that part, but not the best relative to the whole evidence. A related, although different process is at work when one decides to stop collecting evidence at the point where it favours the belief that, on other grounds, one wants to be true. I return to this shortly.

3 *Optimality*

The explanatory force in condition (1) derives from the requirement that the explanandum 'the best' means to accomplish the agent's goal. The enormous success of rational-choice models in economics and other sciences is due to their apparent ability to yield unique, determinate predictions in terms of maximizing behaviour. Although, generally speaking, explanation may take the form of elimination as well as determination,[11] the explanatory ideal in science is always to form hypotheses from which a unique observational consequence can be deduced. In this section I want to consider some difficulties with this view when applied to the social sciences. For one thing, there may be several options that are equally and maximally good; for another, there may be no 'best' option at all. One might retort that these are non-standard cases that, like the problems underlying conditions (2) and (3), only arise in rather perverse situations. This replique is not valid. There exists a strong general argument to the effect that uniquely maximizing behaviour is in general not possible.

Consider first the non-unicity of optimal choice, arising because the agent is indifferent between several options than which none better. There is then no room left for rational choice; yet typically the agent will be able at least to 'pick'

---

[10] Davidson, *Essay on Action and Events*, ch. 2. An alternative account is that of Pears, *Motivated Irrationality*.

[11] R. Ashby, *Introduction to Cybernetics* (Chapman & Hall, London, 1971), p. 130.

one of the options.[12] A fully satisfactory theory would then offer a causal supplement to the rational-choice explanation, by indicating how perceptual salience or some other value-neutral feature of the situation led to one option rather than another being 'picked'. Or, alternatively, one might redefine the choice situation by bunching the top-ranked alternatives into a single option. If I am indifferent between a red umbrella and a blue umbrella, but prefer both to a raincoat, the choice becomes determinate once we have bunched the first two options as 'an umbrella'. This way out, however, may be unavailable if the top-ranked alternatives differ along more than one dimension, since then the indifference between the options could be due to offsetting virtues rather than to value-neutrality.

The presence of multiple optima can create a good deal of embarrassment. General-equilibrium theory, for instance, is not really able to cope with this problem. In the simplest version of this theory, all optima in production and consumption are assumed to be unique. Given some additional assumptions, one can then show that there is a set of prices that will allow all markets to clear when agents optimize. In the more complex version, multiple optima are allowed. The equilibrium concept is correspondingly modified, to mean the existence of a set of prices and a set of optimizing acts that allow market clearing.[13] The difficulty is not that the choice of these acts rather than other optimizing acts would be a pure accident. Rather it is that the indeterminacy is essential for the existence proof to go through. In the actual world, there is no indeterminacy. One optimum will always be chosen. Clearly, if one had a theory that explained which of the maximally good options is chosen (or picked), it would be an improvement over a theory which leaves this indeterminate. Yet it would destroy the existence proof, by introducing a discontinuity in the reaction functions.

In game theory, multiple optima abound. In the wide class of non-cooperative games that have an equilibrium point, many have equilibria that consist of mixed strategies. In any equilibrium point of mixed strategies any actor has many optimal strategies, given that all the others choose their equilibrium strategies. In fact, any pure strategy or linear combination of pure strategies is as good as any other. Why, then, should an actor choose the equilibrium strategy? John Harsanyi argues that the lack of any good answer to this question is a basic flaw in game theory as traditionally conceived. He proposes a substitute solution concept, according to which only 'centroid' or equi-probabilistic mixed strategies are allowed. This corresponds to the idea that when there are several optima, one is chosen at random by 'what amounts to an unconscious chance mechanism inside [the player's] nervous system'.[14] This, of course, is essentially a causal concept.

Consider now the non-existence of optimal behaviour, which can arise in

---

[12] E. Ullmann-Margalit and S. Morgenbesser, 'Picking and choosing', *Social Research*, 44 (1977), pp. 757–85.

[13] See G. Debreu, *Theory of Value* (Wiley, New York, 1959), and many later expositions.

[14] J. Harsany, *Rational Behavior and Bargaining Equilibrium in Games and Social Situations* (Cambridge University Press, Cambridge, 1977), p. 114.

strategic as well as non-strategic situations. A simple case obtains when an agent has incomplete preferences, so that for at least one pair of alternatives x and y it is neither true that he weakly prefers x to y nor that he weakly prefers y to x. If a pair of such non-comparable options are on the top of the agent's preference ranking, in the sense that for each of them it is true that there is none better, it will not be true that there is at least one alternative that is at least as good as all others. In actual cases it may seem hard to distinguish between incomparability and indifference, but the following test should help us. If there is an alternative (perhaps outside the feasible set) that is preferred to x, then it should also be preferred to y if the relation is one of indifference,[15] but this implication does not hold in cases of non-comparability.

As suggested by Sen and Williams, non-comparability may be especially important when our rankings are sensitive to the welfare of other people.[16] Assume that I have the choice between giving ten dollars to one of my children and giving them to another. I may well find myself unable to decide, and, moreover, find that I am equally unable to choose between giving eleven dollars to the first and ten dollars to the second, although I would rather give eleven than ten to the first. This would indicate that I simply am unable to assess the welfare they would derive from the money in a sufficiently precise way to allow me to make up my mind. Yet decisions will usually be made (although in this case paralysis of action is perhaps more plausible than in some other cases,[17]) so for their explanation we must look beyond rational-choice theory.

Preferences can be defined over outcomes or over actions. I shall assume that the latter are derived from the former, so that one prefers an action over another because one prefers the outcome it brings about.[18] I have just discussed the case in which the preferences among actions are incomplete, because the corresponding outcome-preferences are. Action-preferences may, however, be incomplete even when the outcome-preferences are complete, viz. if one is in the presence of uncertainty. Observe first that in condition (1) the notion of 'best' is to be taken in a subjective sense – 'best' relative to the beliefs of the agent. This includes the case of probabilistic beliefs, in which to act rationally means to maximize expected utility. Sometimes, however, it is not possible to establish subjective probabilities on which one can rationally rely on making up one's mind. In decisions concerning nuclear energy, for instance, it seems pointless to ask for the subjective probability attached to the event that a given democratic country some time in the next millennium turns into a military

---

[15] This follows if we make the assumption of consistent preferences (K. Suzumura, *Rational Choice, Collective Decisions and Social Welfare*, p. 8, (Cambridge University Press, Cambridge, 1984), a somewhat weaker requirement than transitivity.

[16] A. Sen and B. Williams, Introduction to *Utilitarianism and Beyond*, ed. A. Sen and B. Williams (Cambridge University Press, Cambridge, 1982), p. 17.

[17] The alternatives are x: give to one child, y: give to the other child and z: give to neither. It may happen that *because* I weakly prefer neither x to y nor y to x, I strongly prefer z to both, perhaps because it would create family trouble if I selected one child without being able to justify my choice in terms of welfare. Yet in the absence of x (or y), I would strongly prefer y (or x) to z.

[18] I do not, of course, deny that actions may be valued for themselves. The assumption is made only for the sake of simplifying the discussion.

dictatorship that could use the reactor plutonium to make bombs.[19] And I believe the same problem arises in many cases of short-term planning as well. In decision-making under uncertainty it is only under very special conditions that we can pick out the top-ranked action. Specifically, this requires that there is one option such that its worst-consequence is better than the best-consequence of any other option.[20] Failing this, rationality is no guide to action, and a fortiori not a guide to explanation of action.

Non-existence of optimal choice may also stem from the strategic nature of the situation. There are two cases: either there is no equilibrium point, or there are several equilibria none of which can be singled out as the solution.[21] The first can arise when the set of alternatives is unbounded or open. In the game 'Pick a number – and the player who has picked the largest number wins', there is no equilibrium set of strategies because the strategy set is unbounded. Hyperinflation sometimes looks a bit like this game. In the game 'Pick a number strictly smaller than 1 – and the player who has picked the largest number wins', there is no equilibrium point because the set is open. One may illustrate this with a variant of the game of 'Chicken', in which the point is to drive at top speed towards a wall and then stop as close to it as possible.

More central, probably, are games that do have equilibria but no unique solution. The standard version of 'Chicken' illustrates this concept. Here two players are driving straight towards each other, and the point is not to be the first to swerve. There are two equilibria, in each of which one driver swerves and the other does not, but there is no way in which rationality alone will help the players converge towards the one or the other. An example of this interaction structure could be some forms of technical innovation, characterized by 'Winner takes all'.[22] The individual firm will have little incentive to invest in R & D if other firms invest heavily, and a strong incentive to do so if others do not. I want to insist that such cases illustrate the non-existence of optimal choice, rather than its non-unicity. When there are multiple equilibria, individual agents cannot toss a coin between the various equilibrium strategies attached to them. True, by coordinating their actions they might toss a coin between the full equilibrium strategy sets, but in that case we have left the domain of individual rationality with which we are concerned here.

Let me pause at this point by drawing a little diagram, to summarize what has been said so far about non-unicity and non-existence of optimal choice.

---

[19] J. Elster, *Explaining Technical Change* (Cambridge University Press, Cambridge, 1983), appendix 1, has a further discussion.

[20] For the proof that in decision-making under uncertainty one can rationally only take account of the best and the worst consequences of each action, see K. Arrow and L. Hurwicz, 'An optimality criterion for decision-making under uncertainty,' in *Uncertainty and Expectation in Economics*, ed. C.F. Carter and J.L. Ford (Kelley, Clifton, N.J., 1972). The proof turns upon the idea that rational choice should remain invariant under an arbitrary reclassification of 'states of nature'.

[21] Recent work has raised a third possibility: even if there is only one equilibrium point in the game, there may be several strategy sets that are 'rationalizable' (B.D. Bernheim, 'Rationalizable strategic behavior', *Econometrica*, 52 (1984), pp. 1007–28; D.G. Pearce, 'Rationalizable strategic behavior and the problem of perfection', *Econometrica*, 52 (1984), pp. 1029–50).

[22] See Elster, *Explaining Technical Change*, pp. 109ff., drawing on P. Dasgupta and J. Stiglitz, 'Uncertainty, industrial structure and the speed of R & D', *Bell Journal of Economics*, 11 (1980), pp. 1–28.

I have been arguing for the following phenomena:

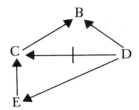

(a) Non-unicity of optimal behaviour, given D and C.
(b) Non-existence of optimal behaviour, given D and C.
(c) Non-existence of optimal beliefs, given E.

Here, D and E have been considered as given. I said above that I did not want to enter into the speculative question whether D could also be subject to rationality criteria, but we surely have to ask this question concerning E. How much evidence is it rational to collect before forming the belief on the basis of which one decides to act? Every decision to act can be seen as accompanied by a *shadow decision* – the decision about when to stop collecting information. The former can be no more rational than the latter, on which it is based, although it may well be less rational if some other things go wrong in the sequence.

In most cases it will be equally irrational to spend no time on collecting evidence and to spend most of one's time doing so. In between there is some optimal amount of time that should be spent on information-gathering. This, however, is true only in the objective sense that an observer who knew everything about the situation could assess the value of gathering information and find the point at which the marginal value of information equals marginal costs. But of course the agent who is groping towards a decision does not have the information needed to make an optimal decision with respect to information-collecting.[23] He knows, from first principles, that information is costly and that there is a trade-off between collecting information and using it, but he does not know what that trade-off is.

It is like going into a big forest to pick mushrooms. One may explore the possibilities in one limited region, but at some point one must stop the exploration and start picking because further exploration as to the possibilities of finding more and better mushrooms would defeat the purpose of the outing. One must decide

---

[23] Since the point is crucial, let me clarify it by means of an analogous example. In the theory of induced factor-bias in technical change, the argument was put forward (C. Kennedy, 'Induced bias in innovation and theory of distribution', *Economic Journal*, 74 (1964), pp. 541–7) that firms optimize with respect to an 'innovation possibility frontier'. Although one may agree, at least for the sake of argument, that an omniscient observer would know which innovations are possible at a given time, it is impossible to see how this would help to explain the behaviour of the firms, since there is no way in which they could acquire the same knowledge. Rational-choice explanations turn upon what the agents *believe* to be the best action, not on an objective conception of the best. Any theory that neglects this constraint lacks microfoundations (W. Nordhaus, 'Some sceptical thoughts on the theory of induced innovations', *Quarterly Journal of Economics*, 87 (1973), pp. 208–19).

on an intuitive basis, i.e. without actually investigating whether further exploration would have yielded better results.[24]

To repeat, this argument does not imply that any decision about when to stop information-gathering is arbitrary. There will usually be many specific pieces of information that one knows it is worth while acquiring. One knows that in order to build a bridge there are some things one must know. These form a lower bound on information-collection. An obvious upper bound is that one must not spend so much time gathering the information that it becomes pointless. If one wants to predict next day's weather, one cannot spend more than twenty-four hours gathering evidence. Sometimes the gap between the upper and the lower bound can be narrowed down considerably, notably in highly stereotyped situations like medical diagnostics. One then has a basis for estimating, with good approximation, the expected value of more information. In many everyday decisions, however, not to speak of military or business decisions, a combination of factors conspire to pull the lower and upper bounds apart from one another. The situation is novel, so that past experience is of limited help. It is changing rapidly, so that information runs the risk of becoming obsolete. If the decision is urgent and important, one may expect both the benefits and the opportunity costs of information-collecting to be high, but this is not to say that one can estimate the relevant marginal equalities.

The upper and lower bounds on information-collection are determined in part by the nature of the problem, in part by one's preferences. When building a bridge with profit as objective and safety as constraint, one will have different bounds than when using safety as objective and profit as constraint. There is nothing wrong, therefore, in the presence of a causal link between D and E, as drawn in the diagram. Note, however, that desires can determine the collection of information in another way, more related to wishful thinking. (Wishful thinking in the diagram is indicated by the line from D to C – blocked in order to indicate that this is not a proper causal influence.) One may stop collecting evidence at the point where the sum total of the evidence collected until then favours the belief that one would want to be true. Sometimes this is clearly irrational, viz. if one is led to stop collecting evidence before the lower bound has been reached. But what if the wish for a certain belief to hold true leads one to collect an amount of evidence well between the lower and upper bounds? Imagine a general who is gathering information about the position of enemy troops. The information is potentially invaluable, but waiting to gather it exposes him to grave risks. He decides to attack when *and because* the net balance of information so far leads him (rationally) to believe that the enemy is highly vulnerable. I am not sure about this case, but I submit that his procedure is not irrational. The wish in this case functions merely as a heuristic device that allows him to make a decision. There is no reason to think that the causal

---

[24] L. Johansen, *Lectures on Macro-Economic Planning* (North-Holland, Amsterdam, 1977), p. 144. Ultimately the argument derives from Herbert Simon. For a strikingly provocative discussion, see also S. Winter, 'Economic "natural selection" and the theory of the firm', *Yale Economic Essays*, 4 (1964), pp. 225–72.

influence of the wish tends to make the decision worse than it would have been had a different device been used.

In short, the only condition one can impose on E is rather vague:

(N) One should collect an amount of evidence that lies between the upper and lower bounds that are defined by the problem situation, including D

Correspondingly, we may impose the following condition on the relation between evidence, belief and desires:

(7) The relation between C, D and E must satisfy (1b), (2b), (3b) and (N)

This concludes my account of rational-choice explanation.

4 *Summary*

Ideally, a fully satisfactory rational-choice explanation of an action would have the following structure. It would show that the action is the (unique) best way of satisfying the full set of the agent's desires, given the (uniquely) best beliefs the agent could form, relatively to the (uniquely determined) optimal amount of evidence. We may refer to this as the *optimality part* of the explanation. In addition the explanation would show that the action was caused (in the right way) by the desires and beliefs, and the beliefs caused (in the right way) by consideration of the evidence. We may refer to this as the *causal part* of the explanation. These two parts together yield a first-best rational-choice explanation of the action. The optimality part by itself yields a second-best explanation, which, however, for practical purposes may have to suffice, given the difficulty of access to the psychic causality of the agent.

It follows from section 3 that even the second-best explanation runs into serious difficulties. It rests on three uniqueness postulates: unique determination of the optimal evidence, of the optimal beliefs given the evidence and of the optimal action given the beliefs and the desires. Each of the links in the chain has been challenged, in the sense that both the unicity and the very existence of optimality have been shown to be problematic in certain cases. The most serious challenge arises at the level of information-gathering, since it will only exceptionally be possible for the agent to determine the marginal cost and benefit of more information. The challenge at the next level arises in cases of uncertainty, i.e. when the evidence does not allow any belief, even a probabilistic one, to be formed. Finally, the link from mental states to action was shown to be problematic, both with respect to unicity and with respect to existence.

Given that one or more of these links fails to yield a unique optimum, the explanation cannot take the form of determination; rather it must consist in eliminating some of the abstractly possible actions. At each level, it is possible to eliminate some of the options in the feasible set. The nature of the problem sets upper and lower bounds on the amount of information one should collect. In cases of uncertainty one should at least not choose an action that has worse best-consequences than the worse worst-consequences of some other action.

In cases of indifference or non-comparability one should not choose an option to which some other alternative is strictly preferred. In games without solutions it is less clear what options are eliminated.

Under the same assumption, the rational-choice explanation must be supplemented by a causal account. At the level of information-gathering one may refer to the fact that people have different aspiration levels. Some people spend ten minutes, others two hours, looking for the best place for mushrooms. In decision-making under uncertainty one may invoke such psychological features as optimism or pessimism to explain why people choose maximax or maximin strategies. When the indeterminacy occurs at the level of action, the explanation may involve perceptual salience (in the case of indifference or non-comparability) or a desire for security (if the maximin behaviour is chosen in games without solution).

Hence rational-choice explanation may fail because the situation does not allow a unique behavioural prediction from the hypothesis that agents behave rationally. But we should not forget that it sometimes fails simply because people act irrationally. They yield to wishful thinking, in the sense of letting their desires determine their beliefs or the amount of evidence they collect before forming their beliefs (assuming that the result is below the lower bound). Or they succumb to weakness of will, in the sense of acting for the sake of a desire which they themselves value less highly than the remaining set of desires. Finally, their intentions and beliefs may be subject to various inconsistencies that are also incompatible with rational choice.

Let me point to a final consequence of this analysis. It has shown that there are many dimensions of latitude in the notion of rationality. Correspondingly, we get more degrees of freedom in our interpretation of other people. In trying to understand each other, we are guided and constrained by the idea that by and large others are as rational as ourselves. The slack in the concept of rationality implies that we are able to understand more, although it also implies that our understanding will be more diffuse.[25]

---

[25] Davidson, *Essays on Actions and Events*, ch. 11.

5

Fishing the Red Herrings Out of the Sea of Moral Responsibility

PETER A. FRENCH

In the mid-seventies, when I was developing the metaphysical foundations in agency theory for the view that corporations should be treated as moral persons, I had the opportunity for an extended discussion of the nuances of the notion of redescription with Donald Davidson. He provided a number of trenchant suggestions that were pivotal in structuring the form my argument finally took. Some months later in the tiny, desolate town of Morris, Minnesota, on the edges of the vast empty prairie, J.L. Mackie, Donald Davidson, and I spent a number of hours discussing Davidson's work on action and events and Mackie's book on causality. (Philosophy is truly a movable feast!) That experience stimulated further work on corporate moral agency. Shortly thereafter I sent Davidson a draft of the paper that later was published as 'The corporation as a moral person.' Davidson wrote back, 'I like it very much. The use you make of my ideas on agency seems appropriate and interesting; more important, I think your view that a corporation simply is irreducibly a moral person is the only view that makes good sense.' In that paper, however, I only scratched on the surface of Davidson's work on agency and its implications for the conditions of moral personhood and the understanding of the variety of interrelated principles that comprise our concept of moral responsibility. This paper is intended to dig a bit deeper.[1]

(1) It has become standard in moral philosophy to explicate the concept of responsibility in terms of the notion of intentional agency. The question, 'What are the essential characteristics of a morally responsible entity?' is regularly translated into a series of issues about the conditions of metaphysical personhood, intentionality, and freedom. It is generally assumed that an adequate understanding of intentional agency will include or, at least, entail the concept of a morally responsible entity and also produce a basic principle of responsibility.

J. L. Mackie has called the prototypical version of that principle the 'straight rule of responsibility.' It says that 'an agent is responsible for all and only [its] intentional actions.'[2] Although he did not endorse this principle without

---

[1] This paper owes much to a series of helpful discussions with my colleague Curtis Brown.
[2] J.L. Mackie, *Ethics: inventing right and wrong* (Penguin Books, Harmondsworth, 1977), p. 208.

modifications, I will refer to it in this pristine form as 'Mackie's Rule.' On Mackie's Rule ascriptions of responsibility are proper only when made about things capable of intentional action, intentional systems. An intentional system may be defined, following Dennett,[3] as a system some of whose behavior can be explained and predicted by relying on ascriptions to the system's beliefs and desires (or hopes, fears, intentions, perceptions, expectations, etc.). It is irrelevant to something's being an intentional system that its behavior also can be adequately explained in a purely mechanistic way. To be an intentional system, as Dennett stresses,[4] an entity need not have any particular intrinsic features that are referred to when it is called intentional. It need not have, for example, any 'real' beliefs or desires. It merely has to 'succumb to an intentional stance' adopted toward it. In other words, it must make sense to ascribe intentional predicates to some of its behavior and that is only to say of it that it has reasons for doing some things, or expects certain outcomes or wants certain ends, or seeks, hopes, etc. The conditions of something's being an intentional system may be more profitably explicated in terms of Donald Davidson's account of agency. It is on his account that I will focus my attention.

For an entity to be treated as a Davidsonian agent it must be the case that some of the things that happen (some events) are describable in a way that makes certain sentences true, sentences that say that some of the things the entity does were intended by the entity itself.[5] This, of course, is remarkably similar to the basic requirements for a first-order Dennett intentional system. An identifying feature of attributions of intentionality is that they are referentially opaque: that on one description of a piece of behavior it is intentional does not entail that it is intentional on all true descriptions of the event. Hence a perfectly good account of a piece of an entity's behavior may be purely mechanistic while at least one true description of that behavior says that the entity acted to bring about some state of affairs, or because of certain expectations, or desires, etc.

As long as there is one true description of the event that says it was intended by the agent, the event is an action of the agent. In this way intentionality is used to sort actions out of the larger category of events. For example, if I dump out a cup of coffee, believing it is tea and wanting to dump out the tea, then dumping out the coffee (though not what I intended) is an action of mine.

Mackie's Rule clearly allows only intended actions as appropriate subjects of responsibility ascriptions. But commonly it is actions, some of which are unintended under the relevant description (though intended under other descriptions), for which we are held accountable. An extension of Mackie's Rule or, rather, a restatement of it in terms of actions seems advisable. We could rephrase the rule to read: 'A person is responsible for his actions.' That appears to be in tune with what Bradley called 'the vulgar notion of responsibility.' The matter of whether or not those actions were intended under the

---

[3] Daniel Dennett, 'Conditions of personhood,' in *The Identities of Persons*, ed. Amelie Rorty (University of California Press, Berkeley, 1976), p. 179.

[4] Ibid., p. 179.

[5] See Donald Davidson, 'Agency,' in *Essays on Actions and Events* (Clarendon Press, Oxford, 1980), pp. 43–61.

relevant description seems to play more of a role in mitigation than in structuring the basic rule of moral responsibility. For example, if I really intended to dump out tea, but mistook the coffee for tea, I might be forgiven or lightly reprimanded and required to make a fresh pot. In more serious matters forgiveness may be harder to garner by appeal to 'intention under a different description,' e.g. 'I didn't know the gun was loaded.'

We might view this as a first shaking of the foundations of Mackie's Rule, but an important link to intentionality is preserved, for it is intentionality ascriptions that drag the doings of entities into the class of their actions while it is for actions (those that are or produce untoward events), in the first instance, that moral responsibility is ascribed.

(2) Moral theorists generally have shown little appreciation for the philosophical and practical consequences of Davidson's account of agency. That is unfortunate, for a number of important things follow from the Davidsonian idea that intentionality is wrapped up in the possibility of redescription.

Whether or not something is an intentional agent depends upon the possibility of describing things that happen or its movements in a particular sort of way: as upshots of the reasons for their occurring. When we describe them by reference to desires, wantings, etc., we describe them as intentional actions. Intentional agents then, or moral persons, come into existence at various levels of description, or, more to the point, via descriptions. Hence whether or not something is a morally responsible entity, i.e. a moral person, is dependent on rules of redescription that allow us to say of a movement of a body that it was, e.g. pitching a baseball or stabbing the person hiding behind the arras. Those rules, or what I have elsewhere called licenses of redescription,[6] are cultural, linguistic, historical inventions.

If a human being were never to do anything that could be properly redescribed as the upshot of its having certain reasons, desires, expectations, etc., no matter what it did, it would not be a member of the moral community. By the same token, if a machine's behavior could be so described, as for example a game playing computer's moves might be attributed to its strategies, then it is a Dennett intentional system or a Davidsonian agent and, using Mackie's Rule, could qualify as a moral person. I have argued that corporations with certain kinds of decision structures, those having not only standard recognizable procedures but also delineatable policies, also satisfy the requirements of Davidsonian agency.[7]

What I have called the Corporate Internal Decision Structure (CID Structure) is really just a redescription license of the required sort. A CID Structure has two elements of crucial interest: (1) an organizational system that delineates stations and levels of decision-making and (2) a set of decision/action recognition rules of two types: procedural and policy. These recognition rules provide the tests that a decision or an action was made for corporate reasons within the corporate decision structure. The policy recognitors are

---

[6] Peter A. French, 'The corporation as a moral person,' *American Philosophical Quarterly*, Vol. 16, Number 3 (1979), pp. 207–16.
[7] Ibid.

particularly relevant to the attribution of corporate intentionality. Borrowing the distinction from Wittgenstein,[8] the organizational structure of a corporation gives the grammar of its decision-making and the recognition rules provide its logic. The CID Structure accomplishes a subordination and synthesis of the decisions and acts of various human beings and other intentional systems into a corporate action, an event that under one of its aspects may be truthfully described as having been done for corporate reasons or to bring about corporate ends, expectations, purposes, etc.

Although Davidson is concerned to explicate human agency, there is nothing in his account that requires that the primitive actions, the moving of bodies that is all that we ever do when we act, must be performed by the entity to whom the relevant intentionality is being attributed. It is just that, for every action, on some true description it is intentional and on another it is a basic bodily movement. In the case of a corporation raising its prices on a product it manufactures, the primitive action might be located in the body of a senior officer, e.g. the writing of a signature on the bottom of a piece of paper. (That is not, of course, really primitive, we should talk instead of his hand moving in a certain way.) There may be a number of intentional descriptions that are true of that event. One may attribute to him the intention of signing the document knowing full well that his so doing has the procedural effect of corporately doing something. At yet another descriptive level, however, it is true (given the CID Structure of his corporation) that the corporation intentionally or deliberately raised the price, that it had certain corporate reasons or purposes for doing so (consistent with its basic policies, including profit maximization) that are quite distinct from any purposes the executive might have had for affixing his signature.

As long as there are primitive acts (body or physical movements) that are being redescribed, there seems to be no built-in restriction on the number (or layers) of descriptions before the focal intentional one is reached or the number of intentional acts performed when a single primitive movement occurs. Each description, of course, must be true and accord with appropriate description rules. We could imagine a situation in which the muscles of a hand contract, pulling a lever, releasing a storage tank of untreated chemical waste, polluting a canal in a residential area and it be true of the lever-puller that his only intention (if he had one at all) was to pull the lever as ordered by his superior. Furthermore, we stipulate that the lever-puller had absolutely no intention of polluting the canal, etc., though that is certainly one of his actions, assuming he intentionally pulled the lever. If he were incapable of doing anything intentionally, suppose he was under a hypnotic trance or that he was really a robot programmed to pull the lever at a specific time every day, then pulling the lever and polluting the canal would not be actions of his. (Under the circumstances, he will probably be excused from the responsibility for it.) What the lever-puller did, however, may be redescribed, if the company in question had adopted certain policies about waste disposal and/or had reasons for (interest in) getting rid of its waste in such a fashion, as Hooker Chemical's intentional pollution of

---

[8] Ludwig Wittgenstein, *Philosophical Remarks* (Basil Blackwell, Oxford, 1975), p. 39.

the canal or Hooker's intentional dumping of waste materials, then the lever-puller's actions or his movements if they were not his actions are corporate actions of Hooker Chemical. The fact that something was done by a robot, then does not entail that it was not an action of whatever programs or controls the robots.

This sort of expansion of what I take to be a Davidsonian account of intentionality raises hurricane signals for many moral philosophers because it entails that the moral community is not, shall we say, metaphysically basic or substantial. Its members are not identified in the way those of natural kinds are. Instead, the moral community is a product of a certain kind of description or, rather, redescription.

(3) Intentionality, the criterion of agency, is intensional, though the expression of agency is extensional. Davidson notes: 'The relation that holds between a person and an event, when the event is an action performed by the person, holds regardless of how the terms are described. Therefore, we can without confusion speak of the class of events that are actions, which we cannot do with intentional actions.'[9] Hamlet intentionally killed the person hiding behind the arras in Queen Gertrude's room, but he did not intentionally kill Polonius, though Polonius was the person hiding behind the arras. Hamlet had no intention of killing Polonius or of orphaning Ophelia. His intentions with respect to the event seem to have been to (1) kill the King and (2) to kill the person hiding behind the arras (who he believed to be the King) and (3) to frighten Gertrude. There is only one event, so Hamlet's intentionally killing the person hiding behind the arras is extensionally identical to Hamlet's killing Polonius. If there were a class of intentional acts, we would be committed to saying that one and the same action, what Hamlet did, was both intentional and not intentional. This would tend to further support our revision of Mackie's Rule in terms of actions rather than intentional actions. If we are trying to specify the class of events for which an agent can be held accountable, we had better focus on a class of events.

Clearly Hamlet was the agent of Polonius' death. Killing Polonius was one of his actions. Should he be held morally responsible for Polonius' death? I suspect that most of us would say yes; even though it was not his intention. It would badly bend the concept of an intentional action to rescue the old Mackie Rule by treating every act done intentionally under some description as intentional. As long as our intuitions are that Hamlet is morally responsible for the death of Polonius, we will have to abandon the idea that persons are morally responsible for only their intended actions.

Consider another example: I know how much you prize a cup of coffee before entering an important meeting. Your cup has been filled with coffee, but you have not yet arrived. I find your cup but think it is filled with tea, which I know you dislike. I dump the contents of the cup down the drain, intending to pour out a fresh cup of coffee for you. You enter as I discover that the coffee pot is dry and you identify the residue in the sink as coffee. Clearly, I intentionally

---

[9] Davidson, 'Agency', p. 47.

dumped the cup believing it was filled with tea. What I did was intentional, though what I did was dump the cup of coffee and I did not do that intentionally. Am I not still responsible for the loss of the coffee? Hopefully, however, you will forgive me because I thought it was tea. Laertes will not forgive Hamlet for killing his father because Hamlet thought the person behind the arras was the King. There seems no reason why he should.

Interestingly, praise or credit and holding morally responsible are not symmetrical in what seem like similar cases. Suppose someone had laced the coffee with arsenic. I think it is tea, dump it, and it is later learned that I saved your life. It is unlikely I will be credited or praised for saving your life, though saving your life was what I did.

More closely parallel to the Hamlet case, suppose that I am passing a lake and see someone drowning. I am convinced that it is X, a dear friend. I toss caution to the winds, dive in, and save the drowning person who, it turns out, is Y, my most bitter and despicable enemy. I tell Y, who offers me a healthy reward, 'If I'd known it was you, I'd have let you sink. The only reason I jumped in was to save X. My intention was to save the person drowning who I thought was X. It was most assuredly not to save you, you swine.' Do I deserve moral praise for saving Y? I think we would be reluctant to extend it, when we know what my intentions were. It would seem that for morally crediting and praising the person is expected to have the specific intentions to do the creditable praiseworthy deed. We hold persons morally responsible or accountable, like Hamlet, however, for untoward events over a much greater range of their actions. I suspect the reason for that is that, despite what Kant would have said, we are much more concerned with controlling and preventing untoward or harmful occurrences than we are with patting people on the back for the good things they do or for examining their mental states when things have gone awry. Again we have reason to endorse the modified version of Mackie's Rule that says that an agent is morally accountable for its actions. Although intentionality allows us to sort actions out of the class of events, it is not central to the attribution of responsibility. At best we may look at intentions in the evaluation of excuses put forth to mitigate penalties. In a way that is what happened on the positive side in the praising cases. Praise is withdrawn if the intentions are inappropriate. Punishment or blame may be lessened if the intentions were good but the result an untoward event. If I am right about this, then praise and blame (affected by consideration of specific intentions) are matters apart from or following after attributions of moral responsibility. (Curtis Brown suggested to me that Ophelia and Laertes may not blame Hamlet quite so much for their father's death upon learning he had no intention of killing the old man, though he is still morally responsible for Polonius' death.)

The notion of responsibility is basically a minimum maintenance and preventative device. Its focus is clearly, as Austin noted, on situations that have gone wrong, on events where harm has occurred, etc. It is more important to curtail such events and identify perpetrators, than to allow the claim 'I never intended that' to end the matter.

(4) Davidson makes a persuasive case against another vestige of the traditional way of distinguishing the members of the moral community from

those with respect to whom responsibility ascriptions are inappropriate.[10] If I lace your coffee with arsenic with the intention of killing you and I succeed, did I not cause your death by poisoning your coffee? The temptation, of course, is to agree, but agree to what? It sounds as if the claim is that I, i.e. the agent, caused something, your death. Most basically, of course, what I caused was my hand muscles to contract in a specific way. That muscle contraction caused the poison to be put in your coffee. The implication is that there are two distinct kinds of causality. Regular event causality, as when contracting hand muscles cause poison to drop in your cup, and agent causality, a special power that intentional agents, that is persons, have to cause parts of themselves, e.g. hand muscles, to do things. Surely if there is such a thing as agent causality, being a person should require having the capacity or power to agent-cause.

Davidson has conclusively demonstrated, however, that agency requires nothing like agent-causation. It should be recalled that primitive actions are basic bodily movements, such as moving a finger. It may well be true that I cause my finger to move in a certain way by contracting certain hand muscles and I do that by making a certain event occur in my brain. It looks as if the movement of my finger, rather than being primitive, is the result of more basic actions. But that is not the case, for doing something that causes my finger to move does not cause me to move my finger. It is moving my finger. Davidson's argument is something of this form: suppose that causing a primitive action is to introduce an event separable from and prior to the action. This prior, distinct event must either be an action or not an action. If it were an action, then the action with which we began (the one we pronounced to be primitive) was not primitive. If it were not an action, then we slip into trying to explain intentional agency by appeal to the obscure, if not utterly senseless, notion of *causing* that is not a *doing*. The whole idea of a special kind of causation that is a mark of agency, a Cartesian mental ability that computers, corporations, and other non-human intentional systems are supposed to lack, is then rendered contentless, useless, and unnecessary. Causation between events perfectly well accounts for intentionality. The relationship between my moving my finger and the arsenic being put in your coffee and your being poisoned is simple event causality. No appeal to a special brand of causation (that is the making of cerebral events occur that is not itself an action of the agent) is required to explain how it is that I am the cause of your being poisoned. As Davidson notes,[11] even if the agent must make certain brain events occur and he is utterly unaware that he has to do that to move his finger, moving his finger is all that he does and he does it under at least one description intentionally, the description of the event as intentionally putting arsenic in your coffee, that is, poisoning your coffee in order to kill you.

It is certainly true that most of us do not know that we are making things happen in our brains when we move our fingers. We may be ignorant of the fact that we have brains, like the Scarecrow in *The Wizard of Oz*. What is needed for action is that the agent know what he does under some description. All he needs to know is that he is moving his fingers or that he is poisoning the coffee, etc.,

---

[10] Ibid., pp. 52–60.
[11] Ibid., p. 59.

for the event to be an action of his under all of its descriptions, including the neurophysiological one.

If Davidson is right, searching for the identifying characteristics of moral persons will not be looking for occult mental powers. A Davidsonian agency account conjoined with the modified Mackie Rule does not exclude non-human intentional systems from membership in the moral community. Mackie's Rule, as modified, however, is far short of adequate to satisfy our intuitions about responsibility.

(5) In its basic form Mackie's Rule holds that the necessary and sufficient condition of being morally accountable for an action is having intended it. Already we have modified the rule to include actions of the agent that were not intended under the relevant description. Having intended *something* is then a necessary condition for moral responsibility, but it is not necessary that the action being targeted have been intentional.

Surely we are not held to morally account for every action we perform. I suppose we are not, but that is probably only because we have adopted some standard exclusionary rules for blaming or punishing, that is rules that allow the appeal that it was unintended to mitigate or even exculpate over a range of cases. The governing factor on the scope of moral responsibility over actions, however, is not intentionality *per se*. The first and foremost concern in the assessment of moral responsibility is, as Austin once said, with the fact that something has gone awry.[12] In other words, we determine first that something went wrong. Then we find out whose actions produced it. That person is morally responsible, but if it were not the person's intention to do that action, mitigating or exculpating excuses are entertained. Austin put this rather well when he identified such words as 'intentionally,' 'deliberately,' and 'on purpose' as 'words of aggravation – words, that is, that not only don't get us out of things, but may actually make things worse for us.'[13] Excuse words like 'inadvertently' and 'mistakenly,' on the other hand, are used to loosen the noose of responsibility, by admitting that it wasn't a good thing to have done, but claiming it not to be accurate to say it was done 'baldly.'[14] In a standard excuse, its maker has to acknowledge the action and that it was untoward, but then tries to avoid the full fury of moral condemnation by pleading some kind of extenuation. Excuses, including those involving lack of relevant intention, seldom fully exculpate.

(6) The first condition of being held morally accountable is to be a member of the moral community. The earlier discussion suggested that all intentional systems be admitted to moral citizenship. That, however, is clearly not consistent with our basic intuitions about responsibility. Dennett maintains that most animals and even some plants can qualify as first-order intentional systems[15] and I have been accused of providing an argument that not only

---

[12] J.L. Austin, 'A plea for excuses,' in *Philosophical Papers* (Oxford University Press, Oxford, 1961, 1970), pp. 175–6.

[13] J.L. Austin, 'Three ways of spilling ink,' in *Philosophical Papers*, p. 273.

[14] Austin, 'A plea for excuses,' p. 176.

[15] Dennett, 'Conditions of personhood,' p. 186.

qualifies corporations for moral citizenship, but admits cats and dogs as well.[16] The fault, however, lies not directly with the Davidsonian agency condition, it lies with reliance on an inadequate account of the concept of responsibility. A somewhat drastic remodeling to satisfy ordinary practice is called for. After we have seen to that we may reexamine the Davidsonian agency condition.

I have elsewhere argued[17] that we are regularly held accountable for things we were willing to have happen when we do things we intend. One way to describe what Hamlet did in Gertrude's room is to say that he orphaned Ophelia. He most certainly had no intention of doing that, but it seems reasonable to say that he was willing to do that, as he was also willing to stab Polonius, if, as it happened, Polonius rather than the King was the person hiding behind the arras. The idea that being willing to do something does not entail intending to do it is embedded in the concept of negligence.

Wayne Davis has provided a nice example that I will borrow and modify.[18] I practice the piano but that disturbs the neighbors and, from past experience, I even know that it does so. I don't intend to disturb them, I'm not that kind of person, though surely I am willing to do so in order to improve my piano-playing skills. I hope that this time I won't disturb them. It would be odd to say that I intend to disturb the neighbors, but I hope that I won't. No one tries not to carry out their intentions or hopes that they won't. Hence, there should be a distinction with a difference between what one intends to do and what one is only willing to do when one intends to do something else. That distinction, however, is not acknowledged as fundamental in ordinary moral responsibility judgments. Generally we are held accountable for doing the things we were willing to do though we did not intend them.

Davidson's theory of agency can, of course, assimilate things done willingly but not intentionally, to the actions of a person because they amount to redescriptions of the person's intentional behavior. Being negligent (understood in terms of being willing without intending) then is usually an action of an agent. Such cases could be covered by Mackie's Rule if it were modified to focus on actions rather than just intended actions. At any rate, we should say that a person can be held morally responsible not only for things done intentionally but for things the person was willing to do, as well.

There are a number of other cases in which things not done intentionally are, nonetheless, more likely than not to land one in the sea of responsibility. J.L. Austin argued that one can distinguish in some cases persons doing things deliberately and on purpose from their doing them intentionally.[19] I suspect that there may be some overlap with cases of willingness, but Austin-type cases are worth at least brief mention. Consider my rushing to get to the airport to catch a plane to Bermuda. I'm off on a well-earned holiday and it's the last flight of the week. I'm running a bit late so I hurriedly back my car out of the

---

[16] Thomas Donaldson, *Corporations and Morality* (Prentice-Hall, Englewood Cliffs, N.J., 1982), p. 22.

[17] Peter A. French, *Collective and Corporate Responsibility*, (Columbia University Press, New York, 1984), chs 10 and 11.

[18] Wayne Davis, 'Intending' (an unpublished manuscript).

[19] Austin, 'Three ways of spilling ink.'

driveway. Then I stop short, seeing my youngest child's favorite doll lying directly in my path. I realize I could get out and move it. But that's precious time. It's just too bad, I've got a plane to catch! I drive over the doll, crushing it, and speed off to the airport. Now, following Austin, it seems right to say that I deliberately drove right over my child's doll. But I did not do it intentionally, that is, it was not any part of my intention to destroy the doll. Of course, I didn't do it unintentionally either. It was an incidental business to my intentions. But I am not only causally responsible for destroying the doll, I should be held to account for it as well. I could try to explain to my child that I just had to get to the airport. She might even accept that by way of not thinking me such a monster. But it shouldn't get me much off the moral hook. Had my intentions involved the doing of something very laudatory or morally commendable, for example, rushing to the aid of an injured friend, the deliberate driving over the doll would be more than likely forgiven or excused. That, however, goes further towards confirming that we can be held morally accountable for what we deliberately but not intentionally do, for otherwise no excusing or forgiving would be sensible.

I suspect that further investigation will show that doing something deliberately but not intentionally is commonly distinguished from being willing to do it. After all, to do it deliberately I must have deliberated about it. I may be described as willing to do things that I have hardly thought about, e.g. disturbing the neighbors when I practice the piano, which I did neither deliberately nor intentionally. At any rate Mackie's Rule needs to be broadened to allow deliberate actions even if they are not intended actions in order to remain consistent with common usage and intuitions. Davidson's agency theory again, however, anchors the required modification. My deliberately running over my child's doll is an action of mine because 'drove over the doll' is a true description of what I did under another description intentionally 'drove out of the driveway.' Responsibility then remains firmly attached to intentionality by merely modifying Mackie's Rule to encompass more than just intentional actions. Collateral or second effects involving the intentional acts of others demand other adjustments to this base principle of responsibility, but the link to intentionality will still be preserved.

(7) Mackie's Rule with all of these alterations I have called the Extended Principle of Accountability or EPA.[20] The modified Mackie Rule or EPA is likely to be viewed as extraordinarily rigid insofar as it admits all of the actions of an agent into the scope of moral responsibility. In other words, as long as a piece of behavior was intended under some description, it is an action of the agent and so something for which the agent can be held accountable. Only a limited range of behavior would be exempt. The latent tyranny of moral responsibility, however, is checked and balanced at the appellate level of excuse evaluation, which is a far more complex business than is often supposed by moral philosophers. What EPA does clearly indicate, however, is that certain popular excuses such as 'I didn't mean that,' 'It was unintentional,' 'That wasn't what I wanted to do,' etc., are not necessarily exculpatory or even mitigatory.

---

[20] French, *Collective and Corporate Responsibility*. ch. 10.

EPA, however, is not adequate for another class of cases in which moral responsibility is commonly assessed. Those are cases in which something untoward occurs that was unintended, unforeseen, not deliberately done, or not willingly done on any true description. An ascription of moral responsibility for such an event, in its first instance, would be inappropriate on EPA. However, if after a period of time the perpetrator fails to change his ways of behaving, etc., that produced or resulted in the untoward event, we often morally reevaluate the earlier event and hold him morally responsible for its occurrence. This is done in full recognition of the fact that at the time the untoward event occurred it was not intended by the agent, nor something the agent was willing to do, etc. It was not an action of the agent. In effect moral responsibility may be assigned specifically because the perpetrator subsequent to the event failed to respond to its occurrence with an appropriate modification of his behavior or habits that had as an outcome the unwanted or harmful event. I have called this the Principle of Responsive Adjustment or PRA.[21]

PRA captures the idea that, after an untoward event has happened, the person(s) who contributed to its occurrence is (are) expected to adopt certain courses of future action that will have the effect in his (their) future conduct of preventing repetitions. We have strong 'moral expectations' regarding behavioral adjustments that correct character weaknesses, habits, etc., that have been productive of untoward events. PRA, however, is more than an expression of such expectations. It allows that when the expected adjustments in behavior are not made, and in the absence of strong evidential support for non-adjustment, the person(s) in question is (are) to be held morally responsible for the earlier untoward event that provoked attention. PRA does *not* assume, however, that a failure to 'mend one's ways' after being confronted with an unhappy outcome of one's actions is strong presumptive evidence that one had originally intended that outcome. The matter of intentions at the time it occurred is closed. If it were not intentional, nothing after the action could make it intentional when it occurred. PRA expresses the idea that a refusal to adjust practices that led to an untoward occurrence is to associate oneself, for moral purposes, with the earlier behavior. In this respect, PRA captures more of the richness of our ordinary action of moral responsibility than EPA by uncovering a way we morally reevaluate persons with regard to some occurrences even when attributions of intentionality to those persons are defeated for some reason or other.

PRA should not be read as suggesting that some future intention can affect a past event, that a future intention as manifested in a future course of notion could have the effect of making something that was done or occurred intentional when it was not intentional or even an action when it happened.

Of particular interest for corporate responsibility would be cases like the crash of a large passenger airplane or the pollution of Lake Superior with asbestors fibers. Airplane crashes are, in fact, rather good examples of the sort of thing on which PRA would focus. In the usual cases, the crash is an event

---

[21] Peter A. French, 'A principle of responsive adjustment,' *Philosophy*, Volume 59, Number 230 (1984), pp. 491–503.

that is not an action. Something went wrong, a malfunction, a mechanical breakdown, etc. Prevention of repetition, however, is a dominating concern.

There is no 'backward causation' in the application of PRA. By intentionally doing something today, however, a person can make something that happened yesterday something for which that person should bear moral responsibility. A person's past is captured in the scope of that person's present and future intentions. PRA insists on that.

F.H. Bradley wrote, 'In morality the past is real because it is present in the will.'[22] PRA provides an expression of this elusive notion. The idea is that adjustments in one's behavior that rectify flaws or habits that have actually caused past evils or routinized behavior that has led to worthy results are required by moral considerations. Put another way, the intention that motivates a lack of responsive corrective action or the continuance of offending behavior affirms or loops back to retrieve the behavior that caused the evil. By the same token, failure to routinize behavior that has been productive of good results divorces that behavior from one's 'moral life.' Intentions certainly reach forward, as J.L. Austin's miner's lamp,[23] but they also may be seen as having a retrograde or retrieval function by which they illuminate past behavior that was not at the time of its occurrence an action of the agent. A present intention to do something or to do it in a certain way can draw a previous event into its scope. Davidsonian agents need not be viewed as purely prospective ahistorical, even abstract, centers of action. They have lives, that is pasts out of which their intentions emerge.

Suppose that Sebastian gets drunk and in a stupor drives his car over Quincy's property. Let us assume that Sebastian had no intention of damaging Quincy's property. Nothing he did when inebriated was intentional. After regaining sobriety and learning of his misadventures, Sebastian, who is not yet an alcoholic, subsequently and quite deliberately returns to the local pub and proceeds to get himself roaring drunk. Sebastian well knows his own past, including the fact that he got drunk on a particular occasion and destroyed Quincy's property. Nonetheless, he embarks upon the same course again. Though he might not have been accessed moral responsibility for the damage he did on the first spree (he was, after all, under the influence) had he subsequently modified his behavior, he did not do so and, by PRA, he has made the crucial early events not an out-of-character happenstance, but very much in character and hence something for which he may be held morally accountable as he may be held strictly or objectively liable for the damage under the law. PRA captures, at least to some extent, the Aristotelian idea that we do not hold people morally responsible for unintentionally 'slightly deviating from the course of goodness'[24] as long as they do not subsequently practice behavior that makes such deviations a matter of character.

The most radical element with respect to PRA surely is that which provides for a retrieval of past unintentional behavior in a present intention to do

---

[22] F.H. Bradley, *Ethical Studies* (Oxford University Press, Oxford, 1876), p. 46.
[23] Austin, 'Three ways of spilling ink,' p. 284.
[24] Aristotle, *Nicomachean Ethics*, tr. M. Ostwald (Bobbs-Merrill, Indianapolis, 1962), p. 51.

something. A more technical account is surely wanted. Act descriptions have a well-known feature that Joel Feinberg called the 'accordion effect.'[25] Like the musical instrument, the description of a simple bodily movement can be expanded in different directions by causal linkages and other associations. For example, the act of pulling the trigger of a rifle might, through a series of redescriptions, be expanded to the description 'the killing of the judge.' Accordions, of course, can be drawn apart in both directions. The description of Sebastian's present act of getting drunk may be associated to his past behavior by the ordinary relations 'like yesterday,' 'as before' or 'again.' It is the case that Sebastian, in our story, intends to get drunk *again*. The action intended under that description clearly retrieves the previous behavior, though it certainly does not make the previous behavior an action at the time it occurred.

Sebastian might counter with the plea that he had not intended to get drunk under any such 'accordioned' description at all. He only intended to get drunk simpliciter. Such a plea, however, can be rejected on the grounds that unless he is of diminished mental capacity or suffering from amnesia, etc., Sebastian's grasp of what he is doing is made within a mental or personal history that is not present-specific. The descriptions of events under which he intends his actions are formed within that history. 'I intended only to get drunk, not to get drunk again' is too restricted an intention for what he is doing. There are limits on excludability by appeal to semantic capacity in intention. If Sebastian quite intentionally makes his way to the pub in order to get roaring drunk, he intentionally goes to get drunk again, or like yesterday, etc., and his doing so affirms the previous episode insofar as it takes it into the description captured in the scope of the intention.

PRA insists that persons learn from their mistakes, that the pleas of mistake and of accident cannot be repeatedly used to excuse frequent performances of offensive behavior. 'It was an accident' will only work if it was not the result of behavior that is repeated after the offending event. 'It was inadvertent or a mistake' will exculpate only if corrective measures are taken to insure non-repetition. Such excuses can be, and often are, reevaluated after the individual's actions have been observed subsequent to the event for which the excuses were offered. But I think it would be wrong to say that in such cases we decide that the individual must have had the relevant intention in the first instance of the offending behavior. We may grant that no error was made at that time in describing the event, but the event takes on a new description in the light of subsequent action.

The application of PRA may be read as saying that a person may be held morally responsible for a previous event to which that person had unintentionally, even inadvertently, contributed, if he or she subsequently intentionally acts in ways that are likely to cause repetitions of the untoward outcome. A strict set of temporal closures need not apply to PRA. For example 'moral enlightenment,' many decades after, may demand reevaluation of an event that was not originally thought to have been bad or harmful and PRA will require moral

---

[25] Joel Feinberg, *Doing and Deserving* (Princeton University Press, Princeton, 1970), p. 134.

accountability of the perpetrator if, after enlightenment, no behavioral adjustments were made.

PRA has another important intuitively appealing aspect. Suppose that we think of all of those things for which a person can be held morally responsible as exhausting that person's moral life, the life which, when regarded as a complete moral biography, can be morally judged or evaluated as Aristotle would have it, 'in a complete life,' against a standard of moral worth or virtue. PRA forces incorporation of originally non-intentional pieces of behavior into a person's moral life because PRA does not let persons desert their pasts. It demands that present and future actions respond to past deeds. It forces us to think of our moral lives as both retrospective and contemporaneous, as cumulative. It does not let us completely escape responsibility for our accidents, inadvertencies, unintended executive failures, failures to fully appreciate situations, bad habits, etc., by simply proffering excuses. The PRA-countenanced response to such pleas in certain cases will be 'Yes, it surely was unintentional, etc., but you have done nothing to change your ways. You have seen the earlier outcome and you have not altered your behavior to guard again recurrence. Hence, you must bear the moral responsibility for the earlier untoward event.' The ordinary notion of moral responsibility then operates over more than isolated intentional acts considered seriatim as the original Mackie Rule implies. The moral integrity of a person's life depends upon a moral consistency that is nurtured by PRA.

(8) PRA is, of course, not divorced from a firm foundation in Davidsonian agency for at least two reasons: (1) It is to subsequent intentional actions of the person that PRA is directed as well as to the earlier unhappy event, and (2) the capacity to respond, response itself (in the relevant moral sense) must be expressed in intentional action. The two principles (EPA and PRA) of moral responsibility that have here been uncovered constitute the superstructure of accountability, supporting Mackie's Rule. EPA captures Bradley's insistence that a deed cannot belong to someone unless it can be properly said to 'issue' from his will[26] and Aristotle's view that virtue and excellence depend upon the voluntary nature of actions. While PRA embodies Aristotle's conviction that persons are 'themselves by their slack lives responsible for becoming men of that kind and men make themselves responsible for being unjust or self-indulgent ...; for it is activities exercised on particular objects that make the corresponding character.'[27]

EPA and PRA together entail that if something is to be counted as a moral person, it must, minimally, be a Davidsonian agent with the capacity or ability to intentionally modify its behavior patterns, habits, or modus operandi after learning that untoward events were brought about by its past pieces of behavior. The modification condition involves, we should expect, the reflexive capacity that Dennett includes in his definition of what he calls 'second-order intentional systems.'[28]

---

[26] Bradley, *Ethical Studies*, p. 31.
[27] Aristotle, *Nichomachean Ethics*, p. 57.
[28] Dennett, 'Conditions of personhood', p. 181.

The term 'responsible' speaks in favor of this view of a moral person. To be responsible is to be able to make a response.[29] (There is a notable archaic use of 'responsible' as an actor who undertakes to play any part required by the company. Someone in the theatre who could answer any call was a 'good all-round responsible.') Understanding 'responsible' in terms of response-able carries the concept further from Mackie's Rule than even PRA takes us. Although to be able to respond one must be an intentional agent, being the person that is able to or must respond may have little or nothing to do with being the entity that caused the untoward event (let alone intentionally caused it). Parents run into this with regularity. A child, whether or not intentionally, breaks a neighbor's window. Who must respond? Who is able to respond? The child's parents. They are not responsible for breaking the window, yet they are response-able. Used this way, moral responsibility associates with tasks, stations, status, etc. Being responsible for x, in this sense, does not necessarily imply that one did x or did x intentionally or did something y intentionally that could be redescribed as doing x. It would be ridiculous, for example, to extend the redescriptions of the parents' act of conception to include the child's wanton breaking of windows. It is enough to assign responsibilities to roles or to task-holders, etc. Many of the moral responsibilities (and the legal responsibilities) of mature moral citizens are, however, of this task or role variety and Mackie's Rule, EPA, and PRA are not separately or in combination adequate to account for this kind of responsibility. Assignment of these responsibilities are, however, made only to intentional agents who are capable of the kind of responses PRA demanded.

(9) How then does the concept of a moral person fare? What entities ought to be included in the moral census? A moral person, we should say, is a Davidsonian agent with the capacity to respond and responsively adjust to moral evaluation. Most mature human beings satisfy these conditions. But animals and other purely first-order intentional systems do not. Corporations, however, are not excluded.

---

[29] Kurt Baier suggested this aspect of responsibility to me in a discussion of corporate responsibility, as did Herbert Fingarette, in another context.

6
Questions About Motivational Strength[1]

IRVING THALBERG

Since Aristotle's time, causal theorists of human behavior have shared an intuitively appealing assumption. It is that, except for our automatic responses and habitual routines, how we act depends upon the strength or feebleness of conative goings-on within us – our desires, aversions, preferences, schemes and so forth. As a convenience I follow many contemporary philosophers in speaking of our 'pro-attitudes' (henceforth abbreviated 'PAs'). The idea seems to be that we are by nature inert. But apparently not just any PA is forceful enough to jolt us out of our torpor. And even when we have a sufficiently robust PA toward doing x, which we are quite able to do, we may do y instead – no doubt because we have a more vigorous PA toward doing y. Thus causal analysts deploy the concept of motivational strength to explain why we do anything at all – and in circumstances where both x and y appeal to us, which we end up doing.

My inquiry into these matters will be guided by a disgracefully naive question: What do causal and any other theorists mean when they rate the strength of our PAs? I hope to learn how our brawniest PA always or usually manages to overcome its flabbier opponents. In my search for answers, I shall often consult the pioneering, deservedly influential work of Donald Davidson. Any occasional misgivings I express toward some of his doctrines should not be read as sniping criticism, but as an attempt to build dialectically upon the impressive foundations he has laid down.

To start with, I should remark – in agreement with Davidson – that PAs are not the only accredited causes of our behavior. There is a role for our *beliefs* about *how* we can get what we desire – or do what we feel like doing – as well as our beliefs about what will happen *if* we get or do the things we want. These cognitive factors blend with our PAs, and both form the 'primary reasons' which, according to Davidson, cause us to do whatever we do for a reason. In his words: 'r is a primary reason why an agent performed an action x only if r

---

[1] I thank John Deigh, Alfred Mele, and my commentator at the Davidson conference, Amelie O. Rorty, as well as several other conferees, for valuable discussion.

consists of a PA of the agent towards actions with a certain property, and a belief ... that x ... has that property'[2] (here and elsewhere I may alter and substitute symbols for uniformity). Davidson's by now familiar example involves someone who flips a light switch. Why does he flip it? Because he has a PA directed at actions with the property of being turnings-on of this lamp – and because he thinks his flipping of the switch has that property. In short, he wants to turn on the lamp; he believes that by flipping the switch he will turn it on; and as a result he flips the switch, thus doing what he has a reason to do.

Strength enters the scenario when Davidson claims that 'Any serious theory for predicting action on the basis of reasons must find a way of evaluating the relative force of various desires and beliefs' – particularly when there is 'weighing of competing reasons.'[3] Davidson also seems to be convinced that serious forecasting will be unable to make use of any causal 'law connecting events classified as reasons with [other] events classified as actions – the classification may ... be neurological, chemical, or physical.'[4] I infer that until we learn to estimate the 'force' of reasons in neurological, chemical, or physical – rather than mentalistic or psychological – terms, it may prove difficult for us to gauge how powerful a reason must be to elicit action, and by how much one reason outweighs another.

I would illustrate Davidson's contrast by recalling that at least the white-garbed scientists among us can easily measure the voltage of neural impulses. They can then investigate whether impulses of a given strength make a synapse fire. All of us can understand the wattage of fluorescent bulbs. We can also see if high-wattage bulbs grow brighter than low-wattage bulbs. The strength of fermented beverages – their alcohol content – is no mystery. It is also measurable independently of how much it affects the coordination, reaction times, and the joviality of people who drink a tumblerfull of the beverage. We deal constantly with physical forces: water pressure in the household plumbing system, air pressure in our bicycle tyres. A crude contraption on my roof indicates how strong the wind is. In these cases again we can discover separately what the degree of strength is, and what effects it has. When the water pressure is low, we find that our bath tub takes longer to fill. If my tyres only have ten pounds pressure, I don't travel as fast as when they are inflated to eighty pounds. When there is only a three-knot breeze, my sailboat remains stationary; but a higher velocity gust will move it. By reference to such examples of physical – including chemical and neural – force, my question is down-to-earth: Are similar stories available to back the claim that powerful PAs do, and weak PAs don't, trigger action? When causal theorists rate your primary reason or PA as strong enough, and mightier than its rivals, what else do they mean but that you acted on it?

Maybe we should simply equate the conative strength of our PAs and reasons

---

[2] 'Actions, reasons, and causes', reprinted in *Essays on Actions and Events* (Clarendon Press, Oxford, 1980), pp. 3–19, at p. 5.

[3] Ibid., p. 16.

[4] Ibid., p. 17. See D. Davidson, 'Paradoxes of irrationality', in *Philosophical Essays on Freud*, ed. R. Wollheim and J. Hopkins (Cambridge University Press, Cambridge, 1982), pp. 289–305, at p. 299.

with their intensity.[5] Paradigms of intensity are the unpleasant and disruptive longings that smokers, alcoholics, and drug addicts experience when deprived of their anodyne. We can estimate this intensity before we see whether and how the person acts. Intensity-strength of our motivational state is measured by how uncomfortable and preoccupied we are. However, I doubt that we can use intensity as a yardstick of conative strength. Most of our PAs and reasons presumably have some strength, yet very few of them are intense, i.e., disagreeable and distracting. More significantly, even if we consider only motivational states which *are* painful and upsetting, we will observe an extremely imperfect correlation between their intensity, so measured, and appropriate behavior – which is alleged to result from their intensity. A long-distance swimmer may be tormented by an urge to give up, and not especially afflicted by her contrary desire to forge ahead; but the upshot may be that she keeps on swimming. Incidentally I think Davidson would concur that more or less intense feelings are unconnected with the strength of our PAs and reasons. He says that in conflict situations, 'where there are good reasons both for performing an action and for performing one that rules it out ... feelings of strife and anxiety are inessential embellishments.'[6]

Perhaps we will get a clearer idea of motivational potency if we reverse field. Why are some conative states too anemic to make us act? Silly wishes, fleeting impulses, whims, and apparently mild cases of wanting, all seem to qualify as 'weak' PAs. Yet when they are allied with suitable beliefs, don't they constitute reasons – albeit neither very good nor conclusive ones – for acting? We can delineate the agent's fancy in a way that 'leads us to see something that [he] saw ... in the action' he contemplated.[7] In what respects, then, aren't such motivational states compelling enough to elicit our behavior? On the basis of what empirical research – analogous to testing the efficacy of variously diluted paint-removers – are causal theorists so confident that wishing and moderate wanting *won't* stir us to act?

Davidson asks a similar question while analyzing the nature of intention.[8] First he says an intention is an 'all-out unconditional judgment' (henceforth abbreviated 'UJ') that some 'action present (or past) that is known [to the agent] by acquaintance' is 'desirable'. Next he inquires: 'what is there to distinguish an intention [so characterized] from a mere wish?' That is, are we right to assume that intending is sufficiently potent to initiate behavior, and wishing is too slack? Why can't an episode of wishing become equally robust, or – what amounts to the same – qualify as an instance of intending? Davidson has a trenchant answer:

> wishes ... that are not consistent with what one believes [possible] ... are ruled out by our conception of an intention. And we may put aside wishes that do not

[5] See the symposia between N. Cooper and J. Benson, 'Oughts and wants', *Proceedings of the Aristotelian Society*, supp. vol. 42 (1968), reprinted in *Weakness of Will*, ed. G.W. Mortimore (Macmillan, London, 1971), pp. 190–215, at pp. 197, 203, 207, 213; 'Further thoughts on oughts and wants', in *Weakness of Will*, pp. 216–32, at pp. 219ff.

[6] 'How is weakness of the will possible?', reprinted in *Essays on Actions and Events*, pp. 21–42, at pp. 33ff.

[7] Davidson, 'Actions, reasons, and causes', p. 3; 'Paradoxes of irrationality', p. 293.

[8] 'Intending', reprinted in *Essays on Actions and Events*, pp. 83–102, at pp. 97–102.

correspond to UJs. ('I wish I could go to London next week': my going to London next week may be consistent with all that I believe [possible], but not with all that I want ... once we put these cases aside, there is no need to distinguish intentions from wishes. For [any remaining] judgment that something I ... can do ... is desirable ... is not a mere wish. It *is* an intention.

Unfortunately this does not seem to explain why a mere wish is unable to propagate deeds. So we might as well resume our investigation of conative states which have such power. How about the UJs which Davidson casts as intentions? They originally surfaced in Davidson's renowned contribution to the ancient debate over *akrasia*: Can it happen – and if it can, *how* can it happen – that our reasons favor one readily available course of action, *x*, yet nevertheless we voluntarily and knowingly pursue another, *y*, instead?

Consider the most elementary sort of case, which Davidson also highlights.[9] *X* and *y* are the only alternatives, and refraining from *x* amounts to doing *y*. Davidson argues that in this and more complex situations, *akrasia* may occur. We may irrationally, but often coolly, do *y*, realizing that *x* is more in line with the reasons we think pertinent and take account of.

But *how* might this happen? One possibility Davidson rules out is that we go against a current *intention* of ours to do *x*. In Davidson's scheme of things, this would be our UJ that *x* is more desirable than *y* (henceforth abbreviated 'UJ(x,y)'; and he regards this conative state as guaranteed to produce *x*ing, given hospitable circumstances. At all events, if you equate our UJ(x,y) with our intention to do *x* rather than *y*, won't you have difficulty maintaining that we have ever acted contrary to our UJ(x,y)? For you would be asserting that we have intentionally done *y* rather than *x*, while intending to do *x* rather than *y*! But you might also interpret this awkward consequence as an omen that unconditional judging is not the same as intending.

However this may be, there are commentators who have challenged Davidson's belief that it is impossible to act against one's UJ, or against one's intention. Robert Audi would allow it to be conceivable that a person 'does *y* intentionally though he judges simply [= unconditionally] that it would better to do *x*'.[10] Alfred Mele is more intrepid.[11] He grants for the sake of argument that our UJ(x,y) constitutes our 'intention to do *x* here and now'. Why, he proceeds to ask, 'should [we] believe that we never act against' this UJ? Mele audaciously offers a counter-instance. He imagines that a college biology student, John, has the 'lab assignment [of] pricking one of his fingers with a needle and [then] examining a sample of his blood'. John 'judges unconditionally' that carrying out his assignment (doing *x*) is better than not doing so (= doing *y*). *Ex hypothesi*, John 'intends to prick his finger' straightaway. Twice John brings the needle into contact with a finger, but he 'stops' each time. What went wrong? Mele furnishes two diagnoses: one is that 'because [John] is weak, he fails to do ... what he intends' to do; the other is that John's 'desire not to harm himself grows stronger' than his intention to follow orders – in fact, his wayward PA waxes 'so

[9] E.g. 'Paradoxes of irrationality', p. 295.
[10] 'Weakness of will and practical judgment', *Nous*, 13 (1979), pp. 193ff.
[11] '*Akrasia*, reasons, and causes', *Philosophical Studies*, 44 (1983), pp. 348ff.

strong that he now wants to refrain from pricking his finger more than he wants to prick it'. Nevertheless John *intends* to pierce it.

I'll come back to the notion of PA strength as 'wanting ... more'. At the moment I should connect Mele's apparent counter-example with Davidson's thesis. As noted above, Davidson would admit that akratic behavior somewhat like John's may occur. But evidently he cannot agree with Mele that John disregarded an UJ(x,y). No; Davidson's view is that during episodes of *akrasia* the agent makes a 'prima facie', 'relational', or 'conditional' judgment: inasmuch as x and y have assorted 'desirable characteristic[s]', or in relation to these characteristics of x and y, x is better or more desirable than y.[12] The most important conditional verdicts are 'all things [reasons] considered' judgments (henceforth 'ATCJs'). In reaching ATCJs, you must take stock of all the pros and cons you find germane to doing either x or y. Although your ATCJ incorporates everything that on balance matters to you with respect to x and y, Davidson discloses that it is by itself powerless to start you moving. He writes:

> Intentional action ... is geared directly to [= is directly caused by] UJs like 'It would be better to do x than to do y'. Reasoning that stops at conditional judgments ... is practical only in its subject, not in its issue [effects].
> Practical reasoning does however often arrive at UJs that one action is better than another – otherwise there would be no such thing as acting on a reason.[13]

Now Davidson could account for our akratic failure to act on our ATCJ that x is better than y (henceforth 'ATCJ(x,y)') by postulating that sometimes our ratiocination just 'stops' there: it does *not* 'arrive at' the corresponding UJ(x,y). Thus we have reasons to do x, but we remain passive, and omit to do x. Yet this may not appear to be an *intentional* failure to do x – or what in this context is equivalent, a case of intentionally doing y. Perhaps in order to dispel such uncertainty, Davidson goes further, and postulates that when we behave akratically, our practical reasoning continues from our ATCJ(x,y) to the seemingly perverse, incongruous UJ(y,x) – which has the strength required to make us do y. Moreover, the PAs and reasons on which we based our ATCJ(x,y) *cause* our UJ(y,x). At least that is how I how I interpret the following remarks of Davidson's:

> Every judgment is made in the light of all [one's PAs and reasons] in this sense, that it is made in the presence of, and is conditioned by, that totality ... this does not mean that every judgment is reasonable, or thought to be so by the agent, on the basis of those reasons.... [We are only] supposing a person sometimes holds that all that he believes and values supports a certain course of action, when ... those ... beliefs and values cause him to reject that course.[14]

This story of UJs, intentions, and *akrasia* puzzles me. Why do UJs not only insure action, but alone 'directly' bring it about? Why would 'there ... be no ...

---

[12] 'How is weakness of the will possible?', pp. 27–42; see 'Intending', pp. 96–102.
[13] 'How is weakness of the will possible?', p. 39.
[14] Ibid., pp. 40ff.

acting on a reason' in the absence of UJs? Why does Davidson assume that their counterpart ATCJs 'cannot be directly associated with actions?'[15] Can my ATCJ(x,y) *indirectly* cause me to act by directly propagating either a normal UJ(x,y) or an akratic UJ(y,x)? What does Davidson mean when he asserts: 'the fact that the action [for which we have reasons] is performed *represents* a further judgement ... [which] must be an UJ' (my emphasis)?[16] Does he mean that if it is true that we did x, it follows logically that we made the UJ(x,y)? Should it not instead be an empirical issue whether an UJ must mediate between our ATCJs and our deeds?

Mysteries remain even if we suppose we are dealing with a factual claim about what kinds of judging are causally necessary or sufficient for action. Is it the straightforward hypothesis that every time people do x intentionally, they first reach the UJ(x,y) – and that, when able to do x, they always do x after making their UJ(x,y)? Not quite. Davidson explicitly denies that 'whenever an agent acts [for reasons] he goes through a process of deliberation ... and draws [unconditional] conclusions'; instead, all the agent 'must have [are PAs] and beliefs from which, had he been aware of them ... he *could* have reasoned that his action was [unconditionally] desirable'.[17]

But how does a '*could*'-be, or even a definitely-would-be UJ manage to cause the agent's behavior? For that matter, when the agent does judge, how will he, or bystanders, discover which *type* of judgment he makes? Does he have to mutter phrases like 'ATC', 'on balance', or 'x is unconditionally better than y'? With regard to 'the kind of judgment that can be the conclusion of ... practical reasoning – that can correspond to an intentional action', Davidson only cautions: 'No weight should be given the word "judgment", ... I do not suppose ... [the agent] necessarily *judges* that it would be good to [do x]'.[18] Despite these enigmas about the allegedly factual claim that only an UJ(x,y) will enable you to do x for reasons, and that UJs work infallibly, Davidson's overall scheme is clear. *Akrasia* is possible because your ATCJ(x,y), which encapsulates your reasons for doing x, may consort with an irrational UJ(y,x). His commentators Audi and Mele provide room for *akrasia* between whatever is the final stage of practical reasoning – an ATCJ(x,y), even an UJ(x,y) – and your intentional behavior. On both sides, the explanation of how it comes about that you voluntarily and knowingly act against your reasoned judgment is in terms of relative strength.

Before I return to that central notion, I want to investigate briefly one of Davidson's premises. He assumes that often – if not always – people who behave akratically judge x better than y, ATC, and at the same time judge y unconditionally better than x. But aren't these judgments – or in technical terms, their propositional contents or objects – logical contraries, thus reducing *akrasia* to 'a simple logical blunder'?[19] Davidson's findings on this subject confuse me. Once he declares that ' "x is better than y, AT ... C" ... entail[s] "x

---

[15] 'Intending', p. 98.

[16] Ibid., p. 98.

[17] Ibid., p. 85.

[18] Ibid., p. 97.

[19] Davidson, 'How is weakness of the will possible?', p. 40.

is better than y"' *simpliciter.*[20] Yet a paragraph earlier we read that an ATCJ(x,y) 'cannot conflict logically with *any* UJ' (my emphasis). These claims about what we judge conditionally and unconditionally seem to be at odds. For suppose the proposition p_1, 'x is better than y, ATC', *does* entail p_2: 'x is better than y'. Then isn't there an unconditional proposition that p_2 may 'conflict ... with'? How about p_3, 'y is better than x' – which cannot be true if p_2 is true? Since, according to Davidson, p_1 entails p_2, it follows that if p_1 is true, then p_2 is, and p_3 is not, true. Therefore the conditional, ATC proposition p_1 does 'conflict ... with' an unconditional proposition, namely p_3. If Davidson wishes to maintain his 'no logical conflict' thesis regarding ATCJs and UJs, he must abandon his 'entailment' thesis. In fact, three pages prior to his remarks on entailment, Davidson asserted: 'we must give up the idea that we can *detach*' UJs from ATCJs. It goes without saying that we cannot validly detach p_2 from p_1 unless p_1 entails p_2.

Davidson's latest word on the topic is that a 'merely conditional [judgment that] in the light of all my [reasons], I ought to do x ... cannot contradict the UJ that I ought to do y. Pure internal inconsistency enters only if I also hold – as in fact I do – that I ought to act on ... what I judge best ... [ATC].'[21] This makes it sound easy to avoid 'internal inconsistency': just repudiate the 'second-order principle that [you] ought to act on what [you] hold ... to be best, [ATC]'.[22] But is this a 'take it or leave it' principle? What is ATC-judging, other than a procedure by which you settle on a course of action that harmonizes with the ATCJ that you arrive at? Can you be *sincere* in your ATC-judging if you declare: 'ATC, I ought to do x; nevertheless, since I do not hold that I ought to act on my ATCJs, I ought unconditionally to do y'? This may not exemplify a 'logical blunder', or a logical 'conflict' between your ATCJ and your UJ. Yet there is at least an apparent pragmatic inconsistency here. Until the situation is cleared up; I think it is premature to accept Davidson's unsupported *dictum* that when you behave akratically, you are making the powerless ATCJ(x,y) as well as the authoritative UJ(y,x).

Whether or not you can simultaneously make both judgments, we should wonder what causes you to reach the irrational UJ(y,x). Davidson's intuitively plausible answer is that even if you have preponderant reasons to do x, chances are that you also have *some* reasons to do y instead. They are bound to be inconclusive, and – in *this* extended sense of our key term – not as 'strong' as the reasons which shaped your ATCJ(x,y). Cogency-strength, however, may not coincide with motivational strength. So it is because your relatively un-cogent reasons for doing y are motivationally heftier that – after judging x superior, ATC, to y – you arrive at your surprise UJ(y,x). Davidson's explanation seems to relocate the source of power. UJs appear to derive their muscle from the muscle of reasons.

Is this analytical progress? Certainly there are welcome specifics. Thus Davidson says 'it is natural to suppose that the strongest [i.e., most cogent] reasons are the strongest causes' of behavior; however, 'a reason that is causally

[20] Ibid., p. 40.
[21] 'Paradoxes of irrationality', pp. 296ff.
[22] Ibid., pp. 296f.

strongest need not be deemed by the actor to provide the strongest (best) grounds for action'.[23] A further disparity he notes is that you cannot be mistaken about whether your reasons to do x are for you more conclusive than your reasons to do y; but you may be wrong about which have more of what it takes to elicit behavior.[24] Hence 'it seems obvious ... that we may think x better, yet [perhaps without realizing it] want y more'.[25]

Apparently reasons are not the ultimate wellsprings of conative energy. Less cogent reasons seem able to prevail over more cogent ones due to the greater force of their PA component. In Davidson's simplest case, where 'the agent does not have the [second-order] principle that he ought to act on what he holds to be best [ATC] ... to explain his [akratic] behavior we need only say that his desire to do what he held to be best, ATC, was not as strong as his desire to do something else'.[26]

One recent commentator, Mele, to whom I referred several pages ago, has further information about what it is for the akratic person to think x better, yet want y more. Elaborating a thesis of Gary Watson's,[27] Mele says:

> 'wants more' has both an evaluative and a motivational use. In the evaluative use, to say that S wants x more than he wants y is to say that he 'prefers x to y or ranks x higher than y on [his] scale of values ...', whereas in the motivational use, it is to say simply that S is more strongly motivated by considerations of x.[28]

Mele adds that what we usually estimate is not 'which of our competing wants has the most motivational force', but rather, 'from the point of view of our own values, which want it would be best to satisfy'. Mele then blames *akrasia* on a 'disparity between [our] wanting more in the evaluative sense [to do x] and wanting more in the motivational sense' to do y.[29] This echoes Watson's talk of a 'divergence between certain kinds of desire and judgments of the good'.[30] Unfortunately the fundamental notion of an agent's 'own values' has been left shrouded in obscurity. Watson has mainly separated our 'own values' from the codes that socialization foists upon us willy nilly. He considers a value our own if we have critically thought it out 'in a cool and non-self-deceptive moment'; and Watson is confident 'we all have [such] more or less long-term aims and normative principles'.[31]

To me this approach to *akrasia* seems overly restrictive. Even if we all carry around our own goals and principles, it is doubtful that whenever we intentionally fail to do what we have conclusive reasons to do, the reasons we flout are linked with these – or society's – norms. Sometimes we face no value

---

[23] *Essays on Actions and Events*, p. xii.
[24] 'Actions, reasons, and causes', p. 18.
[25] 'How is weakness of the will possible?', p. 27.
[26] 'Paradoxes of irrationality', p. 297.
[27] 'Free agency', *Journal of Philosophy*, 72 (1975), pp. 205–20; 'Skepticism about weakness of will', *Philosophical Review*, 86 (1977), pp. 316–39.
[28] '*Akrasia*, reasons, and causes', p. 351.
[29] Ibid., p. 352.
[30] 'Skepticism about weakness of the will', p. 339.
[31] 'Free agency', p. 215.

issue, and yet we act contrary to our appraisal – of what is most convenient, efficient, or maybe just fun. For his part, Davidson thinks at least moral value is inessential to *akrasia*, and wisely urges us to 'dwell on the cases where ... [it] doesn't enter the picture ... or if it does, it is on the wrong side'.[32] *Pace* Watson and Mele, I'm inclined to follow this advice. I would *not* ask: 'How can anyone rank *x* above *y* on her or his scale of (moral or other) values, but nevertheless intentionally do *y*?' I would pursue the more general question: 'How can anyone place *x* above *y* by reference to what s/he prizes, *or any other factors* which shape their ATCJ(x,y) – and yet intentionally do *y*?'

So far I am unpersuaded that we make an explanatory advance if we suppose either (1) that the agent's desire to do *x*, in accord with his (moral or other) values, was less sinewy than his hankering to do *y*, or (2) that 'his desire to do what he held to be best, ATC, was not as strong as his desire to do' *y*.

Will it help if we change idioms and say: 'He wanted to do *x* more, in the evaluative sense; but he wanted to do *y* more, in the motivational sense'? Or how about 'He thought *x* better, ATC, but he simply wanted to do *y* more than he wanted to do *x*'? Perhaps expressions of the 'wants more' family are not mere metaphorical equivalents of the 'strength' terms which we are attempting to understand. Certainly they are popular among causal theorists of action. For instance, in a very recent discussion of *akrasia*, Frank Jackson 'assume[s] that we can measure [= estimate] an agent's wants ... with a *value function* which takes a higher positive value the more something is wanted, and a lower negative value the more [it] is disliked'.[33] Jackson also talks of 'how much I want something', and desires which are 'greater' or 'less'.

It might be profitable to compare 'He wants to do *y* more (less) than he wants to do *x*' with 'He smokes cigars more (less) than he smokes cigarets'. The latter could mean: 'He consumes a larger (smaller) quantity', 'He devotes a longer (shorter) total portion of each day to puffing cigars', or 'He begins smoking a cigar oftener'. By analogy, does someone who 'wants to do *y* more' do a larger quantity of wanting to do *y*? Does he simultaneously have a greater number of desires to do *y* than he has to do *x*? Does he spend a longer amount of time each day wanting to do *y* than he spends wanting to do *x*? Does he oftener suddenly begin wanting to do *y*? All such quantitative literal interpretations of the causal theorist's 'wants more' terms sound ludicrous. These locutions must have been vague surrogates for talk of conative strength.

Our attempt to clarify the nature of motivational force has been conducted mostly within a Davidsonian causal framework. On Davidson's view, only an intention or UJ(x,y) has the zap to make me do *x*. My ATCJ(x,y) somehow cannot bring me to act, although it is normally joined by an UJ(x,y), which does so. When I behave akratically, of course, my ATCJ(x,y) manages to team up with an UJ(y,x). Which of these UJs I reach, and consequently, whether I do *x* or *y*, depends upon the relative power of my reasons for doing *x* and my reasons for doing *y*. Finally, that set of reasons is stronger which has the stronger or 'greater' desire ingredient. The hitch is that to date we have only a vacuous notion of what it is for someone's desire – and *ipso facto* his reasons, his ATCJ

---

[32] 'How is weakness of the will possible?', p. 30.
[33] 'Weakness of will', *Mind*, 93 (1984), pp. 1–18, esp. pp. 3–7.

or his UJ – to be endowed with or deficient in conative force. As things stand, you explain nothing when you say 'He did this rather than that *because* his desire to do so was greater'.

Is the situation so bleak? One thoughtful, explicit reply comes from Gerasimas Santas. He concedes that unless 'we have ways of determining the relative strength of ... conflicting desires independently of ... information as to what action ensues ... the main principle of explanation [*viz.*, that a person 'acts in accordance with the strongest desire'] would be empty'.[34] But Santas believes that certain laboratory experiments with animals

> show that the strength of two conflicting drives or motives – say, the desire for ... food (approach drive) and the fear of the electric shock that accompanies the obtaining of the food (avoidance drive) – increases as the animal approaches the goal, and ... the rates of increase of the avoidance drive is always greater.... In addition it has been possible to determine the initial strength of the approach and avoidance drives (by varying ... the time of deprivation of food or the intensity of the electric shocks).[35]

The laboratory work Santas refers to was conceived and reported – sometimes with co-authors – by Neal E. Miller. Beginning in 1943, Miller *et al.* repeated, with ingenious modifications, a simple procedure with scores of two- or three-month-old albino rats. They withheld food from the rats up to forty-eight hours. Then they trained the rats to scamper the length of an alley, at the end of which food was available. Next they started delivering electric shocks to the unwary creatures either while they dined, or when they were halfway to the food supply. All during its trials, each animal wore a tiny harness linked with a device that would record both its speed and 'the force with which [it] pulled' in either direction at any point on the track.[36] Thus Miller and his colleagues could measure something like the 'strength' of several phenomena. We could ask them: By comparison with the optimal amount and frequency of eating for such rats, how severely undernourished are these creatures? How fast and how hard did they run toward the food, after various periods of deprivation when they had not yet been shocked? Following trials that included shocks? How high was the voltage of each shock? How long did it last? And so on.

What about the strength of conative factors – PAs such as the rats' 'hunger', 'approach', 'fear' and 'avoidance' drives? Miller and his partners frequently describe their results in terms of how powerful these PAs and correlated behavioral 'tendencies' prove to be. Likewise when they define their fundamental notions, make crucial distinctions, and state assumptions. For example, Miller says a 'theoretical analysis verified by experimental work indicates', among other things, that 'strength of the tendencies to approach or avoid varies with the strength of the drive upon which they are based'.[37] When

---

[34] 'Plato's *Protagoras* and explanations of weakness', *Philosophical Review*, 75 (1966), reprinted in *Weakness of Will*, p. 56.

[35] Ibid., pp. 58ff.

[36] 'Experimental studies of conflict', in *Personality and the Behavioral Disorders*, ed. M. Hunt (1944), reprinted in N.E. Miller, *Selected Papers* (Aldine-Atherton, Chicago, 1971), vol. I, pp. 6ff.

[37] Ibid., pp. 6ff.

Miller *et al.* speak of 'tendencies', they do not mean patterns of behavior which tend to recur. Tendencies are treated as distinct phenomena which mediate between PAs and action. We learn, for instance, that 'stronger tendencies *produce* stronger pulls' (my emphasis).[38] Of course hunger or approach drives are distinguished from the withholding of food which creates these drives within the animals – as well as from their resultant behavior, namely their hungrily approaching the food. Similarly with fear or avoidance drives, the shocks which cause the animals to develop such drives, and their ensuing fearful antics. Most important, approach and avoidance drives are assumed to have a degree of power to cause tendencies and behavior. Miller writes:

> To determine the effects of different strengths of avoidance the experimenters divided the rats into groups ... which received a different strength of shock. To determine the effects of different strengths of approach, they further divided ... these groups ... one with a strong ... the other with a weak hunger drive.
> ... The characteristic behavior was to approach part way and then stop. [Where] the animals stopped was determined by the relative strength of the two drives. Stronger hunger or weaker shock [avoidance drive?] caused the animals to come nearer to the goal.[39]

How does Miller get from severity of undernourishment and strength of shocks and pulls, to strength of PAs? Apparently by some 'partial definitions':

> (B) That the animals running to food are being trained to *approach* under the motivation of hunger.
> (C) That the animals running away from shock are being trained to *avoid* under the motivation of fear.
> (D) That greater amounts of food deprivation, up to a limit of at least 48 hours, produce greater *strengths of hunger drive.*
> (E) That greater strengths of electric shock, within the limits used, produce greater *strengths of fear drive.*[40]

Miller's verbal conventions (B)–(E) may be useful for reporting what happened in his laboratory. Yet they hardly provide an answer to my guiding question: 'What is it for our motivational states to have some degree of power to generate behavior?' (B) and (C) beg my question by simply *postulating* that hunger and fear drives *do* result from undernourishment and shocks, and that *these drives* make the animals run toward or away from their source of food. (D) and (E) again beg my question by laying it down that there is a further causal relationship between how severe or strong the undernourishment and shocks are, and how potent the rival hunger and fear drives are. I have no doubt that Miller and colleagues present solid evidence that withholding nourishment and administering shocks caused the rats' approach and avoidance behavior. Miller is surely correct in saying the rats' 'strength of pull ... could be measured in grams'.[41] Certainly the more starved the rats were, and the harder they were

---

[38] Ibid., p. 8.
[39] Ibid., p. 10.
[40] 'Comments on theoretical models', *Journal of Personality*, 20 (1951–2), pp. 90–3.
[41] Ibid., p. 91.

shocked, the harder they tugged. But no evidence is presented that the animals had *drives* which resulted from undernourishment and shocks, and which in turn caused their behavior. Nor is there proof that either the severity of undernourishment and shocks or the 'strength of pull' correspond to these drives' strength – measurable in grams, volts, or what have you. I conclude that Santas was overly impressed by the trappings and jargon of laboratory science when he said the Miller experiments reveal how we can determine 'the strength of ... conflicting drives or motives' in animals. So any questions about whether analogous methods apply to human PAs are moot.

Should we end our attempt to analyze motivational power? Not until we have looked at an alternative theory, suggested by Mele, to some extent by Watson before him, and elaborated in Davidson's latest work on *akrasia*. Recall Mele's anecdote about the biology student, John, who allegedly intended to draw a sample of blood from his finger, and whose 'desire not to harm himself grows stronger' than his intention or UJ, Mele goes on to sketch a different account of what is or isn't strong. He declares:

> *Akrasia*, strictly speaking, is ... a condition of a person['s character] which may be manifested in action ... a ... deficiency in ... strength.
> ... The key to what I am most motivated to do, and hence to what I *do*, lies in my character ... my self-control or deficiency therein [*sic*].
> ... reasons 'do not tell the whole story [of *akrasia*] ... the (psychological) explanation is to be filled in by attending to ... the trait of character.[42]

On this alternative theory, the clash of reasons, their PA components, and UJs, is supplanted by a struggle between *me* – who ranks action *x* above *y* in evaluative or any other terms – and my irrational contrary desire to perform *y*. Unless I vigorously practice 'self-control', won't my desire get the best of *me*? Even if we grant the curious assumption that I somehow must stand up for my values – or more generally for my most cogent reasons – are we any nearer to understanding the notion of conative strength? Is it any more evident how *I* can exercise or lose control of my unruly PA, than it was how one of my PAs or reasons could overpower its rival? It still appears that our only criterion for attributing strength to my UJs, reasons, PAs, or *me*, is what I eventually do. It sounds no less empty if we explain that I akratically did *y* *because* I was deficient in self-mastery, than if we say I did *y* because my hankering to do *y* overwhelmed its higher-valued opponent.

Before we throw in the sponge, we ought to study Davidson's newest analysis of what battles against what during *akrasia*. In the background looms his earlier parody of two ancient models of irrational behavior. Davidson wrote:

> The image we get ... from Aristotle ... is of ... two contestants..... one labelled 'passion' and the other 'reason'; they fight [and passion] wins .... A competing image ... [from] Plato ... is adumbrated perhaps by Dante ... when he speaks of the [akratic] man as one who 'lets desire pull reason from her throne' .... Here

---

[42] '*Akrasia*, reasons, and causes', pp. 360, 366; see Watson, 'Skepticism about weakness of will', pp. 331–8.

there are three actors .... the one who lets desire [win] is ... named 'The Will'. If
The Will is strong, he gives the palm to reason [instead of passion].
    ... the first story [does] not account [for the fact that an akratic agent goes
against *his own* better judgement. His] ... action merely reflects the outcome of a
struggle [between passion and reason] within him. What could he do about it? ...
In the second image, [his] representative, The Will, can judge ... both sides [and]
execute [his] decision. The only trouble is that we seem to be back where we
started. For how can The Will judge one course of action better and yet
[akratically] choose the other?[43]

Now Davidson thinks we need some kind of 'divided soul' model. He argues:

to explain irrationality ... we must assume ... the mind can be partitioned into
quasi-independent structures.
    ... the way could be cleared for explanation ... if we ... suppose two
semi-autonomous departments of the mind, one that finds a certain course to be,
ATC, best, and another that prompts another course ....
    [This] partitioning ... does not correspond ... to ... a battle between ... reason
and passion .... [It requires] organized elements ... operat[ing] on [one] another in
the modality of non-rational causality.[44]

Presumably 'the mind' Davidson refers to is not some incorporeal thinking
device which the agent has, but is the 'mindful' flesh and blood agent himself.
As for 'non-rational causality', my own example would feature two people. I
would imagine that during a circus performance, the laughter of a spectator
next to me becomes 'infectious'. It puts me in a jovial mood. Yet nobody would
say, 'My reason for being mirthful is that he is mirthful.' I'm not amused *at* his
guffaws, or *that* he is entertained. Perhaps by analogy with this type of situation,
Davidson asserts that 'certain mental events take on the character of mere
causes [not reasons] relative to ... other mental events in the *same* mind' (my
emphasis).[45] *Akrasia* would exemplify such non-rational causality if our ATC-
$J(x,y)$ brings about the perverse $UJ(y,x)$ in us – for obviously this ATCJ is not a
reason for that UJ. Had our $ATCJ(x,y)$ operated normally, engendering an
$UJ(x,y)$, could we say it 'rationally produced' a suitable UJ? Would this be a
different 'modality' of causation? No: the causal relationship between an ATCJ
and whatever sort of UJ it calls into being is the same. But sometimes our UJ
matches our ATCJ, which is then a reason as well as a cause.
    Davidson contends that 'Only by partitioning the mind ... can we explain
how a thought [or ATCJ] ... can cause another [an UJ] to which it bears no
rational relation'.[46] His hope of providing an 'internal conflict' account of
irrational behavior was kindled by 'Psychoanalytic theory as developed by
Freud', notably by 'a few very general doctrines central to all stages of Freud's
mature writings' – but *not* including his conjectures about unconscious

---

[43] 'How is weakness of the will possible?', pp. 35ff.
[44] 'Paradoxes of irrationality', pp. 300ff.
[45] Ibid., p. 304.
[46] Ibid., p. 303.

repressed mental activity.[47] Specifically, Davidson underscores three Freudian teachings:

> *First*, the mind contains ... semi-independent structures ... characterized by mental attributes like thoughts, desires, and memories.
>
> *Second*, [these] parts of the mind are ... like people, not only in having (or consisting of) ... psychological traits, but in that these factors can combine, as in intentional action, to cause further events in the mind or outside it.
>
> *Third*, some ... [mental] events that characterize ... various substructures ... must be viewed on the model of physical dispositions and forces when they affect, or are affected by, other substructures.[48]

Davidson's Freudian doctrines seem to clear the way for a somewhat novel diagnosis of *akrasia*. Instead of explaining that one judgement, reason-cluster, or PA of mine overpowered another – or got the best of *me* – we recount the machinations of competing 'departments', 'structures', and similar 'organized elements' which I harbor. What matters now is not *my* initially making the ATCJ(x,y), then adding an UJ(y,x). Now the tension is between entities which constitute 'parts of' me – 'one that finds a certain course of action to be, ATC, best, and another that prompts another course'. But why do they fight? I gather, because their respective 'thoughts, desires', reasons or judgements conflict. Incidentally, I assume that when one of them manages to dominate its rivals, the cogency, plausibility, brilliance – even the specious charm – of its reasons and judgements have no effect upon the outcome. Only its brute strength – its 'physical dispositions and forces' – will enable it to prevail over its competitors. So strength is very much in the picture.

Can Davidson's Freudian theory yield the illumination of *akrasia* and conative energy that we've been looking for? Does it make sense of the idea that considerations which favor my doing *x* may seem more cogent to me, but have less influence upon me than those favoring *y*? Is the strength differential between my own conflicting judgements, reasons, or PAs on a par with the relative strength of separate person-like structures which belong to me but reach judgements, weigh reasons, and have PAs of their own?

I would say we have made theoretical headway, *if* we can manage to spell out what my departments and their warfare have to do with me and my occasional bouts of *akrasia*. An example may spotlight some of the gaps between *their* quarreling and *my* irrationality. Imagine that the structure which, in Davidson's phrase, 'finds ... [x] to be, ATC, best', has been defeated, and I perform action *y*. Shouldn't we echo Davidson's erstwhile misgivings about 'The image we get ... from Aristotle'? For how does Davidson's model connect with *my* going against my own ATCJ? What role did *I* have in Davidson's drama? Could I have aided the structure which made the sober ATCJ(x,y)? Could I have restrained the part of me that disregarded this ATCJ? As a matter of fact, is it altogether intelligible to suppose that parts of me judge, ATC or unconditionally, what *I* ought to do – rather than, for instance, what they themselves should do? Come

---

[47] Ibid., pp. 290ff., 304.
[48] Ibid., pp. 290ff.

to think of it, what sort of actions would be desirable for parts of me – besides various mental capers? Can a *part* of me desire to do the things *I* desire to do – read, travel, meet people?

Along these lines, recall that Davidson stipulated that UJs are intentions. So be it. However, in English and some other languages, when people say of a creature that it intends to ..., any verb phrase they fill the blank with is going to be understood as specifying only *that creature's* action. It is grammatical, and makes literal sense, to report that Sue *wants* Charles to prepare dinner, *hopes* that he will, or *decides* that he ought to. But 'Sue *intends* Charles to prepare dinner' violates syntax, and has no straightforward literal meaning; it must be interpreted non-literally – perhaps as 'She intends to ask (remind, persuade, compel) him to ...'. Clearly the asking, etc., is to be done by her. If this is right, can we suppose that the structure which prompts me to do y has made an UJ that I should perform y? Then we would be supposing that *it intends me* to do y – a decidedly peculiar upshot. So alongside the general problem about why the departments I shelter concern themselves with my behavior, we face specific riddles as to what mental high-jinks they engage in on my behalf. If in fact a structure cannot determine what I do by issuing an UJ, how does it get me to act – either rationally or akratically? How else might it exercise its power over me?

I have another perplexity regarding Davidson's 'divided mind' theory of motivational strength. This time I echo his disparagement of the old tripartite image of *akrasia*. He wondered: 'how can The Will judge one course of action better and yet choose the other?' My variant is: how can my most powerful subdivision neglect the ATCJ of its colleague? A partial answer may be that my structures are not only 'semi-independent' of *me* – insofar as they sometimes operate without my awareness and consent; on occasion their mental goings-on are also not monitored or influenced *by each other*. Indeed, Davidson remarks that although a person's departments inhabit a single mind, the events which unfold within each department can be as 'segregated' as events which 'occur in different minds'.[49] Hence my toughest subdivision may simply be *ignorant* of another's $ATCJ(x,y)$.

But shouldn't this reply baffle us? How can my dominant structure rush to an $UJ(y,x)$ – or whatever it uses to make me act – without first seeking an ATCJ on whether x or y is more desirable? Has Davidson provided us an explanation of *my* akratic behavior at the cost of generating new puzzles about the irrational carryings-on of my strongest department? And even if we are unperplexed by its bizarre doings, have we improved our understanding of its alleged power to determine my actions?

The framework of our inquiry into motivational strength has been a Davidsonian causal theory of action – which explains what people do by reference to their antecedent and contemporaneous mental states. A notion of strength is vital to any such analysis. Presumably the agent who acts must not only have some inclination, hankering, moderate desire, vague reason, or half-hearted intention. Her or his PA must be sufficiently robust. His reason has to be conclusive, his intention firm. What else could overcome his inherent

---

[49] Ibid., p. 300.

sluggishness? And in the very common situation where an agent has two or more incompatible motives, each pressing enough to make him act, isn't it self-evident that the most energetic one will triumph?

The doctrine that we act on our strongest motive has imposing credentials. But as soon as we endeavor to clarify what philosophers of action and drive theorists in psychology mean by motivational strength, we run across one obscurity after another. By contrast, we understand well enough what it is for ocean currents, earthquake tremors, radioactive emissions, electric shocks, and simple tugging or pushing, to be comparatively strong or feeble. In dealing with such non-psychological examples, we can easily discriminate between a phenomenon's strength and its effects; thus it will be an empirical question, sometimes answerable in the negative, whether the strongest causal factor always 'wins out'. We do not contradict ourselves if we deny that the most violent earthquake produces the most damage – or that the arm-wrestler who pushes hardest pins down his opponent's hand. But can we imagine that an agent is more strongly motivated to do x than to do y, and is fully able to do either, but does y? Yet this should be conceivable, if it is an informative factual claim to say the strongest motive prevails.

Despite these troubles, some useful distinctions have emerged – for instance between the alleged power of our motivational states to cause action, and their intensity, cogency, and rank in our scheme of values. But our specific questions about conative power went largely unanswered. I still wonder: Why is wishing too anemic to get us started? Should we equate intending with making an UJ? Are UJs causally – or perhaps logically – necessary and sufficient for 'acting on a reason'? Is it enough that the agent *could* have reached an UJ? Is it impossible to act against one's UJ? Are ATCJs utterly powerless, or simply always weaker than any UJ which contravenes them? Why? Are there entailment and logical incompatibility relationships among ATCJs and UJs? When I behave akratically, what matches strength with what? Do my desires, reasons, UJs and ATCJs go at it – or do I, even parts of me, enter the fray? Until we get some answers, perhaps we should not consider it obvious that motivational strength explains behavior.

7

Davidson on Moral Conflict

FRANK JACKSON

In 'How is weakness of the will possible?'[1] Donald Davidson approaches the problem of akrasia through a discussion of moral conflict. He holds that 'incontinence can only exist when there is conflict in this sense',[2] but allows (rightly) that although the existence of moral conflict is a necessary condition of incontinent action, it is not a sufficient condition. In this paper I will restrict my attention to his treatment of moral conflict.

Davidson says about moral conflict that 'It is astonishing that in contemporary moral philosophy this problem has received little attention, and no satisfactory treatment'[3] This raises the following questions. What is this problem that has been largely overlooked? What treatments are unsatisfactory? What is Davidson's own treatment and is it satisfactory? I will address these questions more or less in this order, and also make some remarks at the end about the implications of what we have said for the interpretation of moral principles – a matter Davidson himself sees as related to what account one should give of moral conflict.

What is the problem of moral conflict?

The problem of moral conflict is the problem of how exactly to characterize it. But first, what is it that we are seeking to characterize exactly?

Davidson quotes an example from Aquinas.[4] In considering whether to commit fornication one faces a moral conflict constituted between pleasure on the one hand and immorality on the other (according to Aquinas). By implication, Davidson also gives two more examples.[5] A case where lying is needed to save a life, and a case where I cannot avoid breaking one of two promises I have made to two different people (Lolita and Lavinia).

---

[1] Reprinted in Donald Davidson, *Essays on Actions and Events* (Clarendon Press, Oxford, 1980).
[2] Ibid., p. 34.
[3] Ibid., p. 34.
[4] Ibid., p. 33.
[5] Ibid., p. 34.

It will be helpful to flesh out one of these examples for later reference. I will refer to the following example as the Anne Frank case. Anne Frank is hiding in the attic of your house. A member of the Gestapo comes to the door and asks you whether anyone Jewish lives in your house. You decide to lie and say no in order to save her life. I am going to assume that this is the right thing to do. Perhaps I haven't said enough to make this indisputably the correct view to take of this case. But I am sure all of you – unregenerate Kantians aside – can think of how to embellish the case so as to make lying indisputably the right thing to do.

(A fair question about cases of this general kind is whether there can be cases where there is no answer – perhaps because some kind of incommensurability arises between the competing considerations – as to what the right thing to do is. It is not, however, a question Davidson pursues, and it is, I think, a question we don't need to pursue in order to make our points.)

I agree with Davidson that it is plausible to think of cases like the Anne Frank case as involving something properly describable as moral conflict. But wherein lies the conflict? Exactly how should we characterize these cases? Davidson makes two preliminary suggestions – or perhaps I should say uses two formulations – to try and get across to us what he has in mind. There are, however, problems with both.

Here is one passsage: 'The situation [of moral conflict] is common; life is crowded with examples: I ought to do it because it will save a life, I ought not because it will be a lie; if I do it, I will break my word to Lavinia, if I don't, I will break my word to Lolita.[6]

The trouble with this as a characterization, even a preliminary one, is that 'P because Q' entails both P and Q. If I ought to do it because it will save a life, and also I ought not to do it because it will be a lie, then it will simultaneously be true that I ought to do it and ought not to do it. And that result is unacceptable. In the Anne Frank case *the* answer is that I ought to lie; in some cases (perhaps) the answer is indeterminate; but in no case is it true both that I ought to do it, and that I ought not do it. Part of the point of saying that I ought to do A is to exclude that I ought to do something other than A.

I must, however, report that what I have declared to be unacceptable is in fact accepted by some writers in moral conflict.[7] I will return to this briefly later.[8] For now I will just say two things. First, I am fairly sure that Davidson would regard the result as unacceptable. He says 'we must give up the idea that we can *detach* conclusions about what is ... obligatory from the principles.'[9] His reason here appears to be precisely that if we did detach, we would get 'I ought to do A

---

[6] Ibid., p. 34.

[7] See, e.g., Bernard Williams, 'Ethical consistency', reprinted in his *Problems of the Self* (Cambridge University Press, Cambridge, 1973); Bas van Fraassen, 'Values and the heart's command', *Journal of Philosophy*, 70 (1973), pp. 5–19; Ruth Barcan Marcus, 'Moral dilemmas and consistency', *Journal of Philosophy*, 78 (1980), pp. 121–36.

[8] For a fuller discussion see my 'Internal conflicts in desires and morals', forthcoming in *American Philosophical Quarterly*, and Earl Conee, 'Against moral dilemmas', *Philosophical Review*, 91 (1982), pp. 82–97.

[9] 'How is weakness of the will possible?', p. 37.

and I ought not do A'; and that's bad. Second, in any case it is clearly a weakness in a preliminary characterization designed to identify a largely overlooked problem that it should require accepting the highly controversial doctrine that 'ought' and 'ought not' are consistent.

Here is another passage, also designed to help us identify our problem cases: 'By a case of moral conflict I mean a case where there are good reasons both for performing an action and for performing one that rules it out (perhaps refraining from the action.)'[10]

There is, I think, no denying that this passage helps us at an intuitive level to identify the essential feature of cases of moral conflict (which, of course, is exactly what it is designed to do). In the Anne Frank case, it makes good intuitive sense to say that a reason for doing what you did, namely, lie to the Gestapo, is that it would save her life[11] – indeed this is an overwhelming reason – and that a reason against – albeit an insufficiently strong one – is that what you did was to lie.

Nevertheless there is a problem, which I will approach by distinguishing between *external* and *internal* reasons for (or against) performing an action. Suppose I am wondering whether to undergo a certain operation. A top surgeon advises me to have it. This is clearly a reason for having it, in a perfectly respectable sense. Now suppose the surgeon elaborates on why she is advising me to have it, explaining that it will enable me to run again. That I am advised by an expert to have the operation is a reason for having it; that it will enable me to run again is also a reason for having it. But there is a big difference, which I will mark by calling the first an external reason for, and the second an internal reason for.

Being told by the surgeon is an external reason for, because it does not add to the value of the operation. It adds to my estimate of the value, but not to the value itself. After all, had the advice not been given, the contemplated action would have been just as good, though I might not have known so. By way of contrast, its enabling me to run again is an internal reason for having the operation, for were it not to do this, the action itself would be of less value.

When I act for an external reason alone, I do not know the corresponding desire which rationalizes my action.[12] I know, or believe, that there is such a desire but do not know which of mine it is. When I act merely because the surgeon has advised it, I believe that there is some desire of mine, presumably to do with my health, which will be satisfied by having the operation, but do not know which desire it is. When she elaborates, I learn that it is my desire to run again.

Is moral conflict a matter of a clash of external reasons for and against, or of internal reasons for and against, an action? I think it is fairly clear that it must be a clash of internal reasons. If one surgeon says yes and another says no, there is a clash of an external reason for with an external reason against; but this seems

---

[10] Ibid., p. 33.

[11] Whether it is that it would save her life or, more strictly, your belief that it would is not important for our discussion.

[12] I here presume at least general agreement with Donald Davidson, 'Actions, reasons, and causes', reprinted in *Essays on Actions and Events*.

to be more an epistemological dilemma than anything else. Thus the suggestion under discussion, as applied to the Anne Frank case, is that there was an internal reason for and an internal reason against what you did. The internal reason for was clearly that it led to her survival. This counts as an internal reason for, because had your action not led to her survival its value would have been much less. But what is the internal reason against? Presumably the lying; but an internal reason against is something such that had it been absent, things would have been better – like an internal reason for, but the other way around – and it is not true that, had lying been absent, things would have been better. Had you not lied, Anne Frank would have been caught and killed. It was lying that secured the great benefit of her survival. A feature of an action that secures a great benefit hardly sounds like a reason against.

An internal reason for going on holiday may be that it will enable you to do a lot of swimming. Why is that an internal reason for? Surely because it has or would have, *all in all*, good results (we all know it can be a bit of a mixed bag). Precisely that is true of lying in the Anne Frank case, lying has, all in all, good results; so how can it be counted a reason against instead of a reason for? (I'll drop the 'internal' from now on.)

The same point can be made about other cases of moral conflict. I am caught in a position (let's suppose through no fault of my own) where I must break my promise to Lavinia or Lolita. Suppose it is my promise to Lavinia that matters more, and so I ought to and do break my promise to Lolita. Clearly, on the preliminary characterization under discussion, this is supposed to be a case of moral conflict because there is a reason against what I ought to do, namely the fact that it involves breaking my promise to Lolita. But *that* is what is needed in the circumstances to secure what ought to be, and what is needed to secure what ought to be sounds like a reason for, not against.

Notice that it is not to the point that lying and promise-breaking are not good in themselves. Most features of actions that we cite as reasons for performing them are not good in themselves. If receiving a smallpox vaccination ensures, and is in the circumstances the only way of ensuring, protection from smallpox, then the fact that a visit to the doctor involves it is a reason for visiting the doctor, but receiving a vaccination is not good in itself. The essence of our puzzle is that lying and promise-breaking *in cases of moral conflict* may be known to ensure, and in the circumstances be essential to ensuring, an overwhelming benefit. How then can their presence fail to be a reason for?

Let me emphasize that I am not going back on my earlier remark that Davidson's preliminary formulation of moral conflict in terms of a clash between reasons for and reasons against makes good intuitive sense. What I have tried to show is that it will need some work to make good philosophical sense out of what makes good intuitive sense.

I have suggested that Davidson's preliminary characterizations of cases of moral conflicts are in one way or another unsatisfactory. This is not a point against his overall contention that there is a problem, quite the reverse in fact. We all know the kinds of cases Davidson has in mind, we all know that they involve conflict in some sense or other; the very fact that his preliminary characterizations face difficulties reinforces his contention that the problem of how exactly to characterize moral conflicts is a *problem*.

Which treatments of moral conflict are unsatisfactory?

Davidson mentions two, I will add a third. Here is the crucial passage: 'Those who recognise the difficulty seem ready to accept one of two solutions: in effect they allow only a single ultimate moral principle; or they rest happy with the notion of a distinction between the prima facie desirable (good, obligatory, etc.) and the absolutely desirable (good, obligatory, etc.).'[13]

I take it that, by a solution in terms of a single moral principle, Davidson means more a dissolution than a solution. He mentions utilitarianism in this connection, and seems to hold that there are no real moral conflicts for the utilitarian. I think this is wrong, but for reasons which I cannot give until near the end of this paper.

I am not sure that I have fully grasped Davidson's objection to treating moral conflict in terms of a distinction between what is prima facie right or wrong (say) and what is absolutely right or wrong. But I take the following objection to be at least consonant with what he says.

Normally when people talk about what is prima facie right or wrong, they mention *types* of actions rather than particular actions:[14] lying is prima facie wrong, promise-keeping is prima facie right, and so on. In short they introduce the predicates 'is prima facie right' and 'is prima facie wrong' as predicates on properties of actions rather than on particular actions.

Now moral conflict arises with particular actions. 'Should I *here and now* break my promise to Lolita or my promise to Lavinia? What should I do in the *particular* circumstances of the Anne Frank case?' How then does a doctrine about types of actions help us characterize the relevant feature of particular actions. The obvious approach would be via the following rule: If act-type T is prima facie right (wrong), then every particular instance of T is prima facie right (wrong). Thus (given that lying is prima facie wrong) your act of lying to the Gestapo in the Anne Frank case will be prima facie wrong. But your act of lying to the Gestapo *is one and the same as* your act of ensuring Anne Frank's safety.[15] Hence your ensuring Anne Frank's safety will also be prima facie wrong. Likewise (given that ensuring safety is prima facie right) your act of ensuring her safety will be prima facie right, but, as it is one and the same as your lying, your lying is also prima facie right. It doesn't sound right to say that your saving her life is prima facie wrong, and that your lying is prima facie right. Moreover the *conflict* in cases of moral conflict has not been captured. Intuitively, the conflict arises because of something bad about the lying and something good about the life-saving. If we construe the appeal to the notion of the prima facie in terms of predication on types, then we can say that lying differs from

---

[13] 'How is weakness of the will possible?', p. 34.

[14] See, e.g., W.D. Ross, *The Right and the Good*, (Oxford University Press, Oxford, 1930), and H.J. McCloskey, *Meta-Ethics and Normative Ethics* (Martinus Nijhoff, The Hague, 1969).

[15] I am here assuming a view that Davidson has argued for in a number of places, e.g. in 'Agency', reprinted in *Essays on Actions and Events*. However, even if it is false that your lying is one and the same event as your life-saving, it is plausible that the two are closely enough related to earn the same moral predicates.

life-saving in that the first is and the second is not prima facie wrong, and the first is not and the second is prima facie right. But then we leave it a mystery wherein lies the conflict in particular cases. Though lying and life-saving, the types, may differ in prima facie status, this particular lying and this particular life-saving, the particular action, cannot. 'They' are one and the same action and so alike in every respect.

What we need is a development of the appeal to the prima facie which does two things together: (1) offers us predicates which apply to particular actions, and yet which (2) allows us to associate something different of the 'wrong' kind with the lying side of things, and something of the 'right' kind with the life-saving side of things. Davidson's theory does exactly this.

But before I discuss his theory I want to say something very brief about a treatment of moral conflict which he does not discuss and which I adverted to earlier. This treatment sees the crucial feature of moral conflict as being the simultaneous obtaining of 'S ought to do A' and 'S ought to do not A'. In the Anne Frank case, it is both true that you ought to lie and that you ought to not lie.

This theory must distinguish among kinds of oughts, it must have a hierarchy of oughts. Otherwise it lacks the conceptual resources to say how moral conflicts ought to be resolved, and, whatever may be the case for some moral conflicts, some are to be resolved one way rather than another. For example, in the Anne Frank case the conflict is to be resolved in favour of lying. But on the theory in question this cannot be expressed by saying simply that your lying has the property of being what you ought to do, *for so does not lying*. What must be done[16] is to distinguish a resolution sense of 'ought' from a non-resolution sense of 'ought'. We might label the first 'absolute' and the second 'prima facie', and so the theory will be in essentials the one we have just been discussing, and the difficulty will be as before: How do we capture the conflict in the particular case? In the resolution sense of 'ought' it is false that your life-saving ought to be done and your lying ought not be done – your lying ought to be done. In the non-resolution sense it is true that your life-saving is what ought to be done and your lying is what ought not be done, but in that sense it is equally true that your life-saving is what ought not be done and your lying is what ought to be done.

Davidson's treatment of moral conflict

Instead of a predicate like 'x is prima facie wrong' of the simple prima facie theory, Davidson works with a more complex predicate like 'x is prima facie wrong given it is a lying'.[17] This affords an immediate application to actual cases of moral conflict, for 'x' is to be replaced by a term for a particular action and not by a name of a type of action. Moreover, his complex prima facie theory

---

[16] And is by Philippa Foot, 'Moral realism and moral dilemma', *Journal of Philosophy*, 80 (1983), pp. 379–98.

[17] And with predicates like 'x is prima facie better than y given x is a promise-keeping and y is a promise-breaking'.

enables us to express the conflict between, for example, the lying and the life-saving in the Anne Frank case. The trouble with the simple prima facie theory was that, though the obvious way of transferring attributions of prima facie value from types to tokens gave 'This act of lying is prima facie wrong', it equally gave 'This act of life-saving is prima facie wrong'. As far as statements about the particular act go, interchanging 'lying' and 'life-saving' does not change truth value. The complex prima facie theory handles the matter straightforwardly. According to it, 'is prima facie wrong given it is a lying' is *true* of the act while 'is prima facie wrong given it is a life-saving' is *false* of the act. Hence interchanging 'lying' and 'life-saving' (in the predicate) can change truth value. (What happens to the simple theory if we use an unobvious way of transferring 'is prima facie wrong (right)' from types to tokens? If we use the rule 'if act type T is prima facie wrong (right), then a token of T is prima facie wrong (right) given it is of type T', we get, of course, Davidson's theory.)

Accordingly, I think that Davidson's account of moral conflict is a clear advance; nevertheless it leaves something obscure. It seems to me that Davidson does not say enough about how to interpret statements of the form 'A is prima facie right (wrong) given it is an F' for it to be clear that the truth values come out the way they must if this theory is to be acceptable. Take, for a change, the Lolita–Lavinia case, where I ought – absolutely, in the 'resolution' sense, all in all, all things considered – to break my promise to Lolita. This is the only way to keep my promise to Lavinia, and that is agreed to be more important. Suppose I do keep my promise to Lavinia; then if the case is to be one of moral conflict, Davidson must hold that what I do, though absolutely right, is prima facie wrong given it is a promise-breaking to Lolita. Is it obvious that this is true? The problem parallels that which arose for the reasons-for–reasons-against characterization of moral conflict discussed earlier. If being a promise-breaking to Lolita is known to be essential and sufficient in the circumstances for what is agreed to be of prime importance, then how does it make an act prima facie wrong?

It might be replied that if all we knew about the act was that it was a promise-breaking to Lolita, we would judge it wrong. And it is true that Davidson says 'There is conflict in this minimal sense [meaning moral conflict] whenever the agent is aware of considerations that, *taken alone*, would lead to mutually incompatible actions' (my italics).[18] This does suggest we analyze 'x is prima facie right (wrong) given it is F' as 'If all we knew about x was that it was F, we should judge x right (wrong)'. I think it is clear though that were such an analysis adopted, this would make the notions of prima facie rightness and wrongness relative to being ... unsuited to account for moral conflict. Consider the following example. There is a card-index box containing one thousand cards, each card containing a specification of a course of action. I do not know what these specifications are, but I do know that all but one is of a quite immoral course of action. I draw a single card out at random. It is the exception, it specifies that I fill in an honest tax return; which I proceed to do. It is obvious that my so doing was not resolving a moral conflict in the sense we are

---

[18] 'How is weakness of the will possible?', pp. 33–4.

concerned with. Yet what I did was right, while being prima facie wrong relative to something I knew about what I did, on the account under criticism; because my action was specified by the randomly drawn card, and had I known only that about it, I should have judged it wrong.

Again, it might be that if all I knew about an act was that it was recommended by Dr A, it would be correct for me to judge it right, and also true that if all I knew was that it was recommended against by Dr B, it would be correct for me to judge it wrong, and moreover true that Dr A recommends for and Dr B recommends against. This is not enough for moral conflict, but only enough for an epistemic dilemma. The point is essentially that made earlier about the unsuitability of a clash of *external* reasons, for the characterization of moral conflict.

There is a way of making clear what I think Davidson leaves obscure, but first we need to notice a distinction between two senses in which a property may contribute to, or diminish from, value.

Properties and value

The value of something depends on its properties. If it is aesthetic value that is in question, it may be properties like shape, line, colour distribution, and so on. Some may be properties of parts of the object, others of the object as a whole, others of the object-in-a-situation; and just which properties (and of exactly what) are of fundamental significance is of course a matter of controversy in aesthetic theory. There is an important point about how we determine the contribution, positive or negative, that a property makes to the value of an object. Suppose we are looking at a relatively attractive building and an architect remarks that it is a pity about the thickness of one of the supporting columns, for it detracts from the aesthetic value of the building. An engineer replies that the thickness of the column does not detract from aesthetic value; quite the reverse in fact, because had the column not been thick, the building would have been a pile of rubble. And a pile of rubble has less aesthetic value than the building, imperfect though it is. The engineer is right (we may suppose) that the thickness of the column adds to the amount of aesthetic value in the world, but he is wrong to suppose that this shows that the thickness of column does not detract from the value of the building – as his remarking that the building is imperfect effectively concedes. The contribution a property makes to the aesthetic value of an object is determined by treating the various distinct properties of the object that are aesthetically relevant as independent, and comparing the value of it with the value of the possible object which has all the same aesthetic properties except for the one in question. The fact that had that property been absent, then, for reasons to do with engineering, or whatever, various other aesthetic properties would have been absent is irrelevant to the contribution that property makes to the value of that object. In short, we don't consider what would have been the case had the property been absent, but the possible object with all the same aesthetically relevant properties save the one in question.

The same is true when it is moral value that is in question. We must distinguish the question as to whether a property of some state of affairs (often a state of affairs which is a possible or actual action) contributes positively or negatively to the moral value of that state of affairs, from whether its presence contributes positively or negatively to the moral value of the world. We answer the first question relative to some delineation of which properties are fundamentally relevant to moral value – for short, which properties are the moral properties – by regarding all the moral properties of the state of affairs as independent, and so determining the contribution a given moral property, P, makes to the state of affairs by comparing the value of the state of affairs with that of a state of affairs exactly alike in moral properties except for P. We 'subtract' P without worrying about what would, because of the contingencies of the situation, have been the case with the other moral properties had P been absent. On the other hand, if we want P's contribution to the value of the world, we must consider what would have been the case had P been absent.

Lying is a property of what you did in the Anne Frank case. Did it add to or detract from value? Two answers, for there are really two questions. It detracted from the value of what you did, because the possible action with the same moral properties except for the lying has greater moral value than the action you in fact performed. It added to the value of the world, because had you not lied what would then have been the case would have been clearly worse. (Anne Frank would have died.) The reason why we earlier found the question of whether lying was a reason for or a reason against so baffling was that we were in effect seeking one answer to two questions which need to be differently answered.

We can now make transparent what was left obscure in Davidson's complex prima facie theory of moral conflict. Consider

(1)   This act is prima facie wrong given it is a lying, where the act in question is your act in the Anne Frank case. (1) might be spelt out as (2) or as (3).

(2)   This act's being a lying diminishes the value of this act.

(3)   This act's being a lying diminishes the value of the world.

If (1) is read as (2), (1) is true; if (1) is read as (3), (1) is false.

My view, therefore, is that provided we read statements like (1) as (2) – and more generally provided we read the predicate 'x is prima facie right (wrong) given it is F' as 'x's being F increases (diminishes) the value of x', rather than as 'x's being F increases (diminishes) the value of the world' – Davidson's theory of moral conflict is correct, and amounts to the following simple and appealing account of it. A moral conflict is a case where an action, or possible action, has a property which diminishes its value and a property which enhances its value. This squares nicely with our intuitive feeling that the conflict in the Anne Frank case is between the lying and the life-saving. This is the literal truth of the matter: the life-saving adds to, and the lying detracts from, the moral value of what you did.

Moral principles

Our account of moral conflict – Davidson's account interpreted in the way I've suggested – assumed a discernment of a set of properties as the moral properties. Which these are is one question for an ethical theory, *another is the rule of decision*. Knowledge of which properties are the moral properties is not alone enough to settle what one ought to do. Consider some reasonably classical form of pleasure utilitarianism. It tells you that the properties you need ultimately to worry about are pleasure and pain. This leaves open, though, *how* you are to worry about them; it leaves open, for instance, whether it is the total of pleasure and pain or the average of pleasure and pain that is crucial in determining what ought to be done. In deciding between two courses of action you know that it is the distribution of pleasure and pain consequent upon them that is said to matter by utilitarians, but if one action gives a higher total, and the other a higher average, of pleasure over pain, you need a rule of decision.[19] Similarly, two prima facie duty theorists might agree in their lists of prima facie duties, while disagreeing in their rules of decision – perhaps one says that a clash between promise-keeping and truth-telling is to be resolved in favour of promise-keeping, and the other says that truth-telling is the more important. We can put the matter in terms of supervenience. Total and average utilitarian agree that any two acts exactly alike in respect to the distribution of pleasure and pain (happiness and unhappiness, ideal good and evil ...) are either both right or both wrong, but may not agree on whether it is right that they both are or wrong that they both are. Similarly prima facie duty theorists who have the same lists of duties agree that two acts that fulfill and violate exactly the same duties are alike in being right or in being wrong, but which they are may be in dispute.

The distinction between moral properties and (moral) rules of decision enables us to see that utilitarians can acknowledge the existence of moral conflicts. True, they will not think much of our examples in this paper, but they will have examples of their own.

Consider a total-pleasure utilitarian faced with hurting one individual, Fred, in order to give pleasure to many. Although he holds that he ought to hurt Fred, he also holds that the value of what he ought to do is diminished by the presence of Fred's pain. For, according to him, Fred's pain is a moral property, and the possible action alike in all moral properties except for Fred's pain is of greater moral value. Hence this is a case of moral conflict for him. By contrast, if what is needed to secure the pleasure to many is a lie, there is no moral conflict. Keeping all moral properties the same except for the lying is, for him, keeping all moral properties the same. Hence the lying does not detract from the moral value of what is done, and so there is no conflict.

The crucial point is, of course, that lying is, according to him, of no significance in itself. It is not just that the complete distribution of pleasure and pain swamps the lying, rather the lying counts for naught when set beside the

---

[19] For some cases see, e.g., Peter Singer, *Practical Ethics* (Cambridge University Press, Cambridge, 1979), pp. 85–8; and the references cited therein, p. 225.

distribution. On the other hand Fred's pain does count because it is a *constituent* in that complete distribution. It may be thought that Fred's pain does not count in itself, because only the total amount of pleasure and pain counts. But Fred's pain is part of what makes up that total, the total is not something separate caused by Fred's pain. By contrast, for the utilitarian, lying only matters inasmuch as it causes pleasure and pain, including possibly Fred's pain.[20]

I am, therefore, disagreeing with Davidson's (passing) suggestion that utilitarianism is incompatible with the existence of moral conflict. Provided an ethical theory's account of which are the moral properties allows a number of separate instances of these properties (Fred's pain, Mary's pleasure ...) to count in themselves for or against moral value, that theory is consistent with the existence of moral conflict. (However, a theory which held that the only moral property was being approved of by God, and whose rule of decision was that – as of any range of possible actions exactly one was approved by God – what one ought do was the one God approved, would be inconsistent with the existence of moral conflict.)

The distinction between the moral-properties part of an ethical theory and the theory-of-decision part enables a useful distinction to be made between two ways of reading a moral principle like

(L) Lying is wrong.

It may be that (L) is part of the theory of decision, saying that any action which is a lying is one that ought not be done. Read thus it is a universal conditional about states of affairs: $\forall x$ [if x is a lying, then x ought not be done], and read thus it is false.

There is another way of reading (L) though, a way which preserves its universal status but makes it part of the delineation of the moral properties. Read thus it says that the property of being a lying always detracts from moral value: $\forall x$ [if x is a lying, then x is the worse for it]. The world may be the better for it, in which case it is a counter-example to (L) read as a part of the theory of decision, but the action is the worse for it.

(L) read in the first way as a universal about actions and a part of the theory of decision is denied by utilitarians, prima facie duty theorists, and indeed by the moral majority. (L) read in the second way as a part of the delineation of moral properties is denied by utilitarians, but accepted by some prima facie duty theorists, and, I think, by the moral majority.

It is important that the distinction between the moral-properties part and the theory-of-decision part of an ethical theory enables us to distinguish these two readings of (L). For without the second reading we have no way of expressing the view of the moral majority about lying (and promise-breaking, injustice, and so on).[21] The moral majority does not think that lying is always the wrong thing to do. But nor is their view captured by saying that most often lying is the wrong thing to do. They grant that Anne Frank cases might be much more common than they are, so that at least half the time lying is the right thing to do; but they hold that it would still be the case that lying was wrong, though justified. (They remark that it would be most regrettable if Anne Frank cases were much more common; but if it were then the case that lying was right, what would be so regrettable?) Their thesis that lying is wrong is a part of their view about which the moral properties are, a matter on which they are typically much more confident than they are on the finer points of the theory of decision. Most of us have some degree of confidence about the kinds of properties we should be worrying about when considering what we morally ought to do, while admitting to considerable bafflement about the right decision to come to in the face of conflicting claims.

8

Rhyme and Reason: Reflections on Davidson's Version of Having Reasons

Annette C. Baier

A reason, according to Davidson, is a mental cause which is a *rational* cause. At the end of 'Paradoxes of irrationality,' he raises the question of whether the characterization he has given of the irrationality of the akratic person, namely as being in a mental state which has a mental cause which is not a rational cause, gives a sufficient condition of irrationality. He answers that it does not, and produces two examples of non-rational mental causation which we would not want to say exhibit irrationality. These are the cases of someone who is led to remember a name by humming a tune, and the case of a person who turns against his former desires and goals and tries to change them. In the latter case, he says:

> From the point of view of the changed desire, there is no reason for the change – the reason comes from an independent source, and is based on further, and partly contrary considerations. The agent has reasons for changing his own habits and character, but those reasons come from a domain of values necessarily extrinsic to the content or values to undergo change.[1]

This outcome, where the rational or reason-caused mental state contrasts not only with the irrational but also with two other sorts of mental states with mental causes, namely the less than rational recall of associated items, and the more than rational judgment on what had previously counted as reasons, might lead one to have some doubts about the adequacy of the initial account of what reasons were, and of what counts as rationality. For we do seem to have reason to welcome the fact that we can use association to recall names, and that we can transvalue values. The mental causes of these happenings, although not rational causes, are like rational causes in that we endorse their working when we reflect on them. If there are reasons that rationality knows not of, not only in the heart, but in the best brains, then we perhaps should try to acquaint rational reason with all those lower and higher reasons. It seems to me that Davidson's version

---

[1] *Philosophical Essays on Freud*, ed. R. Wollheim and J. Hopkins (Cambridge University Press, Cambridge, 1982), p. 305.

of rationality and of what reasons are is ripe for metamorphosis. (For all I know, the transformation or transfiguration has already occurred – 'A nice derangement of epitaphs' suggests that it may have.) So at the risk of merely cheering on a change which is underway I shall point out what those tensions were, in the past Davidsonian views, and also say something about the alternatives open to a philosopher who tries to understand the norms which we recognize as those of reason.

I think we can draw a rough but helpful contrast between those who are fairly confident that they can identify 'the demands of reason,' a reason seen as having sovereign authority (or at any rate an authority excelled only by any divine countermands), and who therefore see any human thinking or acting which is not guided by and obedient to these demands as some sort of normative failure on our part, and those who are much less confident about what reason requires of us, and interested in how its requirements relate to other demands, such as those of love, or of loyalty, or of self-assertion, how its guidelines relate to other guidelines we can identify – those of tradition, custom, animal intelligence, instinct. We could call the first approach rationalist, the second empiricist. (I call it empiricist rather than naturalist because the latter term might be thought to exclude attention to the social and cultural norms to which the norms of reason should be related. 'Empiricist' I take to cover anyone who looks seriously at whatever does guide human thought and action, when, on reflection, it is found acceptable.)

The rationalist, say Leibniz, believes that the demands of reason can be spelled out, and in principle presented in such a way that there is an algorithm for being rational. To be rational is to have sufficient reason for what one does, in thought and in action, and the paradigm reason is a premiss for a deductively valid conclusion. The empiricist, say Hume, is impressed with how few not only of our actual moves but of the moves we approve of fit this model. We do get things right by reciting little verses ('i before e except after c') or multiplication tables to ourselves, we do admire good narratives as well as good arguments, we do approve of those whose action is guided by compassion, even if the compassionate act is akratic, done against the sensible knave's or sensible profit-maker's 'better' judgment. The empiricist looks, like Aristotle in *De Anima*, at how reason coexists with animal intelligence and with vegetative growth and development, as well as with social and political pressures. What practical reason demands may have to be specified only as what the wise person would do and advise, whether or not reasons for that advice can be spelled out. The sovereignty of reason need not be prejudged, for the empiricist. Until we understand better the variety of pressures we operate under, and their interrelation, empiricists will postpone the decision on ultimate sovereignty. Decisions about normative force, of course, cannot all be indefinitely postponed, but we do not in all conditions have to settle constitutional questions of what has highest authority in order to muddle along recognizing a variety of authorities.

Davidson's views about reasons, from 'Actions, reasons, and causes' through 'How is weakness of the will possible?', 'Agency,' 'Freedom to act,' 'Intending,' 'Psychology as philosophy,' to 'Paradoxes of irrationality,' seem to show a strengthening of the rationalist *motif* in his thought, accompanied throughout by an awareness of discordant considerations. The rationalist *motif* intensifies the more reasons are assimilated to premises in arguments, and goodness of reasons to soundness of inferences. I think the most rationalist claims, paradoxically enough, occur in 'Paradoxes of irrationality,' the same paper where those rationalist theses seem on the brink of being *aufgehoben*.

At first reasons were merely motives. 'Actions, reasons, and causes' exhibited a fairly tolerant view of what it took to show oneself to be a rational animal. It was enough to have a 'primary reason' to 'rationalize' one's action, where that was some want along with a belief about how to satisfy it. The want might be a sudden impulse to touch an elbow which presented itself, a yen to drink a can of paint, a claustrophobic need to leave a party, as well as less colorful wishes to get on with one's knitting or do one's duty. (I note, for future purposes, that such primary reasons had to include some want of the agent. Orders, requests, suggestions from others, were not included as possible primary reasons.) Although such reasons were said not just to explain but to justify one's action, that was only in 'a somewhat anaemic' sense of 'justify'. Although practical syllogisms were invoked, it was a passing invocation and one which acknowledged the contrivance needed to present reasons as premises of syllogisms. But by 'How is weakness of the will possible?' reasons settled into being premises, and more than anaemic justifications seem needed for reasons to be good reasons, good enough to ward off charges of irrationality. A rationalist view of reasons as premises, and of rational or reason-guided activity as the making of valid moves from all the available premises, replaces the earlier more tolerant view. This is sustained throughout the progressive versions of the sort of form sound practical inferences might have. Aristotelian syllogisms are replaced by moves from *prima facie* conditionals to derived more 'conclusive' *prima facie* conditionals, and moves detaching the consequent from such a privileged *prima facie* conditional, but throughout these transformations rationality is what is displayed in inference, and irrationality is formally faulty inference. The fault of misconcluding in deductive inferences is distinguished from misconcluding in inferences whose soundness cannot be displayed as solely a matter of their deductive form, but all variants of irrationality are seen as mismoves in inference according to a canonical form.

A question left outstanding in 'How is weakness of the will possible?' is what the relation is of the irrationality which is not inconsistency to that which *is* a matter of drawing a conclusion inconsistent with one's premises. Also left in doubt there was whether the akratic move from 'it would be best for me not to do *a*, since the reasons I have for doing it are outweighed by those against doing it' to 'Nevertheless I am going to do *a*' was an irrational move reducible to logical inconsistency, or whether it involved a different formal fault, or a nonformal fault. Davidson is quite explicit that the move from 'It would be wrong (imprudent, hurtful to my fellows or whatever) to do *a*' to 'I shall do *a*' does not involve inconsistency, since its premiss is a less than final *prima facie* conditional, which is not inconsistent with the unconditional conclusion, the 'all out' intention. He is also quite explicit that there is no algorithm for getting from the less than final 'It would be wrong to do *a*' and 'It would be pleasant to do *a*' and 'It would displease father to do *a*', etc., to the penultimate move 'It would be best not to do *a*'. But about the move from 'It would be pleasant but not best to do *a*' to 'I shall do *a*' we are left in some doubt. The *akrates* has a reason, namely the expected pleasure, to do *a*,[2] but has *no* reason to do *a which he has judged it best not to do*. The latter intention is said to be 'surd'. Is it inconsistent? Is it formally faulty? That remains unclear.

The irrational surdness of 'I shall do *a* because it will be pleasant (or my duty) despite the fact that I believe it would be better not to do *a*' seems still to remain hovering between inconsistency and some other fault when we look at Davidson's clarification, in 'Intending,' of just what it is to intend to do *a*. There we learn that it is to judge that *a* is desirable. An intentional action expresses an implicit 'all-out or unconditional judgment which, if we were to express it in words, would have a form like "this action is desirable".'[3] Davidson's use of 'desirable' is as slippery as J.S. Mill's. Does it mean 'preferred'? It must, presumably, mean both less and more than 'desired,' since one's intentional doing of one's painful duty may be less than desired, and one's intentional embarking on a hedonist's life may not be merely desired, but judged to be desirable and desirably desired. Still, to judge an action desirable is not yet to judge it more desirable than any alternative, so we cannot yet accuse the *akrates*, who judges 'It would be better (more desirable?) not to do *a* than to do *a*; but *a* is good (desirable) and I shall do *a*', of inconsistency in judgment.

What we would need, to reduce the *akrates*' supposed irrationality to inconsistency, is supplied in 'Paradoxes of irrationality,' namely an extra higher-order premiss, the judgment, which apparently is an 'all out' one, not a *prima facie* one, 'I ought to act on my own best judgment, what I judge best or obligatory all things considered'. If that judgment is made, then the *akrates*' irrationality is said to turn into 'pure internal inconsistency'.[4] Davidson goes on:

> A purely formal description of what is irrational in an akratic act is, then, that the agent goes against his own second-order principle that he ought to act on what he holds to be best, everything considered .... If the agent does not have the principle that he ought to act on what he holds to be best, all things considered, then though his action may be irrational from *our* point of view, it need not be irrational from his point of view.[5]

This is interesting, because it now seems that the *akrates* is freed not only from the charge of inconsistency but also from the charge of irrationality if he disavows, or simply doesn't avow, the second-order principle. It is as if Achilles tells the tortoise, 'If you don't accept *modus ponens* you needn't conclude "q" from "If p then q and p".' The *akrates*, even to be irrational, must accept the second-order principle that he ought to do what he judges best all things considered. One might have thought that rationalist irrationality would be shown in rejecting it (as irrationality would also be shown in rejecting *modus ponens*, once offered it), but Davidsonian irrationality shows, at this highpoint of his rationalism, only in both accepting and disobeying this rule. Reasons now have become not merely rational causes, but hyperrationalist or deductivist

[2] D. Davidson, *Essays on Actions and Events* (Clarendon Press, Oxford, 1980), p. 42 n. 25.
[3] Ibid., p. 98.
[4] *Philosophical Essays on Freud*, p. 297.
[5] Ibid., p. 297.

causes. To have reason is to have explicit avowed principles of inference and premisses which constrain one, on pain of inconsistency, to accept a conclusion, or what the reason is reason for. Consistency between first- and second-order judgments requires one to do what is judged best.

What has changed, since the earlier paper on weakness of the will, is that second-order principles have been introduced, and so consistency can now be looked at not merely within the lower-order (or higher-order) judgments, but also across levels. This alone would not tilt the scales in favour of assimilating irrationality to inconsistency, unless the second-order judgments include just the one which Davidson gives – the judgment that one ought to act on one's own best judgment – and unless this yields the all-out judgment that it is desirable so to act. We would then have two all-out judgments that contradict one another – the all-out judgment giving the intention in the irrational act, and the all-out judgment derived from the second-order principle in conjunction with the all-things-considered judgment. Supplying the second-order principle, and what it implies, turns irrational weakness of the will into trans-level internal inconsistency. If an agent avoids endorsing such a second-order principle, her action against her own best judgment can avoid both internal inconsistency and irrationality.

A slight complication in exposition of Davidson now arises. For there is a qualifier in the crucial last quoted passage which I omitted, to bring out the reduction of irrationality to inconsistency. What Davidson actually says is that the person who does not have as his own the principle that one ought to do what one holds to be best, everything considered, need not be irrational from his point of view, 'at least not in a way that poses a problem for explanation'.[6] So far I have abstracted from the Davidsonian project of gearing reasons to causes. It is because reasons are still being construed as rational *causes*, and causal explanation is taken as the paradigm of explanation, that there is any shadow of a problem for the explanation of akratic action. What causes the akratic agent's action, in the case of one who does accept the principle that one ought to do what one judges it is best to do, is not that higher-order judgment, complemented by the spelling out of what is judged best, but some other less 'rational' but equally mental cause, namely the desire for pleasure, or to defy authority, or whatever. In that case there may be an explanatory problem for one who wants to fit reason explanations and causal explanations together in the way Davidson had hoped and perhaps still hopes to do. For the reason in this case is less rational a cause than it would have been had the agent not been akratic. To say that reasons are rational causes, but that the *akrates'* reason are less rational than they might have been, is to suggest that the *akrates'* action-causes might have been more rational causes, and so to raise the question of what determined that they be as they are, less than fully rational. This poses a threat to the hoped for compatibility of natural-law-governed action causes with rationality-governed agents' reasons.

What causal factor is it, which determines whether or not the agent does what she judges it best to do, or does something else? The mere presence in her of

---

6 Ibid., p. 297.

whatever causal factor is the anomalous correlate of acceptance of the second-order principle will not explain that, if the principle can be accepted yet not prevent irrational actions which go counter to it. What causal factor explains whether and when the second-order principle gets power as it presumably has authority? Is that cause a mental cause, and could it possibly be a reason? Can we ask for the reason why an agent's behaviour is controlled by her second-order principle, or is there merely a cause to be found for such conformity? In the earlier article Davidson had said that there was no reason for not being guided by one's all-things-considered judgment, although there was reason (expected pleasure, let us say) to do what in fact can only be done by refusing to be guided by one's best judgment. Presumably the same holds for nonconformity with the new second-order principle. There is no reason to disobey it, but there may be reason to do the act which in fact can only be done by disobeying it. Reasons are for actions under relevant action descriptions, not for events under event descriptions. So the event which is the irrational act has no rational cause in as far as it is an irrational act, contrary to one's best judgment, but has a more or less rational cause in as far as it is motivated. Nor is there any reason, only a cause, why less rational motivation on this occasion won out over the more rational motivation. Are we to say the same when the second-order principle is conformed to – that it is a brute fact that such conformity occurred, that there is no rational cause, no reason, why the second-order principle was obeyed? If so, then rational action becomes as 'surd' as irrational action. If to be 'surd' is for an action to have causes which cannot be fully 'rationalized', paired off with reasons, then action guided by one's all-things-considered judgment, and by any second-order principles conferring authority on it, as much as action against that judgment, becomes 'surd'. If to understand ourselves is to transform every mental cause of our intentional action into a rational cause, then we understand ourselves no better when we act rationally than when we act irrationally, for we can give no reason why reason's claimed authority is, or is not, accompanied on a given occasion by sufficient motivational power. Davidson says, 'In the case of incontinence the attempt to read reason into the behaviour is necessarily subject to a degree of frustration.'[7] The frustration comes about as much from the attempt to find rational *causes* as to find *rational* causes, and spreads from incontinence to continence.

In 'Paradoxes of irrationality' Davidson tries to explain how irrationality can come about by postulating 'quasi-independent sub-systems' within a person at the time of the irrationality. The total system of beliefs and desires, along with the endorsed second-order principles which dictate what is to be done when desires conflict, splits into a rebellious sub-system, consisting of the desire whose frustration is advocated by the authoritative principle, accompanied by such beliefs as are relevant to its satisfaction. But there is still no account of when such fragmentation into powerful sub-systems occurs, nor of what decides when the sub-system rather than the main system controls behaviour.

We will only find it puzzling that deliberative reason should fail to control our action if we both see that reason as most authoritative, and expect authorities to

---

[7] *Essays on Actions and Events*, p. 42.

possess preponderant power over other forces. I want to challenge both these presumptions. To begin with the latter, it needs to be remarked that sincerely endorsing a practical principle can make a difference not just to what we do, but to what we say and feel about what we do, and to what further action responses we make to our own previous actions. The 'power' of a second-order principle may lie in the shame or guilt produced by disobedience to it, the felt need to make amends for nonconformity to it, as well as in some conformist action. Even if we take as sincere a person's claim to have accepted a principle only if that acceptance makes some effective difference in her life, that difference may lie in reaction as much as action. Some authorities pass retrospective judgment on what we have done more effectively than they control what we do. They are not therefore shown to be powerless, since their reactions are important, and changed reactions can lead indirectly to changed actions. So even if we require some psychological power in any proper claimant to authority, we do not have to restrict that to power to control actions. There is no need to postulate rebellious sub-systems within the person to explain less than fully rational actions once we see the main system as functioning by negative feedback from our more rational reactions to our less than rational actions.

There may indeed be phenomena which justify the Freudian postulation of quasi-independent sub-systems within the mind, phenomena such as significant slips of the tongue, significant forgettings, and other such apparently teleologically ordered actions and reactions which are not part of a person's avowed plans, purposes, and conscious reactions, but irrational action seems to require no such postulation. The *akrates* simultaneously accepts as her own both the principle which condemns her action and the motive which is indulged. Discrepancy is present, but no conflict between semi-autonomous structures. For the judgmental principle would have no role if there were no possibly conflicting motives to judge, no worthy motives to endorse or unworthy motives to condemn. It cannot be autonomous, since it needs what it judges, what it may be supposed to control, at least indirectly. The lower-level motives have a better chance of semi-autonomy, but they too in a non-selfdeceived person are guided by and in necessary touch with the same beliefs which, to use Hume's words, 'concur' with the higher-level principles – both governor and sometimes rebellious subjects share the same slave spies, the same body of information about facts, causal connections, logical connections, conventional connections. So, when there is conflict of reasons within the *akrates*, or discrepancy between his motive and his judgment on that motive, it is not a conflict between main system and semi-autonomous sub-system.

I now take up the question of whether there is good reason (whatever sort of cause this might involve) to recognize the authority of deliberative reason. Should we trust our all-things-considered judgment as a guide to action, when it is at odds with what we most want to do? Of course there is no point in making such judgments at all unless they are used for some purpose, but, as just noted, we can be guided by them in our reactions rather than our actions, so give them some honest psychic work to do. I do not find it obvious that our 'best judgment' is our best guide to action. As Davidson has noted, we have no algorithm for arriving at an all-things-considered judgment – we just ponder and so somehow 'weigh' the different considerations. It is like guessing the weight of the pig at the fair – not only do we not know how we do it, we have proved ourselves not much good at doing it, if regret is any criterion of a mistaken weighing of reasons. When we consider which of our intentional actions survive as endorsed unregretted actions, given our later experience and reactions to it, do we find that our impulsive and weakwilled actions are more often regretted than our deliberated actions in accordance with what at the time seemed our best judgment? My own answer is 'no', but that may merely show how bad my deliberative judgment is, or how lucky my instincts. (I do not mean to suggest that regret is what has final authority. Retrospective evaluations can be as biased as prospective evaluations and as much in need of revision, if regret is to be any indicator of what is really regrettable.) If others can make less regrettable 'best' judgments, then they may have more reason to trust their deliberative reason, and we may all have good reason to pool our cognitive resources, to reduce the usual discrepancy between the prospective and retrospective deliverances of reason, and of whatever else we have reason to trust.

This brings me to another striking feature of Davidson's account of reasons and rationality, namely its individualism. Not only are reasons assimilated to premisses in valid arguments, but in arguments which are self-contained within one arguer. However capable that one is of producing within himself sub-systems with their own practical syllogisms, the main system, the human person, is seen as an autonomous reasoner. Other people come in to Davidson's account of reasons for actions only to give us a model for causal relations between sub-system and main system, to show us how a mental cause of a mental effect need not be a rational cause, when the mental cause is in one person, the mental effect in another. He likens the outcome of the conflict between a motivating desire and a principle directing the *akrates* to do what she judges it best to do (not to satisfy that desire) to cases of social interaction, seen as causal links between autonomous structures. If your powerful will overcomes my principled resistance to it, your will may cause my surrender, but it cannot be my Davidsonian reason for surrender. So mental causes of mental effects may fail to be reasons, at the interpersonal level. Davidson suggests that we use this as a model for understanding the *akrates*. There too, he suggests, there are mental causes operating across the boundaries between semi-autonomous structures, mental causes which fail to be reasons. When the social interaction is a case of domination, then we are back to something close to Medea's case – the dominated one acts against her own will. The surrender may be intentional, but the act is against her own will rather than just against her own best judgment. Davidson's own example is not of domination but of seduction – someone lures another into his garden by growing there an irresistibly beautiful flower. Here the act of entering is done intentionally, and not against the will of the one seduced. The mental cause, namely the designing will of the flower-grower, is here rather remote from its supposed effect, the other party's entering the garden. I would not call that yet social interaction – that doubtless will develop once the gardener and the flower-seduced visitor meet, but until that meeting all we have is a flower-mediated causal chain linking what for all we know are two hermits who never meet or talk. There is as much 'social interaction' between Robinson Crusoe and the shellfish whose shells he picks up on the beach – had those fish not chosen those waters, he would not have done just what he did.

If we take a really social interaction, and one neither between dominator and dominated nor between reclusive flower people, we may indeed find mental causes having fairly direct effects across person-boundaries. If the social interaction is someone trying to change another person's mind by offering persuasive arguments, then that person may change her mind about what to do, without really changing her mind about what she thinks it best to do, and so act akratically. But what decides her is the reason the other presents so persuasively or temptingly. It might even be a threat which the other presents. If I decided that it is best all things considered not to go out tonight to see a particular movie but to stay home and work, and my friend not only points out how good the movie is claimed to be, but also says 'I'm beginning to think you just don't want to go out with me, and that I'd better look for another steady companion,' then the costs of staying home working are increased as well as vividly presented. The costs may not be increased enough to lead to the conclusion 'all things considered, threat included, it is better to go to the movie,' but it could well lead to a decision to go to the movie although it would be better not to. The threat may decide the action, accompanied by this judgment: 'Such manipulative appeals to friendship should be ignored – it would be better to stick with my original decision, but I don't have the strength to do this.' Such social interaction, where the 'cause' of the decision to go to the movie is the whole case the friend presents, is a case of intentional action against one's better judgment but not against one's will, and surely here the cause would be cited as a reason. We can use this as a model for understanding akratic action, but it does not show us that mental non-reasons can cause action, merely how the reasons causing action are sometimes not seen by the agent as her best reasons. The reasons the friend presents are reasons for the decider – their being voiced by another makes no difference to their status as reasons. The will or wishes of another can be one's reason for doing something, and for doing it even when that involves going against one's better judgment. They can also be one's reason for revising one's version of one's better judgment, as would occur if I had judged, 'All things considered, my work is less important than my relation to this friend, so I should do what he wants and not endanger the friendship.'

Why did Davidson think that social interaction would typically provide clear cases of mental causes which were not rational enough causes to count as reasons? Was it just the result of his anti-social example of social interaction? Suppose the gardener gave a direct invitation to enter, instead of saying it only with flowers, and that the invitation was accepted. Would the invitation count, for Davidson, as a reason, or would it, as much as the devious flower-growing intention, count as a mental cause which is not a reason? I think that, for Davidson, the direct invitation is as much a non-reason for the one who accepts it as is the unsuspected designs of the dumb or shy gardener who did his luring with flowers. In the case of the direct invitation, Davidson must transform that into the invitee's *belief* that she has indeed been invited and her *wanting* to accept. This is not because the invitation cause is mediated by the understood physical expression of that invitation before it gets its mental effect, since Davidson has never stipulated that mental causes, to be rational causes, must be the *proximate* causes of their rational effects. Presumably neuro-physiological events always mediate between reason causes and their rational effects. It is not the indirectness of the causation, but the fact that it involves two brains, which seems to disqualify it, for Davidson, as rational causation. So even in cases of more social and less devious interpersonal action, the responder's reason will not be the first party's act. The reason for answering will not be the other party's question, but one's desire to answer what one believes is a question addressed to one. If Davidsonian reasons must be internal to the person whose reasons they are and whose actions they rationalize, then of necessity all interaction, however direct, exhibits mental causes which are less than reasons. The question cannot be the reason for answering, the prompter's cue cannot be the reason for the actor's picking up that cue, nor the police order to pull over the motorist's reason for pulling over. Such apparent reasons for responsive actions, to become Davidsonian reasons, have to be recast to be absorbed into one agent's beliefs and desires.

This seems to me not the way we in fact identify reasons. If asked his reasons the motorist will normally say not 'I thought he ordered me to,' but 'He ordered me to.' Facts, not beliefs as such, are cited as reasons. What about the desire component in a Davidsonian reason? Suppose I go to the movie because my friend wants me to. Can his want guided by my knowledge of how to satisfy it serve as my primary reason, or must that be my want to do what he wants? Davidson must say the latter. No one would want to deny that when a question, an order, or an expressed wish of another serves as the apparent reason for my action, I must be aware of the question, the order, or the wish. The question is rather whether my reason is my awareness of it, or is rather what I am aware of. We talk as if it were the latter, and we do not normally feel the need to specify motivating desires plus guiding beliefs in order to give reasons. Factors such as common knowledge, willingness to reply to polite questions, respect for police power and the wish not to lose one's friends are presupposed in ordinary reason explanations, and both explanatory and justificatory reasons emerge against that taken-for-granted background. In a Davidsonian primary reason, all that implicit individual psychological background is to be spelled out, but not the equally important social psychological and real-world background. In ordinary reasons, we take normal shared non-deviant motives and knowledge for granted, and give as reasons whatever is special to the case in question, the particular fact, the special ignorance or forgetting, the sudden urge, the friend's insistence. There is a presumption that anything given as a reason will be something not unknown to the one for whom it is a reason, but that does not make the knowledge or the awareness into the reason. It is *what* we take to be true and desirable, not our so taking it, which serves us as reasons.

I have no quarrel with Davidson's suggestion that we look at interaction to understand intentional action, only with the implication that what we find there will typically be mental non-reason causes of intentional action, which help us to understand only less than rational action. Coercion, trickery, obedience to authority figures, friendly persuasion, advice, suggestion and countersuggestion, prompting, invitation, seduction, are all interpersonal influences on action which obviously have provided us with our language for trying to describe individual decision and weakness of the will. But they seem to present us with the array of sorts of reason a person may have for acting (that one has no choice, that it is authoritatively commanded, that wise people think it best, that others are so acting, that the instructions are to do this, that it is inviting, or irresistible) not an array of mental non-reasons. Davidson wants reasons to be mental causes, and wants to characterize irrationality as having a mental, so a reason-like, cause of one's action which nevertheless fails to have the right 'logical relation' to its effect to be a rational cause, and he looked to social interaction for a model of that sort of mental cause. But social interacion can give us our model of rationality as well as irrationality. Not only is it not irrational to do something because the prompter tells one that is one's next verbal move, or because the police order one to do it, or the law demands it, or because one's priest counsels it, or one's friend wants it, it is not *non*-rational either. All those facts may provide good reasons for action. If we want to find irrationality at the social level, as a model for irrationality at the individual level, we can indeed find that too. Suppose a society sets up a supreme court or an ombudsman, to do a specific job – to settle disputes at lower levels, to look into grievances still outstanding when the rest of the legal machinery has done its work properly, then provides no reliable procedures for the implementation of the decisions of these meta-authorities, so that what happens goes against their authoritative edicts. That seems a good case of social irrationality, and a case parallel to making idle retrospective judgments on one's actions, not accompanied by appropriate follow-up action. Or one may set up a 'government', then give it no power to act. This would parallel cultivating a practical reason which never guides one. Most procedures are at least somewhat unreliable, at both the individual and the social level, and there need be nothing inexplicable about their occasional failure to achieve the rational functioning which is their point. Irrationality is the occupational hazard of non-automata who aim at rationality.

The methodological individualism which constrains Davidson's account of reasons, leading him to distort or at least unnaturally regiment reasons into psychological states of the ones they are reasons for, may as previously suggested have its roots in the conviction that an inference must go on all in one head, and that seeing the force of reasons is seeing what logically follows from them. Reasons, he says, must have 'appropriate logical relations' to what they explain.[8] If acting on reasons is practical inference, and inference is a single-minded operation, then both reason-premises and what conclusion they are reasons for must be in that one mind. I see no good reason to think that there are no cooperative inferences, nor to think that what anyone infers from must be the content of a previous psychological state of the inferer. ('Immediate inferences', such as inferring the dog's intent to attack from its facial expression, is not first noting the expression then inferring its significance.) But I suspect that it is because Davidson wants moves from reasons to what they are reasons for to be valid inferences, and thinks premises and conclusion must be entertained within one mind, that Davidsonian reason causes have to be psychological states of the person whose psychological state is their rationalized effect.

---

[8] *Philosophical Essays on Freud*, p. 298.

Davidson does not tell us in so many words what are these 'appropriate logical relations' between reasons and what they are reasons for, but, as we have seen, they seem to be entailment relations. After his earlier noncommittal version of the irrationality of the *akrates* as located in his mismove, which was, however, not necessarily an inconsistent move, to an all-out intention which goes against his own best judgment, Davidson in 'Paradoxes of irrationality' seems to wish to treat that mismove as one which is plain inconsistent with the *akrates'* own second-order principle that he ought not act against his own best judgment.

Even if we could assimilate all the norms of reason to the consistency-demanding constraints of formal logic, that would not really show us how reason can be much of a guide to us, since, even if we adopt the higher-order principle to be logical, to avoid inconsistency, inconsistency is too easily avoided for its avoidance to be much of a guide to action, let alone to guide us in retrospective judgments. To mend his ways the accused *akrates*, confronted with the formalist regimentation of his move, can as easily say 'Then it cannot be that I accept all and only those premisses,' as say 'I see I must revise my practical conclusion.' After the event, he may stick by this claim, bound by consistency not to revise his version of his endorsed practical principles. We need to combine the virtue of consistency with that virtue of reasonableness which enables us to revise our judgments, to take back or contradict our earlier judgments when they prove too epistemologically costly to maintain. The reasonable person will be willing to show less trust in her own powers of deliberation, if their record is bad, and to be less condemnatory of counter-to-deliberative-reason impulses, if their record is no worse than that of deliberative reason. What matters most is the ability to revise, to reduce the discrepancy between prospective and retrospective judgments by awareness of the limitations and the bias to be expected from each. We are unlikely to get that ability unless we reason together, pooling our perspectives. Coordinating our judgments with those of other people, past and present, helps us to achieve that coordination between our own present and future viewpoints which the reasonable person strives towards. As at the interpersonal level we aim not at agreement at all costs, but at reasonable and consistent ways of handling disagreements, so also within the person, we want not cross-temporal consistency of judgment as much as a consistent and consistently revised policy for revising our judgments.

That policy may call for some revision of our inherited rationalist assumptions about which of our capacities are most trustworthy. Akratic action is a typically rationalist philosophical topic. Empiricists, faced with apparent discrepancy between intentional action and avowed reasons for it, whether that be inconsistency or some other sort of inappropriateness, will worry as much about what might be wrong with our discernment of our reasons as with what might be wrong with our ability to follow them. Both faults are to be expected, and present no paradox. What reason is there, when we think a bit about our own evolution, individual and collective, into rational animals, to suppose that our ability to systematize should equal our ability to see reasons, or that our ability to see all our reasons clearly should outstrip our ability to act in accordance with them?

I have drawn attention to three features of Davidson's account of reasons –
its intellectualism, its individualism, and its intolerance of uncertainty over
which moves *are* mismoves, which guide is our best guide. But I began by saying
that in this one paper, 'Paradoxes of irrationality', Davidson both intensifies his
rationalist construal of reasons and shows his awareness that other than
rationalist or formalist norms are in operation when we recall correctly by
moving from tune to name, and when we transvalue our values wisely. Both
when we do less than logic and when we do more than logic we can act well, and
endorse the way we act. But only if we free ourselves from the need to see all
norm-governed and disciplined moves as if they were inferences within one
head, and all inferences as valid in virtue of their form, and all formally valid
inferences ones whose premises entail their conclusions, can we say, as I think
we should say, that we can have good reason for our pre-logical moves and for
our translogical moves, individual and collective, as well as for our inferences,
have as good reasons for our material as for our formal principles of inference,
and have as good reasons for our non-entailed as for our entailed inferential
moves. If 'with good reason' is to be a term of commendation, then we need a
version of reason which relates those sufficient reasons which are given in
premises which entail their conclusions to those which do not, and which put
reasons given in any sort of premiss of an inference in proper relation to those
reasons which are mere reminders, and to those reasons, individual and social,
which re-form the minds they are reasons for.

My paradigm empiricist, Hume, pointed out that not all useful associative
thought moves are constrained enough to count as inferences, and that not all
evidence-constrained (so inferential) moves in thought are deductively valid
'demonstrations', and that the most important reflective endorsings or refusals
to endorse, those which 'turn habits into rules', are neither demonstrations nor
inferences nor mere understandable associative swerves of the fancy. They fail
to be captured in any of these epistemological nets. They, the fundamental
principles for those who listen to reason or good Humean sense, are reflective
revisions both of habits of animal-intelligent goal-pursuit and of social
convention, and so of all the belief-formation and action-guidance strategies we
inherit from those two parents of rationality. Hume describes this crucial
mental operation by the rationalist term 'reflection', a turning of an operation
on itself to test it for that Cartesian and Leibnizian 'integrity' which is shown by
successful self-application, but he gives it an interpersonal, social, and
proto-Hegelian sense. It is *we* who have to ask if our habits, including those of
inference, of reason-giving, and of retrospective judgement, can justify themselves when turned on themselves, we whose reason-motives must survive their
own survey. Hume thought he had shown that intellectualist individualist habits
failed the reflective test, but new forms of rationalism and individualism keep
turning up. They, of course, are not the only policies to fail – equally
unsuccessful would be the policy of acting on impulse, or of intelligent
goal-pursuit unconstrained by any social rules, or of social rules untested by
freedom of individual expression. The policies of belief-formation, of the
correction of sentiment, and of action-guidance which Hume thought passed
his test employed culture as well as nature, tradition as well as passion, social

inventiveness and criticism as well as social conformity, imagination as well as logic, rhyme as well as reason.

Following reason includes following the argument where it leads, but it may also involve following the narrative, following the clues, following the rules and the spirit of those rules, following the precedent of examining and perhaps revising the rules, and of restricting the area where they are needed, and keeping up the tradition of examining the connection of the algorithms to the looser guides. Following reason includes following the precedent of examining our version of reason, and of its relation to what it presumes to govern. Like all claimants to authority, its legitimacy rests on the informed consent of the governed. Like all claimants to authority, it sometimes fails to control even those who acknowledge its legitimate authority. There is no paradox in the fact that we often act contrary to reason, and there may be providence in our tendency often to act contrary to our current version of reason. The difference the possession of reason makes to us is to be found as much in our questions about what its demands are, and about why and how they are to be heeded, as in any meek conformity to some version of those demands. As it protects us against uncritical conformity to collectivist demands, and from bondage to unreflective passions, so it can protect us from insufficiently reflective versions of itself. The benefit of individual rationality is that it enables us to keep a critical eye on the forms being taken by human custom, human institutions, human intelligence, and human desire. The price of individuality and rationality is eternal vigilance over the individualist and the rationalist lurking in each of us.

9

Reply to Annette Baier: Rhyme and Reason

DAVID PEARS

Annette Baier starts from two remarks made by Donald Davidson in his paper, 'Paradoxes of irrationality'.[1] He seems to have meant the two remarks as minor additions to his theory of human action, but she takes them as signs that there is something radically wrong with the theory. According to her, it is too calculative and, in a certain sense, too rationalist. That is her argument in the first half of her paper, and in the second half she develops a different account of reasons for actions, designed to correct what she regards as his excessive rationalism and to give the emotions their due.

That summary over-simplifies her strategy in two different ways. One is that it omits her suggestion that Davidson's ideas may be moving in the direction that she recommends, and that the two points, which he seems to have regarded as minor additions, are really signs that a major change is beginning in his ideas about reasons for actions. Another thing omitted from my summary is her claim that the tensions in his theory are produced by his adherence to the view that reasons for actions are causes.

I cannot possibly do justice to all these interesting suggestions in a few minutes and so I shall merely try to set up some kind of framework for the discussion of the first half of Baier's paper. I shall do this by repeating the two points which Davidson probably regarded as minor ones, commenting on them and trying to discover whether they really do show that his theory is in trouble, or on the move to avoid trouble.

(1) The first of Davidson's two points is that non-rational mental causation is not necessarily irrational. He uses two very different examples to illustrate it. One is a simple case of association: I hum a tune and it reminds me of a name. Here the humming of the tune is a mental cause of the recollection but not a reason for it, at least not in the sense of 'my reason for it'. Nevertheless, this is not a case of irrationality.

His second example is more complicated. I set out to change my own

---

[1] *Philosophical Essays on Freud*, ed. R. Wollheim and J. Hopkins (Cambridge University Press, Cambridge, 1982).

character by taking a certain course of action. There are several ways in which this might come about. Davidson focuses on to a case in which my reason for changing my present character is based on a value that I do not yet accept. In this special case the value that produces the change, if indeed it does produce it, is extrinsic to my present character and so, though it operates as a cause in my development, it does not operate as a reason for it.

Let me make some quick comments on these two examples. The first one is non-controversial. Perhaps it would have been better to choose a case in which the mental cause was not an action, like humming a tune, but a passive event: e.g. the name of a place occurs to me and it brings back the name of a person. But that is a minor point. The main point is that associations of this kind, which are, as Davidson says, very common, are indisputably examples of mental causation which is not irrational but only non-rational.

However, his second example is more controversial. Would it not be more plausible to say that I have to accept the new value before I can be dissatisfied with my present character and so before I will set about changing it? True, my dissatisfaction will be based on a value extrinsic to its target, the part of my present character that I want to change, but it will not be based on a value extrinsic to my whole character. So a case can be made for saying, contrary to Davidson, that the value, or its acceptance, is not only the cause of the action that I take but also my reason for it.

Before I go any further, it may help if I put Davidson's remarks in their context. They occur at the end of an article in which his aim has been not to define irrationality but to explain how it occurs. The irrationality with which he is concerned is, of course, internal irrationality, and his examples of this kind of irrationality are clear cases of akratic action. His question is, 'How can this sort of thing happen?' The explanation that he offers is that it happens because human agents are often divided against themselves. One internally rational system operates on another which, without that interference, would also have been internally rational. That is how *akrasia* occurs.

The explanation evidently requires a criterion for drawing the boundaries between different systems within a single person. Davidson's criterion involves non-rational causation: he draws a systemic boundary between a mental cause and its mental effect when the former does not produce the latter rationally, or at least not wholly rationally. Notice that this is less than the requirement that it produce it irrationally, or partly irrationally.

I have two reasons for making this point about the context of Davidson's remarks. First, the context raises a question about which I shall have more to say later: 'Is it really the way to draw systemic boundaries?' Second, it helps to explain his view of his other example (the controversial one): he is impressed by the fact that the value operates from outside the part of my character that I want to alter so that, in a certain sense, the change originates in a different system. The controversy mentioned just now begins when we ask whether this different system has to be another part of my character.

(2) Davidson's second problematical remark is quoted on p. 119 of Baier's paper. It is not quite complete. Let me quote the whole passage before commenting on it:

A purely formal description of what is irrational in an akratic act is, then, that the agent goes against his own second-order principle, that he ought to act on what he considers to be best everything considered. It is only when we can describe his action in just this way that there is a puzzle about explaining it. If the agent does not have the principle that he ought to act on what he holds to be best, everything considered, then, though his action may be irrational from *our* point of view, it need not be irrational from his point of view, at least not in a way that poses a problem for explanation. For to explain his behaviour, we need only say that his desire to do what he held to be best all things considered was not as strong as his desire to do something else.[2]

Baier interprets these remarks as the expression of a theory of reasons for actions which is too calculative, a theory according to which the only ground for an accusation of irrationality would be inconsistency. She comments, 'it now seems that the *akrates* is freed not only from the charge of inconsistency but also from the charge of irrationality, if he disavows, or simply doesn't avow, the second-order principle. It is as if Achilles tells the tortoise, "If you don't accept *modus ponens*, you needn't conclude 'q' from 'If p then q and p'."'

I am not convinced by this interpretation of Davidson's remarks. Baier is quite right to stress the importance of accepting the appropriate second-order principles, but Davidson is not denying it. His point is only that the difficult thing is to explain internal irrationality, but that, if it becomes clear that an agent is not being internally irrational, because he does not accept the appropriate second-order principle and is, therefore, externally irrational, that difficulty vanishes. There is no suggestion that there is nothing wrong with external irrationality, or even that it does not need to be explained. The point is simply that the special difficulty of explaining internal irrationality does not arise in this kind of case, because there is no internal irrationality.

My interpretation of Davidson's remarks fits the context in which they were made, which was, as I said, an attempt to explain how the kind of internal irrationality that we call *akrasia* can occur. The main point of his earlier article, 'How is weakness of the will possible?',[3] had been that the *akrates* is not guilty of any logical inconsistency when he takes another drink against his own better judgement before driving home from a party (my example). He is not guilty of any logical inconsistency even though, according to Davidson, his unconstrained intentional action indicates that he judged it better to take another drink. For this perverse outright value-judgement is not logically incompatible with the relativized value-judgement which preceded it, 'In relation to everything that I know about my situation and all the considerations of value that I see to be relevant to it, it is better *not* to take another drink.' Nevertheless, it is irrational and its irrationality is still difficult to explain.

Davidson is, of course, assuming that the agent accepts the appropriate second-order principle, which in this case is the Principle of Continence. He accepts it and yet he goes against it and that is what is difficult to explain. The main point of the earlier article was that it is not so difficult to explain as the

---

[2] Ibid., p. 297.
[3] Reprinted in *Essays on Actions and Events* (Clarendon Press, Oxford, 1980).

flouting of *modus ponens*, which would involve him in logical contradiction. Naturally, if he rejected *modus ponens*, his irrationality would not disappear, but it would become external rather than internal.

Davidson's later article, 'Paradoxes of irrationality', is an attempt to answer the question, 'How can internal irrationality ever occur?' Although no logical contradiction is involved, it is still difficult to understand the phenomenon of *akrasia*, and an explanation is needed. His answer is going to be that it occurs because the agent is divided against himself and a mental cause operates non-rationally and so, according to Davidson's criterion, across a boundary between two systems within him. Notice again that this criterion is less than the requirement that the mental operate irrationally.

In the example introduced just now the mental cause of the akratic action is the desire for another drink. This desire is, of course, a reason for taking another drink, but not a rational reason for taking one against the relativized value-judgement, 'In relation to everything that I know about my situation and all the considerations of value that I see to be relevant to it, it is better *not* to take another drink.' So the mental cause has to operate *in part* as an *irrational* reason. How does it succeed in extending its influence beyond its rational authority? Davidson attributes its success to the fact that it is operating across a systemic boundary, or, to spell out his criterion for this kind of operation, non-rationally. Notice yet again the difference between the irrationality of the performance and the non-rationality that is adduced to explain it.

All this is against the background of the assumption that the agent really does hold the Principle of Continence. But suppose that he denies that he ought to act on what he holds to be best everything considered, or suppose that he merely withholds his assent. What then? Davidson shares the generally accepted view that the agent is then externally irrational, an abnormal case, the kind of person who, in general, does not aim at the internal rationality which the rest of us struggle to achieve. Consequently, when his action fails to meet the standards of internal rationality, we have no difficulty in explaining the failure: he is a non-starter in this particular competition. Of course, this fact, in its turn, needs to be explained, but that is another story.

At this point in the exposition of Davidson's views, it is necessary to go back to his actual words. He says of this agent that 'though his action may be irrational from *our* point of view, it need not be irrational from his point of view, at least not in a way that poses a problem for explanation.' This strikes me as a slightly paradoxical way of making a valid point. It is slightly paradoxical because the agent does hold premisses given which it *is* internally irrational to take another drink. The valid point is that he does not recognize that it is internally irrational, and this is not just because of some failure of awareness in the particular case – that would be a type of *akrasia* – but because he does not accept the appropriate second-order principle of internal rationality and is, therefore, externally irrational. What he does not accept is the Principle of Continence, which is constitutive of internal rationality in action.

I do not think that Davidson's remarks indicate that his theory of reasons for actions is quite as calculative as Baier takes it to be. He is simply focusing on to internal rationality and he is so far from denying the importance of external rationality that he explicitly takes it for granted that his akratic agent is externally rational. He has to be externally rational, if he is to qualify as akratic. However, I do agree with Baier to this extent: within the field that Davidson does try to cover, the internal rationality of an agent's deliberative history, there is more to be said about episodes that are not calculative, or, at least, not calculative in any simple way. It often happens that there is no single measure for the values that guide a piece of rational deliberation, and emotion and reason cooperate in a way that ought to be explained, and that would be a long and difficult task.

I need not take it up here. Nor do I need to take up Lewis Carroll's question, whether someone who does not subscribe to a second-order constitutive principle of internal rationality can be forced to subscribe to it by an argument based on a third-order principle. Carroll gives a negative answer, because the recusant might not accept the third-order principle. That is very interesting, but in real life, confronted by a second-order recusant, we would certainly take a different line. For example, we would point out the disastrous consequences of rejecting the second-order principle that is constitutive of internal rationality in action, and the recusant would not be in a position to reply that he might achieve satisfactory results by luck. That is an appropriate response when the agent *occasionally* lapses in his observance of the Principle of Continence – and it is, in fact, made by the type of akratic agent mentioned just now, who is, incidentally, *the only type recognized by Davidson* – but it is not a response that can be made by a tortoise who rejects the Principle of Continence.

What is worth asking here is whether in real life we distinguish between different kinds of rejection of second-order principles. There is, I think, one distinction that we do draw between different cases and, because it is relevant to Baier's discussion of Davidson's views, I shall mention it.

On the one hand, we sometimes encounter people who have not yet acquired the principles of a certain kind of reasoning. If someone is old enough to speak and has not yet accepted the Principle of Continence, it is unlikely that he ever will accept it. However, perfectly sane people may not yet have grasped the elementary principles of probabilistic reasoning and we do not have to take such a pessimistic view of their future development.

On the other hand, we encounter people who, in spite of their general acceptance of a constitutive principle of internal rationality, occasionally flout it deliberately. Davidson maintains that, when someone flouts the Principle of Continence in this way, he will necessarily support his action with a perverse singular value-judgement, which, he hopes, will turn out to be true by good luck. I doubt that this is the only possible type of conscious *akrasia*, but will not argue the point here. I want to draw attention to another, quite different possibility: the agent may believe that on this particular occasion irrational action would be *intrinsically* better than rational action.

That would be an occasional rejection of the Principle of Continence and in this respect it would be like *akrasia*. But it would be a rejection of it in favour of an independent, higher value, and in this respect it would be unlike *akrasia*. The agent's idea would be that internal rationality is not always paramount. For example, he might think it better to stay on at a party *precisely because it would really be rational to leave it.*

This case has something in common with Davidson's controversial example of the person who sets out to change his own character. Both agents appeal to values that are extrinsic to their ordinary patterns of deliberation. However, there is also an interesting difference between them. Davidson's agent appeals to a specific value which he must at least be on the verge of accepting, but my agent appeals to the value of a general holiday from internal rationality, whatever specific precepts it would support in his particular case on that particular occasion.

Finally, let us return to the firmer ground of ordinary *akrasia*. Here I have a doubt about Davidson's systemic explanation, a doubt which is less extreme than Baier's and which, if correct, would lead to a modification of his explanation rather than a rejection of it.

In the straightforward example of *akrasia* introduced earlier the agent takes another drink simply for pleasure in spite of the fact that this reason has been defeated in his deliberation and remains defeated and he knows that this is so. Davidson's question is 'How can this happen?' and his answer is that the thought of the pleasure of another drink is a mental cause which does not operate as a reason.

I think that he means that the mental cause does not operate as a *rational* reason and not that it does not operate as a reason at all. For the agent acts for pleasure, knows that he is acting for pleasure and knows that in so doing he is being partly irrational. So it cannot be quite right to criticize Davidson on the ground that in his theory a mental cause which operates in part irrationally is not to be regarded as a reason in respect of that part of its operation but only as a cause that is not a reason. True, it is irrational or surd at that point in its operation, but not, therefore, not a reason. The agent would say, 'Of course, it's irrational, but my only reason for taking another drink was pleasure,' and there is really nothing in Davidson's theory which would *force* him to reject or rewrite this confession. His problem – a big one – is to explain how this kind of thing can happen, given that reasons normally belong to an internally coherent system.

However, it must be admitted that Davidson courts misinterpretation in his development of this part of his theory. For he says more than once that, when a mental cause is operating irrationally, it is operating as a cause that is not a reason. As I said, I think that he means that it is operating as a cause that is not a rational reason, but unfortunately he does not say so. Consequently, he gives the impression that the agent would actually be wrong to say, 'It's irrational but my only reason for taking another drink was pleasure' – wrong because reasons are necessarily rational.

What Davidson needs at this point is a pair of easily confused but in fact quite different distinctions. First, he has to distinguish between a mental cause which operates non-rationally and a mental cause which operates as a reason. Then, among mental causes that operate as reasons, he has to distinguish between those that operate rationally and those that operate irrationally.

This brings me round full circle to the first of Davidson's two problematic remarks. One of his two examples of a non-rational mental cause was humming a tune. Here the subject obviously would not say that his humming the tune, or the tune itself, was his reason for recollecting the name. So it seems that in this passage Davidson's concern is with mental causes that are not operating as reasons, rational or irrational. That was the interpretation that I suggested earlier. True, the point is rather obscured by his second, controversial example, of the person who changes his character in conformity to a value that he has not yet accepted. However, it is not clear exactly how this example is to be taken. So I think it fair to conclude that in this passage he really is concerned with causes that are not operating as reasons at all. These are non-rational causes and they are quite unlike the mental causes of *akrasia*.

The second distinction does not come into play until we bring in mental causes operating as reasons. The operations of these mental causes may be rational or irrational. An example of the latter kind is provided by the agent who says, 'It's irrational, but my only reason for taking another drink was pleasure.'

Davidson's explanation of the occurrence of this kind of internal irrationality is that there are two different systems within the agent. But what exactly is it that would lead us to draw a boundary between two different systems in this type of case? As I pointed out earlier, Davidson's criterion for such a division is the non-rational operation of a mental cause. It is a conceptual truth for him that, when a mental cause operates non-rationally, it operates across a systemic boundary.

Now the point of making this a conceptual truth is that it is going to provide a foundation for an account of *akrasia* with considerable explanatory power. The internal rationality of the agent's main system is upset by a sub-system operating, from its own point of view, in an internally rational way.

But, as I have argued elsewhere,[4] it surely cannot be necessary to postulate a separate internally rational sub-system every time a mental cause produces its effect *non-rationally*. It is far more plausible to restrict the scope of this kind of theory to cases where a mental cause operates as a reason but produces its effect *irrationally*. That is certainly what happens when the guest's desire for another drink stops the intervention of the Principle of Continence and so cuts a way through to its own gratification.

Here I am assuming, as Davidson does, that the agent is aware of the irrationality of his action (and, in Davidson's theory, aware of the irrationality of the outright value-judgement that supports it – though I would not accept this part of his theory). We may, of course, drop this assumption and suppose that the agent's desire in some way succeeds in making him unaware of the irrationality of indulging it. Then the desire in its operations based on the sub-system will be playing an even bigger role. The theory gets its explanatory power from the fact that in both kinds of case the sub-system is internally rational.

Davidson's critics may say that I am changing his theory rather than interpreting it. For he does often take the two distinctions in a single stride, moving straight from non-rationality to rationality and omitting irrational reasons. Perhaps this is connected with his tendency, often remarked by his critics, to tie reasons too closely to rationality, because he fears that excessive loosening of this knot would make it impossible for people to understand each other's reasons.

---

[4] *Motivated Irrationality* (Oxford University Press, Oxford, 1984), ch. V.

I do not really know to what extent I am changing his theory. But I do know that the change, if there is one, does not amount to a withdrawal of the claim that reasons are causes. So I do not agree with Baier's view that the tension in his theory is produced by that claim. It is produced by a failure to preserve the two distinctions that I have separated, and by a related failure to choose the right criterion for a systemic boundary. But these are points that can be corrected without any alteration in the main structure of his theory.

10

Deception and Division[*]

DONALD DAVIDSON

Self-deception is usually no great problem for its practitioner; on the contrary, it typically relieves a person of some of the burden of painful thoughts the causes of which are beyond his or her control. But self-deception *is* a problem for philosophical psychology. For in thinking about self-deception, as in thinking about other forms of irrationality, we find ourselves tempted by opposing thoughts. On the one hand, it is not clear that there is a genuine case of irrationality unless an inconsistency in the thought of the agent can be identified, something that is inconsistent by the standards of the agent himself. On the other hand, when we try to explain in any detail how the agent can have come to be in this state, we find ourselves inventing some form of rationalization that we can attribute to the self-deceiver, thus diluting the imputed inconsistency. Self-deception is notoriously troublesome, since in some of its manifestations it seems to require us not only to say that someone believes both a certain proposition and its negation, but also to hold that the one belief sustains the other.

Consider these four statements:

(1) D believes that he is bald.
(2) D believes that he is not bald.
(3) D believes that (he is bald and he is not bald).
(4) D does not believe that he is bald.

In the sort of self-deception that I shall discuss, a belief like that reported in (1) is a causal condition of a belief which contradicts it, such as (2). It is tempting, of course, to suppose that (2) entails (4), but if we allow this, we will contradict ourselves. In the attempt to give a consistent description of D's inconsistent frame of mind, we might then say that since D both believes that he is not bald and believes that he is bald (which is why (4) is false) he must then believe that he is bald and not bald, as (3) states. This step also must be resisted: nothing a person could say or do would count as good enough grounds

*© Donald Davidson.

for the attribution of a straightforwardly and obviously contradictory belief, just as nothing could sustain an interpretation of a sincerely and literally asserted sentence as a sentence that was true if and only if D was both bald and not bald, though the words uttered may have been 'D is and is not bald'. It is possible to believe each of two statements without believing the conjunction of the two.

We have the task, then, of explaining how someone can have beliefs like (1) and (2) without his putting (1) and (2) together, even though he believes (2) *because* he believes (1).

The problem may be generalized in the following way. Probably it seldom happens that a person is *certain* that some proposition is true and also certain that the negation is true. A more common situation would be that the sum of the evidence available to the agent points to the truth of some proposition, which inclines the agent to believe it (makes him treat it as more likely to be true than not). This inclination (high subjective probability) causes him, in ways to be discussed, to seek, favor, or emphasize the evidence for the falsity of the proposition, or to disregard the evidence for its truth. The agent then is more inclined than not to believe the negation of the original proposition, even though the totality of the evidence available to him does not support this attitude. (The phrase 'inclined to believe' is too anodyne for some of the states of mind I want it to describe; perhaps one can say the agent believes the proposition is false, but is not quite certain of this.)

This characterization of self-deception makes it similar in an important way to weakness of the will. Weakness of the will is a matter of acting intentionally (or forming an intention to act) on the basis of less than all the reasons one recognizes as relevant. A weak-willed action takes place in a context of conflict; the akratic agent has what he takes to be reasons both for and against a course of action. He judges, on the basis of all his reasons, that one course of action is best, yet opts for another; he has acted 'contrary to his own best judgment'.[1] In one sense, it is easy to say why he acted as he did, since he had reasons for his action. But this explanation leaves aside the element of irrationality; it does not explain why the agent went against his own best judgment.

An act that reveals weakness of the will sins against the normative principle that one should not intentionally perform an action when one judges on the basis of what one deems to be all the available considerations that an alternative and accessible course of action would be better.[2] This principle, which I call the Principle of Continence, enjoins a fundamental kind of consistency in thought, intention, evaluation and action. An agent who acts in accord with this principle has the virtue of continence. It is not clear whether a person could fail to recognize the norm of continence; this is an issue to which I shall turn presently. In any case, it is clear that there are many people who accept the norm but fail from time to time to act in accord with it. In such cases, not only do agents fail to conform their actions to their own principles, but they also fail

---

[1] I discuss weakness of the will in 'How is weakness of the will possible?', in *Essays on Actions and Events* (Clarendon Press, Oxford, 1980).

[2] What considerations are 'available' to the agent? Does this include only information he has, or does it also embrace information he could (if he knew this?) obtain? In this essay I must leave most of these questions open.

to reason as they think they should. For their intentional action shows they have set a higher value on the act they perform than their principles and their reasons say they should.

Self-deception and weakness of the will often reinforce one another, but they are not the same thing. This may be seen from the fact that the outcome of weakness of the will is an intention or an intentional action while the outcome of self-deception is a belief. The former consists of a faultily reached evaluative attitude, the latter of a faultily reached cognitive attitude.

Weakness of the will is analogous to a certain cognitive error, which I shall call *weakness of the warrant*. Weakness of the warrant can occur only when a person has evidence both for and against a hypothesis. The person judges that, relative to all the evidence available to him, the hypothesis is more probable than not; yet he does not accept the hypothesis (or the strength of his belief in the hypothesis is less than the strength of his belief in the negation of the hypothesis). The normative principle against which such a person has sinned is what Hempel and Carnap have called *the requirement of total evidence for inductive reasoning*: when we are deciding among a set of mutually exclusive hypotheses, this requirement enjoins us to give credence to the hypothesis most highly supported by all available relevant evidence.[3] Weakness of the warrant obviously has the same logical structure (or, better, illogical structure) as weakness of the will; the former involves an irrational belief in the face of conflicting evidence, the latter an irrational intention (and perhaps also action) in the face of conflicting values. The existence of conflict is a necessary condition of both forms of irrationality, and may in some cases be a cause of the lapse; but there is nothing about conflict of these kinds that necessarily requires or reveals a failure of reason.

Weakness of the warrant is not a matter simply of overlooking evidence one has (though 'purposeful' overlooking may be another matter, and one that is relevant to self-deception), nor is it a matter of not appreciating the fact that things one knows or believes constitute evidence for or against a hypothesis. Taken at face value, the following story does not show me to have been self-deceived. A companion and I were spying on the animals in the Amboseli National Park in Kenya. Self-guided we did not find a cheetah, so we hired an official guide for a morning. After returning the guide to Park Headquarters, I spoke along these lines to my companion: 'Too bad we didn't find a cheetah; that's the only large animal we've missed. Say, didn't that guide have a strange, high-pitched voice? And do you suppose it is common for a man in these parts to be named "Helen"? I suppose that was the official uniform, but it seems strange he was wearing a skirt.' My companion: 'He was a she'. My original assumption was stereotyped and stupid, but unless I considered the hypothesis that the guide was a woman and rejected it in spite of the evidence, this was not a simple case of self-deception. Others may think of deeper explanations for my stubborn assumption that our guide was a man.

Suppose that (whatever the truth may be) I did consider the possibility that the guide was a woman, and rejected that hypothesis despite the overwhelming

---

[3] See Carl Hempel, *Aspects of Scientific Explanation* (The Free Press, New York, 1965), pp. 397–403.

evidence I had to the contrary. Would this necessarily show I was irrational? It is hard to say unless we are able to make a strong distinction between lacking certain standards of reasoning and failing to apply them. Suppose, for example, that though I had the evidence, I failed to recognize what it was evidence for? Surely this *can* happen. How likely an explanation it is depends on the exact circumstances. So let us insist that there is no failure of inductive reasoning unless the evidence is taken to *be* evidence. And could it not happen that though the evidence was taken to be evidence, the fact that the totality of evidence made some hypothesis overwhelmingly probable was not appreciated? This too could happen, however unlikely it might be in a particular case. There are endless further questions that the tortoise can ask Achilles along these lines (there being as many gaps that unhappy reasoning may fail to close as happy reasoning must). So without trying to specify all the conditions that make for an absolutely clear case of weakness of the warrant, I want to raise one more question. Must someone accept the requirement of total evidence for inductive reasoning before his or her failure to act in accord with the requirement demonstrates irrationality? Several issues are embedded in this question.

We should not demand of someone who accepts it that he or she always reasons or thinks in accord with the requirement, otherwise a real inconsistency, an *inner* inconsistency, of this kind would be impossible. On the other hand, it would not make sense to suppose that someone could accept the principle and seldom or never think in accord with it; at least part of what it is to accept such a principle is to manifest the principle in thinking and reasoning. If we grant, then, as I think we must, that for a person to 'accept' or have a principle like the requirement of total evidence mainly consists in that person's pattern of thoughts being in accord with the principle, it makes sense to imagine that a person has the principle without being aware of it or able to articulate it. But we might want to add to the obvious conditional ('a person accepts the requirement of total evidence for inductive reasoning only if that person is disposed in the appropriate circumstances to conform to it') some further condition or conditions, for example that conformity is more likely when there is more time for thought, less associated emotional investment in the conclusion, or when explicit Socratic tutoring is provided.

Weakness of the warrant in someone who accepts the requirement of total evidence is, we see, a matter of departing from a custom or habit. In such a case, weakness of the warrant shows inconsistency and is clearly irrational. But what if someone does not accept the requirement? Here a very general question about rationality would seem to arise: whose standards are to be taken as fixing the norm? Should we say that someone whose thinking does not satisfy the requirement of total evidence may be irrational by one person's standards but not (if he does not accept the requirement) by his own standards? Or should we make inner inconsistency a necessary condition of irrationality? Is it not easy to see how the questions can be separated, since inner consistency is itself a fundamental norm.

In the case of fundamental norms the questions cannot be clearly separated. For in general the more striking a case of inner inconsistency seems to an outsider the less use the outsider can make, in trying to explain the apparent aberration, of a supposed distinction between his own norms and those of the person observed. Relatively small differences take shape and are explained against a background of shared norms, but serious deviations from fundamental standards of rationality are more apt to be in the eye of the interpreter than in the mind of the interpreted. The reason for this is not far to seek. The beliefs etc. of one person are understood by another only to the extent that the first person can assign his own propositions (or sentences) to the various attitudes of the other. Because a belief cannot maintain its identity while losing its relations to other beliefs, the same proposition cannot serve to interpret particular attitudes of different people and yet stand in very different relations to the other attitudes of one person than to those of another. It follows that unless an interpreter can replicate the main outlines of his own pattern of attitudes in another person he cannot intelligibly identify any of the attitudes of that person. It is only because the relations of an attitude to others ramify in so many and complex ways, logical, epistemological, and etiological that it is possible to make sense of some deviations from one's own norms in others.

The issue raised a few paragraphs back, whether irrationality in an agent requires an *inner* inconsistency, a deviation from that person's own norms, is now seen to be misleading. For where the norms are basic they are constitutive elements in the identification of attitudes and so the question whether someone 'accepts' them cannot arise. All genuine inconsistencies are deviations from the person's own norms. This goes not only for patently logical inconsistencies but also for weakness of the will (as Aristotle pointed out), for weakness of the warrant, and for self-deception.

I have yet to say what self-deception is, but I am now in a position to make a number of points about it. Self-deception includes weakness of the warrant. This is clear because the proposition with respect to which a person is self-deceived is one he would not accept if he were relieved of his error; he has better reasons for accepting the negation of the proposition. And as in weakness of the warrant, the self-deceiver knows he has better reasons for accepting the negation of the proposition he accepts, in this sense at least: he realizes that conditional on certain other things he knows or accepts as evidence, the negation is more likely to be true than the proposition he accepts; yet on the basis of a part only of what he takes to be the relevant evidence he accepts the proposition.

It is just at this point that self-deception goes beyond weakness of the warrant, for the person who is self-deceived must have a *reason* for his weakness of the warrant, and he must have played a part in bringing it about. Weakness of the warrant always has a *cause* (everything has), but in the case of self-deception weakness of the warrant is self-induced (one *did* it oneself). It is no part of the analysis of weakness of the warrant or weakness of the will that the falling off from the agent's standards is motivated (though no doubt it often is); but this is integral to the analysis of self-deception. For this reason it is instructive to consider another phenomenon that is in some ways like self-deception: wishful thinking.

A minimal account of wishful thinking makes it a case of believing something because one wishes it were true. This is not irrational in itself, for we are not in general responsible for the causes of our thoughts. But wishful thinking is often irrational, for example if we know why we have the belief and that we would not have it if it were not for the wish.

Wishful thinking is often thought to involve more than the minimal account. If someone wishes that a certain proposition were true, it is natural to assume that he or she would enjoy believing it true more than not believing it true. Such a person therefore has a reason (in a sense) for believing the proposition. If he or she were intentionally to act in such a way as to promote the belief, would that be irrational? Here we must make an obvious distinction between having a reason to be a believer in a certain proposition, and having evidence in the light of which it is reasonable to think the proposition true. (Sentences of the form 'Charles has a reason to believe that *p*' are ambiguous with respect to this distinction.) A reason of the first sort is evaluative: it provides a motive for acting in such a way as to promote having a belief. A reason of the second kind is cognitive: it consists in evidence one has for the truth of a proposition. Wishful thinking does not demand a reason of either sort, but as just remarked the wish that *p* were the case (e.g. that someone loves you) can easily engender a desire to be a believer in *p*, and this desire can prompt thoughts and actions that emphasize or result in obtaining reasons of the second kind. Is there anything necessarily irrational in this sequence? An intentional action that aims to make one happy or to relieve distress is not in itself irrational. Nor does it become so if the means employed involve trying to arrange matters so that one comes to have a certain belief. It may in some cases be immoral to do this to someone else, especially if one has reason to think the belief to be instilled is false, but this is not necessarily wrong, and certainly not irrational. I think the same goes for self-induced beliefs; what it is not necessarily irrational to do to someone else it is not necessarily irrational to do to one's future self.

Is a belief deliberately begot in the way described necessarily irrational? Clearly it is if one continues to think the evidence against the belief is better than the evidence in its favor, for then it is a case of weakness of the warrant. But if one has forgotten the evidence that at the start made one reject the presently entertained belief, or the new evidence now seems good enough to offset the old, the new state of mind is not irrational. When wishful thinking succeeds, one might say, there is no moment at which the thinker *must* be irrational.[4]

It is perhaps worth noting at this point that both self-deception and wishful thinking can at times be benign. It is neither surprising nor on the whole bad that people think better of their friends and families than a clear-eyed survey of the evidence would justify. Learning is probably more often encouraged than not by parents and teachers who overrate the intelligence of their wards. Spouses often keep the family on an even keel by ignoring or overlooking the lipstick on the collar. All these can be cases of charitable self-deception aided by wishful thinking.

---

[4] In 'Paradoxes of irrationality' in *Philosophical Essays on Freud*, ed. Richard Wollheim and James Hopkins (Cambridge University Press, Cambridge, 1982), I assumed that in wishful thinking the wish produced the belief without providing any evidence in favor of the belief. In such a case the belief is, of course, irrational.

Not all wishful thinking is self-deception, since the latter but not the former requires intervention by the agent. Nevertheless they are alike in that a motivational or evaluative element must be at work, and in this they differ from weakness of the warrant, where the defining fault is cognitive whatever its cause may be. This suggests that while wishful thinking may be simpler than self-deception, it is always an ingredient in it. No doubt it very often is, but there seem to be exceptions. In wishful thinking belief takes the direction of positive affect, never of negative; the caused belief is always welcome. This is not the case with self-deception. The thought bred by self-deception may be painful. A person driven by jealousy may find 'evidence' everywhere that confirms his worst suspicions; someone who seeks privacy may think he sees a spy behind every curtain. If a pessimist is someone who takes a darker view of matters than his evidence justifies, every pessimist is to some extent self-deceived into believing what he wishes were not the case.

These observations merely hint at the nature of the distance that may separate self-deception and wishful thinking. Not only is there the fact that self-deception requires the agent to *do* something with the aim of changing his own views, while wishful thinking does not, but there is also a difference in how the content of the affective element is related to the belief it produces. In the case of the wishful thinker, what he comes to believe must be just what he wishes were the case. But while the self-deceiver may be motivated by a desire to believe what he wishes were the case there are many other possibilities. Indeed, it is hard to say what the relation must be between the motive someone has who deceives himself and the specific alteration in belief he works in himself. Of course the relation is not accidental; it is not self-deception simply to do something intentionally with the consequence that one is deceived, for then a person would be self-deceived if he read and believed a false report in a newspaper. The self-deceiver must intend the 'deception'.

To this extent, at least, self-deception is like lying; there is intentional behavior which aims to produce a belief the agent does not, when he institutes the behavior, share. The suggestion is that the liar aims to deceive another person, while the self-deceiver aims to deceive himself. The suggestion is not far wrong. I deceive myself as to how bald I am by choosing views and lighting that favor a hirsute appearance; a lying flatterer might try for the same effect by telling me I'm not all that bald. But there are important differences between the cases. While the liar may intend his hearer to believe what he says, this intention is not essential to the concept of lying; a liar who believes that his hearer is perverse may say the opposite of what he intends his hearer to believe. A liar may not even intend to make his victim believe that he, the liar, believes what he says. The only intentions a liar must have, I think, are these: (1) he must intend to represent himself as believing what he does not (for example, and typically, by asserting what he does not believe), and (2) he must intend to keep this intention (though not necessarily what he actually believes) hidden from his hearer. So deceit of a very special kind is involved in lying, deceit with respect to the sincerity of the representation of one's beliefs. It does not seem possible that this precise form of deceit could be practiced on oneself, since it would require doing something with the intention that that very intention not be recognized by the intender.[5]

In one respect, then, self-deception is not as hard to explain as lying to oneself would be, for lying to onself would entail the existence of a self-defeating intention, while self-deception pits intention and desire against belief, and belief against belief. Still, this is hard enough to understand. Before trying to describe in slightly more and plausible detail the state of mind of the self-deceived agent, let me summarize the discussion up to here insofar as it bears on the nature of self-deception.

An agent A is self-deceived with respect to a proposition p under the following conditions: A has evidence on the basis of which he believes that p is more apt to be true than its negation; the thought that p, or the thought that he ought rationally to believe p, motivates A to act in such a way as to cause himself to believe the negation of p. The action involved may be no more than an intentional directing of attention away from the evidence in favor of p; or it may involve the active search for evidence against p. All that self-deception demands of the action is that the motive originate in a belief that p is true (or recognition that the evidence makes it more likely to be true than not), and that the action be done with the intention of producing a belief in the negation of p. Finally, and it is this that makes self-deception a problem, the state that motivates self-deception and the state it produces *coexist*; in the strongest case, the belief that p not only causes a belief in the negation of p, but also sustains it. Self-deception is thus a form of self-induced weakness of the warrant, where the motive for inducing a belief is a contradictory belief (or what is deemed to be sufficient evidence in its favor of the contradictory belief). In some, but not all, cases, the motive springs from the fact that the agent wishes that the proposition, a belief in which he induces, were true, or a fear that it might not be. So self-deception often involves wishful thinking as well.

What is hard to explain is how a belief, or the perception that one has sufficient reasons for a belief, can sustain a contrary belief. Of course it cannot sustain it in the sense of giving it rational support; 'sustain' here must mean only 'cause'. What we must do is find a point in the sequence of mental states where there is a cause that is not a reason; a specific irrationality by the agent's own standards of rationality.[6]

Here, in outline, is how I think a typical case of self-deception may come about: in this example, weakness of the warrant is self-induced through wishful thinking. Carlos has good reason to believe he will not pass the test for a driver's licence. He has failed the test twice before and his instructor has said

---

[5] One can intend to hide a present intention from one's future self. So I might try to avoid an unpleasant meeting scheduled a year ahead by deliberately writing a wrong date in my appointment book, counting on my bad memory to have forgotten my deed when the time comes. This is not a pure case of self-deception, since the intended belief is not *sustained* by the intention that produced it, and there is not necessarily anything irrational about it.

[6] The idea that irrationality always entails the existence of a mental cause of a mental state for which it is not a reason is discussed at length in 'Paradoxes of irrationality'.

discouraging things. On the other hand, he knows the examiner personally, and he has faith in his own charm. He is aware that the totality of the evidence points to failure. Like the rest of us he normally reasons in accord with the requirement of total evidence. But the thought of failing the test once again is painful to Carlos (in fact the thought of failing at anything is particularly galling to Carlos). So he has a perfectly natural motive for believing he will not fail the test, that is, he has a motive for making it the case that he is a person who believes he will (probably) pass the test. His practical reasoning is straightforward. Other things being equal, it is better to avoid pain; believing he will fail the exam is painful; therefore (other things being equal) it is better to avoid believing he will fail the exam. Since it is a condition of his problem that he take the exam, this means it would be better to believe he will pass. He does things to promote this belief, perhaps obtaining new evidence in favor of believing he will pass. It may simply be a matter of pushing the negative evidence into the background or accentuating the positive. But whatever the devices (and of course these are many), core cases of self-deception demand that Carlos remain aware that his evidence favors the belief that he will fail, for it is awareness of this fact that motivates his efforts to rid himself of the fear that he will fail.

Suppose Carlos succeeds in inducing in himself the belief that he will pass the exam. He then is guilty of weakness of the warrant, for though he has supporting evidence for his belief, he knows, or anyway thinks, he has better reasons to think he will fail. This is an irrational state; but at what point did irrationality enter?

There are a number of answers that I have either explicitly or implicitly rejected. One is David Pears' suggestion that the self-deceiver must 'forget' or otherwise conceal from himself how he came to believe what he does.[7] I agree that the self-deceiver would *like* to do this, and if he does, he has in a clear sense succeeded in deceiving himself. But this degree and kind of success makes self-deception a process and not a state, and it is unclear that at any moment the self-deceiver is in an irrational state. I think self-deception must be arrived at by a process, but then can be a continuing and clearly irrational state. Pears' agent ends up in a pleasantly consistent frame of mind. Luckily this often happens. But the pleasure may be unstable, as it probably is in Carlos' case, for the pleasing thought is threatened by reality, or even by just memory. When reality (or memory) continues to threaten the self-induced belief of the self-deceived, continuing motivation is necessary to hold the happy thought in place. If this is right, then the self-deceiver cannot afford to forget the factor that above all prompted his self-deceiving behavior: the preponderance of evidence against the induced belief.

I have by implication also rejected Kent Bach's solution, for he thinks the self-deceiver cannot actually believe in the weight of the contrary evidence. Like Pears, he sees self-deception as a sequence the end product of which is

---

[7] See David Pears, 'Motivated irrationality', in *Philosophical Essays on Freud*, and Pears' contribution to this volume. The differences between my view and Pears' are small compared to the similarities. This is no accident, since my discussion owes much to his earlier article and to his paper in this volume.

too strongly in conflict with the original motivation to coexist with an awareness of it.[8] Perhaps these differences between my views and those of Pears and Bach may be viewed as at least partly due to different choices as to how to describe self-deception rather than to substantive differences. To me it seems important to identify an incoherence or inconsistency in the thought of the self-deceiver; Pears and Bach are more concerned to examine the conditions of success in deceiving oneself.[9] The difficulty is to keep these considerations in balance: emphasizing the first element makes the irrationality clear but psychologically hard to explain; emphasizing the second element makes it easier to account for the phenomenon by playing down the irrationality.

At what point in the sequence that leads to a state of self-deception is there a mental cause that is not a reason for the mental state it causes? The answer partly depends on the answer to another question. At the start I assumed that although it is possible simultaneously to believe each of a set of inconsistent propositions, it is not possible to believe the conjunction when the inconsistency is obvious. The self-deceived agent does believe inconsistent propositions if he believes that he is bald and believes he is not bald; Carlos believes inconsistent propositions if he believes he will pass the test and believes he will not pass the test. The difficulty is less striking if the conflict in belief is a standard case of weakness of the warrant, but it remains striking enough given the assumption (for which I argued) that having propositional attitudes entails embracing the requirement of total evidence. How can a person fail to put the inconsistent or incompatible beliefs together?

It would be a mistake for me to try to answer this question in a psychologically detailed way. The point is that people can and do sometimes keep closely related but opposed beliefs apart. To this extent we must accept the idea that there can be boundaries between parts of the mind; I postulate such a boundary somewhere between any (obviously) conflicting beliefs. Such boundaries are not discovered by introspection; they are conceptual aids to the coherent description of genuine irrationalities.[10]

We should not think of the boundaries as defining permanent and separate territories. Contradictory beliefs about passing a test must each belong to a vast and identical network of beliefs about tests and related matters if they are to be contradictory. Although they must belong to strongly overlapping territories, the contradictory beliefs do not belong to the same territory; to erase the line between them would destroy one of the beliefs. I see no obvious reason to suppose one of the territories must be closed to consciousness, whatever exactly that means, but it is clear that the agent cannot survey the whole without erasing the boundaries.

It is now possible to suggest an answer to the question where in the sequence of steps that end in self-deception there is an irrational *step*. The irrationality of

---

[8] See Kent Bach, 'An analysis of self-deception', *Philosophy and Phenomenological Review*, 41 (1981), pp. 351–70.

[9] Thus I agree with Jon Elster when he says that self-deception requires 'the simultaneous entertainment of incompatible beliefs': *Ulysses and the Sirens* (Cambridge University Press, Cambridge, 1979), p. 174.

[10] I discuss the necessity of 'partitioning' the mind in 'Paradoxes of irrationality'.

the resulting state consists in the fact that it contains inconsistent beliefs; the irrational step is therefore the step that makes this possible, the drawing of the boundary that keeps the inconsistent beliefs apart. In the case where self-deception consists in self-induced weakness of the warrant what must be walled off from the rest of the mind is the requirement of total evidence. What causes it to be thus temporarily exiled or isolated is, of course, the desire to avoid accepting what the requirement counsels. But this cannot be a *reason* for neglecting the requirement. Nothing can be viewed as a good reason for failing to reason according to one's best standards of rationality.

In the extreme case, when the motive for self-deception springs from a belief that directly contradicts the belief that is induced, the original and motivating belief must be placed out of bounds along with the requirement of total evidence. But being out of bounds does not make the exiled thought powerless; on the contrary, since reason has no jurisdiction across the boundary.

Part II
Event and Cause

The Semantics of Action, Event, and Singular Causal Sentences

Ernest LePore

The concept of an event plays a prominent role in Davidson's philosophy. He regards the mind–body problem as the problem of the relation between mental events and physical events;[1] his discussions of explanation assume that the entities explained are events; causation he treats as a relation between events, and he takes actions to be a species of events, so that events make-up the very subject matter of action theory. His central claim is that events are concrete particulars – that is, unrepeatable entities with a location in space and time. He does not take for granted that there are events, but *argues* for their existence and for specifics about their nature. Though there is no substitute for a careful reading of his papers on these topics, in particular, the section 'Event and Cause' in AE, I hope that the discussion below presents some of Davidson's views about events in a way that aids in reading the essays which follow. I begin with some examples of claims requiring events.

In 'Causal Relations,' Davidson argues that events are the relata of causal relations, the causes and effects themselves [AE:149–162]. He arrives at this conclusion by arguing that the most plausible interpretation of singular causal statements like (1):

(1) The shortcircuit caused the fire

Treats them as having the form of two place predicative statements, with their singular terms, in this case 'the shortcircuit' and 'the fire,' functioning as event-designating singular terms.

In the early pages of 'The Individuation of Events,' Davidson argues that a satisfactory theory of action must employ literal talk of the same action under different descriptions, and that we must therefore assume the existence of

---

[1] Donald Davidson, *Essays on Actions and Events* (Clarendon Press, Oxford, 1980), pp. 207–24. Hereafter AE.

actions – a species of event; otherwise, we could not make sense of the following kind of talk:

> Jones managed to apologize by saying, 'I apologize'; but only because, under the circumstances, saying 'I apologize' *was* apologizing [AE:164–5].

He also argues that we cannot make sense of explanation and causation without positing events:

> Last week there was a catastrophe in the village. In the course of explaining why it happened, we need to redescribe it, perhaps as an avalanche .... And when we mention, in one way or another, the cause of the avalanche, we apparently claim that though we may not know such a description or such a law there must *be* descriptions of cause and avalanche such that those descriptions instantiate a true causal law. All this talk of descriptions and re-redescriptions makes sense, it would seem, only on the assumption that there are *bona fide* entities to be described and redescribed [AE:165].

Davidson does not see how to provide a satisfactory account of explanation and causation which can avoid talk of description and redescription, and he does not see how to make sense of this talk without positing events.

This list is not exhaustive, but, as with all of Davidson's arguments for positing events, each presents the opponent of events with a challenge. Some take up the challenge by trying to show how to regiment all singular causal statements into a form which represents the causal relation with a sentential connective rather than a predicate.[2] This regimentation thus retains causation while eliminating the need for events in virtue of having causes corresponding to sentences rather than singular terms. Under this construal causation is relationship between facts, states of affairs, or whatever one thinks can correspond to a complete sentence. Some authors try to show how to avoid the notion of the same action under different descriptions.[3] Others try to provide a general way to avoid talk of description and redescription in explanatory and causal accounts.[4] Earlier we noted that Davidson thinks the mind–body problem is most perspicuously discussed in terms of events.

> ... The most perspicuous forms of the identity theory of mind require that we identify mental events with certain physiological events; if such theories or their denials are intelligible, events must be individuals [AE:165].

Yet others argue that although some versions of the identity theory require the identification of mental events with physical events, other versions only require that we identify mental *attributes* with physical ones.[5]

---

[2] J.L. Mackie, *The Cement of the Universe: A Study of Causation* (Oxford, 1974), chap. 10; Terence Horgan, 'The Case Against Events,' *The Philosophical Review*, 1978; R. Trenholme, 'Doing Without Events,' *Canadian Journal of Philosophy* 8, 1978.

[3] Alvin Goldman, *A Theory of Human Action* (Englewood Cliffs, 1970); Horgan, ibid.

[4] J. Kim, 'Noncausal Connections,' *Nous VIII* (1974); Horgan, ibid.

[5] David Lewis, 'An Argument for the Identity Theory,' *The Journal of Philosophy*, 1966; Wilfred Sellars, 'Empiricism and the Philosophy of Mind,' in H. Feigl et al. (eds) *Minnesota Studies in the*

Whether one finds arguments of this sort or their rejoinders convincing is not crucial, I think, for demonstrating the theoretical need to posit events. I believe this because I take Davidson's strongest arguments for the existence of events and their nature to be his semantic arguments [AE:105–80]. These arguments also have their critics,[6] but these criticisms I find least convincing because they derive from a basic misunderstanding of Davidson's arguments. Therefore, I will focus on Davidson's semantic arguments for the existence and nature of events. I am comfortable with this restriction because most of the papers in the ensuing section are on the semantics of action, event, and singular causal sentences.

Any semantic theory for a language must embody a distinctive view of the relationship between language and reality. Davidson's conviction all along has been that a semantic theory, by virtue of providing a view about this relationship, will provide substantive and illuminating answers to the various metaphysical questions about the nature of reality.[7] In particular, it will require events to explain the semantic (logical) form of action, event, and causal sentences. But to see why we first need to see how Davidson extracts an ontology from semantics.

According to Davidson, an adequate semantic theory for a language L will take the form of a truth theory for L which issues in theorems satisfying Convention (T) for every sentence S of L.

(T) S is true in L iff p,

where p can be replaced by a sentence which states conditions under which S is true.[8]

Consider the English sentence:

2. John hit Bill.

One obvious candidate for its truth condition is (3):

3. 'John hit Bill' is true iff John hit Bill.

Philosophy of Sciences, I (Minneapolis, 1956); Herbert Feigl, 'The "Mental" and the "Physical",' ibid., II (Minneapolis, 1958); and Hilary Putnam, 'Psychological Predicates,' in W. Capitan and D. Merrill (eds) *Art, Mind and Religion* (Pittsburgh, 1967). Indeed, until Davidson this was a pretty common view since people did not want to talk about the identity being between mental and physical *substances*.

[6] Bennett (this volume); Horgan, ibid.

[7] Cf., in particular, 'The Method of Truth in Metaphysics,' in *Inquiries into Truth and Interpretation* (Clarendon Press, Oxford, 1984). Here after, ITI.

[8] Cf. essays (1)–(5) in ITI. Also, although I assume Davidson's conditions of adequacy on a semantic theory, this does not weaken the metaphysical points I want to support. Even if truth is not, contra Davidson, the basic semantic concept, any semantic theory must say something about the relationship between language and reality, and although ontological commitments may be relative to which basic semantic categories one embraces, the kind of argument expounded here works for any semantic theory.

(3), by itself, does not establish any metaphysical hypotheses about events. We might think that (2) could not be true, unless there is a hitting by John of Bill, that there could be no hitting, unless there is an action of which John is the agent, that this action is an event which causally results in another event, namely, Bill's being hit. And, there is a great deal of support for this inference in the ways in which we ordinarily speak. We can say John hit Bill and he did *it* in the bedroom. We can say that the hit John gave Bill was so hard it *caused* Bill's lip to bleed, and so forth. Although these sorts of considerations lend an intuitive support for positing events, these inferences to events do not follow from (3) alone, since it apparently does not posit any event.

In (3), on the left hand side, language is mentioned, and on the right hand side, language is used. In this sense (3), 'hooks up' language with reality. But this hook-up remains silent on the nature of reality; it simply tells us that the English sentence (2) requires for its truth that John hit Bill. So, although we might intuitively call many sentences of form (2) action or event sentences (as in, 'The rock broke the window'), nothing so far justifies any ontological inferences on this basis. However, this is not the entire story, and as more of it unfolds we begin to see why Davidson finds so much metaphysical bite in his semantics. To see why, we need to see a bit more about Davidson's approach to a theory of meaning.

Davidson believes that adequate semantic theories must be finite [ITI].[9] This means that its axioms and rules of inferences (logical and non-logical) must be finite in number. If all action or event sentences took the form of (3) (simple singular terms flanking simple 'action' or 'event' predicates), no difficulties would arise in satisfying this constraint, since we could simply list all the appropriate truth conditions, assuming there are only finitely many simple predicates and singular terms. But if we try to deal with an infinite fragment of English, we would be forced to read semantically relevant structure into the sentences, since a recursive procedure seems the only way to generate infinitely many sentences from a finite vocabulary, 'to oil the wheels of the semantic theory'. For example, let L consist of the finitely many sentences of form (2) plus any sentence we can construct by adding the following syntactic rules:

If R and S are predicates of L then so is R~'and' ~S. If R is a predicate – complex or simple – of L, then 'someone'~R~'someone' is a sentence of L,

where '~' is read as 'concatenated with'. Standard Tarskian truth conditional semantics for languages like L introduce a semantic relationship *satisfaction* such that for any predicate 'Q' of L the following semantic axiom holds:

(4) For any ordered pair (x,y), (x,y) satisfies the predicate 'Q' iff x Q's y.

---

[9] He attaches great importance to the requirement that a semantics should *not* be characterized such that it could not be mastered (stated) in a finite period of time. Given that the number of sentences in a natural language is, in general, denumerably infinite, a semantics for a particular natural language must show how an infinity of meanings (truth conditions) is derivable from a finite number of semantic primitives; otherwise, the language, so Davidson has argued, would not be learnable. See his 'Theories of Meaning and Learnable Languages,' in [ITI:4–15] for details.

Axiom (4), together with a standard quantifier semantic axiom for 'someone,' given usual rules of inference, issue in correct truth conditions for every sentence of L. However, a close look at (4) shows that, again, *nothing in the semantics* requires positing events, and therefore, *mutatis mutandis*, nothing in the semantics says anything about the nature of events. Let the ordered pair in (4) be (John, Mary) and let 'Q' be 'hits' then one instance of (4) reads that (John, Mary) satisfies 'hits' iff John hits Mary. To draw any ontological conclusions about hittings, i.e., what they are or include, from this instance of (4) certainly goes beyond anything the semantic theory says, requires, or implies. However, Davidson came to recognize that there are semantic features of our language that, though perhaps they do not require, provide us with good reason to countenance events until a better account is formulated [AE:180].

Consider sentences like:

(5) John hit Bill at 6 p.m.
(6) John hit Bill at 6 p.m. in the bedroom.
(7) John hit Bill at 6 p.m. in the bedroom with the stick.
(8) John hit Bill at 6 p.m. in the bedroom with a stick after the rainstorm.

It is not clear that there is any specifiable limit upon the number of kinds of adverbial modifiers which can sensibly be attached to distinct action (event) sentences. If no such limit exists, then treatment of each distinctively modified sentence as involving a distinct primitive relation will offend against the condition that a semantic theory be finite [cf. ITI:3–16]. We simply could not list each assignment of truth conditions. If there is no upper bound on the number of predicate adverbial modifiers we can tag on to (2), then if we treat each addition of an adverbial modifier as introducing a new predicate with a new number place, we introduce infinitely many predicates, each requiring its own special satisfaction clause. For example, the ordered triple (John, Mary, 6 p.m.) satisfies the predicate 'hit ... at ...' iff John hit Mary at 6 p.m. Thus, unless some structure can be read into this potential infinitude of 'action' predicates, a finite (based) semantic theory for this language is not possible.[10]

A slightly different, but related, worry is that sentences, (2), and (5)–(8), involve at least intuitively a common semantically significant element – 'hit'. Our semantic theory can articulate this element by seizing upon the common contribution of this predicate. It is not a typographical accident that that word occurs in each sentence in the list.[11] This common element is not, however, acknowledged in the treatment of adverbs suggested in the above example 'hit ... at ...,' for here the predicate is treated as an unstructured, primitive relation. The further thought is then that this semantically significant common element is what explains, or figures essentially, in any truth conditional account of

---

[10] This, plus simplicity, and unity of other arguments for events, are *together* very powerful. If events will do *all* these different things, then even if *no one* argument for them is conclusive, the arguments put together may be *very* compelling [AE:136].

[11] Part of what we must learn when we learn the meaning of any predicate is how many places it has, and what sorts of entities the variables that hold these places range over. Some predicates have an event as place, some do not [AE:119].

sentences like (2), and (5)–(8), and which is lost if we postulate an infinite number of unstructured primitive relations.

On the basis of considerations of this sort, Davidson has put forth a proposal which reveals the common elements in these sentences, issues in the correct semantic truth conditions, and, validates the requisite implications, e.g., that (8) implies (7), (7) implies (6), and so forth. Moreover, he does this in a way that meets the finiteness requirement and that makes in this case the intuitive inferences a matter of logical form alone. His idea, roughly, is to assign semantic structure to sentences like (2), and (5)–(8), in such a way that they are 'revealed' as harboring existential quantifiers with these quantifiers ranging over events: thus, an extra place, for each bound variable, is introduced into each of the relations *apparently* involved in (2), and (5)–(8). Thus, (3) becomes:

(9) 'John hit Bill' is true in English iff there is an e such that e is a hitting of Bill by John.

or, formally:

(10) 'John hit Bill' is true in English iff (Ee)Hit(John,Bill,e).

Adverbial modification is treated as the conjunction of the surface predicate with an appropriate relation between an entity and the time, place, or other sorts of items specified by the modification. Prepositions are viewed as the standard surface embodiments of these relations, for example, the truth conditions for (5)–(8) become:

(11) 'John hit Bill at 6 p.m.' is true in English iff (Ee) (Hit(John, Bill, e) & At (6 p.m.,e))
(12) 'John hit Bill at 6 p.m. in the bedroom' is true in English iff (Ee) (Hit(John,Bill,e) & At(6 p.m., e) & In(the bedroom,e)).
(13) 'John hit Bill at 6 p.m.. in the bedroom with the stick' is true in English iff (Ee) (Hit(John, Bill,e) & At(6 p.m., e) & In(the bedroom,e) & With(the stick, e)).
(14) 'John hit Bill at 6 p.m. in the bedroom with the stick after the rainstorm' is true in English iff (Ee) (Hit(John,Bill,e) & At(6 p.m., e) & In(the bedroom,e) & With(the stick, e) & After(the rainstorm, e)).

In this proposal, the common element, the three place relation, is revealed. The inferences among these sentences are immediately revealed as valid in virtue of simplification. Requirements of finiteness, in point both of primitive vocabulary and of inferential axioms, are tidily met. And, most importantly, each sentence is assigned its correct truth condition.[12]

---

[12] It is an interesting question what the truth theory for the language consisting of sentences like (2), and (5)–(8), and which has (3), and (11)–(14) as consequences, will look like. Here is not the place to elaborate on these details. However, it is useful to see part of what this theory might be. It will consist of base clauses for each of the finitely many primitive predicates. For example, it will have base satisfaction clauses for the three place predicate 'hit' and the two place predicate 'at': an ordered triple (x,y,z) satisfies the predicate 'hit' iff Z is a hitting of y by x, and an ordered pair (x,y)

Several points are noteworthy. One is that quantification over entities together with ascribing to them spatial, temporal, instrumental, directional, and a host of other sorts of relational properties, requires that these entities be concrete, unrepeatable, particulars – at least as these predications are normally understood within first-order semantics.[13] The position officially endorsed by Davidson is that these entities are events. But why *events* [AE:136]? Although these kinds of predications lend some (I would say strong) support to the view that the quantifier ranges over events, another argument in Davidson can be used to further support his ontological claim.[14] Consider sentence (15):

(15) A shortcircuit caused a fire.

Statements of this form are causal statements. It is important to note that variable polyadacity, the main feature which motivated introducing the quantifier and new argument place into action (event) sentences, holds for causal statements as well. Thus all of the following are well formed sentences of English.

(16) A shortcircuit caused a fire at 6 p.m.
(17) A shortcircuit caused a fire at 6 p.m. in the bedroom.
(18) A shortcircuit caused a fire at 6 p.m. in the bedroom after the rainstorm.

Since there is no obvious upper bound on the number of adverbial modifiers we can attach to the causal predicate, in assigning truth conditions to these sentences we will need to read semantically relevant structure into them. Taking the lead from our account for action (event) sentences, a good candidate for the truth condition for (16) is (19):

(19) 'A shortcircuit caused a fire at 6 p.m.' is true in English iff (Ee) (Shortcircuit (e) & (Ee') (Fire(e') & At(6 p.m., e') & Caused (e,e'))).

Informally, there is an e which is a shortcircuit and there is an e' which is a fire, and e' occurred at 6 p.m. and e *caused* e'.[15] Again, although not conclusive,

---

satisfies the place predicate 'at' iff y is at time x. Also, there will be clauses for each singular term. 'Bill' refers to Bill; '6.' refers to 6., and so forth. There will be a recursive clause for 'and' of the sort described above. There will be a standard semantic clause hooking satisfaction up with truth, and rules of inference licensing the derivation of each truth condition from the semantic axioms — base and recursion clauses. This is sketchy, but for our purposes it need not be any clearer. For details about the theory, the nature of its derivations, the need for finiteness and other technical and philosophical issues surrounding truth theories, see my articles 'What Model Theoretic Semantics Cannot Do?' *Synthese* 54, 1983, pp. 167–87, and 'In Defense of Davidson,' *Linguistics and Philosophy* 5, 1982, pp. 277–94.

[13] For an attempt to give an alternative reading to these predicates, see R. Chisholm's *Person and Object*, LaSalle, Ill., 1976, pp. 115–130. Cf. also AE:168.

[14] ... the problems we have been mainly concerned with are not at all unique to talk of actions; they are common to talk of events of any kind ... the problem of variable polyadacity – though we can take to be a mark of verbs of action – is common to all verbs that describe events [AE:120].

[15] Several points of interest: some readers might find (16) ambiguous between one reading which has the shortcircuit at 6 p.m. and the other which has the fire at 6 p.m.. Also, someone might want to argue that e and e' could be identical. These points are irrelevant to the one I am trying to make.

what stronger evidence could one adduce for treating the quantifiers in the truth conditions for these various sorts of sentences as ranging over events than that they range over entities which stand in causal relations, as well as having spatial and temporal properties, and so forth? Until a better account is forthcoming, it is reasonable to countenance events, and to see semantics of action, event and causal sentences as committing us to them. [It is important to add here and stress that Davidson's account is not piecemeal, make-shift, or *ad hoc*, but very comprehensive, simple, elegant, and general. It deals with a lot of different things in a *unifying* way. That is a huge virtue for any theory.]

The arguments sketched above are Davidson's, but they are not presented in the way he standardly argues for events. In 'The Logical Form of Action Sentences,' for example, Davidson seems to be more concerned with getting the correct logical form for these sentences rather than their correct truth conditions. But, so I and Davidson, would argue, (cf., his 'In Defense of Convention T' [ITI:65–76]), these are one and the same project. In laying bare the conditions under which the sentences of some infinite fragment of English are true, we as a matter of course lay bare their logical form. However, it is more illuminating to present Davidson's arguments for events (and their subspecies – actions) via the assignment of truth conditions than in terms of logical form, since the latter route often encourages readers to think syntactically rather than semantically. When we focus on the implications among sentences rather than on their truth conditions, we are more inclined to devise rules for assigning syntactic forms to these sentences and to devise rules for licensing these inferences on the basis of these forms. This way of proceeding obscures ontological commitments, because it encourages us not to think semantically. When we couch the debate in terms of finding the semantically relevant structure which will 'oil the wheels of the semantic theory,' there is no danger of myopia. But this is not so much a change in project as a difference in emphasis.

One last point on logical form: Davidson distinguishes analysis from logical form.[16] (20) below may be true, but Davidson denies that its right hand side gives the logical form of 'John knows that snow is white'; rather he would say that it provides an analysis of its meaning.[17]

(20) 'John knows that snow is white' is true iff John believes that snow is white, it is true that snow is white, and John is justified in believing that snow is white.

Many readers of Davidson wonder just how sharply he can draw this distinction between logical form and analysis, especially since Davidson thinks that (10)

---

[16] Cf. 'Truth and Meaning', in ITI and 'The Logical Form of Action Sentences,' in AE.

[17] It does, of course, give truth conditions (assuming it adequate). So, if not all conditions cast light on logical form. ... we need not view the difference between 'Joe believes that there is life on Mars' and 'Joe knows that there is life on Mars' as a difference in logical form. That the second, but not the first, entails 'there is life on Mars' is plausibly a logical truth; but it is a truth that emerges only when we consider the meaning analysis of 'believes' and 'knows' [AE:106]. Cf. also ITI:131, AE:143.

gives the logical form of (2) and not an analysis of (2). One might complain that (10) looks like an analysis in as much as it apparently tells us that (2) harbors conceptual resources, for example, quantification over events, that it does not wear on its sleeve. What after all is analysis if not giving non-circular necessary and sufficient conditions for the particular expression (or concept) in question? And, is not (10) doing this for (2)?

Here I see further advantages in describing Davidson's project as providing a semantics for English instead of describing it as providing the logical forms for its sentences (even though these projects may be equivalent). As I understand Davidson, both (20) and (10) give analyses for the sentences mentioned on the left hand side of their biconditionals in as much as both tell us that there are conceptual resources harbored by the mentioned sentences which the assignment of truth conditions makes manifest. But there is a difference! The kind of structure (or analysis) (10) provides 'oils the wheels of the semantics' in a way that the structure (or analysis) manifested by (20) does not.[18] There is no apparent analogue to the variable polyadacity problem for knowledge sentences which forces us to read the kind of structure in to these sentences in the way that the problem forces us to read semantic structure into action, event, and singular causal sentences. If an analogous problem should arise, then an assignment of truth conditions like (20) might be warranted. To sum up, if the sentence mentioned on the left is not identical to the sentence used on the right (where the truth theory is couched in the object language itself), then we have an analysis. But only analysis which moves the semantics towards satisfying Convention (T) is warranted. I turn now to some metaphysical concerns.

The semantic arguments we have examined are intended to support positing events. What about causal relations? Does having a satisfaction relationship between objects and causal predicates like 'hit' in (4) commit us to the existence of the relationship of hitting? And, because we introduce the predicate 'causes' in explicating the truth conditions of sentence (16) via (19), does this commit us to the existence of causal relationships? Yes and no. If (John, Bill) satisfies the predicate 'hit' iff John hit Bill, then there is a relationship hitting which obtains between John and Bill. And, if the ordered pair of events (e,e') satisfies the predicate 'causes' iff e causes e', then of course there is a causal relationship between e and e'. But there is a difference between the claim that there are events and the claim that there are causal relationships. This difference is easy to understand.

That there are events is true, according to Davidson, in the strong ontological sense of this claim because the semantics requires quantification over these

---

[18] It does not just 'oil the wheels ...'. The structure, referential, satisfaction, and quantification clauses *are* the wheels. 'Admittedly there is something arbitrary in how much of logic to pin on logical form. But limits are set if our interest is in giving a coherent and constructive account of meaning: we must uncover enough structure to make it possible to state, for an arbitrary sentence, how its meaning depends on that structure, and we must not attribute more structure than such a theory of meaning can accommodate' [AE:106]. 'I am not concerned with the meaning analysis of logically simple expressions in so far as this goes beyond the question of logical form. Applied to the case at hand, for example, I am not concerned with the meaning of "deliberately" as opposed, perhaps, to "voluntarily"; but instead I am interested in the logical role of both these words' [AE:105].

entities. However, we provided no reason for quantifying over causal relations, just the causes and effects. The events e and e' satisfy the causal relational predicate 'causes' because e causes e'. But this alone does not imply there are causal relations. In this sense, Davidson doesn't see the same sort of need to posit relations or properties.

One last point on ontological commitment. Davidson is ontologically committed to events in virtue of the truth conditional semantics for English requiring quantification over them. In addition, the various satisfaction clauses which hook up events to various predicates tells us a great deal about the nature of these entities. What more, if anything, needs to be said in order to make these entities respectable? I would think nothing. Yet some metaphysicians, e.g., Quine, subscribe to the doctrine 'no entity without identity'. Davidson apparently accepts this doctrine and in several places tries to provide individuation criteria for these particulars [AE:124, 164]: his official doctrine is that two designating expressions refer to the same event iff the event referred to by the one designator has the same causal ancestry and same causal consequences as that referred to by the other designator [AE:179].[19]

Why does Davidson provide an individuation criterion for events? Why has the semantics not told us enough, and if not it, why not Leibniz' Law? Davidson is not seeking identification criteria (if by this is meant some method for *telling* when one event is identical with another) [AE:172]. His concerns, as Quine's, are metaphysical and not epistemological. Another reason some philosophers seek individuation criteria is on reductionist grounds. If the necessary and sufficient conditions for event identity were required to be non-circular, then in a sense the conditions could be viewed as providing a reduction of one category to some other. For example, suppose we individuated events in the way Lemmon does according to their spatial and temporal properties [AE:124–125]. There is a temptation to read this as a reduction of events to some more basic ontological category, space–time zones or physical objects. In this sense, events would not be part of the basic ontological make-up of the world. Whether this reading is plausible, what is important is that Davidson should not be read in this way either. For him, events are part of the basic ontological make-up of the world. For Davidson, events constitute an ontic category which is distinct from substances or continuants. His semantic arguments establish this. But why then do events require an individuation criterion? I believe that his reason is rather simple.

'Same' in 'same causal ancestry and same causal consequences' does not mean for Davidson merely qualitative similarity: rather he means 'identical'. This apparently requires that we be given identity conditions for causes and effects. Davidson faces an apparent problem here since he holds that causes and effects are also events. Circularity seems to threaten: to know whether an event referred to by one designator is identical to that referred to by another, we have to establish whether there is identity of causal ancestry and causal consequences, which is itself a matter of establishing whether there is identity of sets of events. But this appearance of problematic circularity is illusory.

---

[19] However, cf. Davidson's reply to Quine in this volume where he seems to be embracing a different criterion.

Consider material objects: one standard ground for the individuating material objects is spatio/temporal continuity. Two designators refer to the same material object just in case their referents have the same spatial and temporal continuities. But we fix a spatial/temporal framework by identifying and reidentifying other material objects! Such circularity as there is here is unavoidable given that material object is a basic category of classification of particulars; a 'non-circular' account could only be given if the individuation conditions for material objects could be given in terms of some other, independent, category of particulars. Likewise, the defense against the 'circularity' charge brought against Davidson's proposal for the individuation conditions for events is simply that it ignores the possibility that the category of event, too, is basic. For such a category, as the material object case shows, the discerned degree of 'circularity' is unavoidable. Put somewhat differently, the motivation for Davidson's search for an individuation criterion is best understood as a defense of events by showing that as basic ontological entities they are in no worse shape than material objects. So that if events are a suspect ontic category, then so are material objects. Yet there has not been the same degree of resistance towards material objects as there has been towards events. Davidson's lesson is that this scepticism is equally powerful, or weak, in both cases [AE:137]. Moreover, although learning that two events are identical just in case that they have the same causal ancestry and consequences may not help us in *telling* when two events are identical, or in *reducing* events to a more basic ontological category, and although there may be a degree of circularity in the statement of the individuation criterion, the same causes and same effects criterion does tell us something important about events. It locates events in a conceptual space. It tells us that whatever an event is, it plays an important role in causation. It is the sort of thing that can stand in causal relations. This enough is to distinguish events from many other ontic categories.[20]

[20] I would like to thank Peter Klein, Barry Loewer, Larry Lombard, Brian McLaughlin, Chris Swoyer, and especially Donald Davidson for their help.

11

Events and Reification

W.V. QUINE

When Frege introduced quantification, he illuminated three subjects: logic, language, and ontology. The bound variable of quantification clarified ontology by isolating the pure essence of objective reference, leaving all descriptive content to the predicates. The quantifiers clarified language by resolving the grammatical anomaly of the false substantives 'everything' and 'something'. And quantification was the very making of logic, rendering it a substantial branch of science.

When Russell defined singular description, he further illuminated those same three subjects: logic, language, and ontology. One logical and linguistic insight was the dispensability of singular terms in favor of predicates and variables, and another was the rich productivity of contextual definition. Furthermore, one saw how singular terms might be legitimized even when shorn of unwelcome ontological commitments.

A third contribution that likewise impinges on those same three subjects – logic, language, and ontology – is Davidson's theory of adverbs, in which he quantifies over events.[1] I shall examine it and consider what lessons can be drawn from it regarding the nature of reification generally and the purposes served by it.

Davidson's problem of adverbs was how to accommodate them in predicate logic. Taking an example of his, we begin with 'Sebastian walked.' It consists of a general or one-place predicate 'walk' and a singular term 'Sebastian', of which the general term is predicated. Or perhaps we should picture a two-place predicate and two singular terms, one for Sebastian and one specifying a time: 'Sebastian walked at t'. But then what of 'Sebastian walked slowly at t'? Do we need a new two-place predicate 'walked slowly at'? And what if we want to say 'Sebastian walked slowly and aimlessly at t'? or 'Sebastian walked slowly and aimlessly in Bologna at t'? The adverbs and adverbial phrases can be multiplied and concatenated without end. It would be an abdication of logical analysis to accept every such adverbial modification of every verb as a distinct and

---

[1] D. Davidson, *Essays on Action and Events* (Clarendon Press, Oxford, 1980), pp. 166ff.

irreducible predicate. A language with a limitless basic lexicon is absurd, as Davidson has stressed. It could not be learned.

Ajdukiewicz presented grammar neatly in terms of categories of functors.[2] A verb is a functor that attaches to one or more singular terms to form a sentence. An adverb such as 'slowly' is a functor that attaches to a verb to form a longer verb. An adverb such as 'very' is a functor that attaches to an adverb or adjective to form a longer adverb or adjective. This is all very well, but it does not contribute to our present project, namely, adaptation to standard predicate logic. Functions can indeed be generated in set theory, and set theory can be formulated in standard predicate logic with membership as the primitive predicate; but the trouble is that Ajdukiewicz's functors do not express functions. A function applies to objects to yield objects. His functors attach to expressions that are mostly not names of any objects, to form expressions which again need not name objects.

There is a premium on providing for the adverbs within the clear and elegant structure of classical predicate logic if we reasonably can. It admits just truth functions, quantification, and predicates of one or more places with variables attached. Identity is accommodated as one of the two-place predicates, and constant singular terms and function signs are easily paraphrased, in context, to fit the scheme. The logic of this close-knit but powerful branch of language is susceptible of familiar proof procedures that are demonstrably complete. Furthermore, thanks to Tarski, the structure lends itself to a straightforward recursive definition of satisfaction and truth. Davidson was concerned to handle adverbs in these congenial terms.

Let me return now to his point about the impenetrability of a language with an unlimited basic lexicon; for he has made it also in other connections.[3] He applied it to something of mine about belief and other propositional attitudes, where I had propounded a series of belief predicates with increasing numbers of places. Along with the dyadic case 'x believes S', where S is a sentence, I recognized the triadic case 'x believes P of y' where 'P is a one-place predicate, and the tetradic case 'x believes P of y and z' where P is dyadic, and so on without end. It was a way of separating out the objects that were referred to *de re*, or on their own merits, rather than as a manner of speaking. Davidson saw these as an infinity of belief predicates, and cited the impossibility of an infinite lexicon.

There was really no such difficulty in my belief predicates, for we can construe belief uniformly as a two-place predicate relating believers to sequences of arbitrary lengths. Tarski was confronted with the same situation, in his definition of satisfaction that is dear to Davidson's heart and mine, and his expedient was the same: he treated satisfaction as a two-place relation borne to open sentences by sequences.

As applied to the predicate 'walk' and its modifications, however, Davidson's point about unlimited lexica holds. It cannot be circumvented by resorting to sequences, for there are no appropriate objects to make sequences of. The

---

[2] Kazimierz Ajdukiewicz, *The Scientific World Perspective and Other Essays* (Reidel, Dordrecht, 1978), pp. 95–109.

[3] D. Davidson, *Inquiries into Truth and Interpretation* (Clarendon Press, 1984), pp. 13ff.

relevant multiplicity now is a matter of adverbs 'slowly', 'aimlessly', 'in Bologna', and so on, and these are not names; there is no talk of corresponding objects.

In this contrast between the two situations there is already a glimmering of what will emerge increasingly as we proceed; namely, the part that reference to objects can play in making structure amenable to standard predicate logic. Because the various complements of my belief construction referred to objects, I was able to make a sequence of them, which, being an object in turn, could figure as one of two arguments of a two-place belief predicate.

In this there is a hint of a solution of the Sebastian problem as well: why not reify? We might reconstrue the adverbs 'slowly', 'aimlessly', 'in Bologna', and so on, as singular terms, each naming a strange new object, and then form sequences of these objects. We would then take 'walks', like 'believes', as a two-place predicate relating men and other animals to sequences. The sequences consist now of these strange new objects, as many or few as desired, along perhaps with the time t. Thus 'Sebastian walked slowly and aimlessly in Bologna at t' becomes:

$$\text{Walk (Sebastian, } <t, \text{slowly, aimlessly, in-Bologna}>)$$

relating Sebastian to the sequence of a time and three newly reified objects. But I shudder at the thought of infesting my well-swept ontology with these ugly new objects. Happily there are better ways.

An easy way of eliciting a modicum of standard structure from the Sebastian example has been staring us in the face all along: we can convert the stacked adverbs into an explicit conjunction of sentences.

(1) Sebastian walked slowly at t and Sebastian walked aimlessly at t and Sebastian walked in Bologna at t.

Objective reference has contributed here again to the extracting of standard logical structure; for it is thanks to the references to Sebastian and t that we were able to convert here to sentential conjunction. It is only by having tied the three conjoined reports to the same agent, Sebastian, and the same time, supposed short, that we can be seen to have been reporting the same walk in all three clauses.

This step has illustrated once more the contribution of objective reference in exposing standard logical structure, but it does not solve the adverb problem. The third clause of the conjunction could indeed be freed of its adverbial structure by saying simply that Sebastian was in Bologna at t, but the adverbs 'slowly' and 'aimlessly' are not thus easily to be dissociated from their verb

It was the fixed reference to Sebastian and t, throughout, that enabled us in (1) to resolve 'slowly and aimlessly in Bologna' into its three components, distributed through a conjunction of three sentences. What further fixed reference can we find, or stipulate, that will enable us to split 'walked slowly' in turn into its components distributed through further conjunction? In answer Davidson posited something that could be said to be a walk *and* to be slow.

(2) ∃x[x is a walk and x is slow (for a walk) and x is aimless and x is in Bologna and x is at t and x is by Sebastian].

Here is his solution. The threefold conjunction has become sixfold and the adverbs have become predicates. All is resolved at last into lexicon and predicate logic.

The line of reasoning that led him to the solution may not have been what I have been recounting, but I wanted to highlight what it is that objective reference or reification contributes. It contributes the link between clauses, a link that may be needed to reinforce the loose association afforded by mere conjunction and other truth functions.

Let us pause for another example, in which to begin with there is no overt reference to objects, not even Sebastian or Bologna or t.

Erupteth brightly, noisily and disastrously.

I mean it as a sentence, but have left the verb without a subject to keep it impersonal, as if to say *erumpit*. Reification of an eruption enables us to adapt the sentence to predicate logic in Davidson's way.

∃x(x is an eruption and x is bright and x is noisy and x is disastrous).

The four elements of the original sentence thus fall into four sentences loosely joined by conjunction, but the reference to an eruption, recurring in each component, continues to link them as required.

Adverbs that are modifiers of verbs are thus converted into predicates. 'Slowly' gave way to 'slow', 'aimlessly' to 'aimless', 'brightly' to 'bright'. But what about adverbs that modify adverbs or adjectives? One thinks first of 'very', but it involves an independent problem, not peculiar to adverbs. It is a problem shared by what I have called syncategorematic adjectives[4] and what philosophers now call attributives. They are adjectives such as 'mere', 'would-be', or 'poor' as in 'poor player': adjectives whose attributive use (in the grammarians' sense of 'attributive') cannot be analyzed as conjunction (in the logicians' sense of 'conjunction'). Analysis of syncategorematic adjectives is a large topic, on which I defer to Wheeler and others.[5]

What of further adverbs, likewise modifiers of adverbs or adjectives but free of the syncategorematic character of 'very'? Examples are not easily come by. One example is the parenthetical 'as a walk' in (2). Perhaps they can be adapted to predicate logic by unsystematic paraphrase case by case. At any rate Davidson's analysis pertains specifically to adverbs in their primary and abundant use, namely, as categorematic modifiers of verbs.

In illustration of that analysis we witnessed the positing of a walk and an eruption. They are events, one would say. That category is broad enough to

---

[4] W.V. Quine, *Word and Object* (The Technology Press of M.I.T., Cambridge, Mass., 1960), p. 103.

[5] Samuel C. Wheeler III, 'Attributives and their modifiers,' *Nous* 6 (1972), pp. 310–34.

cover all the examples that are apt to worry us. It is a familiar category, but still it invites further clarification. How are events individuated? Davidson proposes this standard: events are identical if and only if they cause and are caused by all and only the same events.

(3) $x = y \longleftrightarrow \forall z$ (z causes x.$\longleftrightarrow$. z causes y:
    x causes z.$\longleftrightarrow$.y causes z).

He concedes that it has an 'air of circularity,' but protests that it is not a circular definition, since there is no identity sign in the definiens.[6]

True, it is not a circular definition; but its air of circularity does not end there. Thus consider, first, this simpler proposal for the individuation of events:

(4) $x = y$.$\longleftrightarrow$ $\forall z(x \in z$.$\longleftrightarrow$.$y \in z)$.

Again the definiens contains no identity sign, and indeed it justly defines identity, for events and other things too; but it does not individuate them. And why not? Because, in quantifying over classes z, it makes sense only insofar as classes make sense, and hence only insofar as classes are individuated. But are classes not individuated to perfection by the law of extensionality, which equates classes whose members are identical? No; this law individuates classes only to the degree that their members are individuated. Since (4) explains identity of events by quantifying over classes of events, it individuates events only if the classes of events are already individuated, and hence only if events are already individuated. Here is the circularity of (4) – not as a definition but as an individuation. The circularity of (3) is similar but more direct: it purports to individuate events by quantifying over events themselves.

An interesting point emerges regarding impredicative definition, that is, definition of something by appeal to a totality that includes or depends on the thing that is to be defined (3) and (4) are examples. There have been mathematicians from Russell and Poincaré onward who espoused a constructivist philosophy and banned impredicative definitions, alleging a kind of circularity. Such was Russell's so-called vicious-circle principle in the early years of his theory of types. Unlike Poincaré and the other constructivists, however, Russell presently found the ban intolerable and eased it with his axiom of reducibility, not appreciating that he thereby lifted the ban altogether.[7]

For my own part, I welcome impredicative definitions. I have remarked that there is nothing wrong with identifying the most typical Yale man by averaging measurements and tests of all Yale men including him. But we now observe that impredicative definition is no good in individuation. Here a difference between the impredicative and the predicative emerges which is significant quite apart from any constructivist proclivities. We can define impredicatively but we cannot individuate impredicatively.

In events as thus far conceived there is also another cause for discomfort, apart from individuation. It is a case of indigestion: events intrude as foreign

---

[6] *Essays on Action and Events*, p. 179.
[7] W.V. Quine, 'On the axiom of reducibility,' *Mind* 45 (1935), pp. 478–500.

matter. We are comfortable with our spatiotemporal regions and the stuff that fills them, the bodies and their extrapolations into the gerrymandered, the diffuse, the very large and the very small; but the events are conceived to be none of these.

This is not a fatal drawback. Classes offend in the same way and more so, but we reluctantly tolerate them because of the indispensable role that numbers, functions, and other classes play in natural science. However, I question whether in the case of events we are driven to these two major concessions, one to do with imperfect individuation and the other to do with heterogeneity. I hope we can do better.

A physical object, in the broad sense in which I have long used the term, is the material content of any portion of space–time, however small, large, irregular, or discontinuous. I have been wont to view events simply as physical objects in this sense. If Sebastian chews gum all the way across Bologna, and no longer, that event of his chewing and that event of his walking have been for me identical; they take up the same place–time.

We might break this tie by a spatial narrowing of the events, limiting the chewing to Sebastian's head and the walking to his legs. But Davidson blocks this strategy with another example: a ball that was simultaneously rotating and heating up.[8] The rotating had certain effects on the surroundings, and the heating had other effects. Can we say that its rotating is its heating up?

I am not put off by the oddity of such identifications. Given that the ball's heating up warms its surroundings, I concede that its rotating, in this instance, warms the surroundings. I am content likewise to conclude that Sebastian's gum-chewing got him across Bologna, if it coincided with his walk. These results seem harmless to science, for they imply no causal connection between warming and rotation in general, nor between locomotion and chewing gum. But the ball example raises also a more stubborn problem: if it is rotating rapidly and heating slowly, can we say that the event is both rapid and slow?[9] Perhaps we must retreat after all to a more complex version, construing an event as the pair of a physical object in my sense and a distinctive set of some sort. Jaegwon Kim and Richard Martin have ventured on somewhat such lines.[10] Such a construct could still be accommodated in the ontology that I have accepted, which comprises physical objects, classes thereof, and so on up.

The problem of individuation of events would seem to be dissolved now by the assimilation of events to physical objects or to some sort of constructs upon physical objects. For physical objects are well individuated, being identical if and only if spatiotemporally coextensive.

Yet it has been felt that physical objects, bodies in particular, are poorly individuated. Who can aspire to a precise intermolecular demarcation of a desk? Countless minutely divergent aggregates of molecules have equal claims to being my desk. True enough; but this circumstance attests only to the

---

[8] *Essays on Action and Events*, pp. 178ff.

[9] Here and elsewhere I am indebted to auditors at Brown University. A remark by Stanley G. Clarke in Ottawa also prompted an improvement elsewhere, and a critical reading by Burton Dreben led to several.

[10] See Davidson, *Essays on Action and Events*, pp. 129, 170.

vagueness of the term 'desk', or 'my desk', and not to that of 'physical object'. Each of these visually indiscriminable candidates for the status of being my desk is a distinct physical object, individuated by the requirement of spatiotemporal coextensiveness.

Vagueness of boundaries has sparked philosophical discussion in the case of desks because of their false air of precision. Mountains meanwhile are taken in stride; the thought of demarcating a mountain does not arise. At bottom the two cases really are alike; our terms delimit the object to the degree relevant to our concerns. In the case of the mountain we care about the summit, its altitude, its immediate approaches, and perhaps whether to reckon some subordinate summit as part of the same mountain or as a lesser neighbor. We are indifferent to area, population, and the boundary of the base. The mountain is no particular physical object; any one of a vast number would serve. The desk is to be viewed similarly; the cases differ only in degree.

Are we then to withhold the term 'physical object' from the very things that have been its prototypes – desks and mountains? Yes and no. A certain adjustment is required, and the place where I would make it is in the interval between formal logic and the terms to which it is applied. Consider, to begin with, the classical notion of the extension of a general term. The extension of the term 'desk' is conventionally thought of as the class of its denotata, thought of as physical objects. Realistically we may recognize rather an *extension family*, as I shall call it. It is a family of vaguely delimited classes, each class being comprised of nested physical objects any of which would pass indifferently for one and the same desk. When we bring formal logic to bear on discourse of desks, then, we adopt the fiction that the extension is some one arbitrary and unspecified selection class from that family of classes; it selects one physical object from each. Similarly, and more obviously perhaps, for mountains. This strikes me as the reasonable way to accommodate vagueness: not in a logic of vagueness, but in the account of the application of a logic of precision.

These questions of demarcation carry over to events. Sebastian's walk is perhaps to be identified with a pair whereof one component is the temporal segment of his body over the period while he was walking, and there are then the vague limits of his body to reckon with, on a par with those of the desk. The accommodation is the same. Another event, an explosion, is comparable rather to a mountain: the nub of it is well placed, but its perimeter is as may be.

Physical objects, despite the vagueness of terms that denote them, are individuated to perfection by spatiotemporal coextensiveness. No wonder: our conceptual apparatus of space, time, and physical objects is all of a piece. Space–time is a matrix that stands ready to cast objects forth as needed in the course of introducing logical order into one or another branch of science or discourse.

We have examined the workings of reification in the logicizing of adverbs. In the light of those observations, I want now to speculate on the function of reification in general and in principle. I shall begin by considering the relation of scientific theory to sensory evidence.

How do we muster sensory evidence for or against a theory? We formulate a deviously related question as to the outcome of a proposed experiment or observation and then we so situate ourselves that the stimulation of our sensory receptors will trigger our answer to *that* question – 'Yes' or 'No'. The theory is thereby sustained, for the time being, or shaken.

On the one hand there is the set of theoretical sentences that is under fire. On the other hand there is the observation sentence, as I call it, that is subject to a verdict by dint of sensory stimulation. Where complexity comes is in the relation of the set of theoretical sentences to the observation sentence. They are connected by a network of intervening sentences, variously linked in logical and psychological ways. It is only here that we have to pry into the sentences and take notice of names, predicates, and objective reference, as Davidson well argued in 'Reality without reference.'[11] What are related are sentences first and last; terms intrude only along the way, in the interrelations of the sentences. Sentences, not terms, are the termini – the *termini ad quos et a quibus*. One thinks of Davidson again with his semantical focus on truth conditions of sentences. Terms are the means to a sentential end. I want to see more clearly how terms and objective reference contribute to that end of relating sentences to sentences. What we have seen in connection with adverbs may afford some leads.

Consider, then, an observation sentence. To fit the typical scientific situation it should perhaps treat of a galvanometer, a pointer reading, a blue liquid in a test tube, or the like, but a homelier example will be more convenient:

A white cat is facing a dog and bristling.

The scientific theory that is being tested is perhaps ethological. This observation sentence, true to form, is one that we will directly assent to or dissent from when suitably situated and visually stimulated. It is in its global susceptibility to visual triggering, and not in its mention of two creatures, that its observationality consists. Its referential aspect belongs rather to its devious connections with the ethological theory to which it is meant somehow to bear witness. How the referential aspect contributes to that connection is now the question. Let us begin by so rephrasing the sentence as to mask its referential function. Just as we say 'It's raining' or 'It's getting dark' without meaning to refer to any object, so we might say 'It's catting' in the sensible presence of a cat. Our observation sentence, 'A white cat is facing a dog and bristling', then goes noncommittally into adverbs:

It's catting whitely, bristlingly, and dogwardly,

Reference, then, is what emerges when we regiment the sentence to fit predicate logic, which is the chosen mold of our scientific theory. Analogously to the earlier example of the eruption, our sentence becomes:

(5) $\exists x(x$ is a cat and x is white and x is bristling and x is dogward).

I am not conjecturing about the genesis of reference, as I have done elsewhere, nor am I proposing a rational reconstruction of its genesis. I am

---

[11] Reprinted in *Inquiries into Truth and Interpretation*.

concerned rather with scientific theory and observation as going concerns, and speculating on the function of reference in the linking of whole observation sentences with whole theoretical sentences. I mean predicate logic not as the initial or inevitable pattern of human thought, moreover, but as the adopted form, for better or worse, of scientific theory.

Reification of the cat has adapted our observation sentence to predicate logic, but nothing as enduring as a proper cat is needed for that purpose. The briefest stage of a cat will suffice. The identity of a cat over time, in its going and comings, is a further refinement that is called for at the level of scientific theory where causal chains are being traced. Reification of the briefest trace of cat sufficed for adjectivizing the adverbs: extrapolation to proper cats is wanted for further theoretical purposes. But the utility of the reification is basically the same in both cases: a forging of links between sentences or clauses. The effect is visible in (5), in the recurrence of 'x' from clause to clause, and it is no less evident in the case of the enduring cat. In pursuing causal connections at the crudest level we want to say this sort of thing:

If something that a cat eats causes him discomfort, he takes increased care to sniff things before he eats them.

The 'if-then' here is truth-functional, as loose as conjunction; and then the required tightness of connection is imposed by the recurring reference to an enduring cat – just as the required tightness of connection was imposed on conjunction, in earlier examples, by recurring reference to a walk or an eruption.

Space–time is the matrix on which we can draw for all our reifications of concrete objects, however small or large, diffuse or irregular. The efficacy of reification in forging links between clauses and sentences has become evident from our examples. In Davidson's case it linked clauses of conjunction to take the place of adverbial connections. In the case of enduring physical objects it links clauses and sentences according to causal connections. It could be said, going a step beyond Voltaire, that if things had not existed they would have had to be invented. And indeed we have found it fruitful to press our reifications beyond space and time. We posit abstract objects – numbers, functions, classes – and our natural science would be a pretty sorry affair without the loyal support of that ghostly host. Here again the utility of the reifications ultimately lies, we may be sure, in superimposing firm connections upon the looseness of truth functions.

Deviant logicians have espoused strict conditionals and various brands of relevance logic to add tensile strength to the truth-functional connectives, but standard predicate logic gains the required strength through reification. Clauses are bound together by shared anaphora to a quantifier. Whitehead and Russell long ago cited the quantified conditional as their defense of the material conditional against its critics,[12] and I am now suggesting that this mode of

---

[12] Alfred North Whitehead and Bertrand Russell, *Principia Mathematica*, vol. 1 (second edition, Cambridge University Press, 1925), pp. 20ff.

bonding the loose clauses of truth functions is the basic technical service of reification itself.

In talking thus of the uses of reification I would not seem to impugn the reality of walks, eruptions, cats, or other physical objects, or even of numbers, functions, and classes. Let us identify our ball game and keep our eye on the ball. It is clear, surely, in the relation of science to sensory evidence, that sentences rather than terms are the gross termini – *ad quos et a quibus*. Objects of reference are invoked in between. In considering how they help to forge links between sentences of high theory and observation sentences, I am no more questioning their reality than I am questioning the reality of the sensory receptors that feed the *terminus a quo*.

There is nevertheless an inescapable methodological lesson here, which has somewhat the air of skepticism or nihilism on first encounter. It is the lesson of what I call proxy functions. It hinges on the fact that scientific theory consists of sentences, presumed true, and that what are contingent on sensory evidence are also sentences. Terms figure only as nodes in the network of sentences and consequently their references could be shuffled or reconstrued at will without disturbing the connections. Thus suppose any arbitrary one-to-one transformation imposed on our ontology, and suppose every term, every predicate, reinterpreted to conform to the ontological shift. No word of any sentence is changed; words are merely reinterpreted. Observation sentences remain associated with the same stimulation patterns as before, and the relations of these sentences to those of the scientific theory remain undisturbed.

This reflection is a reflection on epistemology, or the theory of scientific evidence, and not on the nature of the world. It tells us that scientific evidence is a matter of sensory stimulation and the structure of the network of sentences. The nature of the world is another question, and a no less interesting one. It is to be answered in natural science, not in the theory of evidence for natural science; and robust realism is then the order of the day. In our methodological sophistication we appreciate that a reshuffled ontology would fit all evidence just as well, but it would not fit it any better. Predictions proceed and are confirmed apace, and we cannot ask for more.

12

Reply to Quine on Events[*]

DONALD DAVIDSON

It's a pleasure to be replying to a paper of Quine's, a pleasure for many reasons. One reason is that it almost always has been the other way around, and here is my chance to return the compliment; another is, of course, that there is always so much to learn from Van: he not only makes familiar points sound new. He can make them new. Now I confess that some of the novelty in replying to a paper of Van's is reduced by the fact that his paper comments from time to time on work of mine; but then I can console myself by noting that some of Van's comments concern earlier comments of mine on his work. That is the end of that particular regress; as I say in the dedication to *Inquiries into Truth and Interpretation*,[1] Quine is for me (as for many others) 'without whom not'. (I leave it to those who know more Latin than I to translate this back into Latin.) Anyway, we can continue the sequence of comment on comment on comment in the other direction *ad libitum* if not *ad infinitum* and I certainly hope we do.

Quine is right, of course, about the reasons I became interested in events and adverbial modification, though his remarks on how the connections between sentences can offset the apparent failure of single sentences to convey all we want put some old problems in a new light for me. Along with all the agreement, though, I also sense a difference in emphasis. Like Quine, I am interested in how English and languages like it (i.e., all languages) work, but, unlike Quine, I am not concerned to improve on it or change it. (I am the conservative and he is the Marxist here.) I see the language of science not as a substitute for our present language, but as a suburb of it. Science can add mightily to our linguistic and conceptual resources, but it can't subtract much. I don't believe in alternative conceptual schemes, and so I attach a good deal of importance to whatever we can learn about how we put the world together from how we talk about it. I think that by and large how we put the world together is how it is put together, there being no way, error aside, to distinguish between these constructions. As Quine pointed out, adverbial modification happened to be the

*© Donald Davidson
    [1] D. Davidson, *Inquiries into Truth and Interpretation* (Clarendon Press, Oxford, 1984).

problem that first led me to think about events, and part of the reason for this in turn was an interest in actions, and in particular what it could mean to say that two actions are one, especially since the sentences that many of us were thinking of as 'describing' actions apparently contained nothing like a singular term or description referring to an action. But I soon found a welter of closely related problems. Obviously there had to be some close connection between verbs and their nominalizations, between 'die' and 'death', and hence between sentences like 'Mozart died in 1791' and 'Mozart's death occurred in 1791'. (These do not have the same truth conditions.) There was also the fact that we use the definite and indefinite articles with verb nominalizations, say that one event is identical with another, quantify over events, and count events under sortals. Causal talk too turned out to be involved. There was also the problem of causal verbs like 'kill' and the transitive form of 'break', along with the question how the transitive and intransitive forms of certain verbs are related. (This is an obvious problem only when the intransitive form is not elliptical for the transitive form.) I mention all these problems that are related to the semantics of certain verbs and adverbs only because I want to stress the importance, if one is interested in the semantics of natural languages, of looking for a theory that fits all the relevant phenomena. We have to take the problems one at a time, but we shouldn't be happy ending up with solutions that can't be embedded in a unified theory.

One important consequence of holding that our natural languages embrace our major conceptual tools (they are 'universal', as Tarski said) is that we must be able to explain a language by using that same language (well, almost). If we add this idea to Tarski's demand that a theory of truth end up able to prove, for every sentence of the language under study, a biconditional of the form 's is true iff 'p' where 'p' is replaced by a translation of s, we end up requiring that our biconditionals, our T-sentences, be, in Quine's happy word, 'disquotational'. Disquotational T-sentences are an ideal which the vagaries of grammar make hard to achieve. But the ideal has its value nevertheless.

One application of the ideal is this: as long as we do our best to explain a language in (almost) the same language we cannot make sense of the idea that the logic of the object language differs from the logic of the theory of that language. The merits I find in predicate logic are not just the ones Quine mentions: that it is what science ('for better of worse', Quine says) uses, and that we know how to produce a theory of truth for a language with the structure of predicate logic. A further merit that interests me is that if we can recognize this structure in a language we can give a disquotational semantics for it: we can use it to explain itself.

These remarks have some applications to the semantics of verbs and adverbs. Anthony Kenny long ago raised the problem of the variable polyadicity (as he called it) of verbs of action, the fact that 'Eve ate', 'Eve ate an apple', 'Eve ate an apple in the Garden of Eden' seem to treat 'ate' as a one-place, two-place, and three-place predicate in turn – with no end in sight.[2] If this were all there were to the problem, then as Quine points out it would be possible to treat 'ate' as a

---

[2] Anthony Kenny, *Action, Emotion and Will* (Routledge & Kegan Paul, London, 1963).

permanently two-place predicate, true of persons and sequences. Quine explains that 'slowly' might then have to be taken as naming some entity; but I think this is hasty. For as Quine says, 'slowly' is to adverbs what 'slow' is to adjectives: it cannot stand alone. It is a syncategorematic adverb. A slow runner may be a fast five-year-old, and slowly crossing the Atlantic may be rapidly rowing the Atlantic. It all depends on the comparison class. Mention of the comparison class, however, provides the reference needed to turn 'slowly' into 'slow in the class of Atlantic crossings', thus giving the multi-grade predicate idea another lease on truth, though also making overt reference to events (crossings). But this way of treating 'slow' and 'slowly' already bothers me. For suppose a slow runner is a runner slow in the class of runners. Then a T-sentence for a sentence containing the phrase 'slow runner' will have to iterate 'runner' on the r.h.s. of the biconditional, once to insure that we can infer that what holds of the slow runner holds of the runner, and once to help describe the class in which the runner is slow. But if the word 'runner' requires reference to the class of runners here, it is hard to think why it does not elsewhere. Yet if the semantics of any predicate regularly requires reference to the class it defines, and we stick to the disquotational mode, an endless regress starts: each attempt to give the semantics of a simple predicate leads to a complex predicate containing the simple as part. Perhaps we must settle for reference to classes when it comes to the syncategorematic adjectives and adverbs, but I hope not.

Of course turning verbs like 'runs' into two-place predicates true of runners and sequences won't work anyway, for reasons Quine made clear. The trouble isn't only the non-existence of appropriate entities, it's the work done by all those little prepositions and their cohorts. Thus there would be no telling, from the fact that Eve ate the sequence >the apple, the Garden of Eden< whether she ate the apple *in* the Garden of Eden or *outside* the Garden of Eden. The difference between eating in and eating out here is still the difference between two relations and two predicates though both of the predicates have only two places.

Quine mentions that I once criticized one of his treatments of sentences about propositional attitudes on the ground that it called for an infinite basic vocabulary; and he has replied once before. In 'Intensions revisited' he wrote, 'Critics of that paper ["Quantifiers and propositional attitudes"][3] reveal that I have to explain – what I thought went without saying – that the adoption of a multigrade predicate involves no logical anomaly or any infinite lexicon.... As for the use of quotation, it of course is reducible by inductive definition to the concatenation functor and names of signs.'[4] That was not as sweet in tone as the present remarks, but in the earlier reference he named no names. In any case, I stand corrected. Well, half corrected. For I was one who had also criticized Quine's suggestion on quotation, and for the fun of carrying on the War of the Quotes ('You quote me and I'll double-quote you'), I think there is

---

[3] W.V.O. Quine, 'Quantifiers and propositional attitudes', in *The Ways of Paradox* (Random House, New York, 1966).

[4] W.V.O. Quine, 'Intensions, revisited', in *Theories and Things* (Harvard University Press, Cambridge, Mass., 1981), p. 114.

still the same trouble with the present suggestion. For if we add the name of a sign to our basic vocabulary, we must add a name of that name in case we ever need to refer to it, and then the name of that name .... This is really a trivial matter, however, since the difficulty could be overcome by using descriptions of the items in the lexicon (e.g., 'the thirty-first item in the lexicon') instead of names.

Indeed, is there anything wrong with treating 'believes' as a multigrade predicate true of people, sentences (open and closed), and sequences of objects believed to satisfy the sentences? As Quine pointed out, this would make 'believes' much like Tarski's satisfaction, which relates languages, sentences (open and closed), and sequences of objects geared to the free variables in those sentences if any. Perhaps too like. For 'satisfies', as applied to a language L, is a predicate that can't, on pain of contradiction, belong to L, while 'believes' must, to do its dubious work, be in both metalanguage and object language. The threat of paradox seems clear, especially if we take 'knows' instead of 'believes'.

There may be natural ways around this threat. Something else worries me more, and will bring me back to an earlier and more directly relevant point. If the T-sentence for 'Ralph believes of Ortcutt that he is a spy' says this sentence is true if Ralph believes 'x is a spy' is satisfied by the sequence >Ortcutt<, then we seem to be assuming that Ralph's belief concerns, not Ortcutt and spying, but expressions, satisfaction, and a sequence. It may now be explained to me that what is on the right of the biconditional is not supposed to mean what the sentence mentioned on the left does. The word 'believes' on the right isn't the same word as the word mentioned on the left that has the same spelling. O.K. Now I want the word 'believes' on the right explained, just as Tarski explained 'satisfaction'. Tarski did it, of course, with a recursion which brought our understanding of 'satisfies' down to our understanding of numerous non-multigrade predicates. It would be wrong to ask semantics to reduce the familiar 'believes' to something else, but it seems to me appropriate to ask for an explanation of the new semantical predicate 'believes', presumably by a recursion using the old predicate 'believes'. It is not obvious to me that this can be done.

I turn now to Quine's comments on what sorts of things events are and how they are to be individuated. He says my suggested criterion for individuating events is radically unsatisfactory, and I agree. I accepted it only tentatively, but stressed that I thought it was about as good a criterion as we have for physical objects. Quine has made clearer to me what was wrong with my original suggestion, and I hereby abandon it. In the essay in which I put my suggestion forward I considered Quine's alternative: events, like physical objects, are identical if they occupy the same places at the same times. I rejected it (again tentatively) because I thought one might want to hold that two different events used up the same portion of space–time; and also because I thought the boundaries of events were even less clear than the boundaries of objects. The first concern is perhaps overdone; I speculated that we might identify the rotation of the sphere with its heating up by realizing both events were identical with the history, during that period, of the constituent particles. Quine's criterion is neater, and better, since it does not need a scientific theory to back it up.

On the matter of vagueness of location, Quine notes, as I did, that the center of an explosion locates it much as the summit of a mountain locates *it*, the outer edges remaining vague. But Quine goes on to point out that the vagueness in the spatiotemporal boundaries of objects and events as normally sorted does not compromise the clarity of his principle of individuation. This is true, and it brings home a mild paradox. One might have thought that where counting has a clear application, individuation has to be at its best, since we must be able to tell one from two. Yet Quine's clear principle for individuating objects yields no way of counting, while the different and undoubtedly less clear principle that individuates tables, does fairly well when it comes to counting. Perhaps it is obvious that individuating items in a grand category like events or objects is quite different from individuating kinds within those categories, such as desks or people; I had not fully appreciated this.

I may also have made the mistake of thinking that if objects and events are both individuated by spatiotemporal location, we must identify events with objects. But Quine makes us see that this is a separate matter. For events and objects may be related to locations in space–time in different ways; it may be, for example, that events *occur* at a time in a place while objects *occupy* places at times. It is easy, though, to question the distinction. If a wave crosses an ocean, that is an event from the point of view, so to speak, of the ocean. But the wave is also an object in its own right, keeping to a general shape while rapidly exchanging waters. Examples like this are easy to multiply. A lenticular cloud, unlike other clouds, stands still relative to the surface of the earth while the flow of wind on which it depends carries newly condensed particles of water into its defining area while subtracting others by vaporization. From the point of view of the air which contains it, the lenticular cloud is an event; from the point of view of the mountains which caused it, the cloud is an object.

These difficulties in deciding between objects and events are, however, generated by identifying space–time content with space–time content. Grammar allows no such confusion. The undulations of the ocean cannot be identified with the wave or the sum of waves that cross the sweep of ocean, nor can the complex event composed of condensations and evaporations of endless water molecules be identified with the lenticular cloud. Occupying the same portion of space–time, event and object differ. One is an object which remains the same object through changes, the other a change in an object or objects. Spatiotemporal areas do not distinguish them, but our predicates, our basic grammar, our ways of sorting do. Given my interest in the metaphysics implicit in our language, this is a distinction I do not want to give up.

13

Actions and Events Despite Bertrand Russell

JAMES D. McCAWLEY

In this paper, I continue my longstanding practice of denouncing Russell's 1905 account of definite descriptions[1] whenever I have an audience of philosophers before whom to denounce it. (I also denounce it before audiences of nonphilosophers when the occasion arises, though not with quite as much prophylactic fervor.) I should remark at the outset that I share the commonly held judgement that Russell's analysis represented a major advance in philosophical logic. Russell's treatment of definite descriptions has been described as 'a paradigm of philosophical analysis', and I readily grant that it deserved that status. It deserved to hold that status for five, maybe even ten years, but not for the forty-five years that elapsed before Strawson published the first serious challenge to it.[2] The fact that Russell's analysis went unchallenged so long cannot be attributed to any philosophical or scientific breakthrough that had to be achieved before Russell's account could be disputed; indeed, there is nothing in Strawson's 1950 paper that could not in principle having been written in 1910 by Strawson's grandfather. The only plausible explanation that I can see for the length of time that Russell's analysis enjoyed near-universal acceptance is the conjunction of Russell's intimidating presence and the endemic myopia among English-speaking philosophers that made it possible for them to fail to notice the vast majority of tokens of the word *the* that they heard, read, or produced, and the serious problems that they pose for Russell's analysis.

While the description of Russell's analysis as 'a paradigm of philosophical analysis' antedates Thomas Kuhn's use of the word 'paradigm' in the senses that it has in his writings, it can be seen from a 1980s vantage point to have been a serendipitous choice of words, in that Russell's analysis has for the community of philosophical logicians the role of one of the components of a Kuhnian paradigm, namely that of what Kuhn more recently has come to call

---

[1] Bertrand Russell, 'On denoting', *Mind*, 14 (1905), pp. 479–93.
[2] P.F. Strawson, 'On referring', *Mind*, 59 (1950), pp. 320–44.

an EXEMPLAR:[3] a prestigious problem-solution, regularly taught to neophytes in the field as an example of good problem-solving and a model after which new problem-solutions should be patterned.

I list below some assumptions and policies that form part of the Kuhnian paradigm for the community of philosophical logicians.[4] These assumptions and policies are of relevance to the remainder of this paper by virtue of their all being reflected in the fine details of Russell's analysis of definite descriptions and all having been involved in the Oscar-sized supporting role that Russell's analysis has played in Donald Davidson's research on actions and events.

(i) Quantification is unrestricted. That is, there is a single set (the 'universe of discourse') that serves as domain for all individual variables. (In the alternative view, that of restricted quantification, each variable must be supplied with a specification of what its domain is, and variables normally do not have the whole 'universe of discourse' as domain; each quantifier combines with two propositional functions, one giving the domain of the variable and one whose truth in that domain is at issue.[5] In unrestricted quantification, restrictions of the domain are simulated by the use of propositional connectives, e.g. 'All Fs are G' is represented as $(\forall x)(Fx \supset Gx)$, and 'Some Fs are G' as $(\exists x)(Fx \wedge Gx)$.)

(ii) Only an existential quantifier and a universal quantifier are admitted as full-fledged quantifiers. This policy is a practical (not logical, of course) consequence of (i), since only universal and existential quantifiers allow plausible analyses in which propositional connectives simulate restrictions on the domain. For example, there is no plausible way to analyze 'Most Fs are G' as 'Most x' combined with Fx, Gx, and propositional connectives.

(iii) For syntactically well-formed propositional expressions, falsehood is the only alternative to truth. This assumption is readily visible in Russell's formula for 'The king of France is bald', in which he has simply conjoined three terms, each corresponding to one of the three ways in which the sentence could fail to express an unqualifiedly true proposition:[6]

---

[3] Thomas Kuhn, *The Structure of Scientific Revolutions*, 2nd edn (University of Chicago Press, 1970).

[4] In 'Kuhnian paradigms as systems of markedness conventions', in *Festschrift for Rulon Weils*, ed. A. Makkai and A. Melby (Jupiter Press, Lake Bluff, Illinois, 1985), I defend a revisionist conception of 'paradigm', in which the paradigm of a community is the set of 'markedness principles' that define the respects in which activity within the community can be 'unmarked' (= normal, available without cost) or 'marked' (= non-normal, available only at some cost). Note that with this conception of 'paradigm', acceptance of a paradigm does not imply a commitment to engage only in 'normal' activity, only a commitment to pay the costs (e.g. to offer justifications) for any non-normal activity.

[5] Not all advocates of restricted quantification agree that it is a propositional function that gives the domain of a variable. Anil Gupta, *The Logic of Common Nouns* (Yale University Press, New Haven, 1981), argues that the domain of a bound variable is given by a 'common noun expression' and that such expressions are not reducible to propositional functions.

[6] Following my standing policy of charitable misrepresentation, I have given the second term in (1b) in a form that fits its common paraphrase *No one else is king of France*, rather than the more usual form $(\forall y)(KFy \supset y = x)$. If contraposition is in general valid, the two versions are logically

(1) a. The king of France is bald.

    b. $(\exists x)KFx \wedge (\forall y)(y \neq x \supset -KFy) \wedge Bx$

((1a) is clearly false when there is one and only one king of France and that individual is not bald. The remaining two cases, that in which there is no king of France and that in which there is more than one, actually differ from the first case, and from each other, in the respects in which they make (1a) anomalous, though (1b) in each case comes out simply false; when there is no king of France, (1a) is not clearly false, and even if it is taken to be false it has the additional anomaly of expressing a commitment to the existence of a king of France, and when there is more than one king of France, (1a) has the quite distinct anomaly of not in itself sufficing to specify to which king of France it alludes.)[7]

(iv) Mass nouns are either ignored entirely or analyzed away in terms of count nouns, e.g. *All blood is red* is given an analysis in which the mass noun *blood* is analyzed away in terms of a count noun expression such as *quantity of blood*. The tactic of ignoring mass nouns entirely is by far the more common practice. Russell's analysis of definite description fails miserably when applied to noun phrases whose head is a mass noun, e.g. on the assumption that the parts of a quantity of milk are themselves quantities of milk, the presence in the refrigerator of a container of milk, which would often serve to establish the truth of (2), would serve to establish the falsehood of the corresponding Russellian formula, which would come out false because of the falseness of the 'uniqueness term' (not only is the whole quantity of milk in the refrigerator, but so also are its parts, which are themselves milk):

(2) The milk is in the refrigerator.

(v) The values of the variables are taken to be non-overlapping. This policy is easy enough to follow if you operate, as most logicians and even many philosophers of language do, with universes of discourse that have only persons

---

equivalent; see *Everything that Linguists Have Always Wanted to Know About Logic (But Were Ashamed to Ask)* (University of Chicago Press, Chicago, and Basil Blackwell, Oxford, 1981), pp. 50–4, however, for some serious doubts about the general validity of contraposition.

[7] Later in this paper, I will dispute the standard assumption that existence of a king of France is necessary for the use of *the king of France* to be normal. The difference between failure of the 'existence' and of the 'uniqueness' conditions is brought out clearly by a device that colloquial American English provides for the expression of external negation:

    i.A: The King of France is bald.
    B: Bullshit – there's no king of France.

    ii.A: The senator from Illinois is bald.
    B: *Bullshit – there are two senators from Illinois.

While Russell's British English may have lacked this means of expressing external negation, it surely had other means of expressing it.

and numbers as their members.[8] It can't very well be followed if you admit e.g.
quantities of blood as values of your variables: a quantity of blood generally can
be divided up into two or more smaller quantities of blood, and when you
reanalyze *blood* as *quantity of blood* in a quantified NP, you thereby commit
yourself to a semantics in which the same thing is counted more than once: any
particular quantity of blood is then not only itself a value of the variable but also
a part of many other values of the variable. You can get away with that if you
follow policy (ii) and admit only existential and universal quantifiers, but (as is
pointed out by Parsons)[9] it completely messes things up if you want to talk
about quantifiers such as *most*: to get a plausible semantic account of *Most blood
is red*, you have to insure that no blood gets counted twice. (For *all* and *some*, the
semantics does not suffer if things get counted twice; policies (ii), (iv) and (v)
reinforce each other.)

(vi) The denotations of predicates are classical (as opposed to fuzzy) sets:
any entity either unqualifiedly is or unqualifiedly is not a member of any given
set – degrees or dimensions of membership in a set are not recognized.

(vii) Identity is taken to presuppose existence, e.g. John can't be looking for a
specific unicorn, it is claimed, unless a unicorn exists which John is looking for.

(viii) Pragmatics is dismissed as an ungentlemanly enterprise.

I maintain that all of these characteristics of 'standard quantificational logic'
compound the difficulty of analyzing actions and events and divert the attention
of philosophers from real problems to pseudo-problems. Policy (i) is responsible for much of the opposition to admitting actions and events as values of
variables. When every entity that is ever allowed as a value of any variable
becomes a value for all variables, as it does under a policy of unrestricted
quantification, there is reason to subject one's universe of discourse to a strict
immigration policy: the riff-raff that one allows in won't confine themselves to
the ontological slum in which one might think they belong[10] but will be free to
mingle with the ontological aristocracy. Worries about how to accommodate
ontological riff-raff are particularly common in discussions of non-existent
possible individuals, as typified by Quine's rhetorical question 'How many
possible fat men are standing in that doorway?' If non-existent possible
individuals are to be admitted as members of a Russellian universe of discourse,
only by a judicious choice of the properties assigned to them can they be kept
from lousing up the truth conditions of quantified expressions to which they
should be irrelevant. That problem can be avoided in a system of restricted

---

[8] There are in fact interesting cases of overlap even within the domain of persons, e.g. the
possibly distinct persons corresponding to the two cerebral hemispheres of a commisurotomized
patient. A number of works of science fiction deal seriously with imaginable cases in which the
individuation of persons is problematic, e.g. John Varley, *The Ophiuchi Hotline*; Robert Sheckley,
Crompton Divided; Algis Budrys, *Rogue Moon*.

[9] Terry Parsons, 'An analysis of mass terms and amount terms', *Foundations of Language*, 6
(1970), pp. 362–88, at p. 372.

[10] These words should not be taken as implying that I find slums of either the ontological or the
urban variety objectionable. I regard both kinds of slums as valuable resources that should be
conserved rather than destroyed. I happily admit my status as an ontological slumlord.

quantification by allowing as domain-defining expressions only expressions that restrict the values of the variable to one 'sort', with sort membership being an 'essential' property (an entity belongs to the same 'sort' in all worlds in which it exists), and in the evaluation of a quantified proposition in any world, admitting as values of the variable only individuals that exist in that world and have in that world the property expressed by the domain expression. The number of possible fat men standing in the doorway in the real world will then be identical to the number of real fat men standing there.

Policy (iii), which is manifested in the conjoined expression in Russell's formula (1b), is responsible for a minor detour into irrelevancy in 'The individuation of events', where Davidson says that when we 'ask for an explanation of why *the* avalanche fell on the village last week ... we are now asking not only why there was at least one avalanche, but also why there was not more than one.'[11] Davidson is saying here that when we ask why the avalanche fell on the village last week we are asking why Russell's formula for *The avalanche fell on the village last week* does not come out false. But that misrepresents the meaning of the question. You can explain why the avalanche fell even if you have no clue as to why no other avalanches fell or even if you do not know WHETHER any other avalanches fell.[12] To take a parallel case: AN accident occurred at 56th Street and Lake Park Avenue last Tuesday because with the torrential rain that was coming down, some driver was sure to fail to see the stop sign. THE accident (e.g. the one reported on page 23 of the *Tribune*, though there may well have been others that we didn't hear about) occurred because with the torrential rain that was coming down, THE driver failed to see the stop sign and collided with a car that was turning into the underpass. The proposition that no other accidents occurred is relevant not to accounting for why the accident occurred but only to identifying which accident we are accounting for the occurrence of.

Policy (vi), the failure to admit fuzzy sets, is partly responsible for the willingness of many philosophers to attribute temporal and spatial identity to events that differ at least in the degree to which various times and locations can be held to be involved in them, as in Davidson's example, 'Suppose that during exactly the same time interval Jones catches cold, swims the Hellespont, and counts his blessings'.[13] Davidson offers this as a case in which three distinct events would be identical in spatiotemporal location. However, unless one

---

[11] 'The individuation of events', reprinted in *Essays on Actions and Events* (Clarendon Press, Oxford, 1980), p. 171.

[12] Sentences like *If an avalanche falls next week, it will kill many persons* are difficult to analyze within standard quantification theory without employing non-existent possible events in a way that even I (cf. note 10 above) find objectionable. The analysis demanded by standard quantification theory is:

$(\forall x)(x$ is an avalanche $\supset (x$ falls next week $\supset x$ kills many persons))

If this is to be semantically non-vacuous, we have to recognise a set of 'possible avalanches', each having the property that if it falls next week it will kill many persons. But that means admitting avalanches as existing prior to the events responsible for their existence. See my *Everything that Linguists Have Always Wanted to Know*, p. 268, for an alternative, and to my thinking more plausible, account of such sentences.

[13] Davidson's reply to Lemmon, reported in *Essays on Actions and Events*, p. 125.

insists on imposing sharp boundaries on the events, it is not a very plausible example of identity. Catching a cold never has the same sharp temporal boundaries that swimming the Hellespont does: Jones starts swimming the Hellespont the instant he pushes off from the one shore and finishes the instant he touches down at the other shore, but his catching of the cold doesn't have the former instant as a clear beginning and the latter instant as a clear finish; indeed, it is not clear that one ever finishes catching a cold. The whole of Jones' body and also the water immediately around him is involved in the spatial location of his swimming, with his arms and legs and the surface of his body directly involved and the rest of his body going along for the ride, while it is his respiratory organs that are most directly involved in the catching of the cold, his arms and and legs being involved only peripherally. And while the counting of blessings has temporal boundaries nearly as sharp as those of swimming the Hellespont, it is located physically in the parts of Jones that do his thinking, which are not the same parts that do the swimming.[14] A better instance of spatiotemporal identity between distinct events is provided by the case of Austinian locutionary and illocutionary acts, e.g. if Fred apologizes to Ethel by saying to her 'I apologize', Fred's locutionary act of saying 'I apologize' to Ethel will have the same spatiotemporal location as his illocutionary act of apologizing to her.

The sharp boundaries that classical set theory forces one to assume are available only through arbitrary choices, and (as in the cases discussed by Schelling)[15] we prefer to draw boundaries where boundaries already exist,[16] whether in the form of a river or in the form of the epidermis that bounds a person's body. When fuzzy set theory is assumed, the arbitrariness of these

---

[14] Davidson's policy on the location of mental events is: 'The event took place where the person was' ('The individuation of events', p. 176). The difficulty in applying that policy is in specifying precisely the location of the person. One can always identify the location of the person with the location of his (entire) body, but that is only a makeshift, to be resorted to simply to avoid getting into the fine details of spatial location. Some aspects of this question are discussed insightfully by Anna Wierzbicka ('Mind and body from a semantic point of view', in *Notes from the Linguistic Underground* (Syntax and Semantics 7), ed. J. McCawley (Academic Press, New York, 1976), pp. 129–57; 'Ethno-syntax and the philosophy of grammar', *Studies in Language*, 3 (1979), pp. 313–83), who deals in detail with sentences (such as *John kissed Mary on the cheek*) referring to events that affect a person (and not just his body) but are localized at a limited region of his body. Wierzbicka and also Gerard Diffloth ('Body moves in French and Semai', *Papers from the 10th Regional Meeting* (Chicago Linguistic Society, Chicago, 1974), pp. 128–38) note that languages differ regarding what can be treated as part of a person in such syntactic constructions as the ethical dative (e.g. whether the clothing that he is wearing or the car that he is driving can count as part of him). Symbiotic arrangements between human beings and machines (especially computers) further complicate the problem of locating events spatially, e.g. what is the location of the event of Beatrice computing the mean reaction times in her latest experiment if she does it via a telephone connection to a computer mainframe twenty miles away? See in this connection Dennett's intriguing suggested answers to the question 'Where am I?' under various exotic but imaginable circumstances (Daniel Dennett, 'Where am I?', in *Brainstorms* (Bradford Books, Cambridge, Mass., 1978), pp. 310–23).

[15] Thomas Schelling, *The Strategy of Conflict* (Harvard University Press, Cambridge, Mass., 1960).

[16] This preference can be subsumed under Grice's maxim of manner. (H.P. Grice, 'Logic and Conversation', in *Speech Acts* (*Syntax and Semantics* 3) , ed. P. Cole and J. Morgan (Academic Press, New York, 1975), pp. 45–58).

choices is at least more apparent, and we are more likely to think twice about making them.

In many instances where the individuation of events is controversial, a consideration of their (fuzzy) spatiotemporal extent provides reasons for taking them to be distinct. For example, Davidson, in discussing examples as in (3), conflates a blow with an event of striking the blow:[17]

(3) a. Peter struck John.
    b. Peter struck the blow which blinded John.
    c. The blow which blinded John was struck by Peter.

For example, in arguing that these sentences require an analysis that 'acknowledge[s] an ontology of events', he says 'a sentence like "John struck the blow" is about two particulars: John and the blow ... striking is predicated alike of John and the blow.' But the blow and the event of striking it do not have exactly the same spatial location: the blow is located primarily in the contact between Peter's fist and John's head, secondarily in the trajectory of Peter's fist, while the event of Peter's striking the blow is located in Peter's mind and in all of his movements in delivering the blow, fully as much as in the spatiotemporal region in which the impact occurs.[18]

The above discussion of the blow and the event in which Peter struck the blow suggest that in the realm of events, overlapping particulars, which are ruled out by policy (v), may be a common occurrence. If so, one should be particularly wary of applying Russell's analysis of definite descriptions to events, since overlapping particulars give rise to serious failures of Russell's analysis. Under Russell's assumptions, (4) is a valid argument:

(4) a is the X
    $b \neq a$
    Therefore, b is not an/the X.

However, instances of (4) in which a and b overlap are not in general valid, for example, the argument in (5) is invalid:

(5) 1010 E. 59th St., Chicago 60637 is the office address of Leonard Linsky.
    Dept. of Philosophy, University of Chicago $\neq$ 1010 E. 59th St., Chicago 60637.
    Therefore, Dept. of Philosophy, University of Chicago, is not the office address of Leonard Linsky.

---

[17] 'The individuation of events', p. 175.

[18] The difference to which I allude here is confirmed by differences in what properties can be predicated of the blow or of the event:

The blow/*event struck John in the nose.
The blow/*event was forceful.

While the two addresses are distinct,[19] they are not disjoint, and it takes disjointness, not mere distinctness, to get a valid analogue to (4). Of course, in the realm of Russell's examples (a realm that Russell's successors have not greatly enriched), there was no distinctness without disjointness, i.e. the persons and numbers that were assumed as values of variables were disjoint if distinct. Thus, to give an analogue to Russell's (6a) a chance of working correctly in cases involving overlapping particulars, it would have to be revised to (6b):

(6) The A is B.
   a. $(\exists x)(Ax \wedge (\forall y)(y \neq x \supset -Ay) \wedge Bx)$
   b. $(\exists x)(Ax \wedge (\forall y)(y \text{ disjoint } x \supset -Ay) \wedge Bx)$

Note that since 'y disjoint x' is a stronger condition than 'y≠x', the second term in the conjunction in (6b) is true in more cases than is its counterpart in (6a), and thus (6b) will be true in more cases than will (6a).

The suggested revision of Russell's analysis suffices to defuse a type of argument that has often been wielded against analyses in which understood performative verbs represent 'the illocutionary force of' sentences. For example, Gazdar, starting with the observation that *That was a good movie* has the illocutionary force of commending, says that the advocate of a performative analysis is then forced to posit *commend* as the understood performative verb; he proceeds to show that that leads to horrible consequences.[20] However, the performative analysis actually requires only that illocutionary forces be represented in deep structure by clauses of the form 'I V you S', with V a performative verb; it doesn't choose among the different things that all are 'the illocutionary force of the sentence' (cf. the different things that are 'the office address of Leonard Linsky'). Gazdar assumes that if commending is the illocutionary force of a given sentence, then nothing else can be, which is preposterous precisely because illocutionary forces can overlap. An act is not any less one of commending a movie in virtue of being one of asserting that the movie was good, nor vice versa, and there is nothing inappropriate about describing commending and asserting as each being 'the illocutionary force of' a given sentence. Commending is not disjoint from asserting, and thus, under an analysis of *the* on the lines of (6b), from the proposition that the illocutionary force of S is commending, it does not follow that the illocutionary force of S is not asserting, though since commending *is* disjoint from requesting, it does follow that the illocutionary force of S is not requesting.[21] Thus, in a performative analysis, the underlying performative verb of *That was a good movie* could be taken to be *assert*.

---

[19] A fact relevant to the appreciation of (5) is that 1010 E. 59th St., Chicago 60637, is the address of the building that houses the offices not only of the University of Chicago's philosophy department but also of its linguistics, classics, and English departments. In addition, some of the philosophers have offices in an adjacent building.

[20] Gerald Gazdar, *Pragmatics* (Academic Press, New York, 1979), p. 28.

[21] The case where different overlapping illocutionary forces can all correctly be described as 'the illocutionary force of' a given sentence must be distinguished sharply from true cases of multiple

Another example of the invalid argument in (4) is (7):

(7) The place where Fred lives is New York City.
Manhattan ≠ New York City.
Therefore, the place where Fred lives is not Manhattan.

I am forced to accept the conclusion that New York City and Manhattan can both be 'the place where Fred lives' without being identical, but since that accords perfectly with the way in which *the* is normally used, I do not find that objectionable. I note though that it does force one to be extra careful not to treat definite descriptions as if they were proper names. While I object to most of the details of Russell's analysis of definite descriptions, one of the few points on which I side with him is that definite descriptions make a significantly different contribution to logical form than do proper names.

Actually, (7) suffers from an additional defect besides simple invalidity. In the transition from the first premise to the conclusion, the ground has shifted in one of the fashions described by Lewis.[22] Lewis's approach to discourse pragmatics relies on 'scorekeeping': the setting and changing of values for a set of parameters (the 'score') that affect the possibilities for using and interpreting sentences in the given discourse. For example, thresholds for the applicability of inexact predicates are part of the 'score', and whether an occurrence of *The table is flat* is true or false depends not only on facts about the table but on how much deviation from pure planarity the score allows *flat* to take in. If the score is changed in the middle of the discourse (e.g. if one of the participants introduces more stringent standards of flatness), *The table is flat* can change from being true to being false, in virtue of the standards of flatness being changed from ones that the table meets to ones that it doesn't meet. *The place where Fred lives is New York City* is an appropriate thing to say only relative to a score in which things at the same taxonomic level as New York City are admitted as places where someone lives. (Whether it can be TRUE only relative to such a score is a separate question and a much harder one to answer.) The first premise and the conclusion in (7) thus require different scores, but what intervenes between them does not suffice to change the score, so that a person who utters (7) commits a foul in the language game that he is playing.[23]

---

illocutionary forces, e.g. where a sentence consists of two parts, each having its own illocutionary force:

I apologize for spilling my wine, and I promise that I won't let it happen again.

In this case one can speak of apologizing being the illocutionary force of the first conjunct and promising being that of the second conjunct; here it does not make sense to speak of anything as being the illocutionary force of the whole sentence.

[22] David Lewis, 'Scorekeeping in a language game', *Journal of Philosophical Logic*, 9 (1979), pp. 339–59.

[23] We don't say that Fred lives in two places, Manhattan and New York, just as we don't say that *That was a good movie* has two illocutionary forces, commending and asserting. Counting presupposes that the things counted don't overlap. Scorekeeping serves to enforce this presupposition: the score will exclude from the count the entities at higher and lower taxonomic levels that the entities counted overlap with.

We can then in a sense rehabilitate (4): if we restrict the notion of validity to stretches of argumentative discourse in which the score remains constant, then we can claim that (4) is valid after all, in that all apparent instances of invalidity of (4) require a midstream change of score. Note, though, that we can perform that supposed rescue of Russell's analysis only at the cost of changing the nature of the enterprise from pure semantics to pragmatics: 'score' is an inherently pragmatic notion.

Before turning to another class of examples that force the analysis of *the* into pragmatics, I wish to explore some cases of overlapping particulars that arise in the realm of actions and events. Consider the familiar question of whether the stabbing of Caesar by Brutus and the killing of Caesar by Brutus are identical.[24] We may have to do here with two overlapping actions and/or with two overlapping events, and we have to allow for the possibility that identity of actions might not be equivalent to identity of corresponding events. Whether Brutus' action of stabbing Caesar is identical to his action of killing Caesar depends on whether the killing involved anything more ON BRUTUS' PART than merely stabbing Caesar. The sort of thing that it might involve is monitoring by Brutus, e.g. Brutus might have committed himself to the execution of a feedback loop in which stabbing is to be repeated until it is judged that the wounds administered are mortal:

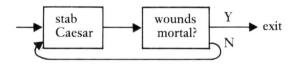

A single execution of the instruction 'stab Caesar' may suffice to produce the desired mortal wound(s), but even in that case, execution of the entire program consists not just of executing the instruction to stab Caesar but also of doing the monitoring that sanctions exiting. Considering the central role that monitoring plays in a broad range of things that are unqualifiedly actions, the neglect to which action theorists have subjected monitoring is unjustified. The cook's part in his action of boiling an egg, for example, consists largely in overseeing the work that the flame does (e.g. watching that the flame does not go out and that

---

Among the entities that could in principle be described as *the place where Fred lives* is 'the universe'; indeed, for any sentence S, if there is any place that can be described as 'the place where S', then the universe can be so described, because no location *y* meets the condition '*y* disjoint U', where U is the universe. This fact, which Davidson touched on in his reply to Lemmon (p. 125), poses no major difficulty: events can differ in location even though there is a place that is 'the location of' all of them, just as long as some places that are 'the location of' one of them are not the location of the others. Note, though, that in a normal discourse the score would never be such that the universe *would* be described as 'the place where S', since that would mean the score was set so as not to provide for the drawing of any distinctions of location. The discussion of the Hellespont example above took the context to be such that the score called for the drawing of fine distinctions in spatiotemporal location.

[24] Following standard philosophical practice, I will make the dubious assumption that the foul deed was perpetrated by Brutus all by himself.

the water does not boil away, and determining when the egg is fully cooked and thus to be removed from the flame). Davidson makes the error of assuming that actions of stabbing Caesar and of killing him would have to be non-overlapping if distinct: 'But this reasoning [an argument by Jaegwon Kim] is futile if, having stabbed Caesar, Brutus has a different action YET to perform (killing him)' (emphasis added).[25] The stabbing may have the starring role in an action of killing but not be the whole of the action, in which case what the killer has yet to do is not to kill Caesar but to finish killing him. As in the New York/Manhattan example, the action of stabbing Caesar is distinct from the action of killing him but, because of overlap, we do not say that Brutus did two things, stab Caesar and kill him.

The above flowchart may actually be a more correct description of *murder Caesar by stabbing him* than of *kill Caesar by stabbing him* – we do not reserve use of the word *kill* for cases in which the agent monitors the effects of his action on the victim. In cases where the agent's act results in the victim's death but the agent does not engage in the above sort of monitoring, the agent has killed the victim and his action of stabbing him is presumably identical with his action of killing him, since the actions involved in the stabbing and in the killing are in that case identical. That still leaves open the possibility that the EVENT of the agent stabbing the victim and the event of his killing him are distinct. A consideration of the use of time adverbs provides evidence that they are indeed distinct, that the event of A killing B includes as a proper part the event of B dying, while the event of A stabbing B (even stabbing him mortally) does not. Consider the by now overly familiar example in which a murderous husband on Friday evening puts in the orange juice that he knows his wife will drink on Saturday morning a poison that is sufficiently slow acting that the wife does not die from its effects until Sunday evening, by which time the husband has already absconded to Brazil. Calling the murderer Fred and his ill-fated spouse Amy, let us evaluate the truth of various combinations of *Fred killed Amy* with time adverbs:

(8) a. Fred killed Amy last Friday. (F or indeterminate)[26]
    b. Fred killed Amy last Saturday. (F)
    c. Fred killed Amy last Sunday. (F)
    d. Fred killed Amy last weekend. (T)

The time adverbs that make the sentence true appear to be precisely the ones that refer to a time interval that contains both Fred's act and its lethal consequences on Amy.

Recognizing that Fred's action of killing Amy can be a proper part of the event of Fred killing Amy makes it easier to accept the uncomfortable conclusion that Davidson draws about a similar case: 'Suppose I pour poison in

---

25 'The individuation of events', p. 171.

26 This example may exhibit the same sort of indeterminacy in truth value that *Turkey is in Europe* does. The fact that only (8a) and not (8b) or (8c) can be taken as indeterminate rather than flat-out false suggests that the temporal location of the event is a fuzzy set of instants, with the time of the action belonging to it fully and the times of the effects belonging to it only to lesser extents.

the water tank of a spaceship while it stands on earth. My purpose is to kill the space traveller, and I succeed: when he reaches Mars he takes a drink and dies.... We are driven to the conclusion that I have killed the traveller long before he dies.'[27] This is a fine conclusion to draw about the agent's action of killing the traveller and does not prevent one from drawing a different conclusion about the event of his killing the traveller.

Back to definite descriptions now. Davidson seems to strongly prefer existential quantifiers to definite description operators as the understood quantifier in the various examples in which he invokes actions and events as values of variables. I suspect that part of the reason for this policy is an adherence to Russell's analysis of definite descriptions, with its 'uniqueness' term, which would allow the formula for (9) to come out true only if only one eruption of Vesuvius ever occurred:

(9) Vesuvius erupted in 79 AD.

I maintain that (9) is in fact ambiguous, having one reading appropriately paraphrased in terms of an existential quantifier, as suggested by Davidson, and one appropriately paraphrased in terms of a definite description, though not one that conforms to Russell's analysis. The 'definite description' interpretation of (9) is the one that alludes to an eruption of Vesuvius that is already under discussion and says that that eruption occurred in 79 AD. Russell's formula is inadequate as an analysis of that interpretation in just the same way in which it is inadequate as an analysis of (10):

(10) The dog is barking.

The Russellian formula for (10) implies that there is only one dog. An advocate of Russell's analysis must thus either accept that implication or alter the formula. The most obvious possible response of the former type is to claim that (10) is used properly only relative to a 'universe of discourse' that includes only one dog. The problem with that move is that a Russellian universe of discourse is supposed to provide domains for ALL the bound variables in the discourse, and it is easy to construct sentences involving *the dog* understood as in (10) but combined with material whose analysis requires bound variables having more than one dog among their possible values:

(11) a. The dog likes all dogs.
      b. The dog was barking at another dog.
      b'.The eruption of Vesuvius was more catastrophic than all the previous eruptions of Vesuvius.

The Russellian formula for (11b) is self-contradictory (the 'uniqueness term' for *the dog* implies that there isn't any such thing as 'another dog'); and relative to a universe of discourse in which there is only one dog, the formula for (11a) is true under the same conditions as that for a sentence that clearly has different truth conditions, namely *The dog likes itself*. The only obvious way to implement

---

[27] 'Event and Discourse', p. 177.

the second possible response to the problem of (10) is to add material to the pristine Russell formula, e.g. replace 'x is a dog' by a formula corresponding to 'x is a salient dog'. The problem with that proposal is that if that substitution is to yield plausible truth conditions, the formula for 'x is a salient dog' (or whatever) would have to have an interpretation that varied with context in a way that is not provided for in standard quantification theory. Rover need not remain 'salient' throughout an entire discourse but can flit back and forth between salience and relative non-salience, in the sense that (as pointed out especially clearly by Lewis)[28] *the dog* can pick out a different dog in the second sentence of a discourse than it did in the first sentence, e.g. (with subscripts indicating purported coreference):

(12) While I was walking the dog$_1$, another dog$_2$ started barking at us. The dog$_2$ was so big that he gave my dog$_1$ a real fright.

The second Russellian response to the problem of (10) thus brings in a term that can be interpreted only in terms of pragmatics and thus violates policy (viii). Bringing in such a predicate as 'is salient' is a roundabout way of making the interpretation of definite descriptions a matter of pragmatics to begin with. I will now sketch a more straightforwardly pragmatic account of definite descriptions. Suppose that one recognizes not only a universe of discourse in Russell's sense but also what I call a CONTEXTUAL DOMAIN:[29] the set of objects whose identities are taken as 'mutual knowledge' of the participants in the discourse at the given point in the discourse. The universe of discourse, as usual, supplies the values for ordinary bound variables, while the contextual domain provides referents for definite descriptions.[30] The notion of 'salience' alluded to in the last paragraph does not correspond to a predicate that can appear in formulas but is rather a relation among the members of the contextual domain, varying as the discourse progresses, that is used in assigning referents to definite descriptions, e.g. the referent of any particular occurrence of *the dog* will be the most salient member of the contextual domain at the particular point of the discourse that has the property of being a dog.[31]

---

[28] 'Scorekeeping in a language game'.

[29] Confusingly, John Lyons, *Semantics* (Cambridge University Press, Cambridge, 1977), p. 508, uses the term 'universe of discourse' for what I have called 'contextual domain'. 'Universe of discourse' would indeed be a reasonable thing to call a contextual domain if it weren't that most logicians use the term to denote something quite different.

[30] Two qualifications have to be added to this simplified sketch. First, the universe of discourse serves as a default source of referents of definite descriptions when nothing in the contextual domain meets the description; I thus take what for Russell were paradigm cases of definite descriptions (e.g. *the smallest prime number*) to reflect rather a backup mechanism that is employed when normal means of interpreting definite descriptions fail. Second, in the case of expressions like *most of the students*, in which a quantifier is combined with a plural definite description, it is the contextual domain that provides the set that gives the values of the bound variable.

[31] I would in fact maintain that what is relevant to the assignment of a referent to *the X* is not the *truth* of the various propositions X(a) but rather their status as mutual knowledge, e.g. in Keith Donnellan's celebrated example ('Reference and definite descriptions', *Philosophical Review*, 75 (1966), pp. 281–321), what is relevant to the choice of Smith as the referent of *the man in the corner with the martini in his hand* is not whether Smith actually has a martini in his hand but whether the participants in the conversation take the proposition that Smith has a martini in his hand as mutual knowledge.

A contextual domain can have among its members not only dogs but also eruptions of Vesuvius or entities of any other sort. The 'definite description' interpretation of (9) says of the most salient eruption of Vesuvius in the contextual domain that it occurred in 79 AD. The members of the contextual domain, incidentally, need not be individuals. The serious problems with attempts to extend Russell's analysis to plural definite descriptions can be avoided by e.g. taking the referent of *the dogs* to be the most salient set of dogs that is a member (NB: a member, not a subset) of the contextual domain. Note that there is no assumption that the members of a set belonging to the contextual domain belong themselves to the contextual domain; this allows e.g. for the possibility that you and I take the identity of the set of dogs in my neighbor's apartment as mutual knowledge even if we do not have mutual knowledge of the identity of any particular dog in that set or even of how many members the set contains.

I turn now to another policy inherent in the Russellian analysis that deserves more dissent than it has so far received, namely the policy (vii) of assuming that definite descriptions carry an existential commitment. Here too the treatment in terms of contextual domains allows dissent from the policy to be given some substance. Davidson takes up a case that provides some grounds for such dissent in 'Eternal vs. ephemeral events'.[32] In his discussion of variants of *Sebastian strolled in Bologna at 2 am*, Davidson considers the case in which a secret society to which Sebastian belongs chooses by lot each night someone who is to take a stroll that night along a certain path. He observes, 'Then we might say that had the cards fallen out differently, another person would have taken *that* stroll.' We could of course also say *the stroll*, or perhaps *the fateful stroll*, in that case, but indeed we could say that even if no one takes the stroll: 'Due to Sebastian's sudden attack of appendicitis and his inability to recruit a substitute, no one took the fateful stroll in Bologna on May 11, 1975'.

Existence of a unique individual having the property of being an X JUSTIFIES the use of *the X*, but only in virtue of something that it shares with many cases in which either no individual or more than one has that property: it provides a means of identifying an individual, irrespective of whether such an individual exists. A common case of identities that are established independently of existence occurs in recipes that involve optional ingredients. For example, a recipe whose list of ingredients includes '2 tbsp minced shallot (optional)' can say 'Add the salt, the ginger, and *the shallot*'. Failure to distinguish between the existence of objects and the existence of identities for (possibly non-existent) objects has caused much confusion in discussions of 'non-referring expressions'. The ambiguity in (13) is not between a reading that implies the existence of unicorns and one that doesn't; indeed, neither reading implies that there are unicorns:

(13) Harry is looking for a unicorn.

The so-called 'referential' interpretation of (13) merely presupposes that an identity for a unicorn has been established, e.g. Harry has concluded that one

---

[32] 'Eternal vs. ephemeral events', in *Essays on Actions and Events*, p. 197.

particular unicorn, to which he may even have given a name, the way that a certain possibly non-existent aquatic beast has been christened 'Nessie', is responsible for the chewed-up geraniums, and he intends to catch that particular unicorn, not just any old unicorn that might wander into his garden. There is nothing self-contradictory about (14):

(14) Harry will never catch the unicorn that he's looking for, because that ($\neq$ such a) unicorn doesn't exist.

The unicorn that he's looking for is a definite description based on a 'referential' interpretation of the object of *look for* but doesn't imply the existence of any unicorn, only that a particular unicorn identity is established as mutual knowledge; such an identity has to exist as mutual knowledge for *That unicorn doesn't exist* to be interpretable. This can easily be accommodated in the contextual-domain approach, since there is no need to take membership in the contextual domain as implying existence. This of course allows for the possibility of non-existent entities being the referents of definite descriptions in sentences that purport to refer to the real world. But that is required anyway, in order to accommodate such sentences as (15):

(15) Harry is afraid of the unicorn that he is looking for.

Definite descriptions don't imply existence – they just give the illusion of doing so when they are combined with predicates that imply the existence of the entities that they are predicated of, as in (16):

(16) Harry wounded the unicorn that he was looking for.

I will close this paper with a brief comment on an aspect of policy (v) to which Davidson, to his credit, has not conformed: the sub-policy of not even worrying about questions of individuation and of panicking when such worries become unavoidable. One of the most memorable segments in 'The individuation of events' is on the last page, where Davidson points out that individuation is not in general any more intractable a problem for events than it is for physical objects, and suggests, though without giving details, that physical objects pose the same sorts of individuation problems that have made some philosophers leery of admitting events into their ontologies. There are in fact a great profusion of banal examples in which it is unclear what exactly is included in a physical object. When we speak of a car colliding with a truck, do the drivers and the cargo count as parts of the objects that we speak of as colliding? When we discuss the artistic merits of a statue, is the pedestal on which it stands part of the object about which we express aesthetic judgements? How exactly are items to be counted in determining whether one is entitled to stand in the checkout line that is reserved for '8 items or less'? I conjecture that these questions have no fixed answers and that pragmatic considerations (i.e. Lewis's 'scorekeeping') resolve the questions differently in different contexts, just the way that they resolve indeterminacy in what counts as the location of an event. On the question of individuation, as on many other questions relating to actions and events, Davidson's work has been refreshing for its wealth of novel insight, and occasionally exasperating for the reverence that Davidson has displayed for a scheme of analysis that represents a formidable obstacle to the achievement of those insights. If Davidson's *Essays on Actions and Events* needs a subtitle, I would propose 'Despite Bertrand Russell'.[33]

[33] For valuable comments on the version of this paper that I read at the Rutgers Davidson conference, I wish to thank Emmon Bach, Terry Parsons, Barbara Hall Partee, Jeff Pelletier, and especially my commentator, Alex Orenstein.

14
Adverb-Dropping Inferences and the Lemmon Criterion

Jonathan Bennett

Introduction

Davidson did us a service in reviving the idea of events as concrete particulars, and commanding our attention by his theory about how to regiment adverb-dropping inferences – that is, ones where the conclusion differs from the premise only in omitting a restrictive adverbial phrase.[1] If we are to use ordinary simple logic to explain why from 'He comforted her with a few words' we can validly infer 'He comforted her', Davidson argued, we'll have to treat it as an inference from:

> There was a comforting: it was by him, it was of her, and it was done with a few words

to:

> There was a comforting: it was by him, and it was of her.

And thus an exercise of logical regimentation leads us to say that there was *a comforting*, thus including events in our ontology.

Most of the criticisms of this seem to me to rest on misunderstandings, and to be perfectly meetable,[2] though one by Eddy Zemach does call for work on Davidson's part.[3] But a more serious difficulty than any of these has not been noticed. It is my topic in this paper.

---

[1] Donald Davidson, 'The logical form of action sentences', in his *Essays on Actions and Events* (Oxford University Press, New York, 1980), pp. 105–22.

[2] For example, those in J.A. Fodor, 'Troubles about actions', in *Semantics of Natural Language*, ed. D. Davidson and G. Harman (Reidel, Dordrecht, 1972), pp. 48–69; and Bruce Aune, *Reason and Action* (Reidel, Dordrecht, 1977), pp. 29–31.

[3] Eddy M. Zemach, 'Events', in *Philosophy of History and Action*, ed. Y. Yovel (Reidel, Dordrecht, 1978), pp. 85–95.

First, a little scene-setting.

Sometimes the dropping of an adverb takes you from truth to falsity – as in the move from 'He is nearly qualified', to 'He is qualified' – and Davidson's treatment has nothing to say about these. His theory applies only to adverbs that can validly be dropped; neither it nor any weakened version of it has a word to say about the likes of 'nearly qualified' and 'allegedly impotent'.

Montague and others have devised a kind of theory that treats of all adverbial modification, and then within that large framework adds details about the two species – those of restrictive and unrestrictive adverbs, i.e. ones that can and ones that cannot be validly dropped.[4] I don't know whether to prefer this treatment to Davidson's, other things being equal. Davidson's theory uses less logic than the other, but has a larger ontology. Is that a stand-off? Davidson's theory has to treat restrictive adverbial modification as *sui generis*, rather than as one species within a theoretically unified genus; this is *prima facie* a demerit, but is it really one? I can't answer these questions; and I mention this whole matter only to sketch in some background.

Verb-dependent adverbs

Davidson's theory in its simplest form cannot always be applied even to restrictive adverbs, i.e. to ones that *can* be validly dropped, because it doesn't apply when the adverb in question is (as I shall say) *verb-dependent*. If John walked from Belgium to Turkey last summer, then he journeyed from Belgium to Turkey last summer. Davidson will say, then, that there was a walk and there was a journey; and now I add the important fact that according to him the walk *was* the journey – a single protracted event involved leg movements etc. and also covered a lot of the earth's surface etc. Now let's try a Davidsonian treatment of the statement that:

> John journeyed slowly from Belgium to Turkey.

The simplest Davidsonian treatment of this would say that it means

> There was a journey: it was by John, it was from Belgium to Turkey, and it was slow,

and merely by dropping the clause 'and it was slow' we get the conclusion that John journeyed from Belgium to Turkey. That may seem all right, but if John's journey was his walk then we have trouble. For our premise includes the statement that the journey was slow; but if the journey was the walk it follows that the walk was slow. And then, re-applying the equation of walking slowly with being the subject of a slow walk, we get the result that:

---

[4] Richard Montague, 'English as a formal language', in his *Formal Philosophy* (Yale University Press, New Haven, Conn., 1974), pp. 188–221, especially pp. 210–13; Terence Parsons, 'Some problems concerning the logic of grammatical modifiers', *Synthese*, 21 (1970), pp. 320–34; Romane Clark, 'Concerning the logic of predicate modifiers', *Nous*, 4 (1970), pp. 311–35.

John walked slowly from Belgium to Turkey.

But if he walked at thirty miles a day, this is just false, although it is true that he journeyed slowly. It's obvious what the source of the trouble is: the adverb 'slowly' is verb-dependent to such a high degree that it may be truthful with one verb and not with another, even if the two pick out one and the same event.

Davidson mentioned this problem in his original paper on adverb-dropping inferences, and placidly set it aside:

> The problem is not peculiar to talk of events, however. It appears equally when we try to explain the logical role of noun-dependent adjectives in 'Grundy was a short basketball player, but a tall man' .... The problem of dependents is indeed a problem about logical form, but it may be put to one side here because it is not a problem for event sentences alone.[5]

On the face of it, that is right. And Davidson can even strengthen it a bit. He can say that a grasp of noun-dependent adjectives such as 'short' can help us to understand verb-dependent adverbs such as 'slowly': once we see that the facts about 'short man' and 'short basketball player' have to do with the difference between 'short, for a basketball-player' and 'short, for a man', we can understand the difference between 'journeyed slowly' and 'walked slowly' by equating it with that between 'slow, for a journey' and 'slow, for a walk'.

But there is trouble, all the same. Granted that adjectives are often used noun-dependently, many are not. And so there is plenty of work to be done by a treatment of adjective-dropping inferences in terms of the idea that 'It is an [adjective] [noun]' has the form:

It is [adjective] and it is a [noun].

To say that something is a rectangular brick is to say that it is rectangular and is a brick: obviously, if a rectangular brick is an F it is a rectangular F, whatever F may be. And so on, for hosts of other adjectives. But where adverbs are in question, the analogous claim may not be true.

Whether it is true depends upon what sort of item an event is, i.e. on what event-identity statements are true. The trouble with 'slowly' arose only because we assumed that John's walk was the very same event as his journey. Drop that assumption and the troublesome argument won't go through and then we can safely take 'John journeyed slowly' to mean that there was a journey of which John was the subject and which was slow. Before I get deeper into that, let's stand back and look more generally at the question of event identity.

Event identity: Davidson, Kim, Lemmon

Davidson has made one proposal about this, and has looked at others. The one he has made is just that where events are in question x is y just in case all and

---

only the causes and effects of x are causes and effects of y.[6] Whether or not it is covertly circular, as is sometimes alleged, this 'same causes and effects' condition is certainly not helpful: it doesn't resolve *any* of the controversies over particular cases of event identity. For example, when the Titanic went down in icy waters there was a certain event:

E_1 the Titanic's going down

and there was the event:

E_2 the Titanic's going down in icy waters,

and there is dispute over whether this is one event or two. The 'same causes and effects' criterion is not challenged by any of the disputants, which shows how poor a peace-maker it is. Those who think that E_1 is not E_2 say that the large loss of life was caused by the latter but not the former, and they appeal to the reasonableness of saying:

What caused the large loss of life was not merely the Titanic's sinking but its sinking in icy waters.

Their opponents, who hold that E_1 is E_2, say that this strikes us as plausible only because we hear it as a statement not about which *event caused* the large loss of life but rather about which *fact explains* it.[7] The 'same causes and effects' criterion is a wheel which turns, whatever the other wheels are doing; and so it is not a revealing part of the mechanism. It certainly has no bearing on the problem which is my chief topic.

Now let us look at two other occupied positions. They stand at opposite ends of a continuum of possible views about the individuation of events.

One is a proposal by Alvin Goldman and Jaegwon Kim.[8] It rests on the idea that in theorizing about particular events we should refer to them through nominalizations of sentences made up of (1) a noun phrase and (2) a verb phrase and (3) a dating adverb. An example would be:

---

[6] Donald Davidson, 'The individuation of events', in his *Essays on Actions and Events*, pp. 163–80.

[7] Neither side in this debate has attended properly to the difference between perfect and imperfect nominals, and to how that affects one's intuitions about examples. The example using '... not its sinking but its sinking rapidly' is less plausible in the form '... not merely its loss but its quick loss', and the main difference is that in the former version the phrase 'sinking rapidly' forces one to read 'sinking' as an imperfect nominal, whereas 'loss' is perfect. This entire debate is transformed when the perfect/imperfect difference is given due weight, and attention is paid to Vendler's thesis that imperfect nominals name facts and perfect ones name events (Zeno Vendler, 'Facts and events', in his *Linguistics in Philosophy* (Cornell University Press, Ithaca, N.Y., 1967), pp. 122–46. See also Noam Chomsky, 'Some remarks about nominalization', reprinted in *Logic and Grammar*, ed. D. Davidson and G. Harman (Dickenson, Encino, Cal., 1975). In this part of my paper I have had to write as though, like everyone else, I thought one could discuss Davidson versus Kim without giving a central place to Vendler. In my forthcoming book on events I shall have room to sort all this out properly.

[8] Jaegwon Kim, 'Events as property exemplifications', in *Action Theory*, ed. M. Brand and D. Walton (Reidel, Dordrecht, 1976), pp. 159–77.

(1) John (2) journeyed from Belgium to Turkey (3) in the winter of 1983.

From this we get the sentence nominal:

John's walking from Belgium to Turkey in the winter of 1983.

The general form of this, according to Kim, is:

SUBSTANCE's having PROPERTY at TIME

and he offers to individuate events, when they are designated in this manner, through the principle that any two such expressions stand for the very same event if, but only if, they involve the same substance, the same property, and the same time. That leads to such conclusions as that John's *journey to Turkey* last winter was not his *journey from Belgium to Turkey* last winter, because although the substances and times are the same the properties – journeying to Turkey, and journeying from Belgium to Turkey – are different.

The other clear proposal is due to John Lemmon who, in comments on Davidson's first adverbial paper, suggested that event x is event y just in case x has exactly the same spatiotemporal location as y.[9] Lemmon remarked that this treats the individuation of events as being like that of bodies. Whereas Kim maps events onto substance–property–time triples, Lemmon maps them onto substance–time pairs (nearly enough). So long as John's verbing$_1$ at time T is located exactly where John is at T, it will follow that if he verbs$_1$ at T and verbs$_2$ at T his verbing$_1$ will be identical with his verbing$_2$. Not only will his walk from Belgium to Turkey be identical with his journey from Belgium to Turkey, but it will also be identical with his development of strong leg-muscles, if this occurred at the same time.

Event identity: the middle ground

Those are the extremes: Kim's events are sliced very thinly, while Lemmon's are thick. And nobody has yet staked out a clear intermediate position. Such a position would presumably say that two nominals refer to the very same event if they pick out the same substance, the same time, and properties which have to one another some relation R weaker than identity (Kim) and stronger than joint instantiation by S at T (Lemmon). The literature contains only two ideas about what R might be.

One, which has occurred to a number of philosophers, is that R is the relation that holds between two properties if one of them contains or entails the other.[10] According to this, R does not hold between journeying and walking,

---

[9] John Lemmon, Comments on 'The logical form of action sentences', in *The Logic of Decision and Action*, ed. N. Rescher (University of Pittsburgh Press, Pittsburgh, Penn., 1967), pp. 96–103.

[10] Judith Jarvis Thomson, 'Individuating actions', *Journal of Philosophy* 68 (1971), pp. 774–81; Monroe C. Beardsley, 'Actions and events: the problem of individuation', *American Philosophical Quarterly*, 12 (1975), pp. 263–76.

because you could do either without doing the other; but R does hold between walking and walking to Turkey, because you can't have the latter property without having the former. So John's walk is his walk to Turkey, but his walk is not his muscular development.

R on this account of it is a reflexive relation, so that it holds wherever identity does (and sometimes where it doesn't). The theory built on it will therefore endorse all Kim's identities (and some that Kim does not accept). This is what the middle-position theorist wants.

The danger is that this way of individuating events will turn out to slice them as thickly as Lemmon does. Consider the event of John's *going* to Turkey: our middling position identifies that with his walk to Turkey and his journey to Turkey, because walking there and journeying there each entail going there; and so the walk must after all be identified with the journey since each is identified with the going. And this can be generalized: let P_1 and P_2 be any two properties that substance S has at time T, then consider the property of having-either-P_1-or-P_2. The latter is entailed by each of the others, and so ... well, you can easily see where the argument goes. This supposedly intermediate criterion turns out to lie at one of the extremes, carving events as thickly as Lemmon's criterion does.

This collapse might be averted if there were no such item as the property of having one or other of two properties (and no such item as the property of having both of them, for that yields the same difficulty by a different route). But I don't think that anyone has tried to stiffen this middle-strength position by adding the starch of a suitably restrictive theory of properties, and I am not optimistic that it can be done.[11] The only published attempts to do it that I know of have not been promising.

The other published try for an intermediate position is Lawrence Lombard's.[12] He wants to tie event identity to a relation R that holds between any property and itself and also between any two properties that are interrelated thus and so in true total science. The versions of this that I have seen are hard to evaluate, however, and I can't usefully discuss the thesis until I get a clearer idea of just what it is. Still, I report Lombard's idea with respect: the idea that something causal might help to individuate events after all, but not through Davidson's unhelpful principle, deserves to be pursued.

No friend of events is entitled to turn his back on this problem. If there is an answer to the question of where the truth lies on the Kim-to-Lemmon continuum, we need to know what it is. (To say that there is no answer, I think, implies giving up events, at least for purposes of regimenting adverb-dropping inferences.) If the events theorist continues to square up to the problem, then, what are his options? I agree with Davidson that the data which make Kim's end

---

[11] In her comments on an earlier version of the present paper, Alison McIntyre offered a way of arming the middling position against this kind of attack. It puts two further constraints on the R relation: one simply bans disjunctive event properties; the other says something about part–whole relations between events, its intent apparently being to ban the promiscuous formation of conjunctive properties. I have doubts about this; but it is a fresh, original proposal which deserves to be published by its author and then properly discussed.

[12] Lawrence Brian Lombard, 'Events', *Canadian Journal of Philosophy*, 9 (1979), pp. 425–60.

of the continuum plausible are really about facts rather than events. So if the events theorist can't develop a tenable position midway between Kim and Lemmon, he ought to go with Lemmon and say that a sentence nominal of the form:

> x's verbing at T

is just one name for the totality of x's monadic states and processes at time T, and that other names for the very same entity are generated by all the different verb phrases which are also true of x at that time.

Lemmon: preliminary remarks

It's easy to find fault with this account of what an event is. It may seem obvious that:

> John's walk caused his muscular fatigue

could be true when it is false that:

> John's poetry lesson caused his muscular fatigue,

even if the walk and the lesson were both done by John at the same time and therefore counted as the same Lemmon event. But a friend of the Lemmon criterion can say that the lesson *is* the walk, that it *did* cause the fatigue, and that our resistance to the 'lesson caused' sentence comes from our hearing it as saying that the lesson caused the fatigue by virtue of its being a lesson. Of course *that* is false (the Lemmonist says), but it is also more than the sentence itself actually says. Does this seem stubborn and unreasonable? Well, it differs only in degree from moves that must be made in defending any middling position against Kim. Here is an example.

The iceberg drifted south-west: any middling theorist will say that this was *one* drift whose features included a southward vector towards the equator and a westward one towards the international date-line. Such a theorist must therefore say that:

> The iceberg's journey towards the date-line caused its melting

could well be true; and he must explain our resistance to this by saying that we hear it as meaning that the drift caused the melting by virtue of its mentioned feature (its westward vector), whereas really it means only that the drift caused the melting by virtue of *some* of its features.

Davidson has always kept his distance from Kim's end of the continuum, but apart from that he has taken no particular stand. His examples always suggest that he is entertaining some intermediate position, but he has never tried to stake one out; and he has always treated the Lemmon criterion with respect, never flatly rejecting it. In a reply to Quine at the Davidson conference, indeed, he joined Quine in going out to Lemmon's end. That sets him up nicely for the points I want to make, but I shan't inist on holding him to it. His more usual attitude of rather relaxed agnosticism, apparently assuming that his decision about Lemmon wouldn't much affect the rest of his theorizing about events, is also unsuitable, as I shall show.

Lemmon: the fatal difficulty

In a nutshell, if the Lemmon criterion is adopted then Davidson's treatment of adverb-dropping inferences collapses, thus depriving his ontology of concrete particular events of one of its best-looking supports. If John walks and learns at the same time, and if his walking is his lesson, then no inference of the form:

> John walks adverbly at T, so he walks at T

can be handled in the simple Davidsonian manner, namely by taking the premise to mean:

> There is a walking: it is by John, it occurs at T, and it is F,

where F is an adjective corresponding to the original adverb. Or, rather, that can't be said unless it is equally true that:

> John learns adverbly at T

and, more generally, that:

> John verbs adverbly at T

for every verb such that John verbs at T. In short, the simple Davidsonian treatment will work only for adverbs that truly modify every verb that fits the subject at the given time. The upshot is that virtually every adverb must be treated on a par with a noun-dependent adjective, having the form of 'x is useful as a muckraker', 'x is clean for a pig', 'x is slow for a walk', rather than of 'x is cubic', 'x is made of lead', 'x is radio-active'.

As I have just indicated, we'll get an adjective that is monadically applicable to the Lemmon event – i.e. predicable of it under any of its names or descriptions – if we can find one that goes truthfully with every verb that fits the subject at the time. There are cases of this. For example, if while John walked in Bologna he also verbed, then (whatever 'verb' may stand for) he did at that time verb in Bologna; and so we could say that his walk, understood as a Lemmon event, was in Bologna – this being true of it under each of its many descriptions.

But why drag in the event at all? Why not express the original sentence as saying that at the relevant time John walked (and John verbed etc.) and *John* was in Bologna? Any adverb that corresponds to an adjective which can be applied monadically to a Lemmon event will also correspond to one that can be applied monadically to *the subject of* the event. This lets us handle those adverb-dropping inferences without needing events as subjects of predication.

In that example, the adverb 'in Bologna' goes over into the adjective 'in Bologna', said of John; but in other cases things are trickier than that, and my general claim is just that when an adverb goes with all the relevant verbs it will correspond to *some* adjective that is true of the subject. Consider, for example,

John walked through Bologna between T and T*.

Read this in the weak sense in which if while walking through Bologna John also verbed, then he verbed through Bologna – e.g. he chewed gum through Bologna and sang the Marseillaise through Bologna and so on. (On another reading of it, 'He walked through Bologna' implies that he got through Bologna *because* he walked; but that's verb-dependent and thus irrelevant to my present topic.) Now, the adverbial 'through Bologna', taken in the weak sense I have proposed, is not verb-dependent, and so it corresponds to an adjective which is applicable to John in respect of the relevant time. But we can't say:

John walked and John was through Bologna

because the second clause is not English. Never mind. *Some* fact about how John related to Bologna during that period is the source of the truth of all those adverbial uses of 'through Bologna'; and it's of no importance that I don't know exactly how to word that fact in English. What matters is something I offer as obviously true, namely:

> 'John walked through Bologna between T and T*' – when construed so that 'through Bologna' is not verb-dependent – conjoins the statement that John walked during that interval with *some* statement about John's spatial relations with Bologna during that interval.

And so again we can handle the adverb-dropping inference without predicating anything of John's walk.

Temporal adverbs

Temporal adverbs need separate treatment. Part of the Davidson program is to account for the fact that:

John walked in Bologna *at midnight*

entails:

John walked in Bologna.

Davidson will handle this with help from:

> There was a walk etc. and it was at midnight;

apparently we can predicate being-at-midnight of the walk under any of its descriptions: it wasn't at midnight only *qua* walk, but also *qua* verbing generally. No monadic fact about John can generate all those truths. We derived adverbs from the fact that John was in Bologna, but we shan't derive any from the fact that John was at midnight: there is no such fact.

But this is not a good reason for reverting to a Davidsonian handling of temporal adverbs. It would be better to treat them as operators on sentences. Tense logic shows how useful it is to treat tenses as sentence operators, so that 'John will walk' means 'F(John walks)', where F is a futurity operator on temporally incomplete propositions. A treatment which works well for 'in the past (present, future)' can hardly be bad for 'at noon last Wednesday' and 'tomorrow morning' and 'throughout the seventeenth century'.

I don't say only that a Davidsonian treatment of temporal adverbs is not mandatory, because there is a legitimate alternative. I contend that the Davidsonian treatment is unacceptable. Here is why

Set time and tenses aside for a moment. It's clear that some adverbial modification *is* best treated in terms of operators on sentences. We are familiar with this fact as one that Davidson can adduce in explaining many of the adverbs that are not validly droppable – e.g. 'allegedly' and 'possibly' – but it extends to some that are validly droppable as well, e.g. 'notoriously'. Davidson could explain the entailment running from:

> Streicher notoriously used race prejudice for political purposes

to:

> Streicher used race prejudice for political purposes,

by saying that the former means something of the form:

> There was a use by Streicher ... etc., and it was notorious.

But it is not obviously worse to explain the entailment by saying (i) that the former means

> It is notorious that: Streicher used ... etc.

and (ii) that the operator 'It is notorious that: ...' cannot take us from a falsehood to a truth. Don't say that the sentence-operator treatment is worse because it invokes a fact (ii) about the meaning of 'notoriously'. It *does* involve knowing that it is one of the operators F such that if F(P) is true then so is P; but someone offering a Davidsonian treatment must be relying on that very same information about 'notoriously', for otherwise he would not know to handle 'He notoriously ... etc.' differently from 'He allegedly ... etc.'

So we need a sentence-operator treatment of adverbs in our repertoire in any case; it is clearly right in many cases where a Davidsonian treatment won't work; it seems all right in plenty of cases where a Davidsonian treatment *could* be employed; and it can be smoothly extended to do all the work for temporal adverbs.

I conclude that temporal adverbs ought not to be handled in Davidson's manner. If (a) the sentence-operator treatment were not already a going concern, and were attractive only as a way of handling temporal adverbs, and (b) the event approach had already earned its keep because some adverbs couldn't be handled without it, then we ought to prefer the Davidsonian procedure, quantifying over events. If one but not both of (a) and (b) were true, there would be a level contest between the two treatments of temporal adverbs. But in fact (a) is false; and we have yet to find evidence that (b) is true, i.e. to find work that can satisfactorily be done with events and not otherwise. So, on the present showing, we have a confrontation in which an independently valuable sentence-operator treatment competes with an event treatment which is to be introduced just for this one purpose. That is no contest.

Why the difficulty is fatal

Now here is a more serious challenge.[13] I have argued, in effect, that by the Lemmon criterion all the adverbs that Davidson wants his theory to handle go over into either:

1 predications on the subject of the supposed event; or
2 sentence operators; or
3 noun-dependent predications on events.

If I am right about that, then that abolishes what I have called 'the simplest' version of Davidson's program, in which adverbs go over into simple monadic predications on events. But does it challenge the whole program? Apparently not, for I have left 3 above, and that *is* an execution of the program. Davidson always intended his theory to deal with, among other things, the entailment from:

> John walked quickly etc.

to:

> John walked etc.

and he presumably knew that he would have to handle this with something like:

> There was a walk etc. and it was quick-for-a-walk,

---

[13] Until this final challenge is met, the present paper doesn't amount to much. I didn't see how important the challenge is until I was forced to do so by Alison McIntyre's comments. This is the biggest of several contributions she made to improving the thinking in this paper.

in which the final clause relates the walk in a certain way to the concept *walks* or the property of walking or the class of walks or some such. That was a complication, but not a gap in the theory; for Davidson could still handle the above entailment by attributing to 'John walked slowly' the form:

> There was a walk: it was by John and it had relation R to (walk),

where '(walk)' stands for the property of being a walk (or the like); and then simple logic provides the entailment to 'John walked', for when the second conjunct is dropped we are left with:

> There was a walk: it was by John,

which is to say that John walked.

Davidson thought that only some of his adverbs would involve such relatings of events to concepts or properties, and expected many to be treatable as monadic predications on events. So my argument offers him a little surprise. But does it offer more than that? I shall argue that it does, and that if Davidson sides with Lemmon he should drop his theory about how to regiment adverb-dropping inferences.

I shall rely on a principle that I also used in adjudicating between sentence-operators and events. The version of it that I now want goes as follows:

> We ought not to accept any proposal of the form: 'If we add Fs to our ontology we can handle x in simple logic; so let's add Fs to our ontology', if x can be brought within the scope of simple logic without the ontological addition, using only analytic devices that we are strongly committed to anyway.

In our present context, the relevant analytic device is *the use of dyadic predicates to relate particulars to properties in ways other than mere instantiation.* (In all of this, replace 'properties' by 'concepts' or 'classes' or 'verb-meanings', *mutatis mutandis*, if you wish.) That device lets us assign to 'John walks slowly' the logical form of a relating of *John* to the property of walking (i.e. being a walker). We don't have to say that:

> *The walk* was *slow for a walk*

which relates the walk in a certain way to the property of being a walk, because we can instead say that:

> *John* was *slow in his capacity as a walker,*

which relates John in a certain way – a different way, of course – to the property of walking. Similarly, the statement that:

> John played the violin incompetently

can be assigned the form of:

> John played the violin and he was incompetent *qua* violin-player,

which is to assert that John played and that a certain relation held between him and a certain property; and this is all we need to explain the entailments that Davidson wants explained.

Objection: 'In your endeavor to keep events out of the picture you have had to invoke a suspiciously wide variety of relations between things x and properties P. To handle 'John walked quickly' you have to suppose that all the specific ways of having the property of walking are on a speed-correlated scale and that John's specific way of having the property is in the upper half of the speed scale. To handle 'John walked with the aid of a stick' you have to say something to the effect that John used a stick to help him to have the property of walking. And so on. Isn't this evidence that you have started off on the wrong foot?'

I reply that this kind of complexity and disunity will be equally present in a Davidsonian treatment of the same materials. When I treat 'John walked with the aid of a stick' as saying that John walked and that a certain fancy relation held between him and the property of walking, Davidson must treat it as saying that there was a walk by John and that a certain fancy relation held between that walk and the property of being a walk. It's a different relation from mine, and of course a different property; but I see no reason to think that a Davidsonian treatment can offer more real unity of treatment, less complexity, a less cluttered conceptual landscape, than mine can. Of course he can stay at the level of abstractness that he associates with the vague phrase 'logical form', saying that 'He walked with the aid of a stick' has the logical form:

> There was a walk: it was by him, and it had R to the property of being a walk

(or to the class of walks, or whatever), and that it is no concern of his what relation R is. But I can and do say the same.

That's enough of a reply, but something else may be worth adding. It is that this same disunity or variety is obviously present in the whole range of noun-dependent adjectives, even where the question of events doesn't arise. Think of the differences amongst:

> It is a small elephant
> She is a superb violinist
> He is a facile speaker

These have in common that each states a relation between a thing x and a property P, but there are many differences – some of them deeply structural – amongst the relations. The first compares an object with the members of a certain class; the second compares an object with a certain ideal for a class; the third ... well, I'm not sure how best to describe what that does. Our language uses dependent adjectives or adverbs for profoundly various purposes, united only by the bare fact that in each of them a dyadic predicate relates a thing in *some* way to a property – some way other than instantiation, that is. That this should be true of my proposed handling of verb-dependent adverbs is better evidence that my proposal is right than that it is wrong.

I conclude, then, that if Davidson espouses the Lemmon condition for event identity, he ought to say of the cases of adverbial modification that he hoped to treat in his theory that they all fall into one or other of three categories:

1 predications on substances;
2 operators on whole sentences;
3 relatings of substances to properties.

Since these are all forms that we have to employ anyway, we aren't enlarging our repertoire if we invoke them to help us with adverbial modification. And with their aid we can bring within the scope of first-order logic all the entailments Davidson is interested in.

Incidentally, in all my examples so far the particular is said to instantiate the property as well as to have the other relation to it: a small elephant is an elephant, a facile speaker is a speaker, and so on. But lots of noun-dependent adjectives don't imply that the particular instantiates the property, though they do relate it to the property in some other way – as in 'fake Rembrandt', 'fictional bastard', and so on. The relations between particular and property become ever more various and hard to capture in a phrase.

But a relating of particular to property clearly *is* what these all have in common; and there is no obstacle to extending this to cover not only noun-dependent adjectives but also verb-dependent adverbs. From which I conclude that if Davidson adopts the Lemmon criterion he ought not to account for any adverbs in terms of predications on events; and so he will be committed to relinquishing one of his two main arguments for having an ontology of events.

15

A Decompositional Approach to Modification

JERROLD J. KATZ, CLAUDIA LEACOCK AND YAEL RAVIN

1 *Introduction*

In this paper we present a decompositional theory of modification in natural language. The special character of a decompositional theory is that it bases its account of compositional meaning on the structure revealed in analyses of the senses of syntactic simples. We will argue that a decompositional approach succeeds where non-decompositional approaches fail, because exposing the complex sense structure of syntactic simples provides the elements required to state the laws governing the contribution of the meaning of modifiers to the meaning of their heads. Theories that do not take decompositional structure into account can be shown to lack the power necessary to state these laws.

Non-decompositional theories base their treatment of the semantics of natural languages on applied predicate logics, so that predicate constants correspond directly to the syntactic simples of a language. On such theories, it is a logical fact that English has one syntactic element 'starve,' denoting the concept of dying from lack of food, but no corresponding syntactic element for the concept of dying from lack of water. In contrast, a decompositional theory claims that the lack of correspondence is a historical accident with no semantic significance. Further, non-decompositional theories cannot properly distinguish between sentences like 'the nurse injected the medicine painstakingly,' and 'the nurse injected the medicine painlessly.' Although the adverbials are syntactically alike, they are quite different semantically: one adverbial refers to the manner in which the injection was administered; the other refers to the sensation that the injection caused in the recipient. In representing the sense of 'inject' as a complex concept of a process whereby an agent forces a liquid into the body of a recipient, a decompositional theory provides formal apparatus to distinguish the way the action of forcing is done from the effects of the forcing on the recipient. Exposing semantic structure thus enables us to describe how sentences take modification in different ways. It also gives a more comprehensive account of compositional structure. The meanings combined to form the meaning of syntactic complexes are now the semantic elements in the decompositional structure of syntactic simples.

The most problematic aspect of current treatments of modification is how attributives operate on the meaning of their heads. We believe that there is no acceptable solution to this problem within any framework that does not expose decompositional structure. Davidson addresses the problem in 'The logical form of action sentences':

> Susan says, 'I crossed the channel in fifteen hours.' 'Good grief, that was slow.' ... Now Susan adds, 'But I swam.' 'Good grief, that was fast.' We do not withdraw the claim that it was a slow crossing; this is consistent with its being a fast swimming. Here we have enough to show, I think, that we cannot construe 'It was a slow crossing' as 'It was slow and it was a crossing' since the crossing may also be a swimming and it was not slow, in which case we would have 'It was slow and it was a crossing and it was a swimming and it was not slow.' The problem is not peculiar to talk of actions, however. It appears equally when we try to explain the logical role of the attributive adjectives in 'Grundy was a short basketball player, but a tall man,' and 'This is a good memento of the murder but a poor steak knife.' The problem of attributives is indeed a problem about logical form, but it may be put to one side here because it is not a problem only when the subject is action.[1]

As Davidson points out, Grundy would be short and tall, and the knife poor and good. Davidson sees no way to handle such attributive modifications in his system, but he recognizes that an account of modification must at some point come to grips with them. He thus shelves the problem of attributives on the grounds that it goes beyond the study of action sentences. But it is hard to see why the fact that the problem is more general than Davidson's chosen topic should be a reason for ignoring it in an explanation of the semantics of action sentences. Examples like 'Grundy shoots baskets well but too poorly to play pro ball' show that the same 'logical inconsistencies' appear in adverbial modification as well. This direct relation to action verbs should by itself be enough to keep the problem from being put to one side.

Before we look at how a decompositional theory handles the 'attributive paradox' in cases of adjectival modification, we should review the manner in which semantic markers represent complex structures of senses. Semantic markers, like phrase markers, are complex formal symbols whose orthography represents complex grammatical structure under conventions which interpret the representation relation. Semantic markers are written in the form of parenthesized expressions to distinguish them from other kinds of markers in grammatical notation. Semantic markers take the form of tree structures with labelled nodes, like phrase markers, but the branching structure represents sense qualification rather than syntactic subcategorization. A semantic marker of the form (M) represents a complex concept c^* as being built up out of the

---

[1] The logical form of action sentences,' in *The Logic of Decision and Action*, ed. N. Rescher (University of Pittsburgh Press, Pittsburgh, 1967), pp. 81–120, at p. 82 (reprinted in D. Davidson, *Essays on Action and Events* (Oxford University Press, New York, 1980)).

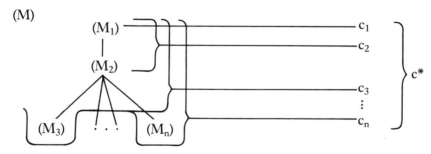

(M)

component concepts c_1, ..., c_n and the qualification relations among them. If we were to adopt Aristotle's concept of being human as the sense of the word 'human,' then c^* would be this concept, and the constituent branch structures shown in (M) would represent the concept's internal structure. c_1 would be the concept of a physical object, c_2 the concept of being an animal, and c_3 the concept of being rational. The concept of an animal is formed by qualifying the concept of a physical object, and the concept of a rational animal from qualifying the concept of an animal. The superordinate relations among the concepts c_1, ..., c_n and hence, derivatively, between the English words 'physical object,' 'animal,' and 'rational animal' that express them, are given by the branching braced in (M): c_1 is superordinate to c_2, c_2 superordinate to c_3, ..., c_{n-1}, and c_n; but, for example, c_3, ..., c_{n-1}, and c_n are not superordinate to one another.[2]

Component semantic markers in a complex semantic representation can be of the form (M′), where the *categorized variables* written to the right and slightly

---

[2] It should be noted here that Janet Fodor's criticism that semantic marker notation cannot handle superordinate relations (J.D. Fodor, *Semantics, Theories of Meaning in Generative Grammar*, (T.Y. Crowell Co., New York, 1977)), is mistaken. She writes:

> What must be faced is that the ultimate components of meaning are atomic in the sense that they are not components themselves decomposable into other smaller components, but are nevertheless internally complex in the sense that they CONTAIN other smaller components. Though the concept of being colored cannot intelligibly be SUBTRACTED from the concept of redness, it is nevertheless contained therein, and this fact must somehow be recorded. This is the way in which decomposition stops short before all significant semantic relations have been captured. At least some relations between concepts must be captured in a different fashion (p. 150).

Fodor simply fails to see that some primitive semantic markers can have complex branching structure and thereby represent an atomic sense with internal conceptual structure. To take her example, the concept of being red might be represented by the primitive semantic marker:

(Color)
|
(Red)

The sense of the word 'red' is represented by this complex semantic marker. But the symbol '(Red)' does not occur by itself. Thus, according to semantic theory, 'the concept of being colored cannot intelligibly be SUBTRACTED from the concept of redness.' Given that the superordinate concept of being a color is part of the structure of the concept of being red, it is represented as 'contained therein.' Hence, it is simply false to claim that decompositional representation fails to capture superordinate relations.

(M′) $((M_i)_{[F_1]\ [F_2]}\quad [F_n])$
                                         $(X),\ (X),\ldots,(X)$
                                         $<>\ <>\quad <>$

below '(M_i)' formally relate the senses of subjects, direct objects, etc., to the
sense of a verb, verb phrase, etc., in whose representation '(M_i)' occurs.
These variables are substitutions symbols to be replaced by semantic representations of subjects, direct objects, etc., in applications of the projection
principle.[3] The categorizations appearing in brackets over the variable are
syntactic or semantic symbols that pick out semantic representations to replace
the variable. For example, if F_i is the grammatical function [NP,S], then
semantic representations of the subject of the sentence can replace the
categorized variable, and if F_i is the semantic function for the agent concept,
then semantic representations of the particular agent concept in the sense of the
sentence can replace the categorized variable.[4] The projection principle says
that a semantic representation R can replace an occurrence of a categorized
variable V only if R has the syntactic or semantic categorization expressed in the
function F_i of V. The angles under the categorized variables state semantic
selection restrictions: the replacement of an R that has the appropriate
categorization takes place just in case R meets the semantic selection restriction
in the angles under V.[5]
    The categorized variables occurring in a complex semantic marker also
determine the argument places of the predicate that the marker represents: the
number of places is the number of distinct categorized variables occurring in
the semantic marker.[6] The semantic representation replacing a variable is the
term appearing in the argument place that the variable determines. The heavy
parentheses enclosing a variable represent the fact that the place is referential.[7]
    We can now turn to the 'attributive paradox' in the case of adjectival
modification. We may work with the example appearing in Davidson's discussion quoted above, namely (1).

(1) This is a good memento of the murder but a poor steak knife.

We take the sense structure of 'memento' and 'knife' to be roughly as
represented by the semantic markers (2) and (3), respectively.[8]

---

    [3] J.J. Katz, *Semantic Theory* (Harper & Row, New York, 1972), pp. 104–16.
    [4] J.J. Katz, *Propositional Structure and Illocutionary Force* (Harvard University Press, Cambridge,
Mass., 1980), pp. 77–87.
    [5] J.J. Katz, *Semantic Theory*, pp. 104–16.
    [6] J.J. Katz, *Propositional Structure and Illocutionary Force*, p. 68.
    [7] Ibid., pp. 63, 97, 101–5, 107–12, and 116–17.
    [8] See J.J. Katz, 'Semantic theory and the meaning of "good"', *Journal of Philosophy*, 61 (1964),
pp. 739–66 for a more detailed discussion of evaluative modification. We are leaving the selection
restrictions blank in almost all the semantic markers in the text in order for them to be easier to
present and read. In certain cases, we provide the semantic marker(s) that a selection restriction
requires a semantic representation to contain.

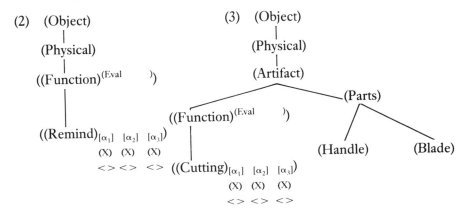

The evaluation is left undetermined by the meaning of 'memento' and 'knife', though it is determined in the case of a noun like 'bonanza.' The evaluation in sentences like 'that's a good knife,' 'that's a bad knife,' etc., is provided by attributive adjectives when their sense combines with the sense of nouns to form the sense of a complex noun phrase. Thus, the (Eval) node is left unspecified in the dictionary entry for nouns such as 'knife' and 'memento.' The projection rule introduces the values provided by the adjectives into representations of the decompositional structure of the nouns. The structures of the complex noun phrases of (1), 'good memento' and 'poor knife,' are represented by (2′) and (3′), respectively. (2′) represents a positive evaluation of the referent of 'this' in (1), saying that it adequately serves to remind. (3′) represents a negative evaluation of the referent of 'this' in (1), saying that it does an inadequate job of cutting. As (2′) and (3′) do not display semantic markers from the same antonymous n-tuple[9] immediately dominated by the same node, their conjunction does not represent an inconsistent sense.

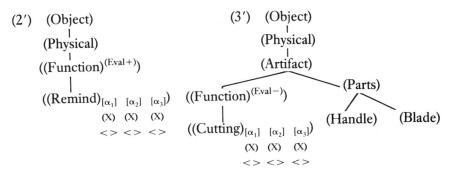

---

[9] Two semantic markers, $(M^{(i)})$ and $(M^{(j)})$, belong to the same antonymous n-tuple if they have a common base and different superscripts. The base represents concepts in the same domain, and the superscripts indicate incompatible elements within the domain. See Katz, *Semantic Theory*, p. 52 for a detailed analysis.

Our treatment explains why concepts devoid of either function or other aspects susceptible to evaluation (such as role) cannot be combined with attributives. Expressions such as 'good height' or 'good width' are semantically deviant without a contextually supplied standard of evaluation because the decompositional structures of 'height' and 'width' do not contain an evaluation concept. They become fully meaningful only when a standard of evaluation is supplied, as in 'good height for playing basketball' and 'good height for a coal miner.'

'Memento' and 'knife' have different sense structures since a memento is not by definition an artifact or something having parts. The marker (Eval) forms part of the representation of the decompositional structure of the nouns, figuring as a superscript within the representation of the element specifying the standard of evaluation. Its placement within the (Function) node captures an important fact about the semantic nature of nouns: the senses of 'knife' and 'memento' express evaluations only in terms of knives and mementos having a function, not in terms of knives or mementos being physical objects or having parts. Thus, 'that's a good knife' means that the knife cuts well, and 'that's a good memento' means that the memento adequately reminds. Hence, there is no inconsistency in (1) because the two adjectives operate on different elements in the sense structure of the nouns. The appearance of inconsistency is an artifact of frameworks in which adjectives are simply conjoined to nouns.

Example (4) is treated in the same way.

(4) Grundy was a short basketball player but a tall man.

The relative adjectives, 'short' and 'tall,' express a comparison in size between Grundy and the average member of a specified class. In forming the compositional meaning of (4), the meaning of 'basketball player' goes into the meaning of 'short' to specify one comparison class, and the meaning of 'man' goes into the meaning of 'tall' to specify the other. The adjectives determine the approximate position of the subjects in relation to the average height in the class. The property measured is determined by the meaning of the adjective – 'short' and 'tall' place concepts on a scale of relative height ('expensive' and 'cheap' on a scale of relative cost, etc.). A decompositional approach interprets (4) to mean that Grundy's height falls below the height of the average basketball player and exceeds the height of the average man. Since the property of height acquires different evaluations depending on whether it is measured relative to the category of men or to the category of basketball players, the relative nature of the modifiers would be lost, without the decompositional structure of the nouns that provides the contrasting categories.

We have sketched how a decompositional approach treats adjectival modification. The aim of this paper is to extend this treatment to adverbial modification. A semantic theory of modification must cover both, since the phenomenon of modification is a uniform one. Indeed, many noun–adjective combinations can be paraphrased with verbs and adverbs. 'This is a good knife,' for example, is synonymous with 'this knife cuts well.'

In the next two sections, we consider the treatment of adverbials within two non-decompositional theories, namely, that of Davidson and that of Thomason and Stalnaker.[10] We show that the apparatus in such theories gives rise to problems in the case of adverbial modification similar to those just discussed in connection with adjectival modification. In the final section we show how a decompositional theory can solve these problems for adverbials in the same manner that it solves them for adjectivals. We outline a general theory of modification based on decompositionality.

2 *Davidson's theory*

In 'The logical form of action sentences,' Davidson seeks 'to give an account of the logical or grammatical role of the parts or words of [action] sentences that is consistent with the entailment relations between such sentences and with what is known of the role of those same parts or words in other non-action sentences'.[11] The emphasis is on action verbs and their adverbial modifiers. Davidson classifies adverbial modifiers into three categories. The first class contains adverbials which impute intention, such as 'deliberately.' This class of adverbials operates on noun phrases that specify the agent. The second class contains attributive adverbials, like 'slowly,' which modify the verb's specification of an action. Davidson dismisses this class from his discussion for the reasons mentioned in section 1. The third class includes adverbials denoting time, place, and instrument. Davidson develops a detailed notation to represent the role of this class in the logical form of action sentences.

Davidson begins by looking at nominalizations and pronominalizations of action verbs. How can 'it' be represented in the logical form of 'Jones did it'? In Davidson's example, 'it' represents the buttering of a piece of toast, but in a standard account of such sentences there will be no argument place for the singular term expressing the event of buttering. Davidson's solution is to posit

---

[10] We have not considered the type of logic-based theory where the treatment of modification would be based on Carnapian meaning postulates (R. Carnap, 'Meaning postulates,' in his *Meaning and Necessity*, enlarged edn (University of Chicago Press, Chicago, 1956)). The reason for narrowing the scope of the present study is that there has been no coherent proposal of this type. We believe that this is not an accident but due to the problem of how to use meaning postulates in compositional constructions. But our reasons for thinking that this type of logic-based theory would not be adequate go beyond the problem just cited. We will ultimately conclude that the logic-based theories considered in this paper fail because they do not countenance enough logically significant structure. It is always an interesting question whether theories which severely restrict themselves in the structure they countenance can account for as much as those which countenance more. Our complaint against Carnapian logic-based theories, however, is the opposite: they countenance too much structure as significant for questions of compositional meaning. For these theories, any and all necessary connections into which expressions enter count as features of their meaning. There is no way to distinguish those deriving from sense from those deriving from mathematics or metaphysics. (See J.J. Katz, *Cogitations* (Oxford University Press, New York, in press), for a full statement of this criticism.) Since this is the case, if it turns out that the decompositional theory put forth here deals with the semantics of adverbial modification successfully, we can dismiss Carnapian logic-based theories.

[11] 'The logical form of action sentences,' p. 81.

an extra argument place for events. The logical form of every action sentence now contains one more argument place than it might seem to contain. For example, 'kicked' is a three-place predicate with a kicker, a kickee, and a kicking. This notation, as Davidson shows, can capture a number of entailment relations.

But there are some putative entailment relations that the notation does not capture because the notation is based on the standard restriction of logical vocabulary to logical particles. Davidson rejects any liberalization of logical vocabulary that would include elements that emerge on a meaning analysis, such as the factive element in the sense of 'know.' He writes:

> Admittedly there is something arbitrary in how much of logic to pin on logical form. But limits are set if our interest is in giving a coherent and constructive account of meaning: we must uncover enough structure to make it possible to state, for an arbitrary sentence, how its meaning depends on that structure, and we must not attribute more structure than such a theory of meaning can accommodate.[12]

This is a purely theory-internal argument for specifying which elements contribute to the logical form of sentences. The argument suggests that the semantics of the language can be tailored to fit the notation of a theory. But why should a theory of meaning for natural languages be arbitarily limited by the strictures of an artificial system?[13] The linguistic issue cannot be how much a particular theory can accommodate, but how much there is in the language to be accommodated. If a theory is too weak to accommodate what is in the language, then the theory should be changed. Taken to its logical conclusion, Davidson's argument would justify any theory, no matter how weak.

Owing to his theoretical framework, Davidson has to claim that meaning analysis of syntactic simples plays no role in the logical form of sentences. He writes:

> I am not concerned with the meaning analysis of logically simple expressions in so far as this goes beyond the question of logical form. Applied to the case at hand, for example, I am not concerned with the meaning of 'deliberately' as opposed, perhaps, to 'voluntarily'; but I am interested in the logical role of both these words.[14]

---

[12] 'The logical form of action sentences,' p. 82.

[13] There is, of course, a prepackaged answer to this question, viz., the limitation is not arbitrary because any attempt to go beyond it involves the notion of meaning which Quine has shown to be untenable in 'Two dogmas of empiricism' (W.V. Quine, *From a Logical Point of View* (Harvard University Press, Cambridge, Mass., 1953)). This is perhaps what Davidson has in mind when he motivates his introduction of the paradigm '*s* is T if and only if *p*' to replace '*s means p*' on the grounds that we thereby avoid becoming 'enmeshed in the intensional' ('Truth and Meaning,' *Synthese*, 17 (1967), pp. 304–23). But there is a rebuttal to this prepackaged answer which is that Quine's argument depends on the erroneous assumption that the tenability of meaning and other linguistic concepts rests on the possibility of providing substitution tests for them (see Quine, *From a Logical Point of View*, pp. 27–32, p. 56). This rebuttal is spelled out in a number of publications, most recently in J.J. Katz, *Language and Other Abstract Objects* (Roman & Littlefield, Totowa, New Jersey, 1981).

[14] 'The logical form of action sentences', p. 81.

The claim is that the logical role of both of these adverbials is solely to denote intention. Other adverbials denoting intention, such as 'maliciously,' would presumably share the logical role of 'voluntarily' and 'deliberately.' Thus, the principle entailments Davidson can derive from his representation of the logical form of 'Jones did it maliciously' are ones such that Jones's doing it was intentional. Other entailments, such as that 'maliciously' entails evil intention, cannot be derived.

The exclusion of decompositional analysis from his theory forces Davidson into a contradiction:

> we need not view the difference between 'Joe believes that there is life on Mars' and 'Joe knows that there is life on Mars' as a difference in logical form. That the second, but not the first, entails 'there is life on Mars' is plausibly a logical truth; but it is a truth that emerges only when we consider the meaning analysis of 'believes' and 'knows.'[15]

Thus Davidson grants that the meaning difference between the syntactic simples 'believes' and 'knows' determines entailment differences. But this contradicts Davidson's claim that such entailment relations are independent of logical form. Since entailments, on Davidson's account, are supposed to reflect logical form or truth conditions, how can there be entailment differences which correspond to no difference in logical form or truth conditions? Either logical form and truth conditions never coordinate with entailment, or they always do. Davidson cannot have it both ways.

Davidson's theory claims that each action verb contains an extra argument place filled by the event variable x. Thus (5) has (6) as its logical form.

(5) Jones buttered the toast in the bathroom with a knife at midnight.
(6) $(\exists x)$(buttered (Jones, toast, x))
    & (in (bathroom, x)) & (with (knife, x))
    & (at (midnight, x))

Davidson can now derive the entailment relations he wants, i.e.: Jones buttered the toast, and Jones buttered the toast with a knife, etc. But the derivation is made possible by introducing an argument place in the representation of action verbs, one which Davidson himself describes as a place 'that they do not appear to [contain].'[16] A decompositional theory, as we will show, can save the appearances. It can say that every action verb contains exactly the number of argument places that it appears to.

For the class of adverbial modifiers that impute intention, such as 'deliberately,' Davidson correctly claims that intentionality 'bears a special relation to the belief and attitudes of the agent ... but does not mean that the agent is described as performing any further action'.[17] As the logical form for sentences with intentionality adverbials Davidson proposes 'It was intentional of x that p.'[18] Yet Davidson would give different logical forms for verb structures that

---

[15] Ibid., p. 82.
[16] Ibid., p. 92.
[17] Ibid., pp. 94–5.
[18] Ibid., p. 95.

contain decompositional intentionality and for synonymous verb structures where intentionality is expressed by a syntactically independent adverbial. If an adverbial denoting intention is in construction with a verb, Davidson would represent intentionality in his account of logical form. If the concept of intention is included in the sense of a verb, then Davidson would not represent intentionality in the logical form. The synonymous sentences 'Jones killed himself intentionally' and 'Jones committed suicide' will be marked non-synonymous because Davidson's theory gives them non-equivalent logical forms. Again, the view that meaning analysis of syntactic simples does not contribute to logical form turns a historical accident (whether intentionality is expressed in two words or one) into a logical fact.

A corresponding difficulty for Davidson is that sentences like (7) and (8) cannot be marked as inconsistent.

(7) Grundy is a tall man and a midget.
(8) Jones sipped his milk with one huge gulp.

A decompositional theory is needed to represent the concept of tallness in the sense of 'tall man' and the concept of shortness in the sense of 'midget' as joint predications. Finally, although Davidson's theory acccounts for entailment relations like those from (9) to (10), and (10) to (11), it cannot account for ones like (11) to (12) because the semantic structure of syntactic simples is unavailable.

(9) Jones sipped a glass of milk before going to bed.
(10) Jones sipped a glass of milk.
(11) Jones sipped.
(12) Jones drank.

A decompositional theory accounts for entailments like (11) to (12) because it can represent the concept of 'drink in small quantities' as part of the sense of 'sip.' This will be shown in the final section.

3 *Thomason and Stalnaker's theory*

In 'A semantic theory of adverbs' Thomason and Stalnaker attempt to provide the foundations for 'a general semantic theory of adverbs.'[19] They discard Davidson's theory as 'explicitly narrow in its scope [because] adverbs such as "slowly", "greedily", "carefully" and "intentionally" [are] excluded; and we suspect it may prove even more narrow than he anticipated'.[20] The authors feel that Davidson's theory fails to explain the ambiguities in sentences containing adverbials. They see the focus of a general theory of adverbials as representing ambiguities that rise from the scope of adverbials. Rejecting Davidson's use of

---

[19] R.H. Thomason and R.C. Stalnaker, 'A semantic theory of adverbs,' *Linguistic Inquiry*, 4 (1973), pp. 195–220, at p. 196.
[20] Ibid., p. 196.

the logical operator of conjunction to attach adverbials to predicates, they introduce a more powerful device of intensional logic – abstraction – to express scope differences. Using abstraction, they develop two or more formal representations for English sentences that contain both an adverbial and a complex predicate, that is, a predicate containing conjunction, disjunction, quantifiers, etc.

Thomason and Stalnaker divide all adverbials into two categories on the basis of scope differences: *sentence modifiers*, whose scope includes the sentence as a whole, and *predicate modifiers*, whose scope includes the predicate only. The authors suggest four tests for assigning adverbials to these categories. An adverbial is a predicate modifier only if it fails all four tests and a sentence modifier if it passes at least one. Most adverbials in English turn out to be sentence modifiers on these tests.

Thomason and Stalnaker discuss the scope of adverbials in sentences containing complex predicates in connection with examples like (13):

(13) Reluctantly, John bought gas and changed the oil.

They claim that such sentences have two different readings and are therefore ambiguous. On one reading of (13), the scope of the adverbial is distributive over the conjunction, and the sentence can be paraphrased as 'John reluctantly bought gas and John reluctantly changed the oil.' On the second reading, the scope of the adverbial is collective, and the sentence can be explained as 'it was doing both that John disliked – say, because it cost too much – while he was not reluctant to do either separately.'

The authors claim that 'such formal differences of scope frequently correspond to distinctions with which speakers of English are familiar and which are expressed in English in a variety of ways.'[21] This may be so; nonetheless, these two readings do not correspond to two *senses* of (13). 'Reluctantly' specifies a mental disposition of John's, the agent, while he was performing the actions. Whether his disposition was caused by the combination of the two actions or solely by the first (and carried over to the second) or mostly by the first and only slightly by the second is not expressed by the sentence. Moreover, the sentence provides no semantic grounds for speculation about whether John would have been equally reluctant had he only to buy gas or change the oil. These hypothetical conditions merely reflect different situations that can satisfy the truth conditions of the sentence. The apparent ambiguity vanishes when the adverb is properly understood to attribute a mental disposition to the agent in performing the actions.[22]

---

[21] Ibid., pp. 199–200.

[22] Another apparent ambiguity is presented by S. McConnell-Ginet, 'Adverbs and logical form: a linguistically realistic theory,' *Language*, 58 (1982), pp. 144–84, in an attempt to improve on Thomason and Stalnaker's theory. According to the author, the following sentences differ in cognitive content:

(1) Reluctantly, Joan instructed Mary.
(2) Reluctantly, Mary was instructed by Joan.

'It has often been noted that [(2)] can be interpreted as attributing reluctance to Mary, whereas [(1)] unambiguously attributes reluctance to Joan' (p. 145). But 'there is no way to represent the

So evident is it that scope formalism predicts sense ambiguities where none exist that Thomason and Stalnaker themselves admit that their abstraction operator manufactures ambiguities:

> In many cases like these there seems to be no difference in meaning between the two scope readings of a single English sentence, even though the strategy of formalization predicts the existence of two such readings. In such cases, the absence of a difference in meaning may be ascribed to particular semantic properties of the lexical items appearing in the example.[23]

They seem to regard this situation as acceptable, offering no account of what these mysterious semantic properties are, nor any explanation of why we need such properties when the absence of a difference in meaning is predicted more simply by not assigning multiple scope.

Just as Davidson's use of logic forced him to arbitrarily reject part of a sentence's truth conditions as not pertaining to its meaning, so Thomason and Stalnaker's use of logic forces them to predict ambiguity where sentences are unambiguous. Instead of treating this situation like any other case of false prediction, Thomason and Stalnaker offer *ad hoc* explanations. When predicted ambiguities are not found in natural language, they find no fault with their theory: 'It may happen that one expression of English may be represented by more than one expression of our formalized language. There is much evidence to suggest that the formal operation of abstraction is hardly ever represented explicitly in English, and so is a plentiful source of such ambiguities.'[24]

Since Thomason and Stalnaker's formal apparatus is so plentiful a source of ambiguities that are not in English, why is it that they do not drop abstraction in favor of formal apparatus that does not cause trouble? The answer, we believe, is that their approach, like Davidson's, is limited to the apparatus in logic-based theories, and such referential apparatus characteristically transmutes situations in the world that satisfy the truth conditions of a sentence into distinct senses of the sentence. Referential apparatus does not suffice for handling such aspects of sense structure. The phenomenon of multiplicity of sense requires apparatus appropriate for individuating *senses*.

The trouble that Thomason and Stalnaker encounter with their use of abstraction is nothing new. A similar use of quantificational apparatus on the part of McCawley caused similar trouble.[25] McCawley claimed that 'John and Harry went to Cleveland' is ambiguous between the senses 'each went

---

non-synonymy of actives and passives with passive-sensitive adverbs if these adverbs are translated as sentence operators of the sort which Thomason and Stalnaker discuss' (p. 154).

McConnell-Ginet's claim that the approach of Thomason and Stalnaker cannot handle adverbials in general rests on allegedly ambiguous sentences like (2). However, these sentences are by no means clearly ambiguous in the language. Mary seems no more reluctant in (2) than she is in (1). Adverbials describing mental states such as 'reluctantly' or 'willingly' seem to modify the state of mind of the agent (see section 4 of this paper). Note examples like: 'Obediently, Mary was instructed by Joan,' which are deviant.

[23] 'A semantic theory of adverbs,' p. 200.

[24] Ibid., p. 212.

[25] J. McCawley, 'The role of semantics in a grammar,' in *Universals in Linguistic Theory*, ed. E. Bach and R. Harms (Holt, Rinehart & Winston, New York, 1968), pp. 152ff.

separately' and 'they went together'. Harnish has criticized this use of conjunction on the same basis that we have criticized Thomason and Stalnaker's treatment of (13), observing that 'John and Harry went to Cleveland' means nothing more than that John and Harry traversed some distance and arrived in Cleveland.[26] Possibilities like John's reluctance being caused mostly by the buying of gas and only slightly by the changing of oil parallel possibilities like John and Harry travelling together part of the way to Cleveland and separately the other part of the way.

Furthermore, the same mistake of treating sense phenomena with referential apparatus is made in some of Chomsky and Jackendoff's arguments for the Extended Standard Theory. Katz criticizes them as follows:

> The Chomsky–Jackendoff account claims that, in the pair 'Everyone in the room speaks two languages' and 'Two languages are spoken by everyone in the room,' the active sentence is two-ways ambiguous: between a sense on which it means that each person speaks the same two languages, and a sense on which it means that each person speaks two but not always the same two. But why not say, instead, between a sense on which it means each person speaks a different two, and one on which it means each person speaks two but not always a different two? Why not a three-way ambiguity combining these? Why not as many different senses are there are combinations possible for *n* people and *m* languages? This will lead to the embarrassing consequence that the sentence 'Every one of the seventeen people in the room speaks twenty-eight languages' is many more ways ambiguous than the sentence 'Every one of the eleven people in the room speaks sixteen languages' – and to the even more embarrassing consequence that the sentence 'Everyone in the room speaks infinitely many languages' is infinitely many ways ambiguous.
>
> Where and how is one to draw the line? The Chomsky–Jackendoff proposal allows only arbitrary decisions. No principle for drawing the line at one point can be given that is not matched by other principles, no better and no worse, for drawing it at the other points. This is because, in fact, there are not different senses to be separated. There is just a range of circumstances under which such sentences would be true; they could, with equal justice, be divided anywhere, so far as matters of grammar are concerned. The object NP of 'Everyone in the room speaks two languages' is not ambiguous because its truth conditions encompass the case of sameness of language and cases of non-sameness, any more that the subject NP of 'A parent can be too protective of his or her children' is ambiguous because its truth conditions encompass over-protective mothers and over-protective fathers.[27]

We believe that Thomason and Stalnaker, like McCawley, Chomsky, and Jackendoff before them, confuse the sense property of *ambiguity* with the reference property of *vagueness* or *indeterminateness between the different situations that will satisfy a truth condition*. We think that this confusion is due to the fact that their theoretical framework, lacking apparatus appropriate for representing sense structure, forces them to use inappropriate apparatus from the theory of reference.

---

[26] R.M. Harnish, 'Logical form and implicature,' in *An Integrated Theory of Linguistic Ability*, ed. T.G. Bever, J.J. Katz, and D.T. Langendoen (Thomas Y. Crowell, New York, 1976).

[27] J.J. Katz, 'Chomsky on Meaning,' *Language*, 56 (1980), pp. 1–41, at pp. 27–8.

After the discussion of the ambiguity of adverbials in sentences containing complex predicates, Thomason and Stalnaker proceed to discuss adverbials which modify the sentence as a whole and not just the predicate, such as 'possibly,' 'probably,' and 'unfortunately.' Thus, in (14) the adverb 'necessarily' modifies the proposition expressed by the sentence:

(14) 'Necessarily, nine is an odd number.'

Thomason and Stalnaker observe that 'necessarily' creates an opaque context, as is shown by the argument:

>   Necessarily nine is odd.
>   Nine is the number of the planets.
> _____
>   Therefore, necessarily the number of the planets is odd.

This leads them to claim that opacity is a test for classifying adverbs as sentence modifiers: 'Only if an adverb is a sentence modifier, can it give rise to opaque contexts everywhere in a sentence in which it occurs.'[28] The example chosen by the authors to support this test is (15):

(15) On a number of occasions the President of the United States has died in office.

'On a number of occasions' is said to be a sentence modifier because (15), which is true, yields a false sentence, (16), on substitution:

(16) On a number of occasions Richard Nixon has died in office.

The example is puzzling for several reasons. Will the same test classify 'on a number of occasions' as a predicate modifier in a sentence where substitution is valid, such as 'On a number of occasions the President has travelled to Europe' (valid substitution: 'On a number of occasions Richard Nixon has travelled to Europe')? Thomason and Stalnaker are unclear on this point. Be this as it may, their test is wrong in that it makes any adverbial that modifies 'The President of the U.S. has died' a sentence modifier. This has the consequence that the adverbials in sentences like 'The President has died painfully' and 'The President has died in his car' turn out to modify the sentence, when they clearly modify only the predicate. Thus almost all adverbials become sentence modifiers according to this test, and the category becomes proportionately less interesting.

Here, as in the case of the ambiguity of complex predicates, Thomason and Stalnaker's theory predicts distinctions not found in English sentences. There does exist in English a distinction between sentence modifiers and predicate modifiers. A good example of an adverb truly ambiguous in this respect is pointed out by Thomason and Stalnaker: '"Happily" is ambiguous, having one

---

[28] 'A semantic theory of adverbs,' p. 203.

sense (roughly equivalent to "fortunately") that is a sentence modifier and another (roughly equivalent to "gladly") that is a predicate modifier.[29] However, in order to determine, in cases of true semantic ambiguity, whether an adverb is a sentence adverb, a predicate adverb, or both, one has to examine the meaning of the adverb. Since Thomason and Stalnaker reject, like Davidson, semantic decomposition, they have no access to the source of adverbial ambiguity.

Not only is the substitution test too strong, in that it declares adverbials such as 'on several occasions' and 'in some restaurants' as sentence modifiers, it is also too weak, as it fails to detect some true sentence modifiers. As Thomason and Stalnaker themselves note, an adverb such as 'actually,' while modifying propositions rather than predicates, is transparent. To account for all other sentence modifiers, the authors suggest three more tests, all yielding the same puzzling results. The second test, for example, says that only sentence modifiers can 'give rise to quantifier scope ambiguities in simple universal or existential sentences.'[30] The test classifies 'frequently' as a sentence modifier on the grounds that '"Frequently someone got drunk," contrasts with "Someone got drunk frequently" (on one reading of these sentences).'[31] According to the authors, 'the semantic difference can be explained only on the assumption that "frequently" is capable of modifying the sentence "someone got drunk," and hence is a sentence adverb.'[32] By this test, 'quickly' will also be a sentence modifier, for 'Quickly someone volunteers' and 'Someone volunteers quickly' contrast in the same way as the 'frequently' sentences. However, 'quickly' must be classified as a predicate modifier because Thomason and Stalnaker cite its antonym, 'slowly,' as a clear case of a predicate modifier throughout their article. The tests are therefore not consistent in their predictions. They are too strong in classifying most adverbials as sentence modifiers. Finally, the situation becomes more confusing when Thomason and Stalnaker say they are not even sure the tests are sufficient: 'Though it is strong prima facie evidence that an adverb is a predicate modifier if it fails all four tests, we have no conclusive criteria that will prove it is not a sentence modifier.'[33]

---

[29] Ibid., p. 205.

[30] Ibid., p. 203. The third test relies on the first two. It says (on p. 204) that an adverbial is a sentence modifier if it 'includes within its scope an adverb or adverbial that has already been shown to be a sentence modifier, and if the whole rest of the sentence is within the scope of that sentence modifier.' Our discussion of the first two tests is applicable to this test. The fourth test (on p. 205) classifies an adverbial as a sentence modifier if 'one [can] paraphrase the sentence by deleting the adverb and prefacing the resulting sentence by *It is Q-ly true that.*' The authors claim that the test holds for their paradigm cases. Thus, 'Sam frequently sucks lemons' can be paraphrased as 'It is frequently true that Sam sucks lemons.' This confusion of the sentence type with a statement about the occurrences of its tokens is discussed in footnote 32.

[31] Ibid., pp. 203–4.

[32] Ibid., p. 204. There is a further problem with classifying 'frequently' as a sentence adverb. 'Frequently' is an adverb representing a parameter of temporal specification. It does not modify the predicate or the sentence as a whole but rather specifies the temporal conditions under which the sentence is true. 'Frequently someone got drunk' means that it was often true that someone got drunk. Because the sentence type itself cannot be either true or false, 'frequently' expresses the ratio of true to false tokens of the sentence. By accepting 'frequently' as a sentence modifier, Thomason and Stalnaker blur the distinction between terms that refer to tokens and are therefore metalinguistic and terms that are truly linguistic and modify the meaning of sentences they occur in.

[33] Ibid., p. 206.

Like Davidson's theory, Thomas and Stalnaker's fails to explain anomaly. They admit that their theory cannot rule out such sentences as 'John is slowly tall' or 'John slowly ignored the music.'[34] We observe that the reason for this failure is that the decompositional structure on which the anomaly rests is not accessible. The sense of the constituent modified by a rate adverbial like 'slowly' has to contain a concept of process or action in order for there to be a compositional combination with the sense of such a modifier. This is discussed below.

Thomason and Stalnaker discard some insights of Davidson's. Whereas Davidson carefully distinguishes adverbials modifying the agent's mental state from adverbials modifying the action, Thomason and Stalnaker dismiss this distinction, claiming that the adverbial ambiguously modifies different parts of the complex predicate. Similarly, they discard Davidson's classification of adverbials into time modifiers, place modifiers, and instrument modifiers. Davidson's exclusion of sentence modifiers from his discussion is appropriate, as such modifiers operate on propositions as a whole, and are, therefore, different from adverbials in action sentences. Thus Thomason and Stalnaker's theory, which is an attempt to improve on Davidson's, not only does not do so, but it introduces new problems.

4 *A decompositional theory*

In the first section of this paper we showed how a decompositional theory handles attributive adjectives in complex noun phrases. We showed that there are advantages in such a theory over non-decompositional theories. For example, a decompositional theory is not forced to incorrectly predict that (1) is inconsistent.

(1) This is a good memento of the murder but a poor steak knife.

The theory can correctly represent the modified noun phrase because it associates the sense of 'good' and 'poor' with different components in the internal semantic structure of the noun. In the present section we show how to extend the decompositional treatment to adverbial modification. Explaining modification on a decompositional theory is explaining how the sense of modifiers fits into the decompositionally exposed structure of the sense of its head to form a compositional sense for the entire modifier–head construction. This compositionally emergent sense is a new predicate whose meaning is more specific than the meaning of the head in virtue of the contribution of the meaning of the modifier. The compositional meaning of 'kill with a knife' is a case in point. (17) is a representation of the sense of the head 'kill' and (18) is a representation of the sense of its modifier 'with a knife.' (19) is a representation of the compositional meaning of 'kill with a knife.'

(17) represents the concept of killing as an action of the agent's which results in the recipient's death. (17) will distinguish the sense of 'kill' from that of a

---

[34] These examples are from ibid., p. 218.

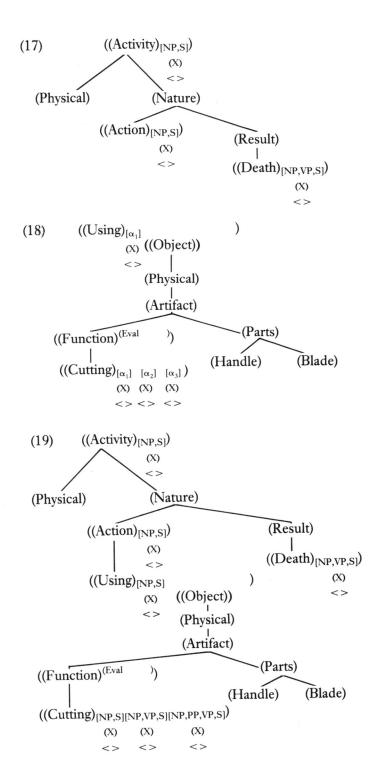

(17)   ((Activity)[NP,S])
                 (X)
                 < >

  (Physical)   (Nature)

          ((Action)[NP,S])
             (X)   (Result)
            < >   ((Death)[NP,VP,S])
                           (X)
                           < >

(18)   ((Using)[α₁]   )
           (X) ((Object))
          < > |
             (Physical)
              (Artifact)

((Function)^(Eval   )   (Parts)
     |
   ((Cutting)[α₁] [α₂] [α₃])   (Handle)   (Blade)
      (X) (X) (X)
     < > < > < >

(19)   ((Activity)[NP,S])
             (X)
            < >

  (Physical)   (Nature)

       ((Action)[NP,S])   (Result)
          (X)   ((Death)[NP,VP,S])
         < >   (X)
    ((Using)[NP,S]   )   < >
         (X) ((Object))
        < > |
          (Physical)
           (Artifact)

((Function)^(Eval   )   (Parts)
    |
                  (Handle)   (Blade)
((Cutting)[NP,S][NP,VP,S][NP,PP,VP,S])
      (X)   (X)   (X)
     < >   < >   < >

verb like 'murder' by the absence of a semantic marker representing the agent's intention to bring about the recipient's death in performing the action,[35] and distinguish the sense of 'kill' from that of a verb like 'gun down' by the absence of a semantic marker representing the action as firing a gun at the recipient. (18) represents a two-place predicate concept in which the agent of an action is related to the instrument of the action. The agent is left unspecified, but the instrument is specified as a knife. This latter specification is accomplished by having the representation of the noun 'knife,' as shown in (3), dominated by a node representing the sense of the preposition 'with.' That the sense of 'with' is the concept of an action performed with an instrument, as represented in (18), can be seen from the fact that expressions of the form 'with NP' are ambiguous: they can mean either by means of NP or accompanied by NP. 'Jones was killed with his dog' can mean either the dog was used to kill Jones or the dog and Jones were killed together. This account of the sense of 'with' is by no means idiosyncratic. Quirk and Greenbaum classify 'with' in both the instrumental category, as in 'someone had broken the window *with a stone*,' and in the accompaniment category, as in 'I'm so glad you're coming *with us*.'[36] All verbs can take the accompaniment modification, and all action verbs can take the instrument modification as well. Therefore, action verbs will often yield ambiguous predicates when modified by expressions of the form 'with NP.' The accompaniment sense of 'with' does not occur in our example, 'kill with a knife,' because an expression like 'Jones and his knife were killed together' is anomalous.

The derived semantic representation (19) is formed by the projection principle in application to the representations (17) and (18) for the verb 'kill' and its modifier 'with a knife.' In semantic theory there are three projection operations. One is the *embedding* of a semantic representation into another semantic representation by an operation of substituting the first for an occurrence of a categorized variable in the second. This operation was discussed in section 1. The second operation is a *conversion* of a semantic representation into another semantic representation, as for example, in the case of the interaction between the sense of a grammatical particle like negation and the sense of an expression in its scope. The third projection operation, which handles modification, is an *attachment* of the semantic representation of the modifier to the semantic representation of its head. The character of this operation is a consequence of the way in which branching structure in semantic markers represents a complex sense as a superordinate sense qualified successively by concepts that thereby give rise to the subordinate senses making up the complex sense. Such branching structure is what the attachment operation achieves.

Since the attachment that has to be accomplished by explicit compositional steps in cases of multi-word combinations like 'kill by shooting with a gun' is already there, fully accomplished, in the decompositional structure of a single lexical item like 'gun down,' the semantic representation of the latter tells us

---

[35] Katz, *Propositional Structure and Illocutionary Force*, pp. 69–77.

[36] R. Quirk and S. Greenbaum, *A Concise Grammar of Contemporary English* (Harcourt Brace Jovanovich, New York, 1973), pp. 159–60.

what the result of an attachment operation looks like. Thus, if there were a single lexical item 'knife down' in the way there is a single lexical item 'gun down,' the item would have the semantic representation (19). But, due to historical accident, English does not contain a lexical item 'knife down.' The sense is expressed by the multi-word combination 'kill by stabbing with a knife,' and hence, it is compositionally formed from the senses of 'kill,' 'by stabbing,' and 'with a knife.' Accordingly, (19) is the result of an operation of attaching (18) to the node labelled (Action) in (17).

Attachment is brought about by a projection principle with one of two operations, *appending* or *merging*. In appending, the topmost semantic marker of the semantic representation of the modifier is appended to an occurrence of a superordinate semantic marker in the semantic representation of the head. Whether a semantic marker is superordinate to another is also given in the *redundancy rules* of the dictionary.[37] (M_i) is superordinate to (M_j) just in case there is a redundancy rule of the form $(M_j) \rightarrow (M_i)$. Appending is formulated in (P′), where (M_m) is the semantic representation of the modifier and (M_h) is the semantic representation of its head:

(P′) If there is a semantic marker (M_i) in (M_h) which is superordinate to the topmost semantic marker in (M_m), *viz.* (M_j), attach (M_m) to (M_h) by making (M_j) a daughter of (M_i).

Appending occurs when a verb contains a node that can dominate the topmost node of the modifier. All (Action) nodes dominate a (Using) node because the former represent a concept that is superordinate to the concept represented by the latter. The attachment of 'with a knife' to 'kill,' forming 'kill with a knife,' discussed above, is an example of appending. In contrast, the semantic representation of a state verb like 'believe' contains no (Action) node to which (Using) can be appended because state concepts do not contain action concepts.

In the second attachment operation, merging, the topmost semantic marker of the semantic representation of the modifier is merged with an occurrence of that semantic marker in the semantic representation of the head. Merging is formulated in (P″):

(P″) If there is a semantic marker (M_i) in (M_h) which is the same as the topmost semantic marker in (M_m), attach (M_m) to (M_h) at this common semantic marker, merging redundant semantic markers.

(P″) operates on the semantic representations of adverbials whose structure is identical to part of the representation of the verbs they modify. The rule merges identical markers, and what is left of the adverbial representation then hangs off the representation of the verb. The semantic representation of the verb must contain a semantic marker that is identical to the topmost node of the semantic representation of the modifier if merging is to occur. When there is no such

---

[37] Katz, *Semantic Theory*, pp. 44–6, 99–100.

semantic marker, as in the case of the verb in an expression like 'believe with a knife,' the expression will be semantically anomalous. The failure of the projection principle to attach means that no derived semantic representation is assigned to the full expression. This marks 'believe with a knife' as semantically anomalous.

Consider another example: attachment of 'by stabbing' to 'kill,' to form 'kill by stabbing,' is an instance of merging. (17) represents the meaning of 'kill' and (20) represents the meaning of 'by stabbing.'[38]

(20)

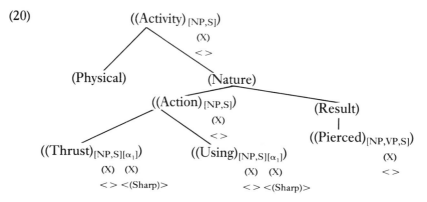

When the projection principle (P″) attaches the semantic representation in (20) to that in (17), the representation of the new predicate, 'kill by stabbing,' is formed, as shown in (21).

(21)

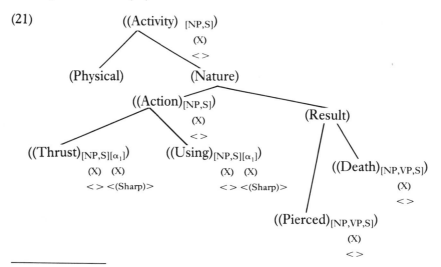

---

[38] The semantic representation of 'by stabbing' is identical to that of 'stab.' This is so because the semantic function of the preposition 'by' is to introduce the concept of activity to the adverbial, if needed. In the case of 'stabbing,' however, the representation of the verb already contains an (Activity) node, which therefore merges with the representation of 'by.'

The identical markers, like (Activity), (Nature), and (Result), have merged. All other semantic markers remain. When dominating nodes merge, their daughter nodes become sisters. For example: (Death) and (Pierced) are now sister nodes dominated by (Result). Unlike the conjunction principle of Davidsonian theories, the projection rule shown here does not require positing an extra argument place representing the event. Thus the only argument places which a decompositional theory has to posit are the standard ones for agent, recipient, and instrument.

Semantic anomaly results when the nodes in the semantic representation of a verb and its adverbial modifier can neither merge nor append. 'Kill by dreaming' is such an anomaly. Since 'dreaming' is a mental activity, its semantic representation cannot merge with the (Activity) node in the semantic representation of 'kill,' because the latter contains (Physical) and the representation of 'dream' contains (Mental). There is no possibility of appending either, because the topmost node in the representation of 'dream' is as high in the superordinate structure as the topmost node in the representation of 'kill.'

We can now show how synonymous expressions can have a single semantic representation regardless of the complexity of their respective syntactic structure. 'Kill by stabbing' is synonymous with 'stab to death.' Both have (21) as their semantic representation. The representation of 'kill by stabbing' results from the merging of (17) and (20). The representation of 'stab to death' results from appending the representation of the modifier 'to death' to the representation of the head, 'stab.' The representation of 'to death' has (Result) as its top node which merges with the (Result) node in the semantic representation of 'stab' (shown in (20)).[39]

Since decompositional theories can identify the same complex structure in the sense of both multi-word combinations and lexical items, the difference between lexical items and multi-word combinations can be treated as a matter of historical accident and rather than as a matter of logic. For example, such theories can give the same semantic representation (22) to synonyms like the single lexical item 'strangle'[40] and the multi-word combination 'kill by compressing the throat and causing choking,' as shown in (22) overleaf.

Theories like Davidson's, on the other hand, would represent 'strangle' as a single logical element and 'kill by compressing the throat and causing choking'

---

[39] It might appear that only one operation is necessary for the projection principle, namely the merging operation which merges identical markers in the semantic representations of the head and modifier. However, this reduction of operations would force us to add extra semantic structure to the representations of modifiers. For example, in order to attach a rate modifier, such as 'quickly' (see (33)), to an action verb, we would have to posit an (Activity) node as the topmost node of the semantic representation of the modifier in order to allow merging with the (Activity) node of the semantic representation of the verb. Consequently, the theory would predict ambiguity where none exists because it would require a different semantic representation for the same modifier depending on the type of verb it is attached to. In order to attach 'quickly' to a process verb such as 'die,' the topmost node of the semantic representation of 'quickly' would have to be (Process) in order to allow merging with the (Process) node of the semantic representation of the verb. Thus modifiers such as 'quickly' would have at least two semantic representations, hence two senses. Since having only one operation for the projection principle leads to this false prediction, we posit two operations of the projection principle.

[40] By definition, strangling is an act that results in the death of a victim. When the choking does not bring about such death, the act is only an attempted strangling.

(22)

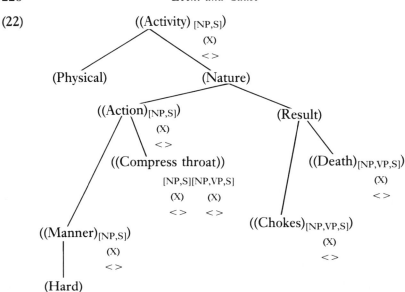

as a conjunction of logical elements, thereby failing to account for the synonymy of the expressions.

The sense of 'strangle' specifies the manner in which the action is performed; that is, this action is performed with a certain amount of strength. This is illustrated in the semantic representation of 'strangle.' As in the case of instrument modification, we posit that the (Manner) node appends to an (Action) node in semantic representations. Thus a decompositional theory predicts that any action can be modified by a manner adverbial. Similarly, the semantic representation of 'kill brutally' is formed by appending (Manner), the topmost node of the semantic representation of 'brutally,' to the (Action) node in the semantic representation of 'kill.'

A decompositional theory also captures the semantic property of analyticity in sentences such as (23).

(23) The man who strangled Bill killed him.

Informally, a sentence is analytic when the sense of one of its terms includes the sense of its main predicate together with the terms occupying the argument places of the main predicate. This is a generalization of the familiar Kantian definition of analyticity as containment of the predicate concept in the subject concept. The generalization is made in order to accommodate analytic transitive sentences like 'Mary marries those whom she weds.' On this informal definition, (23) is marked as analytic because the sense of 'the man who strangled Bill' in (23) includes the sense of the main predicate 'kill,' and its terms – 'the man' and 'Bill.'

A decompositional theory formally defines analyticity by means of a subtree relation. The tree structures of semantic markers represent complex concepts as constructed out of a base concept with qualifications that give rise to more specific concepts. The semantic markers representing these more specific concepts are subtrees of the tree representing the complex concept. A complex concept entails all the concepts that are subtrees of it. In order to specify the subtrees of a complex concept, we define the formal relation of the 'same-rooted subtree of.' It is generally intuitively clear when one structure is a same-rooted subtree of another. For example, in the case of a semantic marker of the form (M), its branches of the form (24), among others, are same-rooted subtrees of the marker, whereas its branches of the form (25) are not.

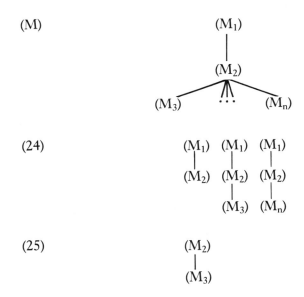

(M)

(24)

(25)

We take (M_i) to be the same-rooted subtree of any semantic marker whose topmost node is (M_i), including the semantic marker (M_i) itself. We do this to bring sentences like 'A killing is an activity' and 'A knife is an object' under the definition of analyticity.

A simplified version of the definition of analyticity is the following: a sense of a sentence is analytic if and only if the semantic representation of its main predicate is a same-rooted subtree of the semantic representation of one of its terms, T_i, and the representations of the terms occupying the argument places of the main predicate, $T_j, ..., T_n$, are same-rooted subtrees of the representation of terms occupying the argument places of T_i. $T_j, ..., T_n$ correspond sequentially to the terms of T_i. Somewhat more formally, the definition of analyticity is as follows: A sense is analytic in case its semantic representation is of the form (i):

(i) $P_{T_1}, \ldots, _{T_n}$

and some T_i, $1 \leqslant i \leqslant n$, which is of the form (ii),

(ii) $P_{t_1}, \ldots, t_m$

is such that $P_{x^1}, \ldots, _{x^n}$ is a same-rooted subtree of $P_{x^1}, \ldots, _{x^m}$ and each of $T_1, \ldots, T_{i-1}, T_{i+1} \ldots T_n$ is a same-rooted subtree of the corresponding term in $t_1, \ldots, t_m$. Under this definition, sentence (23) is marked as analytic. The semantic representation of 'kill' is a same-rooted subtree of the semantic representation of 'strangle,' and the representation of the terms occupying the argument places of 'kill' are, sequentially, same-rooted subtrees of the representations of the terms in the argument places of 'strangle.' Similarly, 'the man who strangled Bill performed an action' and 'the man who strangled Bill brought about Bill's death' are marked analytic as well, assuming appropriate representations of these sentences.

A second case of sense inclusion, analytic entailment, is illustrated in (26).

(26) (a) Jones strangled the bachelor at the stroke of midnight.

 (b) Jones killed the bachelor.
 (c) The bachelor is male.

Like analyticity, analytic entailment is defined using the same-rooted subtree relation. A simplified version of the definition of analytic entailment is the following: A sense analytically entails another sense in either of two cases. The first case of entailment is when the semantic representation of a sense, the entailed sense, is a same-rooted subtree of the semantic representation of another sense, the entailing sense, and for each semantic representation of a term in the entailed sense, T_j, there is a semantic representation of a term in the entailing sense, T_i, such that T_j is a same-rooted subtree of T_i. A somewhat more formal definition of this case of analytic entailment is as follows: A sense s^1 analytically entails a sense s^2 in case the semantic representations of s^1 and s^2 are such that the predicate of s^2, $P^2_{x^1}, \ldots, _{x^n}$, is a same-rooted subtree of the predicate of s^1, $P^1_{x^1}, \ldots, _{x^{n+k}}$, and also each of the terms in s^2, $T^2_1, \ldots, T^2_n$, is a same-rooted subtree of one of the terms in s^1, $T^1_1, \ldots, T^1_{n-k}$. The sense of the conclusion (26b) is included in the sense of the premise (26a). As can be seen from (17) and (22), the semantic representation of (26b) will be a same-rooted subtree of the semantic representation of (26a). Therefore, by the above definition, (26b) is entailed by (26a).

The second case of analytic entailment is when the semantic representations of two senses are such that one sense, the entailed sense, is analytic *and* the semantic representation of its including term is a subtree of the semantic representation of one of the terms in the representation of the entailing sense. And more formally: A sense s^1 analytically entails a sense s^2 in case the semantic representations of s^1 and s^2 are such that the latter is analytic (i.e. satisfies the definition given above), and the including term T^2_i is a subtree of some term in $T^1{}_1$, ..., $T^1{}_{n+k}$. The sense of (26c) is marked analytic and the semantic representation of its including term, 'bachelor,' is a subtree of the semantic representation of 'bachelor' in (26a).[41] Hence, (26a) is marked as analytically entailing (26c).

With the logical vocabulary expanded to include all of the vocabulary of the language, decompositional theories can capture the entailment differences between (27) and (28) without generating the logical contradiction implicit in Davidson's treatment:

(27) Joe believes that there is life on Mars.
(28) Joe knows that there is life on Mars.

(28), but not (27), entails that there is life on Mars because 'knows' is factive, whereas 'believes' is not. Given access to the decompositional structure of the syntactic simple 'know,' we can represent factivity in terms of a truth predicate internal to the sense of 'know.' The predicate has its argument place filled with the sense of the complement sentence when the sense of the verb phrase is formed.[42]

Expressions like 'free gift' are semantically redundant. Redundancy is also defined by means of the subtree relation: the sense of a head–modifier combination is redundant if and only if the representation of the sense of the modifier is a subtree of the representation of the sense of the head.[43] Such is the case with 'murder,' which has the concept of intention as part of its meaning. Decompositional theories predict that the predicate 'murder intentionally' is redundant, while 'kill intentionally' is not, because the representation of the intention in the representation of the adverbial is already contained in the representation of 'murder' (29).[44]

(29)

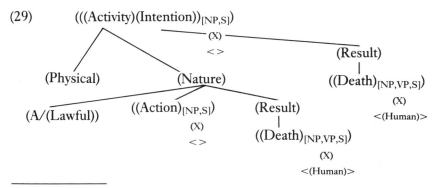

---

[41] As noted above, a semantic marker is a subtree of itself.

[42] The structure that fills the argument place is specified by the categorization variable for the complement sentence. The categorization variable will have the form [S,S,VP,S].

[43] Redundancy is sometimes used to emphasize a component of decompositional structure, as in 'free gift.' Redundancy then serves to stress the fact that no charge will be made. This feature of use further demonstrates the existence of the decompositional structure.

[44] Murder is by definition unlawful. The negation operation on (Lawful) is represented by A/. Thus the semantic representation of unlawful is (A/(Lawful)).

As Davidson points out, intentionality adverbials differ from the adverbials we have been discussing because the former operate on noun phrases that specify the agent. Since we agree with Davidson's distinction, we posit that (Intention) figures alongside (Activity), thereby sharing its categorized variables, as is shown in the semantic representation of 'murder' (29).

Decompositional theories can also mark contradictory senses, for example, in (30).

(30) Jones killed Bill unintentionally for money.

Reason adverbials indicate conscious motivation leading an agent to undertake an activity, and therefore their representations have (Intention) as their topmost node. The adverbial 'for money' is an example of a reason adverbial introducing the concept of intention into the meaning of the predicate. The representation of the modifier 'for money' has (Intention) as its topmost node, whereas the representation of the modifier 'unintentionally' is (A/(Intention)). The operator 'A/(M)' represents an exclusive alternation of all the semantic markers in the antonymous n-tuple to which (M) belongs, except for (M) itself.[45] A decompositional theory marks a sense as contradictory when its semantic representation contains two members of the same antonymous n-tuple dominated by the same node. Thus (30) is marked as contradictory because it is represented as expressing both intention and lack of intention of the same activity.

The sense of (31) contains both the concept of intending, from the semantic structure of 'promise,' and the concept of not intending, from the semantic structure of 'insincerely.'

(31) Jones insincerely promised to pay his college loan.

But (31) is clearly not contradictory. A decompositional theory can treat (31) as non-contradictory by distinguishing between the concept of purpose and the concept of intention. The concept of purpose is the concept of the objective of an *activity*, depicting what the act is structured to accomplish. Since purpose is part of the activity's structure, we posit that the (Purpose) node is dominated by the (Activity) node of a semantic representation (as, for example, the purpose of a promise is to undertake to do something). The concept of intention, on the other hand, is the concept of the objective of the *agent*. In a sincere promise, the speaker's intention is the same as the activity's purpose, while in an insincere promise the speaker's intention differs from the purpose. The intention in an insincere promise is the speaker's objective not to do what is promised.

As with intentionality adverbials, the representation of state adverbials figures alongside an (Activity) node and shares its categorized variables. These adverbials describe the state of the agent while performing an action. 'Reluctantly' is a state adverbial, as is shown in the semantic representation of 'kill reluctantly' (32).

---

[45] Katz, *Semantic Theory*, pp. 157–71.

(32)

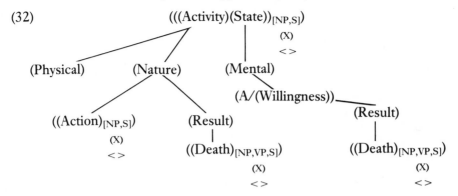

Since the semantic representation of 'reluctantly' figures at the top of the tree structure, it modifies the agent but not the action. Similarly, in (13) the modifier refers to the agent, not to either of the actions.

(13) Reluctantly, John bought gas and changed the oil.

As noted above, Thomason and Stalnaker's theory predicts that (13) is ambiguous. A decompositional theory can avoid making such predictions by attaching the representation of state modifiers directly to the representation of the agent as in (32).

Finally, a decompositional theory has the apparatus to treat rate adverbials such as 'slowly' in a consistent manner, while Thomason and Stalnaker's treatment leads them to inconsistency, as also noted. 'To kill quickly' is represented in (33).

(33)

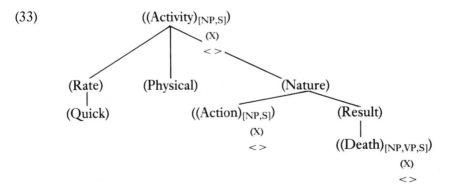

The sense of 'quickly' modifies both the action and the result of the activity. This is clear from the fact that when the agent peforms the action quickly but the death of the recipient is slow, the truth conditions of 'kill quickly' are not met. Therefore, the semantic representation of 'quickly' is appended to the topmost node of the semantic representation of 'kill,' i.e., it attaches to the

(Activity) node. This attachment also shows that every activity can be modified by rate adverbials.

We can summarize our discussion of the semantics of modification as follows: In sections 1 to 3 we presented a set of problems concerning modification. We diagnosed these problems as all stemming from a failure to take the decompositional structure of syntactic simples into account. This failure is inherent in all theories which do not analyze the meaning of syntactic simples. In section 4 we presented solutions to these problems based on a decompositional approach. We showed that taking decompositional structures into account solves all the problems in one stroke. In addition, we showed how our proposal can explain semantic properties and relations of adverbial constructions, such as ambiguity, synonymy, anomaly, analyticity, analytic entailment, redundancy, and contradiction. These solutions and explanations provide a strong argument for a decompositional approach to modification.

16

Underlying Events in the Logical Analysis of English[*]

TERENCE PARSONS

1 Introduction

The purpose of this paper is to explore the idea that many sentences of English can be assigned logical forms that make reference to, or quantify over, events, states, and processes. This idea was first proposed by Hans Reichenbach,[1] and was worked out in some detail by Donald Davidson.[2] As an illustration, the sentence:

(1) Mary saw John

could be assigned the form:

(2) *(Ee)[Seeing(e) & Agent(m,e) & Object(j,e)]*,

in which the variable *e* ranges over events, *Seeing(e)* means that *e* is an event of seeing, *Agent(m,e)* means that Mary is the agent of that seeing event, and *Object(j,e)* means that John is the object of the seeing.[3] This logical form is considerably more complicated than the symbolization that is normally taught in logic texts, which is simply:

(3) *S(m,j)*.

---

[*] This is a version of a paper presented to the conference at Rutgers on the philosophy of Donald Davidson. The paper is in part a reaction to work by Emmon Bach, Michael Bennett, David Dowty, and Barbara Partee – and, of course, Donald Davidson. In addition to the persons named elsewhere, I wish to acknowledge indebtedness to Brian Skyrms and Peter Woodruff.

[1] *Elements of Symbolic Logic* (The Free Press, New York, 1947).

[2] *Essays on Actions and Events* (Clarendon Press, Oxford, 1980).

[3] This is slightly different from Davidson's original proposal, in which all three conjuncts were combined into one single three-place predicate. For most of this paper, this difference is irrelevant; see section 6 for some ways in which the difference might be important.

The two forms are not incompatible, however, for we can just view (2) as a more refined version of (3). We do this by treating the traditional formula, $S(x,y)$, as a crude form which fails to display certain logical structure, the structure in question being that of:

(4) *E(e)[Seeing(e) & Agent(x,e) & Object(y,e)].*

But (2) is obviously much more complicated than the traditional symbolization, and one might naturally wonder whether – and why – the additional complication is necessary or desirable. The goal of this paper is to explore the idea that the more complicated forms are indeed desirable, because they allow one to account for certain phenomena that go unexplained by simpler theories of logical form.[4]

One phenomenon that Davidson's account handles in a nice way has to do with certain adverbial modifiers (certain adverbs together with certain prepositional phrases functioning adverbially). Davidson's idea was that these modifiers appear in logical form as predicates of events, so that a sentence such as:

(5) Agatha sang softly in the shower

would be assigned the logical form:

(6) *(Ee)[Singing(e) & Agent(a,e) & Soft(e) & In(the shower,e)].*

One advantage of this method of symbolization is that it accounts for the fact that sentence (5) entails each of the following sentences:

(7) Agatha sang softly,
(8) Agatha sang in the shower,
(9) Agatha sang.

For the logical forms of each of these are the same as the logical form associated with (6), with one or more conjuncts dropped out. With the given method of symbolization, the inferences are valid in the ordinary predicate calculus. The method accounts similarly for the fact that both (7) and (8) entail (9), and that the conjunction of (7) and (8) does *not* entail (6). I know of no significantly different approach to logical forms which accounts for these facts.

The appeal to events (and perhaps also to states and processes; see below) is not merely a logician's invention. Our language contains numerous common nouns that seem to apply to these things. Nouns such as 'accident' and

---

[4] I take a *theory of logical form* to be any theory which associates 'forms' with sentences in such a manner that logical relationships among sentences can be described solely in terms of relationships among those forms. Usually such a theory will also say something interesting about the way in which the truth or falsehood of the whole form associated with a sentence depends on the things in the world associated with the parts of the form associated with the sentence, and usually this will be relevant to the account of logical relationships given by the theory. I do not suppose that there is any unique correct theory of logical form. Indeed, if there is one correct theory then there must inevitably be many different (though equivalent) theories.

'marriage (ceremony)' appear to be true of EVENTS; nouns such as 'matrimony' appear to be true of STATES, and nouns such as 'evolution' seem to apply to processes. We even have systematic ways of producing these nouns; for example, the gerund 'killing' (in the construction 'a killing') seems to be a common noun that is derived by a regular process from the noun 'kill'. One theoretical issue has to do with how the referents of such nouns are related – if at all – to the entities that are appealed to in the semantical account of sentences which contain only the associated verbs. A tempting idea is that the nouns in question have exactly the meanings of the predicates which occur in the logical forms that – according to the view being explored – are associated with the corresponding verbs. Consider, for example, the following inference:

(10a) In every burning, oxygen is consumed.
(10b) Agatha burned some wood.
(10c) Oxygen was consumed.

The first sentence appears to contain a quantification over burnings; the second and third do not. Yet there must be some relation among them, for the argument that they make up is valid. In the theory being explored, the second and third sentences are assigned logical forms which *do* involve quantification over burnings, and the argument comes out valid in the ordinary predicate calculus. The logical forms are (ignoring tense, and simplifying somewhat):

(11a) *(e)[e is a burning → (Ee')[e' is a consuming & Object(oxygen.e') & In(e,e')]].*
(11b) *(Ee)[e is a burning & (Ex)[x is wood & Agent(Agatha,e) & Object(x,e)]].*
(11c) *(Ee)[e is a consuming & Object(oxygen,e)].*

Note that the verb, 'burn,' in (11b) and the noun, 'burning,' in (11a) both receive exactly the same representation in logical form. Additional evidence for the close relationship of explicit and implicit event talk is the fact that (12a) seems to entail (12b), and the only thing that prevents (12b) from entailing (12a) is that (12a), unlike (12b), seems to presuppose that the '*Star Spangled Banner*' was only sung once (during the relevant times in question):

(12a) After the singing of the '*Star Spangled Banner*,' they tossed the coin.
(12b) After the '*Star Spangled Banner*' was sung, they tossed the coin.

If 'after' stands for a relation between events, then the 'underlying event' approach can easily account for this relationship.[5] Probably there is some way of handling phenomena of this sort within more usual frameworks, such as a typed intensional logic, but the naturalness of the underlying event approach makes it at least worth exploring.

The layout of this paper is as follows. In section 2 I will discuss briefly the underlying ontology of events, states, and processes that will be presupposed in

---

[5] For some of the details see T. Parsons, 'Modifiers and quantifiers in natural language', *Canadian Journal of Philosophy*, supp. vol. 6 (1980), pp 29–60.

this paper, as well as some of the terminology that will be used in connection with these 'things'. Section 3 then presents rules for assigning logical forms to the simplest kinds of sentences under discussion. This section should at least be skimmed before proceeding to sections 4 through 6, though mastery of its details will not be essential for most purposes. The rest of the sections are mostly independent of one another. Section 4 contains a brief discussion of perceptual verbs which take events and processes as objects; it can be skipped entirely without loss of comprehension. Section 5 is taken up with a discussion of adverbials of Manner, Location, Instrument, Direction, and Motion. And the last section, section 6, contains a discussion of the individuation of events from the point of view of the theory developed previously. This section could probably be read on its own, though strictly it presupposes the material in sections 2, 3, and 5.

In an earlier paper[6] I discussed how quantified NPs (such as 'every woman') might fit into a framework like the present one, and I included a discussion there of certain temporal adverbials. That material will not be repeated here, and it will not be presupposed.

2 *The underlying ontology*

The account to be discussed presupposes that in addition to individuals and times, there are events, processes, and states (or 'states of affairs'). It is convenient to have a generic term to stand indifferently for events, processes, and states; I will follow Emmon Bach in using the term 'eventuality' for this purpose.[7] But the differences among events, processes and states will initially be important. As illustrations, I suppose that:

(1) Agatha is a doctor

reports a state (or reports that a state of a certain kind holds),

(2) Agatha ran

reports a process, and

(3) Agatha made a sandwich

reports an event. Eventualities usually have agents, and may also have objects. If Mary builds a bookcase then there is a building event of which she is the agent and the bookcase is the object. If she runs for a while then there is a process which has her for an agent and which has no object. If she is a doctor then there is a state (of affairs) of being a doctor which has her as agent and which also

---

    [6] Ibid.

    [7] E. Bach, 'Topics in English Metaphysics' in 'On Time, Tense and Aspect: An Essay in English Metaphysics', in R. Bauerle, C. Schwarze, A. von Stechnow (eds) *Meaning Use and Interpretation* (de Gruyter, New York, 1983).

lacks an object. The eventualities appealed to here are all 'individual' as opposed to 'generic'. For example, people sometimes speak of 'the state of being a doctor' as a state which many different people could be in. This is not the notion of state being utilized here. For present purposes Mary's state of being a doctor is a different state than John's state if he is also a doctor; both are different states of the same kind, that is, both states are in the extension of the common noun 'doctor.'

In the case of events, we can typically identify subparts which have a special significance for the present theory: an event often has both a development portion and a culmination. For example, if Mary builds a bookcase then there is a period of time during which the building is going on – the development portion – and then (if she finishes) a time at which the bookcase finally gets built, the time of culmination.

I do *not* suppose that every event has a culmination. If Mary begins building a bookcase but is struck down by lightning when three-quarters finished, then there is an event which is a building, which has her for an agent, which has a bookcase (an unfinished one) as object, and which never culminates. This idea is important for an analysis of the progressive, but it will not be pursued in this paper.[8]

Might there be events which have culminations but which lack development parts? Perhaps. In Zeno Vendler's classic discussion of eventualities[9] he employs four categories: *states* (our 'states'), *activities* (our 'processes'), *accomplishments* (events of the sort illustrated above), and *achievements*. Achievements are supposed to be something like instantaneous events; examples are Agatha's winning the race, and John's finishing the exam. Although these eventualities have causal antecedents, those antecedents are not supposed to be part of the eventuality itself in the way in which Agatha's building actions are part of her building of the bookcase. I am not sure whether there are any such things, but if there are they would be classified in the present account as events which have culminations but which lack development portions.[10]

There is an enormous literature on the 'Aristotelian' categorization of verbs of natural language into 'event'-verbs, 'state'-verbs, etc., with a wide variety of

---

[8] I think that Michael Bennett (in 'A Guide to the Logic of Tense and Aspect in English', *Logique and Analyse*, 20 (1977), pp. 491–517), uses *completion* in much the same way that I use the term *culmination*, except that where I will appeal in certain cases to *events* that do not culminate, he would not call these unculminated ('incomplete') things 'events'; he would reclassify them as 'activities' (my 'processes'). I use the notion of unculminated events to explain certain problems about the progressive in English in 'An improved theory of the progressive in English' (summer 1984 draft).

[9] *Linguistics in Philosophy* (Cornell University Press, Ithaca, N.Y., 1967).

[10] A test for an 'achievement verb' is supposed to be that it does not take the progressive. The trouble with the test is that most so-called achievement verbs *do* take the progressive. For example, 'win' is supposed to be a paradigm achievement verb, but 'Agatha is winning' is clearly a grammatical sentence of English. The question then arises as to whether the verb 'win' that takes the progressive is the same as the so-called achievement verb 'win', or only a homonym which means something like 'be in the lead'. I will remain neutral on this issue.

tests proposed for marking these distinctions. At best these tests form clusters, but they rarely coincide. There is also little agreement as to whether the distinctions originate in the world, as Aristotle seems to have thought, or are artifacts of our language, as Whorf would hold. I have little to contribute here in a direct way. Clearly, the approach under discussion supposes that we can distinguish, in a rough way at least, between events, processes, and states. The hope is that a theory which presupposes this distinction can simultaneously help to clarify it by filling in some of the details regarding its relationship to our language. In fact, in another paper[11] I make a suggestion that considerably simplifies the approach, by viewing processes as just special kinds of events, leaving us with a basic two-fold division of events and states. For present purposes, however, I will use the more traditional three-fold (or four-fold) distinction.

In the following sections I will be using certain symbols. I will always use e and e' as variables that range over eventualities. I will use $Cul(e,t)$ to mean that e is an event which culminates at t. I will use $Hold(e,t)$ to mean that the eventuality in question is holding at t, i.e., that e is a state and e's agent is in state e at t, or e is a process which is going on at t, or e is an event which is in development at t. For simplicity, I will suppose that if e is an eventuality then the set of times at which e holds forms a continuous open interval, and I will further suppose that if e culminates it does so at the end of that interval (that is, at its least upper bound). This presumes that there are no 'gappy' eventualities, that is, that eventualities do not hold for a while, then fail to hold for a while, and then hold again.[12] It is undoubtedly artificial in other ways as well, but it seems best to explore the theory initially with a simple picture in mind.

3 An initial fragment

3.1 Syntax

The fragment of English to be discussed in this paper will be developed in stages. In this section I give the syntax and logical forms for its simplest sentences. This part consists solely of sentences which consist of a name plus an intransitive verb, or a name plus a transitive verb and another name, where the verb is either in its present or past tense form, or else is tenseless and is preceded by 'will'. (I will occasionally speak of 'will' plus an untensed verb as the 'future tense' form of the verb.) The sentences will be ones like:

---

[11] See note 8 above.

[12] The only problem that I know of that this is relevant to has to do with the truth value of a sentence such as 'Mary is running', uttered at a time in the middle of her workout when she is taking a rest. There seems to be two different ways to take the sentence; in one way the answer is *yes*, and in the other way the answer is *no*. The same phenomenon is illustrated by the question 'Is someone sitting there?', accompanied by a pointing at an empty seat. I would account for the *yes* answers to these questions by supposing that the running (or the sitting) is an extended gapless process that holds even during the 'lulls'. This is not a substantive claim, but rather an explanation

John left.
John leaves.
John will leave.
Mary saw John.
Mary sees John.
Mary will see John.

The syntax could be presented in many different forms, corresponding to many different theories in linguistics concerning the proper form for a syntactic theory. I will choose a format that is similar in style to Montague Grammar. I use this format only because it is a convenient one to use when stating semantical rules. The resulting system of syntax-plus-semantics could be readily converted into other forms that are more popular in the linguistics literature.[13]

The syntactic categories that will be used in this section are:

NAME	('Proper Noun')
VERB	('Verb')
VP	('Verb Phrase' or 'Predicate')
CL	('Sentential Clause')
S	('Sentence')

I will suppose that we have available certain information that will allow us to further subcategorize examples of these categories. For example, 'walk' is an *intransitive* VERB; it is also a *process* VERB. Notions such as these could be represented in many different ways, such as by means of *features*.[14] In order to avoid getting bogged down, I will simply assume that this information is represented in some perspicuous way, and is available for the formation and translation rules to use when necessary.

To generate sentences, we begin with a vocabulary classified into parts of speech:

NAMES: Agatha, John, the burglar, the house
VERBS: run, leave, drive, alert, see

Clearly there is some idealization here, for 'the car' is not a proper noun of English. I will frequently take liberties of this sort in the interests of having a variety of examples to deal with, assuming that the lists above may be extended in obvious ways.

We will be making sentential clauses by combining NAMEs with VPs, so first we need to know what VPs are. The first two rules tell us this.

---

of how I intend the technical term *hold* to be understood. The *no* answer to these questions arises, I think, only in contexts in which it is clear that extended 'nonhomogeneous' processes are not what is at issue.

[13] 'Grammar, generative semantics interpretive semantics', in *Montague Grammar*, ed. B. Partee (Academic Press, New York, 1976).

[14] As introduced in N. Chomsky, *Aspects of the Theory of Syntax* (MIT Press, Cambridge, Mass., 1976).

R1: An intransitive VERB all by itself constitutes a VP.

R2: A transitive VERB plus a NAME make a VP.

So R1 tells us that 'run' (as in 'Agatha runs') is a VP, and R2 says that 'see John' is a VP.

R3: A NAME plus a VP makes an untensed CL.

This rule lets us make infinitival CLs, such as 'Agatha run' and 'Agatha leave the house.' These clauses will be used in forming certain more complex sentences using perceptual verbs, such as 'John saw *Agatha leave the house*' (in section 4 below).

Ordinary main clauses of English always contain tenses, and so we have the next to last rule of this section:

R4: If A is an untensed CL then the past, or present, or future tense version of A is a tensed CL.[15]

So now we have tensed Cls, such as 'Agatha left the house' and 'John will run.' We need one final rule which will convert clauses into sentences (i.e. CLs into Ss):

R5: A tensed CL may be converted to an S without change of spelling.

This rule tells us, for example, that 'John ran' functions both as tensed CL and as an S. At this stage, the import of this rule is primarily semantic. Its significance will be discussed below.

3.2 Logical forms

The semantics for the fragment of English that is being developed will be given indirectly. I will give rules which show how to associate a *logical form* with each well-formed constituent of the fragment, and I will suppose that these logical forms are themselves given a semantical treatment. But I will not discuss the semantical interpretation in any great detail. There are many different well-known ways to do this (all of them controversial); instead of choosing sides, I will just say enough to indicate whatever is special about the approach I am using.

The logical symbolism that I will employ is essentially a three-sorted version of the ordinary predicate calculus with predicate abstraction. Corresponding to

---

[15] See Parsons, 'Modifiers and quantifiers in natural language', for a brief account of the past, present, and future tense forms of sentences. This account must be carefully given, so as to abide by the 'sequence-of-tense' rules of English (ibid., notes 22 and 26). It is essential in an expanded fragment to allow that-clauses to be quantified in, just like ordinary NPs, so as to account e.g. for the proper generation of both 'John believed that Mary would win' and 'John believed that Mary will win'.

each of the three 'sorts' is a style of variable. I suppose that x, y, z, ... are variables that, in the intended interpretation, range over individuals, that t, t', ... range over moments of time, and that e, e', ... range over eventualities. I assume nothing out of the ordinary about individuals or times; eventualities will be discussed throughout. I will use the Greek letter λ to make 'lambda-abstracts' in the usual way, so that if A is a formula then $\lambda x A$ stands for a property of individuals, $\lambda e A$ for a property of eventualities, $\lambda t \lambda x A$ for a relation between times and individuals, and so on. I assume that we have an ordinary rule for abstract elimination/introduction, so that, e.g., $\lambda x[P(x)\ \&\ Q(x)](a)$ is equivalent to $P(a)\ \&\ Q(a)$, and $\lambda t \lambda e[Hold(e,t)](e',t')$ *is equivalent to* $Hold(e',t')$. If such notation is unfamiliar, the reader may either take some of the following details on faith, or may check a standard text such as Dowty.[16]

In a full development of English there would be need for a detailed theory of nonextensional contexts. I suppose that the language of logical forms contains, at least potentially, the resources to handle such contexts. However, almost none of the proposals discussed in this paper involve nonextensional contexts, and so I have found it convenient to ignore them.

The first step in associating logical forms with items of English is to do this for the individual vocabulary items. Given the meager fragment that we have so far we only need to specify that each NAME has associated with it an individual constant of the logical symbolism, and each VERB has associated with it a one-place predicate of eventualities (NOT a predicate of people or things, as in the usual approach). To make translation more perspicuous I will indicate the translation of each simple item of English into the logical symbolism by writing the item itself followed by an asterisk. Thus 'Agatha*' will be some individual constant of the logical symbolism, and 'alert*' will be a one-place predicate of eventualities. The ultimate intent is that when a semantics is given for the logical symbolism, 'Agatha*' will be assigned the woman, Agatha, as denotation, and 'alert*' will be assigned the property of being an alerting. Recall that *alert*(e)* is to be read '*e is an alerting*', not '*e alerts*'. To keep this obvious I will usually turn translations of verbs into their gerundive forms, writing *alerting*(e)* instead of *alert*(e)*.

Each rule of the syntax will now be expanded to include directions for translating its constructions into logical form; the directions will show how to produce the translation of the output of the rule given the translations of its inputs. The expanded rules are as follows:

R: An intransitive VERB all by itself constitutes a VP. Its translation as a VP is the same as its translation as a VERB.

R2: If A is a transitive VERB and B is a NAME than AB is a VP, and $(AB)^* = \lambda e[A^*(e)\ \&\ Object(B^*,e)]$.

So, by R2, 'leave the house' is a VP, and its translation, '(leave the house)*', is $\lambda e[leaving^*(e)\ \&\ Object(the\ house^*,e)]$. This is a complex predicate which is true of any eventuality if and only if that eventuality is a leaving whose object is the house.

---

[16] D. Dowty, *A Guide to Montague's PTQ* (Indiana University Linguistics Club, Indianapolis, 1978).

R3: If B is a NAME and A is a VP then BA is an untensed CL,
and:
if A is a Process or Stative VP then (BA)* =
$\lambda e\lambda t[A^*(e)$ & $Agent(B^*,e)$ & $Hold(e,t)]$;
otherwise, if A is an Event VP then (AB)* =
$\lambda e\lambda t[A^*(e)$ & $Agent(B^*,e)$ & $Cul\ (e,t)]$.

Here we have a change of category; any CL is going to translate into the logical symbolism as a relation between eventualities and moments of time. Crudely put, the translation of a CL will relate an eventuality and a time just in case the eventuality is of the sort picked out by the clause, and either it is a process or state that holds at the time in question, or it is an event which culminates at that time. For example; the untensed CL:

Agatha run

will, by R2 and R3, translate as:

$\lambda e\lambda t[running^*(e)$ & $Agent(Agatha^*,e)$ & $Hold(e,t)]$,

which relates any eventuality and time just in case the eventuality is a running whose agent is Agatha and which holds at the time in question. (If one or more of the inputs to a rule is itself an abstract, I suppose that abstract elimination applies whenever possible, so as to keep the translations simple.)

R4: If A is a tenseless CL then the past, present, and future forms
of A are tensed CLs, where:
Past (A)* = $\lambda e\lambda e(Et')[t'<t$ & $A^*(e,t')]$,
Pres(A)* = A^*,
Fut(A)* = $\lambda e\lambda t(Et')[t'>t$ & $A^*(e,t')]$.

(Comment on this rule will be postponed until after R5.)

Recall that our original goal was to produce for each simple sentence of English a logical form that says that *there is* an eventuality of a certain sort; for example, 'Agatha runs' is supposed to say '*There is* a running whose agent is Agatha'. So far this is not what we have; we have instead a logical form which stands for a relation between eventualities and times. Our last rule is designed to correct this situation:

R5: If A is a CL then #A# is an S, where (#A#)* =
$\lambda t(Ee)A^*(e,t)$.[17]

The hatches in #A# are there simply to distinguish A, functioning as a sentence, from A functioning as a CL; in practice I will almost always leave them off. The point is that our goal is to produce an S which has as its

---

[17] Although we want to end up with a logical form which says 'There is an eventuality of such and such a kind', it is important to postpone adding the quantifier, 'There is', until an advanced stage of sentence construction, so that we can expand on the 'such and such a kind' part, e.g. by the addition of modifiers. But *sometime* we need to put the quantifier on; this is the role of R5.

translation a predicate of times. The intended application of the theory is this: that *if A is an S then any given utterance of A is true if and only if the translation of A is true of the time of utterance.* Thus if I say 'Agatha ran' then what I say will be true if and only if the following is true of the time of my utterance:

$$\lambda t(Ee)(Et')[t' < t \text{ } \& \text{ } running^*(e) \text{ } \& \text{ } Agent(Agatha^*,e) \text{ } \& \text{ } Hold(e,t')],$$

that is, if and only if there is some time prior to the time of my utterance at which an eventuality holds that is a running whose agent is Agatha.

The tense rules given above require some comment. I will divide the comments by tense and by verb category.

PAST/EVENT: The rule for the past tense of an event sentence seems to be just right. We never use the past tense to report an event which has not yet culminated, even though it has been 'going on' for some time; on the other hand, it is always appropriate to use the past tense after the event has culminated.

PAST/STATE: The rule in question allows for a past tense state sentence to be true even if the present tense version is also true. That is, if Agatha has believed for some time now that Henry once betrayed her, then it is true to say that 'Agatha believed that Henry once betrayed her' even if she *still* believes it. I think that the rule is correct, and that our reluctance to say that Agatha believ*ed* something when she still believes it is to be explained by a kind of Gricean implicature; the present tense statement is usually more relevant, and so the use of the past misleadingly suggests the falsehood of the present. It is clear that this is only an implicature, however, since it is correct to say, 'Yes, she believed it; in fact she still does.'

PAST/PROCESS: A use of the past tense version of a Process sentence (such as 'Mary walked') seems to carry an implication that the process in question is *over*, even though the rule given does not require this. This problem can be solved by the revised treatment of process verbs given in the paper mentioned in note 8; I will simply ignore it here.

PRESENT/STATE: The present tense rule for stative sentences seems correct and unproblematic.

PRESENT/EVENT: The usage that is captured by the rule is the 'reportive' present, in which the present tense is used to report an event which is culminating at the time of utterance. An example is the sports announcer's exclamation: 'And Mary wins the race!' This usage is rare, and the rule in question explains why: it is never correct to use the present tense in its reportive sense with an event verb except at the exact moment of culmination of the event. In English the present tense is often used in other senses, such as the dispositional ('Agatha builds houses') sense. There is no treatment of these other uses in this paper.[18]

---

[18] Michael Bennett (in pp. 495–6) suggests that this analysis of the reportive present tense version of event sentences cannot be right since 'if someone says that John built a house last month, no one asks on which day and at what time he did it.' This is a serious objection, and I am unsure about what to say in response. I think that the peculiarity has less to do with the tense than it has to do with the temporal adverbials 'on' and 'at'. The difficulty is not confined to the present or past tense, nor is it confined to event verbs; it is equally peculiar to ask for the precise moment at which Mary will love Carlos (as opposed to the precise moment at which she will start to love him).

PRESENT/PROCESS: This is similar to the case of present tense event sentences; the present treatment is inadequate, but it can be improved by the revised treatment in the paper mentioned in note 8.

FUTURE/STATE/EVENT/PROCESS: In all cases the use of 'will' seems to carry with it an implication to the effect that the eventuality in question has not yet started to hold, and so it will lie entirely in the future. This is only an implication, since we can say things like: 'Of course I'll believe you; I already do, and I have no reason to stop,' or, 'Sit down and I'll make lunch; it's almost done already.'

There are a host of problems regarding the behavior of tenses in natural language; I have only said enough here to indicate that the rules given above are at least on the right track. For the time being, the rules given above provide a foundation for the discussion which follows.

4 *Perceptual verbs*

Is the generation of untensed CLs just a superfluous step along the road to generating tensed clauses, or are they needed for some other purpose? James Higgenbotham suggests[19] that these clauses appear on their own in certain sentences containing perceptual verbs, sentences such as 'John saw *Agatha leave the house*.' Suppose that in such a sentence the verb 'see' is treated as an ordinary transitive verb which picks out events (seeings) whose agents are people and whose objects are certain other events. A rule based on Higgenbotham's idea is the following:

R6: If B is a perceptual VERB and A is a nonstative tenseless CL
then BA is a VP, and (BA)* =
$\lambda e[B^*(e)$ & $(Ee')(Et')[A^*(e',t')$ & $Object(e',e)]].$[20]

Coupled with our earlier rules we can now generate sentences such as 'John sees Agatha run,' with the translation:

$\lambda t(Ee)[seeing^*(e)$ & $Agent(John^*,e)$ & $Hold(e,t)$ &
$(Ee')(Et')(running^*(e')$ & $Agent(Agatha^*,e')$ & $Hold(e',t')$ &
$Object(e',e))].$

This is true of a time if there is a seeing which holds at that time whose agent is John and whose object is a running which has Agatha as agent and which holds sometime. Notice that this translation does not require that the time of the seeing be identical with the time of the running. This is because it is possible to see (hear, notice, ...) someone run at a time that is later than the time at which

---

[19] 'The logic of perceptual reports: an extensional alternative to situation semantics', *Journal of Philosophy*, LXXX (1983), pp. 100–27.
[20] The actual statement of the syntax needs to be a little more complicated. In particular, if A begins with a pronoun, the pronoun takes the accusative case, and if A is in the progressive or the passive then the copula 'be' must be dropped.

the running takes place, because of the delay in light or sound reaching the percipient. If precognition is possible, an event may even be seen before it occurs. The fortuneteller who says 'I see you marrying a rich man' may be guilty of fraud, bad science, or even violations of our conceptual scheme, but the sentence *is* well formed, and it has a clear meaning, and it does not say that the marriage is taking place at the time of the seeing.[21]

The rule prohibits the formation of sentences whose objects are statives. It is not good English to say 'John saw Mary believe that snow is white.' And this is not just because believing is not the sort of thing that is susceptible to observation. It is equally bad grammar to say 'I saw the book be between the pencil and the cup.' It would appear that states are not among the proper objects of perception. Which is not to say that we cannot have knowledge about them based on perception – for you can see *that* the book is between the pencil and the cup.

Seeing that something is the case is quite different from seeing an event or process on which the seeing-that is based. Roughly speaking, you typically see *that* something is the case by combining knowledge of part of what you see with other knowledge that you have. For example, John knows (*de re*) that the man before him is Mary's uncle, and sees the man before him fall down. He may in this case know that Mary's uncle fell down, even though the man's being Mary's uncle is not part of what he sees. John has combined his nonvisual knowledge that 'he' is Mary's uncle with knowledge based more directly on perception – that 'he' fell down – and the result is what we might call indirect perceptual knowledge: he sees that Mary's uncle fell down. Given that Mary's uncle is also Fred's father, we may also infer that John saw Fred's father fall down, though not that he saw *that* Fred's father fell down. Tenseless clauses together with perceptual verbs do not create opaque contexts as that–clauses do. Our rules already sanction this; from '(John saw Cicero speak)*' and 'Cicero* = Tully*' we may infer by the ordinary laws of identity that '(John saw Tully speak)*'[22]

---

[21] This may be a different notion of *seeing* than the normal one, but the verb in question does enter into the construction being discussed.

[22] The analysis described here may call to mind recent work by Jon Barwise and John Perry in what they call 'situation semantics'. They too take the semantics of untensed clauses to be a matter of some importance. They also cite Davidson's original paper as a source for some of the ideas in their semantics, and they suggest that their *situations* are the same sorts of things as the things that Davidson says should be quantified over in the analysis of ordinary sentences ('Semantic innocence and uncompromising situations', *Midwest Studies in Philosophy*, 6 (1981), pp. 387–404, at p. 400). And Barwise at one point in discussing the analysis of the sentence 'Austin saw a man [get] shaved in Oxford' criticizes another view for giving us 'no way to assert that Austin saw a certain event', thereby suggesting that in situation semantics it will be *events* that are at least sometimes the objects of perceptual verbs ('Scenes and other situations', *Journal of Philosophy*, LXXVIII (1981), pp. 369–97, at p. 385). His analysis of *a sees B*, where b is an untensed clause, even resembles the form that is given by rule R6; it is:

(Es)(a sees s & s supports the truth of B).

However, this gives the wrong impression. Although there are some points of similarity, the two analyses differ in both form and content. (Higgenbotham presupposes this in his discussion in 'The logic of perceptual reports'. The following discussion may be taken as justification for his doing so.

The points made below should be tempered by the realization that 'situation semantics' is a theory undergoing a great deal of change, and it may be that it will change in a direction that will bring it closer to the underlying event approach.)

First let us compare them for form. We can initially bring them closer together by supposing that Barwise's term for *seeing* encodes the sort of structure used in Davidson's sort of analysis, that is, by supposing that:

$$a \; sees \; \epsilon$$

abbreviates:

$$(Ee')[seeing^*(e') \; \& \; Agent(a,e') \& \; Object(e,e')].$$

Then the analysis of *s sees B* given by Rule R6 above simplifies to:

$$(Ee)[a \; sees \; e \; \& \; B^*(e)],$$

which looks very much like Barwise's proposal. (I have suppressed all references to times to facilitate the comparison.) The only remaining step in getting the two analyses to have identical forms would be to suppose that Barwise's *e supports the truth of B* is a heuristic abbreviation for the $B^*(e)$ of Davidson's sort of theory. But this is not the case at all. The phrase *e supports the truth of B* is an abbreviation all right, but it is an abbreviation for a complex recursive definition whose form differs enormously from the fairly simple forms of $B^*(e)$. (See Barwise, 'Scenes and other situations', for a sketch.)

The analyses differ also as to substance, since the kinds of situations that Barwise and Perry appeal to in analyzing these sentences are quite different from the events under discussion in the present theory. Let me explain. Suppose that Mary shoots John, and that this is the one and only time in her life that she ever shoots anybody. Then consider the two different analyses of the sentence 'Agatha sees Mary shoot John' (again, ignoring times):

SIT.SEM: $(Es)[Agatha^* \; sees \; s \; \&$
                         $s \; supports \; the \; truth \; of \; Mary \; shoots \; John].$

EVENTS: $(Ee)[Agatha^* \; sees \; e \; \&$
                         $shooting^*(e) \; \& \; Agent(Mary^*,e) \; \& \; ...].$

Then according to the event approach there is exactly one event which satisfies the complex second conjunct of the analysis, namely, the event of Mary's shooting John. But according to the situation semantics analysis there are a host of situations which satisfy the second conjunct of *its* analysis. These include all of the various situations which have Mary's shooting of John as part (in a sense of 'part' to be spelled out by Barwise and Perry).

The analyses differ in their first conjuncts as well. According to the event approach there will typically be many different events seen by Agatha at the time in question. In addition to seeing Mary shoot John, she may also (simultaneously) see a fly land on Mary's nose. But on the situation semantics approach there is only one situation seen by Agatha at any given time, and that is, roughly speaking, the maximal complex situation which occupies the whole of her visual field at the time in question (Barwise, 'Scenes and other situations', p. 394).

Further, these differences in the conjuncts of the analyses do not cancel each other out. It is true that on both analyses there is a single thing (situation or event) which makes true the existential quantification. But on the event approach this is an event which can be seen not just by Agatha, but also by other observers on the scene. (This follows from the fact that both of the following sentences can be true:

Agatha saw Mary shoot John,

and:

Samantha saw Mary shoot John,

though there is only one shooting of John by Mary.) Yet on the situation semantics approach the situation which makes true the existential quantification is a situation which no one but Agatha can

5 *Adverbials*

5.1 Classification

I take *adverbials* to include adverbs, such as 'carefully,' prepositional phrases, such as 'with a knife,' and also certain other phrases that function adverbially, such as 'after Mary left.' For the purpose of this work I will divide adverbials into three main categories: intensional, temporal, and certain others which I will call 'normal nontemporal adverbials'. Intensional adverbials are those that create nonextensional contexts; they include examples such as 'necessarily,' 'probably,' 'happily' (in one of its uses), 'in a dream,' 'according to Samantha,' and so on. I will not propose an account of intensional adverbials. Such adverbials raise all of the problems that are typical of intensional contexts in general, and many ways of dealing with these problems are well known. I think that the 'underlying event' approach gives no special insight into these problems, nor does it create any special hindrances.[23]

Temporal adverbials include 'at 3.00,' 'during Lent,' 'after Mary left,' 'Thursday' (as in 'They will arrive Thursday'), and so on. I have discussed the relationship of some of these to the 'underlying event' approach elsewhere,[24] and I will not repeat that discussion here. Suffice it to say, I think that these constructions are of the utmost importance, and that the surface has barely been scratched where they are concerned.

The adverbials that will be discussed in some detail in this work are those of:

MANNER:	'slowly,' 'carefully,' ...
LOCATION:	'there,' 'in the park,' 'by the tree,' 'at the corner,' ...
INSTRUMENT:	'with a knife'
DIRECTION:	'toward Fred' (as in 'looked toward Fred'), 'at Mary' (as in 'looked at Mary'), 'across the room' (as in 'looked across the room'), ...
MOTION:	'into the room' (as in 'walked into the room'), 'at Mary' (as in 'threw the ball at Mary'), 'across the room' (as in 'walked across the room'), ...

I call all of these *normal nontemporal* adverbials. Note that many such adverbials seem to fall into more than one category. For example, 'at' forms adverbials of location when its usage overlaps that of the German 'zu', but it forms adverbials of direction or motion when its usage overlaps that of the German 'nach'. I

---

see – in normal cases anyway – since other observers will have slightly different visual fields than Agatha (Barwise, 'Scenes and other situations', p. 390).

Added March 1985: I have just encountered a paper by Frank Vlach (F. Vlach, 'On Situation Semantics for Perception', *Synthese*, 54 (1983), pp. 129–52), which makes most of these points and more besides. A somewhat different analysis of perceptual statements is given in more recent work by Barwise and Perry (J. Barwise and J. Perry, *Situations and Attitudes* (MIT Press, Cambridge, 1983)). However, the authors intend to modify that analysis in future work (J. Perry, personal communication), so commentary on it would be premature.

[23] This is discussed in Parsons, 'Modifiers and quantifiers in natural language'.

[24] In ibid.

suppose that these different uses correspond to different senses of the word. Perhaps they all have some underlying unity, but I will not discuss that issue in this work.

For the most part these are the adverbials that were discussed in Davidson's 'The logical form of action sentences'. His proposal there was to treat these adverbials as contributing predicates of events to the logical forms of the sentences in question, so that the sentence:

Mary walked slowly through the park with a cane

would have a form something like:

(Ee) (e is a walking by Mary & e is slow & e is through the park & e is with a cane).

Davidson specifically exempted two classes of adverbials from this treatment. One is a class epitomized by 'deliberately', the class of intensional adverbials. These adverbials cannot consistently be given the treatment in question because of failures of substitutivity. From:

(1) Mary deliberately shot the spy,

and

(2) The spy = the prime minister,

it does not follow that:

(3) Mary deliberately shot the prime minister.

(Or at least there is an interpretation of the sentences according to which (3) does not follow from (1) and (2).) But if we were to treat 'deliberately' as contributing a predicate of events, as above, then this inference *would* be sanctioned.[25] The intensional adverbials need some different kind of treatment.

Davidson also refrained from applying the analysis to 'attributives', such as 'slowly'. Here is his commentary:

> suppose we take 'Jones buttered the toast slowly' as saying that Jones's buttering of the toast was slow; is it clear that we can equally well say of Jones's action, no matter how we describe it, that it was slow? A change in the example will help. Susan says 'I crossed the Channel in fifteen hours.' 'Good grief, that was slow.' … Now Susan adds, 'But I swam.' 'Good grief, that was fast.' We do not withdraw the claim that it was a slow crossing; this is consistent with its being a fast swimming. Here we have enough to show, I think, that we cannot construe 'It was a slow crossing' as 'It was slow and it was a crossing' since the crossing may also be a swimming that was not slow, in which case we would have 'It was slow and it was a crossing and it was a swimming and it was not slow.'[26]

---

[25] See Davidson, 'The logical form of action sentences'.
[26] Ibid., pp. 106–7.

This reasoning used to convince me, but now I am not so sure. For one thing, the argument assumes that one and the same event is both a swimming and a crossing, which is something that would be denied by many event theorists. But even granting this, I think the apparent anomaly is only apparent: the swimming (that is, the crossing) can indeed be both slow and not slow if the word 'slow' has a different extension in the two conjuncts. And it seems clear that 'attributives' work in this way. Just consider this response to 'Is he working slowly?': 'Well *yes*, because he's only turning out three pieces per day, but *no* because they are all custom cut.' Here we haven't changed the word modified by 'slowly', as in Davidson's example, but we get an 'inconsistent' evaluation anyway. The truth of the matter seems to be that *evaluative* or *degree* words change extension with context. Their extension is usually determined by an implicit comparison class (*short for a basketball player, tall for a man*), and the noun or verb that is modified by the word in question usually makes a major contribution to the determination of that class.[27] This explains why we are inclined to say that the crossing was a slow crossing and not a slow swimming. But this explanation presupposes that the logical form of 'x is a slow crossing' is 'x is slow & x is a crossing', and indeed I see nothing wrong at all with this as the logical form. Similarly, for adverbials I see nothing wrong with analysing 'Agatha runs slowly' as *There is a running whose agent is Agatha and which is slow.*

5.2 The basic rule for adverbials

The idea sketched above seems simple enough, but it might be implemented in many different ways. The point of this section is to give an implementation that will provide a background for the consideration of some of the peculiarities of adverbial modifiers.

As a guide, notice that normal nontemporal adverbials, unlike intensional ones, all have the capacity of occurring in nontensed clauses. For example, all of the following are well formed:

> John watched [Mary walk *slowly* across the street].
> He saw [her cut the chicken *with a knife*].
> She saw [him look *at Fred*].
> He heard [the vehicle stop *by the corner*].

Intensional adverbials cannot occur in such clauses; the following are not English sentences:

> *Mary heard [*possibly* Agatha sing].
> *Mary saw [*according to John* Agatha run].

---

[27] But the word that is modified does not *determine* the comparison class, as it would have to for the operator approach to provide a good account of these modifiers. This is why I now doubt the operator approach for words like 'tall', though not for words like 'former'. In this connection see M. Siegel, 'Measure adjectives in Montague Grammar', in *Linguistics, Philosophy and Montague Grammar*, ed. S. Davis and M. Mithun (University of Texas Press, Austin, Texas, 1979). Note also that evaluative and degree words appear alone in predicates without modifying anything at all, so their analysis cannot presuppose that they modify something.

The following sentences could have different structures attributed to them; I suppose that when they are interpreted grammatically the intensional adverbials that they contain are part of the containing sentence, not part of the embedded untensed clause:

He saw [her stop] *according to Mary.*
He heard [Agatha sing] *in a dream.*

These examples suggest that normal nontemporal adverbials should get into clauses before tenses are put on. The following rule satisfies this constraint by generating such adverbials within the VP itself:

R7: If A is an adverbial and B is a VP then BA is also a VP, and
$(BA)^* = \lambda e[B^*(e) \ \& \ A^*(e)]$.[28]

In a more complete study we should allow adverbials to occur in parts of sentences other than at the end; we should be able to have:

Slowly he crept across the floor,
He slowly opened the door.

Apparently very little is known about the possible locations of adverbials in sentences, and the effects of their various locations on semantic interpretation.[29] Following Jay Keyser[30] I will presuppose the following *Principle of Transportability*:

PT: Adverbials may be moved from their source locations to other appropriate locations within clauses, without affecting semantic interpretation.

I will leave the task of specifying the appropriate locations to those with better linguistic skills than mine.

As an illustration of how rule R7 operates, let us generate 'walk slowly'. We already have that the translation of 'walk' is 'walking*'. Rule R7 takes this and 'slowly' as inputs and pumps out 'walk slowly', with the translation:

$\lambda e[walking^*(e) \ \& \ slow^*(e)]$.

---

[28] Since the logical forms of transitive and intransitive verbs are exactly the same in the present theory (i.e. they both yield one-place predicates of eventualities) we could simply have adverbials modify the verbs themselves. This would solve a type-proliferation problem in R. Montague, 'The proper treatment of quantification in ordinary English', in *Approaches to Natural Language*, ed. J. Hintikka, J. Moravcsik, and P. Suppes (Reidel, Dordrecht, 1970), pp. 221–42. I have not done this here because it would complicate somewhat the statement of the syntax. (E.g. the unmodified rules would yield things like 'Mary hit softly John'.) This could easily be altered.

[29] See R. Jackendoff, *Semantic Interpretation in Generative Grammar* (MIT Press, Cambridge, Mass., 1972).

[30] Review of Sven Jacobson, *Adverbial Positions in English Language*, (MIT Press, Cambridge, Mass., 1968), pp. 357–74.

Whereas simple adverbs stand for properties of eventualities, I assume that prepositions stand for relations between things and eventualities. A preposition plus its object will become an adverbial by the following rule:

R8: If P is a preposition and N is a NAME then PN is an adverbial, and $(PN)^* = \lambda e[P^*(N^*,e)]$.

For example, rule R8 combines 'in' with 'the park' to produce the prepositional phrase 'in the park', with translation $\lambda e[In^*(the\ park,\ e)]$; then our rule R7 would combine this with 'walk', yielding the VP 'walk in the park', whose translation would be:

$$\lambda e[walking^*(e)\ \&\ In^*(the\ park,e)].^{31}$$

As stated, rule R7 may reapply to its own output, so that after forming 'walk slowly' from 'walk' and 'slowly' it can then combine this result in turn with 'in the park' to yield 'walk slowly in the park'. A great advantage of this treatment is that it automatically yields certain inferences that are difficult to capture with other approaches. For example, consider the sentence:

(i) It landed clumsily in the back yard.

A double use of R7 will produce this sentence with the following translation (ignoring the past tense):

$$\lambda t(Ee)[landing^*(e)\ \&\ Agent(it^*,e)\ \&\ Cul(e,t)\ \&\ clumsy^*(e)\ \&\ in^*(the\ back\ yard,e)].$$

Then the translation of (i) will automatically entail the translations of (2)–(4) by means of the ordinary rules of the predicate calculus:[32]

(2) It landed clumsily,
(3) It landed in the back yard,
(4) It landed.

Likewise, (2) and (3) will each automatically entail (4), though their conjunction will not.

In the more conventional 'operator' approach,[33] these results could only be achieved by means of the introduction of special rules. For example, suppose that (1) is represented as:

(1a) *In the yard [Clumsily[Land]](it).*

---

[31] We might want to complicate the analysis somewhat and allow adverbials to have time-slots as well. E.g. we might want to say that there was a walking by Mary which was in the park at 11.05 a.m., but not in the park at 11.07 a.m. I am not sure about this.

[32] I.e. the translation of (1) is true of a time only if the translations of (2)–(4) are.

[33] Such as that employed in Montague, 'The proper treatment of quantification in ordinary English'.

Then not only will a special rule be needed to drop off outside operators to get:

(2a) *Clumsily[Land](it)*, and then
(4a) *Land(it)*,

we would need an even more special rule which would get us from (1a) to:

(3a) *In the yard[Land](it)*.

5.3 Nonextensionality

On the usual treatments, adverbs are thought to create nonextensional contexts. For example, consider the following argument:

(A) Mary drives slowly,
(B) Everyone drives when and only when they smoke,

so:

(C) Mary smokes slowly.

The inference is clearly invalid, and the second premise appears to state that 'drive' and 'smoke' have the same extension. If so, substitution of coextensive predicates in the context 'Mary ———slowly' does not necessarily preserve truth; that is, 'slowly' creates nonextensional contexts.

On the present approach, this reasoning is incorrect. Note that the logical form attributed to the above argument is this (taking t to represent the moment of utterance):

(A') *(Ee)[driving*(e) & Agent(Mary*,e) & Hold(e,t) & slow*(e)]*,
(B') *(x)(t)((Ee)[driving*(e) & Agent(x,e) & Hold(e,t)] ⟷ (Ee)[smoking*(e) & Agent(x,e) & Hold(e,t)])*,
(C') *(Ee)[smoking*(e) & Agent(Mary*,e) & Hold(e,t) & slow*(e)]*.

Clearly this argument is invalid in the ordinary predicate calculus. The trick is to observe that on the present analysis 'drive' and 'smoke' yield predicates of eventualities, not of people, and so *the second premise does not establish that they are coextensive*; it only says that an eventuality of the one kind holds when and only when one of the other kind holds.

But didn't I note at the beginning of this paper that the present analysis is *consistent with* the ordinary logic textbook analysis of predicates, which treats 'drive' and 'smoke' as predicates of individuals? Yes, but *these* predicates are not the ones that have been substituted for one another in (A)–(C) above. Perhaps an analogy will help here. Suppose for sake of argument that the predicates 'has a mother' and 'has a father' are coextensive. We can easily produce a context in which they may not be intersubstituted without guaranteed preservation of truth-value; it is the following:

(D) Mary *has a mother* who was born wealthy,

versus:

(E) Mary *has a father* who was born wealthy.

Should we then conclude that we are dealing here with nonextensional contexts? No, for when we display the (ordinary logic textbook) analysis of these sentences we see that we have *not* intersubstituted the predicates in question at all. For the predicates are those displayed by:

(F) *x has a mother = (Ey)(y is a mother of x)*,
   (G) *x has a father = (Ey)(y is a father of x)*.

And the former predicate, for example, does not occur at all in the analysis of (D):

(D') *(Ey)(y is a father of Mary & y was born wealthy)*.

Likewise, the logic book predicate *x drives* has, on the present analysis, the form:

(Ee)[driving*(e) & Agent(x,e)],

and this simply does not occur as a unit in the logical forms attributed to the sentences under discussion.

There are other false hints of nonextensionality lurking in the data, often arising out of the ambiguity manifested by many adverbials. For example, the adverb 'happily' may be used either as an adverb of manner, as in:

> She ran happily down the street,

or as a sentence adverb, as in:

> Happily, the war ended soon after it began.

The former sentence indicates that Mary ran in a happy manner; the latter does *not* indicate that the war ended in a happy manner. The sentence adverb 'happily' *does* create non-extensional contexts; this argument, for example, is invalid:

> Happily, the spy was shot,
> The spy = the best volleyball player in camp,

so:

> Happily, the best volleyball player in camp was shot.

'Carefully' is another adverb which manifests such an ambiguity.

Even within the category of adverbials treated here, ambiguities can give rise to false alarms. For example, Jerry Fodor gives the following objection to Davidson's analysis.[34] According to Fodor, the following sentence is ambiguous:

>   John aimed his gun at the target.

It can either tell us what it was that John aimed his gun at – the target – or it can tell us where John was when he did his aiming – he was at the target. But, says Fodor, Davidson's analysis offers only a single paraphrase, namely (ignoring times, and using the version of the theory given above):

>   *(Ee)[aiming*(e) & Agent(John*,e) & Object(his gun*,e) & at*(the target*,e)].*

True, there is only one form to be associated with the sentence, but the ambiguity of the English sentence may not be a structural one. The ambiguity can easily be explained if the preposition 'at' is already ambiguous. And it is. It has one sense which is roughly *in the direction of*; in this sense it translates into German as 'auf'. And it has another sense which is roughly *in the close vicinity of*; in this sense it translates into German as 'zu', 'an', 'auf', or 'in'. If the original ambiguity were structural, it would be peculiar for this to affect the lexical translation of the adverb itself.

Ambiguity also provides an answer to some puzzles raised by Hector Castañeda in response to Davidson's original paper.[35] (My example will be slightly different from Castañeda's.) Suppose that this is true:

>   I flew my kite over city hall.

Its logical form will be something like:

>   *There is a flying which has me as agent, my kite as object, and which is over city hall.*

But this entails:

>   *There is a flying which has me as agent and which is over city hall.*

which appears to be the analysis of:

>   I flew over city hall.

---

[34] 'Troubles about actions', in *Semantics of Natural Language*, ed. D. Davidson and G. Harman (Reidel, Dordrecht, 1972).

[35] 'Comments', in *The Logic of Decision and Action*, ed. N. Rescher (University of Pittsburgh Press, Pittsburgh, 1967).

The answer, as Davidson points out in another connection, is that the transitive verb 'fly' which applies to kite-flyings and the intransitive 'fly' used of people have different meanings, so that the 'flying used in the analysis of the first sentence is only a homonym for the 'flying*' used in the analysis of the second.[36] I will return to this issue in section 6 below.

5.4 From A to Z among the pines

In the ordinary logic text treatment, 'Mary walked to Chicago' is symbolized using a two-place predicate for *walk-to*, and its relation to the one-place *walk* is problematic. In the present treatment the problem is solved by treating 'walk' as a one-place predicate of eventualities, and conjoining to this a formula containing a two-place predicate representing 'to' that relates eventualities to things. A similar problem arises for certain constructions that traditionally have seemed to require even more than two places.

The standard logic text treatment for 'John walked from A to B' and for 'John stood between A and B' would normally require *three*-place predicates:

Walks-from-to(x,y,z)

and:

Stands-between(x,y,z).

How are these additional places to be treated within the present theory?

The answer is VERY SIMPLY – though the treatment of 'from … to …' will not be the same as 'between'. A clue to the treatment of 'from … to …' is to note that both of these prepositions can occur singly, as in:

walk to Chicago

and:

run screaming from the house.

Further, there seems to be a logical relationship between the 'from … to …' construction and its parts, since from:

Mary ran from the house to the barn

one can infer both:

Mary ran from the house

---

[36] Davidson actually suggests that the one might entail the other, though not as a matter of logical form. But his example involved flying a spaceship, not flying a kite, and this might be another sense.

and:

Mary ran to the barn,

whereas the former sentence does not follow from the latter ones, either singly or in conjunction. (This is what prevents us from analysing *Walk-from-to(x,y,z)* as *Walk-from(x,y)* & *Walk-to(x,z)*.)[37] This pattern should by now be familiar, and the proposed solution should surprise no one: a sentence containing 'from ... to ...' is simply a sentence with two adverbials, just like 'Mary walked slowly in the park'. Specifically, both 'from' and 'to' are ordinary prepositions of direction or motion, and a sentence such as:

John walked from the house to the barn

is to be symbolized (ignoring times and culmination) as:

(Ee)[walking*(e) & *Agent(John*,e)* & *from*(the house*,e)* & *to*(the barn*,e)]*.

No new rules are needed, and the inferences noted above are handled automatically.

The preposition 'between' is different, for it seems to require two distinct objects all by itself; the sentence 'Mary stood between the door' is not sensible. My view is that the problem with 'between' has nothing to do with its being an adverbial. Let me explain. In the use under discussion, to say that Mary stood between the trees is exactly the same as saying that she stood *among* the trees, except that the use of 'between' implies that there were two trees, while the use of 'among' implies that there were more than two – or at least that it is not known that there are only two. Now 'among' occurs most normally in constructions where it takes a *group* object, such as 'the trees'. A natural idea then is that 'among' relates an eventuality to a *set* or *group* of things, so that:

Mary frolicked among the pines

would include as part of its translation:

... *among*(the pines*,e)* ...,

in which 'the pines*' denotes a group of pines. I suggest that 'between' should receive the same treatment, so that:

John stood between the pines

would contain as a part:

... *between*(the pines*,e)* ...,

---

[37] For an extended discussion of these constructions within the framework of intensional logic, see D. Dowty, *Word Meaning and Montague Grammar* (Reidel, Boston, Mass., 1979).

with (perhaps) a meaning postulate or weaker convention that says:

between*(s,e) → *s has exactly two members.*

What then of:

John stood between A and B?

In this context, 'A and B' should denote a group or set whose members are the individuals A and B. This will explain the symmetry of the 'objects' of 'between', that is, it will explain the principle that if 'x As between B and C' then 'x As between C and B'. This suggestion requires additional rules to handle group NPs, but they are needed already to handle locutions unrelated to adverbials, such as 'The delegates assembled' and 'Mary and Carlos are twins'.

5.5 Conjunctions

Reiterations of rule R7 yield adverbials that are conjoined in logical form. In English, on the other hand, adverbials are only occasionally strung together with explicit conjunctions. Is this the same thing, or different? That is, is the sentence:

Kim ran into the room, across the floor, and out through the window

to be treated as the result of three applications of R7, as in:

Mary walked slowly across the park with a cane

or should it receive a different treatment? The question seems to boil down to the issue of whether or not the former sentence entails that there was one single eventuality which is correctly characterized by all three locutions, 'into the room', 'across the floor', and 'out through the window'. However, so little has been said so far about the nature of eventualities that it is hard to confront this question head on in this case. We can only look at indirect evidence based on other cases.

My suggestion is that explicit conjunction 'at the surface' is not a case of reiteration of R7, but is instead a result of something like the old CONJUNC-TION REDUCTION transformation. That is, the sentence above is short for:

Kim ran into the room, and ran across the floor, and ran out through the window,

where there is no entailment to the effect that it was one and the same running in every case. The implication that there was one running in question is only that: an implication. And even the implication seems to be absent in certain related cases. For example, if we say:

Juanita drove to the store and to the laundromat,

we would not normally take this to imply that there was only one driving that took place.

An insistence that surface conjunction must always be conjunction of adverbials leads to the following problem, discovered by John Wallace.[38] Consider the sentence:

> Mary hit the 8-ball into the side pocket and the 9-ball into the corner pocket.

If this were treated as containing a conjunction of adverbials, then part of its logical form would be:

> ... *Object(the 8-ball*,e)* & *into*(the side pocket*,e)* & *Object(the 9-ball*,e)* & *into*(the corner pocket*,e)* ...

But notice that this is logically equivalent to what you get by interchanging the two 'into*' clauses. And rearranging these two clauses yields the logical form for the logically independent sentence:

> Mary hit the 8-ball into the corner pocket and the 9-ball into the side pocket.

This is clearly wrong. The difficulty can be avoided by taking the CONJUNC-TION REDUCTION approach mentioned above, which allows there to be two distinct hitting events.

6 *Individuating events*

The foregoing account makes ample appeal to events, and one would be happier if these entities were better understood. At the moment, we cannot say too much more than that events are whatever it is that will work in the theory that has been given. But that may be quite a bit, for the theory does put some definite constraints on what events are to be. In this section I will address certain issues that have been much discussed in the literature concerning events and their individuation. But instead of trying to settle some of these issues by abstract philosophical argumentation, I will focus on what events would have to be like in order for the theory given here to be a good one. I will focus particularly on issues that have to do with the 'individuation' of events.

Davidson has made much of the fact that events commonly have alternative correct descriptions. One and the same event can be a moving of an arm, a stabbing of Caesar, a killing of Caesar, a murder, a deplorable (or laudable) action, and so on. Or so Davidson thinks. Others would hold that some of these descriptions cannot (or at least are not) redescriptions of the same event, but are rather descriptions of different but closely related events. The moving of the

---

[38] 'On what's happening' (Lithograph draft, 1966).

arm, though involved in the stabbing, is not literally the stabbing itself. Similarly, the stabbing is not the killing, though it is the cause of the killing, or perhaps part of the killing. Perhaps the killing is a murder, but some would not even admit this, unless it were thought that 'to kill' and 'to murder' are synonymous. Most people would allow that any one of these events might be deplorable.

When are two different descriptions descriptions of the same event? The question may be addressed a bit more clearly if we distinguish among various kinds of event descriptions. We sometimes describe events by using gerunds that derive from verbs, and adjectives that derive from normal nontemporal adverbs. The phrase 'slow crossing' is of this sort. I will call a description involving such words a *core* description. Alternatively, we can use nouns and adjectives that are not so derived. The noun 'accident' is not derived from any verb, and when we call an act 'right' this does not derive in any obvious way from an adverb. We also use certain special verbs which are not derived from action verbs, and whose subjects are taken to be events; an example is the verb 'occur' in 'The accident occurred at 3.00 on Friday'. Descriptions using these sorts of words will not be core descriptions.

Everybody agrees that events can have alternative descriptions when the descriptions use non-core terminology. My killing of the bank guard was an accident; it occurred at 3.00 on Friday; it was the right thing (or a deplorable thing) to do in the situation. Without the ability to redescribe events in such ways as these it would be hard to appeal to an already partially understood ontology of events in our theory. The controversies come with the core descriptions. These are of two sorts. One has to do with expansion and contraction of core descriptions. Suppose that I butter the toast slowly with a knife. Do the descriptions 'My buttering of the toast', 'My slow buttering of the toast' and 'My buttering of the toast with a knife' refer to the same event or to different though intimately related ones? For simplicity, assume that I only buttered the toast once (since otherwise the first description may not refer at all). Then the account given above *forces* the answer that the descriptions all describe the same event. That is, it does so in conjunction with the following two background assumptions:

(1) if I only buttered the toast once, then there is only one buttering which has me as agent and the toast as object, and
(2) the noun 'buttering' in the phrase 'My buttering of the toast' is the same as that used in the translation of the verb 'butter' given above, the genitive '*My* buttering' indicates that I am the agent of the buttering, the phrase 'of the toast' indicates that the toast is the object of the buttering, the meaning of 'slow' is the same as that used in the translation of 'slowly' given above, and the meaning of 'with' in 'My buttering of the toast with a knife' is the same as that used in the translation of 'with' in 'I buttered the toast with a knife'.

These are things that I have been taking for granted throughout this paper; they are needed explicitly to make the case that the descriptions in question are coextensive.

Regarding expansions/contractions of core descriptions the theory sides with Davidson and against some of his critics; at least some alternative descriptions that are related in this way must be descriptions of the same events. But there is another class of cases where the theory and Davidson sometimes part company. I have in mind certain alternative core descriptions which employ distinct gerunds. Here are some examples:

I kill Caesar by stabbing him. Is my stabbing him the same event as my killing him?

I pay my bill by writing a check. Is the check-writing the same event as the bill paying?

I kill some people by pouring some poison in their water supply. (They drink the water much later.) Is the pouring of the poison the same event as the killing of the people?

I signal by waving my arm. Is the signalling the same as the waving?

In all of the cases described above, Davidson wants to say that the events are the same,[39] whereas others wish to say they are different. What does the theory given above say?

The theory says different things in different cases. Let us start with a case congenial to Davidson. Suppose that I murder the bank guard. Then what of the alternative descriptions: 'My killing of the guard' and 'My murdering of the guard'? Well, the theory does not entail that these are coextensive, even given that there was only one killing and only one murdering. But the theory will say this if given a certain natural supplement, which is to add the principle that every murder is a killing. It will then follow that my murdering of the guard is identical with my killing of the guard. But why would we want to assume that every murder is a killing; isn't that just to beg the question at issue? No, there is an independent motivation. The motivation is that the supplemented theory automatically yields a host of inferences that the unsupplemented version does not yield. This is why I speak of *the theory* siding with Davidson here; *this* theory – perhaps unlike other theories – needs *this* supplementation in order to do its job of explaining uncontroversial inferences. The inferences are those such as that:

I murdered the guard with a shotgun at 3.00 in the bank

entails:

I killed the guard with a shotgun at 3.00 in the bank,

This and a host of others are all accounted for just by supposing that every murder is literally a killing, and then plugging this supposition into the theory. One result of this is to agree with Davidson that sometimes a core description can describe the same event as another which employs a different gerund.

But sometimes the theory disagrees with Davidson. Suppose that I pour the poison into the water supply, and thereby kill the people, and suppose for the

---

[39] See *Essays on Actions and Events*.

sake of argument that the pouring and killing are the same event. Since they are the same event, they have the same objects. It follows that I have poured the people into the water supply and killed the poison. Further, I have killed the people into the water supply, whatever that means.

It should be pointed out here that Davidson's original view is immune to this particular counterexample.[40] For his original idea as to how to analyze sentences did not involve splitting off the agent and object from the type of event. That is, instead of using three one-place predicates to symbolize 'Mary sees John':

(Ee)[Seeing*(e) & Agent(Mary*,e) & Object(John*,e)],

Davidson used a single three-place relation:

(Ee)[Seeing*(Mary*,John*,e)],

in which *Seeing*(x,y,z)* is to be read: *z is a seeing of y by x.* This fuses the 'of John' and 'by Mary' to the gerund, and prevents the reshuffling of agent and object that leads to the problem. However, this only means that more ingenuity is required to create problems. (This was noted by John Wallace.)[41] Suppose that I pay my bill by writing a check, and suppose, *pace* Davidson, that the check-writing *is* the bill paying. Then, since I have paid my bill with a check, I have written a check with a check. But I wrote the check with a pen, not with a check. Something is wrong here.

If Davidson and the theory disagree they cannot both be right. So a defender of the theory would do well to ponder the reasons that Davidson has for his views. His original reasons, at least, had to do with the 'logic of excuses'. Here is an illustrative quote from Davidson:

> 'I didn't know it was loaded' belongs to one standard pattern of excuse. I do not deny that I pointed the gun and pulled the trigger, nor that I shot the victim. My ignorance explains how it happened that I pointed the gun and pulled the trigger intentionally, but did not shoot the victim intentionally. That the bullet pierced the victim was a consequence of my pointing the gun and pulling the trigger. It is clear that these are two different events, since one began slightly after the other. But what is the relation between my pointing the gun and pulling the trigger, and my shooting the victim? The natural and, I think, correct answer is that the relation is that of identity. *The logic of this sort of excuse includes, it seems, at least this much structure: I am accused of doing* b, *which is deplorable. I admit I did* a, *which is excusable. My excuse for doing* b *rests upon my claim that I did not know that* a = b.[42]
> (My emphasis)

The 'logic' of this sort of excuse then seems to require four things (according to Davidson):

---

[40] Actually the original proposal does lead to the consequence that I kill the people into the water supply, but this might be filtered out on grounds of ungrammaticality, or for some other reason.

[41] 'On what's happening'.

[42] *Essays on Actions and Events.*

(a) I admit that I did *a*, where *a* is acceptable.
(b) $a = b$.
(c) I (now) admit that I did *b*, and *b* is deplorable.
(d) I did not know that $a = b$.

It seems to me, however, that clause (b) is irrelevant, and that (d) is not correctly formulated. For we can find cases where this sort of excuse fails entirely, even though all of (a)–(d) are satisfied. Just consider a case in which the agent freely admits that he knew all along that he was doing *b*, but that clauses (a)–(d) are all true. Clearly the 'excuse' would be no excuse at all. How could this happen? Well, suppose that he knowingly pointed the gun and pulled the trigger and also knowingly shot the victim (perhaps intentionally and with malice). Suppose also that he now asserts that the pointing/pulling (which, for the sake of Davidson's example, we suppose to be 'acceptable') was the same event as the shooting, but that he did not know this at the time. That is, he knew that he was shooting the victim, but he thought at the time that this was a different act, perhaps a consequence of the pointing/pulling, or perhaps a larger event of which the pointing/pulling was only a part. So clause (d) is satisfied, as well as (a)–(c). Yet the 'excuse' does not work. What the clauses above have left out is that the agent should *not know* at the time of acting that he was doing *b*. That is, we need:

(e) I did not know that I was doing *b*.

The absence of (e) could be easily overlooked because of the presence of (d). But (d) is merely (normally) symptomatic of (e), it does not entail (e).

But once we have added (e), neither (b) nor (d) is any longer necessary. It is both necessary and sufficient for the excuse (in the presence of (a) and (c)) that I was unaware that I was doing *b*. But then the rationale for the inclusion of (b) disappears, and with it goes Davidson's reason for holding that the logic of excuses requires various instances of event identity.

Or does it? It appears now that perhaps something vital has been left out. What is left out is the connection between *a* and *b*. The pattern of excusing seems in fact to have two elements. One is the part that (perhaps) lets you avoid blame on the grounds that you did not know what you were doing (e.g. you did not know that you were shooting the victim). The other part explains how it was that you came to do this thing without realizing that you were doing it. Davidson's suggestion is that the trick is to explain how you came to do something that you knew you were doing (e.g. you were pointing the gun and pulling the trigger), and then add that this was the very same event as the one that needs explanation. But the obvious comment here is that all sorts of relations short of identity might work as well in the explanation. Certainly it would be just as good an explanation to explain that shooting the victim is an unforeseen *causal consequence* of the pulling and pointing. Or that the shooting had two parts, the first part being the pointing/pulling and the second part, namely the motion of the bullet, being an unforeseen causal consequence of the first part. I am not endorsing these proposals, I am merely pointing out that there are alternative ways to understand the logic of excuses that do not force on us Davidson's views about event identity. And so I think that the theory sketched above concerning the logical forms of sentences is not refuted by examples of this sort. If the theory is true, however, we must distinguish certain events that we or Davidson might otherwise think identical. The check-writing case gives one clear example of this. Whether the poisoning case does this depends on how the theory of logical form is formulated; in Davidson's original version the theory does not force us to distinguish the poison-pouring from the killing, whereas in the revised version discussed throughout this paper, it does. The rest of this section deals with the question of which version of the theory is better.

I have mentioned several times the contrast between the original account that Davidson gave, and the present form of that account. In the original account, the notions of agent and object were amalgamated into the predicate associated with the verb, whereas in the present account they are independent one-place predicates (see illustration above). There are two reasons for changing to the present version. One has to do with grammar, and the other with inference.

GRAMMAR: Notice that in the original account, the places of subject and predicate are treated quite differently than the places of NPs that are objects of prepositions. But this is to focus on a distinction that is idiosyncratic to certain languages, including English. In Latin, for example, the instrumental preposition 'with' can be omitted entirely, so that in the Latin version of 'Mary cut the bread with a knife' there may be no prepositions at all; the positions of subject, object, and instrument are all indicated equally by case markings. And even in English we vacillate over the treatment of indirect objects, sometimes indicating an indirect object by means of word order, as in 'John gave *Mary* the book', and sometimes using a preposition, as in 'John gave the book *to Mary*'. There seems to be no principled reason to single out subject and direct object (and perhaps indirect object) for special treatment in the semantic theory.

INFERENCE: A second reason for separating subject and object from the verb in logical form has to do with inference. The key issue here, as Davidson points out,[43] has to do with logical relationships between transitive verbs and their corresponding intransitive forms. I will discuss two such relationships, epitomized by the inferences:

(A) Mary drove her new Chevy to Chicago
[therefore] Mary drove to Chicago

and:

(B) Agatha sank the *Bismarck*
[therefore] The *Bismarck* sank.

I assume that both are valid inferences, and the issue is simply how to capture them within a theory of logical form.[44]

---

[43] *Essays on Actions and Events*, p. 126, fn. 13.

[44] One might object to the inference in (A) on the grounds that Mary could have driven her Chevy to Chicago *by remote control*, without herself driving to Chicago. I think that there is a sense of 'drive', meaning roughly 'guide', in which the inference does not go through. But since in this sense the transitive and intransitive verbs are only homonyms, the theory does not endorse the inference. I also think that there is another sense of 'drive' in which the inference is valid; this is the sense that is at issue in the body of the paper. If I am wrong, and there is no such sense, then the theory will not have the application under discussion.

Regarding the former inference, it is already captured by the theory. That is, it is already captured by the theory together with one auxiliary assumption: that the transitive verb 'drive', as it is used in (A) above, is the same verb as the intransitive verb 'drive' that is used there. On that assumption the logical form of 'Mary drove her new Chevy to Chicago' entails the logical form of 'Mary drove to Chicago' by the ordinary rules of predicate logic.

Is this sort of inference always correct? The worry has to do with apparent counter-examples illustrated by (B) above; why don't we follow the pattern of (A) and infer from 'Agatha sank the *Bismarck*' that 'Agatha sank'? In fact, the theory as presently formulated will yield this unwanted inference, if the 'sank' in the two sentences is the same. But a slight emendation of the theory will avoid this incorrect consequence, and yield a host of other correct inferences as well.

Consider these three sentences:

(i)   Agatha broke the window with a stick.
(ii) The stick broke the window.
(iii) The window broke.

It seems quite plausible that these sentences can all be made true by exactly one event: a breaking of the window by Agatha using a stick. It seems clear, at least, that the first sentence entailment is automatically yielded by incorporating into the present theory an idea that has been in the linguistic literature for some time now. The idea is that NPs which occupy the position of OBJECT or INSTRUMENT in 'deep structure' can appear in the position of SUBJECT in 'surface structure'.[45] In present terms, the subject of a sentence should be indicated in logical form by *one* of the notions *Agent*, *Object* or *With*, depending on the kind of verb and what else is in the sentence. The suggestion is that we modify rule R3 so as to allow *Object* or *With* to replace *Agent* in some cases.[46] This automatically yields the result that sentence (i) entails sentence (ii), which in turn entails (iii). Furthermore, suppose we apply this idea to a sentence such as 'The *Bismarck* sank', translating the subject of that sentence using *Object* rather than *Agent*. Then this yields the correct result that 'Agatha sank the *Bismarck*' entails that 'The *Bismarck* sank'. Further, it automatically allows us to *escape* from the fear that 'Agatha sank the *Bismarck*' will entail 'Agatha sank', since the former will treat Agatha as agent, and the latter will treat her as object.

Again, the motivation for doing all this is to capture in a systematic way certain inference patterns among English sentences. And again there are consequences for the identity conditions for events, this time in the direction of identifying events in certain controversial cases. In particular, we will now be forced to maintain that, in certain circumstances, Agatha's breaking the window (with a stick) is identical with the stick's breaking the window, and this is

---

[45] See R. Stockwell, P. Schachter, and B. Partee, *The Major Syntactic Structures of English* (Holt, Rinehart & Winston, New York, 1973).

[46] As indicated, for example, in ibid., pp. 59ff.

identical in turn with the window's breaking. Likewise, we are forced to conclude that the *Bismarck*'s sinking is the same event as Agatha's sinking of the *Bismarck*. This, I gather, will be congenial to Davidson, though not to some others.[47]

---

[47] The most widely discussed example in the area of event individuation is the question of whether Brutus' stabbing of Caesar is the same event as his killing of Caesar. The present analysis sheds no light at all on this issue. (This is perhaps fortunate, since the data are so unclear here.) A popular suggestion from the Generative Semantics era is that 'kill' actually has a rather complex semantical representation, something on the order of 'do something which causes —— to die', and that the complications of this analysis can be used to explain some of the unclarities in the data – such as the difficulty in saying exactly when a killing takes place (is it the time of the doing, or the time of the dying?). Such complex representations can be represented more straightforwardly in the underlying events framework than in other frameworks, since the underlying event framework already has a notion of 'doing something' – namely, being the agent of an eventuality. (See Dowty, *Word Meaning and Montague Grammar*, for an attempt to deal with this type of analysis within an orthodox intensional logic.)
Added March 1985: I am now persuaded by considerations such as those in Z. Vendler, 'Agency and Causation,' *Midwest Studies in Philosophy*, IX (1984), pp. 371–84, that even 'Agatha sank the Bismarck' needs to quantify over two things in its logical form: Agatha's sinking of the Bismarck, and the Bismarck's sinking. Such forms should be attributed to all of the transitive 'causatives' of English, such as 'Agatha walked the dog'. (I am still not sure about 'Agatha killed Henry'.) I believe that this complication does not affect any of the arguments given elsewhere in this paper.

17
How Not to Flip the Prowler: Transitive Verbs of Action and the Identity of Actions

Lawrence Brian Lombard

In 'The logical form of action sentences', Donald Davidson proposed a semantic analysis of certain sentences containing transitive verbs of action.[1] This analysis can be, and has been, subjected to criticism from two fronts. One front is semantical; it has been claimed that the analysis is not adequate to the semantic facts. The other is metaphysical; it has been argued that the analysis is inconsistent with certain claims of identity concerning actions that Davidson has in other contexts expressed belief in. In this paper, I want to suggest a pattern of analysis for sentences containing transitive verbs of action that is Davidsonian both with respect to his semantic interests and with respect to what I take to be the obvious truth of his intuitions concerning the identity of actions.

1 Davidson's original analysis

The targets of Davidson's proposal are sentences such as 'Shem is kicking Shaun', sentences of the form:

(1) a is φing b,

where 'a' is replaced by a name or description of a person (or an agent of some other species), 'b' is replaced by a name or description of a thing that is affected by something the agent in question does, and 'φ' is replaced by a transitive verb (or verb phrase) of action. While it is perhaps unclear just exactly what the

---

[1] In *The Logic of Decision and Action*, ed. N. Rescher (University of Pittsburgh Press, Pittsburgh, 1967), pp. 81–95 (reprinted in Davidson's *Essays on Actions and Events* (Oxford University Press, New York, 1980)).

extension of the term 'transitive verb of action' is, Davidson's proposal is clearly meant to apply to those instances of (1) that imply that the agent a is doing something (intentionally or not) to the patient b. Thus, 'kill', 'melt', 'throw', 'move', and 'sink' clearly qualify as transitive verbs of action (though all of these except for 'throw' and 'kill' have intransitive senses as well), while 'is', 'become', 'see', and 'own' do not. Perhaps a close approximation to the right characterization of the idea of a transitive verb of action is this: they are those verbs and verb phrases, 'ϕ', which are such that the fact that a is ϕing b implies that b undergoes genuine (and not merely relational or mere Cambridge)[2] change.[3]

There were two motives for Davidson's offering of an analysis of sentences of the form (1). The first is that such an offering is part of the larger Davidsonian project of showing how the truth conditions of sentences belonging to a natural language depend upon their parts and their structure in a way embeddable in a Tarski-type, first-order, recursive, and extensional theory of truth. The second motive is that of providing a reason for thinking that there are such entities as actions. Any such philosophically appropriate reason must, by my lights, be a deductive argument whose premise is some obviously true and commonsensical claim (e.g., Jack fell down, Smith flipped the switch) and whose conclusion is that there are actions. The validity of that argument is defended by an inductive argument, an inference to the best explanation of the fact that the premise means what it in fact does mean, where that fact is revealed at least in part by the logical relations the premise bears to other claims, and where that explanation shows that the premise also entails that there are actions.[4]

Davidson's proposal is that sentences of the form (1) have the semantic structure of:

(2) $(\exists x)\phi$ing(a,b,x),

that is, there is a ϕing of b by a, where 'ϕing' in (2) is a three-place relational expression true of an agent, a patient, and an action just in case the action is a ϕing that is performed by the agent to (or on) the patient.[5]

Among the sentences whose logical properties are to be explained by this analysis are ones generated from transitive action sentences by the addition of certain adverbial modifiers.[6] Such longer claims entail simple transitive action sentences, and that fact is explained as a matter of ordinary simplification. Thus the fact that 'Jones is buttering the toast with the knife' entails 'Jones is buttering the toast' is explained, since those two claims' analyses are, respectively:

---

[2] For a characterization of relational or Cambridge change, see my 'Relational change and relational changes', *Philosophical Studies*, 34 (1978), pp. 63–79.

[3] This characterization, however, presupposes a claim to be made later on about the meaning of sentences containing transitive verbs of action. And if it is on the right track, it is clear why Davidson's analysis and the one I consider just after that must be mistaken.

[4] For a more fleshed-out version of this account of what it is to be a philosophically relevant reason for thinking that entities belonging to a given kind exist, see my *Events: a metaphysical study* (Routledge & Kegan Paul, London, 1986), ch. I.

[5] See 'The logical form of action sentences', p. 92.

[6] Not attributives, e.g., 'slowly', or intentionals, e.g., 'deliberately'.

(3) (a) (∃x)(Buttering (Jones, the toast,x) ∧ With (the knife,x))
     (b) (∃x)Buttering (Jones, the toast,x),

where 'With (the knife,x)' means 'x is performed with the knife'.

If (2) is the correct analysis of (1), that is, the best explanation of the semantic features of sentences of that form, then (1) implies that there are such things as φings of b by a. And Davidson takes that to imply, in turn, that there are actions.

2 *Intransitives and shortened transitives*

Davidson's original analysis is offered, in part, as an account of how certain *longer* sentences containing (sentences of the form)[7] 'a is φing b' entail 'a is φing b'. But it is also true that 'a is φing b' entails some *shorter* sentences; and if the original analysis is correct, it should not stand in the way of an explanation of these other logical relations.

Consider the following two sentences:

(4) (a) Smith is cleaning the house
     (b) Smith is mowing the lawn.

These two clearly entail, respectively,

(5) (a) Smith is cleaning
     (b) Smith is mowing.

This is so, because the sentences in (5) are ellipses of sentences of the form 'a is φing something'. It is absurd to suppose that Smith might be cleaning and yet not be cleaning something. Thus we have an explanation, in terms of the rule of existential generalization, of the fact that 'a is φing b' entails 'a is φing something':

(6) '(∃x)φing(a,b,x)' entails '(∃y)(∃x)φing(a,y,x)';

and there is, for many transitives, a 'deletion rule' permitting one to shorten 'a is φing something' to 'a is φing'. The verbs in (5) are 'shortened transitives'; they are the same verbs that appear in (4), only their direct objects are deleted. It should be noticed that this explanation works for it does *not* suppose that the shortened transitive, 'a is φing' is to be understood as:

(7) (∃x)φing(a,x).

If (7) were the analysis of 'a is φing', we would have no explanation of the entailments in question, since three-place relational claims do not, on the basis

---

[7] Since confusions are not likely to be generated, I will sometimes not bother to distinguish, except when necessary, sentences of the form 'a is φing b' from the sentence schema 'a is φing b'.

of their form alone, entail two-place relational claims; the appearance of 'ϕing' in (7) and (2) is an orthographic accident. The explanation here, however, insists that when 'a is ϕing b' does entail 'a is ϕing b', the same three-place transitive verb of action is involved.

Consider now these sentences:

(8) (a) Jones is flying the spacecraft
    (b) Jones is moving his car

and their 'shortened' counterparts:

(9) (a) Jones is flying
    (b) Jones is moving.

In one sense of the verbs in (9a–b), the sentences in (8) do entail their counterparts in (9), for they are ellipses, as in (5), and their verbs are shortened transitives. In that sense, 'fly' means 'pilot', and 'move' means 'change the spatial location of'. The same explanation that accounts for the entailment of the sentences in (5) by their counterparts in (4) (existential generalization and deletion) also explains the entailment by the sentences in (8) of their counterparts in (9), in one sense of those counterparts.[8]

But in another sense, the sentences in (9) are *not* ellipses and are not entailed by their counterparts in (8). This is so, for in this other sense, 'Jones is flying', for example, does not mean 'Jones is piloting something'; it means, rather, that Jones is flapping. In this sense, the sentence does not mean that Jones is the agent of a piloting. In this, intransitive sense, 'fly' means 'move through a gaseous medium by flapping', and 'move' means 'change spatial location'. When in 'a is ϕing', the verb 'ϕ' has its intransitive sense, 'a is ϕing b' does not entail 'a is ϕing'.[9] One need not sink in order to sink a ship. (Causes need not be like their effects in this way.) So, when 'a is ϕing' is understood intransitively, it is not implied by 'a is ϕing b'; when 'ϕ' is understood as a shortened transitive, it is.

It should be noted here that the transitive and intransitive senses of sentences of the form 'a is ϕing' (when such a sentence has both) are not, I believe, independent of each other. This despite the fact that 'a is ϕing (trans.)' neither entails nor is entailed by 'a is ϕing (intrans.)'. There is, after all, a common element in 'Jones is moving (his car)' and 'Jones is moving (changing location)'; and it is not, I contend, an orthographic accident that 'moving' appears in both. If this common element is to be kept track of, it cannot be the case that the transitive sense of certain verbs is represented by a three-place relational predicate true of agents, patients, and actions, while their intransitive sense (if such exists) is represented by a two-place relational predicate true of things and the changes they undergo. And this suggests that there is something wrong with

---

[8] I do not claim that, for every transitive verb, there is a shortened transitive inferrable from the transitive by means of the deletion rule.

[9] Of course, not every transitive verb has an intransitive counterpart. 'Kill', for example, has no intransitive sense; so there is no sense in which 'a is killing b' fails to entail 'a is killing'.

the suggestion that (2) has the structure of (1). For it seems reasonable to suppose that 'a is φing' when understood intransitively means that a is undergoing an event of the type 'φing'.

3 *Abandoning the original analysis*

The metatheory in which an analysis of transitive action sentences is to be embedded is supposed to construe the target sentences as involving only first-order quantification; there are to be no quantifiable variables in predicate positions. But 'a is φing b' does entail the following:

(10) (a) a is doing something
     (b) an action is being performed
     (c) b is being acted on.

Second-order quantification, if permitted, would explain how (1) entails (10 a–c); construe (1) as (2) and (10 a–c), respectively, as:

(11) (a) $(\exists F)(\exists y)(\exists x)F\text{-ing}(a,y,x)$
     (b) $(\exists F)(\exists z)(\exists y)(\exists x)F\text{-ing}(z,y,x)$
     (c) $(\exists F)(\exists z)(\exists x)F\text{-ing}(z,b,x).$[10]

In addition, one of Davidson's reasons for proposing his analysis was to give an argument for the existence of actions. One can grant, however, that if (2) were the correct analysis of (1), then it would follow that if a is φing b there is a φing of b by a. But how does that show that there are actions? How is the inference from (1) to:

(12) $(\exists x)\text{Action}(x),$

i.e., there is at least one thing that is an action, to be validated? Construing (1) as (2) won't by itself turn the trick.[11]

We can explain the entailments in question without recourse to second-order quantification by abandoning (2) as an analysis of (1) in favor of one along the following lines:

(13) $(\exists x)(\text{Action}(x) \wedge \phi\text{ing}(x) \wedge \text{Agent}(a,x) \wedge \text{Patient}(b,x)),$

where:

(14) (a) Action(x) =df x is an action
     (b) φing(x) =df x is a φing (in the transitive sense)
     (c) Agent(a,x) =df a is the agent of x (x is done by a)

---

[10] The deletion rule used above is also needed.
[11] The entailment of (12) by (1) can be explained by adding 'Action(x)' as a conjunct to (2), where 'Action(x)' means 'x is an action'. But this won't solve the problem of the entailment of (10a) and (10c) by (1).

(d) Patient(b,x) =df b is a patient of x (x is done to b).[12]

In the light of this analysis of (1), (10a–c) would be rendered, respectively, as:

(15) (a) $(\exists x)(\text{Action}(x) \wedge \text{Agent}(a,x))$
   (b) $(\exists x)\text{Action}(x)$
   (c) $(\exists x)(\text{Action}(x) \wedge \text{Patient}(b,x))$.

And 'a is ϕing' (in the shortened transitive sense) would be rendered as:

(16) $(\exists x)(\text{Action}(x) \wedge \phi\text{ing}(x) \wedge \text{Agent}(a,x))$,

and 'a is doing something to b' as:

(17) $(\exists x)(\text{Action}(x) \wedge \text{Agent}(a,x) \wedge \text{Patient}(b,x))$.

And the entailment of all these claims by (1) is easily explained. So we have a reason for abandoning Davidson's original analysis of (1), an analysis containing one relational expression joining agent, patient, and action, in favor of (13), which detaches these elements of transitive actions from each other and which treats each separately.[13] This alternative analysis, however, is not without its problems.

4 The alternative analysis and the identity of actions

Suppose that on some occasion Jones flips the switch and thereby turns on the light, illuminates the room, and alerts the prowler. According to the alternative analysis of transitive action sentences (13),

(18) (a) Jones is flipping the switch
   (b) Jones is alerting the prowler

should be construed, respectively, as:

(19) (a) $(\exists x)(\text{Action}(x) \wedge \text{Flipping}(x) \wedge \text{Agent}(\text{Jones}, x) \wedge \text{Patient}(\text{the switch},x))$
   (b) $(\exists y)(\text{Action}(y) \wedge \text{Alerting}(y) \wedge \text{Agent}(\text{Jones}, y) \text{ Patient}(\text{the prowler}, y))$.

And according to Davidson and others,[14] if, as is the case here, Jones alerts the prowler (illuminates the room and turns on the light) by flipping the switch,

---

[12] A version of this suggestion is proposed by Terence Parsons, in his 'Modifiers and quantifiers in natural language', *Canadian Journal of Philosophy*, supp. vol. 6 (1980), pp. 29–60, and his 'Underlying events in the logical analysis of English', this volume. Parsons' version does not contain the conjunct 'Action(x)'.

[13] Hector Castañeda has also given reasons for separating agent and patient in his 'Comments on D. Davidson's "The logical form of action sentences"', *The Logic of Decision and Action*, pp. 104–12.

[14] See, for example, Davidson's 'Actions, reasons, and causes', reprinted in his *Essays on Actions and Events*, pp. 3–19; and G.E.M. Anscombe's *Intention* (Basil Blackwell, Oxford, 1959).

then his flipping of the switch and his alerting of the prowler (and his illuminating of the room and his turning on of the light) are one and the same action. That is, there is exactly *one* action that Jones performs on that occasion which is a flipping of the switch, a turning on of the light, an illuminating of the room, and an alerting of the prowler.

However, Terence Parsons has most persuasively shown that we cannot both have (13), the alternative analysis, and the identity of the flipping of the switch and the alerting of the prowler.[15] He has shown that from those assumptions an absurdity can be deduced. Parsons' argument is as follows. On the assumption of (13) and the identity in question, we get that there is an action that is both a flipping of the switch and an alerting of the prowler, a claim that is to be understood as

(20) $(\exists x)(\text{Action}(x) \wedge \text{Flipping}(x) \wedge \text{Agent}(\text{Jones},x) \wedge \text{Patient}(\text{the switch},x) \wedge \text{Action}(x) \wedge \text{Alerting}(x) \wedge \text{Agent}(\text{Jones},x) \wedge \text{Patient}(\text{the prowler},x)).$

By dropping redundant conjuncts, rearrangement, and simplification, we get, as entailed by (20):

(21) $(\exists x)(\text{Action}(x) \wedge \text{Flipping}(x) \wedge \text{Agent}(\text{Jones},x) \wedge \text{Patient}(\text{the prowler},x)).$

But according to the alternative analysis, (21) is a rendering of:

(22) Jones is flipping the prowler!

And (22) must be true if the alternative analysis, (13), of sentences of the form (1) is correct and there is some action performed by Jones that is both a flipping of the switch and an alerting of the prowler. In a similar way, one can also infer that Jones is alerting the switch, flipping the room, and illuminating the prowler. And if Smith signs a check by moving his right arm, then the alternative analysis along with the identity of Smith's check-signing and arm-moving will entail that Smith signs his right arm and moves the check. And all this is, of course, quite absurd.

It might be thought that this result is the effect of the separation of agent, patient, and action demanded by the alternative analysis, and that if we returned to Davidson's original analysis, with a single, three-place transitive action verb relating agent, patent, and action, the problem can be avoided. But this is only superficially so. John Wallace has shown that the problem will arise with (2) taken as the analysis of (1), though in slightly different form.[16] Suppose that, in one action, Smith by striking the cue ball in a certain way pockets the 8-ball into the side pocket and the 9-ball into the corner pocket. Then, according to the usual way of representing action sentences with prepositional phrases in the style of (2), we get:

---

[15] See his papers mentioned in note 12, above.
[16] That Wallace has shown this is reported by Parsons in 'Modifiers and quantifiers in natural language', p. 36.

(23) (a) (∃x)(Pocketing(Smith, the 8-ball,x) ∧ Into(the side pocket,x))
    (b) (∃y)(Pocketing(Smith, the 9-ball,y) ∧ Into(the corner pocket, y)).

But Davidsonians about the identity of actions will insist that there is, on that occasion, exactly *one* action performed by Smith that is both a pocketing of the 8-ball into the side pocket and a pocketing of the 9-ball into the corner pocket. Thus,

(24) (∃x)(Pocketing(Smith, the 8-ball,x) ∧ Into(the side pocket,x) ∧ Pocketing(Smith, the 9-ball,x) ∧ Into(the corner pocket,x)).

But (24) entails:

(25) (∃x)(Pocketing(Smith, the 8-ball,x) ∧ Into(the corner pocket,x))

and:

(26) (∃x)(Pocketing(Smith, the 8-ball,x) ∧ Into(the corner pocket,x) ∧ Into(the side pocket,x)).

That is, (24) entails that Smith hits the 8-ball into the corner pocket, which he does *not* in fact do, and that he hits the 8-ball into both the corner pocket and the side pocket, which he *cannot* do.

    Wallace's argument, of course, just adds insult to the injury already inflicted on (2) due to its inability to explain certain inferences. With respect to Parsons' argument, however, it clear that something must be given up: either (13) as an analysis of (1) or the identity of some flippings and alertings (and similar identities). Parsons evidently sees much in (13) to recommend it and so prefers to give up the identities. My preference, however, is to retain what seem to me to be obviously true claims of action identity and to give up the alternative analysis.[17] But unless there is some reason, independent of the fact that the analysis is inconsistent with the identities, for giving up the analysis, no straightforward defense of such identities is likely to be persuasive. However, I do believe that there is such a reason for rejecting (13) (as well as (2)) as an analysis of transitive action sentences, and that is that (13) (as well as (2)) fails to explain what transitive action sentences mean.

    What made it possible to derive (22)? In order to explain certain logical relations involving action sentences with transitive verbs (without recourse to second-order quantification), it was deemed necessary, correctly I believe, to split Davidson's transitive action verbs into separate components. On (13), however, such verbs are split into a predicate of entities true of them just in case they are actions, an expression relating actions and their agents, an expression relating actions and their patients, and a predicate true of actions if and only if they belong to certain 'transitive action types'. But according to Davidson,

---

[17] I argue for such identities in 'Actions, results, and the time of a killing', *Philosophia*, 8 (1978), pp. 341–54. In that paper, I also defend a version of the verb-splitting analysis of transitive verbs of action that I discuss in section 5, below.

myself, and others, an action performed by an agent on a given occasion may belong to more than one transitive action type. So, one and the same action may be both a flipping and an alerting. But, by Leibniz's Law, if 'y is a patient of x' expresses a genuine, non-intensional relation (which it surely does), then any patient of an action, x, is a patient of any action identical with x. So, if b is a patient of x and x is a φing (a transitive action type), and x is also a ψing, then b must be a patient of a ψing. So, the prowler, patient of the alerting, must be a patient of the flipping as well.

Now while all this is, I contend, true, the alternative analysis goes on to permit one to infer, from the fact that the prowler is a patient of a flipping, that that action is a flipping of the prowler. And this is the inference to be blocked. The alternative analysis (13) cannot block it, for it makes no connection between what happens to a patient of an action and the patient it happens to: according to (13) what happens to any patient happens to every patient. If we understood what transitive verbs of action mean, however, we will see why that isn't so.

What seems right, though it's unfortunate to have to put it this way, is that Jones' action *qua* a flipping has the switch and not the prowler as patient and *qua* an alerting has the prowler and not the switch as patient. His action, insofar as it affects the prowler, is an alerting but not a flipping. This way of putting the matter should remind one of what one says about attributives: this thing is small for an elephant but large for a mammal. That is, *qua* elephant it is small, *qua* mammal it is large. Of course, though we have no clear idea how to deal semantically with '*qua*'-nouns and attributives, it is obvious that no solution to those problems can be correct if it requires that the thing that *qua* elephant is small and the thing that *qua* mammal is large are different things.

My inclination in the case of actions is the same. The action that affects the prowler and the one that affects the switch are the same action. What is needed is an understanding of transitive action sentences that explains what it is for an action to be a flipping insofar as it affects the switch, but not insofar as it affects the prowler. This can be gotten, I believe, by giving an analysis of sentences involving transitive verbs of action that avoids altogether the use of transitive verbs of action. In that way, we can tie flippings to switches and alertings to prowlers (and not the other way around), while also having some flippings be alertings.

5 *Transitive actions and transitive action sentences*

Transitive actions, that is, the actions whose performance make sentences of the form 'a is φing b' true, belong to the transitive action types they do because of their effects. Transitive action verbs are 'causal' verbs. The attempt to say what it is for a verb, 'φ', in a sentence of the form 'a is φing b', to be causal by saying that such a sentence is equivalent to 'a is causing b to be φed', however, is defective. If, for example, Jones coerces Smith into melting the chocolate, then while it is the case that Jones is causing the chocolate to be melted he is not melting the chocolate (even though he gets the chocolate melted). This attempt, however, is not very far from being right. Clearly, if a is φing b then a is causing b to be φed. The problem is with the converse. But counterexamples to the converse arise only when 'multiple agency' is a feature of those counterexamples. Multiple agency is introduced when something else must be done (either by a or by another), in addition to 'what a does' (e.g., coerce Smith, pull the trigger, etc.), in order for b to be φed. Thus, for example, suppose that the King poisons the Queen's tea, and that the Queen drinks the tea and thereby dies. Here the King does do something that is a cause of the Queen's being killed; however, if we are inclined to say that the King killed the Queen, I think that that is a clear extension of the meaning of 'kill'. There is, after all, an important difference between such a case and a case where the King himself cuts the Queen's head off. In the latter case, the King kills the Queen *by* cutting her head off. In the former case, however, there is *no* action that the King performs such that *by* performing it he kills the Queen. The poisoning of her tea only makes it possible for some other action (*viz.* the Queen's drinking of her tea) to cause her death; indeed, the Queen kills herself by drinking the tea. Of course, we will want to hold the King responsible for the Queen's death; and in that extended sense we may say that the King kills the Queen. But in the 'primary' sense of transitive verbs of action, 'a is φing b' is not true unless there is some action that a performs such that *by* performing it a causes b to be φed.

An action is a φing of its patient by its agent only if it causes its patient to be φed. No action is a flipping unless something is flipped; and no action is a sinking of a ship unless a ship is sunk.[18] It should be noticed that terms of the form 'b's being φed' are ambiguous. In one sense, the 'state' sense, they denote states of b. In that sense, 'b's being φed' seems related to the sentence 'b is φed'; 'the door's being closed', in that sense, refers to a state of the door, the obtaining of which makes 'the door is closed' true. The state in question is that which consists in the door's being such that it is surrounded by the door's frame; it obtains when the door is shut. The state sense of such terms should be distinguished from the 'process' sense which some expressions of that form possess. The process sense of 'b's being φed' is related to the sentence 'b is being φed'. In the process sense, however, such an expression is 'relational'. To be φed, in this sense, is to undergo a change that terminates in being φed in the state sense, where that change is one that is brought about. For the door to be closed (in the process sense), for example, is not merely for it to be closed (in the state sense); nor is it merely for it to come to be in the state of being closed. It is, rather, to come to be in the state of being closed as a result of the performance of an action of closing the door. In the case of transitive verbs having an intransitive sense as well, there is a difference between b's being φed and b's φing (in the intransitive sense). A door may close without being closed (in the process sense); it may close all by itself, without there occurring any action or event which causes it to be closed.[19] So, for b to be φed in the process sense is for there to be a change in b which (i) is caused by an action (a φing of b) and (ii) terminates in b's being φed in the state sense.

---

[18] A does not φ b unless b is φed. I do not, however, insist that a does not φ b *until* b is φed. See my paper ibid. for more on this and on related matters.

[19] Though, of course, there must be an event that terminates in the door's being in that state.

The change in the patient of an action may be such that there is a simple predicate already in the language that is true of the patient just in case it undergoes that change. Sometimes the predicate is the intransitive counterpart of a transitive verb of action. Thus, for example, for the ship to be sunk (in the process sense) is for the ship to undergo a change terminating in the ship's being sunk (in the state sense), where that change is caused by someone's (or something's) sinking of it. And the ship's change just is its sinking; the ship sinks as a result of a sinking of it. Sometimes, however, the transitive verb of action has no intransitive form; in the case of the victim's being killed, the intransitive in question is 'dies'. In other cases, there just may be no convenient and simple intransitive verb true of b just in case b undergoes a change terminating in its being φed. 'Becomes alert' may be the best that can be done in the case of what happens to the prowler as a result of Jones' alerting of him. And 'undergoes a change terminating in its being φed' may have to do in other cases. Whether or not there is such a simple verb or verb phrase true of such a change is not the issue. What is important is that to be φed in the process sense is to undergo a change, caused by an action of φing, that terminates in being φed in the state sense, and to φ something is to cause that thing to undergo such a change.

The crucial problem with (13) was that it could not block the inference from 'action x is a φing one of whose patients is b' to 'x is a φing of b'. That inference can be blocked by giving an analysis of sentences containing transitive verbs of action that eschews transitive verbs of action and ties the characterization of actions as belonging to this or that type to considerations concerning the patients of actions and what happens to them. This can be done, I believe, by supposing that sentences of the form 'a is φing b', when they have their primary sense and where 'φ' is a transitive verb of action, have the semantic features of:

(27) $(\exists x)(\exists y)(\exists z)$(Action(x) $\wedge$ Agent(a,x) $\wedge$ Event(y) $\wedge$ Subject(b,y) $\wedge$ State(z) $\wedge$ Subject'(b,z) $\wedge$ Being φed(b,z) $\wedge$ Terminates(z,y) $\wedge$ C(x,y)),[20]

where:

(28) (i)   Action(x) =df x is an action
      (ii)   Agent(a,x) =df a is the agent of x
      (iii) Event(y) =df y is an event
      (iv)   Subject(b,y) =df b is the subject of y (b is the thing that undergoes y)
      (v)   State(z) =df z is a state
      (vi)   Subject'(b,z) =df z is a state of b[21]
      (vii) Being φed(b,z) =df z is b's being φed (in the state sense)
      (viii) Terminates(z,y) =df y terminates in z
      (ix)   C(x,y) =df x is a cause of y.

---

[20] Since it is the primary sense of transitive verbs of action that is at stake, a conjunct should be added to (27) to rule out multiple agency; such a clause would say that there is no further action, performed after or simultaneously with x that is a cause of y. Alternatively, the clause could require that the action, x, is such that *by* performing it, the agent causes the patient to be φed. In any case, I have omitted this additional clause from (27) for simplicity's sake.

[21] I am not inclined to think that the sense in which a thing is the subject of an event is different

That is, 'a is φing b' means 'a is the agent of an action that causes a change in b that terminates in b's being φed'. This proposal attempts to exploit the causal character of transitive verbs of action and to articulate the idea that actions belong to the transitive action types to which they in fact belong in virtue of the changes they produce in their patients. And it constitutes another example, I believe, of the Davidsonian theme that the concept of causation plays a crucial and central role in the theory of action.[22] It remains, then, to test (27) to see whether or not it does the work that (2) and (13) did not do.

6 *Testing the analysis*

Action sentences of the form 'a is φing b' entail sentences of each of the following forms:

(29) (a) there are actions
    (b) a is doing something
    (c) a is doing something to b
    (d) a is φing (shortened transitive)
    (e) an action is being performed on b (b is being acted on)
    (f) b is being φed.

And the analyses of these are, respectively, as follows:

(30) (a) $(\exists x)\text{Action}(x)$
    (b) $(\exists x)(\text{Action}(x) \wedge \text{Agent}(a,x))$
    (c) $(\exists x)(\exists y)(\exists z)(\text{Action}(x) \wedge \text{Agent}(a,x) \wedge \text{Event}(y) \wedge$
        $\text{Subject}(b,y) \wedge \text{State}(z) \wedge \text{Subject}'(b,z) \wedge$
        $\text{Terminates}(z,y) \wedge C(x,y))$
    (d) $(\exists x)(\exists y)(\exists z)(\exists w)(\text{Action}(x) \wedge \text{Agent}(a,x) \wedge \text{Event}(y) \wedge$
        $\text{Subject}(w,y) \wedge \text{State}(z) \wedge \text{Subject}'(w,z) \wedge \text{Being } \phi\text{ed}(w,z) \wedge$
        $\text{Terminates}(z,y) \wedge C(x,y))$
    (e) $(\exists x)(\exists y)(\exists z)(\text{Action}(x) \wedge \text{Event}(y) \wedge \text{Subject}(b,y) \wedge$
        $\text{State}(z) \wedge \text{Subject}'(b,z) \wedge \text{Terminates}(z,y) \wedge C(x,y))$
    (f) $(\exists x)(\exists y)(\exists z)(\text{Action}(x) \wedge \text{Event}(y) \wedge \text{Subject}(b,y) \wedge$
        $\text{State}(z) \wedge \text{Subject}'(b,z) \wedge \text{Being } \phi\text{ed}(b,z) \wedge \text{Terminates}(z,y) \wedge$
        $C(x,y))$.

And (27) obviously entails each of (30a–f), thereby validating the entailment by (1) of each of (29a–f).

As for Parsons' prowler-flipping, the following can be said. We are supposing, with Davidson, that there is just one action that Jones performs and that it is both a flipping of the switch and an alerting of the prowler. To say this is to say:

---

from the sense in which a thing is that which a state is a state of. If I am right about that then 'subject' and 'subject'' express the same relation.

[22] See the Introduction to Davidson's *Essays on Actions and Events*.

(31) $(\exists x)(\exists y)(\exists y')(\exists z)(\exists z')$(Action(x) $\wedge$ Agent(Jones,x) $\wedge$ Event(y) $\wedge$ Subject(the switch, y) $\wedge$ State(z) $\wedge$ Subject'(the switch,z) $\wedge$ Being flipped(the switch,z) $\wedge$ Terminates(z,y) $\wedge$ C(x,y) $\wedge$ Event(y') $\wedge$ Subject(the prowler,y') $\wedge$ State(z') $\wedge$ Subject'(the prowler,z') $\wedge$ Being alerted(the prowler,z') $\wedge$ Terminates(z',y') $\wedge$ C(x,y')).

From (31), by rearranging conjuncts, simplifying, and generalizing we can derive (32):

(32) $(\exists x)(\exists y)(\exists y')(\exists z)(\exists z')(\exists w)$(Action(x) $\wedge$ Agent(Jones,x) $\wedge$ Event(y) $\wedge$ Subject(w,y) $\wedge$ State(z) $\wedge$ Subject'(w,z) $\wedge$ Being flipped(w,z) $\wedge$ Terminates(z,y) $\wedge$ C(x,y) $\wedge$ Event(y') $\wedge$ Subject(the prowler,y') $\wedge$ State(z') $\wedge$ Subject'(the prowler,z') $\wedge$ Terminates(z',y') $\wedge$ C(x,y')).

But all this means is that Jones is flipping something and that his so doing causes a change in the prowler, that one of Jones' flippings affected the prowler. It does *not* mean that Jones is flipping the prowler. That claim would be represented by (33):

(33) $(\exists x)(\exists y)(\exists z)$(Action(x) $\wedge$ Agent(Jones,x) $\wedge$ Event(y) $\wedge$ Subject(the prowler,y) $\wedge$ State(z) $\wedge$ Subject'(the prowler,z) $\wedge$ Being flipped(the prowler,z) $\wedge$ Terminates(z,y) $\wedge$ C(x,y)).

And (33) is manifestly not derivable from (31), for there is no way to infer from (31) that the prowler undergoes a change that terminates in his being flipped. He does undergo a change, a change caused by Jones' flipping of something; but he doesn't get flipped, the switch does.

Wallace's billiard-ball case can be handled similarly. To say that Smith gets the 8-ball into the side pocket is to say that Smith does something which causes the 8-ball to undergo a change that terminates in its being in the side pocket; and in the same action he gets the 9-ball into the corner pocket. Thus:

(34) $(\exists x)(\exists y)(\exists y')(\exists z)(\exists z')$(Action(x) $\wedge$ Agent(Smith,x) $\wedge$ Event(y) $\wedge$ Subject(the 8-ball,y) $\wedge$ State(z) $\wedge$ In(the side pocket,z) $\wedge$ Subject'(the 8-ball,z) $\wedge$ Terminates(z,y) $\wedge$ C(x,y) $\wedge$ Event(y') $\wedge$ Subject(the 9-ball,y') $\wedge$ State(z') $\wedge$ In(the corner pocket,z') $\wedge$ Subject'(the 9-ball,z') $\wedge$ Terminates(z',y') $\wedge$ C(x,y')),

where 'In(w,z)' means 'z is a state of being in w'. And it is obvious that (34) does not imply that the 8-ball gets into the state of being in the corner pocket. We can, of course, infer from (34) that Jones did something to the 8-ball that resulted in something's being in the corner pocket. But that is both true and harmless.

It has sometimes been argued that identities such as that of Jones' flipping of the switch and his alerting of the prowler and of some killings and some shootings run afoul of the fact that in cases where such identities are asserted Jones alerts the prowler *by* flipping the switch and the murderer kills the victim *by* shooting him.[23] According to such arguments, the 'by'-relation relates actions, but cannot relate identical actions since it is an asymmetric and irreflexive relation; Jones does not flip the switch by alerting the prowler or alert the prowler by alerting the prowler. But (27) helps, as Patrick Francken has argued, to refute this objection to such claims of action identity.[24] The asymmetry and irreflexivity of the 'by'-relation, (27) suggests, is the asymmetry and irreflexivity of the *causal* relation. But what 'by' relates are not actions, but the *effects* of actions. Jones' action has at least two effects: the switch flips and the prowler becomes alert. But these are not merely effects of a common cause, Jones' action. Rather, the latter effect is a more remote effect of the action than the former and has the former as a more immediate cause. Jones' action causes the prowler to be alerted because his action causes the switch to flip, which in turn is a cause of the prowler's being alerted; thus Jones alerts the prowler by flipping the switch. Effects are related by the 'by'-relation as they are more and less remote effects of an agent's action.

It thus appears that we can have an analysis of sentences involving transitive verbs of action that is both in the spirit of the semantic and ontological goals Davidson wanted to be achieved by semantic analysis and compatible with what I take to be the obviously correct intuitions Davidson has concerning the identity of actions. We can do this, I believe, only by incorporating into such an analysis some results of reflection on the metaphysics of action. Readers of Davidson's work, however, will not be surprised at the close connection between semantics and metaphysics. Moreover, the resulting analysis of sentences involving transitive verbs of action is only slightly more semantically complex and metaphysically rich than Davidson had originally anticipated.[25]

---

[23] See, for example, Alvin Goldman's *A Theory of Human Action* (Prentice-Hall, Englewood Cliffs, N.J. 1970), p. 5.

[24] In his unpublished paper, 'The by-locutionary argument' (Wayne State University, mimeographed).

[25] I here express my thanks to Michael McKinsey for his helpful advice concerning an earlier draft of this paper.

18

Causal Relata

David H. Sanford

Is the explanation of someone's action by reference to the beliefs and desires that motivate the action a species of causal explanation? Who would deny it? It is difficult to remember now, more than twenty years after of the publication of 'Actions, reasons, and causes,' how many influential philosophers did deny it. That article's main purpose was accomplished with such success and its morals so widely accepted that a student who begins reading in the philosophy of the mind with current work and then works backwards to 1963 has to work back still further to understand its enormous effect.

'Actions, reasons, and causes' is the earliest of the essays in *Essays on Actions and Events*.[1] Davidson's 'Introduction' represents several of his later essays as completing, continuing, specifying, and correcting various parts of the first paper. 'Causal relations' repeats some of the points about causation made in the first paper and shows how they fit with newly articulated views on the logical form of causal statements and the relation, not always that of reference, between sentences about events and events. The distinction between entailing a causal law and entailing that there is such a law is made more vivid by being accompanied by a serious proposal for what the logical form of a causal law might be. Other suggestions in 'Causal relations,' although widely accepted, are also widely questioned. Davidson's adaptation of a Fregean argument to show that 'cause' ought not to be treated as a sentential connective, and his remarks about Mill's confusion of a whole cause with cause wholly specified, provoke diverse reactions. I will display my own reactions presently.

The last section of 'Causal relations' distinguishes two questions: What is the logical form of causal statements? and How should the causal relation be analysed? Failure to appreciate this distinction, Davidson claims, leads to misguided theorizing about the nature of a mysterious sentential connective often called the *causal conditional*. Causes are events, causal relations hold between events, and the analysis of the causal relation is the analysis of 'an ordinary two-place predicate in an ordinary, extensional first-order language.'[2]

---

[1] Clarendon Press, Oxford, 1980. All page references to Davidson's writings will be to this book.
[2] 'Causal relations,' p. 161.

Davidson does not attempt, nor shall I attempt here, to provide an analysis of the causal relation.

Immediately after he draws this distinction, Davidson considers several examples challenging the views that the search for a sentential causal connective is misguided and that the causal relation relates only events. 'The collapse was caused,' for one example, 'not by the fact that the bolt gave away, but by the fact that it gave way so suddenly and unexpectedly.'[3] Davidson deals with this and similar examples by distinguishing straightforward singular causal statements from rudimentary causal explanations. Explanations, he says, typically relate statements, not events. There is provocation enough in this remark for a series of articles, but I am primarily concerned here with what the causal relation relates.

Are only events proper causal relata? While some conceptions of event are broader than others, I want to entertain the inclusion of items as proper causal relata that are counted as events by only the broadest conception.[4] The suddenness of the bolt's giving way, I suggest, can be causally related, be a cause, of the collapse. The bolt's giving way is an event. The suddenness of the bolt's giving way, or the bolt's giving way being sudden, although intimately connected with the event of the bolt's giving way, is something different from that event and is not naturally regarded as an event on its own. Let us call it, for now, an *event aspect*. Event aspects, I suggest, are proper causal relata. I do not mean to deny that events are also proper causal relata. Neither do I mean to suggest that there are several distinct species of causal relation to be distinguished by differences in ontological status between their relata. I suggest, rather, that it is useful to regard the causal relation as a single relation that can relate items of distinguishable kinds including events and event aspects.

Bad philosophers imitate. Good philosophers steal. From this it does not follow, alas, that philosophic theft generally, not even the theft of good philosophy, is itself good philosophy. I steal my central thesis from Fred Dretske who developed it in a series of writings including 'Contrastive statements'[5] 'The content of knowledge,'[6] and 'Referring to events.'[7] I also help myself to work on this topic by Jaegwon Kim and Peter Achinstein. Kim provides an alternative account of the phenomena of emphasis and contrastive focusing that Dretske attends to.[8] Achinstein criticizes Dretske's account, Kim's alternative, and several others.[9] Achinstein's statements of various views he wants to reject have been a great help to me in formulating a view I want to accept. And of course I steal freely from Davidson. A bit of theft at the end of

---

[3] Ibid., p. 161.

[4] Philip Peterson of Syracuse University has such a conception in his theory of complex events.

[5] *Philosophical Review*, 81 (1972), pp. 411–37.

[6] In *Forms of Representation*, ed. B. Freed, A. Marras, and P. Maynard (Elsevier, New York, 1975), pp. 77–93.

[7] *Midwest Studies in Philosophy*, 2 (1977), pp. 90–9.

[8] 'Causation, emphasis, and events,' *Midwest Studies in Philosophy*, 2 (1977), pp. 100–3.

[9] *The Nature of Explanation* (Oxford University Press, Oxford and New York, 1983), ch. 6. 'The causal relation,' pp. 193–217. An earlier version of this chapter appears under the same title in *Midwest Studies in Philosophy*, 4 (1979), pp. 369–86. See also Achinstein's 'Causation, transparency, and emphasis,' *Canadian Journal of Philosophy*, 5 (1975), pp. 1–23.

the paper is somewhat perverse, for I apply some of the morals Davidson teaches about quantifying over events to undermine the primary status as causal relata Davidson gives to events.

Discussions of the topics of the logical form of causal statements and the extensionality of causal contexts usually treat the same few examples. Imagine then that the curtain rises on a number of familiar characters playing their familiar roles. Low red and blue lights convey earlier and later hours of the evening. At ruddy dusk, stage right, Socrates drinks hemlock. Smith, who weighs twelve stone, slips and falls. In the distance, the Titanic sinks. Oedipus, full of dark foreboding, clings to Jocasta ignorant of an awful description under which his clinging falls. Not all is tragedy and death; there are also scenes of domestic comedy. Standing naked and disgusted before her mirror, Flora regrets her rough toweling. Sebastian strolls. Jones, attempting to conceal his midnight gluttony, repairs to the bathroom to butter toast. In the darkened center of the stage, a tiny, sudden flame would have appeared if only someone had scratched match M.

Let us start by ringing changes on one of Davidson's examples.

> Did you say that she fried herself on the beach at noon? No: *dried*, not *fried*. Flora *dried* herself on the beach at noon. Oh, you say that Dora dried herself on the beach at noon? No, no: *Flora*, not *Dora*. *Flora* dried herself on the beach at noon.

These are examples of one species of what Achinstein calls non-semantical emphasis. There is no difference in meaning or in truth value as different components of the following sentence are stressed or emphasized:

> Flora dried herself on the beach at noon.

The same changes of emphasis, however, can have a more profound effect when the sentence is embedded. For example,

> I doubt that *Flora* dried herself.
> I doubt that Flora *dried* herself.
> I doubt that Flora dried *herself.*

In the first case, I doubt that the drying was of or by Flora. (I suspect it was of someone else.) In the second case I doubt that Flora's activity is accurately described as drying. (Perhaps I believe she was dry to begin with, or perhaps I believe that although she started out wet she used so damp a towel that it could not have dried her.) In the third case, if I admit that Flora was dried, I doubt that she was solely responsible for her drying. (She has become accustomed, this season, to receiving help in drying off; and several members of the beach crowd are eager to provide it.) The three sentence tokens beginning with 'I doubt that ...', word-for-word identical but differing in contrastive stress, appear to have different truth conditions.[10]

---

[10] Accepting the appropriateness of Achinstein's semantical/non-semantical terminology, in an earlier version of this essay I said that the three sentence tokens also appear to have different

In 'Referring to events,' Dretske concentrates on causal contexts. It was, we assume, Flora's drying herself with *coarse* towel that caused those awful splotches to appear on her skin. It was not *drying* herself with a coarse towel, as opposed, say, to merely rubbing herself, that caused the splotches to appear, nor was it drying *herself* with a coarse towel, in contrast to being dried by someone else, that caused them to appear. Something that happened on the beach, something that happened at noon, caused the splotches to appear, but probably neither the toweling's being on the beach nor its being at noon played a causal role in the production of the splotches.

Dretske's suggestion that the emphasis-sensitivity of causal contexts accounts ultimately for emphasis-sensitivity generally ought not be dismissed merely because one can think of an emphasis-sensitive context with no obvious causal basis. If the ambitious program Dretske starts in *Knowledge and the Flow of Information* is completed successfully, it will reveal many currently unobvious causal connections.

Dretske holds that event aspects, event features, event facets, event properties, or, as he sometimes says, event allomorphs, are causal relata.[11] This view is attractive to me, and I have a hard time understanding why philosophers want to resist it. Perhaps some other claims of Dretske are taken as essential to his central thesis, so qualms about these other views transfer to the central thesis. I shall question several claims of Dretske in order to show that their rejection is consistent with admitting event aspects as causal relata.

In 'Referring to events,' Dretske writes, 'Events fragment into a multiplicity of causal entities, just as pieces of clay can fragment into a mulitiplicity of statues. The reason for this fragmentation is that causes (and, I might add, effects) are *facets* or *features* of events, not the events themselves.'[12] In a recent article, Ted Honderich claims that 'Causes strictly speaking are individual properties of ordinary things.'[13] It is this teapot's weight – his example – an individual property of this teapot, that flattens a napkin. Honderich and Dretske each want to replace events as basic causal relata with something else. Their candidates are similar but distinct. I do not see how the suddenness of the bolt's giving way can easily be regarded as an individual property of an ordinary thing. It is easier to regard it as an individual property of an ordinary event. We need not choose between Dretske's and Honderich's favored causal relata, and we need not choose between these and ordinary events. As I have announced already, I do not want to deny that events themselves are causes. Another collapse, in the next state, was caused not by the suddenness or unexpectedness of the bolt's giving way, but simply by the bolt's giving way, an event.

The examination of Dretske resumes. Dretske tells a story about someone, let's call him Stanley, who loses his wallet in a restaurant just before the check

---

meanings. I am grateful to Richmond Thomason for questioning this unreflective remark. If one's theory of meaning allows for differences of truth conditions, because, for example, of differences in relevant contrasts, without differences in meaning, then I have no reason to insist that these examples involve any differences in meaning.

[11] Peterson's theory classifies these as non-compound complex events.

[12] pp. 96–7.

[13] 'Causes and *if p, even if x, still q,' Philosophy,* 57 (1982), p. 293.

arrives.[14] It is the time of the wallet loss, just before the waiter arrives with the check, rather than place of the loss, the restaurant, that causes suspicion. Stanley's losing his wallet *just before the check arrives* causes suspicion. Stanley's losing his wallet *in the restaurant* just before the check arrives does not cause suspicion. In 'Referring to events' Dretske succumbs to a temptation he resisted earlier in 'Contrastive statements.' He looks for a way to regard two phrases, word-for-word identical but differing in emphasis, such as:

> Stanley's losing his wallet in the restaurant *just before the check arrives*,

and:

> Stanley's losing his wallet *in the restaurant* just before the check arrives,

as referring to different things, to different event aspects or allomorphic events. You don't have to accept this in order to accept event aspects as causal relata.

There is a habit – I've got it myself – always to seek unity, unified accounts, and single explanatory principles. Let us call it, in remembrance of Thales, the Milesian Urge. Holding that there is just one basic element satisfies the Milesian Urge, whether the element be water, air, or fire. Holding that there is a single species of causal relata satisfies it as well, whether the species be events, aspects of events, or individual properties of ordinary things. When one admits that there is a diversity of items, the Milesian Urge prompts one to seek an underlying or overlying unity. So here, one persuaded that events are not the only causal relata will be tempted to look for a single, all-encompassing species of causal relata of which events are a subspecies. There will be time enough for such a search after we understand better the diversity we hope to unify. The fact that many philosophers shun such diversity and struggle against so-called ontological proliferation attests to the strength of the Milesian Urge.

Who were Shem and Shaun the living sons or daughters of? That's not my question. My question is: What does 'Shem and Shaun' refer to here? Consider the following response: If the phrase refers to Shem, it does not refer to Shaun; and if it refers to Shaun, it does not refer to Shem. There is no principled way to choose one rather than the other. The phrase does not refer either to Shem or to Shaun but to the pair. Neither Shem nor Shaun is the same as the pair to which each belongs; and since the phrase refers to the pair, it does not refer to either member.

This response has been fashioned to assume openly that if the phrase refers at all, it refers to exactly one thing. For any x and y, if it refers to x, and if x is not identical to y, then it does not refer to y. The example of an explicitly conjunctive phrase has been chosen to make this assumption appear as a foolish manifestation of the Milesian Urge. Why assume referential singularity in cases of obvious multiplicity? I shall question the assumption of referential singularity in cases of apparently less obvious multiplicity.

---

[14] 'Referring to events,' pp. 94–6.

Reference is perhaps not the most apt term for the topic at hand. Applying a lesson Davidson repeats in several articles, we should remember that 'Stanley lost his wallet' and 'Flora dried herself' can be true without there being reference to a particular event in either case. Stanley might have lost his wallet, found it, and lost it again. Flora might have splashed in the waves a number of times and dried herself after each aquatic episode. Although 'Stanley's losing his wallet in the restaurant just before the check arrives' may not refer to a particular event, a particular losing of his wallet, I see no harm in saying that the phrase refers to Stanley's losing his wallet. Or we may say instead that it is *about* Stanley's losing his wallet. The phrase is about a lot of other things as well. It is about the location of the losing, in the restaurant; it is about the time of the losing, just before the check arrived (if there were several losings, presumably there were also several checks); it is about the person who lost the wallet, Stanley; it is about what he has lost, his wallet.

Emphasis emphasizes. Emphasis of different portions of the phrase in question directs attention toward different things the phrase is about. The differently emphasized phrases are each about exactly the same things, although different ones of these same things receive prominence from different emphases.

When differently emphasized phrases are embedded in a larger context, the results can differ in meaning and truth conditions. Stanley remembers that (*P*) Mildred left her notebook in my office this morning. Emphasize different components of (*P*), 'Mildred left her notebook in my office this morning', and you get different more specific statements about what Stanley remembers. After listing four different ways (*P*) can be emphasized, Dretske makes the following suggestion: 'When we embed the proposition (*P*) into a context such as "S remembers ..." we automatically embed one of these allomorphs into this context; or, if no allomorph is indicated or understood, the resulting statement is ambiguous.'[15] Peter Achinstein considers a second way of regarding the embedding of unemphasized propositions. If a sentence such as 'Socrates' drinking hemlock at dusk caused his death' contains no emphasis, and does not lack unique truth-value because of ambiguity, it might 'be understood as if *all* the words in the cause-term are emphasized; it is to be understood as implying that all aspects of the event (implicit in its description) were causally operative.'[16] Armed with the disjunction of these two alternatives, Achinstein points out unwelcome consequences of several attempts to paraphrase contrastively emphasized causal statements. If the paraphrase in question is true, then an unemphasized causal sentence is true. But if it is ambiguous, it isn't true, for it lacks a definite truth value; or, if it is understood rather as emphasized everywhere, it still isn't true in most cases, but false. The paraphrase in question, which contains or implies an unemphasized causal sentence, is in trouble in either case.

Achinstein and Dretske overlook a plausible alternative. An unemphasized sentence can be unspecific without being ambiguous. (Trading on ambiguity

---

[15] Ibid., p. 92.
[16] *The Nature of Explanation*, p. 206.

involves shifting from one specific reading to another. Remaining unspecific, on the other hand, involves no such shift; it merely avoids specificity.) According to Achinstein's second alternative, an unemphasized causal sentence can be regarded as a conjunction of all the sentences that result from emphases on different parts of the embedded sentence. According to the alternative Dretske and Achinstein both neglect, it is the corresponding disjunction. A disjunction can typically be true in several different ways, but this does not make it ambiguous. Neither is an existentially quantified statement such as 'Someone left a dead cigar in the begonia' ambiguous merely because Joe, Bernie, and David each might be the lone culprit. Emphasizing a part of an embedded sentence need not remove ambiguity in order to increase specificity, to single out something as relevant. Emphasis in causal contexts singles out something as causally relevant.

Davidson says it is a confusion to think every deletion from the description of an event represents something deleted from the event described. On the view I advance, it is no confusion to think that deletion from a phrase about an event often represents a deletion from the things the phrase is about. 'Flora's drying herself with a coarse towel' is about, among other things, what she dried herself with, a coarse towel. 'Flora's drying herself' is not about this, although it is still about Flora and her drying herself, as was the first phrase, and although all of Flora's drying may have in fact been with a coarse towel.

Smith slipped, fell, and died. His fall killed him. Did his weighing twelve stone, or 168 pounds, also kill him? If we change Smith's weight in this example to 368 pounds, there will be more conversational point in mentioning the causal relevance of Smith's weight to his death. Smith's fall, with Smith weighing, as he did, 368 pounds, was no more efficacious in killing him than Smith's actual fall. It does not follow from this that if Smith's fall killed him then his weighing 368 pounds, or his fall being of someone weighing 368 pounds, did not also causally contribute to his death. It does not follow, at any rate, without the assumption I want to reject, that only events are causal relata.

One argument of Davidson's concerning parts of causes appears to be a lapse. 'It cannot be that the striking of this match was only part of the cause, for this match was in fact dry, in adequate oxygen, and the striking was hard enough.'[17] What prevents us from constructing parallel arguments, each showing that something else cannot be only part of the cause? 'It cannot be that the dryness of this match was only part of the cause, for this was the dryness of a match that was in fact struck, hard enough, in adequate oxygen.'[18] If we assume that only events can be causal relata, then it is reasonable to hold that the only cause in this example is the striking. Abandon this assumption, and I see no good reason not to count the striking's being hard enough, its being of a dry match, and so forth, as distinguishable causes of the match's lighting. Allowing parts of causes, in this fashion, should not prevent us from drawing Davidson's important distinction between causes and the features we hit on for describing them.

---

[17] 'Causal relations,' pp. 155–6.
[18] Gerald Vision makes a similar point in 'Causal sufficiency,' *Mind*, 88 (1979), pp. 105–10. Also see M. Glouberman, 'Complete causes,' *Logique et Analyse*, 94 (1981), pp. 231–44.

If the dryness of the match is counted as part of the cause of its lighting, this sounds dangerously close to saying that the fact that the match was dry was part of the cause. There are stylistic grounds for avoiding *fact that* locutions in causal statements, and no obviously good grounds for using them; but I think an examination of Davidson's argument concerning *fact that* can teach us something about our general topic. Here is a version of the argument. Substitute for 'the match was dry' the logically equivalent 'the class of all things such that they are self-identical and the match was dry is identical to the class of all self-identical things.' Substitute for the first term in this identity statement the coextensive 'the class of all things such that they are self-identical and platinum does not tarnish' to obtain 'the class of all things such that they are self-identical and platinum does not tarnish is identical to the class of all self-identical things.' Make a final substitution of logical equivalents to obtain 'platinum does not tarnish.' If the fact that the match was dry was part of the cause, and if each of these substitutions preserves truth, then the fact that platinum does not tarnish was part of the cause. I have tried here to be faithful to the argument Davidson constructs with regard to his example, '(2) *The fact that* there was a short circuit *caused it to be the case that* there was a fire.' In the course of the argument, Davidson says, 'Surely also we cannot change the truth value of the likes of (2) by substituting logically equivalent sentences for sentences in it. Thus (2) retains its truth if for "there was a fire" we substitute the logically equivalent "$\hat{x}(x = x$ & there was a fire) $= \hat{x}(x = x)$".'[19] Stylometric analysis of Davidson's prose could make us suspect this 'surely,' for he does not habitually use this slippery adverb to lubricate the passage from premisses to conclusion. A still stronger reason for suspecting irony, to my mind, is that (2) does not retain its truth when the indicated substitution is made. If there is some irony here, however, Davidson suffers the common fate of ironists.

Despite what many logic textbooks teach, you can't generally show an argument to be invalid by showing that it has an invalid form. You can't show that the above substitution of logical equivalents is invalid merely by showing that it is an instance of an invalid move. I think it is instructive nevertheless to construct a bad argument form of which our present argument is an instance.

Two predicates are logically equivalent if and only if they both apply in exactly the same logically possible worlds. From this definition of *logically equivalent predicates* it follows that if Fx and Gx are logically equivalent, then for any x, Fx if and only if Gx.

To see that this is an invalid argument, consider the following predicates, each logically equivalent to the others according to the definition supplied:

> x is Nero's fiddling while Rome burned.
> x is Rome's burning while Nero fiddled.
> x is the simultaneity of Nero's fiddling with Rome's burning.
> x is Nero, who fiddled while Rome burned.
> x is Rome, which burned while Nero fiddled.

---

[19] 'Causal relations,' p. 153.

The list could be continued. Although these predicates all apply in just the same possible worlds, they do not apply to the same things. Truth is not generally preserved when 'Nero's fiddling while Rome burned' is replaced by 'Rome's burning while Nero fiddled' or by 'Nero, who fiddled while Rome burned' or by one of the others.

When propositions are viewed as zero-place predicates, the above definition of *logically equivalent predicates* yields a standard definition of *logically equivalent propositions*: they are true in exactly the same logically possible worlds. Are logically equivalent propositions always about the same thing? I don't see why they should be, any more than logically equivalent predicates are always true of the same things.[20]

'The class of all things such that they are self-identical and there was a fire is identical to the class of self-identical things' is about a number of things in addition to a fire. 'The fact that there was a short circuit caused it to be the case that the class of all things, et cetera' says that the obtaining of a certain class-identity is caused to be the case. The original sentence says an occurrence of a fire is caused to be the case. A fire is something different from a class-identity. That's why the substitution in question does not preserve truth.

Before calling for renewed research into the nature of a sentential causal connective, I would rather include facts along with events, event aspects, and individual properties as proper causal relata. And instead of doing this, I would rather avoid fact-talk altogether when discussing causation. Facts and declarative sentences are made for each other, while causal relations obtain independent of sentences. The examples we have been considering of substitutions of logically equivalent expressions in causal contexts, besides bearing on what one can or cannot do with fact-talk, show something about how causal sentence constructions indicate causal relevance.

We have considered three ways of regarding sentences that embed unemphasized phrases. Dretske says they are ambiguous. Achinstein adds that the embedded phrase can be understood to be emphasized in every possible way. I add that the unemphasized sentence can be regarded as unspecific. Now I want to add another alternative, for many causal sentences that embed unemphasized phrases are understood in a fairly specific way. Much of this understanding is no doubt due to background beliefs about causal plausability and causal independence, but some of it is due to linguistic constructions other than emphasis. 'Socrates drank hemlock at dusk. This caused his death.' Our fairly specific understanding of this claim is due in part to its structure, I think, in addition to our prior beliefs about the causal irrelevance of the time of day when poison is ingested. The presumption that the time of drinking was not part of the cause of Socrates' death can be cancelled by emphasis. 'Socrates drank hemlock *at dusk*. This caused his death.' Besides increasing specificity by directing attention, emphasis can shift specificity by redirecting attention.

Although the sentence that results from the first substitution in Davidson's argument is a complicated mouthful, I will transform it syntactically and also

---

[20] For a point of the same kind developed from a different angle, see Jon Barwise and John Perry, 'Semantic innocence and uncompromising situations,' *Midwest Studies in Philosophy*, 6 (1981), pp. 387–403.

use emphasis in an attempt to shift its indication of causal relevance back to that of the original statement '*The fact that* there was a short circuit *caused it to be the case that* there was a fire.'

> The fact that there was a short circuit caused it to be the case that the class of all self-identical things is identical to the class of all things x such that *there was a FIRE* and x is self-identical.

If you are persuaded that substitution of logical equivalents need not preserve truth because it can change the subject-matter, grant for the sake of argument that this particular substitution, with the help of emphasis, preserves truth because it does not change the subject-matter. What happens now when we substitute a coextensive term such as 'the class of all things x such that Nero fiddled and x is self-identical'? This does change the subject-matter and thus fails to preserve truth. What is said to be caused, in an extraordinarily round-about way, is the occurrence of a fire. The appropriate place to substitute a coextensional expression, if we are concerned with such substitution in causal contexts, is for the predicate *is a fire*.

Consider the following two statements, one more specific than the other:

> Shem and Shaun quarrelled, then one kicked the other.
> Shem and Shaun quarrelled, then the first kicked the second.

Substitution of the coextensive 'Shaun and Shem' for 'Shem and Shaun' in the first sentence preserves truth, and it obviously doesn't in the second sentence. The order of the names makes no difference in the first sentence but does in the second, so substitutions in the second sentence should be made only for single names. The greater specificity of the second sentence requires more specific substitutions.

The same point holds, I suggest, for all the examples we discussed earlier. Emphasis in causal contexts locates or relocates a causal relatum. Once a causal relatum is indicated, an expression referring to it can be replaced by another expression referring to it.

Consider now the following argument by Achinstein:

We begin by supposing that

> (5) Socrates' *drinking hemlock* at dusk caused his death

is true. The emphasis in (5) indicates that some feature of the situation – the hemlock drinking – was causally efficacious. Let us assume that 'Socrates' drinking hemlock at dusk' refers to a particular event, and that it refers to the same event no matter which words, if any, are emphasized within it. That is,

> (6) Socrates' drinking hemlock at dusk = Socrates' *drinking hemlock* at dusk = Socrates' drinking hemlock *at dusk*.

If singular causal sentences are referentially transparent in cause-positions, then from (5) and (6) we may infer

> (7) Socrates' drinking hemlock *at dusk* caused his death.

But (7) is false, since it falsely selects the time of the drinking as causally efficacious; it states that the event's being at dusk is what caused Socrates to die. Since we can infer a false sentence from a true one by substituting expressions referring to the same event, I conclude that singular causal sentences are referentially opaque, i.e., not transparent, in the cause-position. A similar argument, given in Section 9, shows that they are referentially opaque in the effect-position as well. Hence singular causal statements such as (1) and (5) are not relational.[21]

If you want to reject this conclusion, as Davidson, Dretske, and I all do, you do not have to deny the identities of (6) so long as you accept the view, as Achinstein puts it, that features of the situation can be causally efficacious. The argument does not tell against the view that causation is a relation, although it may tell against the view that all causal relata are events. We can understand Achinstein's term 'cause-position' more precisely than he intends. Given a sentence of the form

[   ] caused his death,

we need not agree that the cause-position is always indicated accurately by the brackets. What can grammatically fill the blank is not always what the resulting sentence says is a cause of death. Emphasis can narrow or restrict the cause-position, and change of emphasis in otherwise identical sentences can shift the cause-position in the statement. The expressions within the brackets in the next two sentences are about just the same things, yet the sentences make different causal claims because the different emphases single out different aspects as occupying a narrowed cause-position.

[Socrates' *drinking hemlock* at dusk] caused his death.
[Socrates' drinking hemlock *at dusk*] caused his death.

Socrates' drinking being a drinking of hemlock is a cause of Socrates' death. This event aspect, no matter how it is described, is a causal relatum. If (5) is opaque, this does not entail that the more explicitly relational causal statement (5) indicates is also opaque. Once the cause-position is accurately and precisely specified, substitution of coreferrential expressions in the cause-position preserves truth.

I cannot deal fully here with ontological qualms that many feel about listing the likes of event aspects among causal relata.[22] Achinstein admits that we can use emphasis among other devices to focus on an aspect of an event. He insists,

---

[21] *The Nature of Explanation*, p. 194. In his friendly and supportive comments on this paper at the Davidson Conference, Arnold Koslow suggested that this argument of Achinstein's could be attacked along another line. The opacity of (5), says Koslow, does not show that causation is a relation any more than the opacity of statements of strict implication show that implication is not a relation. Perhaps Achinstein could resist this analogy by claiming that the apparent opacity of implication statements is due to carelessness about the use/mention distinction.

[22] Steven E. Boër calls events-allomorphs 'creatures of darkness' in 'Meaning and contrastive stress,' *Philosophical Review*, 88 (1979), p. 272. For a critical discussion of Boër's positive treatment of contrastive stress, see Achinstein, *The Nature of Explanation*, pp. 201–3.

however, that 'we need not be referring to any *entity* in so doing. One can use the expression "drinking hemlock" by itself, or in a prominent position in the sentence, or with emphasis, to focus upon a particular aspect of the event without thereby referring to an entity which is that aspect'.[23] Achinstein would rather deny that singular causal statements are relational than hold that event aspects are causally related. I believe that Davidson's treatment of reference to events shows us the way to refer to event aspects in good conscience.

Davidson asks rhetorically 'Are there good reasons for taking events seriously as entities?' and answers 'There are indeed.'[24] I agree, but would respond differently to the word-for-word identical question with the last word stressed: Are there good reasons for taking events seriously as *entities*? Here emphasis narrows a term's sense. When Achinstein says that, in focusing on event aspects, 'we need not be referring to any *entity*,' his emphasis makes a difference. Anything and everything is something, but we can refer to lots of things that are not *things*, not *entities*. The aphorism of Quine connecting *entity* and *identity* Davidson says is more obvious still in reverse: No identity without an entity.[25] It is not so obvious to me. Those whose ontological scruples are most severe will quantify over times, for example, will say that this and that occurred at the same time, while that and the other occurred at different times. Do they thereby take *times* seriously as *entities*? They would do better, I think, to give up the notion that there is no identity, no clear-headed quantification, without an entity. When Davidson recommends that we take events as entities, that we take them seriously, I think he means no more than this:

> It is impressive how well everything comes out if we accept the obvious idea that there are things like falls, devourings, and strolls for sentences ... to be about. In short, I propose to legitimize our intuition that events are true particulars by recognizing explicit reference to them, or quantification over them, in much of our ordinary talk.[26]

I propose that we recognize emplicit reference to event aspects in some of our ordinary talk. There is something about Sebastian's stroll that makes me uneasy, and something about it that makes you uneasy. It is perfectly proper to ask whether the aspect responsible for your uneasiness is the same as or different from the aspect responsible for mine. Different aspects of one event can have diverse effects and diverse causes. Whatever caused Sebastian to stroll at two in the morning can be different from what caused him to stroll slowly and different again from what caused him simply to stroll. We need not conclude from this that Sebastian's stroll is somehow different from his slow stroll and from his stroll at two in the morning. We should admit rather, that his stroll's being at two in the morning is something different both from the stroll itself and from the stroll's being slow, and that they are all distinct causal relata.

---

[23] *The Nature of Explanation*, p. 203.

[24] 'The individuation of events,' p. 164.

[25] Ibid., p. 164.

[26] Ibid., p. 166. See my 'Knowledge and relevant alternatives: comments on Dretske,' *Philosophical Studies*, 40 (1981), pp. 379–88, for a brief discussion (p. 380) of how Davidson's practice of quantifying over events can be used to respond to an argument of Dretske's concerning scope differences in 'The content of knowledge.'

19

Aspectual Actions and Davidson's Theory of Events

HECTOR-NERI CASTAÑEDA

My purpose here is manifold. To begin with, I am anxious to promote a most important sub-category of action – *aspectual action* I have called it – that has been hitherto seriously neglected. Aspectual actions play a fundamental and irreducible role in our deontic structures, be they moral obligations, legal claims, official duties, commitments grounded on promises, etc. This can be fully appreciated through a discussion of the most profound paradox of deontic logic recently discovered by James Forrester. The best solution to this paradox requires the enrichment of our conception of action, but not the enrichment of deontic principles: the solution falls very gracefully within my standard solution in one fell swoop to all but one of the so-called deontic paradoxes. (The exception is Lawrence Powers' Susie Mae Example.[1]) Forrester's Deontic Paradox of Aspectual Action furnishes some justification for Donald Davidson's claim that the modalities of actions are best treated by means of logical conjunction. Furthermore, Forrester's paradox highlights a most important methodological moral, namely: that we must work on *complex data*, at least data complex enough to show the conceptual patterns we are interested in. Aspectual actions have so far been neglected because of a widespread tendency to work with simple data. Indeed, both the present limitations and points in favor of Davidson's insightful view of the logical form of action sentences cannot emerge within his perspective, which is narrowly limited exclusively to *realized* or *performed action*. For them to emerge we need the complexities that accrue to the combination of action with deontic modalities. When we rise to the level of obligations we find two initial dimensions of complexity: (a) obligatory actions may remain unperformed, (b) obligatory actions may have as grounds of obligation actions, which need not be obligatory, but are performed

---

[1] See Lawrence Powers, 'Some deontic logicians', *Nous*, 1 (1967), pp. 381–400. This paradox has to do with the defeasibility of obligations. For its simplest solution to it see Hector-Neri Castañeda, *Thinking and Doing: the philosophical foundations of institutions* (Reidel, Dordrecht, 1975, paperback 1982), pp. 232ff.

by the very same obliged agent. That is, actions, even when unperformed, may function either as mere circumstances of obligation or as essential deontic foci of obligatoriness. Only on these complications can we build the stage on which aspectual actions can play their crucial roles.

1 *James Forrester's profound deontic paradox of aspectual action*

Forrester's original example of gently murdering slightly is at bottom a variant of the so-called deontic paradox of the Good Samaritan. But it is more intriguing and more informative. It arises from the combination of deontic modalities with the adverbial modalities of actions.[2] Consider:

> John McNewton has decided to act immorally by murdering Smith, who has raped his girl friend Ann. We all grant, including John, that killing is morally wrong. But John is, nevertheless, all set to murder Smith. He asks us to take that as a *non-negotiable fact*. Furthermore, none of us is a moral utilitarian, or a moral hedonist; yet we all recognize that we have a moral duty to minimize suffering. Against this background we have:

(1) It's not true that John McNewton ought morally to murder Smith.
(2) If John McNewton murders Smith, however, then he ought morally to murder Smith gently.
(3) John McNewton will in fact murder Smith.

Hence, from (2) and (3) by *modus ponens*:

(4) John McNewton ought morally to murder Smith gently.

Now, we also have:

(SO) If X doing A *implies* X doing B, then X's obligation Mly to A *implies* X's obligation Mly to B. (Where 'Mly' is an adverbial modality of the deontic operator, that is kept constant throughout the inference.)
(5) John McNewton murdering Smith gently *implies* John McNewton murdering Smith.

Therefore, from (4), (5) and (SO):

(6) John McNewton ought morally to murder Smith.
(7) Obviously, (6) contradicts (1).

---

[2] James Forrester came upon his exciting paradox in the course of a very protracted discussion in a 1982 Summer Seminar sponsored by The National Endowment for the Humanities. Forrester was testing my proposition/practition view on which I have been able to build the most comprehensive and yet the simplest deontic logic. This is just one episode that shows the great value of NEH's seminar program. For me it has been the loveliest and most effective Socratic experience in philosophical midwifery. After this essay was written Forrester published his paradox in 'Gentle Murder or The Adverbial Samaritan', *Journal of Philosophy*, 81(1984), pp. 193–7.

2 *The largest-scope solution*

Originally Forrester offered his example as a case in which it seems invalid to apply *modus ponens* to a deontic statement that *appears* to be of the form *If p, then Ought(q)*. His ultimate purpose was then to claim that of course there is nothing wrong with *modus ponens*, but that perhaps the problem arises because deontic premise (2) is only apparently of the relevant form *If p, then Ought(q)*, but is really of the form *Ought (if p, then q)*. This solution may be called the *Largest-Scope Solution*. Initially at least the following seems not only an effective stopper of the paradox, but also a nice and simple view:

> ECOL. *Exegetical Canon about Ordinary Language*. The modality *ought* has always the largest scope in the formulas in which it occurs outside the scope of negation.

Some philosophers have flirted with this solution. Yet even a cursory canvassing of the facts of normative experience shows that ECOL is false.

The Largest-Scope Solution is, of course, irrelevant if (2)–(4) above constitute a valid example of an *internal* form of *modus ponens*, namely:

(IMP) p and Ought (if p, X to do A); therefore, Ought (X to do A).

Patently, the grip of Forrester's paradox is quite tight if we can establish that the Largest-Scope Solution is a failure because premise (2) above has precisely the form it appears to have, to wit: with the ought-judgment in the consequent. Moreover, for a philosopher who holds that in general *Ought (if p, X to do A)* is equivalent to *if p, then Ought (X to do A)*, the pressure of Forrester's paradox should seem to be utterly suffocating. This is exactly my situation.

On reflection, there is no reason at all to suppose that all true ordinary conditional ought-judgments should conform to the above canon (ECOL). And as one would expect, the idea that unnegated *oughts* have the largest scope wherever they occur has been fostered by a widespread tendency to theorize on simple examples, like (2) above. But even the examination of some slightly complex examples reveals that the modality *ought* is a model of logical orderliness, respectfully occupying positions within all logical connectives. Just consider:

(11) Anthony ought Rly (= by virtue of the rules R regulating his job) to do the following:
   (a) open his office to the public at 9 a.m., and
   (b) inform the main office as soon as possible, if he won't open his office to the public at 9 a.m., and
   (c) answer the mail if and only if he has no unfulfilled orders.

Let us abbreviate the deontic prefix *Anthony ought R ly to do the following as Or*. Then (11) has the form:

(11F) Or(a&b&c).

Evidently, in (11) we have an *ought*, an *ought Rly*, an *ought Rly to do the following*, and Or with the largest scope, governing the conjunction (a)&(b)&(c). But it is also evident that (11) implies:

(12) Anthony ought Rly to open his office to the public at 9 a.m.
    & he ought Rly to do this: inform the main office if he won't open his office to the public at 9 a.m.
    & he ought Rly to do this: answer the mail if and only if he has no unfulfilled orders.

Undoubtedly, sentence (12) does no violation to English grammar or to our normative experience; yet it is of the form:

(12F) Or(a) & Or(b) & Or(c).

In (12) *ought Rly* does not possess the largest scope, but lies within the scope of conjunction. Furthermore, (12) implies:

(13) Anthony ought Rly to open his office to the public at 9 a.m.
    & (if he won't open at 9 a.m., he ought Rly to inform the main office as soon as possible)
    & (he ought to answer the mail, if and only if there are no unfulfilled orders).

In (13) we have *ought Rly* within the scope of conditional and biconditional connectives, it being of the form:

(13F) Or(a) & (if p, then Or(inform)) & (Or(answer), iff q).

This form (13f) is required to account naturally for the fact that from (11) and (14) below we can infer (15):

(14) Anthony has no unfulfilled orders today, but today he won't open his office to the public (because he has juror duty to perform).

Therefore:

(15) Anthony ought Rly to answer the mail today, although he also ought Rly to inform the main office that he won't open his office to the public.

That is, the following argument form is valid:

> Or(a) & (if p, then Or(inform)) & (Or(answer), iff q);
> q & p.
> Therefore, Or(answer) & Or(inform).

Let us ponder the situation carefully. It is not only a local intuition that the arguments below are all valid:

(A) (11),(14); therefore, (15).
(B) (12),(14); therefore, (15).
(C) (13),(14); therefore, (15).

There is, further, the underlying rationale that the involvement of *oughts* with *ifs* and *only ifs* is precisely to connect circumstances of obligation to obligations, so that an agent can infer from given circumstances the particular obligations he has acquired. This is just what the above inferences illustrate. In (A) and (B) we have an internal *modus ponens*, whereas in the case of (C) we have external *modus ponens*. They are in harmonious tandem, because they are interwoven by the implications connecting (11) to (12) to (13). Thus, even if these are not logically equivalent, we have at least that:

(D) *Ought (if p, X to do A)* implies *if p, X ought to do A*, where the indicative (propositional) variable 'p' denotes a circumstance and the infinitive variable 'X to do A' denotes an action practically considered.

   In brief, the situation of our friend John McNewton is an ordinary one. Therefore, it really makes no difference whether in premise (2) we have an *ought* with larger or with smaller scope. If *ought* is, as it clearly seems, restricted to the consequent, then the contradiction between (1) and (7) follows as we derived it; on the other hand, if *ought* has larger scope and governs the whole conditional, as The Largest-Scope Solution proposes, then the contradiction has to be mediated by an additional step involving (D) above.
   This tightens the grip of Forrester's example. We must seek for a solution, but of course, we must look for a solution that can be embedded within an account of the logical interactions between deontic operators and logical connectives.

3 *Forrester's paradox covers all aspects of action*

We must appreciate fully the pervasive nature of the difficulty embodied in Forrester's example. This difficulty covers *all* adverbial modalities of actions: the ways of doing an action, the degrees of the characters of an action, the intensity of the activity, etc. Yet the problem is MUCH more general. Purely external aspects of an action that are in no way connected with the action in any degree of intimacy, but are connected with it as loosely as you may wish, also illustrate the difficulty Forrester has pointed out with McNewton's obligation to murder gently. Just consider the following:

(16) John ought not to enter Luke's house.
(17) If John enters Luke's house, he ought, then, to enter it without having read the newspaper.
(18) John will in fact enter Luke's house.

Therefore,

(19) John ought to enter Luke's house without having read the newspaper.

By principle (SO) it seems that (19) implies:

(20) John ought to enter Luke's house.

Palpably, (20) is a wrong conclusion from (17) & (18).

Obviously, we should seek for a fruitful solution to Forrester's paradox, i.e., a solution that blends smoothly with the solution to the other deontic paradoxes.

4 *The proposition/practition distinction*

In the preceding examples we have dealt with a most important elementary complexity: one that has escaped the great majority of deontic logicians, namely: the contrast between the *circumstances* of obligation, expressed characteristically in the deontic forms under consideration by means of indicative clauses, and the *actions deontically considered*, expressed by means of infinitive clauses. The distinction holds irrespectively of whether the circumstances are within or without the scope of deontic operators. The distinction is so crucial that we must immediately record that:

(DL'1) A useful sentential deontic logic must be two-sorted.

Let us call the circumstances determining deontic character *propositions*. After all, they must be either true or false. Let us call *practitions* the actions and agent-action structures that are deontically considered, i.e., that are the foci (or subjects) of deontic status. Clearly, as these appear in the scope of deontic operators, they are neither true nor false; they are to be performed. A unifying theoretical move I have made is to postulate that second-person practitions are also the core contents of commanding, entreating, advising, etc., and first-person practitions are the core contents of intending and resolving. For instance, the very same first-person practition is expressed by the infinitive clause *I to A* in my psychological statement *I intend to A* as in my deontic statement *I ought Mly to A*, and it is the same practition which is expressed in my resolution *I shall A*.

Propositions are true or false; practitions are neither. Yet we may consider a practition of the form *X to A* as a modalization of the corresponding proposition of the form *X will A*. In the canonical notation we have been using we may postulate the operator T (from the infinitival sign 'to') and construe the practition *X to A* as the value of *T(X will A)*. One word of caution: there is absolutely NO claim here that infinitive clauses express nothing but practitions: the claim IS that infinitive clauses in the scope of deontic prefixes as in the above examples do express practitions, not propositions.

In sum, the 'if'-clauses in (11)–(13) formulate propositions, and the infinitive clauses ('Anthony ―― to open the office at 9 a.m.', 'Anthony ―― to inform the main office as soon as possible', and 'Anthony ―― to answer the mail') formulate practitions.

Evidently, the following principle is of paramount importance:

(DL'2) Deontic operators (or modalities) have practitions as arguments.

Of course, the mere syntactic contrast between indicative and infinitive clauses within the scope of deontic prefixes is *only* a clue to an important logical contrast. This logical contrast has been exhibited above in the validity of the inferences (A)–(D) above. To put it succinctly, the circumstances in the above examples (11)–(15) can be moved in and out of the scope of *ought*, but the actions that are deontically considered cannot be moved out; moreover, we can infer obligations from the circumstances by internal or external modus ponens; but we cannot infer the obligatoriness of the circumstances.

The most exciting consequence of the proposition/practition distinction is that it delivers the simplest and most unified and comprehensive solution to the well known paradoxes of deontic logic. I will illustrate this with the Good-Samaritan paradox. Interestingly enough, at first sight Forrester's paradox seems to resist the same easy and simple solution. This is why in my opinion it is the most profound paradox of deontic logic. As we shall see, however, in the end it also yields, after a partially Davidsonian treatment of actions, to the simple and easy proposition/practition solution. In the end, Forrester's paradox turns out to be the most exciting species of the Good-Samaritan paradox.

5 *The Good-Samaritan paradox*

An old example of mine that illustrates a sophisticated version of the so-called Good-Samaritan is this:[3]

(GS)Arthur is today legally (morally, contractually) obligated to bandage his employer, Jones; but a week from today Arthur will murder Jones. (It makes no difference whether Arthur or Jones knows today that the former will murder the latter.) Thus, we have:

(21) Arthur ought Mly to bandage the man he will kill a week hence.

(22) *Arthur bandaging a man he will kill a week hence* implies *Arthur killing a man*.

Hence, from (22) by principle (SO) above:

(23) Arthur ought Mly to kill a man.

---

[3] See *Thinking and Doing*, pp. 214ff. Given the background on the above formulation of the Good-Samaritan paradox one could discern an argument of the form *Arthur ought Mly to bandage Jones; Jones = the man Arthur he'll kill a week hence;* therefore, *Arthur ought Mly to bandage the man he'll kill a week hence*. This argument is perfectly valid. A most important feature of deontic logic is the extensionality of *ought* with respect to identity. On this see *Thinking and Doing*, pp. 230ff., 267ff. A little reflection reveals why this must be so. Deontic judgments are concerned with conduct. It is of the utmost importance that an agent who has an obligation Mly to perform an action A on an individual *a* performs A on that individual, regardless of how he comes to think of it, and regardless of whatever other properties the individual may possess. Clearly, whoever, e.g., a professional killer with a contract or an executioner, call him Ronald, is obligated Rly to kill the person who murdered Smith, and this person is the mayor of the city, then Ronald is obligated Rly to kill the mayor, and if Smith was the only Swede in town, then Ronald is obligated Rly to kill the murderer of the only Swede in town, and so on. Thus deontic logic is not so intensional as modal alethic logic. Hence, I disagree with Bas van Fraassen's claim that substitutivity of identity should not be valid in deontic contexts, in his 'The logic of conditional obligation', *Journal of Philosophical Logic*, 1 (1972), pp. 417–38, at p. 424.

Clearly, (23) is an incorrect conclusion to derive from (22), regardless of whether (23) contradicts another precept or not. A contradiction develops easily in case *Mly* is *morally* or *legally*, but it may very well be that Jones is a very punctilious employer and always hires his employees through a contract in which the employee commits himself or herself not to kill him, or at least acknowledges no contractual, moral, legal obligation to kill him or anybody else.

There is a legion of proposed solutions for the Good-Samaritan paradox. Some philosophers have, as should have been expected, adopted a form of Scope Solution. Others have put restrictions on times and places on the actions that are obligatory. Often the idea is that obligations are forward-looking; that is why in the above example Arthur's murder of Jones takes place in the future. Other writers have claimed that a difference in agents is the answer. That is why in the above example Arthur is both the killer and the bandager: the wrong-doer and the good samaritan. Obviously, the wrong doer can also be the victim of his/her wrong-doing. (The reader can toy with the identification of Arthur and Jones.) Other philosophers have tampered with the basic logic of *ought*. For instance, some jettison principle (SO) above; for another instance, so-called conditional or dyadic deontic logics are just one family of results of such tampering. We cannot discuss any of such solutions here. We shall limit ourselves to offering the simplest and most illuminating solution of them all,[4] namely, one that by conforming to the principles already established above builds on the proposition/practition distinction.

The first thing worth pondering is this: premise (22) shows a twofold syntactic and semantic contrast between the verbs *to bandage* and *will kill*. Whereas *bandage* is an infinitive and *will kill* is an indicative. On the other hand, the action of bandaging is the *focal point* of the deontic modality, whereas the action of killing is merely a *circumstance* about the person on whom the action of bandaging ought to be performed. As before, that circumstance can be moved in and out of the scope of *ought*. Clearly, (22) is equivalent to:

(22A) Arthur will kill a man a week hence and he ought Mly to bandage him.

But of course we cannot remove the action of bandaging from the scope of *ought*, preserving meaningfulness – let alone preserving truth.

This requires that we exegesize the above principle (SO). Once we have the distinction between propositions and practitions, the locutions of the form 'X doing A' we have used turn out to be ambiguous: they can represent propositions, but they can also represent practitions. Given our commitment to (DL'.2), it seems most fitting to have the logical implications between deontic judgments run along the implicational network of the practitions on which they are built. Hence, we interpret (SO), even generalize it, as follows:

(SO*) If practition *X to A* implies practition *Y to B*, then *X ought Mly to A* implies *Y ought Mly to B*.

---

[4] For a detailed discussion of the other deontic paradoxes see *Thinking and Doing*, ch. 7. On pp. 236ff. there are bibliographical references to a good number of proposed solutions to different paradoxes.

On this way of putting the principle even the grammar looks truly perspicuous.

With this machinery in hand we can solve the Good-Samaritan paradox easily, without having to give up on the richest and simplest deontic logic. Here is the solution. Doubtless, we still accept:

(21) Arthur ought Mly to bandage Jones, the man he'll kill a week hence.

We also acknowledge the deontically relevant counterpart of (22), namely:

(24) The practition *Arthur to bandage Jones, the man he'll kill a week hence* implies the proposition *Arthur will kill Jones (a man)*.

Of course, we still grant the deontically irrelevant counterpart of (22):

(24′) The proposition *Arthur has bandaged (is bandaging, will bandage) Jones, the man he'll kill a week hence* implies
the proposition *Arthur will kill Jones (a man)*.

The crux of the matter is this: (24) together with (21) and (SO*) cannot yield the deontic judgment *Arthur ought Mly to kill Jones (a man)*. Hence, this propositional route is closed. Obviously, the alternative practitional route required by (DL′.2) is also closed, since:

(25) The practition *Arthur to bandage Jones, the man he'll kill a week hence* does NOT imply
the practition *Arthur to kill Jones (a man)*.

This is all there is to it. Everything fits everything harmoniously: the ordinary syntax, the ordinary semantics, the obvious logical asymmetries between the practitional and the propositional clauses, and the simplicity and richness of the logic.

6 *Enter Forrester's paradox*

The practition/proposition solution to the Good-Samaritan paradox applies with equal ease to Chisholm's Contrary-to-Duty paradox and to other paradoxes.[5] But James Forrester's gentle murders look like a monkey wrench in the midst of the beautiful machinery. Let us focus our logical microscopes with large magnification.

In all the standard deontic 'paradoxes' there are two actions, of which one functions as a deontic focus and the other as a circumstance. The grammar of the formulation of the 'paradoxes' reveals this. Each paradox can be phrased in a canonical form where the action that functions as deontic focus is expressed by an infinitive clause, whereas the circumstantial action is expressed by an

---

[5] See ibid., ch. 7.

indicative clause. We follow those clues and solve the paradox in one step – just as illustrated above in the Arthur example.

The Forrester paradox is more puzzling. In all those examples we confront modalities of actions that are typically expressed by means of adverbs or prepositional phrases, with no canonical indicative tense to anchor the practition/proposition distinction. In each one of them we have, as always, a crucial premise in which *ought* governs a practition expressed by an infinitive clause. But there is a perplexing thing staring at us: the infinite clause in question has JUST ONE INFINITIVE and this infinitive expresses the action that is precisely what by the first premise of the argument is forbidden or not obligatory! We seem to have just one focus of obligation. This is grave. Forrester's paradox is much more serious than the most serious and sophisticated versions of the Good-Samaritan paradox so far discussed in the literature. Furthermore, the problem is here more serious because it appears not merely in the representation of English deontic sentences in the formalism of a proposed deontic calculus: it occurs within English itself. It is more serious, we could add, because it seems to threaten the validity of the most obvious and fundamental principle of inference, namely: good old *modus ponens*.

Let us take stock of the situation and fix our predicament. First, we cannot jettison *modus ponens*; second, we cannot adopt a general Largest-Scope View of deontic operators in order to protect *modus ponens*; third, we must either somehow reject the inference from (2) [*If John McNewton murders Smith, then he ought Mly to murder Smith gently*] and (3) [*John McNewton will in fact murder Smith*] to (4) [*John McNewton ought Mly to murder Smith gently*], or reject straightout the inference from (4) to (5) [*John McNewton ought Mly to murder Smith*].

What shall we do?

7 *Exegesis of the data*

Let us now exegesize the data. A careful exegesis should guide us to the best solution to the problem.

The crux of Forrester's example is this: the adverbial modalities of an action are properties of the action. When the action is *performed* there is one event (or a whole package of events] that have their aspects, their properties, which are expressed by the adverbial modalities. When we treat performed action we deal with one action and *its* aspects; yet in the deontic case above we seem to need to alter our view of the aspects or modalities of action: the action's aspects or modalities are in the deontic context *not* so much aspects of an event, but *actions* for the agent to bring about. Thus, as Forrester's example of McNewton's murdering Smith gently demands, we must carefully and rigorously distinguish between the CORE action of McNewton's *murdering* Smith and the ASPECTUAL ACTION of McNewton's murdering Smith *gently*.

In short, at least for the purpose of securing the logical structure of deontic statements, we must recognize that the aspects of actions are themselves actions – at least under deontic considerations. This is the first moral we must extract from Forrester's paradox. That is:

(A.D1*) We must distinguish between a *core action* and its related *aspectual actions*.

Yet this is not enough to solve Forrester's paradox. We must acknowledge that the actional aspects can themselves on their own be foci of obligation (prohibition, permission, and the like). In Forrester's example, McNewton's core action of murdering is wrong; but somehow his aspectual action of murdering *gently* is not merely right, but morally required. And the two deontic modalities do NOT collide. Thus, here is the second moral we derive from the paradox:

(A.D2*) Aspectual actions are *deontically autonomous* with respect to their core actions.

Of course, as we have already noted in discussing performed actions:

(A.D3*) Aspectual actions are *ontically dependent* on their core actions: in their execution they ride piggy-back on the execution of the core actions to which they anchored.

These are the key elements for the solution of Forrester's paradox. They also yield a fourth moral from Forrester's paradox: a most important semantic moral. We must acknowledge a subtle and, I dare say, hitherto undetected ambiguity in the locution 'to murder Smith gently' *in the deontic context* 'John McNewton ought Mly to murder Smith gently'. We may refer to it as a *deontic ambiguity*. Because of the basic deontic principle (A.D1*), the locution *to murder Smith gently*, in *Arthur ought Mly (is Mly obliged) to murder Smith gently*, represents very compactly TWO actions: the core action of *murdering* Smith and the aspectual action of murdering Smith *gently*. By (A.D2*), the deontic autonomy of the aspectual actions, we must recognize three deontic alternatives:

(i) Both the core action and the aspectual action are obligatory.
(ii) The core action is obligatory and the aspectual action is a mere circumstance.
(iii) The core action is a mere circumstance and the aspectual action is obligatory.

Hence, the locution 'to murder Smith gently' in the deontic context under consideration can express either one of the three deontic situations (i)–(iii). Therefore, that locution can have either of the following senses:

i) to murder Smith and to do so gently;
ii) to murder Smith given that (it being the case that) it will be done gently;
iii) it being the case that one will murder Smith to do it gently.

A lexical comment may be worthwhile. The expressions i)–iii) have deliberately been framed so as to depict principles (A.D1*)–(A.D3*). First, the word 'murder' is not included in the expression denoting the aspectual action; this is crucial, because the aspectual action of doing something gently can ride piggy-back on other core actions, e.g., on the actions of pressing, pushing, pulling, etc. Second, the words 'do so' (alternatively, 'do it') are used as a general signal of the ontic dependence of the aspectual action. Third, the conjunctive construction gives both the core action and the aspectual action equal deontic footing, thus signalling their deontic autonomy.

Under the present exegesis we are construing the *deontic* meaning of 'to murder Smith gently' as conjunctive. Because of the fundamental principle (D.L′1), the infinitive clauses denote, in the canonical notation we have been using, deontically focal practitions. Therefore, in case i) we have a conjunction of two practitions; in case ii) there is the conjunction of the practition involving the core action and a proposition presenting the aspectual action as a circumstance; in case iii) we have the reverse: the practition involves the aspectual action and the circumstance the core action.

8 *A simple and elegant solution to Forrester's paradox*

Evidently, the conjunctive analysis of the practition *to murder Smith gently* allows of handling Forrester's example as a special case of the Good-Samaritan paradox. In this example we confront case iii). This is clear from the facts that McNewton ought Mly not to murder Smith and that it is a mere non-negotiable fact that he will murder Smith. The contradiction, the paradox, arises in the move from *John McNewton ought Mly to murder Smith gently* to *John McNewton ought Mly to murder Smith*. In its derivation by *modus ponens* the former had the locution 'to murder Smith gently' in the appropriate sense (iii). But when the adverbial modality is detached, that infinitive locution acquires the incorrect sense i) – or perhaps sense ii). The considerations we engaged in above in connection with the Good-Samaritan paradox apply here. The mixed practition (iii) implies the realization of the circumstance *McNewton will murder Smith*, but not the validity of the practition *McNewton to murder Smith*.

Obviously, the same holds for *all* the modalities of actions. Just consider another example.

> John ought Mly not to enter Luke's house.
> But if he enters Luke's house he ought Mly to do so without breaking any windows.

Clearly, here our locution 'to do so' is less confusing than the tempting choice 'to enter Luke's house'.

The conjunctive analysis applies to all expressions of modalized actions. In general the formula is this:

> To A qly with (for, by, before, next to, etc.) Y

is to be construed as a conjunction of the form:

To A and to *do* it qly and to *do* it with (for, by, before, next to, etc.) Y.

To this conjunction we apply the proposition/practition distinction, and we are free of all forms of the Good-Samaritan paradox – including the most profound form of them all: James Forrester's paradox.

9 *Davidson's view of the logical form of action sentences*

That Donald Davidson had proposed a conjunctive view of action sentences was mentioned in response to Forrester's example by Anatole Anton.[6] He meant to reinforce Forrester's case by remarking that on Davidson's view there is only one actional conjunct, the others being predications of properties to that action-event, not themselves actions; they lack, therefore, an agent. Thus Anton pointed to the basic element of the solution to Forrester's paradox. My solution adopts this component from Davidson's view of action sentences, but it dispenses with other Davidsonian theses. It may be worthwhile to clarify the situation.

The main features of Davidson's analysis are:

(Di)   *Syntactically*: The introduction of a special variable and a term-place in action expressions.
(Dii)   *Semantically*: The assignment to that variable of a domain of events, with the requisite introduction of a quantifier ranging over such events.
(Diii) *Logically*: The introduction of the modalities and specifications of the features of the action (or event) conjunctively.
(Div)   *Ontologically*: Treatment of those features as properties of the events referred to by the terms occupying the new slots in action verbs.

We palpably need (Diii). But we need something else as well:

(C.P) The conjuncts that specify aspects of the action must NOT be construed as properties of the event introduced by (Dii), but must be construed as *attributions of actions to the agent*, and furthermore the agent can be connected to these *practically*, by means of the practitional copula.

Tenet (C.P) is supported by the introduction of the verb 'do so' or 'do it' in ii) and iii). This is really an anti-Davidsonian thesis.

Davidson's thesis (Dii) is troublesome. Indeed, I have argued that we need concepts of action that are more fundamental than Davidson's concept of action as performed action and occurred event in order to account for the sameness of what one ought to do with what one intends to do but sometimes fails to do. A first concept of this richer sort is an action type. But that is not enough. We need yet another concept of action, namely, action deontically considered, that is, the concept of action as a practition or a practitional function.[7] In any case an

---

[6] See note 2.
[7] See *Thinking and Doing*, chs 6 and 7.

action that is intended but not realized has no event exemplifying it. What one ought to do may also fail to obtain. Hence, the actions that one ought to do are not events.

We can extend our domain of discourse to possible events. But this raises additional questions. In particular there is the problem of explaining in what sense merely possible events can have properties.

Perhaps we can dispense with Davidson's events at least for deontic discourse and its logic. What we need is to enrich the domain of action types and allow that for each modality of an action there is an action type, a dependent one, of course, but one that can be practitionally involved with an agent. Consider, for instance, the following family of actions, understanding action in an intensional sense, viz., as something that one can do intentionally:[8]

A.   To kill;
A1: To kill Romeo;
A2: To kill Romeo with a knife;
A3: To kill Romeo slowly with a knife;
A4: To kill Romeo slowly next to the bed in his apartment in a moment of anger.

In *deontic contexts* these should be analyzed, respectively, as the following conjunctive actions:

A;   A1
A2 = A1 & (to do it with a knife);
A3 = A2 & (to do it slowly);
A4 = A1 & (to do it slowly) & (to do it next to the bed in his apartment) & (to do it in his apartment) & (to do it in a moment of anger).

It is important to see that the actions represented by the parenthetical expressions are actually independent of actions A and A1. One can perform the action of doing it with a knife attached to other actions than killing or killing Romeo, e.g., buttering a slice of bread, oiling a hinge, opening a door, etc.

The (doing it)-actions are, however, dependent in these sense that they are modalities of core actions; but they are not dependent, necessarily, on this or that core action.

I am, therefore, rejecting Davidson's theses (Dii) and (Div). I am keeping the general conjunctive idea captured in (Diii). But I am interpreting the conjuncts as *actions*, NOT as properties of actions, and indeed in some cases as practitions.

I can accommodate non-existing events in my ontology.

I have already proposed that a theory of CO-EVENTUATION, the counterpart of consubstantiation, may solve crucial problems of event identity.[9] But if we can postpone its introduction into action theory we are better off.

---

[8] On this see Hector-Neri Castañeda, 'Intensionality and identity in human action and philosophical method', *Nous*, 13 (1979), pp. 235–60, and Alvin Goldman's reply, 'Action, causation, and unity', *Nous*, 13 (1979), pp. 261–70.

[9] Castañeda, 'Intensionality and identity in human action and philosophical method'.

It is noteworthy, in any case, to see that the idea of a conjunctive view of the aspects of action is independent of (Div).

Is the conjunctive idea independent of the introduction of a special quantifier ranging on events? There are two distinct points here. (A) Is the conjunctive idea independent of the introduction of a new variable-place in action verbs? (B) Is it merely independent of the assignment of events to the new variables?

Problem (A) is obvious. The piggy-back or dependent (do-it)-properties clearly need attachment to something else: the pronoun 'it' central to their expression makes it evident both that the 'it' is a sort of variable and that we must specify what types of entities are its values. Drafting a Davidsonian view to our conjunctive View, we could still take the 'it' in question to be a variable referring back to a Davidsonian event. Then, as noted above, we would want to move up to an ontology of thinkable events, whether real, or possible, or even impossible – as the thinkable events of squaring the circle.

Thus the main question is (B). I propose for the time being to start with the view that 'it' makes a back reference to a core action type.

10 *The modifier view of aspects of actions or events*

One dia-philosophical note is relevant. An alternative to the Conjunctive-Event view of Davidson's other philosophers, most notably Terry Parsons and Romane Clark, have developed the Modifier View of Events and actions.[10] On this view we have a proposition like *John kills Smith* and to this we attach modifiers with encompassing scope, e.g., *Gently (John kills Smith)*, *Slowly (John Kills Smith)*, *(Slowly* (Gently (with a knife (before Josephine (next to some small children (John kills Smith))))))*.

This view has been proposed by Clark as a way of avoiding Davidson's commitment to a new sub-category of particulars, namely, events. Another reason is that this view has nice set-theoretical models – up to a point, however. If the modifiers are of a monotonic kind we can construe them as essentially providing subsets of the sets previously assigned to a formula. But not all modifiers are monotonic. Some are very tricky. For instance, the modifier 'toy' in 'toy soldier' does not yield a subset of soldiers.

Now, the great virtue of the Modifier View is that it provides a graphic account of the piggy-backness of the aspects of actions. The modifiers are represented as leaves of an artichoke core. But the equal status of many modifiers has to be accounted piecemeal by special axioms, rules, or laws.

Davidson's Conjunctive-Event view pictures the equal status of the modifiers as conjuncts, and conjunction, together with disjunction, is the most egalitarian of all the logical operations. One problem is that the Conjunctive View of Davidson's takes even the action kind core to be on equal footing as the aspects of the action: being a killing is a property of the event in the same boat as being done with a knife and being done slowly. The core of Davidson's action is, so to

---

[10] See Romane Clark, 'Concerning the logic of predicate modifiers', *Nous*, 4 (1970), pp. 311–35, and Terence Parsons, 'Some problems concerning the logic of grammatical modifiers', *Synthese*, 21 (1970), pp. 320–34.

speak, the event substrate represented by the event variable: ALL the event properties are equal before the court of event predication. Too much egalitarianism, it seems.

Now, on our analysis of actions, by distinguishing between a core action and piggy-back aspectual actions riding on that core, we capture the main intuition of the Modifier View. By treating the aspects of actions as themselves actions (if this can be sustained till the end) we eliminate the initial ontological commitment to events. By treating all the actions of the package, whether a core action or piggy-back aspectual actions, as being, so to speak, packaged by conjunction, we preserve the basic logical equality of the aspects of an action (core).

But we have other data to illuminate. The data requiring action types as contents of intending, commanding, and of deontic operations go hand in hand with the avoidance to Davidson's (existing) events. The view that modalities of actions are also actions, though piggy-back actions, fits well with the deontic character of the aspectual actions, revealed by Forrester's paradox. The Conjunctive packaging of the aspectual actions explains very nicely the autonomy of the deontic character of the aspectual actions.

> The core action of killing is wrong;
> the aspectual action of doing it gently is obligatory;
> the aspectual action of doing it before persons who love the victim is
> wrong;
> the aspectual action of doing it with a gun is deontically indifferent;
> etc.

The deontic autonomy of aspectual actions has to do with their being capable of accepting the practical operator T (or the practitional copula) generally independently of the other aspectual actions that impinge upon the same core action.

The Modifier View as normally conceived does not include the proposition/practition distinction. But it can incorporate it. Then there will be two types of modifiers, or two types of modification (the counterpart of predication), and presumably it will have to recognize the dominance of practitionhood by some principle assigning to a sentence a practition if one modifier, or one form of modification, is practitional.

Let us suppose, therefore, that the Modifier View is extended by adjoining to it the proposition/practition distinction. Let us signal this distinction by prefixing a modifier with a 'T' to transform it into a practitional component. Then a practition/proposition conjunction of the form *to murder Smith, it being done gently* can be mapped onto the Modifier View as follows: *Gently (T(to murder Smith))*. Clearly, the mapping is isomorphic. Consequently, there seems to be no special gain in the Davidsonian conjunctive thesis. Nevertheless, I still want to claim a significant advantage for it: the conjunctive view requires fewer rules and my rich deontic logic can be adapted to it immediately.

Undoubtedly, we MUST obtain the same implications whatever the view we adopt. The difference will lie on the principles characteristic of each type of view. We need fully developed theories to see how the complexities in one theory correspond to the complexities in another. The rich data we have available now, including the data involving deontic statements focusing on aspectual actions, are rich. We should urge philosophers to develop alternative views so that we can see our rich collection of data illuminated from different quarters and angles.

12 *Conclusion*

To sum up, we have seen how the deontic logic built on the practition/ proposition distinction solves Forrester's serious puzzle nicely, efficiently, and quickly. What we have extended is the base of the deontic logic: we have extended our conception of action to include aspectual, piggy-back actions. But our deontic logic remains the same – except for its show of fruitfulness.

20

Causation and Explanation: a Problem in Davidson's View on Action and Mind*

Dagfinn Føllesdal

Introduction

This paper will largely be critical. However, as Davidson has taught us, in order for there to be disagreement there has to be a lot of agreement. Rather than focusing on the agreement, I will use the opportunity that this meeting offers to state points where I disagree with Davidson or find difficulties in his view, hoping that we may return from here with insight in how Davidson will handle these issues.

My criticism concerns the notions of causation and explanation and their interrelation. It was first presented in a lecture I gave at a meeting on explanation organized by Stefan Körner in Bristol 1973. The lecture was published in Norwegian later that year. A German version appeared in 1979 and an English in 1980.[1] However, all the time I felt a little uneasy, thinking that I might be misunderstanding Davidson. I agree with Davidson that if a person's views come out unacceptable the way one interprets him, this counts against the interpretation. I therefore hope that Davidson will elaborate his view on the issues I find troublesome.

I am not the only one who has these misgivings. I have discovered a number of people who, no doubt independently of me, have raised similar objections.

*I am indebted to Lars Bergström and Bruce Aune for helpful comments. I also thank Donald Davidson who discussed the paper with me in September 1984. He made me see that to do justice to his view I would have to go into several issues that are not discussed here. Unfortunately, time has not permitted me to follow up Davidson's valuable suggestions.

[1] 'Handlinger, deres grunner og årsaker: en ide hos Aristoteles i ny belysning' in *Filosofihistorie, mening og handling: Til Anfinn Stigen på femtiårsdagen 22. oktober 1973* Oslo 1973 pp. 105–11.
——'Handlungen, ihre Gründe und Ursachen' in Hans Lenk (ed.), *Handlungstheorie – interdiszipli-när*, Band 2, Zweiter Halb band (Fink, München), 1979, pp. 431–44.
——'Explanation of Action' in R. Hilpinen (ed.), *Rationality in Science* (Philosophical Studies, Series in Philosophy, Vol. 21) (Reidel, Dordrecht, 1980), pp. 231–47.

First Frederick Stoutland, in 'The Causation of Behavior' (1976) and also in 'Oblique Causation and Reasons for Action' (1980), and in 'Philosophy of Action' (forthcoming).[2] Also, Raimo Tuomela makes similar observations in his book Human Action and Its Explanation (1977)[3] and Ted Honderich in 'The Argument for Anomalous Monism' (1982).[4] Jennifer Hornsby seems to have a similar objection in mind in her review of Davidson's *Essays on Actions and Events* in *Ratio* 1982[5] (I owe this reference to Davidson). Douglas Huff and Stephen Turner raise a related point in 'Rationalizations and the Application of Causal Explanations of Human Action' (1981).[6] However, their argument is different and not one that I can accept. These and related issues are also discussed in Lars Bergström's paper 'Føllesdal and Davidson on Reasons and Causes' (1981)[7] and in a forthcoming paper by Daniel Quesada.[8] The fact that not only I, but also many other philosophers are disturbed by Davidson's position and arguments, makes it appropriate to take them up for discussion at this meeting and hope to get some clarification.

I will begin my paper by presenting and discussing critically Davidson's use of physical laws in action explanation and then go on to consider his full view, which also includes an appeal to what he calls 'heteronomic generalizations'.

Presentation of Davidson's view
Part 1: the use of physical laws in action explanation

1. *One event, several descriptions*

Much of Davidson's work on action and the mind depends on a simple, but often neglected point: that one and the same object, be it an event or anything else, can be described in several different ways. The point is, of course old, and has been made in the theory of action before, notably by Miss Anscombe, to whom Davidson gives credit (e.g. in 'Agency' (1971), p. 59 of the reprint in *Essays on Actions and Events*. Where nothing else is said, all page references in

---

[2] Frederick Stoutland, 'The Causation of Behavior' *Essays on Wittgenstein in Honour of G.H. von Wright (Acta Philosophica Fennica, 28)* (North-Holland, Amsterdam, 1976), pp. 286–325. 'Oblique Causation and Reasons for Action', *Synthese*, 43 (1980), pp. 351–367. 'Philosophy of Action: Davidson, von Wright, and the Debate over Causation' (forthcoming) in Guttorm Fløistad (ed.) *Chronicles* of the Institut International de Philosophie.

[3] Raimo Tuomela, *Human Action and its Explanation* (Synthese Library, Vol. 116) (Reidel, Dordrecht, 1977).

[4] Ted Honderich, 'The Argument for Anomalous Monism', *Analysis*, 42 (1982), pp. 59–64. See also the ensuing discussion between Honderich and Peter Smith, in *Analysis*, 42.4, 43.3, and 44.2.

[5] Jennifer Hornsby, Review of *Essays on Actions and Events*, by Donald Davidson, *Ratio*, XXIV (1982), pp. 87–93.

[6] Douglas Huff and Stephen Turner, 'Rationalizations and the Application of Causal Explanations of Human Action', *American Philosophical Quarterly*, 18 (1981), pp. 213–220.

[7] Lars Bergström, 'Føllesdal and Davidson on Reasons and Causes', in Wlodzimierz Rabinowicz (ed.), *Tankar och Tankefel: Tillägnade Zalma Puterman*, 50 år, 1. oktober 1981 (Filosofiska Studier utgivna av Filosofiska Föreningen och Filosofiska Insitutionen vid Uppsala Universitet, nr. 33), Uppsala 1981, pp. 9–21.

[8] Daniel Quesada, 'Ontological Claims and the Psychology of Propositional Attitudes', manuscript.

the text of my paper are to this book)[9]. Davidson puts this little point to good use to clear up a number of philosophical puzzles.

2. *Instantiation of causal laws*

First, in his classical 1963 paper 'Actions, Reasons and Causes' Davidson uses it to refute the traditional arguments against regarding reasons as causes, which dominated the theory of action in the fifties and early sixties. Davidson argues convincingly that when reasons and actions are appropriately redescribed in a physical vocabulary, they may instantiate causal laws, and thereby be regarded as causes and effects. And once it has been established through such an instantiation that the reason is the cause and the action the effect, then they will remain cause and effect regardless of how they are redescribed. When we instantiate laws, the choice of description is crucial. However, when we state that a causal relation obtains, it does not matter which description we use; the statement that a causal relation obtains is referentially transparent, to use Frege's notion (or more appropriately, Whitehead's, Frege talked about *occurrences* being direct or indirect). Davidson emphasizes *laws*. I do not agree on this, and will come back to that later. However, for a while let us not question *this* part of his view.

Davidson's point is hence that reasons and actions instantiate laws when they are described in a purely physical vocabulary. The laws that are instantiated are accordingly physical laws, formulated in a physical vocabulary. Davidson states in 'Actions, Reasons and Causes' that there are no laws, at least no laws of the strict kind required for causation, that are formulated in the vocabulary which we normally use to describe reasons and actions (p. 15).

3. *Davidson's identity theory*

In 'Mental Events,' (1970) Davidson uses the same point to argue for his identity theory. He proves it from the following three premises:

(i) (Causal interaction between the physical and the mental.) Some mental events are causes or effects of physical events. For example, light rays within my visual field may bring about beliefs in me, and beliefs and desires in me may bring about actions, which have physical aspects.

(ii) (The nomological character of causality)
In order for one event to bring about another, they have to be connected by a strict law.

(iii) (The anomalism of the mental)
There are no strict laws connecting events described in a mental vocabulary with events described in a physical vocabulary.

---

[9] Donald Davidson, *Essays on Actions and Events* (Clarendon Press, Oxford, 1980). The following essays are referred to: 'Actions, Reasons, and Causes' (1963); 'Causal Relations' (1967); 'Mental Events' (1970); 'Agency' (1971); 'The Material Mind' (1973); 'Psychology as Philosophy' (1974); 'Hempel on Explaining Action' (1976)

From these three premises, Davidson's identity theory follows. For, if a mental event *m* is caused by or causes a physical event *p*, then by (i) and (ii), *m* and *p* must both be describable in such a way that under these descriptions they instantiate a strict law. By (iii), the descriptions must be in a physical vocabulary. Hence the mental event *m* must have a physical description, i.e. be identical with a physical event. So, given Davidson's three premises, which I shall return to later, the identity theory is proved, at least for all those mental events that interact with physical events. Davidson points out that in order to establish by this argument his identity theory in full generality, it would be sufficient to show that every mental event is the cause or effect of some physical event, however, he will not attempt this (p. 224).

This argument is given three places in Davidson's *Essays on Actions and Events*: at the beginning and end of 'Mental Events' (1970, pp. 208 and 223) and in 'Psychology as Philosophy' (1974, p. 231). Davidson calls his position 'anomalous monism' since it is a monism where events do not fall under strict laws when they are described in psychological terms (p. 231).

Criticism of Part 1

This ends my presentation of the first points in Davidson that I want to discuss. Let us now turn to the criticism.

4. *Causation versus explanation*

My main misgiving has to do with the fact that *while cause-contexts are transparent, explanation contexts are opaque*. The transparency of cause-contexts was, as we recall, duly noted by Davidson, it was one of his starting-points in 'Actions, Reasons and Causes'. However, the article is primarily about *explanation* of action. In the article, Davidson talks all the time about explanation, but his arguments turn on observations concerning causation, that depend on the transparency of cause-contexts.

Davidson is well aware that explanation contexts are opaque, but he does in my opinion not fully acknowledge the consequences of this for his enterprise. He says:

> The most primitive explanation of an event gives its cause; more elaborate explanations tell more of the story, or defend the singular causal claim by producing a relevant law or by giving reasons for believing such exists. But it is an error to think no explanation has been given until a law has been produced. (p. 17).

There is a lack of precision in the last sentence of this quotation which makes it acceptable when interpreted in one way, but unacceptable when interpreted in the way in which Davidson uses it in his arguments. Davidson holds that we need not have any idea of what the law must be like. As he says on page 17: 'The laws whose existence is required if reasons are causes of actions do not, we may be sure, deal in the concepts in which rationalizations must deal.'

A fairly standard view, which I fully accept, is the following: If I explain B by citing A, if I say 'B occurred for the reason A'' or 'B occurred because A,' then *the manner in which I refer to A and B determines whether what I say can function as an explanation.*

To spell this out more in detail: If one asks, 'Why did B occur?' not every reply of the type 'B occurred for the reason A,' 'B was caused by A,' or 'A was a cause of B' will be an explanation, even if there is in fact a causal law and descriptions of A and B such that A and B under these descriptions instantiate the causal law. Davidson presumably agrees with all this, but he would most likely disagree with my following, more specific claim: To say that A is a cause of B does not contribute to an *explanation* of the occurrence of B unless there is a law which is instantiated by A and B under *approximately* these descriptions. (By 'approximately' I mean that the descriptions 'A″' and 'B″' under which A and B instantiate the law must be such that the person for whom the explanation is intended believes that 'A″' and 'A' are roughly co-designative, and also 'B″' and 'B'.) If the only law that connects A and B is instantiated by A and B only under descriptions that differ radically from 'A' and 'B', then the assertion that A is a cause of B will be more the pronouncement of an oracle than it will be an explanation. (This constraint on descriptions applies in my view to all types of explanation, be it explanation by means of reason or by means of causes.)

This restriction on the kind of laws and vocabulary that are permissible in explanations makes the question of what is to count as an explanation relative to the person, or group of persons, for whom the explanation is intended. An explanation for a child and an explanation for a specialist in the field that the explanation relates to, must satisfy quite different requirements. Also other features of the situation are decisive for whether the explanation is adequate. However, this is as it shall be, these pragmatic conditions on explanations are just part of the general theory of explanation.

If I am right in what I have just said about the constraints placed on descriptions in explanations, Davidson's claim that reasons are physical causes does not answer the question: Why can explanations based on reasons function as explanations? This means that to the extent that our understanding is broadened by coming to know the reason for an action, this broadening must be attributed to a connection between reason and action other than a causal connection of the type discussed by Davidson.

Davidson brings this point up in the latest of his papers on explanation of action, his 1976 paper 'Hempel on Explaining Action.' Davidson says there, with reference to Hempel:

> The difference in our accounts, if there really is one, concerns the exact way in which *laws* are involved when we explain actions by mentioning the agent's reasons.
> There is a weak sense in which laws may be said to be involved which is not in dispute. Hempel holds, and I agree, that if A causes B, there must be descriptions of A and B which show that A and B fall under a law. This is a weak thesis, because if this is the only sense in which laws must be invoked in reason explanations, someone might explain an action by giving the agent's reasons while having no idea what the relevant law was.
>
> ....
>
> It would follow that we can explain actions by reference to reasons without knowing laws that link them. (p. 262)

So far, this is just the view that seems to be Davidson's in 'Actions, Reasons and Causes,' and which I have taken exception to above. Davidson proceeds to point out that this seems to conflict with Hempel's views on laws, which I share, at least as far as this particular issue is concerned:

> Hempel, if I am right, believes that all explanation requires reference, oblique or direct, to relevant known empirical laws. In that case, in order to explain events we must describe them in a way that reveals how laws are applicable.

One should emphasize here that Hempel does not require the law to be known, only that one should believe that there is a law that is instantiated by the cause and the effect under descriptions that are roughly known by the person for whom the explanation is intended. This is probably what Davidson alludes to when he says that according to Hempel the explanation may make oblique reference to the law. Of course, when one passes from everyday rough generalizations to scientific laws, precision increases, and the vocabulary becomes more technical. An explanation that shall be satisfactory for a layman, must state these laws as precisely and intelligibly as possible in a vocabulary that the layman is familiar with. It is on this point that we are left in the lurch by Davidson's appeal to laws that are totally unknown to the layman and to the expert alike.

This ends my criticism of Davidson's appeal to physical laws in action explanation.

Presentation of Davidson's view
Part 2: Heteronomic generalizations

5. Heteronomic generalizations

Davidson's full theory of action explanation includes, however, another important element: According to Davidson, explanations of action have to make use of generalizations of the kind we use in our everyday explanation of action. These generalizations are the 'laws' that we use in rationalization: viz. practical syllogisms, or better, the kind of patterns one finds in the theory of decision making under uncertainty (p. 268, see also p. 16). In these generalizations mental vocabulary, talk about beliefs and desires, is mixed with physical vocabulary, that I use to describe actions. These two kinds of vocabularies are of quite different kinds, according to Davidson, and he therefore calls these generalizations 'heteronomic.' His main point is now that such heteronomic generalizations cannot be strict laws, of the kind needed in order to establish nomic connections. They therefore do not suffice for action explanation, which ultimately has to fall back on physical laws of the kind we discussed earlier.

In the passage immediately following the one I last quoted from Davidson's discussion of Hempel, Davidson alludes to these heteronomic generalizations and uses his appeal to two kinds of laws to belittle the difference between himself and Hempel. He says:

This sounds like a forthright conflict, but in fact I am not sure it is. For on the one hand, I'm not certain what Hempel requires us to know about the relevant law; and on the other hand, I haven't denied that there may be laws far less strict or deterministic that we must know or assume to be true when we explain actions. (p. 262)

However, Davidson's appeal to two sets of laws is not enough to satisfy Hempel's requirements on explanation. While Davidson's first kind of laws, the physical ones, were unilluminative and left us completely in the dark, his second kind, the heteronomic 'laws' or generalizations, have an equally fatal defect, according to Davidson, they are false (p. 263). According to Hempel, as you remember, for an explanation to be satisfactory, the laws appealed to have to be true. I am afraid that again I have to side with Hempel.

Davidson seems to think that his double set of laws will do the trick. One set, the heteronomic ones, will provide the illumination, the other set, the physical ones, will secure the truth. Against this I will maintain that we need one set of regularities, and they have to be both illuminating and true.

My view is that there are such regularities constantly at work in our normal talk about beliefs, reasons and actions, and that they are both as illuminating and as true as they must be for action explanation to work. I will present this view and argue for it at the end of my paper, but I will now first present my criticism of Davidson's position.

Criticism of Part 2

6. *The connection between action explanation and Davidson's arguments for identity theory*

There is an intimate connection between Davidson's view on action explanation and his argument for the identity theory. All the three premisses that he needs for his argument for the identity theory (see Section 3 above) are also required for his view on action explanation.

7. *Acceptance of Davidson's first premiss (The causal interaction between the mental and the physical)*

The first premiss, concerning the causal interaction between the physical and the mental, is the major issue that has to be resolved by any satisfactory theory of action. The theory has to explain how our beliefs and desires can bring about physical events, like my moving my arm. Some philosophers would claim that the interaction, or the bringing about, should not be called causal. This seems to me to be largely a terminological issue, and in 'Explanation of Action' I have argued for calling this interaction causal. What is clear, however, is that, as Daniel Quesada points out in the paper I referred to earlier, only an epiphenomenalist or a Leibnitzian parallelist could want to question this interaction.

The main problems come with the last two premisses. Davidson presents arguments for both of them, and let us now consider these arguments.

8. *Criticism of Davidson's second premiss (The nomological character of causality)*

Let us start with premiss (ii), the nomological character of causality. Davidson's arguments for this premiss are mainly found in 'Causal Relations' (1967). However, that paper is primarily devoted to a discussion of the logical form of causal statements. It is taken for granted that in order for there to be causation there has to be laws that pretty much are of the universal generalization kind. A form that Davidson finds attractive, is a conjunction of a sufficient and a necessary condition (p. 158). Davidson does not try to argue why the notion of causality requires this sort of law rather than e.g. simple 'laws' that state tendencies or propensities. The idea that causal relations obtain only where universal generalizations are instantiated goes back to Hume but is poorly supported by arguments. Natural science rarely makes use of this idea, and in later years science, in particular physics, has been so strongly oriented towards powers, tendencies and propensities that it has caught the attention of philosophers. There is abundant literature on this subject, for a sample see the writings by Cartwright, Dretske, Harré and Madden, and Suppes.[10]

There are several reasons for this trend away from universal generalization. One is a simple formal consequence of the idea that Davidson emphasizes so often, that one and the same object or event can be described in numerous different ways. Under each of these descriptions it may instantiate a different law. These laws may correspond to quite different courses of events, and what will happen will depend on how the different laws should be balanced against one another.

(An example which illustrates this, is the following, which I discuss in 'Quantification Into Causal Contexts' (1965) and which originally stems from Chisholm.[11] Let us suppose that there is a well which is such that anyone who

---

[10] R. Harré, and Madden, E., *Causal Powers* (Rowan & Littlefield, Totowa, N.J.), 1975.
Fred Dretske, 'Laws of Nature' *Philosophy of Science*, XLIV (1977), pp. 248–68.
Patrick Suppes, 'Davidson's Views on Psychology as a Science', manuscript.
Nancy Cartwright, 'The Truth Doesn't Explain Much', *American Philosophical Quarterly*, 17 (1980), pp. 453–7.
——'Do the Laws of Physics State the Facts?' *Pacific Philosophical Quarterly*, 1 (1980), pp. 75–84.
——*How the Laws of Physics Lie* (Oxford University Press, Oxford, 1983).
[11] Roderick M. Chisholm. 'The Contrary-to-Fact Conditional', *Mind*, 55 (1946), pp. 289–307. Reprinted in Herbert Feigl and Wilfrid Sellars (eds), *Readings in Philosophical Analysis* (Appleton, New York, 1949). Dagfinn Føllesdal, 'Quantification into Causal Contexts', in Robert S. Cohen and Marx W. Wartofsky (eds), *Boston Studies in the Philosophy of Science*, Vol. 2: *In Honor of Philipp Frank* (Humanities Press, New York), 1965, pp. 263–74.

drinks from it gets poisoned. Let us further suppose that a severely dehydrated man comes to this well and drinks from it. He will then instantiate the following two 'laws':

> Any severely dehydrated person who drinks water will improve.
>
> Any person who drinks poisonous water will fall ill.

In addition, numerous other laws apply to this person as well, corresponding to his various other properties, his resistance, his access to medical treatment etc. What will happen to him, depends on how all these 'laws' balance out.)

In addition to these formal considerations, there are other reasons for the trend away from laws towards tendencies and dispositions. These have to do with developments in the sciences, which make them less closed and more holistic than they were before.

It therefore seems to me that in order for Davidson to retain his premiss (ii), he has to weaken the notion of law so much as to include regularities that are rather similar to those that we find in decision theory. If so, he will get into difficulties with his next premiss, premiss (iii), the anomalism of the mental. He is faced with a dilemma here: in order to vindicate premiss (ii), he must weaken the notion of 'law', but the more he weakens it, the more trouble does he get in upholding premiss (iii). Since he leaves the notion of 'law' rather vague, he avoids facing the issue, but it is one that has to be dealt with.

9. *Critiscism of Davidson's third premiss (the anomalism of the mental)*

Let us now turn to premiss (iii). Davidson presents a number of arguments for the anomalism of the mental, primarily in 'Mental Events' (1970) and 'Psychology as Philosophy' (1974). However, I find these arguments far from convincing. I can discern two main arguments for this premiss in Davidson's writings. Let us now consider them one by one.

Argument 1: The openness of the mental

One argument that recurs again and again in Davidson's writings is that strict psycho-physical laws are impossible because of the openness of the mental: 'The mental does not, by our first principle (premiss (i) above), constitute a closed system. Too much happens to affect the mental that is not itself a systematic part of the mental.' (p. 224). 'Since psychological phenomena do not constitute a closed system, this amounts to saying they are not, even in theory, amenable to precise prediction or subsumption under deterministic laws.' (p. 239, see also p. 243).

I agree with Davidson that there is a lot of interaction between the mental and the physical and that a satisfactory theory of action must incorporate both realms. However, I find his argument from this to the anomalism of the mental rather impotent. First, there is the following observation by Bergström in the paper which I mentioned in my introduction: 'The fact that a system is open (in the sense, I suppose, that some of its components are influenced by factors outside the system) does not prevent the existence of strict laws describing (parts of) the system. For example, consider an electronic calculator: the numerals displayed are strictly determined by the buttons pressed even though factors outside the system determine which buttons are pressed.' (Bergström, p. 16.)

A more general criticism of Davidson's argument is that, as we noted earlier, the same openness characterizes much of modern physics, and a parallel argument would show that there can be no physical laws. This may be so if 'law' is taken in Davidson's strict sense, but so much the worse for this sense of 'law'.

Argument 2: Indeterminacy of translation

Davidson's second argument for the anomalism of the mental makes use of Quine's doctrine of the indeterminacy of translation. This is a more interesting argument. It is also a much harder one to refute. This is, however, mainly because it is much more difficult to see how it runs. The place where it is most clearly formulated is on pp. 222–3 of 'Mental Events,' but it is also alluded to in other places in that essay and in 'Psychology as Philosophy,' and also on the last few pages of 'The Material Mind.'

The gist of the various arguments is most explicitly expressed in the following passage from 'Mental Events':

> When we use the concepts of belief, desire, and the rest, we must stand prepared, as the evidence accumulates, to adjust our theory in the light of considerations of overall cogency: the constitutive ideal of rationality partly controls each phase in the evolution of what must be an evolving theory. An arbitrary choice of translation scheme would preclude such opportunistic tempering of theory; put differently, a right arbitrary choice of a translation manual would be of a manual acceptable in the light of all possible evidence, and this is a choice we cannot make. We must conclude, I think, that nomological slack between the mental and the physical is essential as long as we conceive of man as a rational animal. (p. 223).

I can agree with much of what Davidson says here, in particular how the constitutive idea of rationality partly controls our evolving theory of the mental. But the argument does not bring out how this makes our theory of the mental *in*determinate rather than just *under*-determinate, like physical theory. The argument also fails to make clear how our theory of the mental is more adversely affected than physical theory by our not having all possible evidence at our disposal.

Davidson is resting his position upon subtle issues here and on arguments which are far from perspicuous. What I most of all hope will come out of our discussion, is a clarification of these matters.

My own view

My main aim in this paper has been to get Davidson to elucidate and amplify points that I find troublesome in his theory of action and mind. Let me end by indicating briefly my own view on the issues I have been criticizing, and thereby provide a contrasting view that may make it easier to pinpoint exactly where the troubles are, in his theory or in mine.

10. *One comprehensive theory of mind and nature, not two separate theories*

I have sketched my view in some other papers[12] and shall here only focus on some points that are particularly relevant for a comparison with Davidson. My view is that our theory of the mental and our theory of nature are both parts of one comprehensive theory which is tested against our experience as a whole. We have hence not one mental theory which maximizes rationality and one physical theory which maximizes something else, e.g. simplicity. A practical consequence of this is that when we ascribe beliefs, desires and other propositional attitudes to a person on the basis of observation of what he or she does and says, we should not try to maximize his agreement with ourselves or his rationality, but we should use all our knowledge about how beliefs and attitudes are formed under the influence of causal factors, reflection and so forth, and in particular our knowledge about his past experience and his various personality traits, such as credulity, alertness, resourcefulness, reflectiveness, etc. Ascribe to him the beliefs and attitudes you should expect him to have on the basis of this whole theory of man in general and of him in particular.

An example used for a different purpose by Patrick Suppes may illustrate the difference between the rationality-maximizing approach and my approach: A young boy who has just entered puberty and has an attractive female teacher may very frequently come up to the teacher after class to ask questions concerning his school work. When asked why he does this, he may answer that he wants to learn and that the teacher is a good explainer. This may be his sincere answer, but using our theory of man, we may give a different explanation of his actions.

Davidson will certainly not disagree with me about this example, but what it shows, is that in understanding man and explaining his actions we need a mixed psycho-physical theory, where in our matrix of explanation we bring together and weigh against one another both mental and physical factors. This is what we normally do in our everyday explanations, and a scientific theory of man must have room for components of both kinds, both mental and physical.

This comprehensive theory is of course under-determined by the evidence, like all physical theory, and there is an element of indeterminacy, but this is not restricted to the mental parts, but permeates the whole theory, built as it ultimately is on our perception and our actions.

---

[12] 'The Status of Rationality Assumptions in Interpretation and in the Explanation of Action,' *Dialectica*, 36 (1982), pp. 301–16.

11. *Wayward causal chains*

Davidson maintains that explaining an action is a two step process: We first rationalize the action, by arguing that given the agent's beliefs and desires, this was the rational thing for the agent to do. We then next show that he actually did it *because* of these beliefs and desires, that his beliefs and reasons physically caused the movements of his body in the appropriate way.

If this were what action explanation amounts to, then I would hold that nobody has ever explained an action so far. Nobody has ever traced the appropriate chain of physical causality from a person's beliefs and desires to his actions. And yet we explain actions all the time.

We are well aware that rationalization of an action does not amount to explanation of action. We know that there may be deviant chains, as illustrated, for example, by Davidson's climber who loosened his hold on the rope because his belief and want to loosen his hold so unnerved him that he did it or the man who stamped on the floor to break a pot (p. 264), or Oedipus who killed the old man who blocked his way when he was en route to kill his father.

It is these wayward causal chains that according to Davidson can never be handled by a psycho-physical theory of action: 'What I despair of spelling out is the way in which attitudes must cause actions if they are to rationalize the action.' This is where we have to appeal to purely physical laws, according to Davidson. In fact, Davidson's main argument for bringing in physical causation in explanation of action, is to account for the 'because' here.

However, I do not think that we reach such an impasse when we seek to improve and refine our psycho-physical theory. We have in practice no difficulty in classifying Davidson's deviant examples as deviant and we can usually tell why they are deviant. Our psycho-physical theory of action is just an attempt to refine and systematize the intuitions that underlie our intuitive classification. It is just because of the mentalistic component that we are able to sort out and classify some examples as deviant, others as standard. It may be difficult ahead of time to think of all eventualities and spell out all conditions that have to be satisfied in order that the reasons shall cause the action in the right way. However, this problem faces us in all areas which are fairly complex and where we do not have a completed theory. And where do we have completed theories?

12. *Prediction of action*

Finally a few words on prediction of action. One of Davidson's arguments against psycho-physical laws is that 'generalizations connecting reason and action are not – and cannot be sharpened into – the kind of law on the basis of which accurate predictions can reliably be made.' Similar remarks abound in his writings. His arguments for this are mainly that the mental does not constitute a closed system. My view on this point is that the same lack of accurate predictions faces us in all spheres where we lack complete information. Patrick Suppes has pointed out that some of the statistical laws in psychology, e.g. in learning theory, are considerably more accurate than those we find in some parts of physics (Suppes manuscript, p. 9). And certainly, the neuro-physiological theory of action is infinitely worse off at present than is our intuitive psycho-physical theory of action. Thinking, as I do, that we do not have two separate theories, one of nature and one of the mental, but one comprehensive theory which comprises both areas, I also find it hard to accept any a priori argument that accurate predictions are in principle possible in a neuro-physiological theory of action but not in a theory that makes use of mental terms.

21

Adverbs and Subdeterminates

Roderick M. Chisholm

Introduction

I will discuss an ontological distinction between two very different types of property. That there are these two types of property is a philosopheme that should be of interest in its own right. It also tells us something about adverbialization – about what it is that adverbs do. I shall illustrate the latter point by reference to Donald Davidson's discussion of adverbs.

Subdetermination

We may say that one property *includes* a second provided only that the first is necessarily such that whatever has it also has the second. And we may say that one property *falls under* another if the first includes the second and the second does not include the first.

D1 P includes Q = Df P is necessarily such that whatever has it has Q
D2 P falls under Q = Df P includes Q; and Q does not include P

Thus brother falls under male, and red falls under color.

Some properties are *subdeterminates* of properties they fall under and some are not. Contrast the property *red* and *brother*. The property *red* falls under *color* and it is a subdeterminate under *color*. The property *brother*, on the other hand, although it falls under the property *male*, is *not* a subdeterminate under *male*.

Being a male is necessary to being a brother but it is something that is short of being a brother. And being colored is necessary to being red but it is something that is short of being red. Hence we have two questions: 'What can you add to the property male to get the property brother? And what can you add to the property color to get the property red?'

We could put the first question by asking how to instantiate the following formula:

$$(male + X) = brother$$

There is an obvious answer and there are several contrived answers. The obvious answer is this: 'Add to the property male the property of having the same parents that someone else has and then you will have the property brother.' Hence we may say:

(male + sharing parents) = brother

But sharing parents is not the only property which is such that, when conjoined with male, it yields a property that is equivalent to the property brother. Here is a partial list of such properties:

(a) (male + sharing parents) = brother
(b) (male + brother) = brother
(c) [male + (non-male or brother)] = brother
(d) [male+ (brother or both non-male and married)] = brother

It is clear that the last three items, unlike the first one, are somewhat contrived.

To see the way in which these answers are contrived, let us introduce two useful abbreviations:

D3 P is a negation of Q = Df P is necessarily such that, for every x, x has P if and only if x does not have Q
D4 P is independent of Q = Df P and Q are so related that (a) neither is necessarily such that if it is exemplified then the other is exemplified, (b) neither is necessarily such that if it is exemplified then a negation of the other is exemplified, and (c) neither is necessarily such that if a negation of the other is exemplified then it is exemplified

Now we may see how the obvious answer to 'What can you add to male to get brother?' differs from the contrived answers. The obvious answer, unlike the contrived ones, provides a value for 'X' – namely, sharing parents – which has these three features: (a) brother falls under it and also under male; (b) it is not included by a negation of male; and (c) it, but nothing that it falls under, is such that the conjunction of it and male is equivalent to brother.

We may see that being a male is 'a member of a co-ordinate pair that is equivalent to brother' and define this expression as follows:

D9 P is equivalent to a co-ordinate pair = Df There are properties Q and R such that: (i) Q is independent of R; and (ii) Q, but nothing that Q falls under, is necessarily such that, for every x, x has both it and R if and only if x has P

Color is not a member of a co-ordinate pair that is equivalent to red. To see this, we have only to consider the formula:

(color + X) = red

and ask: What *can* you add to color to get red? Only the contrived answers work – for example: *red; noncolored or red;* and *red or both noncolored and heavy.*

Now we may say what a subdeterminate is:

D6 S is a subdeterminate under D = Df S falls under D; and S is not
equivalent to a co-ordinate pair

Some references to this distinction

W.E. Johnson discussed 'the determinable' in his *Logic* in 1921 and noted that
the relation of *red* to *color* is quite different from that of subspecies to species.[1]
Franz Brentano had also called attention to this fact and introduced the
expression 'one-sided detachability' to describe it. He gives this example:

> When we compare 'red thing' and 'colored thing' we find that the latter is
> contained in the former, but we cannot specify a second thing that could be added
> to the first as an entirely new element, i.e., one that would not contain the concept,
> colored thing. The red thing is distinguished from other colored things as being a
> red-colored thing.[2]

The point of Brentano's expression 'one-sided detachability' may be suggested by what I have said about male and brother and about color and red.
Brentano would have said that male is related by 'two-sided detachability' to
brother; for male is a member of a co-ordinate pair that is equivalent to brother.
But color bears only 'one-sided detachability' to red: color is not one of two
co-ordinate properties which are together equivalent to red.

Brentano stressed a second case of 'one-sided detachability' – a second case
of subdetermination. This second case makes it clear that the distinction
between those properties that are subdeterminates and those that are not has
important consequences. Consider the property *thinking* – taking 'thinking' in
its Cartesian sense as being equivalent to *being conscious*. It is clear that *thinking*
is a subdeterminate under the property of *being a person*.[3] Being a person is
related only by 'one-sided detachability' to thinking. Thinking is not equivalent
to a co-ordinate pair consisting of personhood and some other property.

Subdetermination or 'one-sided detachability' is also illustrated in the
following passage from Wittgenstein: 'Let us not forget this: when "I raise my
arm," my arm goes up. And the problem arises: what is left over if I subtract the
fact that my arm goes up from the fact that I raise my arm?'[4] The passage

---

[1] W.E. Johnson, *Logic* (Cambridge University Press, Cambridge, 1921), vol. 1, p. 174.
[2] Franz Brentano, *The Theory of Categories* (Martinus Nijhoff, The Hague, 1981), p. 112. The
passage quoted was dictated by Brentano when he was no longer able to see. I believe that the last
sentence does not express what he intended to say and that it should read: i.e., one that would not
contain the concept *red thing*.' See also Brentano's *Versuch über die Erkenntnis*, 2nd edn (Felix
Meiner Verlag, Hamburg, 1970), p. 29. Brentano made this distinction in his lectures on
descriptive psychology given in Vienna in the 1880s and 1890s; see *Deskriptive Psychologie* (Felix
Meiner Verlag, Hamburg, 1982), pp. 12–19, 25, 79–81, E.G. Husserl repeated what Brentano had
said about red and color in *Logical Investigations* in 1900 (Routledge & Kegan Paul, London, 1970),
vol. II, p. 454; but he made no reference to Brentano.
[3] *Theory of Categories*, p. 198.
[4] Ludwig Wittgenstein, *Philosophical Investigations* (Basil Blackwell, Oxford, 1953), p. 161e.

suggests that raising one's arm is a subdeterminate and not a subspecies under having one's arm up.

Other applications of the distinction

Being a brother is a subdeterminate and not a subspecies under being possibly a brother. It is also a subdeterminate and not a subspecies under being a brother or a sister.

Eating lobster is a subdeterminate under eating; and killing a man is a subdeterminate under killing. But eating in a restaurant is not a subdeterminate under eating; and killing in Toledo is not a subdeterminate under killing.

What of being a French teacher? Is this a subdeterminate under being a teacher? If by 'French teacher' we mean a teacher who is French, then the property of being a French teacher is not a subdeterminate under teacher. But if by 'French teacher' we mean someone who teaches French, then the property of being a French teacher is a subdeterminate under teacher.

What of being a small bank robber? If we take the expression 'small bank robber' to mean small robber of banks, then being a small bank robber is not a subdeterminate under bank robber. But if we take it to mean robber of small banks, then being a small bank robber is a subdeterminate under bank robber. (One could also take 'small bank robber' to mean the same as 'bank robber who is small for a bank robber' – where 'small for a bank robber' has as its sense the property of being smaller than most bank robbers. In this case, we could say that being a small bank robber is a subspecies and not a subdeterminate under being a bank robber.)

More about the color example

The senses of the words 'red' and 'color, as they have being taken here, are those that these words have when applied to sensations, appearances or sense-data.

Now I have no doubt about the fact that we *sense* – or *are appeared to* – in different ways. But where Brentano had taken a substantival view of appearing. I have long defended what has been called – and I here emphasize the word – an *adverbial* theory of appearing. But we may have it either way and we will still have our examples of subdetermination.

Consider, then, the following hierarchies of properties:

(A)	(B)
quality	sensing
color	sensing-colorly
chromatic color	sensing-chromatically
red	sensing-redly
bright red	sensing-bright-redly

List (A) is a list of 'phenomenal properties' – properties that may be attributed to sensations, appearances or sense-data, where these are thought of as being individual things. Lists for nonvisual sense-fields may be obtained by replacing 'color' by such terms as 'sound,' 'feel,' 'taste' and 'smell' and then replacing 'red' and 'bright red' accordingly.

Adverbialization

We now turn to the things that Donald Davidson has said about adverbs. Consider his example about Sebastian strolling swiftly in Bologna.[5] Certainly *strolling in Bologna* is equivalent to the co-ordinate pair, *strolling* and *being in Bologna*. But *strolling swiftly* is a subdeterminate under *strolling*. We should note that *strolling swiftly* is not equivalent to the co-ordinate pair, *strolling* and *moving swiftly*. (Suppose Sebastian was strolling slowly from the front to the back of a fast-moving train.) Davidson makes this clear in his discussion of the relation between *crossing the English Channel* and crossing the English Channel slowly.[6]

I have just said that *strolling* plus *being in Bologna* is equivalent to *strolling in Bologna*. But perhaps we should look further at 'being in Bologna.' Note, for example, that there is a certain ambiguity in the expression 'Sebastian waves a flag in Bologna.' Does it apply to the case where Sebastian is standing in Bologna and has extended the flag across the city line into a place other than Bologna? In this case Sebastian is in Bologna, but the flag is not. Or does it apply to the case where Sebastian is outside of Bologna but is extending the flag into Bologna? In this case the flag is in Bologna and Sebastian is not. If the idea is that Sebastian is in Bologna, then waving a flag in Bologna is not a subdeterminate under waving a flag. But if the idea is that the flag is in Bologna, then waving a flag in Bologna *is* a subdeterminate under waving a flag.

These Davidsonian examples suggest an alternative terminology. Instead of saying 'S is a *subdeterminate* under D,' we could say 'S is an *adverbialization of D*.' But it is problematic whether this is suitable for all cases of subdetermination. And it would seem strange to say that *red* is an 'adverbialization' of *red or round* or of *possibly red*.

One common view of adverbs is that they are 'second order' adjectives – where a 'first order adjective is a word having as its sense a property that may be had by an individual thing. A 'higher order' adjective would be an adjective having as its sense some property of a property.[7] Thus Reichenbach said that in the sentence 'Annette is beautiful' one predicates beauty of Annette, whereas in the sentence 'Annette dances beautifully' one predicates beauty of her dancing.[8] But, as our examples indicate, we cannot say generally that, if P is a subdeterminate under Q, then the sense of P is a property that is exemplified by Q. And so it may be, therefore, that not all adverbs are 'higher order' adjectives.[9]

---

[5] Compare Donald Davidson, 'Events as particulars,' *Nous*, 4 (1970), pp. 25–32; see p. 30.

[6] Compare Donald Davidson, 'The logical form of action sentences,' in *The Logic of Decision and Action*, ed. N. Rescher (The University of Pittsburgh Press, Pittsburgh, 1966), pp. 81–103; see p. 82 (reprinted in Davidson's *Essays on Actions and Events* (Clarendon Press, Oxford, 1980)).

[7] Compare Johnson, *Logic*, pp. 102–3, and C.I. Lewis, *An Analysis of Knowledge and Valuation* (Open Court Publishing, La Salle, Ill., 1946), pp. 80–1.

[8] Hans Reichenbach, *Elements of Symbolic Logic* (Macmillan, New York, *The Free Press*, 1947), p. 305.

[9] I am indebted to Ernest Sosa.

Part III
Philosophy of Psychology

Anomalous Monism and the Irreducibility of the Mental

Brian P. McLaughlin

Davidson's views about the relationship between the mental and the physical are the central topic of many of the essays in this section. It will become evident by reading these essays that contributors are not always in agreement about Davidson's arguments for these views, the details of these views, or their truth. I have allowed myself to offer an interpretation of Davidson's views and to present, in broad outline, what I take to be his central arguments. I shall not discuss the views of contributors. But I hope that what I say will help in the study of the many fine essays that follow.

Davidson's views about the relationship between the mental and the physical receive their most complete and detailed expression in his seminal article 'Mental Events'; but various themes are elaborated in 'Psychology as Philosophy', 'The Material Mind', and 'Hempel on Explaining Action'.[1] In presenting his views, I shall draw freely from these articles and others.

Some of the principal tenets of Davidson's position concerning the relationship in question are:

> *Principle of Causal Interaction.* (1) at least some mental events causally interact with physical events [ME:208].
>
> *Anomalous Monism.* (2) every mental event is a physical event; (3) there cannot be strict psychophysical laws; and (4) there cannot be a physical predicate, no matter how complex, that has, as a matter of

---

[1] All of the papers mentioned above appear in *Essays on Actions and events* (Oxford, 1980). In what follows, I shall use the following abbreviations: 'ME' for 'Mental Events', 'PP' for 'Psychology as Philosophy', 'MM' for 'The Material Mind', 'IE' for 'The Individuation of Events', 'R' for 'Comments and Replies', 'H' for 'Hempel on Explaining Action', 'ARC' for 'Actions, Reasons, and Causes', 'D' for 'Criticism, Comment, and Defence', 'CR' for 'Causal Relations', and 'FA' for 'Freedom to Act'; all of the papers in question appear in *Essays on Actions and Events*, and all paranthetical pages references are to that volume.

So as to make for easy reference, there is an appendix at the end of this paper that contains a list of all the numbered claims in the paper; some claims appear under more than one numbering.

law, the same extension as a mental predicate [see ME:214–15, and PP:231].

Supervenience Thesis. (5) mental characteristics supervene on physical characteristics [see ME:214, and MM:253].

Davidson holds the following related thesis concerning the mental itself:

> *Anomalism of the Mental.* (6) there cannot be strict laws on the basis of which mental events can be explained and predicted [ME:208].

This essay is composed of ten sections. In section I, I introduce Davidson's views about events and causation. In II, I briefly discuss the three subtheses of Anomalous Monism. In III, I say what the scope of the mental is in the present discussion. In IV, I present Davidson's argument for (2), and in V, his argument for (6). In VI, I offer an interpretation of Davidson's notion of a strict law. Employing this interpretation, I present an argument for the claim that there cannot be strict psychological laws in VII, and in VIII, an argument for (3). In IX, I introduce Davidson's notion of a constitutive, synthetic, a priori principle and show how it figures in his argument for (4). Finally, in X, I discuss two ways the mental might supervene on the physical and the relationship between these ways of supervening and reduction.

I Events, causation, and nomic subsumption

Let us begin by seeing what Davidson means by 'an event' and by 'causation'. This will help set the stage for what follows. Davidson maintains that events are dated, concrete particulars that can be described in various logically nonequivalent and nonsynonymous ways; that they are the primary relata of causal relations; and that two events are the same if and only if they have the same causes and effects [see IE].[2] He nowhere offers an analysis of the causal relation. But he holds a *nomic subsumption* view of this relation in that he maintains the following necessary condition for causation:

> *Principle of the Nomological Character of Causality.* (7) events related as cause and effect are subsumed by strict laws [ME:208].

The notion of 'a strict law' requires explanation; since there is some controversy as to how it should be understood, I postpone explaining it until section VI. For now it suffices to say what Davidson means by 'a law' and by 'subsumption'.

Davidson claims that there is no nonquestion begging answer to the question as to what a law is. However, he characterizes *laws* as true, lawlike sentences. A

---

[2] In 'Reply to Quine on Events' (this volume, pp. 172–6) Davidson adopts another criterion: two events are the same if and only if they occur in the same space-time region. This criterion is, I believe, compatible with the 'same causes and effects' criterion, given Davidson's views about causation. See section VI below.

sentence is *lawlike* when but only when it is a generalization that is confirmable by its positive instances and which, if true, would support counterfactuals and other subjunctive conditionals.³ Laws can be universalized conditionals, universalized biconditionals, or statistical in form. Lawlikeness admits of degrees since confirmability by positive instances does. The distinction between laws and mere true generalizations is thus vague; though there are clear-cut cases of each [ME:217].

An event is subsumed by a strict law just in case it instantiates the law. Davidson maintains that since laws are sentences, what primarily instantiate them are other sentences. But a description can instantiate a law in virtue of instantiating a component of the law, for example, the antecedent or consequent of the law. According to Davidson, events instantiate laws only relative to descriptions: an event instantiates a law only in virtue of satisfying a description that does. When an event instantiates a law in virtue of satisfying a description *d*, the event instantiates the law under description *d*. Davidson thus maintains that laws subsume events under descriptions [ME:215].

Thesis (1) asserts that at least some mental events causally interact with physical events. For example, the light's striking Paul's eyes may be a cause of his desiring to move his arm; and his desiring to move his arm may be a cause of his arm's moving. Now thesis (1) may seem at odds with (6) and (7). For suppose some physical event causes a mental event. Then, given (7), it seems that there will be some strict law on the basis of which the mental event can be explained and predicted. But (6) denies this is possible.

Davidson maintains that (1), (6), and (7) are nonetheless compatible [ME:215]. He holds that since an event can be explained or predicted on the basis of a strict law only if it instantiates the law, an event is explainable or predictable on the basis of a strict law only under a description. Thesis (6) should thus be understood as asserting that there are no strict laws on the basis of which events can be explained and predicted under mental descriptions. According to (7), if event *a* causes event *b*, there are descriptions of *a* and *b* that instantiate a strict law [ME:215]. But (7) allows that there may be no end of descriptions of *a* and *b* that do not instantiate any strict law. According to Davidson, we cannot conclude from the fact that *a* instantiates a strict law, and the fact that *a* = *b*, that *b* instantiates a strict law [R:154]. The position occupied by 'a' in the context '*a* instantiates a strict law' is intensional: although it is subject to existential generalization, substitutivity of identicals fails to guarantee preservation of truth [R:241–2]. In the contrast, the positions occupied by 'a' and 'b' in the context '*a* caused *b*' are extensional since they are subject both to existential generalization and to substitutivity of identicals. If *a* caused *b*, then *a* and *b* both occurred; and *a* caused *b* however these events are described. Causation is a relationship between events themselves, not events under

---

³ This notion of lawlikeness is similar to Nelson Goodman's, in *Fact, Fiction, and Forecast* (3rd edn, Indianapolis, 1979).

descriptions. Singular causal statements purport to state causal relations between particular events. Davidson maintains that such statements contain an
essential occurrence of 'cause' (or some expression equivalent in meaning)
flanked by singular terms that purport to refer to particular events [R:154–5].
He holds that a singular causal statement of the form 'The P caused the M', for
example, may be true, where 'the P' is a physical description and 'the M' a
mental description, even if the M does not instantiate any strict law under the
description 'the M' or any other mental description. Claim (7) requires only
that there be some descriptions of the M and the P that instantiate a strict law.
Claims (1), (6), and (7) are compatible if mental events can instantiate strict
laws under nonmental descriptions. Davidson maintains they can, and that
these claims are, therefore, compatible.

The above discussion employs the assumption that laws are sentences. This
assumption has been challenged.[4] Some maintain that laws are singular
relations between certain sorts of universals, relations either of identity,
necessary correlation, necessitation, or statistical dependency. For the most
part, the concerns of this essay are independent of whether laws are sentences
or singular relations between universals. (When the concerns are not, I shall say
so.) One can take Davidson's characterization of laws to be a criterion for
counting a sentence as *the expression of a law*. (Though Davidson would maintain
that the criterion is ultimately circular [ME:217].) Talk of sentences instantiating generalizations can be replaced with talk of ordered pairs of events
instantiating lawful relations. Talk of an event's instantiating a law under a
description can be replaced with talk of an event's instantiating a relatum of a
lawful relation. Talk of explaining events under descriptions can be replaced
with talk of explaining events in so far as they instantiate certain event types,
and talk of predicting events under descriptions, with talk of predicting that
certain event types will be instantiated. In what follows, I shall typically speak of
laws as sentences. But, for present purposes, unless I indicate otherwise, what I
say can be recast in terms of talk of laws as singular relations between event
types (or properties). So, for example, (1), (6), and (7) are compatible if mental
events can instantiate nonmental event types that enter into strict lawful
relations.

II *Anomalous monism*

In this section, I shall briefly comment on the three subtheses of the doctrine of
Anomalous Monism. The doctrine is a monism because of (2); and it is an
anomalous monism because of (3) and (4). Davidson sometimes formulates
Anomalous Monism using (2) and (4) [see, e.g., ME:214–5], and sometimes
using (2) and (3) [see, e.g., PP:231]. Since (3) and (4) are different claims, I
have included both in the formulation of the doctrine. As we shall see in section
VIII, (4) figures as a premise in the argument for (3).

---

[4] Fred I. Dretske attacks this orthodox view of laws in 'Laws of Nature', *Philosophy of Science*, 44
(1977), pp. 248–68.

Subthesis (2) asserts a version of *token physicalism*: every mental event token is identical with some physical event token. Davidson maintains that such mental-physical token identities do not imply mental-physical type-type identities since event tokens can fall under many types [ME:212–13]. He allows that physical predicates can be coextensive with mental predicates [ME:215–16]. But such de facto coextensiveness does not suffice for mental-physical type-type identities; and he would deny there are such type-type identities.

Thesis (4) asserts that there cannot be a physical predicate, no matter how complex, that has, as a matter of law, the same extension as a mental predicate. The sort of law in question is a *bridge law*.[5] (Davidson does not himself use the term 'bridge law'.) Bridge laws imply that two predicates (or properties) are necessarily coextensive or that they are necessarily coextensive modulo certain limiting or boundary conditions. (We can leave open the modal force of 'necessarily' here.) One theory can be reduced to another by means of bridge laws. And many standard cases of intertheoretic reduction (e.g., temperature to mean kinetic energy) are cases of reduction via bridge laws. Thesis (4), then, denies that the mental is nomologically reducible (reducible via bridge laws) to the physical. Davidson notes that: 'Of course other forms of reduction are imaginable' [MM:246]. But, as we shall see in section VIII, this is the sort of reduction he must deny is possible in his argument for (3). What nomological reduction consists in is a complex matter. I say more about it in section IX, where I present what I take to be Davidson's central argument for (4).

Thesis (3) asserts that there cannot be strict psychophysical laws. Davidson allows that there may be true psychophysical generalizations [ME:216]. And he allows that there can be true, lawlike psychophysical generalizations. But he maintains: 'these generalizations, unlike those of physics, cannot be turned into the strict laws of a science closed within its area of application' [MM:250]. I discuss the idea of a closed science in section VI, where I say what a strict law is. As we shall see in section IV, (3) figures as a premise in the argument for (2).

Theses (3) and (4) contain the modal term 'cannot'. Davidson speaks of the *impossibility* of strict psychophysical laws [see, e.g., ME:223–4], and says that psychology *cannot* be reduced to physical theory [MM:259]. Moreover, he maintains that (3) and (4) can be established by a priori arguments since whether a sentence is lawlike is an a priori matter [ME:216]. I think it is fair to understand him as maintaining that it is a priori true that there are no strict psychophysical laws and that it is a priori true that no physical predicate has, as a matter of law, the same extension as a mental predicate. For this reason, we may understand the modal force of 'cannot' in (3) and (4) (and in (6) as well) to be that of *conceptual impossibility*. Let us say that something is conceptually impossible if its negation is a priori justifiable. Thus, for example, strict psychophysical laws are conceptually impossible, if it is a priori justifiable that there are no such laws. (Hereafter, I shall typically suppress the qualifier

---

[5] For an early discussion of bridge laws, see Ernest Nagel, *The Structure of Science* (Harcourt Brace and World, New York, 1961), ch. 11. For a recent discussion see Robert Causey, 'Attribute-Identities in Microreductions', *Journal of Philosophy*, 69 (1972), pp. 407–21.

'conceptually' when using 'necessary' and 'possible'.) It should be kept in mind, however, that Davidson thinks the a priori/a posteriori distinction is vague [ME:216], and that he claims not to have a firm understanding of notions of necessity [see, e.g., H:273].

III *The scope of the mental*

Let us see what Davidson means by 'a mental event', 'a mental description', and 'a mental predicate'. He proposes the following criterion for counting an event as mental:

> an event is mental if and only if it has a mental description, or (the description operator not being primitive) if there is a mental open sentence true of that event alone [ME:211].

A mental description or open sentence is a description or open sentence that contains an essential occurrence of a mental predicate. (The requirement that at least one mental predicate occur essentially rules out the possibility of there being a mental description or open sentence that is logically equivalent to a description or open sentence that does not contain a mental predicate.) A mental predicate is a predicate that essentially contains a mental verb whose occurrence in the predicate creates an intensional context. A verb is a mental verb when but only when it expresses a propositional attitude. 'Propositional attitude' can, in principle, be defined by enumeration: the term covers believing, desiring, intending, deciding, hoping, wishing, fearing, and the like [see ME:210–12].

Two points are in order so as to avert misunderstanding of Davidson's criterion for counting an event as mental. First, in adopting it, one is not thereby committed to the view that an event is mental only under a description or only when so described. The position occupied by 'a' in 'a satisfies the open mental sentence 'x is M'' is extensional; and likewise for the position occupied by 'a' in 'a satisfies the open physical sentence 'x is P''.[6]

Second, the criterion may seem too narrow since it is specified in part by appeal to the notion of a verb that expresses a propositional attitude. Davidson himself counts, for example, having bodily sensations, having after-images, and intentional actions as mental events; and, of course, bodily sensations, after-images, and intentional actions are not propositional attitudes [ME:215]. But actually the criterion is too broad rather than too narrow. Every bona fide mental event would be counted as mental by the criterion. But there are intuitively nonmental events that satisfy mental descriptions and thereby count

---

6 Davidson says in one place that: 'The principle of the anomalism of the mental concerns events described as mental, for events are mental only as described' [ME:215]. What Davidson should have said is that the principle of the anomalism of the mental concerns events described as mental, for events can be explained and predicted on the basis of strict laws only as described. See Mark Johnston's 'Why Having a Mind Matters' (this volume, pp. 408–26) for an elaboration of this and a discussion of the relationship between Davidson's views on the anomalism of the mental and freedom.

as mental by that criterion. For example, the event of the ice's melting may satisfy the mental description 'the ice's melting while Flora decides whether to put ice in her drink' thereby counting as mental. As Davidson notes, every event may satisfy some mental description and so count as mental by his criterion. He acknowledges: 'We have obviously failed to capture the intuitive concept of the mental' [ME:212]. However, he says that the breadth of the criterion is no problem given his purpose of showing that every mental event is a physical event [ME:212]. Given this purpose, there would be a problem, he claims, if the criterion failed to apply to some bona fide mental event. But, as he notes, there seems no danger of that. However, as will become clear in section VI, Davidson appeals to the fact that mental events causally interact with nonmental events in his defense of some of the premises in his argument for the claim that every mental event is a physical event. This appeal requires a more restricted notion of mental event than the one he proposes. Perhaps it will suffice here to say that Davidson is primarily concerned with mental events involving propositional attitudes: believings, desiring, intendings, decidings, and the like. Though much of what he says about such mental events unquestionably applies to other sorts of mental events as well.

By 'a strict psychophysical law' Davidson means a strict law that features both mental and physical predicates, by 'a strict psychological law,' a strict law that features only mental predicates. To avert misunderstanding, two points are in order about the notion of a mental predicate.

First, there are intuitively mental predicates that do not count as mental predicates by Davidson's criterion, for example, 'sees *a*' and 'has a toothache'. The second does not contain a mental verb; and while the first does, the occurrence of the mental verb is not intensional. Davidson would acknowledge this [ME:210]. Let it suffice for now to say that it would be important if mental predicates in Davidson's semi-technical sense cannot figure in strict laws since such predicates either are or contain essential occurrences of predicates we use to attribute propositional attitudes and such attributions figure centrally in rationalizing explanations.[7]

Second, some claim that 'cognitive science' or 'scientific psychology' should not employ the mental predicates of 'folk psychology'.[8] Mental predicates in Davidson's sense either are or contain essential occurrences of such mental predicates. Davidson often speaks interchangeably of the psychological and the mental; but he is quite explicit that his discussion of psychology is restricted to that part concerned with propositional attitudes (and so which employs the mental predicates of 'folk psychology') [see, e.g., R:240 and MM:246]. The relationship between 'folk psychology' and 'cognitive science' is a topic of much current interest. This essay is not the place to address that topic; but the ensuing discussion will have bearing on it.

---

[7] For a discussion of how such attributions figure centrally in rationalizing explanations see Brian P. McLaughlin and Ernest Lepore's 'Actions, Reasons, Causes, and Intentions' (this volume, pp. 3–13).

[8] See Stephen P. Stich's *From Folk Psychology to Cognitive Science: The Case Against Belief* (Bradford, Cambridge, Mass., 1983).

IV Davidson's token identity thesis for events

The gist of Davidson's reasoning in favor of token physicalism for events is this: since causation requires subsumption under a strict law, and strict laws are physical laws, events that causally interact with physical events are physical events; and since every mental event causally interacts with some physical event, every mental event is a physical event.

Davidson states an argument for the claim that every mental event that causally interacts with a physical event is a physical event, and then suggests how the argument could be supplemented to yield (2). The argument he states is this[9] [ME:223–4].

(8) Let m be any mental event that causally interacts with some physical event p.
(9) When two events causally interact, there is some strict law that subsumes them.
(10) There cannot be strict psychophysical laws.
(11) There cannot be strict psychological laws.
(12) If a strict law subsumes m and p, that strict law is a strict physical law.
(13) If a strict physical law subsumes two events, then the events are physical events.
(14) M is a physical event.

(15) Every mental event that causally interacts with a physical event is a physical event.

The argument is valid. Premise (14) follows from what comes before. Premise (13) seems fine: if an event is subsumed by a strict physical law, it satisfies a physical description (or instantiates a physical event type) that instantiates a strict physical law (or a relatum of a strict physical law); and that should suffice for its counting as physical. Premise (8) seems a coherent assumption. (Of course, the argument could be sound even if no mental events causally interact with physical events. However, I shall not consider the extent of psychophysical causal interaction here; let it suffice to note that Davidson has persuasively argued that there are various sorts of psychophysical causal interactions [see, e.g., ARC]. Premise (9) is just a recasting of (7), the Principle of the Nomological Character of Causality. Premise (10) is, of course, subthesis (3) of Anomalous Monism. Premise (11) is implied by but does not imply (6). Premise (12) does not follow from (8)–(11) if there could be a strict law that is neither a strict psychological law, a strict psychophysical law, or a strict physical law. The core controversial premises in the argument, then, are (9), (10), (11), and (12).

---

[9] Compare William Larry Stanton's formulation of the argument in 'Supervenience and Psychological Law in Anomalous Monism', *Pacific Philosophical Quarterly*, 64 (1983), p. 75. Mark Johnston provides a similar formulation and then suggests how the argument can be made more general in 'Why Having a Mind Matters' (pp. 413–14). Dagfinn Føllesdal discusses Davidson's reasons for (2) in 'Causation and Explanation: A Problem in Davidson's View on Action and Mind' (this volume, pp. 311–23).

If the argument is sound, it shows that every mental event that causally interacts with a physical event is itself a physical event subsumed by a strict physical law.

Davidson says that to establish (2), given (15): 'it would be sufficient to show that every mental event is a cause or effect of some physical event; I shall not attempt this' [ME:224]. Here is another way (2) might be established. If it could be shown that it is conceptually necessary that strict laws are physical laws and that it is conceptually necessary that every event is a cause or effect of some event, then, given (7), it would follow that it is conceptually necessary that every mental event is a physical event; indeed, it would follow that it is conceptually necessary that every event is a physical event.[10] This conclusion would rule out the conceptual possibility of disembodied spirits that undergo mental events. Some would maintain that such are possible. They deny only that there actually are such.[11] Some maintain that what makes an event a mental event is that it has any one of a certain set of causal roles, and so that if spiritual events can have one such causal role, they can count as mental. But if causation requires subsumption under a strict physical law, then every event that has a causal role is a physical event; and, if every event has at least one causal role, every event is a physical event.

In any case, for any of the above lines of argument for (2) to succeed, it must be possible for a mental event to fall under a physical event type that enters into strict lawful relations, or to satisfy a physical description in virtue of which it instantiates a strict physical law. As Davidson acknowledges, on some accounts of events this is not possible [ME:213]. According to some accounts, the identity of a mental event token with a physical event token would require the identity of a mental and a physical event type. If such type-type identities are impossible, then, according to such accounts, so are mental-physical token identities. Davidson cites a version of Jaegwon Kim's property exemplification account of events as an example [ME:213]. It will prove useful to have a description of that account. According to Kim,[12] an event consists in an n-tuple of object's having an n-adic property or relation at a time or throughout an interval of time. On this view, each individual (monadic) event is a complex structure that is composed of three constituents: a constitutive object, a constitutive property, and a constitutive time. Two (monadic) events are identical if and only if they have the same constitutive object, constitutive property, and constitutive time. Kim draws a distinction between an event's exemplifying a property and its being an exemplification of a property. While an event may exemplify any number of properties, the event itself will be an exemplification of one and only one property, its constitutive property. The constitutive property of an event will be a property exemplified by the constitutive object of the event at the time of the event, not a property

---

[10] Compare 'Why Having a Mind Matters' pp. 412–13.

[11] Jerry A. Fodor argues for the claim that every event is subsumed by a law of a completed physics. See his *The Language of Thought* (MIT, 1975), pp. 1–26. If I understand him, he maintains that this claim is contingently true and not to be established by a priori arguments.

[12] 'On the Psycho-Physical Identity Theory', *American Philosophical Quarterly*, 3 (1966), pp. 231–2.

exemplified by the event itself. Events are property exemplifications because an event is an exemplification of its constitutive property. (Event type is a species of property.) Suppose, then, that mental events have constitutive mental properties, and that physical events have constitutive physical properties. If so and mental properties cannot be identical with physical properties, then mental event tokens cannot be identical with physical event tokens. Moreover, on this view, since events instantiate laws in virtue of their constitutive properties (and instantiate law expressions only under descriptions that contain predicates designating their constitutive properties), mental events cannot instantiate strict physical laws.

Of course, Davidson eschews the notion of a constitutive property of an event. He takes the category of event to be a fundamental ontological category and would deny that an event consists in an object's having a property at a time [see, e.g., IE]. And he would contend that those who maintain that mental events have constitutive mental properties must either deny the Principle of the Nomological Character of Causality or else deny there can be psychophysical causal interactions.

But this is not the place to examine Davidson's defense of his view of events or his defense of the Principle of the Nomological Character of Causality.[13] To do either would take us too far afield of our central concerns. Whether every mental event token is a physical event token thus depends on issues that cannot be addressed here.[14] But I say more about the dispute over the individuation of events in section VI.

However, it is worthwhile noting that there are versions of a property exemplification account of events which allow that mental event tokens can be identical with physical event tokens. I shall illustrate this with one such version. Kim has never proposed necessary and sufficient conditions for a property's being such that it can be the constitutive property of an event. But he has suggested that events instantiate laws in virtue of their constitutive properties.[15] Suppose, then, that constitutive properties are ones in virtue of which events instantiate strict laws. Then if mental properties cannot enter into strict lawful relations, mental properties cannot be constitutive properties of events. What would make an event mental is that it exemplifies a mental property (e.g., the property of being a believing that water is wet). But this leaves open whether mental event tokens can be identical with physical event tokens since it allows that mental events can have nonmental properties as their constitutive prop-

---

[13] John McDowell expresses doubt concerning the Principle of the Nomological Character of Causality in 'Functionalism and Anomalous Monism' (this volume, p. 398).

For a clear presentation of some of Davidson's arguments for his view of events see Ernest Lepore's 'The Logical Form of Action and Event Sentences,' (this volume, pp. 151–61).

[14] The following contributors either express doubts concerning Davidson's token identity thesis or actually challenge the thesis: Terrence Horgan and Michael Tye in 'Against the Token Identity Theory' (this volume, pp. 427–43), Jennifer Hornsby in 'Physicalism, Events and Part–Whole Relations' (this volume, pp. 444–58), and John McDowell in 'Functionalism and Anomalous Monism' (pp. 397–8).

[15] 'Causation, Nomic Subsumption, and the Concept of Event', *The Journal of Philosophy*, 8 (1973), pp. 218–21.

erties. Indeed, on this property exemplification account of events, if every mental event enters into causal relations and all strict laws are relationships between physical properties, then, given (7), every mental event is a physical event.[16]

V The anomalism of the mental

Almost all of the premises of Davidson's argument for (6) are claims that are also premises in the argument for (2). The argument for (6) that he offers is this [ME:223–4]:

(16) There cannot be strict psychophysical laws.
(17) There cannot be strict psychological laws.
(18) If a strict law subsumes a mental event, then that law would have to be either a strict psychophysical law or a strict psychological law.
(19) No strict law can subsume a mental event.
(20) If no strict law can subsume a mental event, there cannot be strict laws on the basis of which mental events can be explained and predicted.
(21) There cannot be strict laws on the basis of which mental events can be explained and predicted.

The argument is valid. Premise (20) seems fine since an event can be explained or predicted on the basis of a law only if the event is subsumed by the law. Premise (19) follows from (16)–(18). Premises (16) and (17) are, respectively, (10) and (11). Premise (18) is new. Since subsumption is description relative, for the antecedent of (18) to be satisfied, a strict law must subsume an event under a mental description. For a strict law to do that it must contain a mental predicate. Premise (18) is false if there could be a strict law that contains a mental predicate but that is not a strict psychological law or a strict psychophysical law. Thus, the only new controversial claim introduced by the argument is (18). Of course, if no strict law can contain a mental predicate, then no event can instantiate a strict law under a mental description. And if no event can instantiate a strict law under a mental description, the Anomalism of the Mental follows. The question at issue here, then, is whether a strict law can contain a mental predicate. Even if no strict law can contain only mental predicates and no strict law can contain both mental and physical predicates, it does not follow that no strict law can contain mental predicates.

My principal topics of concern in what follows will be (4), (16), (17), and claims offered in their support. But I shall briefly comment on (12) and (18) at the close of section VIII. Since claims (16) and (17) contain the term 'strict law' we must see what makes a law strict before considering them.

---

16 Terence Horgan makes this point in 'Humean Causation and Kim's Theory of Events', *Canadian Journal of Philosophy*, 10 (1980), pp. 669–71.

Davidson distinguishes two kinds of laws, homonomic and heteronomic. He says:

> On the one hand, there are generalizations whose positive instances give us reason to believe the generalization itself could be improved upon by adding further provisos and conditions stated in the same general vocabulary as the original generalization. Such a generalization points to the form and vocabulary of the finished law: we may say that it is a *homonomic* generalization. On the other hand there are generalizations which when instantiated may give us reason to believe there is a precise law at work, but one that can be stated only by shifting to a different vocabulary. We may call such generalizations *heteronomic* (emphases Davidson's) [ME:219].

A strict law (or law expression) is a homonomic law (or law expression). Laws (or law expressions) that are not strict are heteronomic. The distinction between homonomic and heteronomic laws is just the distinction between strict and unstrict laws. So it is intended to be jointly exhaustive over and mutually exclusive over the class of laws: every law is one or the other, no law is both.

Davidson's remarks suggest that what makes a law strict or homonomic is a feature of the vocabulary in which it is couched. He elaborates this idea by introducing the notion of *a closed comprehensive theory*. He says:

> I suppose most of our practical lore (and science) is heteronomic. This is because a law can hope to be precise, explicit, and as exceptionless as possible only if it draws its concepts from a comprehensive closed theory. This ideal theory may or may not be deterministic, but it is if any true theory is. Within the physical sciences we do find homonomic generalizations, generalizations such that if the evidence supports them, we then have reason to believe they may be sharpened indefinitely by drawing upon further physical concepts: there is a theoretical asymptote of perfect coherence with all the evidence, perfect predictability (under the terms of the system), total explanation (again under the terms of the system). Or perhaps the ultimate theory is probabilistic, and the asymptote is less than perfection; but in that case there will be no better to be had [ME:219].

The sort of 'ideal' or 'ultimate' theory Davidson describes is the sort many think a completed physics would be. Davidson himself maintains: 'Physical theory promises to provide a comprehensive closed system guaranteed to yield a standardized, unique description of every physical event couched in a vocabulary amenable to law' [ME:223].

I want to offer an interpretation of the notion of a strict law that squares fairly well with Davidson's use of the notion and which will enable me to state explicitly arguments for (16) and (17) which are, I think, suggested by various remarks he makes; nevertheless, I hesitate to attribute these arguments to him. I shall begin by characterizing the notion of a closed comprehensive theory more explicitly. Closure and comprehensiveness require explication. I shall offer an interpretation of each notion in turn.[17]

---

[17] Stanton offers an interpretation of the notion of a closed comprehensive that is different from the one I ultimately settle on. See 'Supervenience and Psychological Law in Anomalous Monism', pp. 74–6.

Let us say that event *A* causally interacts with event *B* just in case *A* is a cause or effect of *B*. Davidson seems to understand closure as follows: a theory *T* is *closed* just in case events within the domain of *T* causally interact only with other events within *T*'s domain.

Davidson claims that psychology is not closed since nonmental events causally interact with mental events [see, e.g., ME:224, PP:231, and R:241]. Of course, biology and chemistry are not closed either. Chemical events that are not also biological events causally interact with biological events; so biology is not closed. And events that are not chemical events (e.g., transmissions of light rays) causally interact with chemical events; so chemistry is not closed. But Davidson maintains that a completed physics is closed [see, e.g., R:241]. (Henceforth, I shall drop the qualifier 'completed'.)

If physics is closed, then any event that causally interacts with an event within the domain of physics is itself an event within the domain of physics. But it might be objected that physics is not closed since, for example, (at least some) mental events are not within the domain of physics and causally interact with events in its domain. Of course, Davidson argues that every mental event that causally interacts with a physical event is itself a physical event. If strict laws are couched in the vocabulary of physics, then, given (7), every event (that enters into causal relations) is within the domain of physics. But if strict laws must be couched in the vocabulary of a closed theory, then whether all strict laws are physical laws will depend, in part, on whether physics is closed. And whether physics is closed is what is at issue.

Of course, Davidson holds that while the various sciences and common sense employ predicates expressing different event types and so provide different ways of typing events, the events that fall under these various types are all within the domain of physics.[18] But recall that on certain property exemplification accounts of events, many events that causally interact with physical events will not have constitutive properties such that they can instantiate laws of physics. I sympathize with Davidson's views about events. But since we have put aside disputes over the nature of events, let us define a notion of closure that leaves open whether events within the domain of a closed theory can causally interact with events outside its domain, but which captures what seems special about physics in the relevant regard.

Let us call any event within the domain of a theory *T* 'a T-event'. Consider, then, the following notion of closure: a theory *T* is *closed** if and only if [for any space-time region *r*, and for any space-time region *r'*, an event that occurs at *r* is a cause (or effect) of an event that occurs at *r'* just in case a T-event that occurs at *r* is a cause (or effect) of a T-event that occurs at *r'*]. This definition is a mouthful (or eyeful). Less precisely, the idea is this: a theory *T* is closed* if and only if two events occurring at space-time regions causally interact just in case two T-events occurring at the same space-time regions causally interact.

Following Jonathan Bennett,[19] let me characterize two opposite ends of a continuum of possible views about the individuation of events. At one end there is the following coarse-grained criterion for event individuation: two events are

---

[18] Jennifer Hornsby discusses problems for this view in 'Physicalism, Events and Part–Whole Relations' (pp. 444–58).

[19] See 'Adverb-Dropping Inferences and the Lemon Criterion' (this volume, pp. 193–206).

identical if and only if they occur at the same space-time region. This coarse-grained criterion was first proposed by John Lemon.[20] Davidson has always viewed the criterion sympathetically [D:124–5]; and in this volume he embraces it.[21] At the other end of the continuum, there is the following fine-grained criterion: two events are identical if and only if they occur at the same space-time region and are instantiations of the same event type. This criterion resembles Kim's proposed criterion for his property exemplification account of events. In fact, Kim has claimed that an event may be understood, on his account, to be the exemplification of an event type at a space-time region.[22] So perhaps the criterion just is Kim's criterion. (It should be noted, however, that Kim would distinguish between an event's being an instantiation of an event type and its instantiating an event type; that is, he would distinguish constitutive from nonconstitutive event types.) There may well be defensible middle ground positions between these two ends of the continuum. As Bennett notes, a middle ground position may require a weaker relationship between event types than identity, but a stronger relationship than coinstantiation. In any case, we need not concern ourselves with where the truth lies on this continuum of possible views about event individuation. The notion of closure* is neutral concerning whether the extreme coarse-grained criterion, the extreme fine-grained criterion, or some middle ground criterion is correct.

The place of occurrence of an event and even the time of occurrence of an event can be problematic. How one handles such problems will depend, in part, on the criterion of event individuation one adopts.[23] But for present purposes, we can simply note that events can occur at scattered space-time regions, and that events can have vague spatio-temporal boundaries [see, e.g., IE:173·9]. Even mental events have at least vague spatial locations: a mental event occurs wherever the individual undergoing the mental event is at the time he or she undergoes the mental event [IE:176]. (The location of the individual will, of course, itself be vague; and so will the time of occurrence of the event.)

While physics may or may not be closed, it seems fair to say that physics is (or promises to be) closed*. Psychology, biology, and chemistry are clearly not (and do not promise to be) closed*.

Let us turn to comprehensiveness. Davidson does not say explicitly what comprehensiveness is; but I shall suggest a characterization that, I believe, squares fairly well with his use of the notion. Let us say that a T-description of an event is a description of that event couched solely in the vocabulary of a theory T. We can, then, define comprehensiveness as follows: a theory T is *comprehensive* if and only if every T-event uniquely satisfies a T-description

---

[20] 'Comments on "The Logical Form of Action Sentences"', in *The Logic of Decision and Action*, ed. N. Rescher (University of Pittsburgh Press, Pittsburgh, Penn., 1967), pp. 96–103.

[21] See Davidson's 'Reply to Quine on Events' (pp. 172–6). Quine provides a masterful defense of the claim that two events are identical if and only if they occur in the same space–time region in 'Events and Reification' (this volume, pp. 162–71). It should be noted that adoption of this criterion does not require acceptance of the view that events are space–time regions.

[22] See 'Events as Property Exemplifications', in *Action Theory*, ed. M. Brand and D. Walton (Reidel, Dordrecht, 1976), pp. 159–77.

[23] See Quine's discussion of problems concerning vagueness in 'Events and Reification' (pp. 167–8).

under which it instantiates a causal law of T that is as explicit and exceptionless as possible. The notion of a law that is as explicit and exceptionless as possible requires explication.

Laws can also be more or less explicit. Maximally explicit laws will not contain ceteris paribus clauses such as, for example, 'other things being equal' or 'under normal conditions'. Such laws may specify boundary conditions; but they will state precisely and explicitly all of the parameters constitutive of the boundary conditions. Davidson allows that a maximally explicit *causal* law may prove to be probabilistic and so not exceptionless. But the possibility of exceptions will not result from failure on the part of the law to state some causally relevant parameter. For such a causal law will state explicitly every causally relevent parameter in the regularity it expresses. Thus, if a physical theory like quantum mechanics is true, then maximally explicit causal laws may fail to be exceptionless. But then physical systems are intrinsically probabilistic, and the probabilisties that ultimately exist would be explicitly described by maximally explicit laws.

A related feature of such causal laws should be stressed: maximally explicit causal laws will not employ certain kinds of *dispositional* or *functional* predicates. I have in mind dispositional predicates that do not explicitly state the causal bases for the dispositions they express, the causal bases that bring about certain characteristics effects. The sorts of functional predicates I have in mind are those that apply to something in virtue of its having a certain causal or counterfactual role but do not state explicitly what that causal or counterfactual role is, or the properties in virtue of which something has that causal or counterfactual role. When such dispositional and functional predicates appear in a causal law, there is always some more explicit causal law that does not contain those predicates. Let us say that a set of terms is *the basic vocabulary* of a closed* comprehensive theory if and only if it is the vocabulary of a closed* comprehensive theory and no proper subset of it is such. The basic vocabulary of a closed* comprehensive theory will not contain dispositional or functional predicates of the sorts in question. (However, we may leave open whether such a basic vocabulary will contain dispositional predicates designating basic or fundamental causal powers.[24])

The foregoing account of what it is for a theory to be closed* and comprehensive is neither as complete nor as precise as one might wish. But I hope it can serve for present purposes. With this understanding of what a closed* comprehensive theory is, then, let us return to the question of what makes a law strict.

Let us say that *the extended basic vocabulary* of a closed* comprehensive theory *T* is a set of terms such that a term is a member of the set if and only if it satisfies the following disjunctive condition: (i) it is part of the basic vocabulary of *T*, or (ii) it is a Boolean combination of terms in *T*'s basic vocabulary, or (iii) it is

---

[24] See Rom Harré and E.H. Madden, *Causal Powers* (Oxford, 1975) for a defense of the view that there are fundamental causal powers. See J.L. Mackie, *Truth, Probability and Paradox* (Oxford, 1973) for a defense of the view that there are no fundamental causal powers. See Alexander Rosenberg 'Dispositions and Properties', *Midwest Studies in Philosophy*, 9 (1984), pp. 77–91 for an attempt to adjudicate the dispute between Harré and Madden and Mackie.

linked via bridge laws with terms in the basic vocabulary of T or Boolean combinations of such terms. We can now say what makes a law strict:

(D) A law is a strict law when but only when it is couched solely in the extended basic vocabulary of a closed* comprehensive theory.

Let us note two points. First, some strict laws are causal laws. But not all strict laws are causal. For example, if the physical predicate employed in a psychophysical bridge law were part of the extended basic vocabulary of a closed* comprehensive theory, then the mental predicate with which it is linked would be too. So such psychophysical bridge laws, if such are possible, would count as strict laws despite the fact that they are not causal laws. This squares with Davidson's use of 'strict law'. Second, we could define a more restricted notion of strict law according to which a law is strict when but only when it is couched solely in the basic vocabulary of a closed* comprehensive theory. In this restricted sense, presumably, only laws of physics count as strict laws. But the more liberal definition of 'strict law' supplied by (D) better fits Davidson's use of the term.

A strict law can rough and so fail to be as explicit and exceptionless as possible [ME:223]. But when a strict law fails to be such, it can be sharpened into one that is such without shifting to a different general vocabulary. One can sharpen a law by adding further provisos. But one can also sharpen a law by replacing predicates in the law with predicates with which they are linked via bridge laws, if the new predicates help make for a more explicit law. Bridge laws license substitution of predicates within laws. The fact that a predicate is reduced via a bridge law to another predicate makes the first part of the same general vocabulary as the second. (I say more about this in section IX.) Thus, this sort of sharpening would not count as shifting to a different general vocabulary. The basic vocabulary of a closed* comprehensive theory will be adequate to express laws that are as explicit and exceptionless as possible. Since strict laws are couched solely in the extended basic vocabulary of a closed* comprehensive theory they either are or else can be sharpened into such laws. Thus suppose physics is such a theory and that chemistry is nomologically reducible to physics. Then chemical laws can be strict despite the fact that chemistry is not itself a closed* comprehensive theory. The reason is that chemical laws can be sharpened into laws that are as explicit and exceptionless as possible by substituting predicates of physics for the chemical predicates nomologically linked to them and, if necessary, by adding further provisos stated in the vocabulary of physics. This sharpening would not count as shifting to a different general vocabulary since chemical predicates would count as part of the extended basic vocabulary of physics. Heteronomic or unstrict laws, in contrast to homonomic or strict laws, are not stated in the extended basic vocabulary of a closed* comprehensive theory. So they cannot be sharpened into laws couched solely in the basic vocabulary of such a theory without shifting to a different general vocabulary.

While we have put aside the issue of whether the Principle of the Nomological Character of Causality is true, some remarks about this principle and the notion of a strict law (as defined in (D)) are in order. Consider the following principle: (P) for any space-time region r, and for any space-time region r', an event occurs at r and causally interacts with an event that occurs at r' only if there is an event A that occurs at r and an event B that occurs at r', and

A and *B* are subsumed by a strict law. On certain assumptions, (P) is equivalent to the Principle of the Nomological Character of Causality, that is, to claim (7). The assumptions are these: (i) events occurring in space-time causally interact only with other events occurring in space-time; (ii) two events are identical if and only if they occur at the same space-time region; and (iii) 'strict law' should be understood as defined in (D). Davidson would accept (i) and (ii). If (P) and (7) are equivalent given (i)–(iii), that tells in favor of (D)'s capturing Davidson's intended notion of strict law. The implication in one direction is trivial. Assume (7) is true. Suppose, then, that (P) is false. If (P) is false, there can be two events that causally interact without there being any strict law that subsumes them. This contradicts our assumptions that (7) is true. So, if (7) is true, (P) is. To see that the implication goes in the other direction, given (i)–(iii), consider the following: assume (P) is true. Suppose, then, (7) is false. If so, then there can be events that causally interact but which are not subsumed by a strict law. The events in question must occur in space-time. For suppose that an event *A* does not occur in space-time. Then, given (ii), there is no distinct event that does not occur in space-time. An event cannot cause itself, so *A* cannot causally interact with any event not occurring in space-time. So *A* cannot causally interact with any event that occurs in space-time. Given (i), *A* cannot enter into causal relations. Thus the events that violate (7) must occur in space-time. Given (ii), these events are identical with any events occurring in the same space-time regions. So events occurring in space-time can causally interact without any events occurring in the same space-time regions instantiating a strict law. But this contradicts our assumption that (P) is true. So, given (i)–(iii), (P) implies (7). We see, then, that on assumptions (i)–(iii), (P) and (7) are equivalent. If (ii) is false because a more fine-grained criterion of event individuation is correct, and if 'strict law' is understood as defined in (D), then (P) is implied by but does not imply (7).

Suppose physics is a closed* comprehensive theory and that the extreme coarse-grained criterion of event individuation is correct. Then the reason that whenever events occurring in space-time causally interact, events within the domain of physics and occurring at the same space-time regions as the events in question causally interact, is just that every event is itself within the domain of physics. Suppose physics is a closed* comprehensive theory and a more fine-grained criterion of event individuation is correct. Then some other explanation must be offered for why whenever two events occurring in space-time causally interact, events within the domain of physics and occurring at the same space-time regions as the events in question causally interact.[25] Since we put aside the issue of event individuation we need not settle this matter here.

---

[25] For one attempt of this sort, see the following papers by Jaegwon Kim: 'Causality, Identity, and Supervenience in the Mind-Body Problem,' *Midwest Studies in Philosophy*, 4 (1979), pp. 31–49; Epiphenomenal and Supervenient Causation' in *Midwest Studies in Philosophy*, 9 (1984), pp. 257–70; and 'Supervenience and Supervenient Causation' *Southern Journal of Philosophy*, 22 (1984), pp. 45–56. I critically discuss the views Kim expresses in these papers in 'Event Supervenience and Supervenient Causation', *The Southern Journal of Philosophy*, 22 (1984), pp. 71–91. Some related issues are discussed by Horgan and Tye in 'Against the Token Identity Theory' (pp. 427–43).

It might be claimed that physics is not a comprehensive theory since physics does not contain causal laws. This raises the issue of what makes a law causal, an issue beyond the scope of this essay. But I want to rule out one reason for thinking that physics does not contain causal laws, namely, the fact that laws couched in the basic vocabulary of physics do not contain causal locutions such as 'cause', 'make happen', 'bring about', or the like. Given Davidson's view of causation, the basic vocabulary of a closed* comprehensive theory would not contain causal locutions. Recall that, for Davidson, such locutions are promissory notes: they imply that there is a strict law but do not imply the strict law. Such promissory notes can be redeemed in the basic vocabulary of a closed* comprehensive theory since such a vocabulary will suffice for the framing of strict laws covering every causal interaction between events within the domain of the theory. As Davidson notes, on his view of causation: 'Unavoidable mention of causality is a cloak for ignorance; we must appeal to the notion of cause when we lack detailed and accurate laws' [FA:80]. By 'detailed and accurate laws' here, I take him to have in mind maximally explicit laws. Such laws will not contain causal locutions. This is not to deny that causal laws can employ causal locutions; not all causal laws are as explicit as possible. (Again, I do not mean to deny that maximally explicit laws may not employ predicates designating fundamental or basic causal properties.) Since the basic vocabulary of a closed* comprehensive theory will not contain causal locutions, statements couched solely in such a vocabulary can imply singular causal statements only with the help of meaning postulates concerning causation. Davidson would insist that one such meaning postulate will be the Principle of the Nomological Character of Causality.[26]

VII The impossibility of strict psychological laws

Davidson does not deny that psychology is a nomothetic science; he even remarks that its laws may be more exact and precise than those of many other sciences (he cites meteorology and geology as examples) [R:240]. But he denies that there can be strict psychological laws. The central line of argument that he offers for this denial goes as follows: psychology is not a closed theory and cannot be nomologically reduced to a closed comprehensive theory; so there cannot be strict psychological laws [R:240]. Davidson acknowledges that, for example, biology is not closed and so is not a closed comprehensive theory; but he refrains from asserting the anomalism of the biological because he does not know how to show that biology is not nomologically reducible to a closed comprehensive theory (though he expresses doubt that it is so reducible) [R:240].

---

[26] In one place, Davidson provides an example of the logical form of a 'full fledged' causal law and employs a causal predicate in the law [CR:158]. However, Davidson provides this example in the context of placing to one side issues concerning the analysis of causation; and the point of the example is just that full fledged causal laws are biconditionals. Strict laws will imply singular causal statements only in conjunction with meaning postulates.

Understanding 'strict law' as defined in (D), we can recast this line of argument for the denial of strict psychological law as follows: there cannot be strict psychological laws since psychology is not itself a closed* comprehensive theory and cannot be reduced via bridge laws to such a theory. Recasting the argument in terms of vocabularies, the argument is this:

(22) Mental predicates cannot be part of the basic vocabulary of a closed* comprehensive theory.

(23) Mental predicates cannot be linked via bridge laws with predicates in the extended basic vocabulary of a closed* comprehensive theory.

(24) Mental predicates cannot be part of the extended basic vocabulary of a closed* comprehensive theory.

(25) If a mental predicate cannot be part of the extended basic vocabulary of a closed* comprehensive theory, there cannot be strict psychological laws.

(26) There cannot be strict psychological laws.

The argument is valid. Premise (25) is true, given what it is for a law to be strict. Premise (24) follows from what comes before, given what it is for a predicate to be part of the extended basic vocabulary of a closed* comprehensive theory. The core controversial claims in the argument are, then, (22) and (23). I shall comment on (23) at the close of the next section. For now, let us focus on (22).

Since psychology is obviously not itself a closed* comprehensive theory the set of mental predicates cannot itself be the basic vocabulary of such a theory. However, even if this is so, it remains an open question whether the set of mental predicates can be a proper subset of such a basic vocabulary. But it cannot, and so (22) is true, if mental predicates are the sorts of dispositional or functional predicates I described earlier, or contain essential occurrences such predicates. The reason is that, as we saw earlier, such predicates cannot be part of the basic vocabulary of a closed* comprehensive theory. Davidson maintains that mental predicates either are or contain essential occurrences of such dispositional expressions. Mental predicates contain essential occurrences of propositional attitude verbs. Davidson maintains such verbs are dispositional and so that mental predicates are [see, e.g., H:273–5]; and such dispositional predicates do not explicitly state all the causally relevant parameters in virtue of which they apply to something. I cannot defend this claim here.[27] But, for present purposes, it suffices to note that if it is true, (22) is true.

VIII The impossibility of strict psychophysical laws

Let us turn to an argument for the (conceptual) impossibility of strict psychophysical laws that is, I believe, suggested by Davidson's texts. The argument is this:

---

[27] See Alex Rosenberg 'Davidson's "Unintended" Attack on Psychology' (this volume, pp. 399–407) for a related discussion.

(27) There cannot be a predicate, no matter how complex, in the extended basic vocabulary of a closed* comprehensive physical theory that has, as a matter of law, the same extension as a mental predicate.

(28) Mental predicates cannot be part of the basic vocabulary of a closed* comprehensive physical theory.

(29) Mental predicates cannot be part of the extended basic vocabulary of a closed* comprehensive physical theory.

(30) If mental predicates cannot be part of the extended basic vocabulary of a closed* comprehensive physical theory, there cannot be strict psychophysical laws.

---

(31) There cannot be strict psychophysical laws.

The argument is valid. Premise (28) is, I believe, correct. Premise (29) follows from (27) and (28). The core controversial claims in the argument are (27) and (30). Claim (30) may be false if there could be a closed* comprehensive theory that contains physical predicates among its basic vocabulary but that is neither a purely physical theory nor a psychophysical theory. I shall say more about (30) shortly; but first I shall comment on (27).

Claim (27) does not imply (4) if there could be a physical predicate that is not part of the extended basic vocabulary of a closed* comprehensive physical theory. Davidson would, I believe, allow that there are such physical predicates. He counts neurophysiological and biological predicates as physical predicates despite the fact that he thinks they may not be part of the extended basic vocabulary of physics. (He says: 'The assumption that biology and neurophysiology are reducible to physics is ... probably false' [MM:246].) I shall put aside the question of whether neurophysiological or biological predicates can be part of the extended basic vocabulary of physics or a closed* comprehensive physical theory and shall count them as physical predicates whether or not they can be. In any case, (4) implies (27). Claim (4) denies there can be psychophysical bridge laws, where 'physical predicate' is understood in its broadest intuitive sense and where it is allowed that such laws may employ combinations (of any degree of Boolean complexity) of physical predicates. There may well be considerations that suffice to establish (27) which do not suffice to establish (4). But Davidson argues for the stronger of the two claims. In the following section, I shall focus on (4). (And I shall put aside the issue of whether a completed physics would be a closed* comprehensive theory.)

It is admittedly unclear what counts as a physical predicate in the broadest sense. So we shall have to rely on our rough and ready understanding of this notion. The distinction between mental predicates (in Davidson's semi-technical sense) and physical predicates (in the broadest intuitive sense) is not exhaustive over the class of predicates. Certain intuitively mental predicates (e.g., 'has a toothache' and 'sees *a*') do not count as mental predicates in Davidson's sense and surely do not count as physical predicates in any sense. Also, the distinction between intuitively mental predicates and intuitively physical predicates seems not to be exhaustive over the class of predicates.

Some envision for scientific psychology theoretical predicates that would not count as mental predicates or physical predicates.[28] Moreover, Thomas Nagel has argued that there could be protomental predicates that are neither mental predicates nor physical predicates.[29] The question arises, then, as to whether mental predicates can be linked via bridge laws to predicates that are not physical predicates even in the broadest sense. If they can and those predicates are part of the extended basic vocabulary of a closed* comprehensive theory, then claims (12), (18), (23), and (30) may be in trouble. Let us say that a predicate is an x-predicate just in case (a) it is part of the extended basic vocabulary of a closed* comprehensive theory, and, (b) it is neither a mental predicate in Davidson's semi-technical sense nor a physical predicate in the broadest intuitive sense. (Intuitive mental predicates such as 'has a toothache' and, perhaps, the sorts of theoretical predicates envisioned by scientific psychology satisfy (b), but it is seems unlikely that they satisfy (a). Protomental predicates, presumably, are to satisfy (a) and (b); they are to satisfy (a) since they are to be part of the basic vocabulary of a fundamental theory of the world. In any case, we need not decide these matters here.) And let us say that a description is an 'x-description' just in case it contains an essential occurrence of an x-predicate. Consider, then, the following: if a mental event can satisfy an x-description under which it instantiates a strict law, (18) is false. Suppose that x-predicates are part of the basic vocabulary of a closed* comprehensive theory. Then if a mental event that causally interacts with a physical event can satisfy an x-description under which it instantiates a strict law, (12) is false. Moreover, if x-predicates can be part of the basic vocabulary of a closed* comprehensive theory and mental predicates can be reduced via bridge laws to x-predicates or Boolean combinations of x-predicates and physical predicates, (23) is false. Finally, if an x-predicate or a Boolean combination of x-predicates and physical predicates appears in a strict x-physical law and also serves as a reductive base for a mental predicate, then there can be strict psychophysical laws even if mental predicates cannot be part of the extended basic vocabulary of a closed* comprehensive physical theory. If so, (30) is false.

I shall not discuss the possibility of x-predicates in any detail for the following reason. Either x-predicates reduce via bridge laws to physical predicates or they do not. If they reduce via bridge laws to physical predicates, then, since reduction is transitive, mental predicates would be nomologically reducible to x-predicates only if mental predicates are nomologically reducible to physical predicates. So if (4) is true, the possibility of x-predicates makes no trouble for (12), (18), (23), or (30). Suppose x-predicates are not nomologically reducible to physical predicates. Then, while (4) does not deny the possibility of mental

---

[28] Johnston discusses the possibility of a scientific psychology in connection with Davidson's position in 'Why Having a Mind Matters', pp. 422–6. In 'Psychological Laws', *Philosophical Topics*, 12 (1980), pp. 248–50, William Lycan argues that Davidson does not succeed in showing that psychofunctional laws are impossible. The point I make below is that if Davidson's argument against the possibility of psychophysical bridge laws is sound, his reasoning can be extended to show that psychofunctional laws are impossible as well.

[29] 'Panpsychism' in *Mortal Questions* (Cambridge University Press, 1980), pp. 181–95. Stanton invokes the protomental to raise difficulties for claim (12) in 'Supervenience and Psychological Law in Anomalous Monism', pp. 78–9.

predicates being reducible via bridge laws to x-predicates or Boolean combinations of x-predicates and physical predicates, Davidson's argument for (4) could be recast as an argument to show this is not possible. To anticipate the discussion in the following section, the reason is that such predicates would express concepts that have nonrational conditions of application and mental predicates cannot be reduced to such predicates. The point to note is that if Davidson's argument for (4) is successful, it can be recast as an argument against the possibility of mental predicates nomologically reducing to combinations of x-predicates and physical predicates. So, I shall focus on (4).

IX *Constitutive principles and nomological reduction*

Davidson remarks: 'nothing I can say about the irreducibility of the mental deserves to be called a proof' [ME:215]. And he acknowledges that his argument for such irreducibility 'may be found less than conclusive' [ME:209]. Actually, Davidson suggests several lines of argument for (4), some more compelling than others. Before presenting what I take to be his central line of argument, I shall set out one line of argument he explicitly rejects.

According to Davidson, we primarily attribute propositional attitudes in the context of interpreting verbal and nonverbal behavior and dispositions to so behave.[30] Propositional attitude attribution is interpretative because propositional attitude attributions embody arbitrary choices; choices that are arbitrary even relative to all possible evidence. (We need not consider here what such choices are.) Thus Davidson maintains that a systematic indeterminacy besets our attributions of propositional attitudes [ME:222]. There will always be at least two interpretation schemes for attributing propositional attitudes and intentional actions to a given individual that differ in at least some of the attributions they imply; and there will be no fact of the matter as to which interpretation scheme is correct. Davidson's frequent references to such indeterminacy may suggest the following argument: if there could be psychophysical bridge laws, interpretation would be determinate; interpretation is indeterminate; therefore there cannot be psychophysical bridge laws. But this argument does not express Davidson's reason for denying the possibility of psychophysical bridge laws. He points out that such indeterminacy leaves open the possibility that the mental predicates in bridge laws can be relativized to an optimal, but arbitrary choice of interpretation scheme [MM:222]. There is a fact of the matter as to what propositional attitudes an individual has and what intentional actions he or she performs relative to a choice of interpretation scheme. So the indeterminacy of interpretation does not show that psychophysical bridge laws are impossible.

Davidson's central line of argument against the possibility of psychophysical bridge laws is that there is a categorial difference between the mental and the

---

[30] See, for example, Davidson's 'Radical Interpretation' *Truth and Interpretation* (Oxford, 1984), pp. 125–40. For excellent discussions of Davidson's views on interpretation see Michael Root and John Wallace's 'Meaning and Interpretation' *Notre Dame Journal of Formal Logic*, 23 (1982), pp. 157–73, and Ernest LePore's 'In defense of Davidson,' *Linguistics and Philosophy* 5 (1982), pp. 277–94.

physical that makes such laws impossible. I shall attempt to say what that categorial difference is and to present the major steps in Davidson's argument that this difference makes psychophysical bridge laws impossible. So as not to disappoint the readers expectations, let me note that I can do no more here than present what I take to be the major steps in Davidson's reasoning; I cannot justify each step; and so important questions will remain.

The line of argument I wish to present is suggested by the following passages:

> to allow the possibility of such laws would amount to changing the subject. By changing the subject I mean here: deciding not to accept the criterion of the mental in terms of the vocabulary of the propositional attitudes [ME:216].
>
> There are no strict psychophysical laws because of the disparate commitments of the mental and the physical schemes [ME:222].

> There cannot be tight connections between the realms if each is to retain allegiance to its proper source of evidence [ME:222].

> Standing ready, as we must, to adjust psychological terms to one set of standards and physical terms to another, we know that we cannot insist on a sharp and lawlike connection between them [PP:238].

Let me shift from talk of mental and physical predicates or terms to talk of the mental and physical concepts expressed, respectively, by such predicates and terms. (Let it be clear that by 'a mental concept', I shall mean a concept expressed by a predicate we use to attribute a propositional attitude. So, for example, the concept of a pain will not count as a mental concept in this semi-technical sense. I shall be concerned here with a proper subclass of the intuitive class of mental concepts.) For a start at interpretation of the quoted passages, then: the different sets of standards to which we are committed in applying mental concepts and physical concepts are set, respectively, by the constitutive principles of the mental conceptual scheme and the constitutive principles of the physical conceptual scheme. The mental and physical conceptual schemes each have their own constitutive principles; and these two groups of principles are disparate, essentially different.[31] The leading idea is that the constitutive principles of the mental have some feature that the constitutive principles of the physical lack. The categorial difference between the mental and the physical consists in this difference between their constitutive principles. And this difference makes psychophysical bridge laws impossible. In a nutshell, the idea is that there cannot be psychophysical bridge laws because the constitutive principles of the mental are different from the constitutive principles of the physical in such a way that concepts from the two schemes cannot be joined so as to constitutively underwrite such laws.

The following questions arise: (a) what is a constitutive principle? (b) what feature do the constitutive principles of the mental have that the constitutive

---

[31] This talk of two different conceptual schemes is compatible with Davidson's position in 'On The Very Idea of A Conceptual Scheme', *Truth and Interpretation* (Oxford, 1984), pp. 183–98. For a discussion of why see [R:243].

principles of the physical lack? and (c) why does this difference between the constitutive principles in question make psychophysical bridge laws impossible? Let us address each query in turn.[32]

Let us begin with some examples of constitutive principles. In the case of the physical scheme, its constitutive principles include (among a vast number of others) ones concerning, for example, the measurement of length, mass, temperature, and time. (These provide 'the simplest possible' illustrations of constitutive principles of the physical [ME:220].) The principles will include ones concerning the transitivity, and ones concerning the asymmetry, of the two-placed relations, longer than, heavier than, warmer than, later than, and so on. And it includes other principles that serve to distinguish the relations in question.

According to Davidson, constitutive principles are synthetic, a priori generalizations. Such principles have a *constitutive status* because they partly govern the application of concepts: they express standards that *partly* determine what counts as a correct or incorrect application of a concept. They thus play a *regulative* and thereby *normative* role in concept application [MM:254]. Constitutive principles are 'sources of evidence' in that they partly determine what can and cannot count as an *internal* reason for believing that a certain concept applies, this being a reason that explains why the concept applies. The principles are relatively a priori in that they have an a priori status relative to our application of concepts to particular cases. The relative a priori status is this: we do not test them against our application of concepts to particular cases, but rather test out applications of concepts to particular cases against conformance to them. The principles function as meaning postulates that express the a priori *descriptive contents* of concepts. The examples of constitutive principles of the physical that Davidson provides are statements proponents of certain versions of the analytic/synthetic distinction would count as analytic. For example, the statement 'If *a* is longer than *b*, and *b* is longer than *c*, then *a* is longer than *c*' would be counted as analytic by such proponents. They would take it as part of the meaning of 'longer than' that it expresses a transitive relation, and so would hold that the statement in question is true in virtue of its meaning. But Davidson calls such principles 'synthetic'. The reason, I think, is just that he does not think there are any analytic statements. He states that he does not understand what it is for a statement to be necessarily true, or analytic, or true in virtue of its meaning [see, e.g., H:273]. And he seems to maintain that the various theories of analyticity do not succeed in explaining the role of constitutive principles in concept application [ME:221].

Davidson maintains that the constitutive principles of the mental conceptual scheme include *the principles of rationality*: principles that specify what makes for consistency and rational coherence. He says:

> Just as the satisfaction of the conditions for measuring length or mass may be viewed as constitutive for the range of application of the sciences that employ these measures, so the satisfaction of conditions of consistency and rational coherence may be viewed as constitutive of the range of application of such concepts as those of belief, desire, intention and action [PP:236–7].

---

[32] Kim addresses each of these questions in 'Psychophysical Laws' (this volume, pp. 369–86).

The role of the constraints of consistency and rational coherence in the application of mental concepts is a large topic about which Davidson has had much to say.[33] The topic cannot be treated adequately here. But one of the leading ideas is this: when we interpret the behavior of an individual we attribute intentional actions to that individual that can be rationalized by citing beliefs (thoughts, opinions, etc.) and pro attitudes (wants, desires, urges, etc.) of the individual. Such beliefs and pro attitudes must, in virtue of their propositional content, provide the individual's rationale for engaging in the course of action in question, where that course of action is propositionally characterized. In interpreting an individual we must attribute intentional actions and propositional attitudes to that individual that it *makes sense* for the individual to perform or to have. And we cannot do that without attributing at least a minimal degree of rational coherence.

Both the constitutive principles of the mental and the constitutive principles of the physical are synthetic a priori principles. Both groups of principles play a regulative and thereby normative role in concept application. Both groups of principles are partly determinative of the range of application of concepts. Thus, as Davidson notes: 'It may be claimed that there are certain regulative or constitutive elements in the application of psychological concepts. This is certainly right; but the same can be said for the application of physical concepts' [MM:254].

Let us turn to (b), then, and ask what the difference is between the constitutive principles of the mental and the constitutive principles of the physical that makes psychophysical bridge laws impossible. The alleged difference is just this: the constitutive principles of the mental include principles that express the *norms* of rationality and no constitutive principle of the physical expresses a norm of rationality.[34] Constitutive principles expressing norms of rationality *express* normative truths: they say what propositional attitudes an individual ought rationally to have given that the individual has others; and they say what an individual ought rationally to do given the individual's propositional attitudes. Such constitutive principles express the norms governing inductive and deductive rationality. They specify normative relations between mental states and events that hold in virtue of relationships between the propositional contents of the states and events. The constitutive principles of the physical, in contrast, do not themselves *express* such normative relationships, even though they play a normative role in concept application. It is unclear what degree of conformance to the norms of rationality is required for possession of propositional attitudes. But to the extent that an individual

---

[33] See, for example, 'Belief and the Basis of Meaning' *Truth and Interpretation* (Oxford, 1984), pp. 141–154, and 'Radical Interpretation'. It should be noted that it is, of course, not ipso facto irrational to believe that Cicero is Cicero and yet believe that Cicero is not Tully, despite the fact that these beliefs are inconsistent. However, I assume here that a suitable consistency requirement can be formulated.

[34] See John McDowell's discussion of the norms of rationality in 'Functionalism and Anomalous Monism' (pp. 388–97). McDowell critically discusses Brian Loar's attempt to provide a functional reduction of the mental via a modified Ramsey method of reduction in *Mind and Meaning* (Cambridge University, 1981), pp. 20–5 See also Davidson's 'Deception and Division' (this volume, pp. 138–48) for an illuminating discussion of some norms of rationality.

diverges from what such norms enjoin, interpretation falters. Davidson maintains that at least a minimal degree of rational coherence is required in order to have propositional attitudes. He holds that in attributing propositional attitudes 'we necessarily impose conditions of coherence, rationality, and consistency. These conditions have no echo in physical theory' [PP:231].[35] A weak reading of his 'no echo' claim seems appropriate: norms of rationality cannot be expressed in physical terms.

Thus consider the following passage:

> If I am right, then, detailed knowledge of the physics or physiology of the brain, indeed of the whole of man, would not provide a shortcut to the kind of interpretation required for the application of sophisticated psychological concepts ... we would have to interpret the total pattern of ... observed (or predicted) behavior. Our standards for accepting a system of interpretation would also have to be the same: we would have to make allowances for intelligible error; we would have to impute a large degree of consistency, on pain of not making sense of what was said or done; we would have to assume a pattern of beliefs and motives which agreed with our own to a degree sufficient to build a base for understanding and interpreting disagreements. These conditions, which include criteria of consistency and rationality, can no doubt be made more objective. But I see no reason to think that they can be stated in a purely physical vocabulary [MM:258–9].

Davidson concludes from the fact that the conditions for the application of psychological concepts cannot be stated in a purely physical vocabulary that: 'There is no important sense in which psychology can be reduced to the physical sciences' [MM:259]. The important sense of reduction is reduction via bridge laws. The reason conditions for the application of mental concepts cannot be stated in a purely physical vocabulary is that the normative relationships that hold among mental states and events in virtue of which they conform to or approximate what the norms of rationality enjoin *cannot be expressed* in a purely physical vocabulary. I suspect many will find this weak 'no echo' claim plausible. But then question (c) looms large: why does the difference in question make psychophysical bridge laws impossible? To see Davidson's answer to this question, some preliminary remarks are in order.

First we must introduce some terminology. Let us say that a concept has *rational conditions of application* just in case its application is governed in part by principles of rationality. A concept whose application is not governed even in part by such principles has *nonrational conditions of application*. Mental concepts have rational conditions of application, while physical concepts have nonrational conditions of application.[36]

Now we must avail ourselves of an idea that is similar to (and inspired by) one Jaegwon Kim proposes in his contribution to this volume.[37] The idea is this:

---

[35] It should be noted that we are sometimes warranted in attributing inconsistent beliefs to an individual, for example, in cases of self-deception and in some cases of weakness of will. Davidson claims that in such cases we must treat the individual's mind as divided. See 'Deception and Division' (pp. 138–48). (See footnote 33 for a qualifying remark concerning the notion of inconsistency.)

[36] This idea was inspired by Kim's discussion in 'Psychophysical Laws' (pp. 378–81).

[37] Here I am indebted once again to Kim's discussion in ibid., (pp. 378–81), though I develop the idea somewhat differently.

bridge laws *transmit* conditions of application for the concept expressed by the reducing predicate to the concept expressed by the reduced predicate. So, if A is a condition of application for the concept expressed by the reducing predicate in a bridge law and C is the concept expressed by the reduced predicate in that law, A is a condition of application for C. I assume that such transmissions go in one direction only. This asymmetry is due to the fact that reduction is asymmetrical; this asymmetry, like the asymmetry of causation and of explanation, does not seem explainable in modal terms. (But nothing in what follows turns on the assumption that such transmissions are unidirectional.)

I said earlier that when a term is reduced via a bridge law to another term, the term is part of the same general vocabulary as the term to which it is reduced. This is because conditions of application for the concept expressed by the reducing term are conditions of application for the concept expressed by the reduced term. In this sense, *nomological reduction is conceptual incorporation.*[38] The function of bridge laws is to incorporate one set of concepts into another. Incorporation can be understood as follows: conditions of application for the reducing concept will be at least nomologically necessary and sufficient conditions of application for the reduced concept; where the modal force of 'nomologically' is whatever the modal force of bridge laws is, a question I continue to leave open. The constitutive principles governing the reducing concept govern (perhaps with a weaker hand) the reduced concept.

Suppose that bridge laws transmit conditions of application. Then if mental predicates can be reduced via bridge laws to physical predicates, the concepts expressed by the mental predicates will have nonrational conditions of application. If mental concepts cannot have nonrational conditions of application, then mental predicates cannot be reduced via bridge laws to physical predicates. Thus, the argument for the impossibility of psychophysical bridge laws that emerges is this:

(32) Mental concepts cannot have nonrational conditions of application.

(33) Physical concepts have nonrational conditions of application.

(34) If one predicate is reduced via a bridge law to another, the conditions of application for the concept expressed by the reducing predicate are conditions of application for the concept expressed by the reduced predicate.

(35) If there can be psychophysical bridge laws, mental concepts can have nonrational conditions of application.

(36) There cannot be psychophysical bridge laws.

The argument is valid. Premise (35) follows from what comes before. Premise (34) is implied by a certain view about the nature of nomological reduction. The view is, perhaps, controversial. But a defense of it is beyond the scope of this essay. Premise (33) seems true. The claim I want to focus on is (32).

---

[38] Tryg A. Ager, Jerrold L. Arronson, and Robert Weingard argue that reduction consists in conceptual incorporation. See their 'Are Bridge Laws Really Necessary?', *Noûs*, 8 (1974), pp. 119–34. I agree with much of what they say, thought I interpret the data somewhat differently.

Davidson seems to maintain that mental concepts must have rational conditions of application, that regardless of what empirical discoveries are made mental concepts must retain their rational conditions of application. Suppose, then, that mental concepts *must* have rational conditions of application. This seems compatible with their also having nonrational conditions of application. If a mental concept must have rational conditions of application, then it cannot have nonrational conditions of application that enjoin applications that could conflict with those enjoined by its rational conditions of application. The reason is simply that a coherent concept cannot have conflicting conditions of application. But why cannot a mental concept have a logically necessary and sufficient rational condition of application and a nomologically necessary and sufficient nonrational condition of application? To assert that there would always be the nomological possibility of conflict in what such conditions of application enjoin is just to deny that there can be nomological connections between the mental and the physical of the sort expressed by bridge laws. But the point at issue is whether there can be such nomological connections. The fact that such conflict is logically possible does not seem to present a difficulty. To show that mental concepts cannot have nomologically necessary and sufficient nonrational conditions of application (assuming they must have logically necessary and sufficient rational conditions of application), it must be shown that such conflict is always nomologically possible. Otherwise, it will not be shown why having a rational condition of application excludes having a nomologically necessary and sufficient nonrational condition of application.

Davidson points us in the direction of an argument to show this [R:241]. Recall that the constitutive principles expressing the norms of rationality express normative truths. Since rational conditions of application are governed by such principles, such conditions of application are themselves normative. Nonrational conditions of application would either have to be nonnormative or else be governed by principles expressing different norms. An argument that conflict is always nomologically possible might attempt to show that when a concept has normative conditions of application, it cannot have nomologically necessary and sufficient nonnormative conditions of application, or nomologically necessary and sufficient normative conditions of application involving different norms. Presumably, the nonrational conditions of application for the concept expressed by a purely physical predicate will be nonnormative. It may well be that the normativity of the mental makes psychophysical bridge laws impossible. But one thing I am unsure about is why a concept with normative conditions of application cannot also have nomologically necessary and sufficient nonnormative conditions of application. This is one reason I am unable to articulate this line of argument further.[39]

I want to gesture in the direction of a related line of argument in favor of (32). In attributing propositional attitudes in accordance with the norms of rationality, an interpreter must make assessments of what propositional attitudes it

---

[39] For a functionalist reply to the claim that the normativity of the mental makes psychophysical bridge laws impossible, see Robert Van Gulick's, 'Rationality and the Anomalous Nature of the Mental', *Philosophical Research Archives*. I elaborate on my worries about (32) in 'Comments on Kim', presented at the Davidson Conference.

makes sense for an individual to have given other propositional attitudes the individual has; and an interpreter must make assessments of what it makes sense for an individual to do given the individual's propositional attitudes. Such rationality assessments seem perspectival: it seems that they can differ somewhat from one interpreter to another.[40] While, to be sure, rational choice theory has sharpened our understanding of rationality, the broad notion of rational coherence Davidson decribes seems essential to interpretation and does not seem to admit of precise conditions of application. This consideration about rationality assessments seems to point to an additional indeterminacy in interpretation. Davidson maintains that there will always be at least two optimal but nonequivalent interpretation schemes for interpreting any individual and no fact of the matter as to which is correct. The consideration just raised concerning the perspectival character of rationality assessments suggests that the set of optimal but nonequivalent interpretation schemes for a given individual may vary from one interpreter to another. If interpretation is indeterminate, then there will be a fact of the matter as to what propositional attitudes an individual has only relative to certain arbitrary choices. If rationality assessments are perspectival in the way suggested, then there will be a fact of the matter as to what propositional attitudes an individual has only relative to certain arbitrary choices and to the rationality assessments of the interpreter. This suggests that the rational condition of application for a mental concept can vary somewhat from one interpreter to another. If this is right, then nonrational conditions of application for mental concepts would have to vary in a corresponding way. But it is difficult to imagine what such nonrational conditions of application would be like. The arbitrary choices involved in interpretation fix certain physical parameters; for example, the environmental context in which the reliability of an individual's beliefs are to be assessed. But it would be question-begging to maintain that various rationality assessments fix different physical parameters. Now the line of argument I am gesturing at admittedly cries out for further articulation. But even if I had more space available, I could not now further articulate it. I leave it open whether it can withstand careful scrutiny.

X Supervenience and nomological reduction

Whether the mental supervenes on the physical is a topic of much current interest.[41] The claim that the mental might supervene on the physical was first made in 'Mental Events' [p. 214]. In 'The Material Mind', Davidson actually

---

[40] See McDowell's illuminating discussion of the perspectival nature of the intentional in 'Functionalism and Anomalous Monism', pp. 394–7. William Larry Stanton discusses the perspectival nature of the intentional in 'Accounting for the Mental Qua Mental' (unpublished); he suggests there, as I do below, that this may involve an additional indeterminacy in interpretation.

[41] The literature is vast, but see especially: Geoffrey Hellman and Frank Thomson, 'Physicalism: Ontology, Determination and Reduction', *Journal of Philosophy*, 72 (1975), pp. 551–64, and 'Physicalist Materialism', *Nous*, 11 (1977), pp. 309–45; Colin McGinn, 'Mental States, Natural Kinds and Psychophysical Laws' in *Proceedings of the Aristotelian Society*, Supp. Vol. LII (1978), pp. 195–220 and 'Philosophical Materialism' *Synthese*, 44 (1980), pp. 173–206; Jaegwon Kim

asserted that the mental supervenes on the physical. He formulated the supervenience thesis as follows:

> it is impossible for two events (objects, states) to agree in all their physical characteristics and to differ in some psychological characteristic [MM:253].

I want to employ a distinction Kim draws between two kinds of supervenience in order to provide two readings of this claim, one stronger than the other.[42] (For my purposes, it makes no difference whether the strong reading is a plausible interpretation of Davidson's intended claim. In fact, I think it is not for reasons I give later.) Availing ourselves of possible world talk, one reading of the claim is this: there is no possible world in which two events (objects, states) in that world agree in all their physical characteristics and differ in some mental characteristic. (The shift from 'psychological' to 'mental' here is harmless.) This reading takes the claim to express what Kim calls weak supervenience of the mental on the physical. This seems the natural reading of Davidson's claim. But (perhaps) another reading is this: no two possible events (objects, states) agree in all their physical characteristics and differ in some mental characteristic. This reading expresses strong supervenience. Strong supervenience implies weak supervenience, but not conversely. In this section, I shall say why Davidson should reject the claim that the mental strongly supervenes on the physical.

First, however, we must consider the notion of strong supervenience in more detail. Let us take the relata of supervenience relations to be properties.[43] Let us mean by 'a physical property' a property expressed by a predicate in the basic vocabulary of the physics true of this world; and let us mean by 'a mental property' an intentional mental property. Suppose, then, that P is the maximal physical property of an event (object, state) that has some mental property M. Given the strong supervenience thesis, the connection between P and M has modal force: necessarily whatever has P has M. Property P is *a strong supervenience base* of M. Strong supervenience bases provide sufficient conditions for the realization of their supervenient properties. The kind of sufficiency

---

'Psychophysical Supervenience', *Philosophical Studies*, 41 (1982), pp. 51–70, and 'Psychophysical Supervenience as a Mind–Body Theory', *Brain and Cognitive Theory*, 5 (1982); John Haugeland, 'Weak Supervenience', *American Philosophical Quarterly*, 19 (1982), pp. 93–103; Terrence Horgan, 'Supervenience and Microphysics', *Pacific Philosophical Quarterly*, 63 (1982), pp. 29–43, and 'Supervenience and Cosmic Hermeneutics', *Southern Journal of Philosophy*, 22 (1983), pp. 19–38; David Lewis, 'New Work for a Theory of Universals' *Australasian Journal of Philosophy*, 4 (1983), pp. 343–77; Ernest Sosa 'Mind–Body Interaction and Supervenient Causation' *Midwest Studies in Philosophy*, 9 (1984), pp. 271–282; and see Johnston's 'Why Having a Mind Matters'.

[42] Kim discusses the distinction between strong and weak supervenience in 'Psychophysical Supervenience as a Mind–Body Theory', and in 'Concepts of Supervenience,' *Philosophy and Phenomenological Research*, XLV (1984), pp. 157–171. Throughout this entire section, I am deeply indebted in obvious ways to Kim's writings on mental–physical supervenience.

[43] This is not entirely uncontroversial. One who maintains there are no properties may take the primary relata of supervenience relations to be some sort of linguistic entity, for example, predicates. However, even if there are no properties and the primary relata of supervenience relations are predicates, many of my central points in what remains of this section will stand. For example, my characterization in the penultimate paragraph of the text of this essay of the central controversy surrounding (32) will stand.

in question will depend on the modal force of 'cannot' in the supervenience thesis. Let us understand this to be at least that of causal impossibility. This implies that it is true in every causally possible world that whatever has P has M. (But it does not, of course, imply that it is a causal law that whatever has P has M'.)

Since P is a maximal physical property it will likely be a stronger property than is required to necessitate M. Many components of a person's maximal physical property are bound to be irrelevant to whether the person has a certain mental property. (For example, the distance between Jupiter and Edward at a given time is a component of Edward's maximal physical property, but it is likely to be irrelevant to whether Edward believes that many are called but few are chosen.) Let us say that property A is weaker than property B if and only if whenever B is exemplified A is, but A can be exemplified without B. If P is a stronger property than is needed to necessitate M, there will be some weaker property than P that also necessitates M and which is such that no still weaker property necessitates M. Such a property is a strong minimal supervenience base (or, for short, a minimal base) for M.

As Kim has noted,[44] strong supervenience of the mental on the physical allows for *alternative minimal physical bases* for mental properties. A given mental property may well have multiple minimal physical bases. Since mental properties are macro-properties relative to their physical bases, the notion of alternative minimal bases provides a way of interpreting the idea that mental properties are *multiply realizable* by physical properties. Each physical realization of a mental property can be a minimal physical base for that mental property. Multiple realizability seems a fairly common trait of macro-properties and their micro-realizations. If the mental strongly supervenes on the physical, multiple realization of the mental by the physical may be viewed as a special case of the multiple realizability of the macro by the micro.

If the mental strongly supervenes on the physical and mental properties are causally possible, physical properties will necessitate mental properties. Now even if laws are relationships between properties, it would be question-begging to assume that physical properties nomologically necessitate mental properties. Still it is unclear why the necessitation relationship would not count as nomological. But in any case, the realization of any minimal physical base for a mental property will necessitate the realization of the mental property. Moreover, consider the disjunction of each minimal physical base for a given mental property. This disjunctive physical property will be necessarily correlated with the mental property: necessarily, something has the mental property if and only if it has the disjunctive physical property. Since the disjunctive physical property is a micro-property relative to the mental property such a correlation may be taken as a micro-reduction of the mental property. If there are infinitely many distinct physical bases for a mental property, then the mental property will be necessarily correlated with a disjunctive physical property with infinitely many disjuncts. And it could turn out that each disjunct itself consists of infinitely many conjuncts. But while such infinitary operations as infinite

---

[44] 'Supervenience as a Mind–Body Theory'.

conjunction and disjunction may be highly dubious where predicates are concerned, they are not obviously so where properties are concerned.[45]

Now if bridge laws are sentences, the claim that the mental strongly supervenes on the physical does not imply that there are psychophysical bridge laws.[46] The possibility of multiple realizability raises the issue of whether there is a physical predicate that expresses a nomologically necessary condition for a mental predicate. Mental properties may have infinitely many physical realizations. And the notion of an infinite disjunctive physical predicate is surely a dubious one. Moreover, even if a minimal physical base of a mental property is finitely specifiable, the specification may prove to be astronomically complex. Two individuals can be alike in every intrinsic physical respect and yet undergo different mental events. What mental events an individual undergoes can depend on relationships between the individual and the environment;[47] in fact, it has been persuasively argued that the social environment of an individual, for example, the language community to which an individual belongs, can partly determine what mental events the individual undergoes.[48] The minimal physical bases for mental properties will in some cases serve as bases for an individual's language community. This raises the issue of whether there can be a physical predicate expressing a nomologically sufficient condition for the property designated by a mental predicate.

But neither of these last two considerations is Davidson's reason for denying that psychophysical bridge laws are possible. In fact, Davidson makes remarks that indicate he would make no appeal to such considerations. He raises similar considerations employing examples involving action, which he takes to be a species of mental event. The considerations are perhaps clearer and more obvious where actions are concerned and Davidson's responses to them can be extended to cases involving propositional attitudes. He says:

> It is often said ... that there cannot be a physical predicate with the extension of a verb of action (for example) because there are so many different ways in which an action may be performed. Thus a man may greet a woman by bowing, by saying any of a number of things, by winking, by whistling; and each of these things may in turn be done in endless ways. The point is fatuous. The particulars that fall under a predicate always differ in endless ways, as long as there are at least two particulars [MM:252].

As Davidson notes there are endless ways that something can acquire a positive charge but 'acquiring a positive charge' is a physical predicate [MM:252]. Consider also the predicate 'is less than three feet from'; this predicate is a respectable physical predicate despite the fact that the property it designates has uncountably many minimal bases. Considerations of multiple realizability do not show that no relatively simple higher-order physical predicate can be found

---

[45] See 'Concepts of Supervenience', p. 172.

[46] Compare ibid., p. 172.

[47] See Putnam, 'The Meaning of "Meaning"', in *Mind, Language and Reality, Philosophical Papers*, vol. II (1975), pp. 215–71.

[48] See Tyler Burge, 'Individualism and the Mental', *Midwest Studies in Philosophy*, 4 (1979), pp. 73–123.

that designates a reductive base for a mental predicate. (By 'a higher order' physical predicate, I mean a physical predicate that designates a physical property that something has only in virtue of its having a more micro physical property.)

Concerning the second consideration, consider the following remark:

> Again, it is said that cultural relativism affects the classification of actions, but not of physical events. So the same gesture may indicate assent in Austria and dissent in Greece. Here we need only increase the frame of reference to a relevant difference: Austria is physically distinct from Greece, and so any event in Austria is distinct from any event in Greece ... Only if we accept an unduly restricted view of the predicates that can be formed using physical concepts are we apt to be attracted by any of these arguments [MM:252–3].

This passage makes it clear that Davidson would not appeal to the fact that two individuals can be alike in every intrinsic physical respect and yet differ in some mental respect in arguing for the impossibility of psychophysical bridge laws. Such laws may employ quite complex physical predicates expressing relational properties. Besides, there may be relatively simple higher-order physical predicates that will do.

Still considerations of the complexity of the physical predicate required for a psychophysical bridge law seem relevant. If, for example, social factors can partly determine what it is for an individual to undergo a mental event of a certain sort, it *may* prove to be the case that any physical predicate expressing a reductive base for the sort of event in question will be astronomically complex. If reduction is a kind of explanation, considerations concerning the discoverability and comprehensibility of the physical predicate required for a psychophysical nomological reduction seem relevant. This raises difficult questions concerning the epistemology of reduction that cannot be addressed here. However, for present purposes, it suffices to note that Davidson makes no appeal to our actual epistemic limitations in arguing that psychophysical bridge laws are impossible. Consider the following remark:

> Even if someone knew the entire physical history of the world, and every mental event were identical with a physical, it would not follow that he could predict or explain a single mental event (so described, of course) [ME:224].

The passage makes it clear that Davidson would not appeal to our epistemic limitations in arguing that psychophysical bridge laws are impossible.

Of course, Davidson holds that bridge laws are sentences. As we saw, if they are, the strong supervenience of the mental on the physical leaves open whether there can be psychophysical bridge laws. But given Davidson's reasons for denying such laws are possible, he should reject the claim that the mental strongly supervenes on the physical. Consider the following: if the mental strongly supervenes on the physical and, as seems quite plausible, minimal physical bases for mental properties are finitely specifiable, there will be universalized conditional psychophysical supervenience generalizations. Such generalizations will support counterfactuals and other subjunctive conditions, and should be confirmable by their positive instances. Such generalizations would not count as bridge law since they are not biconditionals. Moreover, they would not count as strict laws even if their antecedents are stated in the extended basic vocabulary of a closed* comprehensive theory. The reason is that the mental predicates that figure in their consequents will not count as part of the extended basic vocabulary of such a theory in virtue of their being linked via such generalizations with predicates in such a vocabulary. Moreover, it may even count as question-begging in the present context to maintain that such generalizations would count as laws. (Though they would count as laws, given Davidson's criterion for being a law.) So let us call them 'supervenience principles'. Whether or not supervenience principles are laws, it seems fair to say that they transmit conditions of application. The predicates in their antecedents will express concepts whose conditions of application are causally sufficient conditions of application for the concepts expressed by the predicates that figure in their consequents. The conditions of application they transmit may not be completely general conditions of application. The reason is that they may fail to be necessary conditions of application for the concept expressed by the predicate in the consequent.[49] But claim (32) is intended to imply that mental concepts cannot have sufficient nonrational conditions of application. So if the mental strongly supervenes on the physical and the minimal physical bases of mental properties are finitely specifiable, (32) is false. On the other hand, if (32) is true, the mental does not strongly supervene on the physical.

Of course, to deny psychophysical bridge laws are possible Davidson need only deny that mental concepts can have jointly necessary and sufficient nonrational conditions of application. But he should also deny that they can have sufficient nonrational conditions of application; for the view that they can encourages the idea that mental is nomologically reducible. Suppose again that the mental strongly supervenes on the physical and that the minimal physical bases of mental properties are finitely specifiable. Then there will be infinitely many universalized conditional psychophysical supervenience principles. Suchr supervenience principles are not causal laws. But together with causal laws, they can imply other causal laws. Thus, suppose it is a causal law that whenever a P-event occurs, a P*-event occurs. (I omit reference to times.) And suppose that it is a supervenience principle that whenever a P*-event occurs, an M-event occurs. Then it follows that it is a causal law that whenever a P-event occurs, an M-event occurs.[50] Of course, the physical antecedents of psychophysical supervenience principles may be astronomically complex. Moreover, supervenience principles with similar physical antecedents may have quite different mental consequents; and supervenience principles with similar mental consequents may have quite different physical antecedents. But for all of these reasons, it seems wildly implausible that such principles should express brute facts that admit of no explanation.[51] The existence of such a vast and

---

[49] See Colin McGinn's discussion of this in 'Philosophical Materialism', pp. 197–8.

[50] Colin McGinn provides a similar argument in 'Mental States, Natural Kinds and Psychophysical Laws', p. 215; and so does Stanton in 'Supervenience and Psychophysical Law in Anomalous Monism', pp. 72–4.

[51] Compare 'Supervenience and Psychological Law in Anomalous Monism', pp. 77–8.

heterogeneous group of supervenience principles that together with causal laws imply other causal laws would cry out for theoretical systematization. The idea that the mental strongly supervenes on the physical thus encourages the idea that higher-order physical predicates can be found that are nomologically coextensive with mental predicates; and that bridge laws linking higher-order physical predicates with mental predicates can be used to explain psychophysical supervenience principles. On the other hand, if the mental does not strongly supervene on the physical, there cannot be psychophysical bridge laws. And if it could be shown that mental concepts cannot have sufficient nonrational conditions of application, that would show that the mental does not strongly supervene on the physical.

For the reasons given above, Davidson should deny that the mental strongly supervenes on the physical. However, he can affirm the weak supervenience of the mental on the physical: in every causally possible world w, if two events (objects, states) in w are alike in every physical respect, they are alike in every mental respect. That the mental weakly supervenes on the physical does not imply that physical properties can *necessitate* mental properties. If the mental weakly supervenes on the physical, then each mental property will be correlated with a disjunctive physical property, but such correlations will have no modal force. Weak supervenience of the mental on the physical does not imply psychophysical supervenience principles with modal force.

Davidson has illustrated the supervenience relationship with two examples in addition to the mental-physical case, the supervenience of the moral on the nonmoral, and the supervenience of the truth of a sentence on its syntax [ME:214]. The supervenience of the moral on the nonmoral raises issues too much like those concerning the relationship between the mental and the physical to provide insight into the kind of dependency relationship Davidson intends to assert obtains between the mental and the physical. But his second example is quite revealing. As he notes, that truth supervenes on syntax does not imply that truth is reducible to syntax. The supervenience of truth on syntax is surely a case of weak supervenience: in any world, if two sentences in a (suitable) language are syntactically indiscernible, the one is true if and only if the other is true. But obviously the truth value of many sentences can vary from one world to another. Davidson's use of this example further suggests that he has weak supervenience in mind when he speaks of the supervenience of the mental on the physical.[52]

Suppose that two events are identical if and only if they occur at the same space-time region. Then if occurring at a certain space-time region counts as a physical respect, weak supervenience of the mental on the physical, where events are concerned, holds for this reason: any two events in a world that are alike in every physical respect are the same event, and so will have the same mental properties.

Davidson's thesis of token physicalism for events and the thesis that the mental weakly supervenes on the physical comprise, I believe, his physicalist position. Weak supervenience is not a strong enough dependency relation to

---

[52] Kim draws the same conclusion from this example in 'Concepts of Supervenience', p. 162.

warrant the claim that physical characteristics determine mental characteristics. It is consistent with such weak supervenience that physical twins in different worlds can differ mentally. One might believe that p and the other have no propositional attitudes at all. Weak supervenience of the mental on the physical is compatible with there being a world just like the actual world in every physical respect but in which no mental events occur.[53] Thus, this dependency relationship is hardly the sort to inspire the view that mental properties are nothing but physical properties. In this respect, then, Davidson's physicalism is indeed bland, as he himself emphasizes [see ME:214].

If the mental strongly supervenes on the physical, this dependency relationship calls for explanation. Supervenience principles with modal force, if there are such, cannot plausibly be taken to express brute facts that admit of no explanation. Even if one holds, as I do, that propositional attitude attribution is interpretative, there is a strong intuitive pull to the claim that the mental strongly supervenes on the physical. However, this intuitive pull may be the result of unwarranted assumptions. If (32) is true and psychophysical supervenience principles would transmit sufficient nonrational conditions of application to the concepts expressed by the mental predicates in their consequents, then the mental does not strongly supervene on the physical. And if the mental does not strongly supervene on the physical, it cannot be nomologically reduced to the physical. But a fully articulated argument for (32) remains to be given. The central controversy surrounding (32) is whether the mental strongly supervenes on the physical. Whether it does is, I believe, largely a conceptual issue to be decided in a relatively a priori way. But the issue is beyond the scope of this essay.

The foregoing discussion of the central theses of Davidson's position concerning the relationship between the mental and the physical leaves a host of unanswered questions. But my purpose has been served if the discussion is not too far off the mark in identifying the points of controversy surrounding these theses, and if it succeeds in showing why these theses are interesting and important.[54]

Appendix

1. At least some mental events causally interact with physical events.
2. Every mental event is a physical event.
3. There cannot be strict psychophysical laws.
4. There cannot be a physical predicate, no matter how complex, that has, as a matter of law, the same extension as a mental predicate.

---

[53] Compare ibid., p. 159.

[54] Thanks are due to Rutgers University for a FASP leave during which I completed an initial draft of this essay. In addition to the acknowledgements made in particular footnotes, I would like to thank the following people for helpful conversations concerning the issues discussed in this paper: David Benfield, Martin Bunzel, Donald Davidson, Doug Husack, Jaegwon Kim, Peter Klein, Ernest Lepore, Barry Loewer, John McDowell, Colin McGinn, Michael Root, and Robert Van Gulick. Special thanks are due to Terrence Horgan and Irving Thalberg. Finally, I owe an enormous debt to my friend and teacher Larry Stanton for years of conversation about Davidson's views about the relationship between the mental and the physical. I dedicate this paper to his memory.

5. Mental characteristics supervene on physical characteristics.
6. There cannot be strict laws on the basis of which mental events can be explained and predicted.
7. Events related as cause and effect are subsumed by strict laws.
8. Let m be any mental event that causally interacts with some physical event p.
9. When two events causally interact, there is some strict law that subsumes the events.
10. There cannot be strict psychophysical laws.
11. There cannot be strict psychological laws.
12. If a strict law subsumes m and p, that strict law is a strict physical law.
13. If a strict law subsumes two events, then the events are physical events.
14. M is a physical event.
15. Every mental event that causally interacts with a physical event is a physical event.
16. There cannot be strict psychophysical laws.
17. There cannot be strict psychological laws.
18. If a strict law subsumes a mental event, then that law would have to be either a strict psychophysical law or a strict psychological law.
19. No strict law can subsume a mental event.
20. If no strict law can subsume a mental event, there cannot be strict laws on the basis of which mental events can be explained and predicted.
21. There cannot be strict laws on the basis of which mental events can be explained and predicted.
22. Mental predicates cannot be part of the basic vocabulary of a closed* comprehensive theory.
23. Mental predicates cannot be linked via bridge laws with predicates in the extended basic vocabulary of a closed* comprehensive theory.
24. Mental predicates cannot be part of the extended basic vocabulary of a closed* comprehensive theory.
25. If a mental predicate cannot be part of the extended basic vocabulary of a closed* comprehensive theory, there cannot be strict psychological laws.
26. There cannot be strict psychological laws.
27. There cannot be a predicate, no matter how complex, in the extended basic vocabulary of a closed* comprehensive physical theory that has, as a matter of law, the same extension as a mental predicate.
28. Mental predicates cannot be part of the basic vocabulary of a closed* comprehensive physical theory.
29. Mental predicates cannot be part of the extended basic vocabulary of a closed* comprehensive physical theory.
30. If mental predicates cannot be part of the extended basic vocabulary of a closed* comprehensive physical theory, there cannot be strict psychophysical laws.
31. There cannot be strict psychophysical laws.
32. Mental concept (i.e., concepts expressed by predicates used to attribute propositional attitudes) cannot have a nonrational conditions of application.
33. Physical concepts have nonrational conditions of application.
34. If a predicate is linked via a bridge law to another, conditions of application

for the concept expressed by the reducing predicate are conditions of application for the concept expressed by the reduced predicate.

35. If there can be psychophysical bridge laws, a mental concept (i.e., a concept expressed by a predicate used to attribute a propositional attitude) can have a nonrational condition of application.

36. There cannot be psychophysical bridge laws.

22

Psychophysical Laws

Jaegwon Kim

I

The question whether there are, or can be, psychological laws is one of considerable interest. If it can be shown that there can be no such laws, a nomothetic science of psychology will have been shown to be impossible. The qualifier 'nomothetic' is redundant: science is supposed to be nomothetic. Discovery, or at least pursuit, of laws is thought to be constitutive of the very nature of science so that where there are no laws there can be no science, and where we have reason to believe there are none we have no business pretending to be doing science.

At least in one clear sense, therefore, the absence of psychological laws entails the impossibility of psychology as a science. This need not be taken to mean that there can be no scientists, called 'psychologists' or 'cognitive scientists', who study psychological topics and write useful tracts about them. It is to say that whatever else they may be doing that is useful and worthwhile, they will not be producing *psychological theories*, comprehensive and integrated systems of precise general laws, couched in a characteristic theoretical vocabulary, on the basis of which mental phenomena could be explained and predicted. If such theory-based explanatory and predictive activities are what we suppose psychologists *qua* psychologists to be engaged in, recognition of the impossibility of psychological laws would force us to reconsider the nature of psychology as an intellectual enterprise. In what follows we shall touch on this general issue, but our main topic here is the question of the possibility of laws about psychological phenomena.

It is no surprise, then, that Donald Davidson, who has vigorously argued against the possibility of psychological laws, titled one of his papers on this topic 'Psychology as philosophy'. The intended contrast of course is with 'psychology as a science', an unattainable goal if his striking arguments are sound. In advocating the lawlessness of the mental he joins a small but influential group of philosophers who have taken a dim view of the scientific prospects of psychology. Norman Malcom, for example, has produced a set of arguments,

---

[1] In *Philosophy of Psychology*, ed. S.C. Brown (Harper & Row, New York, 1974). Reprinted in D. Davidson, *Essays on Actions and Events* (Clarendon Press, Oxford, 1980).

inspired by broadly Wittgensteinian considerations, against scientific psychology.[2] There are also Quine's disdainful strictures on Brentano's 'science of intention'.[3] In this paper, however, we shall be concerned exclusively with Davidson's arguments contained in a series of three papers, 'Mental events',[4] 'Psychology as philosophy', and 'The material mind',[5] focusing especially on the first of these.

There are reasons for taking Davidson's arguments seriously and trying to get clear about them. The arguments are interesting and challenging, and have fascinated those interested in philosophy of mind; however, there is little agreement as to exactly how they are supposed to work.[6] Many philosophers have an opinion about how successful these arguments are (the published verdicts have been almost uniformly negative thus far), but most appear to feel uncertain about the accuracy of their interpretations, or think that the interpretations fail to make the arguments sufficiently interesting or plausible. Above all almost everyone seems to find Davidson's arguments extremely opaque; it is not difficult to discern the general drift of his thinking or pick out the basic considerations motivating the arguments; however, delineating their structure precisely enough for effective evaluation and criticism is another matter. In this paper I propose a way of looking at what I take to be Davidson's principal argument against nomological psychology. The suggested interpretation is based on a simple leading idea, and will help us piece together a coherent picture of Davidson's overall views of the mental and relate it to a wider context. My aim here is essentially to interpret and expound, not to evaluate or criticize. But obviously I am embarking on this project because I think the argument to be extracted from Davidson is plausible, at least at first blush, and philosophically important. As I hope will become clear, Davidson's argument has far-reaching implications regarding some basic issues about the nature of mind, such as mental autonomy, the possibility of free agency, and the status of commonsense explanations of human actions, and points to a conception of the mental that I find both intriguing and appealing.

Davidson's apparent strategy in 'Mental events' is, first, to establish the following lemma:

---

[2] *Memory and Mind* (Cornell University Press, Ithaca, N.Y., 1977). See also Bruce Goldberg, 'The correspondence hypothesis', *Philosophical Review*, 77 (1968), pp. 438–54.

[3] W.V. Quine, *Word and Object* (The Technology Press of M.I.T., Cambridge, Mass., 1960).

[4] In *Experience and Theory*, ed. Lawrence Foster and J.W. Swanson (University of Massachusetts Press, Amherst, 1970). Reprinted in Davidson, *Essays on Actions and Events*.

[5] In *Logic, Methodology, and the Philosophy of Science*, vol. 4, ed. P. Suppes (North-Holland, Amsterdam, 1973). Reprinted in Davidson, *Essays on Actions and Events*.

[6] The following, I believe, is a representative list of published discussions of Davidson's arguments (I am not including those that primarily focus on 'anomalous monism'): C.Z. Elgin, 'Indeterminacy, underdetermination, and the anomalous monism', *Synthese*, 45 (1980), pp. 233–55; William Lycan, 'Psychological laws', *Philosophical Topics*, 12 (1981), pp. 9–38; Ted Honderich, 'Psychophysical lawlike connections and their problem', *Inquiry*, 24 (1981), pp. 277–303; Brian Loar, *Mind and Meaning* (Cambridge University Press, Cambridge, 1981), pp. 20–5; Robert Van Gulick, 'Rationality and the anomalous nature of the mental', *Philosophy Research Archives*, 1983; William Larry Stanton, 'Supervenience and psychophysical law in anomalous monism', *Pacific Philosophical Quarterly*, 64 (1983), pp. 72–9.

Psychophysical Anomalism:[7] There are no psychophysical laws, that is, laws connecting mental and physical phenomena. In fact, there *cannot* be such laws,

and then use it to argue for the desired general thesis of psychological anomaly:

Anomalism of the Mental: 'There are no strict deterministic laws on the basis of which mental events can be predicted and explained.'[8]

The bulk of 'Mental events' and 'Psychology as philosophy' is devoted to establishing Psychophysical Anomalism, and much of the interest generated by these papers has been focused on Davidson's arguments for this thesis. In contrast the move from Psychophysical Anomalism to the full Anomalism of the Mental is made rather quickly and abruptly, within one short paragraph in 'Mental events'; I shall make some suggestions about how this transition can be understood, but for the moment, and for much of this paper, we shall follow Davidson in concentrating on arguments for Psychophysical Anomalism.

II

Davidson's conception of the psychological is based on *intentionality*. Expressions we use in attributing *propositional attitudes*, such as 'believe', 'fear', 'hope', and 'regret', are taken to constitute the basic psychological vocabulary; psychological laws then would be laws stated in terms of these intentional psychological expressions. Two questions may be raised about this way of understanding the psychological: first, whether it is broad enough to cover 'phenomenal states' or 'qualia', like pains and after-images, and second, whether it applies to the terms of trade of 'scientific psychology' or 'cognitive science' as it is practiced nowadays. These are large questions and cannot be taken up here; the second raises an issue about the relationship between 'commonsense psychology' and systematic psychology, a topic of much current interest,[9] and I shall make below some remarks relevant to it. In any event, the conception of the psychological as intentional does capture a large core of our commonsense psychological vocabulary, and a successful argument for the impossibility of psychological laws on this conception of the psychological would be of great interest and importance.[10] It would show, for example, that familiar explanations of actions in terms of an agent's beliefs and desires could not be nomological explanations backed by laws about beliefs, desires, and the like, as claimed by some writers (e.g., Carl Hempel[11]). And it would imply a

---

[7] The term 'psychophysical anomalism' is not Davidson's.

[8] 'Mental events', p. 208 (pages references to this article are to its reprinted version in Davidson, *Essays on Actions and Events*).

[9] For a sustained recent treatment see Stephen P. Stich, *From Folk Psychology to Cognitive Science* (The M.I.T. Press, Cambridge, Mass., 1983). See also Adam Morton, *Frames of Mind* (Oxford University Press, Oxford, 1980).

[10] Davidson explicitly limits his arguments to intentional mental states, e.g., 'Comments and replies' following 'Psychology as philosophy' in *Essays on Actions and Events*, p. 240.

[11] In the title essay of *Aspects of Scientific Explanation* (The Free Press, New York, 1965).

significant general conclusion: law-based systematic psychology, if such a thing is possible, would have to make a radical break with the framework of our vernacular psychological idioms and truisms, which forms the basis of our shared ability to describe and make sense of our own motives and actions as well as those of our fellow humans, and without which communal human life would be unthinkable.

The initial impression one is likely to get from Davidson's discussion of Psychophysical Anomalism is something like this: we are first offered a long list of features that characterize the mental but not the physical and, conversely, features of the physical not shared by the mental. For example, the mental is intentional and rational but the physical is neither; physical laws are 'homonomic' but what mental generalizations that there are are 'heteronomic'; combining mental and physical terms in a single statement is like mixing 'grue' with 'emerald'; Quinean indeterminacy besets the mental but nothing analogous obtains for the physical; and so on. We are then tempted to ask: does Davidson expect us to infer from these dissimilarities and divergences that there can be no laws connecting the two systems? But how can he? No simple list of differences between the two domains will have any tendency to show that no laws can connect them. When two arbitrary domains are considered, there is no a priori obvious reason to think there are lawful connections between them; nor need there be any obvious reason to think there are none. We would of course expect that any argument designed to show that there are, or that there are not, correlation laws, will make use of some properties of the two particular domains involved. So differences between the mental and the physical must count; but noting them can only be a starting point. The substance of the argument must show why, given just *these* differences, there can be no correlation laws.[12]

To fix the general picture in mind, consider a domain U of objects and two sets, F and G, of properties. For example, think of U as a set of medium-sized material bodies, F as a set of colors, and G as a set of shapes. We may suppose that each object in U has exactly one color in F and one shape in G. Here we would not expect to find regular correlations between colors and shapes; an object of a given color could be of any shape, and vice versa. Thus, we would not expect true generalizations of the form:

(A)   Every object in U with color C has shape S.

Or of the form:

(B)   Every object in U with shape S has color C.

---

[12] After reviewing the differences noted by Davidson between the mental and the physical, Honderich writes: 'Still, we are not given a reason for thinking that [Psychophysical Anomalism] follows from the description of the two domains. As others have asked, what reason is there for thinking that an item which falls in one domain, and whose description then depends on X, cannot be in a lawlike connection with an item in the other domain, whose description then depends on Y? There is no general truth to the effect that there cannot be lawlike connection between items whose descriptions have different necessary connections. ... Davidson remarks that his argument is no proof. It must also be said, I think, that his argument is at least crucially incomplete' ('Psychophysical lawlike connections and their problem'), pp. 292–3. This reaction is typical and understandable. What I intend to do is to help complete Davidson's argument.

But this is not to say that, contrary to our justified expectations, we may not in fact find, say:

(C)   Every red object in U is round.

If this should happen, though, we would surely think it was pure luck, the result of a fortuitous choice of U. Given what we know about colors and shapes, we would not take the truth of (C) as indicating a *lawlike* connection between being red and being round; the truth of (C) is a coincidence, not a matter of law. We are especially unlikely to take it as lawlike if it is the single isolated correlation between colors and shapes; if it were a law we would expect it to be part of a broader system of color-shape correlations.

Turning to the matter on hand, consider the domain to be the set of persons, and F and G to be, respectively, the set of psychological properties and the set of physical properties. Davidson's point is that even if we should find a true generalization of the form:

(D)   All persons with mental property M have physical property P,

we will not, and should not, consider this a *law*. What then is a law? Davidson follows the familiar philosophical usage: a law is distinguished from a 'mere generalization' by these two marks: (1) it can support counterfactuals and subjunctives, and (2) it is confirmable by observation of instances. Our (C) above, about all red things being round, meets neither of these criteria; it fails to back a counterfactual such as 'If bananas were red, they would be round', and the only way it could be confirmed is by an exhaustive examination of all objects in the domain, there being no instance-to-instance accretion of positive confirmation.

It will be important to keep in mind the crucial role that considerations of lawlikeness must play in Davidson's central argument; for the argument is designed to show, not that there can be no psychophysical generalizations of the form (D), but that there can be no psychophysical laws. Davidson is quite explicit on this point.[13] And for good reason; brief reflection will show why this strategy is the only possible one: whether any generalization of the form (D) is true is a contingent empirical matter that can be known only through tedious observation, if at all. No armchair philosophical argument can insure that some statements of this form, by sheer luck or coincidence, will not turn out to be true; it surely cannot do this any more than it can show that a generalization like (C), that all red things are round, is true, or that it is false. Moreover, whether something like (C) or (D) is true is of no philosophical interest; what is of interest is whether, if true, it would be a law. Davidson thinks we can show from the very idea of what it is to be psychological that no generalization of the form (D), whether true or false, can be lawlike. Its being lawlike is independent of its de facto truth or falsity, and hence can be established or refuted by a priori arguments. At least, that is Davidson's view.

---

13 'Mental events', p. 216.

These considerations suggest a clue to the structure of Davidson's argument: *the argument works, to the extent that it does, only with respect to psychophysical laws, and it should fail, more or less obviously, if 'true psychophysical generalization' is substituted for 'psychophysical law' throughout the argument.* What needs to be done, therefore, is to identify the features of the mental and those of the physical that, while tolerating true psychophysical generalizations, are inimical to these generalizations being lawlike. And if this is to be done, the argument must consciously exploit the special characteristics of laws that set them apart from de facto generalizations.

III

The leading idea of Davidson's argument as I see it can be introduced through an analogy. Most of us remember being told by politicians or political analysts that a democratic nation cannot, on pain of damaging its own integrity as a democracy, enter into a genuine treaty relationship with a totalitarian state. We can also imagine something like this said of two religions: the systems are so alien to each other that no regularized and stable relationship between them is possible. The hidden argument here may be something like this: two systems of government or religion are so fundamentally opposed to each other in their basic commitments that a stable and principled relationship cannot be maintained between them on pain of compromising the integrity of one or both of the systems involved. It might be that a democratic state, if it is to honor its treaty obligations to a totalitarian state, must of necessity violate its own commitment to democratic principles. A weaker relationship could be tolerated, but treaty relations are too strict and binding, imposing on the participants obligations that weaker relations do not impose.

Whatever merits the foregoing might have, the structure of Davidson's argument, I believe, is similar: *the mental realm is characterized by certain essential features which would be seriously compromised if there were connections as strong as laws, with their modal and subjunctive force, linking it with the physical realm, which has its own distinctive essential features incompatible with those of the mental.* These features of the mental are essential in that they are *constitutive* or *definitive* of the system of mental concepts; the mental realm cannot sustain their loss and still retain its identity as a mental system. Further, these features are *global* in the sense that they characterize the mental as a system, not primarily individual mental phenomena or concepts in isolation; and similarly for the essential features of the physical. The argument could be run the other way also: given its own commitment to certain constitutive principles not shared by the mental, the physical realm can no more readily tolerate nomological relationships with the mental, without endangering its identity as a physical system. Mere psychophysical generalizations, being weaker than laws, do no harm to either psychology or physics, but laws with their modal force would bring them too close together, leading to a clash of their incompatible natures.

This way of looking at Davidson's argument explains exactly why the argument is supposed to work for psychophysical laws but not for true psychophysical generalizations. True generalizations, unless they are lawlike, are merely accidental and do not signify any deep or intimate relationship between the two realms (recall the case of colors and shapes). But laws are different: nomic connections are strong enough to *transmit*, or *transfer*, the constitutive properties of the physical to the mental, and vice versa, thereby damaging the integrity of the recipient system. Mere generalizations, even if true, do not have this power of transmitting features of one system to the other. We shall try to fill out this preliminary sketch of the argument by giving concrete meaning to this idea of laws 'transmitting' certain features across systems, but a hint of how this can be understood is contained in the observation that laws, in virtue of their modal force, can underwrite certain inferences that mere de facto generalizations cannot sanction.

The skeletal structure of what I take to be Davidson's principal argument can, therefore, be exhibited as follows:

> The mental system has a certain essential characteristic X and the physical system a certain essential characteristic Y, where X and Y are mutually incompatible. Laws linking the two systems, if they exist, would 'transmit' these characteristics from one system to the other, leading to incoherence. Therefore, there can be no laws connecting the mental with the physical so long as the two systems are to retain their distinctive identities.

It is worth pointing out that the argument as sketched has a general interest going beyond its application to the psychophysical case; if appropriate properties X and Y are identified, the argument would apply to any two domains and help establish the conclusion that there could not be lawlike connections between them. In any event, the proposed line of interpretation explains, and is supported by, the following remarks by Davidson: 'If the case of supposed laws linking the mental and the physical is different, it can only be because to allow the possibility of laws would amount to changing the subject. By changing the subject I mean here: deciding not to accept the criterion of the mental in terms of the vocabulary of the propositional attitudes.'[14] Davidson is saying that if there were psychophysical laws we would lose the mental ('change the subject') as characterized in terms of intentionality; such laws would compromise the essential intentionality of the mental.

Two things need to be done to flesh out the skeletal argument: (1) we need to identify one or more essential characteristics of the mental, and do the same for the physical, to play the role of X and Y, that is, to be transmitted, or be compromised, by the supposed laws between the mental with the physical, and (2) we must explain in what sense laws can 'transmit' these characteristics from one system to the other. Let us turn to the first task.

Davidson does not tell us in a general way what he means by 'intentional'; instead he simply tells us that the paradigmatic mental states he has in mind are *propositional attitudes*, that is, psychological states with *propositional content* typically expressed by that-clauses and gerunds (e.g., fearing that the pipes are frozen, being embarrassed about missing his appointment for the second time).

---

[14] Ibid., p. 216.

What then are the crucial features of such states that can be used to fill out Davidson's argument? Consider the following remarks by Davidson:

> Any effort at increasing the accuracy and power of a theory of behavior forces us to bring more and more of the whole system of the agent's beliefs and motives directly into account. But in inferring this system from the evidence, we necessarily impose conditions of coherence, rationality, and consistency. These conditions have no echo in physical theory, which is why we can look for no more than rough correlations between psychological and physical phenomena.[15]

> Just as we cannot intelligibly assign a length to any object unless a comprehensive theory holds of objects of that sort, we cannot intelligibly attribute any propositional attitude to an agent except within the framework of a viable theory of his beliefs, desires, intentions, and decisions.
>   There is no assigning beliefs to a person one by one on the basis of his verbal behavior, his choices, or other local signs no matter how plain and evident, for we make sense of particular beliefs only as they cohere with other beliefs, with preferences, with intentions, hopes, fears, expectations, and the rest. It is not merely, as with the measurement of length, that each case tests a theory and depends upon it, but that the content of a propositional attitude derives from its place in the pattern.[16]

These remarks vividly bring out Davidson's 'holism' of the mental: the mental is holistic in that the attribution of any single mental state to a person is strongly constrained by the requirement that the total system attributed to him of beliefs, desires, fears, hopes, and all the rest be *maximally coherent and rational*. This coherence or rationality maximization condition, on Davidson's view, is an essential feature of the intentional; without it we cannot make sense of ascription of contentful mental states. The holistic character of the mental, as embodied in the principle of rationality maximization, is constitutive of our conception of the mental as intentional; compromising this characteristic of the mental would be tantamount to 'changing the subject' – that is, as Davidson explains, abandoning the intentional conception of the mental. How does one maximize the coherence and rationality of a system of intentional states? This is an age-old issue of great importance to epistemology, moral philosophy, and philosophy of science, and we need not address it in a general way. What we need is a sense of what it is about. To begin, avoiding logical inconsistency and maximizing inductive rationality in one's belief system is obviously important; the internal coherence of the agent's system of preferences e.g., that it satisfy the transitivity condition, is also a factor; we should also check whether the agent's decisions conform to his probabilities and preferences, and whether his feelings and emotions make sense in light of his wants and beliefs; and so on. Davidson's view is, to put it briefly and somewhat simplistically, that either the set of intentional states we attribute to a person satisfies certain minimal standards of rationality and coherence, or else there is no ground for attributing such a system to an agent; in fact, to consider an organism an *agent* is an

---

[15] 'Psychology as philosophy', in *Essays on Actions and Events*, p. 231.
[16] 'Mental events', p. 221.

expression of our willingness to consider it a rational psychological system, that is, to describe its behavior in terms appropriate for assessment in accordance with canons of rationality, and make sense of its decisions and actions as issuing in appropriate ways from its preferences and cognitions. We might add that the point of attributing intentional states to persons is to be able to formulate 'rationalizing explanations' of what they do, and that unless the system of intentional states so attributed is, in certain minimal ways, rational and coherent, no such explanations would be forthcoming. Davidson says that Quine's doctrine of translational indeterminacy is just another facet of this rationalistic holism of the mental; I shall make a few remarks later about how these two theses are related, but I believe we can construct an argument for Psychophysical Anomalism without an explicit reference to, or reliance on, the indeterminacy thesis.[17]

In point of being holistic, however, the mental is not unique; on Davidson's view, the physical, too, is holistic. Interdependence or seamlessness is common to both.[18] The holism of the physical lies in the fact that the physical, too, is characterized by certain 'synthetic a priori laws' which are *constitutive of* our conception of the physical, and which make possible the formulation of precise physical laws. Among them are principles that make physical measurement possible, such as the transitivity of 'longer than' or 'earlier than'.[19] Basic methodological rules governing theory construction and evidence, fundamental principles about space, time, and causality, and so on, may also qualify. Holism as such, therefore, is a side issue; what is crucial is the divergent constitutive principles from which the distinctive holism of each domain arises. As Davidson puts it, 'there are no strict psychophysical laws because of the disparate commitments of the mental and the physical schemes',[20] and 'there cannot be tight connections between the realms if each is to retain its allegiance to its proper source of evidence'.[21]

These two brief remarks by Davidson are especially revealing: the mental and physical are not able to 'keep allegiance' to their respective constitutive principles and at the same time enter into the kind of 'tight connection' signified by the presence of laws linking them. For the two sets of constitutive principles represent the 'disparate commitments' of the two systems, commitments they cannot disown if they are to preserve their identities. What we now need to understand is exactly how the presence of nomological links is inconsistent with each system's retaining its allegiance to its constitutive principles.

If rationality, therefore, is the essential characteristic of the mental in Davidson's argument, what is the essential feature of the physical that will clash with rationality? I believe we can simply take this as the absence of rationality as a constitutive element of the physical. As Davidson says in a passage already

---

17 As Lycan emphasizes in 'Psychological laws', p. 23.
18 'Mental events', p. 222.
19 Ibid., pp. 220–1.
20 Ibid., p. 222.
21 Ibid., p. 222.

quoted, conditions of coherence, rationality, and consistency 'have no echo in physical theory'.

IV

My suggestion is that we try to understand this crucial step in Davidson's argument in terms of the greater inferential strength of laws, compared with de facto generalizations, on account of their modal force. I shall now formulate two specific arguments based on this idea.

Suppose that, on available evidence, the attribution to a person of either of the two mental states, m_1 or m_2, is warranted, and that the principle of rationality maximization enjoins the choice of m_1 over m_2 (we may suppose that the joint attribution of both states contravenes this principle). Suppose further that there are neural states, n_1 and n_2, which are *nomologically coextensive* with m_1 and m_2 respectively; that is, we have laws affirming that as a matter of law, n_1 occurs to an organism at a time just in case m_1 occurs to it at that time; similarly for n_2 and m_2. Now the neural states, n_1 and n_2, being theoretical states of physical theory, have *conditions of attribution*, that is, conditions under which their attribution to an organism is warranted. Such conditions are probably very complex and in some sense holistic; they are probably difficult to articulate, and we are not assuming that they must be observationally accessible. What matters is only that the ascertaining of whether they hold in a given situation is regulated by the constitutive rules and principles of physical theory, not by those of the mental. To say that C_1 is an attribution condition for n_1 must be more than to affirm a mere de facto coincidence of C_1 with n_1 (or with the warranted attribution of n_1); it is to commit onself to a statement with modal force, which for simplicity we may express as follows:

(1)   Necessarily, if C_1 obtains, n_1 occurs.

We also have the psychophysical law:

(2)   Necessarily, m_1 occurs if and only if n_1 occurs,

whence:

(3)   Necessarily, if C_1 obtains, m_1 occurs.

In the same way we have:

(4)   Necessarily, if C_2 obtains, m_2 occurs,

where C_2 is an attribution condition of neural state n_2.

Consider the force of (3) and (4): they affirm that when a certain set of physical conditions holds, a specific mental state *necessarily* occurs, that we *must* attribute to an organism this mental state if those conditions are observed to obtain for it. And this means that the rationality maximization principle as an essential constraint on the attribution of mental states is in danger of being preempted, or seriously compromised, for the determination of whether these physical attribution conditions obtain is not subject to the constraint of this principle. (3) and (4) would permit us to attribute intentional mental states independently of the rationality maximization rule; at least, they would force this rule to share its jurisdiction over mental attributions. In this way, these mental states threaten to escape the jurisdiction of the ruling constitutive principle of the mental, thereby losing their 'allegiance to [their] proper source of evidence'. By becoming so intimately associated with C_1 and C_2, which are under the jurisdiction of physical theory and its constitutive principles, they have in effect ceased to be mental states. For according to Davidson, being subject to the rule of rationality maximization is of the essence of intentional states; without this constraint the ascription of contentful intentional states would be unintelligible.

If something like this captures Davidson's argument, then we should not be able to run it without the assumption that the supposed psychophysical correlations are lawlike; this is the assumption (2) above. It is obvious that if the modality is removed from (2) we can no longer move from (1) to (3), although we could get the nonmodal analogue of (3) stating a de facto coincidence, 'if C_1 obtains, m_1 occurs'. But this is harmless; it exerts no pressure on the rationality maximization principle as a constraint on the attribution of m_1. A de facto conditional like this cannot be taken as stating an attribution condition of m_1 no matter how loosely we construe the notion of attribution condition.

Two points in this argument require further comments. The first concerns the assumption that mental states m_1 and m_2 have *coextensive* physical correlates. This assumption simplifies the argument and enables us to derive a salient and striking conclusion; but it can be weakened. Obvious further cases to consider would be, first, one where neural state n is only sufficient for mental state m and, second, one where n is only necessary for m. However, these do not exhaust all the possibilities, and it will be useful to consider this in a fully general setting. So let L(m, n) be an arbitrary law linking m and n. If this law is properly to be thought of as 'linking' m and n, then the logical form of L (m, n) must generate strong mutual constraints between the attribution of m and that of n. To assume m and n to be coextensive is to set these constraints at a maximum level; if n is only sufficient, or only necessary, for m, the constraint is weaker but still quite strong. Now, the generalized argument for arbitrary L (m, n) would be something like this: If L(m, n) is to qualify as psychophysical law, the attribution of m to an organism must strongly constrain, and be strongly constrained by, the attribution of n to that organism, and to that extent the constitutive principles of one domain extend its regulative powers to the other domain, thereby infringing upon the latter's integrity and autonomy.

The second point concerns the modalities involved in the displayed statements (1)–(4); more specifically, a question can be raised whether the 'nomological modality' of (2) is the same as the modality involved in the statement of 'attribution condition' (1). This raises a host of complex issues which are best avoided here; a short and reasonable way to handle the point would be this: assume that the modality involved in (1) is that of unrestricted logical necessity, and that logical necessity entails nomological necessity. This would imply that the modality of (3) and (4) is at least as strong as the nomological modality of (2); the crucial step would be to argue that this is sufficient to make (3) and (4) a threat to the mentalistic identity of m_1 and m_2. If the likes of (3) and (4) were to hold, that would generate a strong pressure to integrate these affected mental states into physical theory.

We now turn to another way of filling out our skeletal argument. Let p be the statement 'Ypsilanti is within 10 miles of Ann Arbor' and q the statement 'Ypsilanti is within 20 miles of Ann Arbor'. The rule of rationality maximization presumably requires that whenever we attribute to a person the belief that p we must also attribute to him the belief that q. This much deductive closure seems required of any system of beliefs. Consider the following counterfactual:

(5) If S were to believe p, S would also believe q.

This dependency is *grounded in* the principle of rationality maximization; in fact, this principle may sanction a more specific principle enjoining us to attribute to a person all obvious logical consequences of beliefs already attributed to him. That (5) obtains is an important fact about the concept of belief, and is explainable in terms of the essential features of belief as an intentional state, that is, in terms of considerations of rationality and coherence of intentional systems. Suppose now that believing p and believing q have nomological coextensions, B_1 and B_2 respectively, in physical theory. We construe this to mean, or imply, the following:

(6) Necessarily, a person believes p if and only if he is in state B_1.
(7) Necessarily, a person believes q if and only if he is in state B_2.

Inferences involving counterfactuals are tricky; however we may assume that (5), (6), and (7) together yield:

(8) If S were in state B_1, he would also be in state B_2.

Now, (8) is a *purely physical* counterfactual stating a dependency relation between two physical states; it might state a lawful dependency relation between two neurophysiological states involving discharges of large groups of neurons, or something of the sort. The fact that (6) and (7), the supposed psychophysical laws, would enable us to 'read off' a physical law from a psychological law is not the heart of the argument. We get closer to it when we ask *what could possibly ground or explain this physical dependency*.

What then would explain or ground (8)? There are three possibilities to consider: (a) the dependency expressed by (8) is physically fundamental – it is a basic law of physical theory requiring no explanation. This is highly implausible: we would expect fundamental physical laws to connect physical states a good deal simpler than neural correlates of beliefs. (b) (8) is explainable in terms of more fundamental physical laws. In this case, the same physical laws would yield, via (8), (6), and (7), a physical explanation of why the psychological dependency relation (5) holds, and this means that the role of the rationality maximization principle as a ground for (5) has been preempted, and that the concept of belief has effectively been removed from the jurisdiction of this principle. But the concept of belief that is outside the domain of rationality is no longer an intentional concept – not a concept of belief at all. (c) the dependency relation (8), though not regarded as a basic physical law, has no physical explanation. But then we can explain it psychologically in terms of (5) via (6) and (7), as it was originally derived. But this is absurd: to ground a purely physical dependency in considerations of rationality of belief would have to be taken as an intolerable intrusion on the closedness and comprehensiveness of physical theory. Thus, none of the possibilities makes sense, and we must reject the supposed laws such as (6) and (7).

This concludes my attempt to flesh out Davidson's idea that psychophysical laws would bring too close together two systems with their 'disparate commitments'. There are no doubt other, perhaps more plausible, ways of doing so; however, what has been done here, I think, goes some way toward making Davidson's arguments more concrete and more palpable, and in my view not altogether implausible.

One might ask why we could not show, by the same argument, that there could not be laws connecting, say, biological and physical phenomena. The answer is that biology and physics are both physical theories sharing the same fundamental constitutive principles; they are governed not by 'disparate commitments' but one uniform set. I think this would be Davidson's response.[22] If, on the other hand, you believe in the uniqueness of 'vital phenomena' or 'entelechies', you could make up a Davidsonian argument to show the nomological irreducibility of the vital to the physical; your only problem would be to defend the relevant vitalistic premises.

There are some prominent considerations advanced by Davidson, especially in 'Mental events', that have not been made use of in my interpretation. The distinction between 'homonomic' and 'heteronomic' laws is one example; another is his likening of psychophysical laws to the mixing of 'grue' and 'emerald'; I have already mentioned Davidson's approving references to translational indeterminacy. My view is that these do not, at least need not, play a crucial role in the argument. In 'Mental events', the distinction between the two types of laws quickly leads into the discussion of synthetic a priori constitutive principles of physical theory, and this latter idea of course plays a role in my interpretation. I take the reference to 'grue'-like predicates as just a way of illustrating the incongruity that exists, in Davidson's eye, between mental and physical terms, an incongruity that, as we saw, is given a more precise meaning in terms of allegiance to disparate sets of constitutive principles.

V

I shall now briefly consider how Psychophysical Anomalism relates to the Anomalism of the Mental. In 'Mental events', one gets a strong impression that

---

[22] Actually what Davidson says about this is noncommittal: 'I do not want to say that analogous remarks may not hold for some other sciences, for example biology. But I do not know how to show that the concepts of biology are nomologically irreducible to the concepts of physics. What sets apart certain psychological concepts – their intentionality – does not apply to the concepts of biology' (in 'Comments and replies' following 'Psychology as philosophy', in *Essays on Actions and Events*, p. 241).

Davidson intends to infer the latter from the former. The following is the crucial paragraph:

> It is not plausible that mental concepts alone can provide [a comprehensive framework for the description and law-based prediction and explanation of events], simply because the mental does not ... constitute a closed system. Too much happens to affect the mental that is not itself a systematic part of the mental. But if we combine this observation with the conclusion that no psychophysical statement is, or can be built into, a strict law we have the principle of the Anomalism of the Mental: there are no strict laws on the basis of which we can predict and explain mental phenomena.[23]

Davidson seems to be saying that we can infer the Anomalism of the Mental from the two premises: Psychophysical Anomalism and the statement that the mental, as distinguished from the physical, does not constitute a closed system. But how is the inference supposed to work?

I have no bright idea on interpreting this passage to yield a perspicuous and plausible argument. Instead I suggest another way of viewing the situation which, though possibly not Davidson's, is not altogether implausible and which seems to fit the large dialectic plan of 'Mental events'. First, the Anomalism of the Mental can be thought of as being equivalent to the conjunction of Psychophysical Anomalism and the following thesis:

> *Psychological Anomalism*:[24] There are no purely psychological laws, that is, laws connecting psychological events with other psychological events, which can be used to explain and predict these events.

If mental phenomena can be nomologically explained and predicted, then the required laws would have to be either psychophysical or purely psychological. Psychophysical Anomalism says laws of the first kind are not there; Psychological Anomalism says laws of the second kind are not there either. So there are no laws to explain and predict mental phenomena, and this is precisely the Anomalism of the Mental.

Thus, I see the Anomalism of the Mental simply as a conjunction of the two doctrines, Psychological Anomalism and Psychophysical Anomalism. This raises the question where Psychological Anomalism comes from. No readily identifiable argument for it can be found in 'Mental events', although there is no question that Davidson is committed to it. Furthermore, there are passages in this paper that strongly suggest that the mental as an autonomous realm ought to have, or at least can have, its own laws. In particular, I have in mind Davidson's claim that the synthetic a priori constitutive principles of the physical domain are what makes 'homonomic' physical laws possible, and his explicit acknowledgement that the mental domain, too, has its own characteris-

---

[23] 'Mental events', p. 224.

[24] The term 'psychological anomalism' is not Davidson's. Davidson is clearly committed to this thesis; for example, his argument for anomalous monism cannot go through unless it is assumed that there are no purely psychological laws; it isn't enough merely to assume there are no psychophysical laws.

tic a priori constitutive principles. He says, too, that the attribution of propositional attitudes presupposes as a necessary condition a 'viable *theory* ... of beliefs, desires, intention, and decisions'.[25] What is a theory made up of, if not laws? But how can this be reconciled with Psychological Anomalism, or indeed with the Anomalism of the Mental?

I suggest the following line of reconciliation: on Davidson's account the mental can, and does, have its own 'laws'; for example, 'laws' of rational decision making. The crucial point, though, is that these are *normative* rather than *predictive* laws. When Psychophysical Anomalism and Psychological Anomalism deny the existence of laws about the mental, the meaning of 'law' involved is one that is appropriate to physical theory, namely the concept of a law that permits the formulation of nomological predictions and explanations on the basis of precisely characterized and empirically identifiable initial and boundary conditions. It may be recalled that the Anomalism of the Mental only denies the existence of (in Davidson's own words) 'strict laws on the basis of which behavior can be explained and predicted'. Thus, the existence of nonpredictive normative laws or principles is consistent with the Anomalism of the Mental and Psychological Anomalism. But what do these normative laws look like? I already mentioned principles of decision making; rules of deductive and inductive inference, appropriately phrased, should also be among the prominent examples; there may be principles that govern the coherence of emotions, both among themselves and in relation to other propositional attitudes such as beliefs and desires. These are the norms and rules that guide actions and decisions, and form the basis of rational evaluations of our motives, cognitions, and emotions. And I think there is a sense in which these principles serve as an essential basis for a certain special way in which actions and decisions can be understood and made intelligible.[26] The view of psychology that emerges from Davidson is one of a broad interpretative endeavor directed at human action, to understand its 'meaning' rather than search for law-based causal explanations that are readily convertible into predictions; psychology is portrayed as a hermeneutic inquiry rather than a predictive science.

In order to appreciate Davidson's overall aims and strategies in 'Mental events', it is useful to attend to his initial stage-setting. His announced aim, which he likens to Kant's attempt to reconcile human freedom with natural necessity, is to show how psychological anomaly is compatible with determinism. How is it possible for the mental to escape the nomological net of physical theory? How can this happen when mental phenomena apparently enter into intimate causal transactions with physical phenomena? In order to formulate this problem, something like Psychological Anomalism has to be *presupposed*; psychological anomaly is part of Davidson's starting point in 'Mental events' rather than a conclusion to be proved. In the second paragraph of 'Mental events' he says, 'I start from the assumption that both the causal dependence, and the anomalousness, of mental events are undeniable facts'. Thus, three

---

[25] 'Mental events', p. 221 (emphasis added).

[26] This is developed in somewhat greater detail in my 'Self-understanding and rationalizing explanations', *Philosophia Naturalis*, 21 (1984): 309–20.

elements are needed to generate the initial 'Kantian' tension: psychological anomaly, the causal dependence of the mental upon the physical, and physical determinism. The tension consists in our need to answer this question: how can the mental be anomalous (i.e., escape physical determinism) when it is causally dependent on the physical domain governed by strict deterministic laws? How can we protect the anomalousness, and the autonomy, of mind?

As I see it, Davidson's resolution consists in pointing out, first, that the tension arises because psychophysical causal dependence is erroneously thought to require the existence of psychophysical laws, and then showing that there in fact can be no such laws to threaten mental anomaly. His argument for the first point leads to his celebrated defense of 'anomalous monism', a version of the so-called 'token-identity' theory; but from the viewpoint of the overall aims of 'Mental events', anomalous monism is a side issue. In any event, it is assumed in all this that psychophysical laws would make the mental reducible to the physical, effectively destroying its autonomous character. Thus, Psychophysical Anomalism is what safeguards Psychological Anomalism, by insulating the mental from the full impact of physical determinism. This is why arguments for Psychophysical Anomalism occupy center stage in 'Mental events', and why, on the other hand, there are no arguments for Psychological Anomalism. The former is the substance of what has to be established to answer the principal question of 'Mental events'; the latter only a presupposition of that question.

Has Davidson ever offered an independent argument for Psychological Anomalism? I believe he has; his discussion of the problem of empirically confirming Ramsey-style decision theory in 'Psychology as philosophy' can usefully be viewed as just such an argument. But a detailed discussion of this argument is outside the scope of this paper.

VI

In this concluding section I want to try to relate Davidson's views of the mental to a broader context. His initial Kantian tension can be redescribed (by replacing psychophysical causal dependence with psychophysical laws) to yield an inconsistent triad: (1) psychological anomaly, (2) physical determinism, and (3) lawlike linkages between the psychological and the physical. Faced with this triad, Davidson rejects (3), and that is his Psychophysical Anomalism. And the ultimate goal of this move is to insure the autonomy of the mental and the possibility of free agency.[27] It is instructive, I think, to compare Davidson's move with Quine's: Quine, too, would accept (2) and reject (3), where (3) of course is understood to concern the psychological conceived as intentional. In fact, his doctrine of translational indeterminacy can be taken as the denial of the claim that the intentional psychological *supervenes* on the physical; on Quine's view, the fixing of the totality of physical fact does not suffice to fix the intentional. If there were a pervasive network of laws linking the intentional

---

[27] Davidson writes, at the very end of 'Mental events' (p. 225): 'The anomalism of the mental is thus a necessary condition for viewing action as autonomous.' It is no accident that he begins and ends his paper with quotations from Kant.

with the physical, then the intentional would supervene on the physical.[28] Davidson and Quine, however, part company in their reaction to this failure of supervenience: while Davidson takes it as insuring the autonomy of the mental, Quine takes it as showing the illegitimacy of the mental, as witness his well-known disparaging remarks about Brentano: 'One may accept the Brentano thesis [of the irreducibility of intentional terms] either as showing the indispensability of intentional idioms and the importance of the autonomous science of intention, or as showing the baselessness of intentional idioms and the emptiness of a science of intention. My attitude, unlike Brentano's, is the second.'[29] For Quine, reducibility to an extensional physical basis is an essential mark of legitimacy. Davidson sees it as a threat to autonomy.

So there are two choices: the eliminativist physicalism of Quine and the dualism of Davidson. It undoubtedly will strike many readers as at best paradoxical to characterize Davidson as a dualist. I believe, however, that in spite of his anomalous monism, dualism in the form of a commitment to the mental as an autonomous domain is a nonnegotiable premise of Davidson's overall position in 'Mental events'.

From this general perspective, we can also make sense of Davidson's somewhat cryptic remarks in 'Mental events' linking Quine's thesis of translational indeterminacy with his Psychophysical Anomalism.[30] The essential function served by both doctrines is to pry apart the mental and the physical, and show the former to be irreducible, in a crucial way, to the latter. Where Davidson differs from Quine is in his attitude to this irreducibility. His attitude is strongly reminiscent of the dualism of Kant; it clearly is not Cartesian dualism – his anomalous monism is in effect the rejection of the interactionist dualism of the Cartesian variety.

One question remains: is there any reason for favoring this Kantian stance of mental autonomy over Quinean eliminativism? Alchemy and astrology are also irreducible to physical theory; we do not expect to find laws linking alchemical or astrological concepts with those of physics. But that hardly is any reason to champion an autonomous realm of alchemy or astrology! Here a Quinean response seems absolutely appropriate: so much the worse for alchemy and astrology! The irreducibility, nomological or conceptual, of these alleged

---

28 See Quine's reply to Noam Chomsky in *Words and Objections*, ed. D. Davidson and J. Hintikka (Reidel, Dordrecht, 1969), esp. p. 303, where he says: 'Consider, from this realistic point of view, the totality of truths of nature, known and unknown, observable and unobservable, past and future. The point about indeterminacy of translation is that it withstands even all this truth, the whole truth about nature.' I am aware that in 'Mental events', p. 214, Davidson explicitly endorses supervenience of the mental upon the physical, in spite of the nonexistence of psychophysical laws. To make Davidson consistent, however, this supervenience must be taken in a fairly weak sense falling well short of full dependence or determination. I am here using the term 'supervenience' in a stronger sense in which what supervenes is wholly fixed when the supervenience base is fixed. The distinction between 'weak' and 'strong' supervenience and related matters are developed in detail in my 'Concepts of supervenience' in *Philosophy and Phenomenological Research*, ch, 45 (1984), pp. 153–76; a simpler and somewhat sketchier account is included in my 'Psychophysical supervenience as a mind–body theory', *Cognition and Brain Theory*, 5 (1982), and 'Supervenience and supervenient causation', *Southern Journal of Philosophy*, 12, supplement (1984), pp. 45–56.

29 *Word and Object*, p. 221.

30 'Mental events', p. 222.

inquiries to physical theory is conclusive evidence of the hollowness of their pretensions as serious theories of the world. Why should the case of the mental be different? This is a question of critical importance to the status of the mental in our scheme of things.

I think there is an answer, though this may not be Davidson's. The intentional psychological scheme – that is, the framework of belief, desire, and will – is one within which we deliberate about ends and means, and assess the rationality of actions and decisions. It is the framework that makes our normative and evaluative activities possible. No purely descriptive framework such as those of neurophysiology and physics, no matter how theoretically comprehensive and predictively powerful, can replace it. As long as we think of ourselves as reflective agents capable of deliberation and evaluation – that is, as long as we regard ourselves as agents capable of acting in accordance with a norm – we shall not be able to dispense with the intentional framework of beliefs, wants, and volitions. This again sounds Kantian: our commitment to the intentional framework is a reflection of our nature as rational agents, and our need for it arises out of the demands of practical reason, not those of theoretical reason.[31]

---

[31] I am indebted to Akeel Bilgrami, Reinaldo Elugardo, Fred Feldman, Adam Morton, Bruce Russell, Nicholas White, and the members of my seminars in philosophy of mind at Michigan in 1979 and 1982. Brian McLaughlin gave an interesting set of comments on this paper when it was presented at the Davidson Conference; however, they have not been taken into account in preparing the present draft.

23

Functionalism and Anomalous Monism

JOHN McDOWELL

1. Donald Davidson has insisted on the role played by 'the constitutive ideal of rationality'[1] in shaping our thought about propositional attitudes; and he has argued that this makes it out of the question to reduce that aspect of the mental to 'the physical'. In his book *Mind and Meaning*,[2] Brian Loar has undertaken to refute this. Davidson's argument hinges on the claim that the patterns required by rationality 'have no echo in physical theory'.[3] On the contrary, says Loar: 'the very possibility of a functional interpretation shows that claim to be false'.[4]

I propose to grant Loar's argument that the possibility of a functional interpretation of propositional attitudes would permit a kind of 'physicalist' reduction. The upshot is, I believe, to show that a functional interpretation of propositional attitudes is part of what the constitutive role of rationality excludes. This is a straightforward contraposition of Loar's argument against Davidson. Loar thinks he has established that the argument should go in the other direction, by showing the possibility of a functional interpretation of propositional attitudes. He does not dispute the Davidsonian claim that any interpretation could capture propositional attitudes in its net only if it could attribute a constitutive force to rationality; but he sees nothing to stop a functional interpretation doing that. However, what Loar incorporates in his sketch of a functional account of propositional attitudes, under the head of 'rationality constraints', covers at best a fragment of rationality in general. Davidson's point is that no approach congenial to 'physicalist' reduction could do more than that, and (crucially) that that is not enough; and Loar's argument does not refute this claim, but merely ignores it.

---

[1] *Essays on Actions and Events* (Clarendon Press, Oxford, 1980), p. 223.

[2] Cambridge University Press, Cambridge, 1981; for the argument against Davidson, see especially pp. 20–5.

[3] *Essays on Actions and Events*, p. 231.

[4] *Mind and Meaning*, p. 21.

2. It is already indicative of how far Loar is from engaging with Davidson that the '*a priori* rationality constraints'[5] that he aims to incorporate in his picture of mind are restricted to 'internal constraints of rationality on beliefs'.[6] The restriction limits us to structures that must characterize the interior, so to speak, of a rational mind, excluding (for instance) requirements on how a rational mind expresses itself in intentional action. Such requirements do indeed figure in Loar's picture of the mental, but not under the head of 'rationality constraints'. This means that when Loar purports to have dealt with the obstacle which Davidson thinks the constitutive role of rationality places in the way of 'physicalist' reduction, he is ignoring a suggestion of Davidson's to the effect that the obstacle is operative in the latter area too, in a way that comes out when we ask how propositional attitudes must cause behaviour in order to rationalize it.[7]

However, it will be useful to start by going along with Loar's restriction, since it helps us to focus on an area of application for the concept of rationality in which the point at issue is especially clear.

Loar's '*a priori* rationality constraints' are of two sorts: 'L-constraints', covering relations between beliefs which are specifiable in terms of their logical forms,[8] and 'M-constraints', which are modelled on Carnapian meaning postulates.[9] It is the 'L-constraints', then, that relate to what we can naturally call 'deductive rationality'; and this is what I want to begin by focusing on. Deductive rationality is a capacity, more or less perfectly instantiated in different rational individuals, to hold beliefs when, and because, they follow deductively from other beliefs that one holds. If we are careful, it need do no harm to picture a particular instantiation of deductive rationality as a more or less approximate grasp of a normative structure, determining what follows from what and thus what ought to be believed, given other beliefs, for deductively connected reasons. The Davidsonian claim, now, is that this structure (if we allow ourselves that picture) cannot be abstracted away from relations between contents, or forms of content, in such a way that we might hope to find the abstracted structure exemplified in the interrelations among a system of items described in non-intentional terms. And in this case the claim is actually susceptible of something like proof. Someone who denied the claim would find it hard to explain how his position was consistent with the fact that there is no mechanical test for logical validity in general.

Now Loar is clearly not trying to deny this claim. His 'L-constraints' proscribe beliefs of two forms outright, and proscribe beliefs of a finite number of other forms conditionally on the presence of beliefs of related forms. (Alternative versions, about which he is much more doubtful, make conditional positive requirements.) Loar himself stresses that these constraints are quite

---

[5] Ibid., p. 9.

[6] Ibid., p. 9.

[7] See *Essays on Actions and Events*, pp. 79–81. Loar's brief discussion (*Mind and Meaning*, p. 93) of the problem of 'deviant causation' is unsatisfactory by my lights (in a way that I hope will become clear), in suggesting that the problem is to be consigned to purely theoretical considerations, taking over where what is available to 'common sense' leaves off.

[8] *Mind and Meaning*, pp. 71–4.

[9] Ibid., pp. 81–5.

undemanding: they do not, for instance, ensure even a rudimentary proficiency at making, or assessing, inferences (except for the doubtful positive versions, and even those would introduce only the most elementary inferential capacities). Obviously Loar would not dream of suggesting that his 'L-constraints' capture the structure of deductive reason itself – a structure that would reflect what, in general, follows from what.

But Davidson's claim, particularized to the sphere of rationality that we are focusing on, is that it is that structure that 'has no echo in physical theory'; and he argues the irreducibility of propositional attitudes to 'the physical' from the premiss that the structure of reason itself, of which that structure is a part, cannot be matched up to the interrelations within a non-intentionally characterized system of items. Loar takes himself to have undermined the premiss, as particularized to deductive rationality at least, by pointing out that his 'L-constraints' are available, via functionalism, to a 'physicalist' treatment of propositional attitudes. But since the 'L-constraints' are not meant to capture the structure of deductive reason, this involves a misconception of Davidson's premiss, not a refutation of it; and Davidson's argument is left completely unchallenged.

3. I remarked that any particular instantiation of deductive rationality will embody a more or less imperfect grasp of what, in general, follows from what. This variable gap between actual and ideal may make it seem that any constitutive force that can be attributed to this particularization of the concept of rationality could not extend to the structure of deductive reason itself, as I have said that Davidson's argument requires. The idea would be that constitutive force could be ascribed only to some minimally necessary structure, exemplified in the actual psychological economy of anything that could be recognized as a rational mind: exactly the sort of thing that Loar's 'L-constraints' aspire to capture. Some such idea must underlie Loar's misinterpretation of what Davidson claims. I believe it betrays a prejudice about the character of the understanding we can achieve by employing the conceptual apparatus that is governed by the constitutive force of rationality.

Davidson's claim is, in effect, that if someone offered to reflect the patterns required by rationality in a structure described in non-intentional terms, then, in view of the fact that the constitutive concept functions as an ideal or norm, he would be committing a kind of 'naturalistic fallacy'. (The label is suggestive, but unfortunate in implying that there is something non-naturalistic about propositional attitudes conceived as irreducible to anything non-intentional; I shall return to this.) The prejudice I have in mind would preclude giving this thought its proper significance, by inducing a refusal to recognize that it is something with the status of an ideal which is being credited with a constitutive role in governing our thinking about propositional attitudes. To recognize the ideal status of the constitutive concept is to appreciate that the concepts of the propositional attitudes have their proper home in explanations of a special sort: explanations in which things are made intelligible by being revealed to be, or to approximate to being, as they rationally ought to be. This is to be contrasted with a style of explanation in which one makes things intelligible by representing their coming into being as a particular instance of how things generally tend to happen. (In the usual way of formulating the philosophical issue we are concerned with, 'the physical' need do no more than point to the subject matter of those sciences which aim at explanations of the second sort.[10] Loar's weakening of the concept to which, in purported agreement with Davidson, he attributes the constitutive force that shapes our understanding of propositional attitudes, from Davidson's ideal to his own highest common factor of the actual, reflects a determination to assimilate all explanation to the second of these two sorts.

This has a damaging effect, which I can illustrate without lifting the restriction to deductive rationality. With the restriction in force, what is in question is a mode of understanding in which one finds a belief intelligible on the basis of its following deductively (or being intelligibly but falsely thought to follow deductively) from other beliefs that one knows the believer holds. Attaining this kind of understanding requires bringing to bear the notion of deductive consequence, and it must be that notion itself, not some thinned-down surrogate; if we allow ourselves the idea that the relevant explanations work by locating explanandum and explanans within a structure, it must be the ideal structure of deductive reason, not the less demanding sort of structure that could be determined by something on the lines of Loar's 'L-constraints'. Now Loar envisages a theory that would flesh out the admittedly thin structure which his '*a priori* rationality constraints' would impose by adding further functional relations; these further relations, to be established by theoretical inquiry rather than excogitated *a priori*, are envisaged as belonging to 'the part of the theory outside common sense', and hence as not being required to 'correspond to cognitive, intentional, or conceptual relations'.[11] So there is no requirement that anything in the theory outside the 'L-constraints' should even aim to mirror the structures of deductive inferences, let alone amount to expressing the concept of deductive consequence. The result is that outside the sphere of beliefs, or absences of beliefs, that are related as the 'L-constraints' expressly stipulate, a theory such as Loar envisages would not even aspire to deliver a kind of understanding of beliefs, or absences of beliefs, which depends on the thought that other beliefs are deductively cogent reasons for them. And even within that sphere, the undemandingness of the 'L-constraints' – their innocence of any ambition to capture the ideal structure of deductive reason – means that any understanding that such a theory could offer of beliefs, or absences of beliefs, on the basis of beliefs that are as a matter of fact deductively related to them would not be the kind of understanding that I have described. Such a theory would not have the general normative notion of deductive consequence at its disposal; so its explanations could not exploit that notion, but could draw at most on the idea of certain transitions, and refrainings from transitions, that minds are as a matter of fact prone to. By Davidsonian lights, even that formulation is unwarranted; since the idea of rationality is not credited with its constitutive role, there is nothing to ensure that it is minds that the theory is about.

In connection with his '*a priori* rationality constraints', Loar writes at one point of the way in which a theory which embodies them says that beliefs 'ought

---

[10] This is why I have put 'physical' and its cognates in quotation marks. The issue is a live one quite independently of whether 'physics' is reducible to or even interestingly dependent on physics.

[11] *Mind and Meaning*, p. 79.

rationally to be related'.[12] That 'ought' may seem to make room for the distinctive kind of understanding that I am claiming Loar's position cannot countenance, but the appearance is misleading. It is helpful to consider the question *why* beliefs ought rationally to be related as the 'L-constraints' stipulate. In real life we need have no difficulty in answering this question. But a theory of the sort Loar envisages would contain no materials for addressing it. Such a theory would owe no allegiance to 'common sense' apart from the '*a priori* rationality constraints' themselves; and the explanations it yielded would purport to be self-sufficient – there is no room for the suggestion that their explanatory power might be enhanced if we explained the demandingness of the 'L-constraints' in terms of the general notion of deductive cogency. Made within such a theory, the claim that beliefs ought rationally to be related in accordance with the 'L-constraints' would not reflect the conformity of beliefs so related, in particular, to a categorical norm, intelligibly operative in other cases also; obedience to the 'L-constraints' would have, rather, the status of a hypothetical imperative – something without which a system of states could not be recognized as characterizing a rational mind, and so as a system of beliefs, at all. Now it is no doubt correct to attribute that status to Loar's 'L-constraints'. But if we grant an explanatory role to an ideal that transcends them, we can explain why they have that status in terms of the thought that violations would lie outside the boundaries of what is intelligible – a terrain of whose topography we have a pre-theoretical ('common-sense') grasp that outruns anything captured by Loar's '*a priori* rationality constraints'. In Loar's picture, by contrast, 'common sense' is conceived as doing no more than presenting us with the 'rationality constraints', all else being the province of a theory-construction which, having embraced them, lies under no further obligation to respect thoughts expressible in intentional (content-involving) terms. So Loar's 'ought rationally' does not reflect an acknowledgement of the distinctive kind of understanding I have described; this shows up in its being, from the standpoint of a theory of the sort Loar envisages, a brute fact – a sheer inexplicable datum of 'common sense' – that the '*a priori* rationality constraints' mark limits of intelligibility.

When we come to consider applications for the concept of rationality outside the sphere of deductive consequence, it seems no less plain – though proof is no longer in question – that it would be a fantasy to suppose that the full normative force of the concept, in its extra-logical applications, could be captured in a structure specifiable from outside intentional content. Not a fantasy that Loar indulges in: my point is that his response to Davidson reflects, rather, an inability to see that it is the full normative force of the concept to which Davidson attributes a constitutive status.

That actual instantiations of rationality are imperfect would seem to preclude attributing an explanatory role to the ideal, I suggested, if one assumed that all explanation must be a matter of subsuming particular cases under what generally tends to happen. Without that assumption, the variable gap between actual and ideal is unproblematically reflected in features of the different kind of explanation I have described. On the side of the *objects* of understanding, it

---

[12] Ibid., p. 22.

appears in the critical dimension that any explanation of the ideal-involving kind must have. (Whereas if one tries to force explanation by reasons into the other mould, it is hard to see how one can give due weight to the thought that an ability to understand things on the basis of reasons must carry with it a conception of the difference between good and bad reasons.) And there is a no less important implication on the side of the *subjects*: those who attain understanding. The structure of the ideal (if we allow ourselves that picture) cannot be fixed once and for all from outside. Without an external touchstone, there seems to be no ground on which a subject or group could be confident that its own grasp of the structure, from inside, was incapable of improvement, in particular from coming to understand others. Finding an action or propositional attitude intelligible, after initial difficulty, may not only involve managing to articulate for oneself some hitherto merely implicit aspect of one's conception of rationality, but actually involve becoming convinced that one's conception of rationality needed correcting, so as to make room for this novel way of being intelligible. This reflects the fact that, barring a merely dogmatic complacency, someone who aims at explanations of the ideal-involving kind must be alive to the thought that there is sure to be a gap between actual current conception and ideal structure in his own case as well as in others.

4. If we countenance the ideal-involving kind of understanding that I have described, we have at our disposal a clear interpretation of the thought that propositional attitudes figure in a kind of explanation that is *sui generis*. Unsurprisingly, Loar cannot make much of this thought, which appears at two places in his book.

In the first,[13] it is part of an envisaged attempt to occupy a position – 'anti-reductionism' – whose availability Loar in fact doubts: a position that aims to avoid both instrumentalism about propositional attitudes and the 'physicalist' realism of Loar's own approach. Loar's 'anti-reductionist' accepts that the nature of propositional attitudes can be captured by what Loar calls 'the belief–desire theory': a theory formulable in terms of 'counterfactual relations of causation, transition and co-occurrence'[14] between 'physically' characterized ambient circumstances, psychologically characterized events and states, and 'physically' characterized behaviour. Such a theory would, as Loar insists, describe a structure that might in principle admit of 'physical' interpretation. That is why it is a telling objection against this 'anti-reductionist' that he fails to provide what his rejection of instrumentalism requires, a conception of what it would be for 'the belief–desire theory' to be true of a creature; he rejects the conceptually innocuous, and seemingly common-sensical, 'physicalist' view that the theory's truth would be a matter of an appropriate structuring among the creature's literally internal states, but he supplies nothing (except perhaps a quite unpalatable dualism)[15] to serve instead.

By my lights, this attempt to avoid 'physicalist' reduction is indeed half-baked (as Loar in effect argues). If one accepts Loar's assumption about 'the

---

13 Ibid., p. 11.
14 Ibid., p. 22.
15 See ibid., p. 19.

belief–desire theory', one ensures the impossibility of maintaining that explanations in terms of beliefs and desires are in any serious sense unlike, say, explanations in terms of the internal states of a 'physically' described mechanism. But what needs discussing is a quite different sort of opposition to reductionism: one which attributes a special explanatory role to the ideal of rationality, and on that basis rejects the idea that the explanatory power of citing beliefs and desires could be accounted for by anything like Loar's 'belief–desire theory'. This makes '*sui generis*' into something quite different from the rather empty rhetoric it becomes in the 'anti-reductionism' Loar considers.[16]

In its second occurrence in Loar's book,[17] the notion of a distinctive kind of understanding figures as an overblown response to the fact that a capacity to give common-sense explanations of behaviour in terms of desires does not carry over into a capacity to predict behaviour. Against this, Loar proposes a parallel between desires and the forces that are cited in a familiar sort of non-predictive but nevertheless 'physical' explanation. But the idea of a distinctive kind of understanding is not a mere response to the non-predictiveness of the common-sense explanatory scheme. It is recommended independently by Davidson's point about the explanatory role of rationality. And it, or the point that recommends it, constitutes an argument, not confronted by Loar, against his parallel. It is sensible to try to refine the common-sense conception of forces into a tightly predictive theory, not letting go of the concept of a force but making forces susceptible of precise measurement; but we know *a priori*, on the basis of what sustains the idea of *sui generis* understanding, that no such thing is in prospect for the explanatory scheme in which desires figure.[18]

5. On the view I am recommending, we need not be troubled by what appears in Loar's construction as 'a curious gap between ... functional role and truth conditions'.[19] In Loar's picture, the explanatory capacity ('functional role') of a belief is in general separate from that bearing on the world in virtue of which it is true or false: the latter has to be specially secured after the explanatory capacity has been fully accounted for. (Observational beliefs are an exception.)[20] This strange separation issues directly from failure to appreciate

---

[16] The point does not relate exclusively to what happens *inside* a rational mind: the anti-reductionism I envisage would not accept Loar's view that we can make sense of what happens inside the mind as intervening between 'physically' characterized inputs and 'physically' characterized outputs. The idea that the concepts of behaviour and of mental states are on a par (cf. *Mind and Meaning*, p. 11) need not imply that a conception (scarcely a *theory*, on this different view) of a rational mind is not a conception of 'an *isolable* part of what there is'; Loar's argument to the contrary depends on the inputs and outputs being 'physically' characterized. Something else that can lapse is the extraordinary idea that psychological explanation cannot explain behaviour under descriptions involving acting on objects (see ibid., p. 65: 'grasping away' rather than 'grasping an apple'). A remark on p. 88 suggests Loar would object that the agent's beliefs and desires do not explain, e.g., the presence of an apple at the place where he 'grasps away': but one might equally say that his beliefs and desires do not explain the fact that his nerves and sinews are in working order – using the implicit argument, surely absurdly, to push the explanandum still further 'inwards' (away from the agent's involvement with the world).

[17] *Mind and Meaning*, pp. 90–1.
[18] See *Essays on Actions and Events*, p. 219.
[19] *Mind and Meaning*, p. 194.
[20] Ibid., p. 85.

how propositional-attitude explanations are governed by the constitutive ideal of rationality, and it can lapse as soon as that Davidsonian thought is given its proper significance. Even if we restrict attention to cases where the explanatory ideal is deductive rationality, the capacity of one belief to explain another depends on relations that cannot be characterized except intentionally: relations, in this case specified in terms of form, between representational contents. If we let intentionality go, we lose hold of the idea that constitutively governs the explanations; that is the Davidsonian point on which I have been insisting. When we lift the restriction to deductive rationality, what comes into view is a normatively explanatory structure whose detailed ins and outs can no longer be conceived as knowable *a priori*; and now the substance, and not just the form, of a propositional attitude's representational bearing on the world contributes intelligibly to the attitude's explanatory powers.[21]

This does not disrupt the thesis that the explanations in question work by citing causes.[22] No doubt there is nothing normative about the causal nexus as such: in a broadly Humean conception of causation, that is strikingly reflected in the fact that it is by virtue of being an instance of a generalization about how things tend to happen – the sort of thing that figures in the kind of explanation I have contrasted with the ideal-involving kind – that the relation between a particular pair of events is a causal relation at all. It would follow that a singular causal relation always brings with it a possibility in principle that the effect can be given an explanation of that non-ideal-involving kind. But even if we grant a broadly Humean conception of causation (an issue to which I shall return), it would be a mere prejudice to suppose that citing a cause can be explanatory only by exploiting that possibility.

6. I have claimed that Loar fails to challenge Davidson's argument; his idea that he has refuted its premiss betrays a misconception of what the premiss is. This raises an urgent diagnostic question: something deep and gripping must account for such failure even to identify the threat to his position, let alone counter it. It can be only temporarily satisfactory to postulate a prejudice that obscures from view the possibility of genuinely ideal-involving explanations; such a prejudice needs diagnosis itself.

Cartesian dualism is a good starting-point. Like others, Loar values 'physicalism' as a way of avoiding a behaviouristic denial of the inner life without lapsing into a Cartesian picture of it. Now it is certainly true that, knowing what we do about the comprehensive scope of the 'physical' sciences, we cannot find room for a non-'physical' substance in a common-sense conception of the world; so the Cartesian picture of mind strikes us as brazenly non-naturalistic. It is quite intelligible that that should seem to be its basic flaw, and consequently that a 'physicalist' conception of the inner should seem to be exactly what we need instead. But, although I do not of course dispute that the

---

[21] It is to Loar's credit that he concedes that the gap he envisages is curious (unlike some proponents of similar positions, who represent it as sheer common sense). Consider how the idea applies to wants. What a want is a want for has nothing to do with the explanatory capacity of citing it. What, then, is the point of the notion of what a want is a want for? It lies in such facts as that when one gets what one wants, the want ceases to move one. This remarkable suggestion (for which see *Mind and Meaning*, pp. 196–8) seems close to a *reductio ad absurdum*.

[22] *Locus classicus*: 'Actions, reasons, and causes', in *Essays on Actions and Events*.

brazen non-naturalism is a defect, I think this account of the Cartesian picture does not go deep enough; and if we go deeper, this apparent recommendation for 'physicalism' disappears.

What is fundamentally at issue is the pull of the idea that reality is objective, in the sense of being fully describable from no particular point of view.[23] This idea is in tension with a natural intuition to the effect that the mental is both real and essentially subjective. Cartesian dualism results from trying to put these forces in equilibrium: the subjectivity of the mental is (supposedly) accommodated by the idea of privileged access, while the object of that access is conceived, in conformity with the supposed requirement of objectivity, as there independently – there in a reality describable from no particular point of view – rather than as being constituted by the subject's special access to it.[24] Since there is no plausibility in the idea that one could have the appropriate kind of special access to something 'physical', the upshot is the notion of a non-'physical' substance.

This account of what generates the Cartesian picture of the inner suggests that to recoil from Cartesian dualism into 'physicalism' may be to avoid only a superficial defect; it may be that the fundamental flaw is the attempt to force the mental into an objective mould, something still plainly operative in the supposedly healthy position in which this recoil leaves one. The admittedly unacceptable non-naturalism of the Cartesian picture would justify giving up the intuition that the mental is essentially subjective only if that intuition inevitably generated the Cartesian picture. But the Cartesian picture results from the intuition only in conjunction with objectivism. Davidson's thesis of irreducibility also respects the intuition, and in a healthier form: a form in which it is not distorted, as it is in the Cartesian picture, by the pressure towards objectivity. That pressure – which is what accounts, I suggests, for Loar's inability to appreciate Davidson's argument – now takes on the look of a prejudice: deep-seated and tenacious, evidently, but not something to which reason requires us to succumb.

It is often thought that if essential subjectivity poses any threat to an objectivistic conception of the mental, it is a threat restricted to phenomenal or qualitative mental states or events: states or events about which there is an answer to the question what it is distinctively like to be in them or undergo them.[25] But the Davidsonian irreducibility of propositional attitudes – which are not states whose essence resides in their qualitative character – traces back to subjectivity too: not only in that the mode of understanding which they subserve is a matter of comprehending the specific content of a particular

[23] See Thomas Nagel, 'Subjective and objective', in his *Mortal Questions* (Cambridge University Press, Cambridge, 1979), pp. 196–213.

[24] See Bernard Williams, *Descartes: The Project of Pure Enquiry* (Penguin Books, Harmondsworth, 1978), especially at pp. 225–6. Williams's perceptive discussion is flawed, however, by his apparently equating 'objective' and 'third-personal'. A conception of what it is for another person to be in pain is presumably third-personal; it would be disastrously wrong to conclude that such a conception is separable from a conception of how things feel to the other person.

[25] See Thomas Nagel, 'What is it like to be a bat?', in *Mortal Questions*, pp. 165–80. A substantial amount of work has been based on the idea that 'qualia' pose a *special* problem for functionalism; see, e.g., Sydney Shoemaker, 'Functionalism and qualia', *Philosophical Studies*, 27 (1975), pp. 291–315.

subject's outlook on the world, but also – a thought involving a special status for a less individualistically conceived point of view – in that we cannot find any use for a distinction between what makes sense and what could come to make sense to us, if necessary as a result of our learning from those whom we thereby come to find intelligible.[26] Loar's position cannot incorporate either of these considerations, in both cases for reasons we have already touched on: it misses the first because it holds that the explanatory capacity of a propositional attitude is in general independent of its bearing on the world, and it misses the second because, in so far as it deals at all with a distinction between what makes sense and what does not, it is committed to treating the limits of intelligibility as a brute and presumably objective datum.

These considerations bring out a connection between the ideal-involving kind of explanation and the irreducible subjectivity of propositional attitudes. Achieving the kind of understanding for which rationality plays its constitutive role requires a sensitivity to the specific detail of the subjective stance of others, and an openness to learning from it, that is bound to be falsified if one supposes that explanations involving the constitutive ideal work by locating their explananda in a structure specifiable from outside content. Loar conceives the constitutive ideal as just such a structure – misinterpreting, rather than answering, Davidson's claim about the constitutive concept, as I have insisted. His position seems to be the nearest one could come to accommodating Davidson's point within a picture of mind as an element in objective reality.

What makes it seem right to label the Cartesian picture of mind 'non-naturalistic' is not simply that it cannot be embraced within a 'physicalistic' world-view, but rather the conjunction of that with the fact that it purports to represent an aspect of objective reality. Naturalism assures us, we might reasonably say, that the whole of objective reality (in the relevant sense) can in principle be dealt with by the 'physical' sciences. If mental states are irreducibly mental by virtue of an ineliminable subjectivity, there is no violation of that tenet of naturalism in crediting them with a complete and self-sufficient reality. We can conceive the mental as simply a different aspect of (what else?) the world of nature. That is why the phrase 'naturalistic fallacy' is ultimately misleading as a description of what blocks 'physicalist' reduction, although its historical resonances are useful.

Loar suggests, in a passage I mentioned earlier,[27] that what underlies a suspicion of comparing desires to (say) mechanical forces is 'a now unmotivated anti-mentalism': that is, I take it, a refusal to accept the inner life, of the sort characteristic of behaviourism. This seems to me to be just about the reverse of the truth. It is not the irreducibility thesis – which can of course accept 'force' as a lively metaphor for at least some desires – that threatens the inner life, but the objectivism of which Loar's view is a species. Objectivism poses a choice

---

[26] See Davidson's 'On the very idea of a conceptual scheme', in his *Inquiries into Truth and Interpretation* (Clarendon Press, Oxford, 1984), pp. 183–98. Nagel seems to me to miss the full depth of his own point about subjectivity, not only in suggesting that the point is restricted to the qualitative aspects of the mental, but also in espousing a realism that countenances the idea of subjective facts completely beyond our reach.

[27] *Mind and Meaning*, p. 91.

between behaviourism and psychologism: and of course, taking the psychologistic option, Loar's picture of the mental countenances far more than mere behaviour. But the literally internal states and goings-on that it adds to the behaviourist's world-view cannot be recognized as the inner life by any acceptable standard, however undemanding, of what Loar calls 'conservative explication'.[28]

I have emphasized that Loar's failure to meet Davidson's point is quite explicit (though not, of course, under that description); he leaves it perfectly clear that his functionalist picture of mind does not aim to include a characterization from outside content of the structure of rationality in general. It is tempting to suspect that others, in supposing that a functionalism more vaguely delineated than Loar's can accommodate the mental within a wholly objective conception of reality, have allowed themselves to be captivated by what seems to be a mirage: the fantasy of a theory which, unlike anything Loar envisages, would capture structurally the whole normative force of rationality in such a way as to lend itself to 'physical' interpretation. Perhaps I should note that these remarks are critical of functionalism as a theory of propositional attitudes; they do not tell against functionalism as a framework for theory about how sub-personal states and events operate in the control of behaviour, although they do raise a question about what (if anything) that sort of theory has to do with the mind.[29]

7. Davidson's philosophy of mind has two distinctive strands, anomalism and monism (about events); and, although this paper is meant as a tribute to him, it would be disingenuous to slur over the fact that I have been endorsing only the first. Apart from Davidson's argument itself, which I shall come to, there seems to be nothing to be said for the second: no respectable metaphysical impulse, say, which it enables us to gratify. Anomalism itself, or what sustains it, neutralizes any motivation that might be afforded by the ideal of the unity of science. And avoidance of Cartesian dualism is irrelevant; since it is not events but substances that are composed of stuff, one can refuse to accept that all the events there are can be described in 'physical' terms, without thereby committing oneself to a non-'physical' stuff, or compromising the thesis that persons are composed of nothing but matter.[30]

In Davidson's argument itself, monism is represented as following from three premises.[31] One of them – the Anomalism of the Mental – is what I have been

---

[28] Ibid., p. 43.

[29] Proper attention to this contrast subverts both the idea that sub-personal cognitive psychology might supersede 'folk psychology' and the idea that it reveals the hidden depths of something whose surface 'folk psychology' describes in a rough and ready way. (It is important not to be misled by the role of rationality in, e.g., computational accounts of sub-personal processes. The illumination that such accounts can undoubtedly yield is not a product of deeper understanding of the mind. It is rather a matter of understanding the workings of the brain – in a way whose possibility is wholly unmysterious – by modelling them on certain mental processes.)

[30] My general indebtedness to unpublished work of Jennifer Hornsby is particularly prominent here; and see her 'Which physical events are mental events?', *Proceedings of the Aristotelian Society*, 81 (1980–1), pp. 73–92.

[31] *Essays on Actions and Events*, pp. 208–9.

defending. A second – the Principle of Causal Interaction – seems unquestionable.[32] Given the cogency of the argument, then, scepticism about its conclusion should lead to suspicion of the third premiss: the Principle of the Nomological Character of Causality. I should like to end by suggesting that this suspicion really ought to be a Davidsonian thought, even though Davidson himself has not formulated it.

The broadly Humean picture of causation which the Principle embodies may be encouraged by the prejudice about causal explanation which I mentioned above (§5) – something Davidson has done much to show us how to resist. One can reject the prejudice about explanation while retaining the picture of causation, as Davidson's own example makes clear.[33] However, it is a good question what now holds the picture of causation in place. Hume's own recommendation of it is, in effect, that since singular causal relations are not given in experience, there is nothing for causation to consist in but a suitable kind of generality. And this recommendation seems inextricably bound up with a 'dualism of scheme and content, of organizing system and something waiting to be organized',[34] the untenability of which Davidson has done as much as anyone to bring home to us. Without that dualism, there is no evident attraction left in the thought that singular causal relations are not given in experience. Pending an alternative recommendation, the Prejudice of the Nomological Character of Causality, as I shall venture to relabel it, looks like a fourth dogma of empiricism; the third – the 'dualism of scheme and content' – was not, as Davidson once surmised,[35] the last, but we need to be told what claim the fourth has on our acceptance once the third has been dismantled.[36]

---

[32] I may seem to have committed myself to it already, by my remarks in §5. This is not strictly so, in view of note 16 above; but it would be very strange if the causally interconnected psychological systems I envisage were causally disconnected from the 'physical' world.

[33] Davidson's picture of causation is Humean only in making singular causal relations instantiate generalizations; Davidson does not share the Humean aim of reducing the causal 'must' to a mere 'always' (see 'Causal relations', in *Essays on Actions and Events*). I am grateful to Mark Johnston for reminding me of this.

[34] *Inquiries into Truth and Interpretation*, p. 189.

[35] Ibid., p. 189.

[36] I have been helped in trying to improve this paper by Akeel Bilgrami's thoughtful comments.

24

Davidson's Unintended Attack on Psychology

ALEXANDER ROSENBERG

In the 'Comments and replies' section of 'Psychology as Philosophy', Davidson writes:

> discussions of my paper ... made me realize that I had given the impression that I was making an attack on psychology generally, or at least its right to be called a science. That is certainly not what I intended, but I do see how things I wrote could bear that interpretation.[1]

Intended or not,[2] the conclusions of 'The material mind', 'Mental events' and 'Psychology as philosophy' really do seem to give considerable support to the claim that 'psychology' has no 'right to be called a science'. In this paper I set out this argument in the hope that Davidson can show how it misconstrues his conclusions. In doing so, he may shed needed light on how, as a formerly practising experimental psychologist, he believes this discipline and the rest of the social and behavioral sciences should proceed.

I

But first, consider how Davidson himself attempts to clear up this misinterpretation. He begins by noting that his 'arguments are limited in application to branches of psychology that make essential reference to "propositional attitudes" such as belief, desire, and memory, or use concepts logically tied to these, such as perception, learning, and action'.[3] It is worth noting that this

---

[1] In *Essays on Actions and Events* (Clarendon Press, Oxford, 1980), pp. 229–44, at p. 240.
[2] I am among those who must plead guilty to the charge of such misinterpretation, or perhaps misappropriation, of Davidson's arguments to such purposes. See my *Sociobiology and the Presumption of Social Science* (The Johns Hopkins University Press, Baltimore, 1981). Of this work, one reviewer wrote: 'Philosophers will know what is going on here: Donald Davidson meets E.O. Wilson.'
[3] 'Psychology as philosophy', p. 240.

limitation not only encompasses most of psychology beyond instrumental and classical conditioning, but also the rest of the social and behavioral sciences. Whatever the upshot of Davidson's arguments, they will apply to economics, for example. For in economics the crucial variables are 'expectation' and 'preference' and these are but cognates of 'desire' and 'belief'.[4]

In places Davidson notes the general bearing of his conclusions explicitly: 'The nomological irreducibility of the psychological means, if I am right, that the social sciences cannot be expected to develop in ways exactly parallel to the physical sciences.'[5]

A substantial portion of the misinterpretation seems on Davidson's view to stem from his conclusion 'that psychophysical generalizations must be treated as irreducibly statistical in character, in contrast to sciences where in principle exceptions can be taken care of by refinements couched in a homogeneous vocabulary'. Now to say that if Davidson is right psychophysical generalizations must be statistical in character seems itself an understatement of his conclusions. For anomalous monism is the thesis that there are no scientifically useful psychophysical generalizations whatever. It is not merely that such generalizations as we can uncover will be probabilistic at best. In 'Mental events' Davidson writes, 'I want to describe, and … to argue for, a version of the identity theory that denies that there can be strict laws connecting the mental and the physical.'[6] In 'Psychology as philosophy' the 'Principle of the Anomalism of the Mental' is expressed as the thesis that 'there are no strict laws at all on the basis of which we can predict and explain mental phenomena.'[7] It is true that the qualification 'strict' is employed, and that elsewhere the thesis of anomalous monism is called the 'principle that there are no strict deterministic laws on the which mental events can be predicted and explained'. Nevertheless, the thesis is not that there are strict but indeterministic psychophysical laws like those of statistical mechanics.

The parallel Davidson draws between psychophysical statements and generalizations employing the Goodman-predicates, 'grue' and 'bleen', belies such a conclusion. It is not as if psychophysical generalizations had the probabilistic character of the laws of quantum mechanics, a character which limits their predictive powers to certain theoretically identifiable and precisely explainable ranges. Rather, the suggestion of anomalous monism is that mental predicates supervene on so vast and heterogeneous a group of physical ones that no useful factual generalizations about correlations between them are possible at all: 'There may be true general statements relating the mental and the physical, statements that have the form of a law; but they are not lawlike.'[8] If the physical

---

[4] This is perhaps the only respect in which what Davidson has called the 'neo-Wittgensteinian current of little red books' (*Essays on Actions and Events*, p. 261), like P. Winch, *The Idea of a Social Science*, A.I. Melden, *Free Action*, and R.S. Peters, *The Concept of Motivation* (Routledge & Kegan Paul, London, 1958, 1958, and 1961 respectively), were right. All the social sciences are thoroughly intentional. Even as apparently non-intentional disciplines as macroeconomics and avowedly non-intentional theories as Durkheim's macro-sociology have this unavoidable intentional dimension.

[5] 'Psychology as philosophy', p. 230.

[6] 'Mental events', in *Essays on Actions and Events*, p. 212.

[7] 'Mental Events', p. 224.

[8] Ibid., p. 216.

predicates were less heterogeneous, and smaller in number, then useful though cumbersome and quite lengthy generalizations might be constructed. But this would be the denial of anomalous monism. On the other hand, if psychophysic- al generalizations were nomologically statistical in the way quantum mechanical laws are, then the looseness of intentional psychology would be eliminable up to theoretically derived limits or levels set by theories from neuroscience or psychophysics. But this doesn't seem to be Davidson's point at all.

Davidson says that the predictive looseness of psychology is guaranteed by the conceptually 'hermaphroditic character' of its concepts. I take this to mean that it is the holistic nature of the relation among desires, beliefs and actions, the so-called 'desire–belief–action' triangle, which guarantees the looseness of psychology:

> Any effort at increasing the accuracy and power of a theory of behavior forces us to bring more and more of the whole system of the agent's beliefs and motives directly into account. But in inferring this system from the evidence, we necessarily impose conditions of coherence, rationality, and consistency.
>
> These conditions have no echo in physical theory, which is why we can look for no more than rough correlations between psychological and physical phenomena.

But the 'hermaphroditic character' of intentional concepts not only explains the absence of useful psychophysical correlations, it also precludes purely inten- tional laws of the sort a science of psychology requires.

The imprecision of psychological predictions, of projecting a particular action given a brace of belief and desire, is not due to the stochastic character of any intentional nomic generalization connecting them, for psychology contains no such statistical regularities about intentions and actions. Predictive impreci- sion is due to the impossibility of any manageably short psychophysical generalization linking intentional states with non-intentional ones. The fact of anomalous monism explains not only why psychological prediction must remain loose, but also why no useful statistical regularities about intentions and actions will be forthcoming as well. One way of showing this is to advert to the closure of Brentano's intentional science, or more fashionably, to the 'hermeneutical circle', closed against non-intentional penetration.

Yet Davidson seems to describe the situation in the very opposite terms: 'the part of psychology with which I was concerned cannot be, or be incorporated in, a closed science.'[10] Now Davidson means something quite different by 'closed science' than the hermeneuticist. A closed science is one that contains 'homonomic' generalizations, ones 'which may be sharpened up indefinitely by drawing upon further ... concepts: there is a theoretical asymptote of perfect coherence with all the evidence, perfect predicability ... total explanation.' A homonomic statement is 'correctable in its own conceptual domain.' Because of the want of such laws, 'the social sciences cannot be expected to develop in ways exactly parallel to the physical sciences, nor can we expect ever to be able to explain and predict human behavior with the kind of precision that is possible in

---

[9] 'Psychology as philosophy', p. 231.
[10] Ibid., p. 241.
[11] 'Mental events', pp. 219–20.

principle for physical phenomena.'[12] Presumably, though, psychology and the other intentional sciences preserve their scientific status because they can or do incorporate 'heteronomic' laws, not capable of indefinite improvement, but useful generalizations for all that.

Davidson concludes that '"science" being the honorific word it is in some quarters, it would be meretricious to summarize these points by saying that psychology ... is not a science; the conclusion is rather that psychology is set off from other sciences in an important and interesting way.'[13] Now science is indeed an honorific term, but it is one with other suggestions as well. And if in the light of Davidson's arguments it can be shown incapable of even heteronomic generalizations, it seems equally meretricious to say that intentional psychology is a science at all, albeit 'set off' from the others. Let me try to show how anomalous monism precludes even heteronomic, let alone homonomic, generalizations in psychology.

II

As Davidson argued in 'Causal relations' the truth of a singular causal statement requires the truth of a generalization, though not one we already happen to know in most cases. Consider some singular causal statement linking a particular set of beliefs and a particular set of desires of a particular person with a particular action of his. Assume there is an intentional generalization, perhaps unknown, which subsumes these causes and this effect. Doubtless because of the holistic character of the propositional attitudes, this general statement will be incredibly complex and utterly unmanageable. Nevertheless, it will have the following schematic form:

L.   (x) (If x is in belief states B and has desires D, then x does action A)

The propositional attitudes are pluralized to emphasize the holistic character of intentional states. L of course is not a psychophysical generalization, it is a purely psychological or intentional one. Now if explanation proceeds in roughly the way widely supposed, then this generalization together with the antecedent of the singular causal statement should at least in part explain the consequent and justify the causal claim. The trouble is that given the truth of anomalous monism, it follows that this generalization cannot be theoretically entrenched, improved, or even tested in any credible manner. It's not just, as Davidson notes, that intentional generalizations are heteronomic and cannot be indefinitely refined.[14] The trouble is they cannot be refined at all. They are neither heteronomic nor homonomic; they are non-nomic.

In the natural sciences, predictive and explanatory power of generalizations are improved at least very often by sharpening up the specification of the values of causal variables instanced in a particular sequence that the law subsumes. Thus we can improve the precision of our prediction of the pressure of a gas consequent on a change in its temperature if we can improve our measurement

---

[12] 'Psychology as philosophy', p. 230.
[13] Ibid., p. 241.
[14] 'Mental events', p. 224.

of the temperature. If an alcohol thermometer is correct to one degree celsius, and a mercury thermometer to one-tenth of a degree celsius, the latter will enable us to predict the effects of a change in temperature on changes in pressure to an order of magnitude's greater precision. But to do this we need to know that both devices measure the same variable, and we need to know that one measures it more precisely than the other. Moreover, as we pile up alternative means of measuring initial conditions (and explanandum-properties as well) we usually begin to disconfirm our earliest generalizations, and to find ways of improving them.

Thus, the simple gas law:

$$PV = rT$$

gave way to a succession of improvements through the discovery of thermometers that measured temperature within the original range of values for which $PV = rT$ was formulated, and enabled us to measure extreme values of temperature where the ideal gas law is disconfirmed. The more complex equations of state for gases bear important structural similarities to $PV = rT$; and their underlying theoretical explanation also explains why $PV = rT$ works over a restricted range of values. The sequence of improvements both in the explanatory and predictive use of the classical equation of state and in its formulation is due to the existence of a succession of alternative means of measuring pressure, temperature and volume. Indeed, the original equation could not have been discovered or confirmed unless there had been means of measuring these three variables independent of the equation itself.

If anomalous monism is correct there are no prospects for similar improvements in a law like L. For in order to improve our specification of initial conditions we need a means independent of L for identifying these conditions, we need a measuring instrument that will enable us to identify the propositional attitudes of agents independent of each other and their subsequent effects in action. Holism is the thesis that this cannot be done. But anomalous monism is the argument for this thesis. For anomalous monism holds that any type of propositional attitude may be realized by any of a vast and heterogeneous disjunction of brain-states. It in effect rules out the existence of a neurophysiological 'measuring instrument' for intentional states. Of course even if there were such an instrument, the fineness of grain of neural differences and their practical inaccessibility would make their identities with propositional attitudes too baroquely complex to be practically useful in real time. Nonetheless, such a generalization would provide at least theoretically possible access to intentional states independent of L. But anomalous monism denies even this abstract possibility (it says there are no psychophysical laws, not even baroque and inexpressible ones). So it precludes improvement of any kind in the application of L to explanation and prediction of human behavior. Unless of course there are other means of specifying and identifying beliefs and desires besides neuroscientific correlates.

The only other alternative is of course some version of behaviorism. If behavior were a reliable mark of propositional attitudes then generalizations linking behavior to intentional states might provide the measuring instrument we require. But of course behaviorism founders on this very impossibility.[15] The behavioral specification of a desire is always *modulo* the associated beliefs and actions. And beliefs can only be specified in terms of the behavior they lead to if we hold desires constant. This problem of intentional 'contamination' of a behavioral analysis is of course explained in terms of holism. What it means is that there are no non-intentional ways of specifying intentional states, and so no scope for improving a law like L beyond the predictive power of the 'folk psychology'[16] already ensconced in common sense.

III

Science does not require that we begin with what Davidson calls 'closed theory', with unimpeachable homonomic generalizations. Physics was a going, scientific concern before Newton, as was chemistry before Mendeleev. But what is characteristic of science is its capacity to provide generalizations that are improvable beyond what common sense provides. A bit of chemical history will illustrate this. The phlogiston theory of combustion represents a dead end in chemistry not because it was pseudo-science, or because there was something incoherent about the notion of phlogiston. It was a dead end because it did not carve nature at the joints, because its kind terms, 'phlogiston', 'dephlogisticated air', are not as a matter of empirical fact realized in nature. It was replaced by another theory, Lavoisier's oxygen hypotheses. One reason phlogiston theory came a cropper is that there were widely accepted ways of measuring the values of some of its variables, indirect ways, that were independent of phlogiston theory itself. After a certain point it became impossible to improve the theory's powers, or even reconcile it with experiment, without jettisoning these phlogiston-independent means of measuring its causal variables. The refusal to jettison phlogiston, and the concomitant rejection of non-phlogistic measures of the causal variables of combustion, would have condemned chemistry to sterility, would have denied to it the status of a science.

Intentional psychology does not have even the strengths of phlogiston theory, for its causal variables are not subject to any actual or practically possible independent measurement. This means not only that its explanations and predictions are incapable of improvement, but that its theory can shed no further light at all on the true singular causal statements about action and its intentional determinants than 'folk psychology' sheds on everyday affairs. Indeed, our confidence in the truth of intentional claims of any generality is based not on their predictive or explanatory power, but on the fact that they represent propositions as close to analytic in their grounds as any propositions may be.

General statements of L's form, or more restricted versions of L with self-conscious *ceteris paribus* clauses holding all other beliefs and desires constant, are as close to analytic as any statements can be, just because anomalous monism obtains. Because there are no behaviorally or neuroscienti-

---

[15] See ibid., pp. 216–17.

[16] In the sense of Paul Churchland, 'Eliminative materialism and the propositional attitudes', *Journal of Philosophy*, 78 (1981), pp. 67–90.

fically based means of identifying propositional attitudes, we can define such attitudes only by appeal to L and its more restricted versions. General statements about intentional states are true only when they are in effect implicit definitions of the intensional terms describing these states. Because of the anomalousness of these states, there are no explicit non-intentional character-izations of them, and the implicit definitions intentional generalizations provide are all we have to go on in characterizing and actually identifying propositional attitudes. This makes L and any other putative law of intentional psychology analytic if any sentence is.

Being unrevisable need in and of itself be no obstacle to nomological status. It was in fact the recognition of this fact which led to the downfall of the analytic/synthetic distinction. Nevertheless it is a strange science which contains unrevisable generalizations at its periphery, where it comes into contact with the world, instead of at the center of its nomological network. Yet this is the case for intentional psychology. Statements of L's form meet the data directly, for they systematize the lowest level of true singular causal judgments about human action and its causes. Indeed they are employed to identify bodily displacements as actions, and the determinants of these movements as intentional states.

It is an equally strange science whose generalizations we know in advance cannot be entrenched within or even systematically connected to any other theory, known or unknown. Yet this too is a direct consequence of anomalous monism. It's not just that intentional psychology cannot be reduced to non-intentional science. It cannot even be linked to it in a practically useful way. Compare the terms and generalizations of Mendelian genetics. These too are supervenient on the terms and laws of molecular biology, and because of their anomalousness with respect to molecular concepts the Mendelian terms and laws are not systematically reducible to them. Nevertheless, we may improve and correct Mendelian claims, systematically explain their predictive failings and successes, because we can identify and measure the values of the causal variables of Mendelian theory independently of that theory, through the facilities of molecular biology. The latter theory, and other parts of biology for that matter, enable us to locate, identify, and characterize particular Mendelian genes independent of the hereditary effects accorded them in Mendelian theory. Even though we cannot express Mendelian theory in molecular terms, or actually effect the type–type reduction of the former theory to the latter, we can explain in a piece-meal way why its laws obtain on any given occasion, we can explain why they don't obtain on other occasions, we can improve the exactness of its predictions on those occasions where it does obtain, just because we have theoretical knowledge, knowledge that provides non-Mendelian, molecular access to the causal variables of Mendelian theory. To this extent, Mendelian theory is linked to the rest of science. This, combined with its practical predictive utility, is why Mendelian genetics retains an important place in biology, despite its actual irreducibility.

But intentional psychology has neither any prospects of practical predictive improvement, nor any prospects of piece-meal linkage with the rest of science. It has no practical utility beyond that of 'folk psychology'; indeed whatever power it has is parasitic on the considerable practical predictive powers of the psychological theory we all learn through growing up. Intentional psychology is no more powerful as a predictive tool than the psychological theory with which Thucydides explained the behavior of his contemporaries. And it has no prospects of linkage with the rest of science because of anomalous monism.

IV

Perhaps the difference between intentional psychology and Mendelian genetics is only one of degree. Both are anomalous with respect to their supervenience bases, respectively neurophysiology and molecular biology. In the genetic case, the complexity and the heterogeneity of the disjunctions of molecular arrangements is small enough to be manageable in many cases. So the difference may only be that the neurophysiological supervenience base of intentional psychology is just so much more complicated, involves so many more disjuncts, that it is useless even on a piece-meal basis, given the practical constraints on explanation and prediction. If this were the case then intentional psychology's failure would be entirely practical. The impossibility of linking its causal variables to independent measures would reflect the limitations on our intellectual powers to discover and manipulate immensely long and complicated bi-conditionals relating propositional attitudes to brain-states.

It is evident that Davidson does not view the matter in this light. With something like this very parallel between psychology and biology in mind, he writes:

> psychology cannot be, or be incorporated in a closed science. This is due to the irreducibility of psychological concepts, and to the fact that psychological events and states often have causes that have no natural psychological descriptions. I do not want to say that analogous remarks may not hold for some other sciences, for example biology. But I do not know how to show that the concepts of biology are irreducible to the concepts of physics. What sets apart certain psychological concepts – their intensionality – does not apply to the concepts of biology.[17]

Mendelian genetics is not a closed science either. But its generalizations are at least heteronomic, so that it is a practically useful theory that can be linked to a closed science, biochemistry. Anomalous monism prevents intentional psychology from being similarly linked. The fact that we must employ intensional concepts to describe the causes and effects psychology deals with is not the foundation of its irreducibility, it is the consequence of it. It is by content and direction of the propositional attitudes that we must identify them, because no other alternatives are available. Accordingly it is not intensionality that sets intentional psychology apart as different. Unavoidable recourse to intensional and intentional terms is a symptom of the impossibility of linking psychology and any part of science, not its cause.

---

[17] 'Psychology and philosophy', p. 241. I have tried to show that the concepts of biology are irreducible to the concepts of physics in 'The supervenience of biological concepts', *Philosophy of Science*, 45 (1978), pp. 368–86, in 'Fitness', *Journal of Philosophy*, 80 (1983), pp. 457–73, and *The Structure of Biological Science* (Cambridge University Press, Cambridge 1985).

Without this linkage, improvement beyond the explanatory and predictive powers of 'folk psychology' is impossible. And without even the prospects of such improvement, psychology does not have the hope of being a heteronomic science, let alone a homonomic one. The persistence of intentional psychology cannot be justified or explained by calling it a science, an organized body of empirical generalizations that stand a chance of being improved.

There is of course a tradition in the philosophy of social science to which such a conclusion will give aid and comfort. It is the neo-Wittgensteinian movement of the fifties and sixties.[18] These writers inferred from the alleged impossibility of causal connections between reasons and actions to the logical impossibility of a social science, an axiomatized body of general laws explaining and predicting particular actions by nomic subsumption. Davidson's best-known service to philosophy has been to stem the current of little red books, to explode this view with the double-barrel blast of 'Causal relations' and 'Actions, reasons, and causes'. A causal science of human action is after all logically possible. But if anomalous monism obtains, it is just not practically possible. The irony therefore is that the followers of Wittgenstein were right after all, in all but the modality of their claims. I speculate that it is his discomfort with finding himself among such unlikely company that leads Davidson to deny that he has undermined the scientific prospects of intentional psychology.

As Davidson notes, the term 'science' is indeed honorific, honorific enough so that we might still call 'sciences' the social studies which Wittgensteinians urged replace logically misconceived attempts at a naturalistic examination of mind and action. But, like the 'science of history', they would be sciences in name only. In providing factual reasons, instead of conceptual ones, to rule out the naturalistic study of intentionality and its effects, Davidson has shown it to be more than merely 'meretricious to summarize [his] points by saying that psychology ... is not a science'.

---

[18] The current of little red books mentioned in note 4 above.

25

Why Having a Mind Matters

MARK JOHNSTON

I

Those of us who were taught physicalism – the thesis that every event or state is a physical event or state – at the knees of the Australian materialists, were taught certain things about the *status* of the thesis of physicalism. First, of course, we were taught that it was true, but next and almost equally importantly that it was *contingently* true. This was not the mistake that led to the confused talk of 'contingent identity'. Rather it was the seemingly unavoidable admission that although in fact every event or state was a physical event or state, there could have been spirits or disembodied minds. Physicalism was not a necessary truth, not true however the world might have been.[1]

Thirdly and not surprisingly, the Australian materialists held that physicalism was an a posteriori truth. The claim that every event or state is a physical event or state was held to be plausible because of what in a slightly ominous phrase was called 'the shadow of reduction', that is to say the success of physicalist reductions in chemistry, biology and neurophysiology. The Australian matrialists had a lively sense that we could have discovered that people had nothing in their heads with enough physical complexity to plausibly account for the complexity of their mental lives. Indeed, the Australian materialists rejected analytic behaviorism in part because of their realization that no amount of *analysis* of our use of the mental vocabulary could itself deliver the truth of physicalism.[2]

Fourthly, the Australian materialists mostly supposed that physicalism could be plausibly put forward as a type–type identity thesis. D.M. Armstrong and

---

[1] For some papers in this tradition see *The Identity Theory of Mind*, ed. C.F. Presley (University of Queensland Press, St. Lucia, Queensland, 1967).

[2] Cf. D.M. Armstrong's 'The nature of mind', in *The Mind/Brain Identity Theory*,, ed. C.V. Borst (St. Martin's Press, New York, 1970), and J.J.C. Smart, 'Sensations and brain processes', also in Borst. See especially Smart's answer to Objection 7, 'I say the dualist's hypothesis is a perfectly intelligible one.' Smart notes that the argument for physicalism is partly empirical and partly conceptual; the conceptual part is the appeal to Occam's razor to rule out epiphenomenalism and parallelism.

David Lewis (for these purposes an honorary Australian materialist) outlined a schematic argument for physicalism which would yield identifications of *types* of mental states with *types* of physical states on the basis of the identity of their causal role.[3]

Finally, the Australian materialists held that type–type physicalism did not itself undermine the idea that people were capable of free or autonomous action. By and large the Australian materialists supposed that what distinguished free action from mere bodily movements was the right causal ancestry of the bodily movements which were free or intentional acts.[4]

So, in this tradition, physicalism was held to be a true, contingent, a posteriori and type–type identity thesis. And it was widely supposed that type–type physicalism did not threaten the idea that people were capable of free action.

Against this background Donald Davidson's claims in the paper 'Mental events'[5] are startling almost revolutionary. That paper suggests that the Australian materialists were wrong on four out of five counts. First, 'Mental events' purports to offer a relatively a priori argument for a version of physicalism, an argument based on claims about the nature of the mental vocabulary and the right analysis of singular causal statements. So even if one denied any sharp division between the a priori and the a posteriori, it would still be the case that the Australian materialists had radically mistaken the epistemic status of physicalism, locating it at the wrong end of the continuous spectrum from the a priori to the a posteriori. Secondly, none of Davidson's crucial premises, at least as he defends them, seem to be the sorts of propositions that would fail in any possible situation in which there were mental states or events. So it seems that if Davidson's argument were sound nothing could be made of the ordinary idea that there might have been spirits or disembodied minds, whose mental states and events were not identical with physical states and events.

Thirdly, Davidson's paper not only purports to argue for physicalism without appealing to the probable success of physicalist reduction via bridge laws linking the mental and the physical, but more than this, his argument for physicalism depends upon the impossibility in principle of such a physicalist reduction, even to the point of having the non-existence of psychophysical laws as a premiss.

Finally, in 'Mental events', Davidson holds that this anomalism of the mental, the absence of laws linking mental types with mental types or physical types, is a necessary condition for free or autonomous action, thereby implying that type–type identity theories backed by psychophysical lawlike correlations entailed that there is no free or autonomous action.

---

[3] D.K. Lewis, 'An argument for the identity theory', *Journal of Philosophy*, 63 (1966), pp. 17–25, and D.M. Armstrong, *The Materialist Theory of the Mind* (Routledge & Kegan Paul, London, 1968). Smart also wanted a type–type identity theory to avoid having mental types as 'nomological danglers'.

[4] Cf. J.J.C. Smart, *Philosophy and Scientific Realism* (Routledge & Kegan Paul, London, 1963), pp. 120–30.

[5] Reprinted in his *Essays on Actions and Events* (Clarendon Press, Oxford, 1980).

Anomalous monism, Davidson's own version of physicalism, is a token–token event identity thesis. Davidson claims simply that for each particular mental event which enters into causal relations with physical events there is some physical event or other with which it is identical. Events are here understood as tokens, as particulars in the causal network, so that Davidson's physicalism is intended not to involve any identity of mental types with physical types and to be defensible in the absence of such type identities.

II

Let us now turn to Davidson's arguments for these startling claims. Before subjecting those arguments to criticism we should try to cast them in as persuasive a form as we can so that superficial objections do not obscure what is really at issue. Davidson's argument in 'Mental events' can be set out as follows:

P1.   Some mental events causally interact with physical events (the Principle of Causal Interaction).[6]

P2.   If e causes f then there is some strict law statement L and a description of e which falls under the antecedent of L and a description of f which falls under the consequent of L (the Principle of the Nomological Character of Causality).[7]

P3.   There are no strict psychophysical or psychological law statements (the Anomalism of the Mental).[8]

C1.   Every mental event which interacts with physical events has a physical description.

P4.   Any event which has a physical description is a physical event.[9]

C2.   Every mental event which interacts with physical events is a physical event.

In order to establish that every mental event which interacts with physical events has a physical description the argument proceeds by eliminating all but physical laws as the backing laws for singular causal relations. Though the general strategy is clear the argument needs shoring up at several points.

As it stands P4 allows a much more direct route to physicalist monism than Davidson's, a route which in no way relies on claims about laws or the analysis of singular causal statements. Davidson himself notes that his criterion for *mental* events, viz. an event is mental if and only if it has a mental description, counts all events as mental events. Suppose there is a purely physical predicate 'Px' true of two stellar collisions which occurred at different times. Suppose that Jones realized that π is irrational only once in his life. Then according to Davidson the description

ιx (Px & x stands in spatio-temporal relation R to Jones' realization that π is irrational)

---

[6] Ibid., p. 208.
[7] Ibid., pp. 208, 223; see also the paper 'Causal relations', in *Essays on Actions and Events*.
[8] Ibid., pp. 208, 224.
[9] Ibid., p. 211.

will be a mental description because it contains a non-redundant verb of propositional attitude. It will be a definite description of one or the other of the stellar collisions if only one of them stands in R to Jones' realization about π. As Davidson suggests[10] this indicates that there will be a mental definite description for every event given only that there is some mental event spatio-temporally connected to every event, allowing any spatio-temporal route to count as a connection no matter how tortuous. Davidson accepts and exploits the consequence that every event is mental. But he does not note that a parallel trick serves to show that every event is physical.

Suppose all events are spatio-temporally or causally connected to the Big Bang in the weak sense that there is some chain of causal and/or spatio-temporal relations leading from the Big Bang to any given event, of course not the same chain in different cases. Suppose that the big Bang has '$(\iota x)Qx$' as its physical definite description. Then, for example, Jones realizing that π is irrational, intuitively a mental event, will have a physical definite description of the form

$$(\iota y)(y \text{ stands in causal/spatio-temporal relation } R' \text{ to } (\iota x)Qx)$$

and so by P4 will be a physical event. Bizarrely, a minimal condition on the connectedness of the causal and spatio-temporal network combined with Davidson's criteria for mental and physical events suffices to guarantee not only that all events are mental but also that all events are physical.

It is the criterion for being a physical event which must be tightened up if Davidson's physicalism is to be non-trivial. There is a natural strengthening of the criterion. Davidson's argument, if it succeeded, would deliver something which the description trick could not deliver, namely the conclusion that all the mental events in question have definite descriptions which are built up simply out of a predicate occurring in the antecedent or consequent of some strict physical law plus space–time co-ordinates to secure uniqueness. No mention of an origin event or tortuous causal and spatio-temporal relations figures in such descriptions. Let us call such relatively simple physical descriptions *lawful* physical descriptions. The argument from P1–P3 if it worked would show that all the mental events in question have lawful physical descriptions. And this is not trivial. Indeed, if the only lawful descriptions which mental events have are lawful physical descriptions then there is some point in going on to say that mental events just *are* physical events.

But does P3, the claim that there are no psychophysical or psychological laws, along with P1 and P2 yield the conclusion that all mental events which enter into causal relations have (lawful) physical descriptions? It does not and this will be important later on. The argument goes through only if we can eliminate the possibility that there are non-physical lawful descriptions of events. We need a stronger premiss than P3 to do that. For imagine there is some other sort of strict law besides physical law, say pure laws of the ectoplasm or laws relating states of the ectoplasm to physical states. Then it could be that some true psychological or psychophysical singular causal statements are not backed by

---

10 Ibid., p. 211.

physical law but by laws of ectoplasm. So there need be no physical redescriptions of the mental events figuring in such singular causal relations, but only redescriptions employing predicates figuring in the laws of ectoplasm. In fact, when Davidson gives his argument,[11] he assumes that P3 (or more exactly a statement about explanation and prediction which is for him equivalent to P3) is really the stronger principle that there are no strict laws except physical laws. Evidently this stronger principle is what is required. We shall have to investigate whether there is any good argument for this stronger principle and whether there is any plausible candidate for a third sort of law statement including neither physical nor intensional mental terms, a sort of law statement that would do the work of our fanciful laws of ectoplasm (see Section V).

We are now in a position to see that Davidson has understated the generality of his own argument and in several ways. Premiss 1, that some mental events interact causally with physical events, is in one way stronger than is required and in another way weaker than is plausible. Premiss 1 as it stands would be denied by a psychophysical parallelist, so that it seems that Davidson has nothing to say against such a position. But this is not so. Given that Davidson needs to rely on the premiss that the only strict laws are physical laws he could begin with the weaker claim that mental events have causes and effects. It would then follow that all the mental events in question have (lawful) physical descriptions and so are physical events. Parallelism is ruled out by such an argument.

How wide a class of mental events have causes and effects? I think that Davidson's views on event individuation should lead him to say that all mental events have causes and effects. In the paper 'The individuation of events' Davidson maintains that event x is event y just in case x and y have the same causes and effects.[12] There is some confusion about the intent of this statement. Some have taken it as a criterion for determining which event identities hold and have complained that as such it is hopelessly circular.[13] As I understand it this is not what was intended. What could have been quite reasonably intended was the statement of a non-trivial indiscernibility condition for events. A trivial indiscernibility condition would be: event x = event y just in case they have all their properties in common (in the broadest sense of properties). Davidson's indiscernibility condition is non-trivial in that it states that there is no difference between events without a causal difference between them. And this gives a feel for Davidson's view of what events are. They are just items in the causal network. On such a conception of events there is no point in counting more than one event at a node of the causal network.

Davidson's criterion of event identity tells us that there could not be more than one event which does not have causes and effects. If I'm right about the

---

[11] Ibid., p. 224.

[12] In *Essays on Actions and Events*. Barry Taylor explores ways round these arguments in 'States of affairs', in *Truth and Meaning*, ed. G. Evans and J. MacDowell (Oxford University Press, Oxford, 1976). See also J. Perry and J. Barwise, *Situations and Attitudes* (M.I.T. Press, Cambridge, Mass., 1983), pp. 23–6.

[13] See for example, J. Tiles, 'Davidson's criterion of event identity', *Analysis*, 36 (1976), pp. 185–7.

conception of events which motivates the criterion, then, for Davidson, there will be no events which do not have causes and effects. Those gerrymandered sums of events which are too big to cause or be caused by anything will not deserve the name of events. So I think that Davidson should start out with the claim that every mental event has causes or effects, a claim which follows from what he takes to be the right conception of events.

Notice that this conception of events could not plausibly be claimed to be discovered a posteriori or to be contingently true. In any case, the contingency and a posterioricity of *physicalism* is not creeping in here. Though he may not be inclined to put it this way, on Davidson's view it seems relatively necessary and a priori that having a mind matters, i.e. consists in material goings-on.

III

We are left with the following strengthened and more general version of Davidson's argument.

P1′ All *mental* events have causes and effects.
P2   If e causes f then there is some strict law statement L and a description of e which falls under the antecedent of L and a description of f which falls under the consequent of L.
P3   The only strict law statements are statements of physical law.
C1′ Every *mental* event has a lawful physical description, i.e. a description which falls under the antecedent or the consequent of some strict physical law.
P4′ Any event which has a lawful physical description is a physical event.
C2′ Every *mental* event is a physical event.

Notice that if this argument is a good one there is an argument to a more general conclusion that is equally good. Premiss 1′ was defended on the grounds that anything that deserves the name of 'event' has causes or effects, so that instead of P1′ we could begin with the more general claim that every event has causes and effects. We could then simply cross out all occurrences of the term 'mental' in the argument and arrive at the general conclusion that all events are physical. In this way we vindicate Davidson's initially surprising claim that his implausible criterion for mental events, a criterion which counts all events mental, does not vitiate his argument for physicalist monism.[14] The argument is not essentially concerned with mental events as such. It applies directly to all events.

One might still have a residual and somewhat sophisticated worry about Davidson's criterion of the mental. Is Davidson in a position to believe that there are any mental events? Of course his action theory which appeals to mental causes in the characterization of intentional action would come apart if there were no mental events.[15] But one might think that this is just what does

---

[14] 'Mental events', p. 212.
[15] The central claim of 'Actions, reasons, and causes' in Davidson, *Essays on Actions and Events*, is that every intentional action is caused by a belief–desire complex which rationalizes it.

happen if there is not in principle a way of picking out mental events by means of *intrinsic* mental descriptions, i.e. mental descriptions whose mental predicates are associated with *non-relational* features of the events in question. As we now know very well from Twin Earth examples and the like, an event of state does not typically qualify as a particular propositional attitude in virtue of its intrinsic or non-relational features, for two events or states can be duplicates even though the one is an attitude to a particular proposition P and the other is not an attitude to that proposition. So if the best one can do is to demarcate the mental events as those satisfying descriptions built up (without tricks) from propositional attitude verbs, one has good reason to suppose that there are no intrinsic mental similarities between events. Otherwise why not employ these intrinsic mental features or the corresponding predicates in the criterion for mental events? If there are no intrinsic mental features in virtue of which mental events are similar then why suppose that there are mental events in any important sense?

This is a question to which we will return, but first I want to point to further extensions of Davidson's argument, extensions which if pursued dispel the widely held belief that Davidson's position is really a very modest form of physicalist monism – as he says himself 'a bland monism ... not apt to inspire the nothing but reflex ("Conceiving the Art of the Fugue was nothing but a complex neural event" and so forth).'[16] The argument that generates anomalous monism can be extended to generate an exhaustive monism, according to which all facts are physical facts, i.e. consist in physical things having physical properties. To show this we must go beyond Davidson's actual dicta and explore what it is plausible to go on to believe given what he believes.

Someone might think that for all Davidson's argument has shown there could be mental states not identical with physical states and mental properties or types in some sense unreduced. Moreover one might suppose that propositional attitudes, such as believing that π is irrational and wishing it were not, are not events but states. Coming to have such attitudes might be events in that they are changes or alterations but the attitudes themselves do not seem to essentially involve changes.

This worry can be met by pointing out that Davidson's claims that (i) events must be recognized if one is to have an adequate account of singular causal statements and adverbial modification and (ii) events are particular items in the causal network, apply *mutatis mutandis* to states. (*Caveat*: states are not states of affairs, i.e. triples of n-types of particulars, n-adic properties and times; states come into being and pass away, they are destructible and locatable in space and time and they enter directly into causal relations; states of affairs either obtain or do not, those that obtain are facts, facts are not destructible or naturally locatable in space and time. No set and so no fact enters directly into causal relations.)

Just as an event such as a particular explosion might be located as the cause or partial cause of one bridge collapse, another bridge collapse might have as its cause the weakness of one of the bridge's cables. I have little sympathy with the line that treats such a state of the bridge as the weakness of one of its cables as a

---

[16] 'Mental events', p. 214.

very slow event, one with zero change associated with it. But behind this way of talking is a sense that events and states are in some broad sense the same sort of things. This seems right: states like events are items in the causal network, different only if they have different causes or effects.

Furthermore, if there is anything in the Davidson-style argument that you need to recognize *events* in order to exhibit the step from:

> John jogged quickly yesterday

to:

> John jogged yesterday

as an entailment holding in virtue of the logical form of these sentences, then you had better recognize *states* in order to so exhibit the step from:

> John was intensely sad yesterday.

to:

> John was sad yesterday.[17]

The argument of 'Causal relations', that true singular causal statements about events are backed by strict laws in the sense that there are redescriptions of the cause event in terms of the vocabulary of the antecedent of the law and of the effect event in terms of the vocabulary of the law's consequent, ought also to apply to event–state, state–event and state–state singular causal relations. Indeed if there are other sorts of items in the causal network, say full-blooded particulars such as agents or more generally living things, the broadly Humean account of the relation between singular causal statements and lawful regularities ought also to apply to singular causal statements about such full-blooded particulars. (Hence my original statement of P2, neutral as between events, states and full-blooded particulars.) These full-blooded particulars or substances will also be items in the causal network. It will be very plausible to claim that they all have causes and effects. So they, along with states and events, will be shown to be physical by a simple extension of Davidson's argument. Thus we arrive at the view that every particular in the causal network is a physical particular, be it an event, state or substance. This is already a physicalism that is wide in its scope.

What about mental properties or characteristics – mental types? Davidson says they are supervenient on physical properties,[18] but he does not advance any view of what properties are. To get a feel for the situation we have to settle on one or another conception of properties, either taking them as primitive or constructing them as classes of particulars. Taking properties as primitive

---

[17] See 'The logical form of action sentences', 'Events as particulars' and 'Eternal vs. ephemeral events' in *Essays on Actions and Events*.
[18] 'Mental events', p. 214.

seems against the spirit of Davidson's extensional, first-order semantical commitments. Instead it is natural to suppose that Davidson would follow Quine who argues that properties ought to be recognized as the semantic values of abstract singular terms and that they must be given clear conditions of identity, so that much is to be said for identifying properties with classes of particulars.[19] If we do that, then since all particulars, be they events, states or substances, have been shown to be physical particulars there seems to be little point in supposing that there are any unreduced mental properties. Instead it seems that all properties are physical properties.

Something rather striking emerges. The obvious extension of Davidson's argument for events, states and full-blooded particulars will generate the intermediate conclusion that any particular will have a lawful, physical, definite description. But then it follows that for any mental predicate there will be a 'long and unilluminating alternation' of physical predicates drawn from such definite descriptions such that the mental predicate and the complex disjunctive physical predicate have just the same extension. That is, if 'Mx' is a mental predicate then it will have the same extension as some disjunction 'P_1 (x) v P_2 (x) v ...' where all the predicates in the disjunction are physical predicates. If we are restricting ourselves to extensional semantics where the only semantic values for predicates are extensions then it is hard not to regard this as showing the *definability* of any mental predicate in physical terms. Mental property designators can be similarly defined in purely physical terms, e.g.

$$\hat{x}\,(Mx) = \{y{:}y = (\iota z)P_1\,(z)\;v\;y = (\iota z)P_2\,(z)\;v\;...\,\}$$

If properties are just those semantic values that are the denotata of abstract singular terms and we are extensionalists when it comes to semantic values then the mental property $\hat{x}\,(Mx)$ is just a physical property, a class of physical particulars. (The extension to non-monadic mental properties is obvious.)

By natural extensions of Davidson's argument all events, states, substances and properties are physical. What about facts? In 'Causal relations' Davidson employs a version of the so-called Frege argument against the view that facts are the relata of causal relations.[20] In 'Truth and meaning' he uses a similar argument to support the view that facts or more generally states of affairs cannot be the denotata of sentences, unless there are only two states of affairs, the one that obtains, The Fact or The True, and the one that does not.[21] I find these arguments very dubious. Strictly speaking, they do not affect the related question of whether there are facts. As already indicated I think that triples of properties, times and n-tuples of particulars deserve the name of states of affairs. A state of affairs such that its constitutive property is had by its constitutive particular(s) at its constitutive time *obtains* or is a fact. If all

---

[19] Quine reiterates this view in 'Soft impeachment disowned', *Pacific Philosophical Quarterly*, 61 (1980), pp. 450–1. In my doctoral thesis, *Particulars and Persistence* Princeton, 1984, I offer a construction of properties from particulars which is not open to the usual objections made to Quine's view of properties. Adopting that conception would not affect the upshot of the text. It is a conception which would appeal only to those who are used to the strong meat of modality.

[20] See Davidson, *Essays on Actions and Events, op cit.*, pp. 152–3.

[21] 'Truth and meaning', *Synthese*, 17 (1967), pp. 304–23. See n. 12 above.

particulars are physical particulars and all properties are physical properties then all the facts, including mental facts, are physical facts.

Thus anomalous monism is just a halfway house on the road to a very strong form of physicalism indeed. We might call this strong form of physicalism *exhaustive monism*, the view that the physical facts exhaust all the facts. I think that such a position *is* apt to inspire the 'nothing-but' reflex. Certainly to my taste it is a piquant rather than a bland monism.

Exhaustive monism is a natural extension of anomalous monism. In fact it explains away a problem some have raised for anomalous monism. If anomalous monism is really a physicalist monism it had better imply that the mental features of the world are determined by and so do not vary independently of the physical features. The core doctrine behind all forms of materialism or physicalism is that the mental, if there is such a thing, is so determined. In the familiar jargon, the mental supervenes on the physical.[22] But once a broadly physicalist perspective is adopted more local supervenience claims become plausible. For example, if someone is in exactly the same physical states as I am in now then it cannot be that I am now in a certain raw feel state, say pain, and he is not in such a state at the time at which his physical states are exactly like mine now. Such a conditional can be recast as a universal quantification which supports counterfactuals and is projectible to future physical duplicates of me now. Is it not then a psychophysical law which could back some singular statements about causal relations between my present physical events or states and my present mental events or states? Does this not therefore undermine the very argument Davidson offers for anomalous monism[23] breaking it at the point where it is held that only physical laws are available to back singular causal statements?

If one adopts exhaustive monism one can explain the truth of both global and local supervenience conditionals without threatening the argument for anomalous monism. Since all particulars, all properties and all facts are physical, it is no surprise that the physical features of the world determine the mental features. The mental features are just physical features on this view. Similarly it should be no surprise that some particular's having certain mental properties at a time is determined by its having certain physical properties at that time. This will happen whenever the union of the mental properties is a sub-class of the union of the physical properties. In such a case, talking about the mental properties of a thing will be a shorthand way of talking about clusters of the thing's physical properties. All this can be said while plausibly maintaining that the 'definitions' of mental property designators and mental predicates in particularized physical terms do not generate psychophysical laws. Exhaustive monism implies and thereby explains supervenience whereas mere anomalous monism, being restricted to events, is silent on properties and facts and leaves us with a puzzle about the status of local supervenience conditionals.

---

[22] On supervenience see J. Kim, 'Psychophysical supervenience', *Philosophical Studies*, 41 (1982), pp. 51–70. Davidson avows the supervenience of the mental on the physical in 'The material mind', in *Essays on Actions and Events*, pp. 253ff.

[23] W. Stanton discusses this objection in 'Supervenience and psychological law in anomalous monism', *Pacific Philosophical Quarterly*, 64 (1983), pp. 72–9. It also occurs in an unpublished paper on supervenience by Harry Lewis.

IV

I do not say that exhaustive monism is plausible, just that if you accept Davidson's argument for anomalous monism and do not go on to accept exhaustive monism you are left at an unattractive halfway house.

Exhaustive monism is certainly a type–type identity theory – mental types or properties *are* just physical properties on that view. So for what it's worth, Australian materialism is at least vindicated vis-à-vis anomalous monism on that count.

Now exhaustive monism rests on the claim that events, states and substances (if there are any) have causes or effects, on P2, the claim that singular causal relations are backed by laws, on P3′ the claim that the only strict laws are physical laws and on the generalized criterion of the physical. P2 and P3′, as treated by Davidson, seem relatively a priori and non-contingent. We saw that the claim that events, states or substances enter into causal relations is a priori and non-contingent, depending as it does on a conception of these things as items in the causal network. The generalized criterion of the physical is also not contingent and not a posteriori. Thus exhaustive monism, like anomalous monism, is neither contingent nor a posteriori, at least if we take Davidson's attitude to the question of psychophysical laws. So we still have a striking clash with the older physicalist theory.

Exhaustive monism, despite its identification of mental properties with physical properties, does not imply that there are psychophysical or purely psychological laws. None of the physical properties which are the mental properties need figure in any law. Indeed, if Davidson's argument for anomalous monism and the extension of it to support exhaustive monism are sound then in fact none of the physical properties which are the mental properties will figure in any law. Exhaustive monism will then preserve the anomalism of the mental. This is another difference with the advocates of the older theory. By and large they assumed lawlike correlations between the mental and the physical.

Someone might therefore think that in one sense exhaustive monism is still a comparatively modest form of monism since it preserves the anomalism of the mental, keeping the mental beyond the reach of explanation and prediction in terms of strict law. On such a view the strength of a physicalist monism is to be measured not by its scope but by its impact on our conception of ourselves as free agents. Exhaustive monism will then be a weaker form of monism than the older physicalist theories just in case the anomalism of the mental is *required* to minimize the impact of physicalism on our conception of ourselves as free agents. Let us examine that idea.

The very important status which Davidson gives to the anomalism of the mental has not been widely remarked upon. This is surprising since Davidson is in effect claiming that there is a certain usually unnoticed condition for free action, a condition which many disputants on both sides of the compatibilist/ incompatibilist debate had tacitly assumed was not satisfied. (Exceptions are mentioned below.) Davidson says, 'The anomalism of the mental is thus a necessary condition for viewing action as autonomous.'[24] And it is clear from

---

[24] 'Mental events', p. 225.

the context and earlier remarks in which he offers 'freedom' as a synonym for 'autonomy'[25] that he means that the anomalism of the mental is a necessary condition for free action. P.F. Strawson also put forward this condition in a discussion in 1963 with Geoffrey Warnock and James Thomson, a discussion recorded in David Pears' *Freedom of the Will*.[26] The Davidson-Strawson condition depends upon a restrictive view of explanation.

Whereas I have expressed the anomalism of the mental as the claim that there are no psychophysical or purely psychological law statements, Davidson expresses it as the claim that there are no strict law statements on the basis of which mental events can be predicted and explained. The two formulations are equivalent given Davidson's view about explanation and prediction. On that view to predict or explain a mental event on the basis of law is to offer a deductive nomological argument terminating in a statement asserting the existence of that event and describing that event in mental terms. The idea is supposed to be that, e.g., even though there is a deductive nomological argument constituting an explanation of my arm's moving a certain way and even though my arm's moving a certain way is identical with my raising my arm, there is nonetheless no deductive nomological explanation of my raising my arm. Such identities, even when they are known, are excluded from figuring as premisses in the deductive nomological argument (Hereafter DN argument).

I doubt that there is any non-ad-hoc way of stating this constraint and corresponding constraints on the derived laws figuring in the DN argument which will allow DN explanations of things like the flash of lightning which hit 1879 Hall last year while not allowing DN explanations of events such as my raising my arm and my deciding to raise my arm. But suppose we draw the line so that all admissible DN arguments terminated in statements cast in non-mental vocabulary because only non-mental vocabulary figured in the laws and the auxiliary premises. We would then have *some* sense in which mental events could not be 'explained' or 'predicted'. But what is the interest of this way of drawing the line vis-à-vis the question of whether anyone ever acts freely?

Suppose we introduce the notion of q-explanation, where we can for example turn an explanation in Davidson's sense of my arm's going up at x,y,z,t into a q-explanation of my raising my arm at x,y,z,t by adding to the original argument the identity statement:

The thing which is an arm going up at x,y,z,t = the thing which is an arm raising at x,y,z,t

and making the obvious substitution. If the token identity theory is true every mental event and so every action can be q-explained. Isn't the claim that mental events can be *q-explained* the claim that is relevant to the autonomy of our mental lives, not the claim that mental events can't be explained in Davidson's sense? If there are no mental law statements and mental events cannot be explained, in Davidson's sense all that follows is that mental events are not

---

[25] Ibid., p. 207.
[26] *Freedom of the Will*, ed. D. Pears (Routledge & Kegan Paul, London, 1963), pp. 61–7.

susceptible to explanations of a certain syntactic form. But how can that be crucial to the autonomy of our mental lives?

Surely the putative fact that mental events can't be explained in Davidson's restrictive sense is just a matter of the vocabulary we use to describe events, not at all a matter of the extent to which those events are under our control. To see this suppose that a particular eclipse of the sun was the most exciting event Galileo ever witnessed. Given Davidson's sense of a DN explanation there will be no DN explanation terminating with the sentence 'The most exciting event Galileo ever witnessed took place.' But all we have here is an event described in vocabulary unsuited to figure in statements of law. The event is clearly explicable, we simply have to shift to a description of the event in suitable vocabulary. Since one way of doing this is to offer a q-explanation, I submit that a q-explanation can be an explanation on any reasonable construal of that notion. For mental events to be really anomalous they would have to be q-inexplicable, which would contradict Davidson's token identity theory. An anomalous monist might rightly insist that it is only in principle that all mental events are q-explicable. The derivations from true premises exist but we will never recognize many of them as such since we will never be in a position to cite the needed identities for the q-explanations of hosts of mental events. True, but irrelevant to the issue of freedom, unless one is prepared to take the view that it is our ignorance of particular identities which saves our freedom in those cases.

Davidson insists, 'the principle of the anomalism of the mental concerns events described as mental *for events are mental only as described.*'[27] This remark, offered by Davidson as the way out of the contradiction among the token identity theory, the explicability of all physical events and the alleged anomalism or inexplicability of mental events is extremely puzzling. As against the claim that events are mental only as described one would have thought that the context 'x is a mental event' was a paradigm of an extensional context so that three statements of the form:

> The M is a mental event
> The P is not a mental event
> The M = The P

constituted an inconsistent triad. Do we have any more reason to suppose that 'x is a mental event' is an intensional context than we have to suppose that 'x is a non-mental, i.e. physical, event' is? If they are both non-extensional contexts then it is just not true that every mental event is a physical event. At most what is true is a certain linguistic fact, namely that every event with some mental description has some (lawful) physical description. One cannot recover the non-linguistic fact expressed by the identity thesis by going on to say that to be a mental event is just to have some mental description and to be a physical event is just to have some (lawful) physical description. For these claims imply that the contexts 'x is a mental event' and 'x is a physical event' are, after all, extensional contexts.

---

[27] 'Mental events', p. 215. My emphasis.

If this is not bad enough, suppose that there is some sufficient condition for being a mental event (or state); for example, it seems true on any intuitive criterion of the mental that:

If x feels exactly like pain then x is a mental event (or state).

The predicate expressing the sufficient condition *viz.* 'x feels exactly like pain' is intensional if the predicate 'x is a mental event (or state)' is intensional. Otherwise some painful events or states described in physical terms would satisfy the first predicate and not the second, thereby falsifying the conditional. But if 'x is a mental event (or state)' is intensional being satisfied by events only when they are described in mental terms, then no physical identificand for a pain event can feel exactly like pain. Take a particular firing of C-fibres for example. It will not be a mental event so it will not feel exactly like pain. Why? Because it is simply described in the wrong terms. This is decidedly odd. Are we supposed to be able to cure migraines by uttering in a mantra-like fashion 'a firing of C-fibres'? Surely a pain by any other name would feel as bad.

What these oddities suggest is that Davidson has just run together his official criterion 'an event is mental if and only if it has a mental description'[28] with the idea of an event being mental only when or if described in mental terms; as if mentality could be an intermittent or radically contingent feature of an event.

Only when these are run together is it plausible to think that there is much significance in the point that no valid DN argument without mental vocabulary in its premises could terminate in a statement containing a mental definite description. Only if being describ*ed* in mental terms is taken to be the criterion for mental events is it natural to report this feature of DN arguments as amounting to the inexplicability or unpredictability of mental events on the basis of strict laws. For suppose we treat 'x is a mental event' as an extensional context as Davidson's *official* criterion of the mental implies. It will then be very plausible to say that if the φ is explicable on the basis of strict law, where 'the φ' is some physical description of an event, and the φ is a mental event, then some mental event, i.e. the φ, is explicable on the basis of strict law. Given the token-identity thesis, what we've just said for the φ holds for each mental event.

So the anomalism of the mental as formulated by Davidson is just a linguistic feature of certain patterns of explanation which has nothing to do with free action or with any putative threat to freedom stemming from the availability in principle of a complete characterization of the causal network in physical terms. I suggest that we take the claims about the non-existence of psychophysical and purely psychological laws seriously and jettison the related claim about the alleged incompatibility between the existence of such laws and free action.

We thus have no reason to think that exhaustive monism is relevantly weaker than Australian materialism or that the Australian materialists should have denied there is free action just in virtue of believing in lawlike correlations between the mental and the physical. The question I want to pursue is whether Davidson's denial that there are psychological or psychophysical laws, or more

---

[28] Ibid., p. 211.

exactly what is at the back of that denial, implies a view at least as extreme as the denial of freedom. This is the view that having a mind doesn't really matter in the sense that no mental property is a causally relevant feature of any event or state.

V

It may help to consider two pictures of the mind in order to get clear on what is at issue in the dispute over psychophysical laws. On either view a mind is a unified causal basis of intelligent behavior.

Here is a naive view of the mind and of mental states. A mind is either a substance in various mental states and subject to various alterations in those states or a congeries of mental states and events. Either way, what is important is that the mental states in question are *intrinsic* mental states, i.e. they do not involve or include relations to non-mental items, though they may of course be among the terms of such relations. Various minds can be in the same type of mental state. When this is so those minds will share *some* propensity to instantiate certain other types of mental states and certain types of behavior. Of course these shared propensities and hence the causal relevance of being in mental states of the same type are obscured by the fact that the effects within a mind of a particular mental state of a given type will depend on the other mental states which that mind is in. But in the limiting case in which two minds are in mental states of just the same types, are, as we might say, duplicates in all (intrinsic) mental respects, they have just the same causal propensities. The types of intrinsic mental states which a mind instantiates determine the causal propensities of that mind.

On this view of the mind a scientific theory of mind has as one of its goals the classification of the various types of (intrinsic) mental states. If you like, it has to discover the *natural* mental properties, those that need to be cited in a complete inventory of the types of causally relevant features that there are in the world.[29] Its other main goal is charting the characteristic types of causes and effects of such natural mental properties, including types of sensory causes and behavioral effects, in short, to look for psychological and psychophysical laws.

One of the conceptual difficulties facing such a program is that apart from the vocabulary for raw feels we lack in ordinary language any very rich mental vocabulary for characterizing the intrinsic features of the mind. Reports of a subject's propositional attitudes are janus-faced, partly pointing inward towards intrinsic mental states of the subject which are crucial in causally explaining his behavior and partly pointing outward to supposed or desired conditions in the world, the propositions or states of affairs which 'that'-clauses introduce. Such reports are not characterizations of intrinsic states of the reportee's mind, but claims about relations between the reportee and propositions, relations which

---

[29] For more on the distinction between natural properties and semantic values for abstract singular terms, see D.K. Lewis, 'New work for a theory of universals', *Australasian Journal of Philosophy*, 61 (1983), pp. 343–77.

are not determined solely by the intrinsic mental states which he is in (*vide* Twin Earth examples and what some have said about brains in vats). So we must look to an empirical science of the mind for a vocabulary well suited to carving out the natural mental properties. We can no more rely on the vocabulary of the propositional attitudes in doing psychology than we can rely on layman's terminology when doing microphysics.

However, anything that deserves to be regarded as a science of mind will talk about things amounting to entertaining a thought or going through a process of inference, that is, entertaining and manipulating *contents*. Despite the difficulties with the attitudes, a science of mind can accommodate this so long as it characterizes thought-processes in terms of contents which are wholly determined by intrinsic states of the thinker's mind. In Putnam's useful terminology a science of the mind must make sense of and explore the typical causal relations between *narrow* contents (the contents of the attitudes being *wide* in that they are determined in part by states of the world).[30] Hence the talk in psychology and beyond of mental representations, though (I hope) the representationalist idiom is strictly inessential to the idea of contents wholly determined by intrinsic states of mind.

The naive view of the mind developed in this way seems to its advocates a live and largely empirical research program sometimes going on under the head of cognitive psychology. Those type–type materialists who adopt the naive view hope that as psychology carves out the natural types of mental states, neurophysiology will turn up types of physical states which could plausibly be taken to be the mental types. If this turns out to be the situation, e.g. if so-called 'multiple realizability' turns out to be largely appearance rather than reality, say because the physical identificands for the mental types are higher-order physical structural states which can be constituted by states of protoplasm or silicon chips or whatever, then we have an empirical defence of a type–type identity theory.[31]

Contrast this view of the mind and of physicalism with the view which Davidson's argument for anomalous monism motivates and which I take to be the required assumption for Davidson's arguments against psychophysical laws. According to anomalous monism if there are mental properties or types none of them figure in laws. (In the formal mode, no mental predicates figure in any statement of law.) That is, no mental property need be cited in order to account for any truth about singular causal relations between events or states, even if those events or states are intuitively mental events or states. All such truths can be accounted for via appeal to law statements with only physical predicates in them; in the material mode, laws which relate only physical properties. There is then a clear sense in which, according to anomalous monism, no mental properties are causally relevant. In our earlier terminology there are no natural

---

[30] See H. Putnam, 'The meaning of "meaning"' in *Minnesota Studies in the Philosophy of Science*, vol. 7, ed. K. Gunderson (U. of Minnesota Press, 1975).

[31] For a related way of holding to type–type identities in the face of multiple realizability see E. Prior, R. Pargetter and F. Jackson, 'Functionalism and type–type identity theories', *Philosophical Studies*, 42 (1983), pp. 209–22.

mental properties. At most mental properties are just semantic values for abstract singular terms built up from mental predicates (e.g. 'wisdom' from 'is wise'). For suppose instead that mental properties were such that their being instantiated by an event or state was sometimes sufficient to account for the event or state entering into a particular causal relation. Then Davidson's argument by elimination for anomalous monism would break down. Backing physical laws would not in general be required so that we would have no guarantee that every mental event has a lawful physical description. Davidson's intermediate and a priori conclusion that singular causal statements are backed only by purely physical laws implies that in order to account for an event or state entering into a particular causal relation we need only invoke the physical features of that event or state. It follows that it is knowable a priori that the mental properties of an event or state make no difference to the causal relations it enters into. Barring a pre-established harmony of physical overdetermination which allows mental properties to be causally relevant without making any difference to the particular causal relations events and states enter into, mental properties are not causally relevant features of events or states, even if those events or states are mental. Having a mind does not matter causally.

On such a view the attempt to characterize the causally relevant intrinsic states of the mind is idle. We might put what is behind such an anti-psychologistic view of the mind as follows. In ordinary life we interpret each other's behavior, i.e. construe each other's bodily movements, some of them at least, as actions, and attribute to each other batteries of propositional attitudes which make sense of those actions. Idealizing, we may be seen as developing *interpretive theories* of each other, where an interpretive theory is a consistent and relatively complete set of attitude and action attributions developed under the general guiding principle of making sense of the subject of the theory. Unlike the psychologist we do not hypothesize about the hidden mental springs of behavior, we try to rationalize and so see the point of that behavior. What it is for some event or state to be a mental event or state is not for it to instantiate some intrinsic mental property in virtue of which it has a certain pattern of effects. Instead all that matters is that the event or state in question satisfy some propositional attitude attribution made within an adequate interpretive theory. And it will do that if it stands in a complex enough web of causal relations to stimulus events and behavioral events which satisfy other attributions made within the interpretive theory. As we have noted, according to anomalous monism, an event's or state's standing in any such causal relation is not due to its having any intrinsic mental property. For as the anomalism of the mental and Davidson's analysis of singular causal statements together imply, no mental property need be invoked to account for such singular causal relations.

Such *an interpretive view* of mental events and states takes the propositional attitudes as constitutive of the mental. As Davidson says, to be a mental event is just to satisfy a propositional attitude predicate. On the interpretive view talking of natural mental properties of mental events, mental properties which could figure in laws which back singular causation involving mental events, mental properties which our interpretive practice does not make readily accessible to us, all of this, as Davidson says,[32] is just so much changing the subject, i.e. ceasing to really talk about the mental. Surely this is right if what makes something a mental event of state is not its intrinsic features but rather the fact that it stands in a complex causal web having at its fringes sensory and behavioral events, a causal web upon which an interpretive theory can be slapped.

I think it is evident that Davidson needs to appeal to such an interpretive view of mental states and events if there is to be anything to his arguments against psychophysical laws. His dense reflections on this matter[33] turn on the claim that the 'disparate commitments' of interpretation and physical theory mean that there cannot be psychophysical laws. Unless the interpretive view is assumed, it is open to an objector to insist that interpretation is beside the point when it comes to the question of psychophysical laws. The very facts which Davidson emphasizes in his argument against psychophysical laws, for example that interpretation is only globally constrained by a principle of overall charity and that it involves making a web of attributions of attitude none of which considered singly or even in relative isolation has any predictable physical consequence, could just be taken as showing that the vocabulary of propositional attitudes is not made to carve out the natural mental properties which stand in lawlike relations to physical properties. It seems to me that this naive response is the natural one to make here – we must look to an inventive psychology for the vocabulary for the relevant laws.

Behind this response and the naive view which prompts it lies a fundamental intuition about the difference having a mind makes. In so far as we believe such things as that it is the awfulness of pain which *makes* us want it to stop, that it is the *(narrow)* content of our belief that aspirin will help that *leads* us to reach for the aspirin and so on for other qualia and attitudes, we thereby believe that there are natural or causally relevant mental properties. These natural mental properties will generate non-accidental causal generalizations. Though someone might withhold the title of 'strict law' from such generalizations on the grounds that they are not strictly exceptionless and unqualified, I see no reason to suppose that such non-accidental causal generalizations cannot back singular causal statements in accord with the broadly Humean requirement of same cause/same effect. Why must such psychological and psychophysical generalizations be exceptionless and unqualified to back singular causal statements? Surely the non-accidental physical generalizations suited to back ordinary singular causal statements such as 'The dripping of the water into the cold cave caused the stalactite to form.' will not be exceptionless and unqualified either. I conclude that if the naive view is true we will have non-accidental psychological and psychophysical generalizations suited to play the role of our fanciful laws of ectoplasm. They will back singular causal relations between the mental and the physical leaving us without any Davidson-style argument to the conclusion that every cause and effect has a lawful physical description.

---

[32] 'Mental events', p. 216.
[33] Ibid., pp. 216–23.

Thus Davidson's argument for anomalous monism is only as strong as his argument against the naive view. But no such argument is given and this is no surprise if I'm right in maintaining that to abandon the naive view is to abandon the idea that having a mind matters, the idea that much of what we think and do is due to our mental characteristics. Instead of considering the naive view, Davidson adopts the interpretive view as if it were a conceptual truth, something which could not turn out to be false. Hence the surprising result that just on the basis of investigation of the disparate concepts and constraints of physical theory and interpretation we can see that there cannot be psychophysical laws.

By my lights this strategy is mistaken. The interpretive view stands opposed to the naive view, it cannot be true unless the naive view is false. But the naive view is wedded to an empirical program in psychology, whether that program fails or not is an a posteriori matter. For it is an a posteriori matter whether in investigating the causal basis of intelligent behavior we need to recognize causally relevant mental properties. And I take it that ordinary intuition has it that we do in fact have to recognize causally relevant mental properties.

Partly for the fun of it I have organized this paper around a comparison between Australian materialism and anomalous monism. Australian materialism held that physicalism was a true, contingent, a posteriori and, if plausible, type–type identity thesis that did not imply that there are no free or autonomous actions. Part of the fascination for me of Davidson's novel argument in 'Mental events' was that it implied that Australian materialism was wrong on the last four of these five counts. But I suspect now, as I did before struggling with Davidson's stimulating paper, that Australian materialism was wrong only on the first count, the count of truth. If having a mind matters in the sense that mental properties are causally relevant then it seems to me unlikely that having a mind consists merely in exhibiting material states and events. The prima facie support which the naive view gives to emergentism, the view that the natural mental properties which animals exhibit are different in kind from anything found in the insensate world, has yet to be countered.

26

Against the Token Identity Theory

Terence Horgan and Michael Tye

1.   Donald Davidson advocates the thesis that every concrete mental event or state is identical to some concrete neurological event or state. He denies, however, that there are systematic bridge laws connecting mental event-types, or properties, with neurological event-types. He calls this view *anomalous monism*; it is a kind of monism because it posits psycho-physical identities, and it is 'anomalous' because it does not posit reductive bridge laws or reductive type–type identities.[1]

Our primary concern in this paper is to argue against the first component of anomalous monism, viz., the token identity theory. But we shall briefly sketch the alternative theory of mind we advocate: ours is a physicalistic theory which differs not only from Davidson's token identity theory but also from theories such as the eliminative materialism of Rorty and Churchland, Dennett's instrumentalism toward mental language, and Kim's view that mental events are non-physical entities whose causal efficacy is supervenient upon underlying neurological causes.

2.   In accordance with frequent recent practice, we shall use the rubric 'event' in a broad sense to include not merely changes but also states, processes, and the like. Events, as we shall here construe them, are concrete entities, or tokens. If we mean to speak of the types of which events are tokens, we shall explicitly use the term 'event-type'. (Occasionally we shall use the term 'event/state' rather than 'event', in order to emphasize that the entities we are speaking of can have longer-than-momentary duration, and that these entities can be (or have parts which are) relatively static during their duration.)

Ultimately we shall deny that mental events exist. But if they do exist, then for any creature C who has mentality, there is a non-empty set M(C) containing all and only the mental events of which C, at one time or another during his

---

[1] See Donald Davidson, 'Mental events,' in *Experience and Theory*, ed. L. Foster and J. Swanson (Duckworth, London, 1970); also 'The material mind,' in *Logic, Methodology and the Philosophy of Science*, vol. 4, ed. P. Suppes, L. Henkin, A. Joja, and G. Moisil (North-Holland, Amsterdam, 1973) (both essays reprinted in D. Davidson, *Essays on Actions and Events* (Clarendon Press, Oxford, 1980)).

lifetime, is the subject: we shall call this C's *mentality set*. We shall take the contents of M(C) to include not only events of the kind that are apparently posited by common-sense psychology ('folk psychology'), but also mental events of any additional kinds that would be posited by an ideal theoretical psychology. (This assumes, of course, that theoretical psychology *would* posit mental events; again, ultimately we shall reject that assumption.)

For any creature C with a non-empty mentality set M(C), we shall say that a set of events $P(C)_i$ is a *physical causal isomorph* of M(C) (for short, a PCI) iff (1) every member of $P(C)_i$ is a physico-chemical event of which C is the subject, and (2) there is a 1–1 relation R between the events in $P(C)_i$ and the events in M(C), such that (a) each event in $P(C)_i$ is simultaneous with its R-correlate in M(C), and (b) the events in $P(C)_i$ collectively conform to all the causal principles of common-sense psychology and theoretical psychology which govern their respective R-correlates in M(C).

Our argument against the token identity theory goes as follows. First premise: For any creature C with a non-empty mentality set, M(C) is likely to have several distinct PCIs. Second premise: If M(C) has several distinct PCIs, then some events in M(C) have no unique correlate among those PCIs. Third premise: If a mental event e in M(C) has no unique correlate among M(C)'s PCIs, then e is not identical with any of its PCI-correlates (and hence M(C) is not identical with any of its PCIs). Fourth premise: If a mental event e in M(C) is not identical with any of its PCI-correlates, then e is not a physico-chemical event. Conclusion: Any creature with a non-empty mentality set is·likely to be the subject of mental events which are not identical with any physico-chemical events.

The second premise, we take it, is true by definition: if M(C) has several distinct PCIs, then at least one mental event in M(C) has to have more than one PCI-correlate. The fourth premise too is unproblematic: a physico-chemical event which lacks the causal properties of a given mental event e cannot be identical with e: hence, if e is identical with any physico-chemical event at all, that event will have to be one of e's PCI-correlates.[2] So the key premises, the ones that require defending, are the first and the third. Let us consider them in reverse order, since the third can be dealt with more briefly.

3.   In defense of the third premise, we would claim that mental events can be individuated only by means of their causal roles, as specified by the causal principles which constitute the bulk of folk psychology and theoretical psychology.[3] Mental events are the events which 'physically realize' those

---

[2] A radical psycho-physical event-dualist, who claims that some mental events not only are distinct from physical events but also have their efficacy in a way which does not depend upon the efficacy of any 'underlying' physical events, might conceivably claim that certain *other* mental events are identical with physical events but are not identical with their PCI-correlates. For he might claim that a creature's mentality set simply has no purely physical causal isomorphs. But although this is a logically possible position, it is hard to see why anyone would adopt it. Why would anyone who espouses radical dualism regarding some mental events espouse a token identity theory regarding others?

[3] The relevant causal roles, however, evidently will have to include certain causal connections with what goes on within the creature's social environment; they cannot merely involve causal linkages among sensory inputs, behavioral outputs, and internal events. For, our *doppelgangers* on

principles, in a creature's head. So if there often occur 'simultaneous multiple realizations' in a single creature's head at a single time, then there simply are no further, non-functional, principles which could be used to determine which physico-chemical event is really identical to a given multiply realized mental event.

It should be stressed that the claim that mental events are functionally individuated is weaker than full-fledged functionalism: the latter is the view, roughly, that mental terms can be *exhaustively analyzed* functionally. Many philosophers, ourselves included, think that although a purely functionalist approach may be correct as regards cognitive and volitional mental notions (roughly, those which are expressible by verbs of propositional attitude), nevertheless such an approach cannot do full justice to the qualitative or phenomenal aspects of mentality. (It makes sense to imagine that two creatures who undergo functionally equivalent mental events are experiencing 'inverted qualia,' but it makes no sense to imagine that they are undergoing 'inverted beliefs.'[4])

Since we are not assuming functionalism, our defense of the third premise actually applies to token qualia even if one rejects the claim that qualia-terms can be exhaustively analyzed functionally. Our central claim is that *if* a certain psychological theory is true of a given creature C (something which may well depend upon the nature of C's "neural hardware," and not merely upon the functional organization of C's internal events/states), *then* the causal principles of that theory fix the extensions of its mental terms, relative to C. Qualia-lovers should not object to the claim as thus interpreted, for it does not conflict with their main contention, viz., that mental events in creatures whose physical constitution is radically different from ours would not necessarily have the same qualitative content as the functionally equivalent mental events in humans. (Martian pain would not necessarily feel like human pain. Perhaps it would feel like a tickle, or like nothing we can imagine).

We claim that even qualia-loving token-identity theorists must concede that the only way to find the neural event which is allegedly identical with a particular mental event e, in a creature who has the neural hardware to subserve such a mental event, is to locate the neural event which has all the causes and effects which the correct psychology of that creature attributes to e. So even the

---

Putnam's famous planet Twin Earth do not undergo tokens of the type *believing that water is good to drink*, even though we do and even though their internal neural activity is indistinguishable (in its intrinsic features) from ours. Cf. Hilary Putnam, 'The meaning of "meaning"' in *Minnesota Studies in the Philosophy of Science*, vol. 7, ed. K. Gunderson (University of Minnesota Press, Minneapolis, 1975); and Tyler Burge, 'Individualism and the mental,' in *Midwest Studies in Philosophy*, vol. 4, ed. P. French, T. Uehling and H. Wettstein (University of Minnesota Press, Minneapolis, 1979).

[4] Jerry Fodor makes this observation in his *Representations* (Bradford, Cambridge, Mass., 1981), p. 17. One functionalist who makes a serious attempt to accommodate inverted qualia (rather than treating those who talk of inverted qualia as victims of philosophical dementia) is David Lewis; see his 'Mad pain and Martian pain,' in *Readings in the Philosophy of Psychology*, vol. 1, ed. Ned Block (Harvard University Press, Cambridge, Mass., 1980). For a critique of Lewis see Terence Horgan, 'Functionalism, qualia, and the inverted spectrum,' *Philosophy and Phenomenological Research*, 45 (1984), pp. 453–70; also Michael Tye, 'Functionalism and type physicalism,' *Philosophical Studies*, 44 (1983), pp. 161–74.

qualia-lover must concede that if there are several neural events which fit the bill, then there will be no basis for saying that one of them rather than another is identical with e.

4. We turn now to the first premise. We want to defend this premise on the basis of the following general thesis about causation: Quite often there is no such thing as 'the cause' (at a given time) of a particular event; rather, there are a variety of events, some being proper parts of others, which all can legitimately be called 'the cause.' Which event one calls 'the cause' is normally a contextually determined affair, having to do with such matters as the pragmatics of explanation.

This claim is not as new or radical as it might seem. Mill, for instance, held that what we normally call 'the cause' is usually only a part of 'the cause, philosophically speaking' – where the latter is a relatively complex event/state whose occurrence is sufficient, given the laws of nature, for the effect.[5] If one holds Mill's views, then it is natural to add that various different parts of the genuine cause can be called 'the cause' in a particular context – depending upon which parts of the genuine cause are most naturally treated, in context, as 'background conditions.'

Mackie, who is critical of Mill's view that a genuine cause must be sufficient for its effect, claims instead that a cause is an 'INUS' condition of its effect; that is, a cause is an insufficient but necessary component of a condition which is unnecessary but sufficient for the effect.[6] Under Mackie's view too, it is natural to say that more than one INUS condition can properly be called 'the cause,' and that which INUS condition one should pick is often a context-relative affair.

Now Davidson, as is well known, will have none of this. He writes:

> Mill ... was wrong in thinking we have not specified the whole cause of an event when we have not wholly specified it. And there is not, as Mill and others have maintained, anything elliptical in the claim that a certain man's death was caused by his eating a particular dish, even though death resulted only because the man had a particular bodily constitution, a particular state of present health, and so on. On the other hand Mill was, I think, quite right in saying that 'there certainly is, among the circumstances that took place, some combination or other with which death is invariably consequent ... the whole of which circumstances perhaps constituted in this particular case the conditions of the phenomenon ...' (*A System of Logic*, book III, chap. v., 3). Mill's critics are no doubt justified in contending that we may correctly give the cause without saying enough to demonstrate that it was sufficient; but they share Mill's confusion if they think that every deletion

---

[5] Hume, in a well-known passage in *A Treatise of Human Nature*, ed. L.A. Selby-Bigge (Clarendon Press, Oxford, 1888) (2nd edn as revised by P.H. Nidditch, 1978), writes, 'we must reject the distinction betwixt *cause* and *occasion*, when suppos'd to signify any thing essentially different from each other' (p. 171, emphasis in original). Mill's answer is that 'the real Cause is the whole of these antecedents: and we have, philosophically speaking, no right to give the name of cause to one of them exclusively of the others.' See John Stuart Mill, *A System of Logic* (Longman, London, 1961), book III, ch. 5, section 3, p. 214.

[6] J.L. Mackie, 'Causes and conditions,' *American Philosophical Quarterly*, 2 (1965) pp. 245–64; and *The Cement of the Universe* (Oxford University Press, London, 1974).

from the description of an event represents something deleted from the event described.[7]

Davidson's view, of course, is that the man's eating the dish and his subsequent death have descriptions which instantiate a law: hence the eating of the dish is a full and complete cause of the death. The relevant description of the cause is likely to be quite complex: in particular, it will have to include a description of the man's state of health and bodily constitution. (Either that, or else it will include a complex physico-chemical description of the man, specifying properties upon which his state of health and bodily constitution are supervenient.)[8]

But we maintain that this treatment of such cases of causation, far from undermining our claim that several distinct events often can legitimately be called 'the cause,' actually *supports* this claim. For if the crucial factor in causation is the fact that cause and effect have descriptions that instantiate a law, and if we are allowed to make our description of the cause-event so complex that it includes a substantial amount of relevant information about the event's environment (information like the fact that the eating of the dish was an eating by a man with such-and-such bodily constitution and so-and-so state of health), then it seems quite clear that in many cases a variety of *different* events or states can legitimately qualify as 'the cause' of a particular effect.

Suppose, for instance, that one is asking why a particular man, Smith, died as a result of eating the dish when several others who ate the dish did not die. In such a context, one might choose to relegate the eating itself to the role of a 'background condition,' since the others ate the dish too. And, against the relevant background conditions, one might pinpoint Smith's state of health as 'the cause.'

As far as we can tell, such an approach would be perfectly legitimate, given Davidson's treatment of causality. For, when one constructs the relevant description of Smith's state of health at the time in question, one can build into the description the fact that this event/state is the state of a man who is ingesting thus-and-such a substance. This description-expanding move is quite parallel, it seems, to Davidson's move of building a description of Smith's state of health into a description of Smith's eating the dish. In neither case are we describing an event/state whose occurrence is itself irrelevant to the effect: rather, we are describing two different components of the complex event/state which Mill would have called 'the cause, philosophically speaking.' Thus, if Smith's eating the dish and his death have descriptions that instantiate a law, then presumably his being in such-and-such a state of health and his death *also* have descriptions that instantiate a law. Hence if Smith's eating the dish can properly be called 'the cause' of his death, in certain contexts of inquiry, then

---

[7] Donald Davidson, 'Causal relations,' *Journal of Philosophy*, 64 (1967), pp. 691–703, at p. 698.

[8] In order for there to be any plausibility in Davidson's claim that causally related events have descriptions that instantiate a law, we need to understand the rubric 'law' as including not only the relatively simple nomic principles that are ordinarily called the laws of a scientific theory, but also any arbitrarily complex logical consequence of these principles. The 'laws' that underlie garden-variety macro-level causal statements are likely to be very complex indeed; for garden-variety macro-level objects and events have vast numbers of microphysical components, and it is plausible to conjecture that the only truly 'homonomic' science is physics.

Smith's state of health also can properly be called 'the cause' in other such contexts.[9]

Perhaps it will be objected that we have misrepresented Davidson's treatment of causation. One might construe him as claiming that two events are related as cause and effect only if they have purely *intrinsic* descriptions which instantiate a law – that is, descriptions which refer to the events solely in terms of their non-relational features, rather than in terms that include aspects of the events' surroundings. One might then argue as follows:

> Since Smith's eating the fish causes his subsequent death, these two events have intrinsic descriptions which instantiate a law. But there is no causal connection between his state of health antecedent to eating the fish, and his death; for the former event simply has no intrinsic description which, together with some intrinsic description of the death, instantiates a law. (If it did, then we would have a case of causal pre-emption or causal over-determination; but *ex hypothesi*, we do not.) So, even though several different events can perhaps be *called* 'the cause,' relative to different contexts of inquiry, nevertheless it does not follow, on Davidson's picture, that the various different events really *are* causes. For genuine causes and their effects must have intrinsic descriptions which instantiate a law, whereas what are *called* causes need not satisfy this condition: this is because we sometimes single out events which interest us in the circumstances, not bothering to locate the events which *are* the causes more accurately. Thus there is no real context-relativity about genuine causation.

Our own interpretation of Davidson is different from the one which motivates this objection. We take him to be allowing that the relevant descriptions under which a cause and its effect instantiate a law can be partially *non-intrinsic*: i.e., these descriptions can cite features of the described event's surrounding environment, in addition to any purely intrinsic features of the event itself. Our point was that once one allows reference to non-intrinsic features into one's event-descriptions, then it seems that Smith's state of health, immediately prior to his eating the dish, does indeed have a description which, together with some appropriate description of the death, instantiates a law. (Also, the event described is no mere causally extraneous one, whose connection to the death is solely a matter of the non-intrinsic information packed into its description. Rather, this event is a *bona fide* component of the complex event which *does* have a purely intrinsic description under which it is nomically linked to the death.)

We do not insist that our interpretation represents Davidson's actual position. As far as we know, he nowhere explicitly says whether or not law-instantiating event-descriptions must be purely intrinsic in order for the events described to be genuinely causally related to one another. Consequently,

---

[9] One might object that only momentary *changes*, and not longer-lived *states*, can be causes. But many of our ordinary causal judgments seem to contradict this claim. One highly relevant counterexample is the causation of human actions by wants and beliefs. (No doubt, 'the cause, philosophically speaking' must include *some* element of change. Otherwise, why would the effect occur at just the moment it does? But in certain contexts the relevant change-elements are evidently relegated to the background conditions, rather than being included in the event/state we call the cause.)

either interpretation seems consistent with his published discussions of causation.

We do contend, however, that his position must be interpreted our way if it is to be at all plausible. To see this, consider an often-cited garden-variety example of causation: a short-circuit causing a fire. As Mackie would emphasize, it is most implausible to suppose that the short-circuit-event has a purely intrinsic description which, together with a purely intrinsic descriptioin of the fire, instantiates a law. On the contrary, another short-circuit event, intrinsically indistinguishable from the given event, will only be followed by a fire if it too is embedded in an appropriate surrounding environment: an environment in which the electrical insulation is faulty, in which flammable material is present, in which a suitable supply of oxygen is present, and so forth.

Or consider Smith, who died from eating the fish. Another eating-event, intrinsically indistinguishable from the one involving Smith, will be followed by a death only if the relevant surrounding events/states are again present: a certain state of health and constitution on the part of the person doing the eating, his subsequent failure to consume an antidote, and so forth. (Admittedly, things are less clear-cut in this case than in the short-circuit case. One might try arguing that this particular eating by Smith includes, among its intrinsic components, not merely such events as chewings and swallowings, but also certain fatally abnormal digestive processes which would not have occurred but for Smith's constitution and state of health. But such a move, whatever its plausibility, cannot accommodate such blatantly non-intrinsic events/states as Smith's failure to consume an antidote after eating the fish.)

In the face of these considerations, which are easily multiplied with other examples, an advocate of a nomic-regularity view of causation evidently has three alternatives: (1) denying that the short-circuit (or Smith's eating the fish) really causes the fire (or Smith's death), and claiming that the genuine cause is a complex event/state which includes the relevant surrounding events/states as components (the 'Millian move'); or (2) claiming that in the present context the term 'the short-circuit' (or 'Smith's eating the dish') really denotes the relevant complex event, rather than the short-circuit proper (or the eating proper); or (3) allowing that the descriptions under which the short-circuit and the fire (or the eating and the death) instantiate a law can mention non-intrinsic features, features of the event's environment.

Alternative (1), the Millian move, is *prima facie* highly objectionable, because it forces us to say that most garden-variety singular causal sentences are literally false. Furthermore, as the earlier-quoted passage from Davidson makes clear, he himself thinks that Mill was mistaken in denying that the events we ordinarily call causes are genuine causes. Alternative (2) is also *prima facie* highly objectionable; for it forces us to say, counterintuitively, that terms like 'the short-circuit' denote different events within causal contexts than they normally denote. (In the relevant causal context, the short-circuit event evidently must include, as intrinsic components, the surrounding presence of oxygen, the surrounding presence of flammable material, the surrounding presence of faulty electrical insulation, and so on. Similarly, *mutatis mutandis*, for 'Smith's eating the dish'.) Surely Davidson would not wish to be saddled with *this* claim. Thus the only viable alternative, for someone who wishes to hold that causally related events must have descriptions which instantiate a law, is (3). But once (3) is adopted, Davidson's approach becomes vulnerable to our earlier argument for the context-relativity of causation. The reply cited six paragraphs ago becomes unavailable, because that reply rests upon the untenable contention that causally related events must have purely *intrinsic* descriptions which instantiate a law.

So under Davidson's own treatment of causation, as well as under Mill's or Mackie's, it appears that any of several different events/states can legitimately be called 'the cause' (at a time t) of a given effect, and that matters of context will normally dictate the appropriate event to receive this designation. We submit that any adequate treatment of the notion of cause *should* yield this consequence, because it is a feature of our ordinary concept of causation itself.

This feature, not surprisingly, also manifests itself in the domain of the mental. For example, suppose that a subject S in a psychological experiment has been instructed to watch a panel with one green light and one red light, and to say 'red' whenever the red light flashes and 'green' whenever the green light flashes. The red light flashes, and he promptly says 'red.' What event/state would we call 'the cause' of his behavior, at the level of folk-psychological explanation? It depends upon the context of inquiry. In one context we might take for granted that S understands his instructions and wants to co-operate, and so we would most naturally describe 'the cause' as his noticing that the red light has just come on. But in another context we might be interested in providing a more complete folk-psychological explanation: here we would more naturally describe 'the cause' as including not only the noticing-event, but also his current desire to co-operate and his current belief that in order to co-operate he must say 'red' when he sees the red light flash. There is no single, context-independent answer to the question of which folk-psychological event/state constitutes 'the cause' of S's behavior.

Let us now consider the relevance of context-relativity to the first premise of our argument against the token identity theory. That premise can be established on the basis of two subsidiary claims. First, if one decides to say that a set of physico-chemical events within a creature C is a genuine PCI of M(C) provided only that the events in that set satisfy all *context-independent* conditions on the causal relation that must be met in order for the set to count as a PCI of M(C), then there is every reason to believe that M(C) will have numerous PCIs. Second, it is very unlikely that there exists any such thing as a 'general context of psychophysical inquiry' which can narrow down to one the class of genuine PCIs – that is, a context which, independently of any specific explanatory question or problem, generates criteria that tell us which neural event to count as 'the cause' of a given neural event or piece of behavior. If both of these claims can be made good, then we think there is no avoiding the first premise of our original argument. Let us consider the claims in turn.

The first claim is rendered plausible by the lately noted principle that in general there is no single event which can properly be counted as 'the cause,' at a given time, of a particular effect. This principle is dramatically relevant to the human central nervous system, because of its extreme complexity. The nervous system contains tens of billions of neurons, and thousands of billions of synaptic junctures. Thus at any moment there are vast numbers of neuron excitation-states, neuron-firings, inter-synaptic transfers of electrical energy, and the like; and there are even greater numbers of complex event/states which are 'fusions' of these simpler event/states.[10] Hence it is most unlikely that for any given behavioral or neural event, there will be only one event/state which meets all the formal, context-independent conditions for counting as a cause (at a given time) of that effect. On the contrary, often there are likely to be any number of ways to draw the line between the neural activity that belongs to the cause and the neural activity that belongs to the 'background conditions.' And accordingly, when we consider a person's mentality set as a whole, there are likely to be any number of corresponding sets of physico-chemical events which meet all the context-independent conditions for counting as PCIs.

Moreover, the problem of where to draw the line between the cause and the background conditions is exacerbated when one considers the diachronic dimension of complexity. The causal principles of common-sense psychology and theoretical psychology often don't seem up to the task of precisely pinpointing the temporal instant, or temporal interval, when a posited mental event takes place. Thus the range of potential 'physical realizations' of that mental event must be expanded still further, to include events that occur during a variety of eligible instants or intervals.[11] (When *exactly* does the subject S, in the above-described experiment, notice that the red light has flashed? We know that this event occurs after the light flashes and before he says 'red,' but these temporal limits are quite broad in relation to the time-scale of neural activity.).

Yet another exacerbating consideration is the relatively rough-and-ready nature of psychological causal generalizations, particularly those of folk psychology. It is one thing for these generalizations to be specific enough to allow us to distinguish mental events from one another. But it is quite another thing for them to allow us to make fine-grained distinctions among neural events. We can think of a person's mentality set, together with the causal principles of folk psychology and theoretical psychology, as specifying a 'causal grid' which is somehow instantiated by the person's neural activity, his sensory inputs, and his behavioral outputs. This is a coarse-grained grid; i.e., relatively few intermediary events are posited between sensation and behavior, in

---

[10] For a discussion of event fusions, see Judith Jarvis Thomson, *Acts and Other Events* (Cornell University Press, Cornell, 1977). Thomson is quite liberal in the principles of event-construction she adopts, and in the range of events she is willing to call causes of any given event.

One might construe complex events as entities distinct from the fusions of simpler events – for reasons analogous to those that have led some philosophers to claim that an entity like a ship is not identical to the fusion of its parts, but instead has different intra-world and trans-world identity conditions. The points we shall make in the text concerning event-fusions will be equally applicable to these putatively different kinds of complex events. (An example of a physicalist theory that appeals to such events is Richard Boyd's 'compositional materialism.' See his 'Materialism without reductionism: what physicalism does not entail,' in *Readings in the Philosophy of Psychology*, vol. 1, ed. Block.)

[11] Jennifer Hornsby makes a similar point in 'Which physical events are mental events?', *Proceedings of the Aristotelian Society* (1980–1), pp. 73–92; see especially p. 81. Hornsby's attack on the token identity theory is similar in spirit to ours, although our own views on the consequences for physicalism are very different from hers; see section 6 below. For another sort of argument against psycho-physical token identities see John Haugeland, 'Weak supervenience,' *American Philosophical Quarterly*, 19 (1982), pp. 93–104.

comparison to the vast range of intervening neural events. Now, presumably the token identity theorist is prepared to acknowledge that the strictly *internal* features of the causal grid can be multiply realized within a person's head: he believes, however, that there is only one *total* realization – that is, one realization with the right internal–external causal connections (over and above the right internal–internal causal connections). But in light of the context-relativity of what counts as 'the cause,' it is unlikely that this will be so – at least, not as long as we impose no context-specific parameters onto allowable causal relations. Hence the coarse-grained nature of the grid makes it all the more likely that the grid can be fit onto neural activity in various different ways – i.e., that a person's mentality set will have multiple PCIs.[12]

This brings us to our second claim. Is there such a thing as a psycho-physical 'context of inquiry' that yields parameters restrictive enough to always pick out some single neural event as 'the cause' (at a given time, or approximate time) of a particular neural or behavioral effect? We submit that there is not.

The most plausible candidate for such a context is something like 'the context of neurophysiological explanation.' One envisions asking an ideally well-informed neurophysiologist to determine the cause of the particular effect; and one imagines him doing so in light of whatever contextual parameters govern his ordinary day-to-day causal attributions. ,

But there is little reason to believe that he could[not]do what we ask, because the context-dependence of causal attributions is likely to be as much a factor within neurophysiology as it is anywhere else. The neurophysiologist's day-to-day decisions about what counts as part of the cause, and what counts instead as part of the background conditions, normally occur in much more *specific* investigative contexts; hence he will probably be at a loss if we simply ask him, qua neurophysiologist, to tell us 'the cause' of a particular neural or behavioral event.

But suppose, just for the sake of argument, that for any particular neural event or piece of behaviour, our ideal neurophysiologist actually *could* tell us – independently of any specific context of inquiry – which neural event/state he would consider 'the cause.' (We shall use the term 'context N' for the putative general neurophysiological context in which he makes these judgments.) Even if we make this dubious assumption, there are still reasons to think that context N would not narrow down to one the class of event-sets which would count as allowable PCIs of a person's mentality set.

For one thing, our neurophysiologist might well focus exclusively, or almost exclusively, upon so-called 'precipitating causes' – that is, instantaneous or short-lived *changes*, as against more enduring *states*. But if so then it is implausible to suppose that the events he picks out as causes will always be the right ones to identify with mental event/states; for many of the events/states

---

[12] This point is not affected by the fact, pointed out in note 3 above, that the causal grid will likely involve certain kinds of causal connections with events in the creature's social environment – features of the kind which distinguish the creature's mental life from that of his *doppelganger* on Twin Earth, for example.

posited by folk psychology seem clearly to have the status of temporally extended states, rather than instantaneous changes. (This is why we find it more natural, in pre-philosophical usage, to call beliefs and desires 'states' rather than 'events.')

Furthermore, it is entirely possible that the events our neurophysiologist identifies as causes simply will not possess all the causal properties which folk psychology and theoretical psychology attribute to mental events/states. Often our psychological causal principles will attribute several distinct effects to a given mental event/state; and yet it's entirely possible that the ideal neurophysiologist would attribute these effects to *different* neural events – particularly if the events he is focusing on are momentary changes rather than more complex events which including ongoing states as parts.

One might think that if this last possibility came to pass, then the mentality set we attribute to a person simply won't have any PCIs among that person's neural events. But this isn't so, because even if someone's mentality set has no PCI among the neural events which the neurophysiologist picks as causes (in context N), nevertheless that mentality set can still have numerous PCIs among *other* neural events – events which include ongoing states as well as instantaneous changes, and which might be rather complex 'fusions' of simpler kinds of neurophysiological events.

But if we must turn to these other neural events in order to find a PCI of someone's mentality set, this will mean that we were not able, after all, to pare down effectively the range of genuine PCIs by appealing to the putative context N. Rather, we will again face the likelihood that there will be many PCIs rather than just one.

This idea that the neurophysiologist might often find distinct causes, where folk psychology posits a single cause of two different effects, is not just conjectural. Even in our present state of relative ignorance about the neural basis of cognitive and volitional features of mentality, there is reason to suspect that in many cases where we would attribute two different effects to a single mental cause, the neurophysiologist would find it natural to posit distinct neural causes. For there is reason to suspect that talk of distinct causes will already become appropriate when we drop from the explanatory level of folk psychology to that of cognitive science. Stephen Stich has pointed out that in recent years several leading cognitive scientists have become sceptical about the possibility of identifying particular memories and beliefs with 'naturally isolable' parts of the cognitive system – largely because cognitive models which make such identifications do not seem capable of handling the vast amount of non-deductive inference which is involved in the use and comprehension of language. Stich cites Minsky as an example:

> In a ... recent paper Minsky elaborates what he calls a 'Society of Mind' view in which the mechanisms of thought are divided into many separate 'specialists that intercommunicate only sparsely.' (95) On the picture Minsky suggests, none of the distinct units or parts of the mental model 'have meanings in themselves' (100) and thus none can be identified with individual beliefs, desires, etc. Modularity – I borrow the term from Minsky – is violated in a radical way since meaning or

content emerges only from 'great webs of structure' (100) and no natural part of the system can be correlated with 'explicit' or verbally expressible beliefs.[13]

Suppose Minsky's picture is along the right lines. Then in many cases where folk psychology would appeal to a single belief (say) as the cause of two distinct effects, the cognitive psychologist would be likely to appeal instead to two somewhat different subcomponents of the 'great webs of structure.' He would be especially likely to do this if he were operating in a context of inquiry where it is appropriate to focus on relatively narrow 'precipitating causes,' and to relegate much of the relevant cognitive structure to the role of background conditions. And if the cognitive psychologist posits distinct causes where the folk psychologist posits only one, then the neurophysiologist is likely to do so as well – especially if he too is focusing on relatively narrow precipitating causes.

To summarize: In general, any of various different events/states can properly be considered 'the cause,' at a given time, of a particular effect; normally a particular event/state will receive this designation on the basis of contextually specific parameters, involving such matters as the pragmatics of explanation. Consequently, if one considers only the context-independent features of the causal relation, it is very likely that for any creature C with a non-empty mentality set M(C), there will be numerous sets of physico-chemical events which qualify as PCIs of M(C). Furthermore, it is most implausible to suppose that there is such a thing as a general 'context of psycho-physical inquiry' – a context which would restrict allowable causes in such a way as to pare down to one the class of genuine PCIs of M(C). Moreover, even if an ideally well-informed neurophysiologist *could* make the relevant causal judgments, within some 'general neurophysiological context,' it might well turn out that the events he picked as causes would not jointly constitute a PCI of M(C) at all. This could happen if he usually picked out momentary events, rather than relatively long-lived events/states that have the same duration as the more long-lived propositional attitudes in M(C); it could also happen if he sometimes attributed two effects to different neural causes, in cases where folk psychology (or theoretical psychology) attributes both effects to a single psychological cause. And if it did happen, then the putative 'general neurophysiological context' would not be of any use in the attempt to pare down to one the class of genuine PCIs of M(C).[14]

---

[13] Stephen P. Stich, *From Folk Psychology to Cognitive Science: The Case Against Belief* (The M.I.T. Press, Cambridge, Mass., 1983), p. 241. Stich infers, directly from the premise that beliefs and desires (probably) cannot be identified with 'naturally isolable' parts of the cognitive system, that they (probably) do not exist at all. But this inference is too quick, because it ignores the possibility that folk-psychological events are complex fusions of simpler events. For further discussion of this and related arguments in Stich's book, see Terence Horgan and James Woodward, 'Folk psychology is here to stay,' *Philosophical Review*, 94 (1985), pp. 197–226.

[14] James Woodward points out to us that one might attempt to sidestep this argument by making 'the Millian move' – i.e., by taking the cause, in the strict and philosophically relevant sense, to be the mereological sum of all those events which would be cited as cause in various different contexts of inquiry. But the Millian move is particularly inappropriate with respect to the problem of finding the 'right' PCI with which to identify a creature's mentality set. For it seems clear that the Millian cause of a particular effect – say, a particular piece of behavior – often will include a vast array of relatively permanent standing conditions, over and above the temporary neural events/states which identity theorists want to focus upon. (In order for beliefs and desires to generate actions, for instance, the neural linkages between the motor cortex and the muscles must be in good working order; and the muscles themselves must be in good working order; etc. etc.)

The upshot, then, is that for any creature C with a non-empty mentality set, M(C) is likely to have several – even many – distinct PCIs. And this is the principal premise of our argument against the token identity theory.

5. Someone might reply to our argument as follows. If a creature's mentality set has more than one PCI, then we can still adhere to the token identity theory. For, we can simply *stipulate* that M(C) is to be identified with some specified PCI, and not with any others. Such a move, it might be claimed, is comparable to the stipulative identification of numbers with certain specified sets, in the reduction of number theory to set theory; here too there are numerous potential identifications that will work, and we simply pick one by fiat.

One problem with this reply is that no disciplined method has been specified for determining *which* PCI of a creature C's mentality set is to be stipulatively identified with M(C). By contrast, when one reduces number theory to set theory, one is explicit about one's stipulative identities.

Furthermore, this reply is not at all in the usual spirit of the token identity theory. The theory's advocates, like Davidson, think of the relevant psycho-physical identities as objective facts about the world – facts that involve no element of stipulation or decision on our part. Indeed, this view of the matter is so deep-seated that it probably should be considered partially *constitutive* of the token identity theory. Thus the identity-by-fiat approach is better viewed as a new theory, rather than a version of the original one.

How plausible is this non-Davidsonian identity theory? This depends partly upon the available alternatives. If those alternatives include only psycho-physical event-dualism on the one hand, and views like psychological instrumentalism or eliminative materialism on the other hand, then the identity-by-fiat view does have its attractions – notwithstanding the non-trivial problem of specifying which PCI of M(C) is to be the one that shall be identified with M(C). After all, it would be nice to be able to say that mentality is something real, and it also would be nice to avoid dualism. But we shall sketch below a theory which has these advantages, and which also has the advantage of avoiding any appeal to arbitrary stipulation.[15]

Another possible reply to our argument might be this. All the argument really shows is that there is an indeterminacy associated with a mental event's being identical with a certain neural event (n, say). From this it does not follow that the mental event is different from n. Rather, at best our argument merely demonstrates that token–token mental–physical identities are vague.

This reply is entirely unsatisfactory. If anything is clear, it is clear that every object is determinately identical with itself. Now if a mental event m is only indeterminately identical with n, then obviously it is not determinately identical with n. Since n *is* determinately identical with n, it follows that n has a property

---

[15] Paul Benacerraf, in his well-known 'What numbers could not be,' *Philosophical Review*, 74 (1965), pp. 47–73, argues that the availability of numerous possible set-theoretic reductions of number theory shows that numbers cannot be identical with sets at all. If his argument is sound, then presumably a similar argument can be deployed against the psycho-physical identity-by-fiat theory. (One common response to Benacerraf is to say that there really are no numbers, but only sets. We shall claim, somewhat similarly, that there really are no mental events, but only (at most) physico-chemical events.)

that m lacks. Hence, by Leibnitz's Law, m is not identical with n. Generalizing, we reach the conclusion that an appeal to vagueness in mental–physical identities is tantamount to a rejection of those identities.[16]

Furthermore, it seems that the reasoning of the previous section can be harnessed to argue that if a mental event m is 'indeterminately identical' with its correlate in any one PCI of a creature's mentality set, then m is indeterminately identical to each of its other PCI-correlates as well. So, since m can be indeterminately identical to several events that are not identical to each other, one can only conclude, once again, that the putative relation of indeterminate identity is not a species of identity at all.

Perhaps, though, the idea that m is 'indeterminately identical' with n should be taken to mean this: it is indeterminate which physico-chemical event is identical with m, and one way of resolving this indeterminacy is by *stipulating* that m and n are identical. Thus understood, the 'indeterminate identity' view is really just the identity-by-fiat view considered already. We think our own view, to be presented below, is simpler and more natural.

A third possible reply would be to claim that mental events are to be identified with 'fuzzy' or 'indeterminate' neural events – that is, 'fuzzy fusions' of smaller, non-fuzzy neural events. The idea here is that, with respect to any given fuzzy neural event n, there will be at least one neural event n_k such that it is indeterminate whether n_k is a part of n. The events of the token identity theory, then, will have both determinate and indeterminate parts. This position, it may be argued, permits the token-identity theorist to sidestep the problem of multiple PCIs of a creature's mentality set: he can claim that M(C) has only one PCI composed of *fuzzy* physical events, and that this is the PCI that is identical with M(C).

It is worth stressing that this approach is not committed to the view, lately dismissed, that psycho-physical identity statements rest upon a vague or indeterminate species of identity-relation. Vagueness, on the present proposal, attaches to the part–whole relationship and not to the identity relation. Thus token mental events are held to be determinately identical with indeterminately constructed neural events.

One might question whether there could be fuzzy entities generally, and fuzzy events in particular; but we shall not press this point here. Even if the existence of fuzzy events is granted, we think that they cannot be invoked to avoid the reasoning we used in the preceding section. Consider a particular fuzzy event n with which a given mental event/state is to be identified. Consider now a different fuzzy event n' which has the same determinate parts as n plus one more determinate part n_k which had indeterminate status for n. This event n' is different from n since it has a property which n lacks, namely having n_k as a determinate part. Nonetheless, all things considered, the difference between n and n' is quite minute. Hence, given (i) the context-dependence of what counts as 'the cause' of a particular effect, and (ii) the extreme improbability that there exists any such thing as a 'context of psycho-physical inquiry' that will effectively restrict the range of allowable causes for any given behavioral or

---

[16] This argument derives from Gareth Evans, 'Can there be vague objects?', *Analysis*, 38 (1978), p. 208.

neural effect, there is no reason to suppose that n′ is any less worthy a candidate than n for identification with the original mental event.

6. If, as we have argued, the token identity theory is false, then it appears that only two views of the mental remain open: either mental events are classified as non-physical events or mental events are held not to exist. The former view is not as drastic as is sometimes suggested; one can, like Kim, be an event-dualist without being a Cartesian substance-dualist.[17] Still, we prefer not to clutter our metaphysics with peculiar non-physical particulars; and we think that once non-physical events are posited, it will be hard to avoid epiphenomenalism.[18]

Our position, then, is that mental events do not exist. This position may seem to some philosophers to be as counter-intuitive as epiphenomenalism. But, properly understood, it is not – at least, in the form that we accept. Let us distinguish two versions of the view that mental events do not exist. First, there is the eliminative materialism of Feyerabend, Rorty, Churchland, and others.[19] According to this version of materialism, the ordinary psychological statements we make from day to day are no more to be trusted than the statements our predecessors made 'about' witches, caloric fluid, and phlogiston. Radical error infects the former talk just as it does the latter. Thus mental events do not exist, according to the eliminative materialist, for the simple reason that the everyday statements of our folk psychology are, one and all, false.[20]

---

[17] See Jaegwon Kim, 'On the psycho-physical identity theory,' *American Philosophical Quarterly*, 3 (1966), pp. 227–35; also 'Causality, identity, and supervenience in the mind–body problem,' *Midwest Studies in Philosophy*, 4 (1979).

[18] Kim seeks to develop an account of 'supervenient causation,' whereby (i) mental events are supervenient upon underlying physical events, and (ii) mental events inherit the causal efficacy of the physical events upon which they supervene. See his 'Causality, identity, and supervenience in the mind–body problem'; also his 'Epiphenomenal and supervenient causation,' *Midwest Studies in Philosophy*, 4 (1979); and 'Supervenience and supervenient causation,' *Southern Journal of Philosophy*, 22 (1984), Supplement, pp. 45–56. But David Lewis, in 'An argument for the identity theory,' *Journal of Philosophy*, 63 (1966), pp. 17–25, expresses well our own reason for scepticism about a dual-cause approach like Kim's:

The position exploits a flaw in the standard regularity theory of cause. We know on other grounds that the theory must be corrected to discriminate between genuine causes and the spurious causes which are their epiphenomenal correlates. (The 'power on' light does not cause the motor to go, even if it is a lawfully perfect correlate of the electric current that really causes the motor to go.) Given a satisfactory correction, the nonphysical correlate will be evicted from its spurious causal role. (p. 25).

For a detailed critical discussion of Kim's account of supervenient causation, see Brian McLaughlin, 'Event supervenience and supervenient causation,' *Southern Journal of Philosophy*, 22 (1984), Supplement, pp. 71–92.

[19] Paul Feyerabend, 'Materialism and the mind–body problem,' *Review of Metaphysics*, 17 (1963), pp. 49–66; Richard Rorty, 'Mind–body identity, privacy, and categories,' *Review of Metaphysics*, 19 (1965), pp. 24–54; Paul Churchland, *Scientific Realism and the Plasticity of Mind* (Cambridge University Press, New York, 1979); and Paul Churchland, 'Eliminative materialism and propositional attitudes,' *Journal of Philosophy*, 78 (1981), pp. 67–90.

[20] Daniel Dennett, at least sometimes and in some of his writings, seems to take the instrumentalistic view that although everyday folk-psychological statements are worth preserving because of their explanatory and predictive usefulness, nevertheless they are literally false. But at

We reject this version of materialism. We agree with other critics that it is wildly counter-intuitive, and we are entirely unpersuaded by the positive arguments eliminative materialists have given for their position.[21]

A second version of the view that mental events do not exist – the version we accept – consists of two main contentions. First is the contention that ordinary subject–predicate psychological statements about persons and other sentient creatures, statements like (1)–(3), are frequently true.

(1) Smith is thinking of Vienna.
(2) Smith wants some ice cream.
(3) Smith has an itch in his toe.

Predicates like 'is thinking of Vienna', 'wants some ice cream' and 'has an itch in his toe' are frequently satisfied by persons, on our view; they express genuine properties that persons really instantiate. (These are not physical properties, on our view. Still, as Davidson suggests, they are supervenient upon physical properties. Such a supervenience thesis is, we think, much more plausible than a property–property identity theory as a materialist doctrine of properties.)[22]

The second contention is that mental events fall into the same category as smiles, miles, and styles; that is, they are logical fictions whose non-existence is disguised by the misleading grammar of ordinary language. Thus we do not deny that everyday psychological statements which appear to refer to mental events are frequently true. Rather, we claim that any such statement has a logical form which requires no reference to, or quantification over, events.[23]

This second contention would take a good deal more space to defend fully than we have available here. However, it is worth commenting briefly on one sort of statement involving psychological terms which has been widely taken to show that mental events exist, and which is closely relevant to our earlier argument. We have in mind a causal statement-type, of which the following is an instance:

(4) Smith's having an itch in his toe causes Smith's scratching himself.

---

other times, occasionally within the space of a few sentences, he seems to want to say that such statements are true after all. This tension is especially evident in his 'Three kinds of intentional psychology,' in *Reduction, Time, and Identity*, ed. R. Healey (Cambridge University Press, Cambridge, 1981).

[21] For a critical discussion of Churchland's arguments, see Horgan and Woodward, 'Folk psychology is here to stay.'

[22] There is a growing literature on supervenience in relation to materialism. A number of recent papers on this theme are collected in the Spindel Conference issue of *Southern Journal of Philosophy*, 22 (1984). It was Davidson who first suggested the relevance of the concept of supervenience to philosophy of mind; see his 'Mental events' and 'The material mind.' For more on the nature of mental properties, from our point of view, see Terence Horgan, 'Functionalism, qualia, and the inverted spectrum'; and 'Jackson on physical information and qualia,' *Philosophical Quarterly*, 34 (1984), pp. 147–51. Also see Michael Tye, 'Functionalism and type physicalism'; and 'The subjective qualities of experience,' forthcoming in *Mind*.

[23] We also take this view for the theoretical statements of cognitive psychology.

The standard view is that statements like (4), in Davidson's words, 'more or less wear their logical form on their face'; i.e., they have the logical form of a two-place predication, with the gerundives functioning as event-denoting terms.[24] Under this approach statements like (4), if we accept them, immediately commit us to the existence of mental events; and insofar as we reject non-physical particulars they are thus at the root of the problem we have been discussing – viz., finding the 'right' neural events with which to identify mental events.

Our proposed way out of the problem is to give up the token identity theory and further to reject the standard construal of statements like (4). On our view, (4) is to be analyzed as:

(4a) *The fact that* Smith itches in his toe *causes it to be the case that* Smith scratches himself,

where the italicized words have the status of a non-truth-functional sentential connective.[25] Given (4a), no mental event of Smith's itching in his toe is needed. What is true in this one instance is true, we believe, for all true psychological statements which appear, in their surface grammatical form, to denote mental events or quantify over them.[26] Hence it is not necessary to introduce mental events in order to account for the truth of ordinary psychological discourse.

No doubt some philosophers will object to our use of a non-standard regimentation in (4a). This Hempel-minded attitude does not disturb us, however. We are firmly convinced that standard first-logic is inadequate to the task of analyzing ordinary language generally (for example, we see no standard way of analyzing the inference 'Jones almost sang; so Jones did not sing'). Moreover, we view a certain complexity in the logical analysis of ordinary language as a small price to pay for a tenable physicalistic theory of mind. Indeed, given our main argument, we believe it is the price which must be paid if we are to steer a safe course between the Scylla of Event Dualism and the Charybdis of Eliminative Materialism.[27]

---

[24] Davidson, 'Causal relations.'

[25] This is a proposal which Davidson himself considers and rejects (ibid), on the grounds that the causal connective would have to be truth-functional. But we think his argument for this conclusion amounts to a *reductio ad absurdum* of his premises, and that one can block the argument by means of plausible restrictions on substitutivity within causal contexts. See Terence Horgan, 'The case against events', *Philosophical Review*, 87 (1978), pp. 28–47; also 'Substitutivity and the causal connective,' *Philosophical Studies*, 42 (1982), pp. 47–52. The former of these papers discusses truth conditions for sentences containing the causal connective.

[26] For further related discussion see Horgan, 'The case against events,' where it is also argued that we should dispense with events altogether. Also see Terence Horgan, 'Action theory without actions,' *Mind*, 90 (1981), pp. 406–14; Michael Tye, 'The adverbial approach to visual experience,' *Philosophical Review*, 93 (1984), pp. 195–226; Michael Tye, 'Pain and the adverbial theory,' *American Philosophical Quarterly*, 21 (1984), pp. 319–28; and Michael Tye, 'The debate about mental imagery,' *Journal of Philosophy*, 81 (1984), pp. 678–91.

[27] We thank David Benfield, Brian McLaughlin, Simon Blackburn, and James Woodward for helpful comments and discussion.

27

Physicalism, Events and Part–Whole Relations

JENNIFER HORNSBY

1 *Physicalism*

At a certain high level of abstraction, we may think of the physical world as a world of space and time occupied by particular things, among them persisting things (such as a table or a carrot or a person) and events (such as the wind's once blowing, or a wedding, or someone somewhere's contemplating murder). At the same level of abstraction, we may think that singling out particular things is simply a matter of delimiting the regions of space and time that they occupy – of drawing spatio-temporal lines around them, as it were. In order to identify a particular table at a time, for instance, we might suppose that we had only to specify this as the occupier of some determinate region of space at some moment of time. Philosophers have challenged this conception of the identities of particular persisting things (or, as I shall say, continuants). In this paper[1] I shall suggest that some proponents of physicalism employ a similar conception of the identities of *events*, and that this is wide open to a somewhat similar challenge.

According to the position that I shall call *physicalism*, we are entitled to take a certain view of the relations between the entities spoken of by the different sciences and by common sense. Scientists speak about events (among other things). What distinguishes the various sciences from one another is their employment of different vocabularies; they provide different ways of classifying events. Each science introduces some taxonomy of the events in its universe of discourse; the various taxonomies may not overlap or fit together at all neatly; but ultimately there is one common fund of events spoken of in fundamental science; and common sense, though not a science, imposes one more classification on the same set of things as scientists describe in their different terms. Thus physics describes the same events as chemistry, chemistry

---

[1] I have been helped by comments from John McDowell, David Lewis, Michael Smith, Howard Stone, David Owen and David Wiggins.

describes events which include those of neurophysiology ... , and, more generally, the sciences redescribe the same events as we all describe in the course of day-to-day life.[2]

According to this position, then, there need be no more events in the world than a physicist can descry within it. The doctrine is conceived of here as concerned specifically with what *events* there are, because it is commonly supposed that the laws of science speak of events. Given that supposition (which might be modified to embrace states, processes or whatever), physicalism, which is an ontological doctrine about the world's contents, leads naturally to a more substantial metaphysical doctrine abut the world's workings, that 'under their physical descriptions, all events are susceptible of total explanations, of the kind paradigmatically afforded by physics in terms of physical laws and other physically described events'.[3]

An interesting special case of physicalism so understood is Donald Davidson's anomalous monism.[4] The events of which commonsense psychology speaks (mental events) are the very same events as those of which law-seeking scientists speak (physical events). It is held that it does not count against this at all that the taxonomies of commonsense psychology and of the sciences are out of harmony. Indeed Davidson argues from the absence of close relations between scientific and commonsense languages to his thesis of identities between the items that are described in the two languages.

Many philosophers do not give any arguments for physicalism, but take some such position for granted in all their reasonings. My arguments here are meant to expose and criticize an assumption I believe they make. I shall not return until §7 to the argument that Davidson has offered for the position.

2 *Physicalism, part–whole relations and mereological conceptions*

A first reaction to the physicalism just expounded might be this: 'Scientists look at things through microscopes, and we do not. The things they talk about are then much smaller than the things we talk about, and they cannot be the very same things.' This is certainly a naive reaction (we know that the microscopic is not the sole concern of fundamental physics). But there may yet be something right in the reservation that prompts it.

It would be natural to counter the naive reaction by saying: 'Even if the submicroscopic events of the physicists cannot *be* macroscopic events, still they can be *parts* of them. Allow the relation "is a part of" into the scientist's language, and then he will have all the resources needed to build up descriptions of everyday events.' More generally, it will be said that wherever

---

[2] For an explicit defence, see Jerry Fodor, 'Special sciences, or the disunity of science as a working hypothesis', *Synthese*, 28 (1973), pp. 97–115.

[3] This statement is given by John McDowell in his 'Physicalism and primitive denotation: Field on Tarski', *Erkenntnis*, 13 (1978), pp. 131–52.

[4] Donald Davidson, 'Mental events', in *Experience and Theory*, eds L. Foster and J.W. Swanson (University of Massachusetts Press, Amherst, 1970), pp. 79–101 (reprinted in D. Davidson, *Essays on Actions and Events* (Oxford University Press, New York, 1980)).

the events isolated by two different subject matters are associated with different expanses of space and time, we can assert identities between *fusions* of the events isolated by one subject matter (i.e. events composed from the relevant microphysical parts) and the individual events isolated by the other.[5]

This response will be congenial to proponents of the conception of the physical world that was sketched at the outset. It is in fact found in the literature on physicalism.[6] And the same idea that underlies such a response is implicit in the doctrine that tells us that every entity is a (spatio-temporal) part of that whole which comprises (as their 'fusion') all basic physical entities. This sort of physicalism carries with it the idea that part–whole relations obtain between events not only in the cases where we naturally think of events as comprised from other events, and not only in the cases where there are special reasons for seeing events as comprised from other events, but much more generally.

This is the idea that I want to cast in doubt. So I shall begin by describing and criticizing what I call *mereological conceptions* of continuants and events.

3 *Mereological conceptions of continuants*

I shall take it to be definitive of the decision to adopt a mereological conception of things of some kind that one's theory of things of that kind should commit one to the following principle, and that one be committed to allowing it to play some significant role in determining the identities of those things:

(A) (x) (y) $(\exists!z)$ $(z$ is a fusion of x and $y)$

Taken by itself, (A) could hardly constitute a complete theory of things of any sort.[7] But in practice there is no immediate need to speculate what other axioms

---

[5] 'Fusion' as it is used here, and throughout, can be defined in terms of 'part'. (z is the fusion of x and y, if and only if x and y are parts of z, and anything which is a part of z is a part either of x or of y or of something all of whose parts are parts of either x or y.) Nothing then turns on the choice of the word 'fusion' except what follows from our ordinary understanding of 'part' applied to particulars. ('Sum' or 'aggregate' might have been used instead of 'fusion'.)

In any sophisticated treatment 'fusion' will be a multigrade relation, and not the simple two-place one used in (A) (at the start of §3 below). For useful discussion, see R. Eberle, *Nominalistic Systems* (Reidel, Dordrecht, 1970), esp. ch. 2.

[6] See (a) G. Hellman and F.W. Thompson, (i) 'Physicalism', *Journal of Philosophy*, 72 (1975), pp. 551–64, and (ii) 'Physicalist materialism', *Nous* 11 (1971), pp. 309–45; (b) Colin McGinn, 'Philosophical materialism', *Synthese*, 44 (1980), pp. 173–206; (c) Christopher Peacocke, *Holistic Explanation: action, space, interpretation* (Oxford University Press, Oxford, 1979), p. 44.

In (a) and (b), there is an assumption that the notion of parthood can do some work in arriving at physicalism; see note 16 on (a), and note 23 on (b). (c) makes no such assumption, and merely introduces 'parthood' into a statement of physicalism.

[7] As it stands, (A) is suited, in the presence of claims about what there basically is, to say what else there is. For many mereologists, the basic individuals will be point-sized occupants of space–time (or, ultimately, for the reductionist mereologist, the items will be space–time points). Some mereologists believe (with Quine) that an ontology whose members are identified with the contents of spatio-temporal regions (or, ultimately, with spatio-temporal regions) incorporates continuants and events alike; other mereologists (such as David Lewis, for whom point-sized occupants of space time are point-sized bits of *matter*) take such an ontology to incorporate continuants, but hold some different theory of events. By considering (A) separately for the cases of continuants and of events, I mean to cover both of these doctrines, and also a doctrine in which, for the continuant case, the basic individuals are chemical atoms or their constituents.

might be present in a theory containing (A). For my aim is not to establish the falsity of any particular mereological theory, but to demonstrate and trace to their source the problems that (A) will bring to theories in which it is given a substantial role. In this way I hope to establish that there are problems with mereological conceptions (§§3 and 4) which rebound on the defence of physicalism (§§5 and 6).

If commitment to (A) is diagnostic of the mereological conception, then we may enquire first what role if any it will play in a good account of continuants.

If one assumes the existence of the continuants that we ordinarily talk about, then (A) brings existential commitments far beyond any we ordinarily recognize. For instance it guarantees that there is something composed from the Bodleian library and some carrot, and something made up from my copy of *The Structure of Appearance*, Goodman's left arm and your right leg. Such examples, which can of course be multiplied indefinitely, suggest that (A) is simply false of continuants. But some people think that we should not concern ourselves about these weird things; they think that we can treat them as "don't care" cases and need not worry if our theories admit them. Goodman said 'the supposition that bizarre instances demonstrate that two individuals can fail to have a [fusion] betrays a misunderstanding of the range of our variables'.[8]

Anyone who responds in this way to an attack on (A) must then be someone who understands (A)'s variables to range over a domain which includes more than continuants. And it seems he must allow that not everything in the ontology that can be constructed from everyday continuants is itself a continuant. For not every construct from everyday continuants is such that a principled account could be given of what it is for such a thing to persist: no autonomous principle of individuation through time can be specified for objects that are the fusions of some library plus some carrot.[9] But of course (A)'s proponent will now introduce a new term for the items of his ontology – 'material thing', say. And then his claim will be that we are committed to the existence of material things, and that in the presence of axioms asserting the existence of (say) atoms, (A) simply defines the class of material things. He will then say that our ordinary continuant things are to be found *among* the material things, and that all he does in introducing (A) is to effect a certain generalization.[10]

In order to see what is wrong with such a proposal, it is helpful to distinguish the two components of (A), namely (E), which asserts the existence of fusions, and (U) which asserts their uniqueness.

---

[8] See Nelson Goodman, *The Structure of Appearance* (Harvard University Press, Cambridge, Mass., 1951), p. 51.

[9] For connexions between the notion of a continuant, and a principle of individuation (which gives *inter alia* intelligible persistence conditions), made *via* the notion of a sortal concept, see David Wiggins, *Sameness and Substance* (Basil Blackwell, Oxford, 1980). My argument here takes such connexions for granted, and questions whether a mereologist can admit them.

[10] By 'material thing' one may or may not intend what Quine intends by 'physical object'. (See e.g. 'Things and their place in theories'in W.V. Quine, *Theories and Things* (Belknap Press, Harvard University Press, Cambridge, Mass., 1981).) Those who think that the 'contents of portions of space–time' are *material* contents will use a notion of material thing which differs from Quine's notion of physical object in excluding events; cf. note 7.

(E) (x) (y) $(\exists z)$ $(z$ is a fusion of x and $y)$

(U) (x) (y) (z) (w) $[(z$ is a fusion of x and $y)$ & $(w$ is a fusion of x and $y)) \rightarrow (w = z)]$

What the introduction of material things is supposed to help us to see is how (E) can be true. On the other hand, if I can show that (U) fails for material things, then this will have the effect of showing that (A) is not true where the domain is material things.

Counterexamples to (U) may be found wherever two distinct material things exist in the same place at the same time. The notion of 'part' for material objects is a spatial notion to the extent that, if two enmattered objects are in exactly the same place at a time, then at some level of articulation of their parts, they must have exactly the same parts at that time. Thus any case in which there are two objects in a place at a time will be a case where (U) must rule that there could be only one material thing.[11]

The idea that two things can be in the same place at a time is a familiar, if recent, one.[12] The contention is that we have to distinguish (e.g.) between a gold ring and the quantity of gold from which it is made, because the quantity of gold is something that may exist before the ring does and may go on existing after the ring is destroyed. A similar point can be made about almost any continuant and the fusion of the molecules composing it at any particular time. Biological organisms, which survive through complete replacement of their matter, provide particularly vivid examples. And what leads one to distinguish two objects in cases like these is only an application of Leibniz's Law: x exists at t, y does not exist at t; so x is not the same as y.

Of course an advocate of the mereological conception is likely to claim that we misdescribe these cases when we say that we have two things in the same place at the same time. 'We shall see that in fact there are no counterexamples to (U) here,' he will say, 'if we realize that in deciding what parts an object has at any time, it is not enough to decide what its spatial parts are at that time. A violation of (U) would require the coincidence of the whole of something with the whole of something else; and in these examples we learn only that a part of a ring coincides with a part of something else. (U) does not commit one to identifying a fusion that exists after t with a ring which ceases to exist at t, because the imagined fusion in fact has *parts* that the ring lacks – namely temporal parts.'

We are told now that what we naturally regard as an encounter with the ring at a time when we pick it out is really an encounter with a temporal part of the ring. So next the mereologist must show us how we can regard 'the ring at t' as referring to a temporal stage of something. And he must answer the formidable

---

[11] At this point, one has to make some assumption about what will be combined with (A) in a theory. If (say) chemical atoms are taken as the basic individuals, and everything can be seen as some fusion of atoms, then if x and y occupy the same place, they will have as parts exactly the same atoms, and will be identical. (The mereologist may resist such an assumption: see below on temporal parts.)

[12] See e.g. David Wiggins's discussion of Locke in 'On being in the same place at the same time', *Philosophical Review*, 77 (1968), pp. 90–95. And for a discussion of the counterexamples to (U), and argument that they are genuine, see Frederick C. Doepke, 'Spatially coinciding objects', *Ratio*, 24 (1982), pp. 45–60.

objections to the whole idea of continuants as things with temporal parts.[13] But even if a mereologist thinks that he can answer such objections, he will still have to say how he hits on the particular fusion which he wants to equate the ring with. What I cannot understand is how he proposes to dispense here with all considerations that concern the temporal dimensions of the *ring*. Surely he must avail himself of a prior account of the ring's identity and persistence conditions – something supplied from elsewhere, from our ordinary conception of what a ring is – to determine which things are parts of rings. So it seems that even if he persuaded us that we should 'admit as an object the material content of any portion of space–time' (as Quine puts it), he can scarcely claim that the conceptual resources of our ordinary vocabulary for continuants are simply dispensable. But how then can he allow (A) to play a constitutive role in the account of the identities of the continuant things about which we talk?[14]

No doubt the mereologist will want to present objections of his own to the very idea that there could be counterexamples to (U). He may say that he cannot understand how there could be two distinct (non-identical) things, the ring and the fusion, which are so very like one another whenever both exist. But it seems that it is in fact very easy to explain what he professes to find unintelligible. Many of the properties of a thing derive from the disposition of the matter that occupies the space that it occupies; thus things which are spatial co-occupants cannot help but be alike in respect of numerous features that do so derive.

Of course if absolutely all of the properties of any object derived from such features as molecular arrangement at a moment, then there could not be cases of spatial co-occupancy. So it may be that the mereologist will want to redefine the notion of a property of a material thing so that properties depend entirely upon how the matter occupying the space that the thing occupies is disposed at any time. But in fact this notion of property is not the notion of a property that we apply to continuants. Simply examining a portion of matter at a single time cannot tell us everything about what a continuant's properties are. It is in the nature of continuants to persist. The whole continuant *can* be picked out at a time, and what is then picked out is the very thing that endures. We cannot then say that what it is for some continuant thing we have picked out to endure is something quite irrelevant to what it is, and to its identity.[15]

---

[13] Some of the difficulties about regarding continuants as things with temporal parts are brought out by P.T. Geach, *Truth, Love and Immortality* (Hutchinson, London, 1979), pp. 70–1. See also D.H. Mellor, *Real Time* (Cambridge University Press, Cambridge, 1981), esp. ch. 8.

[14] At this point, essentialist considerations may be brought against the mereological conception (see e.g. Wiggins, *Sameness and Substance*, pp. 136ff.). Such considerations are used for the case of events by Richard Boyd in 'Materialism without reductionism', Introduction to Part Two of *Readings in Philosophy of Psychology* ed. N. Block (Methuen, London, 1980), vol. I, pp. 67–106.

Quine, who regards continuants (his 'bodies') as a special kind of physical object (cp. note 10) relies on reinterpreting (say) 'ring' as 'place–time of a ring'. The question I would put to Quine is: How can people's understanding of (say) 'ring', and their abilities to make reference to rings, be accounted for in the terms that the reinterpretation uses?

[15] A more radical suggestion might be made at this point: that we simply eliminate continuants from our discourse. For arguments against that suggestion, see Doepke, 'Spacially coinciding objects'. Doepke also provides more detailed arguments supporting the conclusions of the preceding paragraphs of the text.

This shows that (U) fails for a domain that purports to contain continuants among mereologically conceived things. But (E) failed for a domain that purports to contain only continuants. The conclusion we reach is that (A) cannot hold true for any domain that includes continuants in it at all.

4 *Mereological conceptions of events*

The arguments of the preceding section were intended to serve as a reminder of what seems to be essentially at fault in the mereological approach. We aren't able to describe the world except in the terms (*inter alia*) of the continuant things that we find there; and we cannot replace continuants with mereologically conceived material objects, because we cannot understand continuants' having the properties they do except by making reference to continuants themselves. The predicates that the champion of a mereological conception must take to suffice in determining things' identities do not in fact suffice for the singling out of continuants. Using Quine's distinction between ontologies (stocks of items) and ideologies (ways of characterizing items), we might put the point by saying that a barely spatio-temporal ideology is inadequate to the singling out of the ordinary items in our ontology; continuants can only be identified in the context of a richer ideology suited to them. Once the idea of bare singling out is discredited, we find that the question whether one and the same thing is singled out in this and that distinct ideologies has to be a substantial question.

How much of this has application to events? The physicalism we have begun from acknowledges the possibility of a certain incommensurability between different event ideologies, but it is not led by this into any consequential doubt about whether the very same entities are isolated within different ideologies. This question is sometimes not treated as the substantial one that the continuant case suggests it is.

Consider (A) with its variables taken to range over events. If one assumes the existence of the events we ordinarily talk about, then (A) now guarantees that there is an event of my reading in the library today fused with your writing a letter yesterday, and an event composed from the death of Julius Caesar, the Battle of Hastings and a recent speech by Edward Heath. Examples can be multiplied indefinitely. And again it seems we ought not to be too easily persuaded of the existence of these things.

The mereological conception of continuants was undermined by the thought that it is in the nature of continuants to persist: fusions of things with coherent, intelligible persistence conditions need not themselves have coherent, intelligible persistence conditions. A corresponding thought for the case of events might be that it is in their nature to cause and to be caused. And then the corresponding problem for a mereological conception would be that fusions of things which cause and are caused need not themselves be things which cause and are caused. This surely is a real problem. What on earth can we find to say about the causes and effects of a fusion of events whose parts occured in 44 B.C., in 1066 and in 1984?

Well, those who think that the more bizarre things whose existence (A) guarantees are no great embarrassment will presumably say that we can perfectly well see the theoretical, constructed fusions as playing some role in the causal order; and perhaps they will propose some principle which has the effect that fusions inherit some of the causal properties of their parts – e.g. something like this:

(C)   IF {event c causes event e AND $f = c + d$ AND [NEITHER d occurs later than e NOR d and e have common parts NOR part of e causes part of d]}

   THEN f causes e

(C) would be meant to introduce enough in the way of causal relations between the entities that (A) imports to credit those things with a causal status of their own.[16]

But (C) seems absurd. And certainly adherents of a typical counterfactual account of causation and of a typical regularity account of causation must reject it.

The simple thought behind counterfactual accounts is that if c caused e, then c made a difference to whether e occurred. Can one say then that f – the fusion of c and some arbitrary event d – made a difference to whether e occurred? Well, perhaps this seems innocuous enough. In typical cases, there will be a difference that c makes such that we can know that e would not have occurred unless c had. But if '$-C\square\rightarrow -E$' is true, then, provided that D is independent of E, we shall also have '$-(C \ \& \ D) \ \square\rightarrow -E$'; and this latter counterfactual is exactly what we shall expect to hold if the fusion of events had not occurred then its parts would not have. (I employ David Lewis's terminology here: '$\square\rightarrow$' is the counterfactual conditional; 'C' (or 'E') says that the event c (or e) occurred.) However, such a defence of (C) from a counterfactual theorist would ignore the fact that, in any particular case of c causing e, it cannot be settled by sole reference to whether c actually caused e exactly which counterfactuals obtain. (It depends, for instance, on whether there was a fail-safe mechanism ensuring the production of e in the absence of c.) The difference which c as cause makes to e's occurrence is a quite specific difference. Why should we think that, for any d, the difference made by $(c + d)$ to e's occurrence is such a specific difference

---

[16] (C) is a simplified and slightly modified version of something proposed by Judith Jarvis Thomson in *Acts and Other Events* (Cornell University Press, Cornell, 1977). The complicated antecedent is required because a proponent of (A) will obviously wish to place some restrictions on the possibility of the inheritance by fusions of the causal properties of their parts. One can imagine all sorts of variants on (C), and (A)'s proponent might well suggest something more highly qualified. The arguments that follow do not exploit any of the deficiencies of (C) that have resulted from aiming at something relatively simple.

Hellman and Thompson ('Physicalism' and 'Physicalist materialism') are committed to something like (C), if they agree that events are such as to stand in causal relations. If their characterization of distinctively physicalist doctrines in those papers were correct, then even the physicalist who confined himself to the ontological doctrine of §1 would commit himself to a mereological conception of events.

that we can take the relation between $(c + d)$ and e also to be causal? Where c caused e, the occurrence of e must have actually depended crucially upon the occurrence of e, and although this may ensure some dependence of the occurrence of e on the occurrence of $(c + d)$, it cannot ensure that there is the same actual crucial dependence as in a real case of causation.[17]

Again there are difficulties for someone who tries to combine (C) with a typical regularity theory of causation. Such a theorist takes the presence of an underlying regularity to be a hallmark of cases of causation: he thinks that what distinguishes between a case where e causes f and a case where f follows on e temporally but not causally is that in the first case, but not the second, there is some significant (law-like or lawful) generalization that subsumes e and f.[18] The problem about (C) for such a theorist is that it requires him to accept generalizations of an *ad hoc* and apparently trivial kind as playing a role which he has to insist only significant regularities can really play. Try to imagine some regularity that subsumes, on the one hand, the fusion of Caesar's death and my striking the match, and, on the other hand, the match's lighting. Here you may assume that there is some significant regularity which deals with the particular striking/lighting sequence, and that there are significant regularities which deal with sequences that include Caesar's death and what we normally consider to have been its effects. On that basis, you must imagine an as interesting as possible (death + striking)/lighting regularity. But it is plain that *that* need not be law-like.

These arguments against (C) suggest that within the domain of events (A) is incompatible with any plausible account of the causal relation: the difficulty with (A) now is that it introduces fusions which, having no place in the causal nexus, lack any title to be identified with events. And notice that it is not merely the more bizarre among putative event fusions – those which are strikingly irregular by virtue of their discontinuity, say – which are cast into doubt: even fusions composed from events that are closely related spatio-temporally are undermined. For surely bare spatio-temporal contiguity of the parts of some fusion cannot be what is needed to endow that item with a causal status.

5 *Mereological conceptions of events and physicalism*

Of course events do sometimes stand to one another in part–whole relations. And often there are arguments for seeing events as parts of others, or as fusions of others. These claims are not at issue. But if physicalism is allowed to be at issue, then we should not start with a presumption that exactly those event fusions exist which are required to make physicalism hold true. The physicalist of §2 said that if one imported the relation 'is a part of' into a scientist's

---

[17] This is only a gesture towards an argument. My remarks about causal explanation in §5 below are suggestive of further problems about combining counterfactual accounts of causation with mereological conceptions of events.

[18] I am thinking specifically of the account of causation in Davidson's 'Causal relations', *Journal of Philosophy*, 64 (1967), pp. 691–703 (reprinted in *Essays on Actions and Events*). (This is discussed in §7 below.)

language, he would then have all the resources he needed to build up descriptions of everyday events (mental events, say). And what the arguments against (A) suggest is that there isn't any reason to think that (putative) fusions constructed from events using the relation of parthood need themselves be genuine events.

To be clear how the argument against (A) rebounds on this physicalist's assumption, it is helpful to consider a particular case where the relation of *parthood* might be put to work in defending the claim that the same event makes its appearance in different ideologies. Consider then some arbitrary macro-event *e*. It could be an event of interest to economists – say the Public Sector Borrowing Requirement's dropping by six billion pounds in a certain period. Consider also the (putative) fusion composed from those microphysical events which will be said to 'occupy the very spatio-temporal region that *e* occupies'.[19] Is there any reason to suppose that this fusion has any special claim to the status of event? Is it not on a par with some of the extraordinary putative items that (A) imports, which, in the light of the arguments against (C), we are confident are *not* events? But if the fusion is not an event, it cannot be the same as *e*.

We have no doubt that *e* itself in this example is a genuine event, because *e* is the sort of thing we might be able to learn the cause of: an economist might be able to cite features of *e* which bring it in the scope of intelligible, more or less projectible generalizations. And it need not be in doubt that the microphysical events whose putative fusion is coincident with *e* are also, severally, susceptible of causally interesting descriptions such as figure in counterfactual sustaining generalizations. But we know that in order to discover generalizations in economics, there is no need to investigate the physics of the regions that economic events occupy; and this suggests that it cannot be relevant to economic generalizations which sorts of microphysical events they are that occur in the spatio-temporal regions in which we find events satisfying predicates from economic generalizations.[20] Thus the fact that *e* has an interesting description, in virtue of which we can appreciate its causal status, cannot in itself help to secure any description of the putative fusion (a description using microphysical vocabulary plus the word 'part') which would figure in some counterfactual sustaining generalization. It is surely because the fusion lacks all such descriptions that we feel it lacks any claim to the title of event.

More generally, I should suggest that the reason why we do not tolerate the extraordinary events which (A) would commit us to, and that the physicalism of §1 apparently requires, is that these putative events lack any conceivable value

---

[19] Of course it may be a vague (or even unanswerable) question which microphysical events occur in the spatio-temporal region in which some given economic event occurs. In assuming that the relevant microphysical events could be specified, we make a concession to the physicalist. (For arguments designed to show that there really is vagueness of this kind in the case of some mental events, and that the vagueness creates a problem for the physicalist, see my 'Which physical events are mental events?', *Proceedings of the Aristotelian Society* 81 (1980–1), pp. 73–92.)

[20] Cf. Fodor ('Special sciences'), who says that 'interesting generalizations ... can often be made about events whose physical descriptions have nothing in common'. Fodor himself, in making the point, presupposes that all events have physical descriptions, which is to beg the question at issue here.

to us in giving explanations. This provides a further point of parallel between continuants and events: inasmuch as it is in the nature of continuants to persist, we expect individual continuants to be members of kinds whose instances have intelligible, individuation-sustaining persistence conditions; inasmuch as it is in the nature of events to cause and be caused, we expect individual events to be members of kinds that pull their weight in illuminating accounts of why one thing followed on another. The items which are events, like the items which are continuants, need to be singled out not merely as occupiers of space and time, but by reference to a suitable ideology; and the suitable ideology for events is conditioned by the need to construct an explanatory causal nexus. If we take ourselves to recognize events in nature only as we come to understand their occurrences by finding ourselves in a position to supply explanations, then knowing that our everyday low-grade explanations and our use of concepts in exercising our ability to discern everyday events require only rough and ready generalizations, and nothing like the laws of scientists, we shall be suspicious of any crudely realist theory neutral ontology such as (A)'s advocate purports to describe. If events *e* and *f* are such as to need to be singled out by different ideologies, it will take an impressive argument to show that *e* is nonetheless the same as *f*. Of course if some reductive thesis connects the two ideologies, then that thesis may provide the premise of the needed argument. But no actual argument is given when the word 'part' is introduced into the vocabulary of physics.

6 *Physicalism and mereological conceptions reviewed*

Someone who was sympathetic to the views about continuants outlined here, and who accepted the parallels between continuants and events (such as they are), might think that to the extent to which this conclusion is anti-physicalist it could not be correct. For he might react by saying that the claims about continuants made in §3 do nothing to impugn the spirit of physicalism: why then should the claims about events in §§4 and 5 be thought to present any sort of challenge to any sort of physicalism about them?

Well, if he wishes to defend a doctrine about continuants exactly parallel to the physicalism about events of §1, then he is simply wrong if he thinks that the arguments against mereological conceptions do not affect him.[21] The physicalism of §1 used a distinctive conception of the *physical*, as that which a physical scientist is concerned with; and it made claims of *identity*. If one uses such a

---

[21] Compare here Hilary Putnam's 'Reflexions' on Goodman's *Ways of Worldmaking, Journal of Philosophy*, 76 (1979), pp. 603–18. In that review, Putnam considered anomalous monism (which is discussed at §7 below), and introduced comparisons between continuants and events so far as their physical status was concerned. But I think that Putnam distracted our attention from relevant comparisons in two ways. First, he failed to distinguish between claims about identity and claims about composition: he simply took for granted the mereological conception of continuants discussed in §§2 and 3 above, and found physicalism about continuants quite unproblematic in consequence. Second, Putnam used the phrase 'a particular event E' to denote a (certain) repeatable thing, so that what Putnam calls events are not always the particulars that are at issue here. I agree with Putnam in the point that physicalism about continuants is less controversial than physicalism about events (mental events, say). The rest of the present section is meant to provide an explanation of this point.

conception, and one makes such claims, then as a physicalist about continuants one will say, for instance, that any gold ring is identical with some fusion of gold atoms. But this is just the sort of claim disputed in §3.

If one is clear about this, but still feels that physicalism about continuants survives the arguments against mereological conceptions, then one must have some different version of physicalism in mind – perhaps a doctrine that employs a different conception of the physical, or perhaps a doctrine that gives no special place to identity claims.

It may be that we do use some more relaxed conception of the physical than the physics-based one in assessing physicalism about continuants. Conceiving continuants as macrophysical things, we do not take the fact that they are not the same as fusions of microphysical things to cast any doubt on their status as physical in some sense. Of course when it comes to events also, we might make use of a relaxed conception of what it is to be physical; and then there will surely be some anodyne physicalist position about events for us to turn to. What I have been concerned with, though (in §§1, 2, 4 and 5), is physicalism as we have it in the literature.

But some people will think that even if we take the exacting (physics-based) conception of the physical, and even if we accept that continuants are not the same as anything that is according to that conception physical, still physicalism about continuants holds true. What these people want to say is 'Even if the ring is not the same as any fusion of gold atoms, still it is nothing over and above that fusion'. Now presumably what this means is that the ring and the fusion of gold atoms have the same parts: there may be rings *and* fusions of gold atoms, but there are not ring-atoms and gold-atoms besides. It seems then that where continuants are concerned, it is thought to suffice, in order to establish physicalism, to demonstrate that all continuants are related exhaustively by *parthood* to things in the scientist's world.

This is where the case of events is very different. The claim about *parthood* for continuants is available because, for continuants, it is arguably a sufficient condition of x's being a part of y (at some time) that x occupy some part of the volume of space that y occupies (at that time). The notion of part that is pressed into service, we might say, relies only on the spatial ideology, yet it seems to have enough substance to give content to something properly physicalist. In the case of events, however, the occurrence of one event within the spatio-temporal region in which some other event occurs does not by itself ensure that the one event is a part of the other. In the ordinary way, we see events as parts of others where that enables us better to explain things; support for particular claims about parthood is given by facts internal to some event ideology, and never by purely spatio-temporal facts. Think, for instance, of the kind of thing that would be brought to bear in deciding whether certain events were correctly regarded as parts of the event that caused economic event e.[22]

---

[22] Someone might posit a spatio-temporal notion of parthood, saying that *any* event occurring within the spatio-temporal volume in which an event occurs is a part of that event. But if this stipulation exhausts the content of *parthood*, it is no longer clear that introducing parthood into physicalist theses gives them any distinctively physicalistic content. Perhaps physicists' events occupy the whole of space and time, and perhaps all mental or economic events are spatio-temporal particulars. Is that a doctrine worthy of the name of physicalism? (I do not know.)

This difference between continuants and events, in the contribution that *parthood* can make to physicalist doctrines, is reflected in a difference in our attitudes towards the constructed items that (A) would introduce. Where a fusion is made up of microphysical events, we are not prepared (without further argument) to recognize it as any sort of thing. On the other hand, where a fusion is made up of (say) gold atoms, the mere assertion of the fusion's existence seems less problematic: we know that the fusion is a portion of matter at least, and we may call it a 'material thing' (cp. §3). It is surely our conception of matter, as space-occupying stuff that is more or less indefinitely divisible, which gives us the idea of items made from matter as competing with one another for room in the spatial world, and makes such material things as intelligible to us as they are. If matter so conceived is something that concerns a scientist, and if matter is what all continuants are composed from, then that explains why the notion of *parthood* has a role to play in stating a physicalism of sorts about continuants.

But the absence in the event case of any analogue of the notion of matter (the fact, we might say, that there is no event stuff out of which occurrences are constructed) prevents the physicalist about events from resorting to any doctrine merely about *parthood* to register his convictions.[23] Such a physicalist seems bound to defend *identity* claims. In that case, he must either introduce a conception of the physical different from that of the physicalism of §1, or else he must find some actual argument for identities that does not simply assume a mereological conception.[24]

7 *Anomalous monism*

Davidson does not envisage extending a physical vocabulary with 'part'. And he does give a positive argument for his doctrine.[25]

---

[23] The argument of McGinn ('Philosophical materialism') may gain its plausibility from a failure to appreciate this disanalogy. McGinn defends physicalism by way of the principle that every particular is of some natural kind. Taking artifacts to provide counterexamples to this principle literally construed, he modifies it – adding to it a disjunction with the effect that the principle only requires *parts* of particulars to be of natural kinds. It is a question why we should find the modified principle compelling for the case of events; and another question whether we should be satisfied with the physicalism that could be derived from it in the case of events (cf. note 22).

[24] A comparison of events with continuants has been crucial to my argument insofar as it can be used to support the idea that it is no more plausible that a purely spatio-temporal ideology defines events than that such an ideology defines continuants. One might mention counterexamples to (U) (see §3) in the case of events in a more direct argument for the conclusion about events; e.g. the simultaneous rotating and heating of a metal ball, suggested by Davidson in 'The individuation of events', in *Essays in Honour of Hempel*, ed. N. Rescher (Reidel, Dordrecht, 1969), pp. 216–34 (reprinted in *Essays on Actions and Events*). Such examples help to make it plain that identity questions are not to be settled by reference purely to spatio-temporal facts. (If someone accepts this point in the continuant case, it seems it ought to be easy to persuade him that continuants do not have temporal parts. But for the purposes of my argument, it may be unnecessary to persuade him of that. *Pro tanto* we do not require any exact analogue in the event case of the claim that continuants lack temporal parts; though counterexamples to (U) can still be relevant both where continuants are concerned and where events are concerned.) A full discusssion of event-parts and of comparisons between event-parts and continuant-parts would take me well beyond the considerations used here.

[25] 'Mental events'. Richard Boyd cites considerations similar to those of my §3 as a ground for suspicion of Davidson's event identity claims. See his 'Materialism without reductionism'. But

Davidson employed three premises: (i) there are psychophysical causal interactions; (ii) there are no psychophysical laws; (iii) wherever events are causally related, some law covers those events. He argued that if some mental event causes some physical event (by (i)), then there is no psychophysical law that covers that case of causal connexion (by (ii)). But some law must cover that case (by (iii)), and it must be a physical law, ensuring that the mental event is subsumed by a physical law, and is itself physical.

Notice that premise (ii), which denies psychophysical laws, introduces the idea of a certain sort of incommensurability between different event ideologies, and that it was incommensurability of this sort that gave the lie to the mereological conception (in §5). Given that premise (ii) (as Davidson acknowledges) already seems to cast doubt on the identity of mental and physical events, the real work in Davidson's argument must be done by premise (iii), which Davidson called the Principle of the Nomological Character of Causality. If Davidson's argument for physicalism can stand, then, it seems that the Principle of the Nomological Character of Causality can do what others have relied on some mereological principle to do.

The notion of a law used in the Nomological Principle is not merely the notion of some counterfactual-sustaining generalization that we can use in explanation: if it were, psychophysical laws could be admitted. Rather, since the conclusion of the argument is to be that mental events are physical, and since this has to be established by showing that mental events can be described using the vocabularies in which laws are stated, a law must at least be this: a generalization stated in such vocabulary that what is described in that vocabulary is obviously physical in some sense of physical in which it could not be obvious before the argument was given that mental events are physical. It seems then that we have to envisage laws as concerned precisely with events that scientists describe.

But now we might wonder whether we can use again a version of the naive point that set all these considerations in motion in order to dispute Davidson's crucial premise. If we take a view of events in the brain as related to one another by strict physical laws, then we shall probably be inclined to think of these as microscopic events, detectable only with a neurophysiologist's fine-tuned apparatus. Are these the things that we talk about as a result of our grosser observations of people's impact on the world as they move about it? It will be said that if the brain scientists make more discriminations than we do, then that need only show that we may sometimes have to introduce the relation of *parthood* to ensure that mental events are among the things subsumed by laws. It seems, then, that someone who thinks that all causally related events can be subsumed by laws formulated by scientists will sometimes claim that events we recognize are in fact fusions of the events described in laws.[26] Now I have heard

---

Boyd's argument assumes the existence of composition relations between e.g. neural events and mental events; and I do not think we have to concede so much to the physicalist in raising the question that both Boyd and I would wish to raise. (I note that I should dispute Boyd's eventual conclusion that 'token events ... seem less like stereotypical "individuals", and more like type events – more like "universals"': the conclusion seems to me to rest on a conflation of the *composition* and *realization* relations; and if the conclusion were correct, it might undermine the relevance of the comparisons between continuants and events.)

[26] I have illustrated this point with a particular example, chosen for its relevance in a discussion

it said, in response to the suggestion that this claim may be problematic, that it can easily be defended because we can always construct the necessary fusions from the events of science. But to say this is to suppose that the picture of causation required by Davidson's argument forces on us the mereological conception of events.[27]

I do not mean to suggest that Davidson himself presupposed a mereological conception of events in the way that some physicalists do. Far from it: the Nomological Character of Causality is surely meant to be an independently grounded principle which in its turn could ground a belief that (say) a fusion of physicist's events is the same as some mental event. And if the principle is defensible in its own right, we can dispense with anything like (A) in arguing for identities.

I cannot here discuss the arguments that may be given for the Nomological Character of Causality. But I note that if the Principle were defensible in its own right, we should have a perhaps unexpected disanalogy between continuants and events. We have a disanalogy, because we know that, using the exacting standard of the physical, there is nothing that can make us think that continuants are the same as fusions of microphysical things – nothing, that is, except an illicit importation of the mereological conception. This disanalogy may be unexpected, because we take it that there are dependency relations between items in the category of continuant and event: we take it that many events can be seen as changes precisely of continuants, that mental events, for instance, are changes in persons.

Suffice it to say that burden of proof of the physicalism I began by describing is on its proponent; and that if the physicalist wishes to shoulder this burden by defending the Nomological Character of Causality, then he must not help himself to a mereological conception of events in its defence. If he does, then his principle, and the physicalism it is supposed to support, is unsupported – if not unsupportable.

---

of Davidson, whose concern was mental events. But one could use examples of (non-mental) macroscopic events to make the point. (Consider again the economic event *e* of §5, say, or an avalanche.)

[27] If this were accepted, then one could aim at a stronger conclusion about anomalous monism. Davidson's premise (iii) in fact records the kind of regularity theory considered in §4, where we saw that one who accepts (A) as true of events is obliged to accept something like (C), and also that (C) is incompatible with that kind of regularity theory. What is being suggested now is that this regularity theory may require something along the lines of (A). So it seems that we might come to say that the regularity theory requires something whose rejection it requires.

28

Davidson and Sartre

Esa Saarinen

My aim in this paper is to discuss some interconnections in the thinking of Donald Davidson and Jean-Paul Sartre. My interest will be descriptive and elaborative, rather than critical, in nature: it is my belief that some of the leading ideas of Davidson and Sartre can be used to illuminate one another. The philosophical vocabularies of Davidson and Sartre are quite different, needless to say, but I will make an effort to indicate that there are points of contact which show that, in spite of the difference in traditions and choice of discourse language, the two philosophers do not revolve in separate orbits.

My aim is not to study the *validity* of specific arguments provided by Sartre or Davidson, nor even to study the question whether a given position is *true*. More generally, I am not assigning a conceptual priority to Davidson or to Sartre: the two can be used to illuminate one another, and the conviction that this is a task worth an effort is the methodological cornerstone of the present essay.

Davidson, unlike Sartre, has not explicitly presented a fullfledged philosophy of man. However, Davidson's work on the nature of thought, belief, intention, on the nature of mind in general, as well as his work on radical interpretation, suggest a perspective on man, the character of which, *vis-à-vis* the Sartrean background, I shall try to explicate in this paper. It is my belief that one of the reasons for Davidson's stature as one of the most profound living philosophers is precisely the fact that his work presents us a general and important vision, not just a collection of detailed arguments. It is the philosophy of the human condition in Sartre and in Davidson that we shall consequently tackle.

Sartre's existentialist ontology

I will begin by a brief exposition of Sartre's existentialist ontology.

The key contrast is between the categories of being-for-itself (*pour-soi*) and being-in-itself (*en-soi*). The former category, designed to represent the fundamental character of man, is characterized by radical freedom. ('Freedom' here is used in the somewhat technical sense explicated by Sartre.) Being-for-itself is free to choose itself and the meaning and value of the world in which it finds itself. The exercise of this freedom is the fundamental project of man; he is condemned to be free, forced to carry out the free series of choices his being consists of. Thus for a human being (being-for-itself) existence precedes essence: a human being is forced to constitute his individual essence out of nothingness, to use another key concept of Sartre's. The for-itself is thus condemned to constituting himself and the world by assigning meaning and value on the world and on his own being in it.

These familiar themes of existentialism also bring out key ideas of Sartre's theory of consciousness. It is precisely human consciousness that is at focus in Sartre's discussion of man: essentially, the notions of consciousness and that of being-for-itself are interchangeable. Thus what lies at the heart of human consciousness is radical freedom.

Sartre's other basic category, the category of being-in-itself, stands in sharp opposition to the category of being-for-itself. Being-in-itself ('thing', 'object', 'the world') is ontically given in itself, as complete and static and as pure essence. No nothingness, to be filled by freedom, is involved in its being.

The basic contrast between being-for-itself and being-in-itself in many ways echoes the contrasts between subject and object and between (subjective) consciousness and the (intentional) object of consciousness (what conscious-ness is conscious of). Without going into the details we proceed to discuss a third dimension of Sartre's existentialist ontology: being-for-the-other (*pour-autrui*).

Being-for-the-other emerges when the for-itself encounters another subject, another freedom. In this sense we deal with a social dimension here; but Sartre's chief idea is that the appearance of the other simply brings out another aspect of the very own being of the for-itself. With the appearance of the other, another being-for-itself characterized by freedom, I encounter a new and hitherto hidden dimension of myself: my *being as an object for the other*.

The striking idea here is that since the for-itself carries his objectivized being-for-the-other in his own being, which in turn presupposes the existence of the other, the traditional problem of the existence of other minds does not arise. We may note in passing that this is a characteristic Sartrean move – to avoid epistemological problem-setting by focusing on ontology. Thus the question 'how do we know the existence of the other?' is taken as secondary at best, since my own being carries the other in its very constitution.

From Sartre's point of view, the being of man is intelligible only in the context of the other. The for-itself is therefore not only freedom and a subject, but also an object, that on which freedom is exercised.

As we turn to Davidson, we will find something akin to Sartre's being-for-the-other. Or so I will now try to argue. The main thesis of the present paper runs: in Davidson's highly original and ingenious work, the emphasis is on those aspects of man that relate to his being-for-the-other. In Davidson's philosophy of mind and in his philosophy of the mental the key role is played by the other, in Sartre's terms, rather than anything resembling Sartre's being-for-itself.

Belief in Davidson and in Sartre

I shall approach the matter by first focusing on belief. This is a topic Davidson has discussed in a number of writings. Here is a characteristic paragraph from 'Mental events':

> There is no assigning beliefs to a person one by one on the basis of his verbal behavior, his choices, or other local signs no matter how plain and evident, for we make sense of particular beliefs only as they cohere with other beliefs, with preferences, with intentions, hopes, fears, expectations, and the rest ... the content of a propositional attitude derives from its place in the pattern.[1]

The account of the content of belief, or other propositional attitudes, is empathetically holistic in Davidson. 'The holistic character of the cognitive field', to use Davidson's own phrase,[2] is absolutely fundamental for Davidson's philosophy of mind, as well as for Davidson's proposals concerning radical interpretation, conceptual scheming and other matters of primary interest in Davidson. It is against this background that Davidson's thesis of the impossibility of massive error emerges:

> Global confusion, like universal mistake, is unthinkable, not because imagination boggles, but because too much confusion leaves nothing to be confused about and massive error erodes the background of true belief against which alone failure can be construed. ... To the extent that we fail to discover a coherent and plausible pattern in the attitudes and actions of others we simply forego the chance of treating them as persons.[3]

Thus, for Davidson, to identify a belief is to identify a system, a network of other beliefs, mental acts, intentions, etc. The content of a belief is essentially tied to such an overall pattern, and 'we cannot intelligibly attribute any propositional attitude to an agent except within the framework of a viable theory of his beliefs, desires, intentions, and decisions'.[4]

Davidson's account of belief, and the implication it suggests for the mental in general, stands in striking contrast to Sartre's discussion of belief, in passages such as these:

> Originally then the *cogito* includes this nullifying characteristic of existing for a witness, although the witness for which consciousness exists is itself. Thus by the sole fact that my belief is apprehended as belief, it is *no longer only belief*; that is, it is already no longer belief, it is troubled belief. Thus the ontological judgement 'belief is consciousness (of) belief' can under no circumstances be taken as a statement of identity; the subject and the attribute are radically different though still within the indissolvable unity of one and the same thing.[5]

---

[1] In *Essays on Actions and Events* (Clarendon Press, Oxford, 1980), p. 221.
[2] 'Psychology as philosophy', in *Essays on Actions and Events*, p. 231.
[3] 'Mental events', pp. 221–2.
[4] Ibid., p. 221.
[5] *Being and Nothingness* (tr. Hazel E. Barnes, Methuen & Co., London, 1969), pp. 74–5.

Sartre's perspective on belief is depicted by the general setting of Sartre's philosophy of mind. The discussion of belief is part of Sartre's discussion of 'the immediate structures of the for-itself', in which Sartre sets out to present the basic structures of the ontological category of being-for-itself. Consciousness as freedom and as nothingness escapes each effort to capture its essence; similarly *belief* as a structure embedded in consciousness escapes each effort to capture it from without. When we try to capture the beliefs of the for-itself, as they lie in the immediate setting of the consciousness, we are doomed to failure: what we can capture is the belief-as-objectivized – something that exists 'for a witness' and is 'troubled' in the face of that witness, to use Sartre's words.

The key point of interest for our Davidson-comparison lies in the emphasis of Sartre's discussion. For Sartre, the fundamental feature of belief is in its nature as something *escaping*. It is not the *content* of belief, in any sense natural from the vantage point of the analytic tradition, that is under scrutiny.

For Sartre, the interest of belief does not lie in the nature of belief *attributions* or in the mechanisms underlying belief-*sentences*. At issue is not philosophy of language or problems in the vicinity of it; at issue is the ontology of consciousness and the structure of being-for-itself. It is in this broad setting that Sartre's discussion of belief takes place, and the key features of belief will thus illustrate the key features of subjective (free) consciousness itself:

> On no account can we say that consciousness is consciousness or that belief is belief. ... We have seen that neither belief nor pleasure nor joy can exist *before* being conscious; consciousness is the measure of their being; yet it is no less true that belief, owing to the very fact that it can exist only as *troubled*, exists from the start as escaping itself, as shattering the unity of all the concepts in which one can wish to inclose it.[6]

The overall picture of Sartre's outline of belief is quite different from that presented by Davidson. While Sartre approaches belief as a structure that sheds light on the subjective nature of the for-itself, thus approaching belief from *within*, Davidson's approach is to explicate those characteristics of belief that presuppose an outside viewpoint and that amount to a discussion of belief-as-objectivized. That ever escaping 'witness' that Sartre posits as part of the overall structure of belief, Davidson takes as fixed. To use Sartre's words, Davidson explicates belief *as it appears to the witness* which exists as 'escaping itself' and as 'shattering the unity of all the concepts in which one can wish to inclose it'.

In short, Davidson explicates belief-as-an-object; Davidson takes as fundamental, in his account of belief, the realm of being-for-the-other.

What happens here from the vantage-point of Sartre's existentialism is that, in Davidson, the viewpoint of the other is presupposed. It is the other that tries to *attribute* a belief to somebody, it is the other that attempts to *interpret* the beliefs of somebody, that defines the problem-setting of Davidson's analysis. The paradigm issues of Davidson's, with their emphasis on (belief) attribution and on (belief) interpretation presuppose the viewpoint of the other.

---

[6] Ibid., p. 75.

Language and the mental

Davidson's interest in the attributions of mental acts and in the interpretation of them suggests that language plays a major role in Davidson's account of the mental. This expectation is fulfilled: in Davidson's analysis of the human condition, the status of language is fundamental.

In 'Thought and talk', Davidson formulates his position most explicitly. In that paper, he indeed goes as far as to argue that 'a creature cannot have thoughts unless it is an interpreter of the speech of another'.[7] For Davidson, the ideas of possessing a mind (being a conscious agent) and operating a language are thus intimately and permanently interlocked. Davidson elaborates:

> We have the idea of belief only from the role of belief in the interpretation of language, for as a private attitude it is not intelligible except as an adjustment to the public norm provided by language. It follows that a creature must be a member of a speech community if it is to have the concept of belief.[8]

From the point of view of Sartre's existentialist ontology, this position of Davidson's is fundamentally unacceptable. It is not only that 'belief as a private attitude' *per se* and outside any public norm is intelligible for Sartre; belief as explicated within the individualistic and subjective realm of being-for-itself presents us belief in its most fundamental form. It is that notion of belief, announced by Davidson to be unintelligible, that Sartre explicates.

Inasmuch as belief is taken as a testcase for the workings of the mind, the positions of Sartre and Davidson appear virtually opposite. This immediate impression will have to be educated, however. The reason: Davidson and Sartre are explicating different dimensions of the mental. In Sartre's terminology, Davidson only focuses on being-for-the-other.

Let us consider Davidson's position in more detail. As already noted, language plays a major role in all of Davidson's discussion of the mental. The tendency to approach the philosophy of man in the light of language is characteristic of Davidson.

Thus Davidson sees a fundamental role for language in the identification of finer distinctions in the realm of the mental:

> At this point it will help to turn to a psychological phenomenon one step more abstract – the ability to speak and understand language. We cannot hope in any case to cope with the full range and subtlety of psychological traits without taking account of language, for the finer distinctions among desires and beliefs, thoughts and fears, intentions and inferences, depend on the assumption of a cognitive structure as complex as that of language and cannot be understood apart from it.[9]

Now the key feature of language is in its intersubjective character: inasmuch as my consciousness is interlocked with language it appears in that same

---

[7] In *Mind and Language*, ed. Samuel Guttenplan (Clarendon Press, Oxford, 1975), p. 9.
[8] Ibid., p. 22.
[9] 'The material mind', in *Essays on Actions and Events*, p. 255.

intersubjective light as well. By emphasizing the role of language in any account of the mental, Davidson approaches mental as it appears to the other, within the realm of being-for-the-other.

'Language is not a phenomenon added on to being-for-others,' Sartre emphasizes in *Being and Nothingness*. 'It *is* originally being-for-others; that is, it is the fact that a subjectivity experiences itself as an object for the other'.[10] Language, for Sartre, exemplifies paradigmatically the realm of being-for-the-other. 'Language is therefore not distinct from the recognition of the other's existence'.[11] Thus the more important the role of language in our account of the mental, the more deeply we are into the region of being-for-the-other. This is precisely what happens in Davidson.

However, it is not simply *attributions* of mental states or acts, the theory of meaning of certain types of *sentences*, that Davidson is engaged with. While a great deal of Davidson's analysis does concern issues that are intimately linked with language, Davidson's writings go far beyond a mere treatment of our mental *vocabulary*. It is the mental itself that ultimately interests Davidson.

Davidson's strategy may be construed as follows. His primary target is the nature of the interpretation of the mental, attributions of mental states and acts, the structure of mental vocabulary. But once again he gains insight into this domain that for Sartre represents mental as an object-for-the-other, Davidson proceeds to conclusions about the realm of mental *per se* – about the nature of consciousness itself. Thus, for instance, in the above argument it is 'finer distinctions among desires and beliefs, thoughts and fears, intentions and inferences' that are under scrutiny: key features of the mental, rather than the language of the mental, is thus the object of study.

More explicitly still, in 'Thought and talk' Davidson first writes that 'we have the idea of belief only from the role of belief in the interpretation of language.' Davidson then adds, in the next paragraph, 'Can a creature have a belief if it does not have the concept of belief? It seems to me it cannot.'[12] Thought and talk are interlocked, and thereupon the key nature of the mental is viewed in terms of a shared frame, a community-based entity (language). The mental is taken to involve a fundamental aspect of social origin. Thus Davidson can close his discussion, in 'Thought and talk', with the words of Ulysses: 'no man is the lord of anything.'

No man is the lord of anything in the realm of *language*, but from the viewpoint of Sartre's existentialist ontology, the observation cannot be generalized so as to characterize the mental itself. When we approach the mental we are referred to freedom and to for-itself; and the key point of the for-itself is precisely to be the lord of its being. From the point of view of Sartre's philosophy of consciousness Davidson's thesis, if interpreted as a claim about the mental itself, is fundamentally misguided. Consciousness *is for itself*, and in this realm of absolute freedom there are no constraints of any kind – not, in particular, constraints of social origin. The for-itself does not exist for any entity given from without.

---

[10] *Being and Nothingness*, p. 372.
[11] Ibid., p. 373.
[12] 'Thought and talk', p. 22.

Freedom in Davidson and in Sartre

To emphasize the public, socially accessible aspects of thought, belief and other mental phenomena is for Sartre to *rectify* the mental. That radical freedom Sartre is mostly intrigued by in his analysis of consciousness, that radical freedom which characterizes the category of the for-itself, does not find place in Davidson's discussion.

While Sartre emphasizes freedom as the key feature of consciousness, Davidson's discussion in effect emphasizes the *limitations* of it. This point comes out most strikingly when we observe that a familiar Davidsonian theme of the impossibility of massive error has a backside.

Even though one might think that freedom could be smuggled into Davidson's framework under the covername of *belief* – as Davidson himself emphasizes 'belief can be idiosyncratic' – it is precisely with regard to belief that Davidson emphasizes the constraints imposed by others on me:

> it cannot be assumed that speakers never have false beliefs. Error is what gives belief its point. We can, however, take it as given that *most* beliefs are correct. The reason for this is that a belief is identified by its location in a pattern of beliefs; it is this pattern that determines the subject matter of belief, what the belief is about .... It isn't that any one false belief necessarily destroys our ability to identify further beliefs, but that the intelligibility of such identifications must depend on a background of largely unmentioned and unquestioned true beliefs.[13]

Thus, Davidson concludes, 'we can dismiss *a priori* the chance of massive error.'

But to the extent that my beliefs cannot be mistaken, to the extent that I must be in agreement with the community of others, to that extent my freedom is constrained! To that extent I am under the command of the other. To the extent that my beliefs can be fixed and constrained by the community of others, to that extent I am object-for-the-other, to that extent I have been objectivized. Thus what Davidson is struggling to demonstrate to us will for Sartre represent an emphasis on the object-characteristics of man.

The impossibility of massive error emerges in Davidson as a result of his theory of radical interpretation. Thus the above discussion amounts to this: If we explicate the mental in the context of Davidsonian radical interpretation, then what we encounter is consciousness as alienated, objectivized and rectified; the mental as being-for-the-other.

Freedom escapes Davidson's analysis here, and with it the whole realm of subjectivity and for-itself in Sartre's sense. If thinking (say) is interlocked with interpretation and with speech (language), as Davidson argues it is, thinking, as a form of being-conscious-of, has lost its character as radical freedom.

Davidson's analysis presents us therefore a picture of man as an objectivized other. Man does not define his being in and for himself; the norms, the constraints that he has to adjust himself to are primary for Davidson, and given

---

[13] Ibid., pp. 20–1.

from without: 'a creature must be a member of a speech community if it is to have the concept of belief.' Belief emerges out of 'the role of belief in the interpretation of language' – belief 'is not intelligible except as an adjustment to the public norm provided by language'.

The arguments of Davidson's that aim at showing the unintelligibility of 'belief as a private attitude' – Davidson's main aim in 'Thought and talk' – can be generalized to amount to a demonstration of the unintelligibility of the whole realm of being-for-itself. If beliefs and thoughts and intentions are unintelligible as private attitudes and a creature cannot have a belief, a thought or an intention if it does not have the corresponding concept, then the possibility of my being-for-myself is destroyed. The result would be devastating for Sartre, as the category of subjective being-for-itself is the key characteristic of human consciousness in Sartre's existentialist ontology.

This conclusion in my opinion shows that something fundamental is lacking in Davidson's discussion. Davidson's 'no man is the lord of anything' thesis is misguided as an account of the whole realm of the mental. Likewise, the picture of man that emerges is severely one-sided.

However, once we observe and appreciate the distinction between being-for-itself and being-for-the-other, we can pave the way out here. Indeed, as has already been suggested, Davidson's account of the mental should be taken as an analysis of only those aspects of it that fall within the realm of being-for-the-other. Davidson does not have a theory of subjective aspects of the mental, of that region Sartre labels being-for-itself. As a result, no picture of the mental qua mental, even in broad outline, is to be found in Davidson.

Davidson talks, as we have already seen, about beliefs, thoughts, etc. *per se*; his analysis is set as a theory of the mental itself. This, I propose, is a mistake. An aspectual qualification has to be introduced to Davidson's account of the mental; it is the mental *as it appears for the other* that is under scrutiny in Davidson's writings.

How can these considerations be reconciled with Davidson's remarks on the freedom of the mental? For if the mental, for Davidson, is the mental as it appears to the other, it would seem that from the Sartrean point of view the notion of freedom cannot have any place within the realm of the mental; freedom, for Sartre, is a characteristic of the for-itself, but within the dimension of being-for-the-other we are dealing with the category of the in-itself, the objectivized, rectified being.

Let us look closer into the notion of freedom as it emerges in Davidson.

The very problem Davidson sets to analyse in 'Mental events', let us recall, alludes to freedom. 'I am in sympathy with Kant', Davidson writes, 'when he says it is as impossible for the subtlest philosophy as for the commonest reasoning to argue freedom away. Philosophy must therefore assume that no true contradiction will be found between freedom and natural necessity in the same human actions, for it cannot give up the idea of nature any more than that of freedom.'[14] It is the problem of explaining away the apparent contradiction between freedom and natural necessity (necessity within the realm of the physical) as aspects of one and the same event that Davidson is engaged with.

---

[14] 'Mental events', p. 207.

Inasmuch as Davidson stresses the 'autonomy of the mental' he emphasizes freedom as a characteristic of the mental.

As I read Davidson, there seem to be two ideas involved in his discussion of freedom *vis-à-vis* the mental.

First, there is *freedom for the interpreter*, freedom on the level of the *attribution* of mental predicates. There is the holism of the mental realm, which in Davidson's words 'is a clue both to the autonomy and to the anomalous character of mental'. But freedom, as we encounter it here, is freedom for the other trying to attach a mental predicate on a given subject – freedom of the interpreter. As Davidson stresses, it is a basic feature of the mental that it doesn't provide a unique, determinate interpretation. Because of the holistic and open character of the mental realm, a host of alternative attributions is always in the offing.

Freedom as it encounters us here is something natural and predictable from the point of view of Sartre's existentialist ontology. Since we are dealing with the freedom of the interpreter here, Sartre's discussion applies with full strength – the for-itself is free: in this case, the interpreter.

Freedom as it emerges *via* the interpreter is thus an issue where Davidson and Sartre take a similar stand. There are features relating to the freedom of the interpreter worth a closer look to which I shall return later. Another element of Davidson's notion of the freedom of the mental is of more immediate interest: Davidson's idea that the mental cannot be subsumed under deterministic physical laws.

This point of Davidson's is interesting in our Sartrean context because it reveals a weakness in Sartre's discussion. Sartre lumps together objectivized being-for-the-other of the for-itself and the being of any object whatsoever. As soon as the for-itself is objectivized, freedom disappears and the for-itself is treated analogously to objects in the category of the in-itself. But to treat consciousness-as-an-object and any object whatsoever on a par seems counterintuitive: a more sensitive treatment seems to be called for, one that would allow us to make distinctions relating to freedom within Sartre's object-category. Davidson's discussion suggests us such a treatment.

If we take Davidson to be analysing the mental as it appears to the other and if we accept his line about the impossibility of subsuming the mental under deterministic physical laws, we seem to have an interesting and from Sartre's point of view novel source of freedom to operate with. As a result, we can attach the notion of freedom to the being of the for-itself as an object for the other. This is interesting, because that possibility did not exist for Sartre, for whom objectivizing automatically blocks away freedom. Davidson's discussion will thus make an important amendment to Sartre's analysis.

In 'Mental events' Davidson explicitly acknowledges that on his 'test' of the mental, the distinguishing feature of the mental is not that it is 'private' or that it is 'subjective'.[15] On the contrary, Davidson points out in 'Mental events', 'I say nothing of the supposed privacy of the mental, or the special authority of an agent has with respect to his own propositional attitudes.'[16] It is important to

---

[15] Ibid., p. 211.
[16] Ibid., p. 223.

note that much of the interest of Davidson's analysis depends on his not acknowledging any 'privacy of the mental'. If we do not announce at the outset, as Sartre in effect does, that there is a private or subjective aspect to the mental, it is striking to learn that 'there are no strict deterministic laws on the basis of which mental events can be predicted and explained', even though such laws are assumed to govern the physical world.[17]

Thus there is a systematic rationale for Davidson's disregard of a Sartrean type of freedom, which emerges in ontology and which exclusively attaches to the subjective side of the mental.

Radical interpretation and being-for-the-other

The subjective realm of the mental, that realm Sartre seeks to systematize with his concepts of freedom and nothingness, escapes Davidson's attention. But even if Davidson does not have vocabulary to describe the mental as subjective consciousness, even if we grant that Davidson's writings do not offer us insight into what Sartre calls being-for-itself, it seems to me that Davidson's discussion complements Sartre's analysis in an important way. When taken as an account of the category of being-for-the-other, Davidson's analysis supplies a perspective that reinforces Sartre, and in some ways goes beyond it.

In Sartre's account of being-for-the-other, the key concept is that of *the look* (le regard). The ontological dimension of being-for-the-other appears with the upsurge of the other, under his *look* for which the for-itself is an object. (The concept of look, like that of freedom above, is a technical notion that should not be taken overtly literally.)

The appearance of the other's look brings about a radical shift in my being. With a transformation reminiscent of Hegel's master–slave dialectics, I become a slave for the other:

> I perceive myself to be over there for *the other*, and this phantom-outline of my being touches me to the heart ... With the other's look the 'situation' escapes me. To use an everyday expression which better expresses our thought, I *am no longer master of the situation* ... the appearance of the other, on the contrary, causes the appearance in the situation of an aspect which I did not wish, of which I am not master, and which on principle escapes me since it is *for the other*. This is what Gide has appropriately called 'the devil's part'. It is the unpredictable but still real reverse side.[18]

The theme that Sartre brings up here is elaborated in detail in *Being and Nothingness*: it is a cornerstone of the being of the for-itself as an object for the other that the key notions of freedom, possibility and nothingness now qualify the other. The transformation brought about by the other's look strips me of my freedom.

In the realm of being-for-the-other, freedom thus lies in the hands of the other. This basic Sartrean theme finds an interesting, if partial, counterpart in

---

[17] Ibid., p. 208.
[18] *Being and Nothingness*, p. 265.

Davidson's account of the mental: the mental, as reflected *via* radical interpretation, is a for-the-other concept which leaves a choice for the other (the
interpreter). Radical interpretation is underdetermined in Davidson's doctrine;
the choice and freedom of the interpreter are thus brought into the focus.

One of the most fascinating and persuasive passages in Davidson's analysis
lies in the emphasis he places on the indeterminacy of radical interpretation.
Evidence, no matter how detailed, does not fix interpretation uniquely in the
case of mental states, nor in the case of linguistic meaning. Beliefs a speaker
holds and the meanings he associates with his words are interlocked, and the
same indeterminacy of interpretation hits to the core of both:

> Underlying the indeterminacy of interpretation is a commonplace fact about
> interpretation. Suppose someone says, 'That's a shooting star'. Should I take him
> to mean it really is a star, but that he believes some stars are very small and cold;
> or should I think he means it is not a star but a meteorite, and believes stars are
> always very large and hot? Additional evidence may resolve this case, but there will
> always be cases where all possible evidence leaves open a choice between
> attributing to a speaker a standard meaning and an idiosyncratic pattern of belief,
> or a deviant meaning and a sober opinion.[19]

To apply Davidson's vision in the relevant context of Sartre's existentialist
ontology yields insight as to why my objectivized being-for-the-other sets me at
the mercy of the other's freedom, why 'being-seen constitutes me as a
defenseless being for a freedom which is not my freedom'.[20] As an object of the
other's interpretation my beliefs, intentions, wishes, and ultimately my whole
being, are radically beyond my own command. That aspect of my being we face
here is 'outside my reach, outside my action, outside my knowledge;'[21] no
matter how I try to impose an intended interpretation of my being on the other,
the indeterminacy pointed out by Davidson will leave a logical gap between my
efforts and the interpretation formed by the other. 'Through the other's look I
live myself as fixed in the midst of the world, as in danger, as irremediable. But I
know neither what I am nor what is my place in the world.'[22]

The indeterminacy of interpretation, emphasized by Davidson, finds thus a
natural place in Sartre's existentialist ontology. If we take Davidson's main
target of analysis to be the mental as an object for the other, the picture that
emerges runs as follows: what represents indeterminacy of interpretation for
Davidson turns into freedom in the hands of the other for Sartre.

The converse does not hold. Succintly put, for Sartre it is not just
interpretation that falls within the realm of the other's freedom. Freedom lies
underneath anything and everything that claims an element of value or meaning
as its constituent. Matters of radical interpretation are a subclass of these.

The present analogy links closely with Sartre's discussion of the nature of
language in *Being and Nothingness*. As already observed, language represents
paradigmatically being-for-the-other for Sartre; as Sartre emphasizes, 'In the

---

[19] 'The material mind', p. 257.
[20] *Being and Nothingness*, p. 267.
[21] Ibid., p. 268.
[22] Ibid., p. 268.

intersubjectivity of the for-others, it is not necessary to invent language because it is already given in the recognition of the other.'[23] Keeping these preliminaries in mind, consider now the meaning of language, as described by Sartre:

> the 'meaning' of my expressions always escapes me. I never know exactly if I signify what I wish to signify nor even if I am signifying anything ... For lack of knowing what I actually express for the other, I constitute my language as an incomplete phenomenon of flight outside myself ... As soon as I express myself, I can only guess at the meaning of what I express.[24]

For Sartre, there is thus a strong element of indeterminacy underlying anything I may try to express: this is the theme of the indeterminacy of radical interpretation as brought to an extreme.

In spite of different philosophical vocabularies, there is thus a deep-rooted analogy between Davidson and Sartre in that realm Sartre labels being-for-the-other.

When taken as an account of my objectivized being-for-the-other, Davidson's analysis yields us a motivation for that category which, by the standards of an analytic philosopher, may appear *ad hoc* on the basis of Sartre's discussion alone. Davidson's account can be interpreted as providing an argument for Sartre's key conviction that the other is a permanent structure of my own being – that no account of man can dispense with his being-for-the-other, his 'me-as-an-object'.

Interpretation, in the sense explicated by Davidson, seems a relatively natural concept which philosophically appears less problematic than those notions on which Sartre builds his category of being-for-the-other. I thus propose to look at Sartre's notion of 'me-as-an-object' as relying on something like Davidson's radical interpretation and to seek a partial motivation for that concept in the philosophical ground landmarked by Davidson.

Thus reflected, being-for-the-other loses much of the flavour that otherwise might strike an analytic philosopher as unintelligible. Loose ontological talk of the sort Sartre favours is not easy for an analytic philosopher to countenance. By shifting the attention to interpretation, we remove a source of possible misunderstanding that might otherwise distract us from the insights underlying Sartre's discussion.

Davidson's emphasis on the intimate connection of language and mental states as well as his account of radical interpretation suggest in a schematic form some basic features of the human condition. Inasmuch as the notion of man is tied to something like Davidsonian radical interpretation – and I believe it is – we are forced to the realm of being-for-the-other.

Our proposal would guarantee the systematic interests of being-for-the-other also from the existentialist viewpoint. With the notion of radical interpretation at our disposal, we can explain why being-for-the-other must loom large in an existentialist philosophy that tries to explicate the idea of a human being constantly transcending itself.

---

[23] Ibid., p. 372.
[24] Ibid., p. 373.

Consider the for-itself interpreting his own acts, efforts and psychology. The interpreter and the object of interpretation are one and the same, but under two different ontological modes: the for-itself looks upon itself as an object-for-the-other. The key point is that there remains an all-important ontological gap, safeguarded by the element of indeterminacy pointed out by Davidson between the subject serving as the interpreter and the object of interpretation. Interpretation will always remain at a distance from the object of interpretation.

But if that is the case, interpretation can be reflected as one method of nihiliation – one method I can use to make myself aware of *what I am not*: this is the existential interest of the Davidsonian radical interpretation, I propose.

For, as Arthur C. Danto has pointed out, 'consciousness is … nothingness: not an absolute lack, an unqualified nihility, but a transitive one; a not-this, a not-that, for any given this or that. Put in these terms, Sartre's otherwise perverse formula even makes direct sense: "we are what we are not".'[25] Thus *that which I am not* will be of profound existential import for me as for-itself; in analysing what the for-itself is authentically we are referred to the this or the that which the for-itself is not.

In everyday thinking we are constantly seduced to bad faith as a result of our assuming we *are* so-and-so when in fact that so-and-so is a result of radical interpretation. I am a coward, I may say to myself, believing this is a property of mine given absolutely and from within. But as a mental predicate it qualifies me only as relative to a scheme of interpretation – it qualifies me at a distance only. For as long as radical interpretation of myself always presents a *possibility* at best, we cannot take it as a fixed given. Myself as a coward is a not-this or not-that in the sense intended by Danto. As long as we keep fresh in mind the indeterminacy of radical interpretation, a key source of bad faith is blocked out.

The proposal, therefore, is that the theme of the for-itself as a transitive nothingness, gets a more concrete formulation in the impossibility of the for-itself to be what a radical interpretation presents it as. The point here is that among the pre-given this or that which the for-itself is not, some are more interesting than others. It is not of interest to learn that I am not this table or that tree; but it may be shockingly interesting to learn that I am not the coward I interpret myself as.

The radical interpretation of oneself thus entertains a special status. There is an intimate ontological bridge connecting the for-itself as subjective consciousness to the for-itself-as-interpreted. This bond is fundamental from the point of view of the above proposal and from the point of view of Sartre's own description, in passages such as these:

> Thus my being-for-others – i.e., my me-as-an-object – is not an image cut off from me and growing in a strange consciousness. It is a perfectly real being, *my* being as the condition of my selfness confronting the other and of the other's selfness confronting me. It is my *being-outside* – not a being passively submitted to which would itself have come to me from outside, but an outside assumed and recognized as *my* outside.[26]

---

[25] Arthur C. Danto, *Sartre* (Fontana/Collins, Glasgow, 1975), p. 73.
[26] *Being and Nothingness*, pp. 285–6.

We also get a closer look at authentic being, as it emerges in the existentialist context. 'The existence of the for-itself is ... vertiginous', Peter Caw writes, 'the constant shifting of ground, the repeated encounter with our own otherness, engenders a desire or a nostalgia for the permanence and fixity of the in-itself, and the corresponding fear of the unknown being one discovers oneself to be.'[27] Our present discussion, which tries to disclose the existential import of radical interpretation, reveals one type of man's inherent otherness. For if radical interpretation of myself is always undermined by indeterminacy, in the last analysis it can indicate to me only *what I am not*. If we are conscious of the true character of radical interpretation, we can thus turn that Davidsonian theme to exemplify 'the constant shifting of ground, the repeated encounter with our own otherness' which is fundamental for Sartre.

As a result, we gain insight into the notion of authentic being. This is a theme Sartre does not discuss explicitly in detail, but the idea of nihilization and of otherness allows one possible formulation that Caws has succinctly put in these terms: 'A form of sincerity is ... possible, provided that it rests not on my being what I am but on my not being it and acknowledging *that* – or, better, acknowledging a constant oscillation or "play of mirrors" between being what I am and not-being it.'[28]

This play of mirrors is exemplified by radical interpretation of myself. To the extent that there is an element of indeterminacy at play, to that extent there is also an element of nothingness involved. To that extent is there the possibility of existential authenticity – of 'acknowledging a constant oscillation between what I am and not-being it'.

---

[27] Peter Caws, *Sartre* (Routledge & Kegan Paul, London, 1979), p. 79.
[28] Ibid., p. 80.

29

Rational Animals[*]

DONALD DAVIDSON

Some animals think and reason; they consider, test, reject and accept hypotheses; they act on reasons, sometimes after deliberating, imagining consequences and weighing probabilities; they have desires, hopes and hates, often for good reasons. They also make errors in calculation, act against their own best judgment, or accept doctrines on inadequate evidence. Any one of these accomplishments, activities, actions or errors is enough to show that such an animal is a rational animal, for to be a rational animal is just to have propositional attitudes, no matter how confused, contradictory, absurd, unjustified or erroneous those attitudes may be. This, I propose, is the answer.

The question is: what animals are rational? Of course I do not intend to name names, even names of species or other groups. I shall not try to decide whether dolphins, apes, human embryos or politicians are rational, or even whether all that prevents computers from being rational is their genesis. My question is what makes an animal (or anything else, if one wants) rational.

The propositional attitudes provide an interesting criterion of rationality because they come only as a matched set. It may sound trivial to say that a rich pattern of beliefs, desires and intentions suffices for rationality; and it may seem far too stringent to make this a necessary condition. But in fact the stringency lies in the nature of the propositional attitudes, since to have one is to have a full complement. One belief demands many beliefs, and beliefs demand other basic attitudes such as intentions, desires and, if I am right, the gift of tongues. This does not mean that there are not borderline cases. Nevertheless, the intrinsically holistic character of the propositional attitudes makes the distinction between having any and having none dramatic.

To make the distinction so strong, and to make it depend on language, invites an accusation of anthropocentrism. The complaint is just, but it ought not to be leveled against me. I merely describe a feature of certain concepts. And after all, it is not surprising that our human language is rich in resources for distinguishing men and women from other creatures, just as Eskimos are said to have a vocabulary convenient for picking out varieties of snow. We connive with our language to make it, and us, seem special.

*First published in *Dialectica*, 36 (1982), pp. 318–27. © Donald Davidson.

I promised not to discuss the question whether particular species are rational, but it will be impossible to avoid the appearance of talking of the feats and abilities of beasts because so much discussion of the nature of thought has by tradition centered on the mental powers of non-human animals. I consider this approach as just a colorful (and sometimes emotionally laden) way of thinking about the nature of thought.[1]

Norman Malcolm tells this story, which is intended to show that dogs think:

> Suppose our dog is chasing the neighbor's cat. The latter runs full tilt toward the oak tree, but suddenly swerves at the last moment and disappears up a nearby maple. The dog doesn't see this maneuver and on arriving at the oak tree he rears up on his hind feet, paws at the trunk as if trying to scale it, and barks excitedly into the branches above. We who observe this whole episode from a window say, 'He thinks that the cat went up that oak tree'.[2]

(Malcolm added, we would say the dog was barking up the wrong tree.) Malcolm claims that under the circumstances someone who attributed that belief to the dog might well – almost surely would – be right; he would have exactly the sort of evidence needed to justify such an attribution.

Let me give a preliminary argument designed to put Malcolm's claim in doubt. It's clear that the evidence for the dog's 'belief' depends on taking belief as a determinant of action and emotional response. We are asked to infer from what we see that the dog wants to catch the cat, that he runs where he does because of this desire and a belief about where the cat has gone, and that he is venting his frustration at not being able to follow the cat up the tree by barking, pawing the ground, and so forth. The details do not need to be right, of course. The point is so far obvious: if we are justified in inferring beliefs, we are also justified in inferring intentions and desires (and perhaps much more).

But how about the dog's supposed belief that the cat went up that oak tree? That oak tree, as it happens, is the oldest tree in sight. Does the dog think that the cat went up the oldest tree in sight? Or that the cat went up the same tree it went up the last time the dog chased it? It is hard to make sense of the questions. But then it does not seem possible to distinguish between quite different things the dog might be said to believe.

One way of telling that we are attributing a propositional attitude is by noting that the sentences we use to do the attributing may change from true to false if, in the words that pick out the object of the attitude, we substitute for some referring expression another expression that refers to the same thing. The belief that the cat went up that oak tree is not the same belief as the belief that the cat went up the oldest tree in sight. If we use words like 'believe', 'think', 'intend' while dropping the feature of semantic opacity, we are not using those

---

[1] I have often given talks based on ideas in this paper under the title 'Why Animals Can't Think'. The title was tendentious, since what I argued for (as here) was that only creatures with a language can think. I happen to believe, however, that men and women are alone in having language, or enough language to justify attributing thoughts to them. On the moral issue how we should treat dumb creatures, I see no reason to be less kind to those without thoughts or language than to those with; on the contrary.

[2] Norman Malcolm, 'Thoughtless brutes', *Proceedings and Addresses of the American Philosophical Association*, 46 (1972–3), p. 13.

words to attribute propositional attitudes. For it has long been recognized that semantic opacity distinguishes talk about propositional attitudes from talk of other things.

Someone may suggest that the position occupied by the expression 'that oak tree' in the sentence 'The dog thinks the cat went up that oak tree' is, in Quine's terminology, transparent. The right way to put the dog's belief (the suggestion continues) is 'The dog thinks, with respect to that oak tree, that the cat went up it' or 'That oak tree is the one the dog thinks the cat went up'. But such constructions, while they may relieve the attributer of the need to produce a description of the object that the believer would accept, nevertheless imply that there is some such description; the *de re* description picks out an object the believer could somehow pick out. In a popular if misleading idiom, the dog must believe, under some description of the tree, that the cat went up that tree. But what kind of description would suit the dog? For example, can the dog believe of an object that it is a tree? This would seem impossible unless we suppose the dog has many general beliefs about trees: that they are growing things, that they need soil and water, that they have leaves or needles, that they burn. There is no fixed list of things someone with the concept of a tree must believe, but without many general beliefs there would be no reason to identify a belief as a belief about a tree, much less an oak tree. Similar considerations apply to the dog's supposed thinking about the cat.

We identify thoughts, distinguish between them, describe them for what they are, only as they can be located within a dense network of related beliefs. If we really can intelligibly ascribe single beliefs to a dog, we must be able to imagine how we would decide whether the dog has many other beliefs of the kind necessary for making sense of the first. It seems to me that no matter where we start, we very soon come to beliefs such that we have no idea at all how to tell whether a dog has them, and yet such that, without them, our confident first attribution looks shaky.

Not only does each belief require a world of further beliefs to give it content and identity, but every other propositional attitude depends for its particularity on a similar world of beliefs. In order to believe the cat went up the oak tree I must have many true beliefs about cats and trees, this cat and this tree, the place, appearance and habits of cats and trees, and so on; but the same holds if I wonder whether the cat went up the oak tree, fear that it did, hope that it did, wish that it had, or intend to make it do so. Belief – indeed, true belief – plays a central role among the propositional attitudes. So let me speak of all the propositional attitudes as thoughts.

As remarked above, there may be no fixed list of beliefs on which any particular thought depends. Nevertheless, much true belief is necessary. Some beliefs of the sort required are general, but plausibly empirical, such as that cats can scratch or climb trees. Others are particular, such as that the cat seen running a moment ago is still in the neighborhood. Some are logical. Thoughts, like propositions, have logical relations. Since the identity of a thought cannot be divorced from its place in the logical network of other thoughts, it cannot be relocated in the network without becoming a different thought. Radical incoherence in belief is therefore impossible. To have a single propositional attitude is to have a largely correct logic, in the sense of having a pattern of beliefs that logically cohere. This is one reason why to have propositional attitudes is to be a rational creature. The point extends to intentional action. Intentional action is action that can be explained in terms of beliefs and desires whose propositional contents rationalize the action. Similarly, an emotion like being pleased that one has stopped smoking must be an emotion that is rational in the light of beliefs and values one has.

This is not to deny the existence of irrational beliefs, actions and emotions, needless to say. An action one has reasons to perform may be an action one has better reasons to avoid. A belief may be reasonable in the light of some but not the totality of one's other beliefs; and so on. The point is that the possibility of irrationality depends on a large degree of rationality. Irrationality is not mere lack of reason, but a disease or perturbation of reason.

I assume in this paper that an observer can under favorable circumstances tell what beliefs, desires and intentions an agent has. Indeed, I appealed to this assumption when I urged that if a creature cannot speak it is unclear that intensionality can be maintained in the descriptions of his purported beliefs and other attitudes. Similarly I wondered whether, in the absence of speech, there could be grounds for attributing the general beliefs needed for making sense of any thought. Without defending the assumption that we can know other minds, let me distinguish this assumption from other stronger assumptions. Merely to claim that an observer can under favorable conditions tell what someone else is thinking is not to embrace verificationism, even with respect to thoughts. For the observability assumption does not imply that it is possible to state explicitly what evidence is necessary or sufficient to determine the presence of a particular thought; there is no suggestion that thinking can somehow be reduced to something else. Nor does the observability assumption imply that the only way to determine the existence of a thought is by observing. On the contrary, it is clear that people normally know without observation or evidence of any kind what they believe, want and intend.

Nor does the observability assumption amount to behaviorism. Propositional attitudes can be discovered by an observer who witnesses nothing but behavior without the attitudes being in any way reducible to behavior. There are conceptual ties between the attitudes and behavior which are sufficient, given enough information about actual and potential behavior, to allow correct inferences to the attitudes.

From what has been said about the dependence of beliefs on other beliefs, and of other propositional attitudes on beliefs, it is clear that a very complex pattern of behavior must be observed to justify the attribution of a single thought. Or, more accurately, there has to be good reason to believe there is such a complex pattern of behavior. And unless there is actually such a complex pattern of behavior, there is no thought.

I think there is such a pattern only if the agent has language. If this is right, then Malcolm was justified in attributing thought to his dog only if he believed, on good evidence, that his dog has language.

The view that thought – belief, desire, intention, and the like – requires language is controversial, but certainly not new. The version of the thesis which I want to promote needs to be distinguished from various related versions. I don't, for example, believe that thinking can be reduced to linguistic activity. I find no plausibility in the idea that thoughts can be nomologically identified with, or correlated with, phenomena characterized in physical or neurological terms. Nor do I see any reason to maintain that what we can't say we can't think. My thesis is not, then, that each thought depends for its existence on the existence of a sentence that expresses that thought. My thesis is rather that a creature cannot have a thought unless it has language. In order to be a thinking, rational creature, the creature must be able to express many thoughts, and above all, be able to interpret the speech and thoughts of others.

As I remarked above, this has often been claimed; but on what grounds? Given the popularity of the idea, from the rationalists through the American pragmatists, and even among contemporary analytic philosophers, there is a remarkable dearth of arguments. So far, I have pointed to the dubious applicability of the intensionality test where dumb animals are concerned, and the requirement, if thought is to be present, that there be a rich supply of general (and true) beliefs. These considerations point in the direction of language, but they do not amount to a demonstration that language is necessary to thought. Indeed, what these considerations suggest is only that there probably can't be much thought without language.

Against the dependence of thought on language is the plain observation that we succeed in explaining and sometimes predicting the behavior of language-less animals by attributing beliefs and desires and intentions to them. This method works for dogs and frogs much as it does for people. And, it may be added, we have no general and practical alternative framework for explaining animal behavior. Don't these facts amount to a *justification* of the application of the method?[3]

No doubt they do. But there could remain a clear sense in which it would be wrong to conclude that dumb (= incapable of interpreting or engaging in linguistic communication) animals have propositional attitudes. To see this it is only necessary to reflect that someone might easily have no better or alternative way of explaining the movements of a heat-seeking missile than to suppose the missile wanted to destroy an airplane and believed it could by moving in the way it was observed to move. This uninformed observer might be justified in attributing a desire and beliefs to the missile; but he would be wrong. I know better, for example, not because I know how the missile is designed, but because I know that it moves as it does because it was designed and built by people who had the very desire and beliefs my ignorant friend assigned to the missile. My explanation, while still teleological, and dependent on the existence of propositional attitudes, is a better explanation because it does not attribute to the missile the potentiality for the rich range of behavior that a thinking creature must have.

The case of a languageless creature differs from the case of the missile in two respects: many animals are far more like humans in the range of their behavior than missiles are; and we do not know that there is a better way to explain their behavior than to summon up propositional attitudes. What we need, then, in order to make a case, is a characterization of what it is that language supplies that is necessary for thought. For if there is such a necessary condition, we can continue to explain the behavior of speechless creatures by attributing proposi-

---

[3] This is the position stressed by Jonathan Bennett, *Linguistic Behavior* (Cambridge University Press, Cambridge, 1976).

tional attitudes to them while at the same time recognizing that such creatures do not actually have propositional attitudes. We will be bound to acknowledge that we are applying a pattern of explanation that is far stronger than the observed behavior requires, and to which the observed behavior is not subtle enought to give point.

In the rest of this paper I state the condition for thought that I believe only language can supply, and I marshal considerations in favor of my view. Although I present these considerations as an argument, it will be clear that several steps in my reasoning can be challenged.

The 'argument' has two steps. I think I have shown that all the propositional attitudes require a background of beliefs, so I shall concentrate on conditions for belief. Without belief there are no other propositional attitudes, and so no rationality as I have characterized it.

First, I argue that in order to have a belief, it is necessary to have the concept of belief.

Second, I argue that in order to have the concept of belief one must have language.

Norman Malcolm, in the article mentioned before, makes a distinction similar to the one I want between having a belief and having the concept of a belief, but his terminology differs from mine. I have been using the word 'thought' to cover all the propositional attitudes. Malcolm, however, restricts the application of 'thought' to a higher level of thinking. In his view, the dog can believe the cat went up that oak tree, but it cannot have the thought that the cat has gone up that oak tree. The latter, but not the former, Malcolm holds, requires language. Malcolm makes the distinction by saying one merely thinks (believes) that *p* if one is aware that *p*, but one has the thought that *p* if one is aware that one is aware that *p*. This is close to the distinction I have in mind between believing that *p* and believing that one believes that *p*. The second is a belief about a belief, and so requires the concept of belief. To make a rough comparison: Malcolm holds that language draws a line between creatures that merely think and creatures that have the concept of a thought; I hold that in order to think one must have the concept of a thought, and so language is required in both cases.

Donald Weiss takes issue with Malcolm: Weiss thinks it is possible to make sensible attributions of awareness to speechless creatures.[4] Since I think his example may strike a responsive chord in others, let me paraphrase and then quote him at some length:

Arthur is not a dog but, let us say, a superdog from another planet. Arthur arrives on earth unaccompanied, and here he hatches. He has no commerce with, or knowledge of, other creatures – he is observed through one-way mirrors. He has no language. According to Weiss, we become convinced he has reflective intelligence when we witness this scene:

> One day Arthur comes upon a shiny metal, puts it in the fire, tries to hammer it out – but discovers that it is apparently no more malleable than it was when cold. He tries again more slowly and more methodically – but again the same result.

---

[4] Donald Weiss, 'Professor Malcolm on animal intelligence', *Philosophical Review*, 84 (1975).

The regularity in which Arthur believed – we whisper among ourselves – is not entirely universal. Arthur has discovered an instance that does not conform to the general rule.

Arthur proceeds to walk agitatedly around his living space. He abruptly sits down; just as abruptly he gets up again; he paces forward and back. Once more he sits down, but this time he remains seated. Fifteen minutes pass without change of posture; Arthur's eyes are focused straight ahead. Then suddenly he leaps up and immediately proceeds to pile a large quantity of wood onto his fire. ... He then plunges his newly discovered metal into the fire, and, after a time, withdraws it. He again attempts to hammer it out – and this time he meets with success. Thus apparently satisfied ... he proceeds in a leisurely manner to cook himself a meal.[5]

Weiss says we now have strong evidence Arthur has reflected upon his own beliefs; he is particularly impressed by the fact that Arthur, in response to his state of befuddlement, sits wide-eyed and stock-still, and then veritably leaps to perform the acts that constitute the solution to his problem.[6]

I will ignore the question-begging vocabulary Weiss uses in describing Arthur's movements, for I think Weiss is barking up a right tree: it is essential that we be able to describe Arthur as being surprised. What I think is clear is that if he is surprised, he does have reflective thoughts and, of course, beliefs.

This is not to claim that all thinking is self-conscious, or that whenever we think that *p* we must be aware that *p*, or believe that we believe that *p*, or think that we think that *p*. My claim is rather this: in order to have any propositional attitude at all, it is necessary to have the concept of a belief, to have a belief about some belief. But what is required in order to have the concept of a belief? Here I turn for help to the phenomenon of surprise, since I think that surprise requires the concept of a belief.

Suppose I believe there is a coin in my pocket. I empty my pocket and find no coin. I am surprised. Clearly enough I could not be surprised (though I could be startled) if I did not have beliefs in the first place. And perhaps it is equally clear that having a belief, at least one of the sort I have taken for my example, entails the possibility of surprise. If I believe I have a coin in my pocket, something might happen that would change my mind. But surprise involves a further step. It is not enough that I first believe there is a coin in my pocket, and after emptying my pocket I no longer have this belief. Surprise requires that I be aware of a contrast between what I did believe and what I come to believe. Such awareness, however, is a belief about a belief: if I am surprised, then among other things I come to believe my original belief was false. I do not need to insist that every case of surprise involves a belief that a prior belief was false (though I am inclined to think so). What I do want to claim is that one cannot have a general stock of beliefs of the sort necessary for having any beliefs at all without being subject to surprises that involve beliefs about the correctness of one's own beliefs. Surprise about some things is a necessary and sufficient condition of thought in general. This concludes the first part of my 'argument'.

Much of the point of the concept of belief is that it is the concept of a state of an organism which can be true or false, correct or incorrect. To have the

---

[5] Ibid., pp. 91–2.
[6] Ibid., pp. 91–2.

concept of belief is therefore to have the concept of objective truth. If I believe there is a coin in my pocket, I may be right or wrong; I'm right only if there is a coin in my pocket. If I am surprised to find there is no coin in my pocket, I come to believe that my former belief did not correspond with the state of my finances. I have the idea of an objective reality which is independent of my belief.

A creature may react with the world in complex ways without entertaining any propositions. It may discriminate among colors, tastes, sounds and shapes. It may 'learn', that is, change its behavior in ways that preserve its life or increase its food intake. It may 'generalize', in the sense of reacting to new stimuli as it has come to react to similar stimuli. Yet none of this, no matter how successful by my standards, shows that the creature commands the subjective–objective contrast, as required by belief.

What *would* show command of the subjective–objective contrast? Clearly linguistic communication suffices. To understand the speech of another, I must be able to think of the same things she does; I must share her world. I don't have to agree with her in all matters, but in order to disagree we must entertain the same proposition, with the same subject matter, and the same standard of truth. Communication depends, then, on each communicant having, and correctly thinking that the other has, the concept of a shared world, an intersubjective world. But the concept of an intersubjective world is the concept of an objective world, a world about which each communicant can have beliefs.

I claim, then, that the concept of intersubjective truth suffices as a basis for belief and hence for thoughts generally. And perhaps it is plausible enough that having the concept of intersubjective truth depends on communication in the full linguistic sense. To complete the 'argument', however, I need to show that the *only* way one could come to have the subjective–objective contrast is through having the concept of intersubjective truth. I confess I do not know how to show this. But neither do I have any idea how else one could arrive at the concept of an objective truth. In place of an argument for the first step, I offer this analogy.

If I were bolted to the earth I would have no way of determining the distance from me of many objects. I would only know they were on some line drawn from me toward them. I might interact successfully with objects, but I could have no way of giving content to the question where they were. Not being bolted down, I am free to triangulate. Our sense of objectivity is the consequence of another sort of triangulation, one that requires two creatures. Each interacts with an object, but what gives each the concept of the way things are objectively is the base line formed between the creatures by language. The fact that they share a concept of truth alone makes sense of the claim that they have beliefs, that they are able to assign objects a place in the public world.

The conclusion of these considerations is that rationality is a social trait. Only communicators have it.

30

Animal Interpretation

Richard Jeffrey

1. The seventeenth century's New Philosophy (= early modern science) posed the problem: If we are clouds of particles governed by the laws of dynamics, what does talk about preferential choice have to do with us? The nineteenth-century reduction of phenomenological thermodynamics to classical dynamics provided the analogue of an answer, e.g., explaining how thermodynamical irreversibility can coexist with the time-symmetry of the basic laws of dynamics that govern the detailed motion of the particles while the cloud obeys the asymmetrical phenomenological laws.

It's cloud phenomena that impinge on us. If the Laplacean superman knew the exact point in phase space that represents the current positions and momenta of all the air molecules in this room, he'd have to do an enormous averaging job in order to discover what we're immediately sensitive to: the temperature. The same sort of thing goes for all our senses, except for such stray bits as our sensitivity to single photons in the dark. (But Laplace's superman has become Maxwell's demon, whose inability to pin down points in phase space is a basic fact of quantum theory. The points themselves have become blurs.)

2. *An analogue antithesis to Davidson's anomaly of the mental.* In the 6N-dimensional phase space of an N-molecule gas, positions and momenta of all molecules at one time are represented by some point, to which the laws of classical mechanics assign a definite trajectory, determining all positions and momenta at any time. As time goes by, any cell that represents interval determinations of a point's 6N coordinates is mapped deterministically (in classical mechanics) into increasingly diffuse regions of phase space, somewhat as a neat smoke-ring diffuses throughout the air in a closed room until, after a time, it is a featureless fog. It is a partition of phase space into some such cells that we sense as warmth and cold.

A reduction of psychology to neurology could be dreamt: phenomenological psychological concepts supervene on neurological ones somewhat as the concepts of phenomenological thermodynamics supervene upon dynamical ones in classical statistical mechanics. But psychology is not in the sort of shape that thermodynamics was in when Maxwell began to connect it with mechanics. We lack psychological analogues of the precise, general thermodynamical laws that the nineteenth century had in hand: precise, general psycho-psycho laws. But why would we have them? We're special, quirky, evolutionary artifacts. Blueprints for one of us would fill a library. We're not the sort of thing we can get the intellectual grip on that we have on some gases.[1]

3. The four Fs (feeding, fighting, fleeing, reproducing) apply univocally to a wide range of animals. But what's food for some might poison others; a gesture of submission for some (a sort of smile) might be a threat display for others; and so on. So, e.g., the interspecific concept of food is a functional one, having to do with what will nourish specific organisms at particular stages of their lives. And even for a single species, where one might hope in principle to find a general chemical characterization of what will do as food, the working concept is the functional one.

4. We've all read some ethology. Let's recall the flavor, through an excerpt from *The Evolution of Culture in Animals*.[2]

> in female or hind groups of red deer there is a dominance hierarchy, the leader being the oldest fertile individual. The organization of the group appears to be centered around a system of protection. This is no better illustrated than by Darling's observation that when a group flees they form a spindle-shaped pattern with the leader in the front and the second dominant individual in the rear .... If they pass into a gulley, the last individual will stop and fix the intruder with her eyes while the group disappears. The moment they emerge into sight again, the leader takes up the sentry duty, and the last individual rushes forward to rejoin the group to reform their spindle.

That's a more complex account that 'it's feeding' would be, but as robust against behavioristic strictures when you see it with your own eyes.

5. The ethologist's characterization of the hind group's bodily movements used the behavioristically unacceptable terms 'flee' and (elsewhere) 'move from danger', which point to a functional explanation, in which the functional design is Nature's. Another step is needed, to go from naturally selected behavior that has an obvious point in terms of survival, to preferential choice by the individuals with survival in view:

> To see this it is only necessary to reflect that someone might easily have no better or alternative way of explaining the movements of a heat-seeking missile than to suppose the missile wanted to destroy an airplane and believed it could by moving in the way it was observed to move. This uninformed observer might be justified in attributing a desire and beliefs to the missile; but he would be wrong. I know better, for example, not because I know how the missile is designed, but because I

---

[1] If we were Turing machines, a relevant remark would be 'You can't know your own Gödel number': see Paul Benacerraf, 'God, the devil, and Gödel', *The Monist*, 51 (1967), pp. 9–32. In these terms, what I have in mind is the inscrutability of the blueprints of others.

[2] By John Tyler Bonner (Princeton University Press, Princeton, 1980), p. 91. He refers to F.F. Darling, *A Herd of Red Deer* (Oxford University Press, Oxford, 1937).

know that it moves as it does because it was designed and built by people who had the very desire and beliefs my ignorant friend assigned to the missile. My explanation, while still teleological, and dependent on the existence of propositional attitudes, is a better explanation because it does not attribute to the missile the potentiality for the rich range of behavior that a thinking creature must have.[3]

The same line of argument might be applied to the red deer, with genetic survival in the deer's case playing the role played by the deliberate design for missiles. But the argument would be harder to win, given the deer's vastly richer range of behavior.

6. Here's Daniel Dennett on a related point:

> Suppose … that we adopt the intentional stance toward bees, and note with wonder that they seem to *know* that dead bees are a hygiene problem in a hive; when a bee dies its sisters *recognize* that it has died, and, *believing* that dead bees are a haleth hazard, and *wanting*, rationally enough, to avoid health hazards, they *decide* they must remove the dead bee immediately. Thereupon they do just that. Now if that fancy an intentional story were confirmed, the bee system designer would be faced with an enormously difficult job. Happily for the designer (if sadly for bee romantics), it turns out that a much lower order explanation suffices: dead bees secrete oleic acid; the smell of oleic acid turns on the 'remove it' subroutine in the other bees; put a dab of oleic acid on a live, healthy bee, and it will be dragged, kicking and screaming, out of the hive.[4]

But what is the 'remove it' subroutine? It's no stereotyped sequence of movements fitted for the removal of dead bees, if the cleaning squad is prepared to deal with a live struggler dabbed with oleic acid. Rather, it's a familiar sort of intentional undertaking, aimed at removing the source of a stink, by means attuned to peculiarities of the case at hand.

7. *Ad hoc fitting of means to ends* is what separates Dennett's bees from Davidson's heat-seeking missile. That doesn't class the bees with the missile's designers. The bees fit means to an end that's functionally related to what their aim would be if they were the little scientists of the scenario Dennett rejects. But they needn't be little scientists to justify our intentional stance toward them. They can have desires (eject the stinker) and beliefs (this hivemate stinks) that prompt acts different from the acts our analogous desires and beliefs prompt in us – but the differences are what one would expect, considering the insects that they are and the primates that we are.

8. If the intentional stance is warranted, does it follow that bees are rational animals? Davidson seems to say so:

> Some animals think and reason; they consider, test, reject and accept hypotheses; they act on reasons, sometimes after deliberating, imagining consequences and weighing probabilities; they have desires, hopes, and hates, often for good

---

[3] Donald Davidson, 'Rational animals', reprinted as chapter 29 in the present volume, at p. 473 (reprinted from *Dialectica*, 36 (1982), pp. 318–27).
[4] 'Intentional systems in cognitive ethology', *The Behavioral and Brain Sciences*, 6 (1983), p. 350.

reasons. They also make errors in calculation, act against their own best judgement, or accept doctrines on inadequate evidence. Any one of these accomplishments, activities, actions or errors is enough to show that such an animal is a rational animal, for to be a rational animal is just to have propositional attitudes, no matter how confused, contradictory, absurd, unjustified or erroneous those attitudes may be. This, I suppose, is the answer.

The question is: What animals are rational?[5]

Then bees who desire to get the stinker out of the hive are rational (a little bit, perhaps?), for the list is disjunctive: to have even one propositional attitude is to be rational. We can think bees rational without thinking of them as considering, testing, rejecting and accepting hypotheses, or as acting on reasons, etc., like fuzzy little scientists or bankers. But the matter is not so simple: 'To have a single propositional attitude is to have a largely correct logic, in the sense of having a pattern of beliefs that logically cohere. This is one reason why to have propositional attitudes is to be a rational creature'.[6] Then would an animal have to be a logician, to be rational?

9. *Rational rats.* Let's see how we might come to view a rat as engaged (in effect) in one of the fancier mental activities in Davidson's disjunctive list: weighing probabilities.

A laboratory rat who sees nothing to choose between two food pellets must press lever A or lever B in order to prevent pellet A or pellet B from dropping out of reach right now while the bell is sounding. It sees pellet A as less likely than B to remain accessible after lever pressure prevents immediate disappearance, having seen pellets in each place disappear randomly, throughout its conditioning, with disappearance rates at A and B set at 3:2.

$$
\begin{array}{l}
\text{p,q} \\[4pt]
\text{T } (=\text{p}\vee\bar{\text{p}}) \\[4pt]
\tilde{\text{q}} \\[12pt]
\tilde{\text{p}}
\end{array}
$$

FIG. 1   The odds on p are the ratio $u(T) - u(\bar{p}) : u(p) - u(T)$ of the marginal utilities of p's falsity and truth. Here, odds on p are 3 : 1; on q, 1 : 1.

My thought is that, where p and q are the propositions that the rat eats pellet A and eats pellet B, the rat is indifferent between p and q, but prefers $\bar{q}$ to $\bar{p}$, i.e., it prefers losing access to the pellet it thinks it's less likely to get anyway. As figure 1 indicates, this pattern of preferences indicates that in effect the rat

---

[5] 'Rational animals', p. 473.

[6] Ibid., pp. 475–6.

[7] Ian Hacking, *The Emergence of Probability* (Cambridge University Press, Cambridge, 1975), argues that the concept of probability is only some three centuries old. (But see Daniel Garber and Sandy Zabell, 'On the emergence of probability', *Archive for History of Exact Sciences*, 21 (1979), pp. 33–53, who detect it ca. 200 B.C.) For the preference logic here applied to the rat, see R.C. Jeffrey, *The Logic of Decision*, 2nd edn (University of Chicago Press, Chicago, 1983).

judges p to be more probable than q, even though it has no explicit concept of subjective probability.[7]

This scenario is incoherent if, as Davidson holds, there is no way to identify a p and q for which an animal prefers truth of p to truth of q, unless that animal is a language user.

10. *Malcolm's dog.* To think that the cat it was chasing has gone up a certain oak tree, says Davidson,

> the dog must believe, under some description of the tree, that the cat went up that tree. But what kind of description would suit the dog? For example, can the dog believe of an object that it is a tree? This would seem impossible unless we suppose the dog has many general beliefs about trees: that they are growing things, that they need soil and water, that they have leaves or needles, that they burn. There is no fixed list of things someone with the concept of a tree must believe, but without many general beliefs, there would be no reason to identify a belief as a belief about a tree, much less an oak tree. Similar considerations apply to the dog's supposed thinking about the cat.[8]

But one can agree that the dog simply doesn't have our concept of tree without concluding that the dog has no concept that we can characterize (say, as 'marker a scratcher can disappear up') that applies relevantly to that tree and that cat. I don't see why we can't deploy a terminology apt for characterizing those of the dog's beliefs and desires that concern us without falling into the trap of using terms that would only be apt for people.

11. *Triads.* Davidson continues:

> We identify thoughts, distinguish between them, describe them for what they are, only as they can be located within a dense network of related beliefs. If we really can intelligibly ascribe single beliefs to a dog, we must be able to imagine how we would decide whether the dog has many other beliefs of the kind necessary for making sense of the first. It seems to me that no matter where we start, we very soon come to beliefs such that we have no idea at all how to tell whether a dog has them, and yet such that without them, our confident first attribution looks shaky.[9]

But as I don't think the network story is true of most human thought, I am not troubled by this problem of tracing dense networks of canine beliefs. It seems to me that, underlying the sophisticated sort of talk about preferences that was illustrated in figure 1, are triads like <thirst, water, drink> and <danger, sanctuary, flee>, of which the general form is <desire, satisfier, action>. These desires are rather basic and widespread among animals (e.g., the four Fs). For animals of familiar species (dogs, say), occasions for such desires are recognizable under favorable circumstances, as are their characteristic signs (e.g., thirst, fear, sexual arousal). Linked with recognition of the desire is recognition of potential satisfiers, and of actions appropriate to the first two elements of the triad. There is a dense network, here, but its nodes are nonpropositional, and subdoxastic. A thirsty dog smells water under its nose

---

[8] 'Rational animals', p. 475.
[9] Ibid., p. 475.

and laps it up, unreflectively. But much of my drinking goes that way, too, *mutatis mutandis* (e.g., at water fountains instead of puddles).

My assumption is that our talk of preference is rooted in such prelinguistic soil, and that it's only at the upper levels, where language plays an essential role, that interpretation of doings in terms of preferential choice involves imputation of self-conscious, Davidsonian rationality.

12. Now I am content to understand 'rational', with Davidson, as presupposing the ability to have beliefs about one's own beliefs. I am content to count rats and dogs as nonrational animals. But I still want to interpret many of their doings in terms of wants and expectations, i.e., in terms of desires and beliefs, i.e., in terms of preferences (which involve degrees of belief, i.e., probabilities, as well as desires). I agree that we identify such preference by means of sentences, truth of one of which the animal prefers to truth of the other. But of course I don't mean that rats and cats understand English:

> we need not suppose that the agent would express his beliefs and desires by using the very sentences that we use .... Nor need the agent be a user of any language: often enough, my cat's behavior makes it clear to me that he believes he is about to be fed, or that he desires to be fed, or that he prefers tuna to egg. ... The theory of deliberate action is ours, not the cat's, and the theory can be used to explain some of the cat's actions even though the cat does not understand the theory, just as the cat can digest his food without being a chemist.[10]

13. Davidson holds that an animal can't have preferences between propositions at all unless it has some preferences between preferences (or beliefs about beliefs, etc.).[11] So in identifying the having of propositional attitudes as the mark that sets humans off from dumb animals he is identifying the having of attitudes about attitudes as the mark.

We both see possession of higher-order propositional attitudes as the key to rationality/irrationality, i.e., as what makes sense of applying either term to behavior. We both draw a circle of ir/rationality around human behavior, excluding dumb animals. But I draw a more inclusive circle, of interpretability in terms of first-order preference, around a great range of animal behavior, including many of the doings of mammals and excluding the doings of heat-seeking missiles.

I think that rats and dogs have modest mental capacities. Desires, hopes and hates – yes. But the other items in Davidson's disjunctive list do seem inappropriate to dumb animals because they seem to presuppose the sort of self-consciousness we have when we think of ourselves as having beliefs and desires, e.g., when we find them unsatisfactory for one reason or another, and contemplate changing them.

Might rats, as social mammals, have beliefs about what other rats believe and desire? I don't know why not. Perhaps some of their more nuanced interactions might illuminatingly be viewed in those terms. But, like Davidson, I see no basis for supposing that they have beliefs about their own beliefs and desires. I

---

[10] Jeffrey, *The Logic of Decision*, sec. 4.7.
[11] 'Rational animals', p. 476.

suppose that while they do have beliefs and desires, they are not self-conscious in that way.

14. *From rationality/irrationality to autonomy.* As a term in everyday talk, irrationality suggests craziness of some sort, and that's not what Davidson or I have in mind. I'm inclined to think that the contrast we're marking, between human rationality/irrationality and animal unrationality, is better seen as a contrast between autonomy and automatism. Unreflective preferential choice *is* automatic, in a way. I guess that's why Davidson sees it as inexplicable in terms of belief and desire. To the extent that preferences can be subject to criticism and alteration by their possessor, action in accordance with them can be autonomous even though unreflective. That's why Davidson insists that it's the capacity for belief about its own beliefs that makes an animal rational, even though that capacity is used sparingly.

15. *Conclusion.* I like Mary Midgley's attitude:

> In discussing the central importance of motives, I shall make no special distinction between man and other species, because I think the problem is the same for both. There is nothing anthropomorphic in speaking of the motivation of animals. It is anthropomorphic to call the lion the King of Beasts, but not to talk of him as moved, now by fear, now by curiosity, now by territorial anger. These are not the names of hypothetical inner states, but of major patterns in anyone's life, the signs of which are regular and visible. Anyone who has to deal with lions learns to read such signs, and survives by doing so. Both with animals and with men, we respond to the feelings and intentions we read in an action, not to the action itself.[12]

But I suppose that with lions as with us, there are real inner states that interact with the visible signs, and that these inner states are both mental and electrochemical. I can't prove that lions feel pain. I can't prove that you do, either. But in both cases I cannot doubt it. There's a great step from there to the view that the preference logic illustrated in figure 1 is a useful basis for interpreting lions' doings; but the same goes for us, too.

For the most part we act unreflectively, as do lions. That's no irrationality. What sets us apart from them is what Davidson identifiese as the basis of our rationality/irrationality, or autonomy, i.e., our ability to reflect on our own beliefs and desires. We can have that ability, he argues, only because we have language. I have no quarrel with that. Our difference concerns the interpretation of animal behavior in terms of unselfconscious belief and desire. Where he argues that these can exist only in autonomous animals like us, who are sometimes conscious of their propositional attitudes as such, I have been arguing for the intelligibility of preference in nonlinguistic, unreflective animals.

---

[12] Mary Midgley, *Beast and Man* (Cornell University Press, Cornell, 1978), pp. 105–6.

Bibliography

Achinstein, P., 'Causation, transparency, and emphasis', *Canadian Journal of Philosophy*, 5 (1975), pp. 1–23.

——, *The Nature of Explanation*, Oxford University Press, Oxford and New York, 1983.

Ajdukiewicz, K., *The Scientific World Perspective and Other Essays*, Reidel, Dordrecht, 1978.

Anscombe, G. E. M., *Intention*, Basil Blackwell, Oxford, 1959.

Aristotle, *Nichomachean Ethics*, tr. M. Ostwald, Bobbs-Merrill, Indianapolis, 1962.

Armstrong, D. M., *The Materialist Theory of the Mind*, Routledge & Kegan Paul, 1968.

——, 'The nature of mind', in *The Mind/Brain Identity Theory*, ed. C. V. Borst, St Martin's Press, New York, 1970.

Arrow, K. and Hurwizc, L., 'An optimality criterion for decision-making under uncertainty', in *Uncertainty and Expectation in Economics*, ed. C. F.Carter and J. L. Ford, Kelley, Clifton, N.J., 1972.

Ashby, R. *Introduction to Cybernetics*, Chapman & Hall, London, 1971.

Audi, R., 'Weakness of will and practical judgment', *Nous*, 13 (1979), pp. 173–96.

Aune, B., *Reason and Action*, Reidel, Dordrecht, 1977.

Austin, J. L., 'A plea for excuses', in his *Philosophical Papers*, Oxford University Press, Oxford, 1961, 1970.

——, 'Three ways of spilling ink', in his *Philosophical Papers*, Oxford University Press, Oxford, 1961, 1970.

Bach, E., Topics in English metaphysics (1979 draft).

Bach, K., 'An analysis of self-deception', *Philosophy and Phenomenological Review*, 41 (1981), pp. 351–70.

Barwise, J., 'Scenes and other situations', *Journal of Philosophy*, 78 (1981), pp. 369–97.

Barwise, J. and Perry, J., 'Semantic innocence and uncompromising situations', *Midwest Studies in Philosophy*, 6 (1981), pp. 387–404.

Beardsley, M. C., 'Actions and events: the problem of individuation', *American Philosophical Quarterly*, 12 (1975), pp. 263–76.

Benacerraf, P., 'God, the devil, and Gödel', *The Monist*, 51 (1967), pp. 9–32.

——, 'What numbers could not be', *Philosophical Review*, 74 (1965)

Bennett, D., 'Action, reason, and purpose', *Journal of Philosophy*, (1965), pp. 85–95.

Bennett, J., *Linguistic Behavior*, Cambridge University Press, Cambridge, 1976.

Bernheim, B. D., 'Rationalizable strategic behavior', *Econometrica*, 52 (1984), pp. 1007–28.

Boër, S. E., 'Meaning and contrastive stress', *Philosophical Review*, 88 (1979).

Bonner, J. T., *The Evolution of Culture in Animals*, Princeton University Press, Princeton, 1980.

Boyd, R., 'Materialism without reductionism', in *Readings in Philosophy of Psychology*, ed. N. Block, Harvard University Press, Cambridge, Mass., and Methuen, London, 1980.

Bradley, F. H., *Ethical Studies*, 1876.

Bratman, M., 'Intention and means–end reasoning', *Philosophical Review*, 90 (1981), pp. 252–65.

——, 'Practical reasoning and weakness of the will', *Nous*, 13 (1979), pp. 153–70.

Brentana, F., *Deskriptive Psychologie*, Felix Meiner Verlag, Hamburg, 1982.

——, *The Theory of Categories*, Martinus Nijhoff, The Hague, 1981.

——, *Versuch über die Erkenntnis*, 2nd edn, Felix Meiner Verlag, Hamburg, 1970.

Burge, T., 'Individualism and the mental', *Midwest Studies in Philosophy*, vol. 4, ed. P. French, University of Minnesota Press, Minneapolis, 1979.

Carnap, R., 'Meaning postulates', in his *Meaning and Necessity*, enlarged edn, University of Chicago Press, Chicago, 1956.

Castañeda, H.-N., 'Comments' on D. Davidson's 'The logical form of action sentences', in *The Logic of Decision and Action*, ed. N. Rescher, University of Pittsburgh Press, Pittsburgh, 1967.

——, 'Intensionality and identity in human action and philosophic method', *Nous*, 13 (1979), pp. 235–60.

——, *Thinking and Doing: the philosophical foundations of institutions*, Reidel, Dordrecht, 1975 (paperback 1982).

Caws, P., *Sartre*, Routledge & Kegan Paul, London, 1979.

Chomsky, N., *Aspects of the Theory of Syntax*, MIT Press, Cambridge, Mass., 1965.

——, 'Some remarks about nominalization', repr. in *Logic and Grammar*, ed. D. Davidson and G. Harman, Dickenson, Encino, Cal., 1975.

Churchland, P., 'Eliminative materialism and propositional attitudes', *Journal of Philosophy*, 78 (1981), pp. 67–90.

——, *Scientific Realism and the Plasticity of Mind*, Cambridge University Press, New York, 1979.

Clark, R., 'Concerning the logic of predicate modifiers', *Nous*, 4 (1970), pp. 311–35.

Conee, E., 'Against moral dilemmas', *Philosophical Review*, 91 (1982), pp. 82–97.

Cooper, N. and Benson, J., 'Further thoughts on oughts and wants', in *Weakness of Will*, ed. G. W. Mortimore, Macmillan, London, 1971, pp. 216–32.

——, 'Oughts and wants', *Proceedings of the Aristotelian Society*, supp. vol. 42 (1968), repr. in *Weakness of Will*, ed. G. W. Mortimore, Macmillan, London, 1971, pp. 190–215.

Cooper, R. and Parsons, T., 'Montague Grammar, generative semantics and interpretative semantics', in *Montague Grammar*, ed. B. Partee, Academic Press, New York, 1976.

Danto, A. C., *Sartre*, Fontana/Collins, Glasgow, 1975.

Darling, F. F., *A Herd of Red Deer*, Oxford University Press, Oxford, 1937.

Dasgupta, P. and Stiglitz, J., 'Uncertainty, industrial structure and the speed of R & D', *Bell Journal of Economics*, 11 (1980), 1.28.

Davidson, D., 'Actions, reasons, and causes', repr. in his *Essays on Actions and Events*, pp. 3–19.

——, 'Agency', repr. in his *Essays on Actions and Events*, pp. 43–61.

——, 'Causal relations', *Journal of Philosophy*, 64 (1967), pp. 691–703, repr. in his *Essays on Actions and Events*.

——, *Essays on Actions and Events*, Clarendon Press, Oxford, and Oxford University Press, New York, 1980.

——, 'Eternal vs. ephemeral events', repr. in his *Essays on Actions and Events.*

——, 'Event and cause', repr. in his *Essays on Actions and Events.*

——, 'Events as particulars', *Nous*, 4 (1970), pp. 25–32, repr. in his *Essays on Actions and Events.*

——, 'Freedom to act', repr. in his *Essays on Actions and Events'.*

——, 'How is weakness of the will possible?', repr. in his *Essays on Actions and Events.*

——, *Inquiries into Truth and Interpretation*, Clarendon Press, Oxford, 1984.

——, 'Intending', repr. in his *Essays on Actions and Events*, pp. 83–102.

——, 'Mental events', in *Experience and Theory*, ed. L. Foster and J. Swanson, University of Massachusetts Press, Amherst, and Duckworth, London, 1970, pp. 79–101, repr. in his *Essays on Actions and Events.*

——, 'On the very idea of a conceptual scheme', *Proceedings and Addresses of the American Philosophical Association*, 47 (1974), repr. in his *Inquiries into Truth and Interpretation.*

——, 'Paradoxes of irrationality', in *Philosophical Essays on Freud*, ed. R. Wollheim and J. Hopkins, Cambridge University Press, Cambridge, 1982.

——, 'Psychology as philosophy', in *Philosophy of Psychology*, ed. S. C. Brown, Harper & Row, New York, 1974, repr. in his *Essays on Actions and Events.*

——, 'Radical interpretation', repr. in his *Inquiries into Truth and Interpretation.*

——, 'Rational animals', *Dialectica*, 36 (1982), pp. 318–27, reprinted as chapter 29 of the present volume.

——, 'The individuation of events', in *Essays in Honour of Hempel*, ed. N. Rescher, Reidel, Dordrecht, 1969, pp. 216–34, repr. in his *Essays on Actions and Events*, pp. 163–80.

——, 'The logical form of action sentences', in *The Logic of Decision and Action*, ed. N. Rescher, University of Pittsburgh Press, Pittsburgh, 1967, pp. 81–120, repr. in his *Essays on Actions and Events.*

——, 'The material mind', in *Logic, Methodology and the Philosophy of Science*, vol. 4, ed. P. Suppes, North-Holland, Amsterdam, 1973, repr. in his *Essays on Actions and Events.*

——, 'The method of truth in metaphysics', *Midwest Studies in Philosophy*, 2 (1977).

——, 'Thought and talk', in *Mind and Language*, ed. S. Guttenplan, Clarendon Press, Oxford, 1975.

——, 'Truth and meaning', *Synthese*, 17 (1967), pp. 304–23.

Davis, W., 'Intending', unpublished ms.

Debreu, G., *Theory of Value*, Wiley, New York, 1959.

Dennett, D., 'Conditions of personhood', in *The Identities of Persons*, ed. A. Rorty, University of California Press, Berkeley, 1976.

——, 'Intentional systems in cognitive ethology', *The Behavioral and Brain Sciences*, 6 (1983).

——, 'Three kinds of intentional psychology', in *Reduction, Time, and Identity*, ed. R. Healey, Cambridge University Press, Cambridge, 1981.

——, 'Where am I?' in his *Brainstorms*, Bradford Books, Cambridge, Mass., 1978, pp. 310–23.

Diffloth, G., 'Body moves in French and Semai', *Papers from the 10th Regional Meeting*, Chicago Linguistic Society, Chicago, 1974, pp. 128–38.

Doepke, F. C., 'Spatially coinciding objects', *Ratio*, 24 (1982), pp. 45–60.

Donagan, A., 'Philosophical progress and the theory of action', *Proceedings of the American Philosophical Association*, 55 (1981).

Donaldson, T., *Corporations and Morality*, Prentice-Hall, Englewood Cliffs, N.J., 1982.

Donnellan, K., 'Reference and definite descriptions', *Philosophical Review*, 75 (1966), pp. 281–321.

Dowty, D., *A Guide to Montague's PTQ*, Indiana University Linguistics Club, Indianapolis, 1978.

——, *Word Meaning and Montague Grammar*, Reidel, Boston, 1979.

Dretske, F., 'Contrastive statements', *Philosophical Review*, 81 (1972), pp. 411–37.

——, 'Referring to events', *Midwest Studies in Philosophy*, 2 (1977), pp. 90–9.

——, 'The content of knowledge', in *Forms of Representation*, ed. B. Freed, A. Marras and P. Maynard, New York, 1975, pp. 77–93.

Eberle, R., *Nominalistic Systems*, Reidel, Dordrecht, 1970.

Elgin, C. Z., 'Indeterminacy, underdetermination, and the anomalous monism', *Synthese*, 45 (1980), pp. 233–55.

Elster, J., *Explaining Technical Change*, Cambridge University Press, Cambridge, 1983.

——, *Sour Grapes*, Cambridge University Press, Cambridge, 1983.

——, *Ulysses and the Sirens*, Cambridge University Press, Cambridge, 1979.

Evans, G., 'Can there be vague objects?', *Analysis*, 38 (1978).

Feinberg, J., *Doing and Deserving*, Princeton University Press, Princeton, 1970.

Feyerabend, P., 'Materialism and the mind–body problem', *Review of Metaphysics*, 17 (1963).

Fodor, J., *RePresentations*, Bradford Press, Cambridge, Mass., 1981.

——, 'Special sciences, or the disunity of science as a working hypothesis', *Synthese*, 28 (1973), pp. 97–115.

——, 'Troubles about actions', in *Semantics of Natural Language*, ed. D. Davidson and G. Harman, Reidel, Dordrecht, 1972, pp. 48–69.

Foot, P., 'Moral realism and moral dilemma', *Journal of Philosophy*, 80 (1983), pp. 379–98.

Fraassen, B. Van, 'The logic of conditional obligation', *Journal of Philosophical Logic*, 1 (1972), pp. 417–38.

——, 'Values and the heart's command', *Journal of Philosophy*, 70 (1973), pp. 5–19.

Francken, P., 'The by-locutionary argument', mimeograph, Wayne State University.

Frankfurt, H., 'The problem of action', *American Philosophical Quarterly*, (1978), pp. 157–62.

French, P. A., 'A principle of responsive adjustment', *Philosophy*, 59 (1984), pp. 491–503.

——, 'The corporation as a moral person', *American Philosophical Quarterly*, (1979).

Gazdar, G., *Pragmatics*, Academic Press, New York, 1979.

Geach, P. T., *Truth, Love and Immortality*, Hutchinson, London, 1979.

Glouberman, M., 'Complete causes', *Logique et Analyse*, 94 (1981), pp. 231–44.

Goldberg, B., 'The correspondence hypothesis', *Philosophical Review*, 77 (1968), pp. 438–54.

Goldman, A., *A Theory of Human Action*, Prentice-Hall, Englewood Cliffs, N.J., 1970.

——, 'Action, causation, and unity', *Nous*, 13 (1979), pp. 261–70.

Goodman, N., *The Structure of Appearance*, Harvard University Press, Cambridge, Mass., 1951.

Grice, H. P., 'Intention and uncertainty', *Proceedings of the British Academy*, 57 (1971), pp. 263–79.

——, 'Logic and conversation', in *Speech Acts* (*Syntax and Semantics*, 3), ed. P. Cole and J. Morgan, Academic Press, New York, 1975, pp. 45–58.

Gulick, R. Van, 'Rationality and the anomalous nature of the mental', *Philosophy Research Archives* (1983).

Gupta, A., *The Logic of Common Nouns*, Yale University Press, New Haven, 1981.

Hacking, I., *The Emergence of Probability*, Cambridge University Press, Cambridge, 1975.

Harman, G., 'Practical reasoning', *Review of Metaphysics*, 29 (1976), pp. 431–63.

——, 'Willing and intending', forthcoming in a Festschrift in honour of H. P. Grice.

Harnish, R. M., 'Logical form and implicature', in *An Integrated Theory of Linguistic Ability*, ed. T. G. Bever, J. J. Katz and D. T. Langendoen, Thomas Y. Crowell, New York, 1976.

Harsanyi, J., *Rational Behavior and Bargaining Equilibrium in Games and Social Situations*, Cambridge University Press, Cambridge, 1977.

Haugeland, J., 'Weak supervenience', *American Philosophical Quarterly*, 19 (1982).

Hellman, G. and Thompson, F. W., 'Physicalism', *Journal of Philosophy*, 72 (1975), pp. 551–64.

——, 'Physicalist materialism', *Nous*, 11 (1971), pp. 309–45.

Hempel, C., *Aspects of Scientific Explanation*, The Free Press, New York, 1965.

Higginbotham, J., 'The logic of perceptual reports: an extensional alternative to situation semantics', *Journal of Philosophy*, vol. 80 (1983), pp. 100–27.

Hintikka, J., *Knowledge and Belief*, Cornell University Press, Ithaca, N.Y., 1961.

Honderich, T., 'Causes and *if p, even if x, still q*', *Philosophy*, 57 (1982).

——, 'Psychophysical lawlike connections and their problem', *Inquiry*, 24 (1981), pp. 277–303.

Horgan, T., 'Action theory without actions', *Mind*, 90 (1981).

——, 'Functionalism, qualia, and the inverted spectrum', *Philosophy and Phenomenological Research*, 45 (1984).

——, 'Jackson on physical information and qualia', *Philosophical Quarterly*, 34 (1984).

——, 'Substitutivity and the causal connective', *Philosophical Studies*, 42 (1982).

——, 'The case against events', *Philosophical Review*, 87 (1978).

Horgan, T. and Woodward, J., 'Folk psychology is here to stay', (forthcoming).

Hornsby, J., 'Which physical events are mental events?', *Proceedings of the Aristotelian Society*, 81 (1980–81), pp. 73–92.

Hume, D., *A Treatise of Human Nature*, ed. L. A. Selby-Bigge, Clarendon Press, Oxford, 1888 (2nd edn, as revised by P. H. Nidditih, 1978).

Husserl, E. G., *Logical Investigations*, Routledge & Kegan Paul, London, 1970.

Jackendoff, R., *Semantic Interpretation in Generative Grammar*, MIT Press, Cambridge, Mass., 1972.

Jackson, F., 'Internal conflicts in desires and morals', *American Philosophical Quarterly* (forthcoming).

——, 'Weakness of will', *Mind*, 93 (1984), pp. 1–18.

Jeffrey, R.C., *The Logic of Decision*, University of Chicago Press, Chicago, 1983.

Johansen, L., *Lectures on Macro-Economic Planning*, North-Holland, Amsterdam, 1977.

Johnson, W. E., *Logic*, Cambridge University Press, Cambridge, 1921.

Johnston, M. J., Particulars and Persistence, Princeton, 1983.

Katz, J. J., 'Chomsky on meaning', *Language*, 56 (1980), pp. 1–41.

——, *Cognitions*, Oxford University Press, Oxford, forthcoming.

——, *Language and Other Abstract Objects*, Roman & Littlefield, Totowa, New Jersey, 1981.

——, *Propositional Structure and Illocutionary Force*, Harvard University Press, Cambridge, Mass., 1980.

——, *Semantic Theory*, Harper & Row, New York, 1972.

——, 'Semantic theory and the meaning of good', *Journal of Philosophy*, 61 (1964), pp. 739–66.

Kennedy, C., 'Induced bias in innovation and the theory of distribution', *Economic Journal*, 74 (1964), pp. 541–7.

Kenny, A., *Action, Emotion and Will*, Humanities Press, 1963.

Keyser, S., Review of Sven Jacobson, 'Adverbial Positions in English', *Language*, (1968), pp. 357–74.

Kim, J., 'Causality, identity, and supervenience in the mind–body problem', *Midwest Studies in Philosophy*, 4 (1979).

——, 'Causation, emphasis, and events', *Midwest Studies in Philosophy*, 2 (1977), pp. 100–3.

——, 'Concepts of supervenience', *Philosophy and Phenomenological Research* (forthcoming).

——, 'Epiphenomenal and supervenient causation', *Midwest Studies in Philosophy*, 9 (1974).

——, 'Events as property exemplifications', in *Action Theory*, ed. M. Brand and D. Walton, Reidel, Dordrecht, 1976, pp. 159–77.

——, 'On the psycho-physical identity theory', *American Philosophical Quarterly*, 3 (1966).

——, 'Psychophysical supervenience', *Philosophical Studies*, 41 (1982).

——, 'Psychophysical supervenience as a mind–body theory', *Cognition and Brain Theory*, 5 (1982).

——, 'Self-understanding and rationalizing explanations', paper presented at 1983 International Congress of Logic, Philosophy and Methodology of Science, in Salzburg, Austria.

——, 'Supervenience and supervenient causation', *Southern Journal of Philosophy*, 22 (1984).

Kuhn, T., *The Structure of Scientific Revolutions*, 2nd edn, University of Chicago Press, Chicago, 1970.

Lemmon, J., 'Comments' on D. Davidson's 'The logical form of action sentences', in *The Logic of Decision and Action*, ed. N. Rescher, University of Pittsburgh Press, Pittsburgh, 1967, pp. 96–103.

Lewis, C. I., *An Analysis of Knowledge and Valuation*, Open Court Publishing, La Salle, Ill., 1946.

Lewis, D., 'An argument for the identity theory', *Journal of Philosophy*, 63 (1966), pp. 17–25.

——, 'Mad pain and Martian pain', in *Readings in the Philosophy of Psychology*, vol. 1, ed. N. Block, Harvard University Press, Cambridge, Mass., 1980.

——, 'New work for a theory of universals', *Australasian Journal of Philosophy*, 61 (1983), pp. 343–77.

——, 'Scorekeeping in a language game', *Journal of Philosophical Logic*, 9 (1979), pp. 339–59.

Loar, B., *Mind and Meaning*, Cambridge University Press, Cambridge, 1981.

Lombard, L. B., 'Actions, results, and the time of a killing', *Philosophia*, 8 (1978), pp. 341–54.

——, 'Events', *Canadian Journal of Philosophy*, 9 (1979), pp. 425–60.

——, *Events: a metaphysical study*, Routledge & Kegan Paul, London, forthcoming.

——, 'Relational change and relational changes', *Philosophical Studies*, 34 (1978), pp. 63–79.

Lycan, W., 'Psychological laws', *Philosophical Topics*, 12 (1981), pp. 9–38.

Lyons, J., *Semantics*, Cambridge University Press, Cambridge, 1977.

McCawley, J., *Everything That Linguists Have Always Wanted to Know About Logic (But Were Ashamed to Ask)*, University of Chicago Press, Chicago, and Basil Blackwell, Oxford, 1981.

——, 'Kuhnian paradigms as systems of markedness conventions', in *Festschrift for Rulon Wells*, ed. A. Makkai and A. Melby, Jupiter Press, Lake Bluff, Illinois, 1984.

——, 'The role of semantics in a grammar', in *Universals in Linguistic Theory*, ed. E. Bach and R. Harms, Holt, Rinehart & Winston, New York, 1968.

McCloskey, H. J., *Meta-Ethics and Normative Ethics*, Martinus Nijhoff, The Hague, 1969.

McConnell-Ginet, S., 'Adverbs and logical form: a linguistically realistic theory', *Language*, 58 (1982), pp. 144–84.

McDowell, J., 'Physicalism and primitive denotation: Field on Tarski', *Erkenntnis*, 13 (1978), pp. 131–52.

McGinn, C., 'Philosophical materialism', *Synthese*, 44 (1980), pp. 173–206.

Mackie, J. L., 'Causes and conditions', *American Philosophical Quarterly*, 2 (1965).

——, *Ethics: inventing right and wrong*, Penguin Books, Harmondsworth, 1977.

——, *The Cement of the Universe*, Oxford University Press, London, 1974.

McLaughlin, B., 'Event supervenience and supervenient causation', *Southern Journal of Philosophy*, 22 (1984).

Malcolm, N., *Memory and Mind*, Cornell University Press, Ithaca, N.Y., 1977.

——, 'Thoughtless brutes', *Proceedings and Addresses of the American Philosophical Association*, 46 (1972–3).

Marcus, R. B., 'Moral dilemmas and consistency', *Journal of Philosophy*, 78 (1980), pp. 121–36.

Melden, A. I., *Free Action*, Routledge & Kegan Paul, London, 1958.

Mele, A., '*Akrasia*, reasons, and causes', *Philosophical Studies*, 44 (1983), pp. 345–68.

Mellor, D. H., *Real Time*, Cambridge University Press, Cambridge, 1981.

Midgley, M., *Beast and Man*, Cornell University Press, Cornell, 1978.

Mill, J. S., *A System of Logic*, Longman, London, 1961.

Miller, N. E., 'Comments on theoretical models', *Journal of Personality*, 20 (1951–2), pp. 82–100.

——, 'Experimental studies of conflict', in his *Selected Papers*, Aldine-Atherton, Chicago, 1971, vol. 1, pp. 3–40.

Mish'alani, J. K., 'Rule and exception in morals', *Ratio*, 11 (1969), pp. 107–20.

Montague, R., 'English as a formal language', in his *Formal Philosophy*, Yale University Press, New Haven, 1974, pp. 188–221.

——, 'The proper treatment of quantification in ordinary English', in *Approaches to Natural Language*, ed. J. Hintikka, J. Moravcsik and P. Suppes, Reidel, Dordrecht, 1973, pp. 221–42.

Mortimore, G. W. (ed.), *Weakness of Will*, Macmillan, London, 1971.

Morton, A., *Frames of Mind*, Oxford University Press, Oxford, 1980.

Nagel, T., 'Subjective and objective', in his *Mortal Questions*, Cambridge University Press, Cambridge, 1979, pp. 196–213.

——, 'What is it like to be a bat?' in his *Mortal Questions*, Cambridge University Press, Cambridge, 1979, pp. 165–80.

Nisbett, R. and Ross, L., *Human Inference: strategies and shortcomings of social judgment*, Prentice-Hall, Englewood Cliffs, N.J., 1980.

Nordhaus, W., 'Some sceptical thoughts on the theory of induced innovations', *Quarterly Journal of Economics*, 87 (1973), pp. 208–19.

Parsons, T., 'An analysis of mass terms and amount terms', *Foundations of Language*, 6 (1970), pp. 362–88.

——, 'Modifiers and quantifiers in natural language', *Canadian Journal of Philosophy*, supp. vol. 6 (1980), pp. 29–60.

——, 'Some problems concerning the logic of grammatical modifiers', *Synthese*, 21 (1970), pp. 320–33.

Partee, B., Some structural analogies between tenses and pronouns in English', *Journal of Philosophy*, 71, (1973), pp. 601–9.

Peacocke, C., *Holistic Explanation: action, space, interpretation*, Oxford University Press, Oxford, 1979.

Pearce, D. G., 'Rationalizable strategic behavior and the problem of perfection', *Econometrica*, 52 (1984), pp. 1029–50.

Pears, D. (ed.), *Freedom of the Will*, Routledge & Kegan Paul, London, 1963.

——, *Motivated Irrationality*, Oxford University Press, Oxford, 1984.

——, 'Motivated irrationality', in *Philosophical Essays on Freud*, ed. R. Wollheim and J. Hopkins, Cambridge University Press, Cambridge, 1982.

Perry, J. and Barwise, J., *Situations and Attitudes*, MIT Press, Cambridge, Mass., 1983.

Peters, R.S., *The Concept of Motivation*, Routledge & Kegan Paul, London, 1961.

Powers, L., 'Some deontic logicians', *Nous*, 1 (1967), pp. 381–400.

Presley, C. F. (ed.), *The Identity Theory of Mind*, Queensland University Press, St Lucia, Queensland, 1967.

Prichard, H. A., 'Acting, willing, and desiring', in *The Philosophy of Action*, ed. A. R. White, Oxford University Press, Oxford, 1968.

Prior, E., Pargetter, R. and Jackson, F., 'Functionalism and type–type identity theories', *Philosophical Studies*, 42 (1982), pp. 209–22.

Putnam, H., 'Reflexions' on N. Goodman's *Ways of Worldmaking*, *Journal of Philosophy*, 76 (1979).

——, 'The meaning of meaning', in his *Philosophical Papers*, Cambridge University Press, Cambridge, 1975.

——, 'The meaning of "meaning"', in *Minnesota Studies in the Philosophy of Science*, vol. 7, ed. K. Gunderson, University of Minnesota Press, Minneapolis, 1975.

Quine, W. V., *From a Logical Point of View*, Harvard University Press, Cambridge, Mass., 1953.

——, 'On the axiom of reducibility', *Mind*, 45 (1935), pp. 478–500.

——, 'Reply' to Noam Chomsky, in *Words and Objections*, ed. D. Davidson and J. Hintikka, Reidel Dordrecht, 1969.

——, 'Soft impeachment disowned', *Pacific Philosophical Quarterly*, 61 (1980).

——, 'Things and their place in theories', in his *Theories and Things*, Belknap Press, Harvard University Press, Cambridge, Mass., 1981.

——, *Word and Object*, The Technology Press of MIT, Cambridge, Mass., 1960.

Quirk, R. and Greenbaum, S., *A Concise Grammar of Contemporary English*, Harcourt Brace Jovanovich, New York, 1973.

Reichenbach, H., *Elements of Symbolic Logic*, The Free Press, New York, 1947.

Rorty, R., 'Mind–body identity, privacy, and categories', *Review of Metaphysics*, 19 (1965).

Rosenberg, A., 'Fitness', *Journal of Philosophy*, 80 (1983), pp. 457–73.

——, *Sociobiology and the Presumption of Social Science*, The Johns Hopkins University Press, Baltimore, 1981.

——, 'The supervenience of biological concepts', *Philosophy of Science*, 45 (1978), pp. 368–86.

Ross, W. D., *The Right and the Good*, Oxford University Press, Oxford, 1930.

Russell, B., 'On denoting', *Mind*, n.s. 14 (1905), pp. 479–93.

Sanford, D. H., 'Knowledge and relevant alternatives: comments on Dretske', *Philosophical Studies*, 40 (1981), pp. 379–88.

Santas, G., 'Plato's *Protagoras* and explanations of weakness', in *Weakness of Will*, ed. G. W. Mortimore, Macmillan, London, 1971.

Sartre, J.-P., *Being and Nothingness*, trans. Hazel Barnes, Washington Square Press; NYU, 1969.

Schelling, T., *The Strategy of Conflict*, Harvard University Press, Cambridge, Mass., 1960.

Sen, A. and Williams, B., Introduction to *Utilitarianism and Beyond*, ed. A. Sen and B. Williams, Cambridge University Press, Cambridge, 1982.

Shoemaker, S., 'Functionalism and qualia', *Philosophical Studies*, 27 (1975), pp. 291–315.

Siegel, M., 'Measure adjectives in Montague Grammar', in *Linguistics, Philosophy, and Montague Grammar*, ed. S. Davis and M. Mithun, University of Texas Press, Austin, 1979.

Singer, P., *Practical Ethics*, Cambridge University Press, Cambridge, 1979.

Smart, J. J. C., *Philosophy and Scientific Realism*, Routledge & Kegan Paul, London, 1963.

——, 'Sensations and brain processes', in *The Mind/Brain Identity Theory*, ed. C. V. Borst, St Martin's Press, New York, 1970.

Southern Journal of Philosophy, 22 (1984), Spindel Conference issue.

Stanton, W., 'Supervenience and psychological law in anomalous monism', *Pacific Philosophical Quarterly*, 64 (1983), pp. 72–9.

Stich, S. P., *From Folk Psychology to Cognitive Science: the case against belief*, MIT Press, Cambridge, Mass., 1983.

Stockwell, R., Schachter, P. and Partee, B., *The Major Syntactic Structures of English*, Holt, Rinehart & Winston, New York, 1973.

Strawson, P. F., 'On referring', *Mind*, 59 (1950), pp. 320–44.

Suzumura, K., *Rational Choice, Collective Decisions and Social Welfare*, Cambridge University Press, Cambridge, 1984.

Taylor, B., 'States of affairs', in *Truth and Meaning*, ed. G. Evans and J. MacDowell, Oxford University Press, Oxford, 1976.

Thomason, R. and Stalnaker, R. C., 'A semantic theory of adverbs', *Linguistic Inquiry*, 4 (1973), pp. 195–220.

Thomson, J. J., *Acts and Other Events*, Cornell University Press, Cornell, 1977.

——, 'Individuating actions', *Journal of Philosophy*, 68 (1971), pp. 774–81.

Tiles, J., 'Davidson's criterion of event identity', *Analysis*, 36 (1976).

Tye, M., 'Functionalism and type physicalism', *Philosophical Studies*, 44 (1983).

——, 'Pain and the adverbial theory', *American Philosophical Quarterly*, 21 (1984).

——, 'The adverbial approach to visual experience', *Philosophical Review*, 93 (1984).

——, 'The debate about mental imagery', *Journal of Philosophy* (forthcoming).

——, 'The subjective character of experience', (forthcoming).

Ullmann-Margalit, E. and Morgenbesser, S., 'Picking and choosing', *Social Research*, 44 (1977), pp. 757–85.

Vendler, Z., *Linguistics in Philosophy*, Cornell University Press, Ithaca, N.Y., 1967.

Vermazen, B. and Hintikka, M. (eds), *Essays on Davidson: Actions and Events*, Oxford University Press, Oxford, 1985.

Wallace, J., 'On what's happening', dittograph draft, 1966.

Watson, G., 'Free agency', *Journal of Philosophy*, 72 (1975), pp. 205–20.

——, 'Skepticism about weakness of will', *Philosophical Review*, 86 (1977), pp. 316–39.

Weiss, 'Professor Malcolm on animal intelligence', *Philosophical Review*, 84 (1975), pp. □

Wheeler, S. C., III, 'Attributives and their modifiers', *Nous*, 6 (1972), pp. 310–34.

Wierzbicka, A., 'Mind and body from a semantic point of view', in *Notes from the Linguistic Underground (Syntax and Semantics*, 7), ed. J. McCawley, Academic Press, New York, 1976, pp. 129–57.

——, 'Ethno-syntax and the philosophy of grammar', *Studies in Language*, 3 (1979), pp. 313–83.

Wiggins, D., 'On being in the same place at the same time', *Philosophical Review*, 77 (1968).

——, *Sameness and Substance*, Basil Blackwell, Oxford, 1980.

Williams, B., *Descartes: the project of pure enquiry*, Penguin Books, Harmondsworth.

——, 'Ethical consistency', repr. in his *Problems of the Self*, Cambridge University Press, Cambridge, 1973.

Wilson, G., *The Intentionality of Human Action*, North-Holland, Amsterdam, 1980.

Winch, P., *The Idea of a Social Science*, Routledge & Kegan Paul, London, 1958.

Winter, S., 'Economic "natural selection" and the theory of the firm', *Yale Economic Essays*, 4 (1964), pp. 225–72.

Wittgenstein, L., *Philosophical Investigations*, Macmillan, New York, and Basil Blackwell, Oxford, 1953.
——, *Philosophical Remarks*, Basil Blackwell, Oxford, 1975.
Zemach, E., 'Events', in *Philosophy of History and Action*, ed. Y. Yovel, Reidel, Dordrecht, 1978, pp. 85–95.

Index

Achinstein, Peter 283–4, 287–8, 290–3
action, intentional 3, 10, 15–28, 476
  aspectual 294–310
  as autonomous 418–19
  conjunctive view 306–9
  as conscious 36
  as event 77, 151–2, 306–7, 362
  individuation of 55–6, 59, 268, 273–6,
    279–81, 317
  modifier view 308–10
  non-causalist view 29–43
  overlapping 186–8
  as a practition 306–7
  prediction of 62, 72, 89, 322–3
  properties of 306–8
  psychophysical theory of 321–3, 352
  purpose of 3, 32–3, 36, 43, 55, 232
  as values of variables 179–81, 188
  see also behavior, intentional; causal
    theory of action; explanations,
    rationalizing; generalizations:
    heteronomic; identity theory;
    intentions; justification;
    movements, bodily; physical laws;
    reason for action; responsibility
action, unintentional 10, 42
action, verbs of, transitive 208, 213–15,
    223–4, 265–6, 268–81
  alternative analysis of 273–6
  intransitive 277–8
  and sentences 276–9
  see also causal theory of action
'Actions, Reasons and Causes' (Davidson)
    3–4, 6–9, 11–12, 14–15, 273n, 282,
    313–14, 316, 338, 394n, 407, 413n
  and behavior 44, 48–9, 89–90, 95

  non-causative view 29–33, 38–40, 43
  and reasons 106, 117–18
adverbs 295, 298, 303
  adverbial theory of appearing 327–8
  attributive 213
  intentional adverbs 213–15, 232,
    249–50, 251–2
  theory of 162–5, 168, 172–4,
    193–206, 269–70, 324
  temporal adverbs 201–3, 249
  and underlying events 249–67
  verb-dependent adverbs 194–5, 199,
    205–6
  see also events: individuation of;
    modification: decomposition
    theory
'Agency' (Davidson) 16n, 74, 77, 108n,
    117, 312–13
agent, concept of 36–8, 42, 60, 376–7,
    386
  and moral responsibility 73–4, 76–7,
    79–84, 86–7
  purpose of, see action, intentional
Ager, Tryg A., Arronson, Jerrold L. and
    Weingard, Robert 357
Ajdukiewicz, Kazimierz 163
akrasia 64
  and behavior 91–6, 99–103, 104
  and reason 116, 118–20, 122–4, 127,
    131–6, 139
  see also conflict, moral; self-deception;
    will, weakness of
analysis, logical, see logical form, theories
    of
animals: behavior of 97–9
  as intentional 37, 80–1, 87, 482–4

as rational 473–80, 483–7
Anscombe, G.E.M. 12, 14, 31, 34, 273n, 312
Anton, Anatole 306
application, rational conditions of 357–9, 364–5, 367–8
Aquinas, St Thomas 104
Aristotle 209
  on causation 31, 88
  on language 239–40
  on morality 84, 86
  on reason 16, 117, 142
Armstrong, D.M. 408–9
attitude, propositional 45, 163, 174, 352–6, 362, 366–8, 371, 375–6, 383, 422–4
  and animals 473, 477–9, 483–7
  as causal 4, 6–13, 14–16, 31–2, 35–6, 41, 88–92, 355, 388
  as constituting mental event 336–7
  functional interpretation of 387–94, 397
  as holistic 402–3, 461, 473
  irreducibility of 389, 395–6
  physicalist interpretation of 389, 411, 414
  and psychology 399–400, 402–3, 405–6, 424–5
  and rationality 355–6, 358–9, 387, 473–6, 486–7
  strength of 88, 91–3, 95, 97–9, 101–2
  see also belief; desire; evaluation: reason: primary
Audi, Robert 91, 93
Austin, J.L. 78, 80–2, 84, 182

Bach, Emmon 238
Bach, Kent 146–7
Baier, Annette C. 116–29, 130–7
Barwise, Jon 247n, 290n
behavior, intentional 44–59, 60–2
  as action 60
  materialist view 54–7, 59
  and mental event 45, 48, 51, 100
  prediction of 52, 393, 401–3, 406; *see also* psychology
  reasons for 45–54, 60–62, 65
  see also action, intentional; *akrasia*; causal theory of action; motivation, strength of
behavior, unintentional 48, 83–6
behaviorism 14, 396–7, 403–4, 408, 476
belief 163–4, 461–6, 469

and animals 474–5, 479–80, 483–7
'belief–desire theory' 392–3
  as causal 4–10, 14–16, 31, 60–2, 88–90, 93, 282, 317, 321–2, 355, 401–4, 437–8
  and future-directed intention 12–13, 17–20, 22–3, 26
  holistic approach 461
  and inconsistency 18, 26–7, 62–3, 138–9, 147–8, 356n
  and non-causalist view of action 37–9, 41
  and principle of charity 49, 52
  probabilistic 67, 71
  and rationality 62–5, 69, 148, 376, 380–1, 388, 390–1, 394
  in Sartre 461–3, 465, 469
  and thought 476–80, 485–6
  see also evidence; reason: primary; self-deception; thinking, wishful
'Belief and the Basis of Meaning' (Davidson) 355n
Benacerraf, Paul 439n
Bennett, Jonathan 193–206, 343–4, 477n
Bennett, Michael 239n, 245n
Bergström, Lars 312, 320
Berkeley, George 54
Boër, Steven E. 292n
Bonner, John Tyler 482
Boyd, Richard 435n, 456n
Bradley, F.H. 74, 84, 86
Bratman, Michael 13, 14–28
Brentano, Franz 45, 326–7, 370, 385, 401
Brown, Curtis 78
Buridan, J. 21–2, 24

Carnap, R. 140, 213n, 388
Carroll, Lewis 134
Castañeda, Hector-Neri 256, 273n, 294–310
Causal Interaction, Principle of 398, 410
'Causal Relations' (Davidson) 151, 282–3, 288–9, 318, 398n, 402, 407, 415–16, 430–1, 443, 452
causal theory of action 3–13, 14–16, 44–6, 60–2, 79, 96, 151, 279–81, 313–23, 402, 409–26, 430–4
  arguments against 23–4, 29–33, 37–43, 48–58, 311, 313, 411–14, 416–17
  and causal relation 151, 282–5, 313,

318–19, 332–4, 347, 394
traditional theories 6, 46–8, 52, 88
see also action, verbs of; context;
explanation, rationalizing; laws:
causal; logical form: of causal
statement; motiviation; reason: as
causal
causation 428–38, 450–4
counterfactual account 345, 451–2
and mental event 123–5, 131–3,
135–6, 147, 313, 319–21, 331,
338–9, 412–13
nomological character of 313, 318–19,
332–4, 338, 340, 346–8, 398, 410,
457–8
non-rational 99–101, 116, 118–19,
123–6, 130–6
regularity account 51, 451, 452, 458n
see also events: and cause; explanations,
rationalizing; sentence: causal
Caws, Peter 472
charity, principle of vii, 49, 52–3, 425
Chisholm, R.M. 157n, 302, 318–19,
324–8
choice, *see* explanation, rational-choice
Chomsky, Noam 196n, 219, 385n
Churchland, Paul 404n, 427, 441, 442
Clark, Romane 308
'Comments and Replies' (Davidson)
333–4, 348, 358, 371n, 381n
conflict, moral 104–5
complex prima facie theory 109–11,
112, 114
and particular action 108–10
simple prima facie theory 108–10
and types of action 108–10
see also akrasia; value
consciousness: in Davidson 463–4
in Sartre 460–1, 465–6, 468, 471
context: causal 284–5, 288, 290–1,
314–15, 432–6
contextual domain 178, 189–91
explanatory 314–15
extensional 284, 420–1
non-extensional 45, 243, 249, 254–5
Continence, Principle of 132–4, 136,
139
continuants 446–50, 454–6, 458; *see also*
events
coordination and intentions 23–4
'Criticism, Comment and Defence'
(Davidson) 344

Danto, Arthur C. 471
Davis, Wayne 81
decision theory 67–8, 316, 319, 383–4
and moral conflict 113–15
see also generalizations: heteronomic
decomposition, *see* modification:
decompositional theory
deductive nomological argument 419–21
definitions, impredicative 166
deletion rule 270–1, 272n
Dennett, Daniel 31, 34, 427, 441n
and intentional systems 74–5, 80, 86,
483
deontic paradox aspectual action
294–9, 300–7, 309–10
Largest Scope Solution 296–8, 301,
303
proposition/practition 299–300,
301–3, 305–6, 309–10
Descartes, René 385, 394–7
on behavior 45, 54
descriptions, definite 177–86, 188–9
and events 183–6, 333–4, 410–11,
416
and existence 190–1
and explanations 314–15
mental 45, 48–58, 336–7, 341,
410–12, 414, 420–1
physical 45, 47–8, 51–68, 411–13,
420–1, 424
and pragmatics 189–91
desire: and animals 483–7
as causal 7–8, 10–12, 14–17, 60–2,
88–9, 93, 95–7, 282, 317, 321–2,
402–4
and collecting of evidence 69–72
comparative 21, 96–7, 99, 121, 123
as consistent 63
and future intention 17–18, 20–3,
40–1
and non-causalist view 31–2, 38–9,
42–3
and rationality 62–5, 106, 119, 125,
376, 393
see also attitude, propositional; belief
determinism, physical, and psychological
anomalism 383–4
Doepke, F.C. 449n
Donagan, Alan 57
Dowty, D. 243, 258n, 267n
Dretske, Fred 283, 285–8, 290, 292,
293n, 318, 334n

dualism 439, 441
 Cartesian 385, 394–7, 441
 in Davidson 384–5

Elster, Jon 60–72, 147n
emergentism 426
emphasis, non-semantical 283–5, 287–8, 290–3
error, massive, impossibility of 461, 465
Essays on Actions and Events (Davidson)
 viii, 11, 94–5, 119, 121, 162n, 166–7, 192, 235, 265, 282, 312, 314, 387–8
'Eternal vs. ephemeral events' (Davidson) 190, 415n
evaluation 11–13
 comparative 21–2, 28
 prima facie 11–12, 15, 17
 unconditional 11–12, 15–18, 23
 see also judgment
Evans, Gareth 440n
'Event and Discourse' (Davidson) 188
'Events as Particulars' (Davidson) 415n
events: as causal relata 151–2, 159–61, 282–6, 288–90, 292–3, 332
 and cause 285–7, 332, 347, 411
 as concrete particulars 151, 157, 167–70, 176, 193, 200–1, 238, 308, 332, 408, 416
 conjunctive view, *see* action, intentional: conjunctive view
 event aspect 283, 285–6, 290, 292–3;
  see also action, intentional: aspectual
 event-fusion 435–7, 440, 446–58
 individuation of 160–1, 166–8, 175–6, 181–3, 191–2, 195–200, 206, 264–7, 340, 343–4, 347, 412, 428–9, 447
 modifier view, *see* action, intentional: modifier
 as ontic categories 160–1, 183, 191, 193, 200, 206, 292–3, 309, 340
 and overlap of particulars 183–7
 possible 307–8
 prediction of 333–4, 382, 419
 properties of 285, 290, 339–41, 343–4, 360–4
 reductionist view 160
 semantic theory 153–60, 173–4, 236–40, 243–7, 268–81
 and subsumption by law 332–3, 367

time–space location 167–8, 175–6, 181–3, 344, 347
token identity thesis 338–41
underlying event, *see* logical form: underlying event approach
 as values of variables 180, 188
 see also adverbs, theory of; mereological conception; physicalism; reification
events, mental: anomalism of 44, 51, 313, 319–20, 322–40, 341, 351, 367, 369, 371, 381–4, 397, 400, 409–10, 418–21, 424, 457, 467–8, 481
 as causing physical events 48, 313–14, 317, 331, 339, 410–12, 457
 denial of 427–8, 441–3
 interpretive view 424–6
 irreducibility of 352, 384
 location of 181–2, 344, 429, 435
 nature of 45, 336–7, 413–14, 427–41
 as normative 358
 as physical events 151–2, 167, 176, 314, 337–41, 343, 363, 384, 397, 410–17, 420, 436, 445, 457–8
 relation with physical events 51, 320–1, 331, 333–7, 351–66, 372, 374–5, 383–4, 408–9, 414, 421, 424, 428–9
 see also causation: mental; identity theory; mind, the; supervenience
eventuality, *see* events
evidence 49–51, 58, 64–5, 69–72, 143–6
 and scientific theory 168–71
 total, requirement of 140–1, 146–8
excuses, logic of 263–4
explanation, rational-choice 60–72, 359
 and causation 72
 and optimality 60, 65–71
 and rationality 62–5, 68–9, 72
explanations, rationalizing 151, 311–23, 333–4, 337, 355, 370, 377, 419–22, 424
 as causal 3–8, 10–11, 31, 283, 311, 314–17, 398
 and functionalism 393–6
 primary 9–11, 118
 see also causation; context; generalizations: heteronomic; identity theory
Extended Principle of Accountability (EPA) 82–3, 86–7
Extended Standard Theory 219

extension, strategy of 23–4

facts 125–6, 152, 289–90, 416–17
Feinberg, Joel 85
Feyerabend, Paul 441
Fodor, Janet 209n
Fodor, Jerry 256, 339n, 429n, 445n, 453n
Føllesdal, Dagfinn 311–23, 338n
Foot, Philippa 109n
form, logical, *see* logical form, theories of
Forrester, James 294–6, 298–300, 302–6, 309–10
Francken, Patrick 281
freedom of action 370, 384, 409, 418–21, 465–9
  denial of 422
  in Sartre 459–60, 462, 464–5, 468
'Freedom to Act' (Davidson) 11, 39, 117, 348
Frege, G. 163, 282, 313, 416
French , Peter A. 73–87
Freud, Sigmund 100–1, 122
functionalism 387–98, 429

Gazdar, Gerald 184
generalization: causal 51–2, 425, 435
  existential 34, 270–1, 333
  heteronomic 312, 316–17, 342, 346, 372, 381, 402, 407
  homonomic 342, 372, 381–2, 401–2, 404, 407; *see also* law: strict
  intentional 402, 405
  psychophysical 335, 372–5, 400–3, 425
  universal 318
  see also law
Glouberman, M. 288n
Goldman, Alvin 196, 281n, 307n
Goodman, Nelson 333n, 447
Greenbaum, S. 224
Grice, H.P. 19, 182n
Gupta, Anil 178n

Harman, G. 19
Harnish, R.M. 219
Harré, Rom and Madden, E.H. 318, 345n
Harsanyi, John 66
Haugeland, John 59n, 435n
Hempel, C. 6n, 15n, 140, 315–17, 371, 443
'Hempel on Explaining Action'

(Davidson) 315, 316–17, 331, 336, 354
Higgenbotham, James 246, 247n
Honderich, Ted 53n, 285, 312, 372n
Horgan, Terence 341n, 427–43
Hornsby, J. 55n, 58n, 312, 343n, 397n, 435n, 444–58
'How is Weakness of the Will Possible?' (Davidson) 11, 15–16, 40n, 90, 92–3, 95–6, 99–100, 104–6, 108, 110, 117–18, 120, 132, 139n
Huff, Douglas 312
Hume, David 318
  on causation 6n, 30, 394, 398, 415, 425, 430n
  on reason 117, 122, 128

identity theory 152, 163, 268–81, 313–14, 317, 400, 454–8
  token identity thesis 59, 110, 335, 338–41, 384, 410, 419–21, 427–43
  type–type identity thesis 59, 108–10, 335, 339, 408–9, 418, 423, 426, 427
  see also causal theory of action
impossibility, conceptual 335–6, 361
incorporation, conceptual 357
indeterminacy thesis, see translation, indeterminacy of
individualism, see reason: and individualism
'Individuation of Events, The' (Davidson) 151–2, 181–3, 187, 191, 196, 293, 340, 340, 344, 412, 456n
Inquiries into Truth and Interpretation (Davidson) viii, 154–5, 163, 172
instrumentalism, psychological 392, 427, 439, 441n
'Intending' (Davidson) 8, 12, 16n, 17–18, 19n, 20, 30, 39–41, 90, 92–4, 117, 119
intentions: and action, see action, intentional
  as agglomerative 21–2, 24
  and alternatives 24–8
  conditional 19–20, 22, 25, 27
  future directed 12–13, 17–28, 40–1, 83
  and inconsistency 119
  and morality 73–84
  perspectival nature of 359n
  and the psychological 371, 375–7,

379, 384–6, 402
and purpose 3, 32–3, 36, 232
reductive view 43, 385
and semantics 213–16, 231–2, 250–2
simple 19–20, 22, 25
see also action, intentional; behavior,
intentional; coordination
interpretation, radical 49, 352–66,
461–5, 469–72
irrationality 63, 99–102, 116, 118–22,
126–7, 129, 130–6, 476, 486–7
and inconsistency 119–21, 127, 132,
138, 141–2, 147–8
and self-deception 139–43, 146–8
see also self-deception

Jackendoff, R. 219, 252n
Jackson, Frank 96, 104–15
Jeffrey, R.C. 486
Johansen, L. 69–70
Johnson, W.E. 326
Johnston, Mark 336n, 338n, 351n,
408–26
judgment: all-out, unconditional (UJ) 26,
40–3, 90–4, 96–7, 99–103, 119–20
'all things reasonably considered'
(ATCJ) 92–4, 96, 101–3, 119–23
prima facie 42, 92
justification for action 7, 118

Kant, I. 78, 383–6, 466
Katz, J.J. 207–34
Kenny, Anthony 173
Keyser, Jan 252
Kim, Jaegwon 283
on individuation of events 167, 187,
196–9
on mental events 441
on psychophysical laws 339–40, 344,
347n, 354n, 356–7, 360–1, 365n,
369–86
on supervenience 417n, 427, 441n
knowledge, see evidence: and scientific
theory
Koslow, Arnold 292n
Kuhn, Thomas 177–8, 178n

language 173, 473, 474n
and the mental 463–6, 469–70
and reality 153–4
and Sartre 464, 469–70
scientific 170–1, 172
and thought 476–8, 480, 485–7

see also adverbs: theory of;
modification: decomposition
theory; semantic theory; thought
and language; truth theory of
language
law: bridge law 335, 346, 349–58,
362–5, 367–8, 409, 427
causal 7, 46–8, 52–3, 282, 313–16,
345–6, 348, 364–5
and closed comprehensive theory
342–51, 364, 367
psychological 47–8, 337–8, 341,
348–9, 367, 369, 371, 373, 380,
382, 402, 410–11, 418–19, 421–2
psychophysical 59, 319, 321–3, 331,
335, 337–8, 341, 349–55, 357–8,
362–8, 369–86, 400, 402–3,
409–11, 417–19, 421–6, 457
as sentence 332–5, 362–3
as singular relation between universals
334
strict 332–5, 337–9, 341, 342–8, 349,
364, 367, 382, 400, 411–13, 415,
419, 425
see also causal theory of action;
generalization; physical laws;
reduction: nomological
Leacock, Claudia 207–34
Leibniz, G.W. von 117, 160, 276, 440,
448
Lemmon, John: on adverb theory
197–201, 203–4, 206
on events 160, 344
LePore, Ernest 3–13, 151–61, 340n
Lewis David 185, 189, 191, 409, 429n,
441n, 446n, 451
lexicon, limited 162–4, 174–5
Loar, Brian 387–97
logical form, theories of 185, 192,
235–67
of action sentences 205, 213–15
of causal statement 282–4, 415
Davidson on 158–9, 236–7, 247n,
250–1, 256–7, 262–6, 294–5,
306–8
underlying event approach 237–40,
242–3, 247n, 249–67
see also adverbs, theory of; modification
'Logical Form of Action Sentences, The'
(Davidson) 158, 193, 195, 208,
213–15, 250, 268, 415n
Lombard, Lawrence 198, 268–81
Lycan, William 351, 377n
Lyons, John 189n

Mackie, J.L.: and cause 345n, 430,
  433–4
  on moral responsibility 73–5, 77–8,
    80–2, 86–7
McCawley, J. 218–19
McConnell-Ginet, S. 217n
McDowell, John 340n, 355n, 359n,
  387–98, 445
McGinn, Colin 364n, 456n
McIntyre, Alison 198n, 203n
McLaughlin, Brian P. 3–13, 331–68
Malcolm, Norman 369–70, 474, 478,
  485
man, philosophy of 321
  in Davidson 459, 460–3, 465–6,
    469–70, 472
  in Sartre 459–60, 461–2, 465–6,
    470–2
Marcus, Ruth Barcan 105n
Martin, Richard 167
'Material Mind, The' (Davidson) 320,
  331, 335, 350, 352, 354–6, 359–60,
  362–3, 370, 399, 463, 469
materialism 408–9, 417–18, 421, 423,
  426
  eliminative 427, 439, 441–2
  see also behavior, intentional; ontology,
    materialist
  meaning, theory of 154, 213–5, 285n,
    464
  in Sartre 470
Melden, A.I. 14, 30–1
Mele, Alfred 91–3, 95–6, 99
'Mental Events' (Davidson) 51, 313–14,
  319–20, 331–9, 341–3, 352–4, 359,
  363, 365, 370–1, 373, 375–7, 381–5,
  399–402, 404, 409–15, 418–21,
  425–6, 456, 461, 466–8
mereological conception: of continuants
  446–50, 455–6, 458
  of events 450–4, 457
Midgley, Mary 487
Mill, J.S. 119
  on cause 282, 430–1, 433–4, 438n
Miller, Neal E. 97–9
mind, the 312, 321, 370, 395, 422–6,
  427, 459–72
  autonomy of 384–6, 466–7
  and body 151–2, 374–6, 379–81
  divided, and motivation 99–102, 122,
    356n
  holism of 376–7, 467
  objectivistic conception of 395–7

rationality of 377–9, 388–91
subjectivity of 394–6
see also dualism; events, mental; identity
  theory; psychology
Minsky, 437–8
modification: adjectival 208–12, 222
  adverbial 155–8, 162–5, 193–4,
    212–34, 236, 249–67, 414
  decompositional theory 207–13,
    215–16, 222–34
  non-decompositional theories 207,
    213–22
  see also adverbs, theory of; logical form,
    analysis of
monism, anomalous 314, 331, 334–6,
  338, 384–5, 397–8, 417, 420, 427,
  445, 454n, 456–8
  an exhaustive monism 417–18, 421
  as identity thesis 410, 413–14, 418
  and psychology 400–7, 423–6
  see also ontology, monistic
Montague, Richard 194, 252n, 253n
morality, *see* conflict, moral; responsibility,
  moral
Morgenbesser, S. 28
motivation, strength of 88–103
  and causal theory 88–97, 102–3
  and self-deception 146–8
movements, bodily, actions as 30–3,
  35–6, 54–7, 76, 79, 85, 409, 482–3

Nagel, Ernest 335n
Nagel, Thomas 351, 395n, 396n
naturalistic fallacy 389, 396, 407

obligation 109–10; *see also* deontic paradox
'On the Very Idea of a Conceptual
  Scheme' (Davidson) 353n, 396n
ontology, existentialist 459–60, 462–4,
  466–7, 469–70
ontology, materialist 54–9
ontology, monistic 44–5, 54, 56, 59

'Paradoxes of Irrationality' (Davidson)
  89n, 90–1, 94–5, 100–2, 116–19,
  121, 127–8, 130, 133, 143n, 145n,
  147n
Parsons, Terry 180, 235–67, 273n,
  274–5, 279, 308
Pears, David 64n, 130–7, 146–7
Perry, John 17n, 247n, 290n
Peterson, Philip 283–285

Philosophical Essays on Freud (Davidson) 116, 119, 126

physical laws: and anomalism of the mental 319–20, 338–40, 367, 372, 377, 380–2, 410–13, 418, 457
and closed systems 319–20, 335, 342–4, 346–8, 381
and descriptions of actions 47–57, 59, 312–17, 321–2, 417, 424
and holism of the physical 377
and rationality 377–8

physicalism 409–11, 413–17, 418, 427, 435n, 443, 444–7, 450
mereological conceptions of events 452–4, 457–8
and part–whole relations 446–7, 452–6, 457
token 335, 338–41, 365–6
type–type 409, 423, 426
see also monism, anomalous; reduction: physicalist

plans, and future intentions 14, 23–4
Poincaré, J. H. 166
Powers, Lawrence 294
predicate: logic of 162–5, 169–70, 173–6, 207, 242–3, 253–7, 265–6, 289–90
mental 332, 335–7, 341, 349–53, 357, 362–7, 416
physical 331–2, 335–7, 350–3, 357, 362–3, 365–6, 416
Prichard, H.A. 16n
Principle of Responsive Adjustment (PRA) 83–7
principles, constitutive 353–8, 383
pro-attitude, *see* attitude, propositional
properties 449
mental 59, 416–18, 422–6, 442
natural 422–6
as particulars 415–16
physical 59, 416–18, 423, 425
as primitive 415–16
and subdetermination 324–8
see also values

psychology: anomaly of 370–3, 382–4, 399–406, 410–11
autonomy of 44, 46–7, 51, 370, 382
commonsense/systematic 337, 371–2, 397n, 404, 407, 428, 434–5, 437–8, 441, 445
as extrinsic 49–56
and intention 371
as instrinsic 57–8
irreducibility of 335, 356, 366, 381,
400, 405–6
and neurology 427, 434–40, 481–2
and reasons for action 49–58
as a science 44, 343, 348, 369–70, 383, 399–407, 426
see also law: psychological

'Psychology as Philosophy' (Davidson) 11, 50–1, 117, 314, 319–20, 331, 334, 353–6, 369–71, 376, 384, 399–402, 406

psychophysical, the: anomalism of 371–7, 381–5, 400, 402–3, 409–11
theory of action and event 321–3, 331, 335, 340
see also law

purpose, *see* action, intentional
Putnam, Hilary 423, 428n, 454n

quantification 162–3
existential 156, 178, 180, 188, 288
first-order 12, 272
restricted 178, 180–1
second-order 272
standard logic 178–81, 189
universal 178, 180, 417
unrestricted 178, 180
Quesada, Daniel 312, 317
Quine, W.V.O. 34–5, 446n, 447n, 475
on events 160, 162–71, 172–6, 180, 199–200, 293, 344n, 449–50
on determinacy of translation 320, 377
on intention 370
on meaning 214n
on the mental and the physical 384–5
on properties 416
Quirk, R. 224

'Radical Interpretation' (Davidson) 352n, 355n
rationality 50, 387, 473–80, 486–7
constraints 388–91
deductive 388–91, 394
and functionalism 387–94, 396–7
maximization principle 321, 376, 378–80
principles of 354–6, 358–9
see also explanations, rational-choice; irrationality; reason; self-deception
rationalism, *see* reason: rationalist view
rationalization, *see* explanations, rationalizing
Ravin, Yael 206–34

Index

'Reality without Reference' (Davidson) 169

reason for action 43, 45–6, 116–29, 130–7, 139–40, 320–1
  as causal 3–12, 14–15, 29–33, 39, 120–1, 125–6, 130–1, 137, 313–15, 321–2
  cognitive 143
  and consistency 119–21, 127
  empiricist view 117, 127–8
  evaluative 143
  external 106, 111
  and individualism 123–6, 128–9
  internal 106–7
  and motivational strength 88–99
  as motive 118; *see also* reason: primary
  as premisses 118–20, 123, 126
  primary 4–12, 32, 88, 118, 125
  as rational 50, 116–17, 120, 129, 133–6, 473, 476
  rationalist view 117–29, 130
  and social interaction 123–7
  see also action, intentional; causation; irrationality
reasoning, practical 117, 146, 386
  and causality 14–17, 46–7, 51–2
  and competing reasons 9, 89, 92–3, 99
  as holistic 46–7
  and intentions 23–4, 42–3, 46
  see also generalizations; reason for action
redescription 38, 73, 75–7, 81, 85, 87
  and events 152
reduction: causalist 32–3, 38–40, 43
  nomological 35, 351–2, 356–7, 363–4, 366, 381, 385–6
  physicalist 387–8, 392–7, 408–9, 454
redundancy, semantic 225, 231
reference 169–71, 190–1, 286–7, 293
  and adverbial modification 217–19
Reichenbach, Hans 235, 328
reification 162, 164–5, 168–71
responsibility, moral: for actions 74–5, 80, 86
  of corporation 73, 75–7, 80–1, 83–4, 87
  of intentional agent 73–4, 76–87
  and moral community 80–1
  and willingness 81–2
  see also conflict, moral
Root, Michael 353
Rorty, Richard 427, 441

Rosenberg, Alexander 345n, 349n, 399–407
Russell, Bertrand 162, 166, 170
  on descriptions 177–81, 183–6, 188–90, 192

Saarinen, Esa 459–72
Santas, Gerasimas 97, 99
Sartre, Jean-Paul 459–72
Scheeling, Thomas 182
science, closed 335, 343, 348–9, 404
self-deception 138–48
  as belief 49, 138–40, 145–6, 356n
  and lying 144–5
  see also akrasia; irrationality; thinking, wishful; warrant, weakness of
semantic theory 153–5, 159–60, 162–3, 169, 173–6, 207–8, 214, 240–2, 281
  extensional semantics 416
  as finite 154–6
  situation semantics 247n
  see also adverbs: theory of; events: semantic theory; modification
Sen, A. and Williams, B. 67
sentence 172–3, 464
  causal 152–3, 157–8, 173, 282–92
  illocutionary force 184–5
  lawlike 332–5, 362–3
  and logical form 242–7, 249–67, 268–71, 294–5, 306–8
  and scientific language 169–71
  and syntax 240–2
  truth conditions 269
Shoemaker, Sydney 395n
Siegel, M. 251n
Smart, J.J.C. 408n, 409n
Smith, Peter 53n
social sciences 400–1, 407; *see also* psychology
Stalnaker, R.C. 213, 216–22, 233
Stanton, William Larry 338n, 342n, 351n, 359n, 364, 417n
Stich, Stephen 337n, 437–8
Stoutland, Frederick 44–59, 312
Strawson, P.F. 177, 419
supervenience 332, 359–66, 367, 385, 406, 417, 427, 441n, 442
  and moral conflict 113
Suppes, Patrick 318, 321, 322

Tarski, A. 154, 163, 173, 175, 269
Taylor, Charles 31

Thalberg, Irving 88–103
thinking, wishful 64, 69–70, 72, 142–5
Thomson, R.H. 213, 216–22, 233, 285n
Thomson, Judith Jarvis 197n, 435n,
   451n
thought and language 475–80, 485; *see
   also* attitudes, propositional; belief;
   desire; intention
'Thought and Talk' (Davidson) 50,
   463–6
Tiles, J. 412n
translation, indeterminacy of 320–1, 377,
   381, 384–5
Transportability, Principle of 252
'Truth and Meaning' (Davidson) 416
truth theory of language 153–60,
   169–71, 173–4, 480
   extensional 269
Tuomela, Raimo 312
Turner, Stephen 312
Tye, Michael 427–43

Ullman-Margalit, E. 28
utilitarianism and moral conflict 108,
   113–14

value 106–7, 131, 134–6
   conflicting 140
   and properties 111–15

Van Gulick, Robert 358n
Van Fraassen, Bas 105n, 300n
Vendler, Zeno 196n, 239, 267n
verbs: of action, *see* action, verbs of
   mental 45
Vision, Gerald 288n
volition and cause of action 6, 15–16

Wallace, John 263, 274–5, 280, 352n
warrant, weakness of 140–8
Watson, Gary 95–6, 99
Weiss, Donald 478–9
Wheeler, Samuel C. III 165
Whitehead, A.N. 170, 313
Whorf Benjamin 240
Wiggins, David 447n, 448n
will, weakness of 142, 356n
   as intention 139–40
   and rational choice 64–5, 72, 120
   see also akrasia; self-deception
Williams, Bernard 105n, 395n
Wilson, George M. 29–43
Wittgenstein, L. 6n, 76, 370
   on intention 36–7, 407
   on subdetermination 326–7
Woodward, James 438n
Wright, G.H. von 58n

Zemack, Eddy M. 193